Grounds for Writers

Critical Perspectives for Reading

Jeanne Gunner

Chapman University

Doug Sweet

Chapman University

PEARSON
Longman

New York San Francisco Boston
London Toronto Sydney Tokyo Singapore Madrid
Mexico City Munich Paris Cape Town Hong Kong Montreal

Executive Editor: Lynn M. Huddon
Development Editor: Katharine Glynn
Senior Supplements Editor: Donna Campion
Senior Marketing Manager: Sandra McGuire
Production Manager: Bob Ginsberg
Project Coordination, Text Design, and Electronic Page Makeup:
    Nesbitt Graphics, Inc.
Cover Design Manager: Wendy Ann Fredericks
Cover Designer: Nancy Sacks
Cover Art: Terry Winters, "Range." Photo © Steven Sloman; art © Terry Winters
Photo Researcher: Jody Potter
Manufacturing Buyer: Lucy Hebard
Printer and Binder: RR Donnelley & Sons Company
Cover Printer: RR Donnelley & Sons Company

For permission to use copyrighted material, grateful acknowledgment is made to the
copyright holders on pp. 623–624, which are hereby made part of this copyright page.

Library of Congress Cataloging-in-Publication Data

Gunner, Jeanne, 1954–
    Grounds for writers : critical perspectives for reading / Jeanne Gunner, Doug Sweet.
        p. cm.
    Includes index.
    ISBN-13: 978-0-321-05529-3

1. English language—Rhetoric—Problems, exercises, etc. 2. Report writing—Problems,
exercises, etc. 3. Critical thinking—Problems, exercises, etc. 4. College readers.
I. Sweet, Doug, 1947– II. Title.
    PE1413.G85 2007
    808'.0427—dc22   2007029902

Visit us at www.ablongman.com

ISBN-13: 978-0-321-05529-3
ISBN-10:   0-321-05529-2

12345678910–DOC–10 09 08 07

contents

part one
Rhetorical Theory and Critical Frames   1

8   Reading Critically About Social Values   228

9   Reading Critically About Legal Values   276

12 Reading Critically About the "Other"   395

13 Reading Critically About Domestic Colonization   446

14 Reading Critically About Resistant Voices and Rhetorical Forms   496

alternative tables of contents

Working with a Semiotics Frame

Thematic Units

Gender and Gender Roles

Individualists and Outsiders

Educational Critiques

Conflict and Violence

Rhetorical Focus

Biography and Personal Narrative

Academic Discourse

preface

Grounds for Writers: Critical Perspectives for Reading is a textbook designed for students in college writing courses. Its approach to writing instruction developed with the following assumptions:

- Writing is always a rhetorical act involving a self writing *from* a perspective, *to* an audience, *for* a purpose.
- Perspectives are critical frames, Burkean lenses, that produce knowledge and rhetorical stances.
- Critical perspectives provide useful rhetorical methods—they operate heuristically and help form the frames and foundations of arguments.
- Critical perspectives help writers connect individual experience with social contexts, enhancing rhetorical awareness and agency.

A defining premise of the text is that through rhetorical and theoretical instruction, students can bring critical perspectives not only to their academic writing, but also to their personal, social, cultural, and historical experiences.

The text thus joins the basics of classical rhetoric—the rhetorical elements of author, audience, and purpose and the rhetorical processes of invention, arrangement, and style—with interpretive methods, especially those that reflect the social and cultural turn of contemporary rhetorical theory. Students are taken through a process of (1) developing familiarity with basic rhetorical principles; (2) understanding a critical perspective; (3) considering a given text from that perspective; (4) using the frame to help create (invent) arguments an academic audience would recognize as valid and relevant; (5) addressing this audience in the genres and voices that are likely to have academic authority; and (6) becoming conscious of the values promoted by particular discourses. Students present their ideas in academic discourse and other discursive forms to become aware of how such forms alter their perceptions of reality, how values are created and preserved, how language communities compete and constrain, how individuals exist in relation to social conventions, how issues of status, class, race, and gender operate in daily life and conceptual thought through language use.

Grounds for Writers asks students to consider how all texts, verbal and nonverbal, form and reflect the wider culture, and asks them to use critical perspectives to elucidate the relations of self to others, and self to writing. It supports students in becoming *critical thinkers* in the most socially meaningful sense of that perhaps overused term: students are asked to question systematically from multiple perspectives the ideas and practices that form the content of their daily lives, to develop ability in systematic analysis from specific perspectives, and to do so by engaging in both academic inquiry and active critique of their daily experience. Students will also, we hope, come to understand composing as a greater enterprise than simply the production of an essay. They are asked to develop a range of perspectives on social issues and culture overall, engaging in academic methods of critical thought and its written forms, which can also become ways of thinking about the world beyond the classroom.

This approach supports composing as a complex, recursive process that recognizes reading and writing as mutually inclusive rhetorical activities, both studied as interpretive acts. The critical perspectives in Parts Two through Five require that students do close textual analysis, not of a New Critical order but of a kind that helps illuminate the constructedness of texts—the rhetorical choices and values that guide selection and representation, making out of language a particular vision of the world, one that can be rhetorically analyzed. Composing becomes more than a linear process, since the argument an essay makes carries with it a set of authorial values and beliefs that themselves can be closely read.

Grounds for Writers is designed to complement a range of curricular and pedagogical approaches, including courses focused on the conventions of academic discourse or literature-based writing courses. It is also designed for use in a range of courses. We do not distinguish courses by level: this book addresses the rhetorical practices that are basic to the communication needs of all adult users of the written language of higher education. If basic rhetorical theory applies in all communication, then what a student needs to know to be an effective communicator does not necessarily change with institutional setting. All students in the process of developing their academic writing abilities, whether in research universities or community colleges, advanced composition or basic writing, are fundamentally engaged in studying the same body of knowledge. The rhetorical and critical methods covered in this book are relevant for all college writing students.

We also have designed the text to be open to use from a range of instructor orientations, reflecting the broad nature of English studies itself. Whether you are primarily a literary critic, critical theorist, rhetorician, compositionist, linguist, creative writer, or another type of specialist (or generalist), as a writing instructor you help students look at how texts are put together by authors for some purpose in relation to an audience. Whether the text you study is a literary work, a student essay, or a cultural event, rhetoric is central to your teaching. Because the book's design recognizes the variety of professional training that instructors bring to their teaching, the sections are not sequenced. Chapters within each section can be used in any number or order, and the writing topics are varied in the type of responses they invite. Thus the book supports a range of informed pedagogical approaches.

Features

Grounds for Writers offers several key features.

- Part One gives students the key rhetorical tools they need to read critically and write effectively.

- The four critical frames that comprise Parts Two through Five are introduced simply with a minimal number of terms and concepts.

- The readings, all chosen with student accessibility in mind, are drawn from both academic and popular culture and range from classic authors (Sigmund Freud, Karl Marx) to contemporary voices (Gloria Anzaldúa, bell hooks, Paul Theroux, Nancy Mairs). Each reading is followed by discussion questions that can be the basis of class discussion or assigned as brief writing assignments.

- Each part includes a section showing students how to use the interpretative frame in their writing. Using the film *Jurassic Park*, students see the rich source of interpretation the frames provide. Should an instructor prefer to use a different film or text, the Instructor's Guide provides the needed support.

- The Topics for Writing sections that end each chapter ask students to develop responses that are rhetorically effective and address the interrelationship of author, audience, and purpose. Each part concludes with research-based Writing Projects that ask student to write about contemporary issues from the perspective of the critical frame.

- The chapters are not sequenced and instructors can select among the sections and readings to suit their own classroom goals.

The book builds a variety of topics for written response into each chapter. Students engage in informal, in-class writing ("write-to-learn") as well as formal individual and collaborative writing projects. Written tasks use a range of sources: chapter readings, students' personal knowledge, media, and an array of research approaches. Students are also invited to consider their work metacritically: what are the rhetorical and social implications of the writing they've done? The book addresses academic writing as a subject but also as an object of critical inquiry: we emphasize academic discourse, but we also ask students to question the social purposes and effects of academic discourse.

We've chosen to use the popular film *Jurassic Park* as a well-known text for the sample drafting process in each section. It's one of the most-viewed films of all time, both in and outside the United States, plus its plot is easily recapped (we provide a summary in Part Two, the first critical frame presented—even as we warn that any summary itself involves interpretation). We use the same text as the object of study for all the critical frames covered, illustrating for students how different critical perspectives pose different ways of seeing a single text and can lead to different readings of it; we show each perspective as having different values and offering different rhetorical approaches. However, instructors can use this same approach using a text of their own choice.

We recognize the difficulty of teaching academic writing in a 10-, 15-, even 30-week course structure. We each teach this material in our writing courses, sometimes using only three or four parts of the book, since all the sections engage students in the basic rhetorical work of a composition class. Instructors can select among the sections and use *Grounds for Writers* to suit their own instructional goals and institutional settings. We hope your students find this textbook an engaging and valuable way of actively joining the unending conversation.

The Instructor's Guide is designed to offer teachers a wide range of pedagogical choices and approaches for working with *Grounds for Writers*. In addition to step-by-step suggestions for using discussion and writing prompts, the guide explicitly ties pedagogy to classroom discussion and activities.

Acknowledgments

The authors gratefully acknowledge the comments and suggestions from these reviewers: Rebecca Brittenham, Indiana University, South Bend; Marguerite Helmers, University of Wisconsin Oshkosh; Paul Kameen, University of Pittsburgh; Megan Knight, University of Iowa; Tom Pace, John Carroll University; and Amy Rupiper Taggart, North Dakota State University.

JEANNE GUNNER
DOUG SWEET

Rhetorical Theory and Critical Frames

*Imagine that you enter a parlor. You come late. When you
arrive, others have long preceded you, and they are engaged in
a heated discussion, a discussion too heated for them to pause
and tell you exactly what it is about. In fact, the discussion had
already begun long before any of them got there, so that no one
present is qualified to retrace for you all the steps that had gone before. You
listen for a while, until you decide that you have caught the tenor of the
argument; then you put in your oar. Someone answers; you answer him;
another comes to your defense; another aligns himself against you, to either
the embarrassment or gratification of your opponent, depending upon the
quality of your ally's assistance. However, the discussion is interminable. The
hour grows late, you must depart. And you do depart, with the discussion
still vigorously in progress.*

    *It is from this "unending conversation" . . . that the materials of your
drama arise. Nor is this verbal action all there is to it. For all these words
are grounded in what Malinowski would call "contexts of situations" . . . .*

—**Kenneth Burke** (from *The Philosophy of Literary Form*)

You've just been thrust into an unending conversation. You
probably don't have a clear sense of why the above passage opens this
section of a writing textbook. And you may not know who Kenneth Burke
is.[1] Welcome to college! (Or to this college writing course.)

---

[1]Kenneth Burke (1897–1993) was one of the last successful independent scholars in American culture; beginning with mostly literary criticism, Burke expanded his ideas to connect rhetorical, literary, and philosophical thought. For him, language is always a social "drama," symbols that we put
into action.

Learning how to situate yourself in the many conversations going on in your classrooms, campus, and larger world is what your work in college writing courses is all about. Learning at this level is not a neat matter of being handed a set of concepts that you study, memorize, and plug into a five-paragraph essay, test, or other conventional form. You've entered a social space in which you'll be expected to grapple with new ideas, new levels of complexity. The goal is for you to join the discussion, contributing your own thoughts and reactions and influencing the course of the argument. That is what's exciting about college study: you've become part of a particular kind of meaning-making community. To be an effective participant, you'll need to be able to think critically, inventively, systematically, and resistantly, in your reading, speech, and writing. And one of the central goals of writing classes—and of this textbook—lies in that word *effective*.

To join a conversation effectively, you need some knowledge of rhetoric and rhetorical skills. *Rhetoric* is a term you'll see repeatedly in this textbook. We use it as Burke does in the opening passage: it names the social act of using language, a process of communication in which a speaker or writer produces words, oral or written (or in some cases visual images), to be shared with a listener or reader for a purpose. Typically, the purpose is to establish the speaker's/writer's and text's credibility in order to have the listener/reader/audience act in some way on the speaker's/writer's subject. Being perceived as credible, as speaking and writing with authority, is an essential part of the rhetorical goal of persuasion: we compose in order to be heard, to be part of a conversation, to engage others with our ideas, to have an effect on how our world works.

In college writing, then, you'll be using language in a way that may be new to you. You'll be working with texts—your own and those of other authors, as a writer and a reader—through the conscious use of rhetorical theory. Understanding rhetorical theory helps us become better readers, since we're better able to identify and evaluate different intended effects of a text or conversation—we can judge the credibility of the author and text we're reading, and then decide the degree to which the argument should influence our own beliefs and actions. The major goal of this textbook is to help you enhance your conscious use of rhetorical theory applied to the reading, speaking, and writing you do as part of your daily experience, in the classroom and in other social spaces.

We do have a second goal, and that's to add different types of critical inquiry to the rhetorical knowledge you'll be developing. Academic work in most fields today uses an array of critical theories as a framework for what is studied. The study of literary texts, for instance, might be grounded in feminist theory, Marxist theory, semiotics, or other systematic critical methods. Critical theories are used outside the academic world as well as part of informed public discourse—in discussions of international politics, for example, especially in arguments about globalization, colonialism, or democracy; and in the business world, for example, in marketing departments, as workers seek out cultural trends for use in product development and advertisement. Understanding critical inquiry as part of rhetorical theory prepares us to play an active part in academic and public exchanges, because this understanding helps us see how experience—personal, social, cultural—is constructed in "interested" ways, ways that favor certain values and belief systems. And the more able we are to understand and actively employ critical rhetorical thought, the more *agency*, or power to act and affect others, we're likely to have. The written word is still the main means of persuasion in the academic world, and so we introduce critical frames for their rhetorical value—for their usefulness in helping us create persuasive, or effective, prose. Together, rhetorical and critical theory helps us identify and address the "contexts of situations" that Burke refers to in the opening passage.

In this book we introduce critical frames drawn from psychoanalytic, materialist, postcolonial, and semiotic theories and use these in connection with rhetorical concepts as an approach to critical writing and reading. Rhetoric teaches us how to write effectively in a range of writing situations. As part of rhetorical ability, using critical frames helps us develop ideas, organize them for readers, and identify our underlying values in the writing we produce. Using these frames also helps us effectively evaluate the arguments of others. To this purpose, in the chapter discussions that follow, we talk about writing and reading as an integrated process of rhetorical awareness and planning and critical framing and inquiry. These are the grounds for writing that this textbook continually invokes.

While Parts Two through Four present particular critical frames in connection with fundamental rhetorical issues, this part, Part One, connects the writing process to basic rhetorical theory and to the concept of critical inquiry as rhetorical practice.

The Basics of Rhetoric: Author, Audience, and Purpose

This Chapter's Rhetorical Concepts

- Creating an identity as a writer/speaker
- Understanding how your authorial identity affects your audience; how your audience affects your identity
- Helping your audience to see your writing purpose as credible

Rhetoric, a formal field of study in the Western world since the time of ancient Greece, is the study of how we can use language to understand and influence the beliefs and actions of others. Rhetoric is about being *persuasive*. Its constant focus is to map out a kind of negotiating process that lets us enter and possibly alter social conversations, in speech and written form. Preplatonics, sophists, Plato, Aristotle, Isocrates, Quintilian, Cicero, Augustine: these are some of the major schools and names of ancient rhetorical theory. The basic questions that these ancient rhetoricians sought to answer are essentially the same matters we study today: the relation of thought to language, language to behavior, and how persuasion occurs. Rhetorical theory matters because it embodies assumptions about language (which is at the heart of rhetorical theory), human nature, society, and the relations among these. Rhetorical theories thus are tied to values: one's theory of rhetoric is also one's theory of knowledge, self, and society (to use formal academic terms, rhetoric ties to *epistemology* and *ideology*). If the ability to use language is a defining human feature, then how we can and do use it become very powerful defining features of humans in society as well.

The kind of rhetorically based study of writing presented here is not prescriptive—it does not provide rules for writing sentences, paragraphs, and essays, outlines for preparing research papers, or instruction in grammar. Most rhetorically based writing classes today emphasize the social nature of language use, which follows what can be called "local" rules, conventions that reflect the values of particular social situations. "Rules" thus change as our social locations change, and we therefore need a way to figure out how to speak and write effectively—how to be persuasive—according to the different times we exist in and settings we enter. We need, in other words, a theory of how best to speak and write for a range of different audiences and purposes. The goal of rhetorically based writing instruction is to give you the fundamental concepts of effective communication. It's up to you to do the work of figuring out in each speaking/writing situation which particular uses of language will be effective in each given time and place. And an effective speaker/writer does this by considering rhetorical elements and options.

In this chapter, we'll cover the concepts of **author**, **audience**, and **purpose**, terms that name the main parts of any rhetorical situation, or any act of language-based communication. These are the fundamental theoretical concepts a speaker/writer uses to develop rhetorical effectiveness across the full range of social exchange.

Author: Persona, Stance, and Voice

When we use language, we become speakers, in the form of conversation or prose or even thought. A speaker necessarily represents an identity, or a *persona*. A persona is a localized identity, which is why it is also sometimes called a "mask." This means that as authors we speak/write not as the absolute sum of all our experiences, not as the full "I" we might experience ourselves individually to be, but as a limited identity or set of identities, one(s) chosen for the occasion (chosen by the author and/or imposed from without—by an instructor, boss, or other authority, including social conventions of what constitutes acceptable language, or even laws). We can speak or write as a student, a mother, an authority (in academic prose, often a disembodied, impersonal authority), a questioner, and so on, or as some multiple set of social roles (as a student who is also a Christian, a disabled person, a woman, or other socially recognized identity). To be rhetorically effective, a speaker/writer determines his or her persona not in isolation but in relation to his or her subject and invoked audience (concepts discussed below). Notice the difference in authorial persona in the following two versions of an e-mail message:

> Professor,
>   I wasn't in class today because I had to drive my roommate to a doctor's appointment. You can call me at your convenience with any work I missed.
> Sandy W.

> Professor,
>   I apologize for missing class today. I have gotten notes from a classmate and will be prepared for our next meeting.
> Sandy W.

Same writer, different personas, and so different rhetorical effects. In the first, the writer assumes that the professor will see driving a roommate as a more valid use of the student's time than attending the professor's class (many professors would disagree). And the student also makes any missed work the responsibility of the professor (again, the intended audience is likely to have a very different set of values and sense of professional relationship). The persona the student adopts in the second version is that of the responsible student who apologizes for and has taken steps to minimize the effects of the missed class. The first message is likely to create a negative impression of the writer; the second is likely to be more effective in creating a sense of a student who is attempting to be responsible. Even in a short e-mail, persona is a powerful rhetorical element.

Rhetorically and critically, our *stance*—our position, attitude, bias, or perspective—is a way to name the points of view we occupy whenever we express ourselves. Along with persona, stance is a way of naming who and conceptually where a piece of communication is *from*, and thus what its *context* is. We may or may not be conscious of the specific personas and stances we adopt, but they nonetheless influence how we see reality and affect the ways we present ourselves and our ideas to others (and therefore how this audience perceives us). A rhetorically effective persona and stance require conscious attention to where we're speaking or writing from—our social setting, set of values, sense of identity. In academic writing, for instance, we often create an identity of authority by aligning ourselves with commonly recognized forms of authority—by quoting from scholarly books and articles; from primary, historical, or literary sources; and so on. These sources reveal to a reader that the writer's authority can be trusted, that he or she is familiar with the field and its research conventions and with what counts as persuasive evidence. The types of sources chosen also suggest the author's perspective: a discussion of environmental issues that draws on recognized environmental activists for evidence, for example, immediately positions the writer as someone writing from a particular point of view, one sympathetic to environmental protection measures.

Persona and stance are further established through an author's *voice*. In traditional academic prose, the writer's voice is an academic one, characterized as objective, impersonal, rational. Academic prose has recently become more open to other sorts of voices: personal, collective, or emotional, for example. Reading current academic books and journals, we're likely to encounter such hybrid voices—voices that reflect complex contemporary notions of our multiple identities, the various social roles that we occupy. You might encounter an essay in which the author switches voices in an attempt to convey the complexity of his or her relation to a topic. (The excerpt in Chapter 13 from Victor Villanueva's academic book *Bootstraps: From an American Academic of Color* is an example; Villanueva speaks as a professor, a Puerto Rican New Yorker, a formerly impoverished person, a husband, and from other roles and social locations.) Voice is created by diction, by the words an author chooses to use, which in turn helps create and reinforce the adopted persona.

In the following opening line to an essay published in an academic journal, the author accomplishes many things: he positions himself and creates a persona, an authorial identity; he takes a stance, a position on his subject; and he adopts a voice, a way of addressing the reader:

> This article uses the sociological concept of underlife to explain several aspects of writing instruction.

The sentence does a lot of rhetorical work. Looking at the sentence's persona, stance, and voice, we can infer that the author is

1. an English professor (and he is—his name is Robert Brooke);
2. a professional (writing a professional article);
3. an expert in an academic field (writing instruction, or composition);
4. a researcher/theorist (applying a sociological theory to his composition subject).

In addition, we can ascertain that the author is

5. addressing a specialized audience within the academic world (the words and phrases *article, sociological concept, underlife, explain,* and *writing instruction* together help focus a reader's attention on a "constructed" impression of the author's knowledge and authority to speak, because they ground his persona, stance, and voice in specialized knowledge and a professional community);
6. not using a personal voice; he does not write, "I argue that . . ." or "My research shows . . ." but instead has chosen a disembodied voice ("This article uses . . ."), suggesting an "objective" stance, perhaps to direct the reader's attention away from the researcher and toward the theory employed (he appeals to a specific authority, in this case derived from the usefulness of the sociological concept he is applying to his topic, rather than from personal voice or identity).

As you can see, the author has by his essay's first sentence already made several key rhetorical choices about how to present himself in relation to his subject and audience. In one sentence, he has consciously formed a context for a purpose. Readers will be expected (and will be expecting) to understand where they are and what kind of discussion is about to follow. Creating that expectation is what successful persuasive writers are able to do.

As a student, you are engaged in forms of inquiry and representation of views, and you'll be called upon in your assignments to develop your own persona, stance, and voice, grounded in a body of knowledge being shared by a professional community, to create a recognizable and shared context. These same concerns exist outside the classroom: whenever you speak or write, you're presenting a persona, revealing a stance, and using a voice. You're an author of your words in all communication situations, and thinking about how to present yourself is one major task of being rhetorically effective.

● The Writer's Task

Looking at/for the Author

The first three items listed below are opening lines from academic essays written by students in a range of writing classes; the final two ask you to consider yourself as an author. How has the student in each case—yourself included—established a credible persona, stance, and voice?

1. "Chinua Achebe's unique and rich novel *Things Fall Apart* incorporates numerous aspects of African life, and, more specifically, of the Ibo culture."

   - Who is speaking? How would you describe the author's persona? How does the author create this impression?

   - How would the line be less rhetorically effective if the last seven words were cut (from "and, more specifically" on)?

   - How does the use of the modifiers "unique and rich" help shape the writer's credibility?

2. "In Jack Schaefer's *Shane*, we see a young boy's struggle to choose between the path of the 'strong, silent type,' a symbol of the id, and the routine life of his farmer-father, a representative of Eros."

   - What can we infer about this author's knowledge of the subject, and how?

   - What is the author's stance? Does the author see the text as having a clear meaning provided by the theory the author invokes?

   - Why might the author have chosen to use the all-inclusive "we" voice?

   - Why has the author used specialized vocabulary ("id," "Eros"), and what is the intended effect on the reader?

3. "One thing we all possess in common is a body, and one process we all undergo is having our bodies be made into cultural texts."

   - One can argue that this author has created an assertive persona. How?

   - How is the diction this author uses different from the diction of the preceding example?

   - Why do you think this author does not use specialized vocabulary or much formal diction?

4. Take a look at a recent essay or exam you've written. In the opening paragraph, what impression of yourself have you created? Do you remember who you were trying to *be* in this writing? Would you now consider revising it for different rhetorical effects? How?

5. Define *rhetoric* in a sentence for other students. Create several versions that shift your stance—speak as an authority, a questioner, an advocate, a doubter, or some other persona.

Audience: Creating Community

To enter a conversation effectively, a speaker or writer determines the conversation's context in relation to its *audience*. The audience is whoever you're addressing, whether a real person sitting next to you and listening to your words, or some abstract notion of a reader who will encounter your written words on a page. Because language is a social activity, we always have an audience, even when we talk to ourselves or write alone at a desk. Alone in a room you might talk through a problem you're having, listening to yourself, reacting to how you phrase the issues, approving or disapproving certain parts of the narrative, wincing as you describe something you now wish you hadn't done or said, convincing yourself to adopt some course of action (even if that's a decision not to act and instead to forget all about the matter). We all do this, all the time. It's the self-reflective aspect of consciousness. In the Shakespearean play *Hamlet*, the main character's famous soliloquy (which begins "To be, or not to be: that is the question: / Whether 'tis nobler in the mind to suffer / The slings and arrows of outrageous fortune, / Or to take arms against a sea of troubles, / And by opposing end them?" III, i) is a literary example of this kind of internal exchange. By arguing his options out loud to himself, Hamlet has listened to his own reasoning and has framed his problem (whether or not to seek revenge for his father's murder) in a way that will ultimately end his indecision. While we may not face Hamlet's extreme situation, using ourselves as an audience still often prompts us to powerful decisions.

In every writing situation, you should ask yourself some basic questions about audience.

- Who is the audience you, as the author, are addressing?
- What interests and knowledge are they likely to share?
- What authorial personas, stances, and voices seem appropriate and effective for gaining the attention of this audience?
- What kinds of reasoning and forms of evidence do you expect will have persuasive power in this situation?

Note that the concept of audience works in reverse, too: the audience we address affects how we present ourselves, what we say, and perhaps even what decision/conclusion we reach. We're not only presenting ourselves, but this self-presentation is altered according to how we think this audience may see us, how we want it to see us—our self-image affects how we speak even to ourselves. We might start talking through a problem from a "poor me" stance, only to realize that it's not accomplishing anything productive, and then tell ourselves to stop complaining, take responsibility, make changes (and our audience in this case is probably an idealized notion of the self). An audience, in other words, can encourage or discourage certain personas, stances, and voices. Those with even minimal experience with academic discourse know not to employ "street" language or profanity in most formal presentations; such an approach is unlikely to establish a rhetorically effective voice for the speaker/writer, because the audience is not one likely to be persuaded by it, to see it as a site of authority. Author affects audience, audience affects author, and neither one is static.

Sometimes we might choose to resist the expected, or conventional, self-presentation as a kind of protest or out of a desire to "shock" the audience into some new way of seeing. Consider the valedictorian's speech at a commencement ceremony. The conventional persona, stance, and voice are serious, acknowledging the solemnity of the occasion, perhaps with some light moments injected here and there to keep the audience engaged. But a speaker might purposely adopt a resistant stance, speaking with a voice tinged by anger or sarcasm, perhaps, for a political reason, playing off the audience's conventional expectations to create heightened attention to the speaker's views. Such attention is the result of the speaker anticipating the audience's expectations and using that knowledge to help either adapt to or shift the context.

Talking about the concept of audience makes it seem as if "audience" refers to a unified group of listeners/readers—unfortunately, not a correct impression. "Audience" is a catch-all phrase for listeners/readers of a potentially endless number and infinite variety, in attitudes, beliefs, and biases. And because most academic discourse is in written form, the audience is also absent when we compose. That's one reason we have conventions, patterns of familiar, accepted writing practices, such as forms, or genres (discussed in detail in Chapter 3). The essay is a conventional genre in academic discourse; readers expect it to have an introduction, thesis, logical organization, evidence, and formal voice. Conventions, in other words, work through us and on us; we follow them and they constrain or frame our work accordingly. The lab report used in science courses is another conventional academic genre, as is the research paper. Observing the conventions of academic discourse (or working in some way that acknowledges them by resisting or upsetting them) is a way of establishing an audience *and* an authorial position.

When we say "establishing an audience," we're highlighting the active role the writer plays in creating a context, ideas about who his or her listeners are or who they are desired to be. As a writer, the rhetorical choices we make limit our audience, defining it by its likely areas of interest, the sort of evidence it is likely to expect, the voices it is likely to be open to, and so on. Consider the following excerpts from two different student essay exams in a political science course (the topic asked for specific reasons explaining the remoteness of a Marxist revolution in the United States). They invoke very different audiences, with consequently very different rhetorical effects.

> **Student A:** Marxism will never make it because it calls for the breakup of the family. Do you want the government telling you that you can't live with your parents?

> **Student B:** The deeply entrenched values of American family life would make the final stage of a Marxist revolution—the dissolution of the family unit—difficult to attain.

The authors' personas, stances, and voices reveal their concept of audience; we also see the audience created through sentence style and forms of evidence. Rereading the first response, we can argue that Student A

- invokes a popular audience through casual, conversational diction, informal voice, and an appeal to common family experience;
- positions herself or himself as an adolescent addressing other adolescents ("Do you want the government telling you that you can't live with your parents?").

Because this writing assignment required and presumed an academic context, the student's creation of an adolescent, informal audience seems faulty for the occasion, even if her or his ideas are valid.

Student B, on the other hand, invokes an academic audience, a response much in the same vein as Student A's, but positions herself or himself differently in relation to that audience: Student B uses

- specialized terminology relevant to the academic topic;
- a formal voice and stance;
- an appeal to authoritative textual evidence.

Note that the two students both focus on the topic and make essentially the same point, but because of their rhetorical differences, the responses are unlikely to be read as equally effective in a political science classroom. Student B seems to have a better grasp on both the theoretical nature of the issue and the social context of the conversation (student writing for an academic audience).

A writer's rhetorical choices at every level—subject, purpose, voice, genre—help create the intended audience. As you write, think specifically of the group of readers or listeners you intend to address and try to match your rhetorical choices to your sense of this intended audience's language conventions.

● The Writer's Task

Finding the Audience

In the following opening lines from student essays written for a composition class, what kind of audience do the authors invoke, and how do the authors position themselves in relation to the audience? Read each for the author's chosen persona, stance, voice/diction, evidence, reference, or other rhetorical feature that suggests a certain kind of reader. Are the approaches equally effective for their apparent purposes?

1. "'Civilized man has exchanged a portion of his possibilities of happiness for a portion of security' (Freud 3). Through a psychoanalytic reading of *Shane*, by Jack Schaefer, we can see that the conflict between desire and repression is the conflict between individual satisfaction and social membership, social acceptance.

Thus by our very nature we can never be truly and completely happy—a human fact evident within the novel."

- What assumptions does this author make about you as a reader?
- What kind of evidence for the claim made does this author expect you to find credible?
- What is the rhetorical effect of opening the essay with a quotation from Freud?
- The author addresses the audience collectively—using the all-inclusive "we." What relationship does this use of the pronoun seek to create between author and audience?

2. "Prison sentences can last from days to years, but behind the bars one cannot track the hours spent in jail. A calendar, a clock, a season: these are measurements of time that are not visible in *The Shawshank Redemption*. Only upon a deeper study of the film do we see the semiotic use [the cultural meanings suggested by visual signs] of the absence of indicators of time."

- Do you accept the claim the author makes in the first line? What effect do you think this line has on an audience reading critically?
- How do you see the author attempting to engage you as a reader? How successfully has this author connected with the intended academic audience?
- What revisions might this author make to strengthen the connection with the apparently intended audience—by creating a shared context, for example?

3. "'If there's a will, there's a way'—one of my father's favorite quotes he would say every time I gave up on something. If one has the will to achieve a certain goal, then one can accomplish it, through hard work and determination. Similarly, in chapter two of *Lives on the Boundary* by Mike Rose, he agrees that hard work is needed, but also proposes that the intervention of an educated person is essential for a person to get out of the cycle—a social status cycle— that entraps one in poverty and failure."

- What evidence does this author offer to support his claim that hard work leads to success?
- How does this author create a confused sense of audience—who is addressed in the first two lines, who in the last?
- Analyze the author's stance and voice: how do they weaken and recede after the first line?
- How does the last line, which purports to encapsulate Rose's view on how one rises out of poverty, represent and position us as readers? Do we have an active role in the discussion?

4. Take these same rhetorical issues related to audience and apply them to the brief definition of *rhetoric* (part of "The Writer's Task" section on p. 9) to revise it for different audiences—for a student who is unfamiliar with the concept; as a quiz response (with an instructor as your likely audience); for an academic audience that understands rhetoric only as "empty words."

Purpose: Arguing to Persuade

> As a child I spent many weekends on my Aunt Minnie's farm in Bucks County, Pennsylvania. I have fond memories of family gatherings, tables laden with simple farm-fresh meals, milk still warm from the dairy up the road, and of course, playing on her big red tractor.

This passage appears on a menu for the Red Tractor Café. The authorial persona and stance in this passage are clearly presented: an adult looking back nostalgically on an idealized childhood. The voice is personal, the diction concrete. As readers, we're able to conjure up the scene sensually, seeing, tasting, feeling the homey setting. The rhetoric of the passage invokes a familiar American myth of the heartland, the farm, and the family, and we as the audience can perhaps be persuaded to share in the author's construction of a past that is not ours, to become nostalgic ourselves through memories that are not real, not part of our actual experience. Why might the author attempt to engage us in this rhetorical exercise?

The passage continues:

> I've named our little café in honor of that tractor and have tried to capture a bit of those simple and honest times gone by.

Appearing at the top of the menu's first page, this passage forms what in academic discourse we'd call the introduction. Its thesis—the main point the author wants us to accept—is implied: eat here if you'd like to be able to return to "simple and honest times," before personal conflicts, economic woes, social ills, or other sources of pain and unhappiness existed. The many categories of "comfort food" on the menu, including mom's pot roast, meat loaf, mac & cheese, and lemonade, serve as evidence that through the restaurant's offerings you can experience this happier time. The menu appeals to feelings it helps you construct, then attempts to persuade you to act—in this case, to spend your money at the restaurant.

Like the menu's author (as likely to be a marketing firm as a real person who grew up in Bucks County), we write and speak with rhetorical purpose: from an intention, to an audience, for a goal. The goal, or purpose, is to persuade the audience to accept an idea, perhaps to act on it; to adopt a way of thinking or a belief; to feel that they've been accurately informed; to share an experience. Being conscious of our rhetorical purpose is vital to our *agency*, our ability to influence others, realize our goals, be understood.

That means that purpose (or what in writing classroom convention ultimately becomes a *thesis*) most effectively develops in relation to a thoughtfully selected authorial persona and audience. The claims a writer or speaker can credibly make depend on contexts and available bases of knowledge. The effective writer selects from these in relation to the values he or she assumes the particular intended audience endorses. Purpose, in others words, or an argument intended to persuade, cannot be determined in a rhetorical vacuum, in some simplified "here's what I think" way, at least if the author or speaker truly intends to seek a hearing for his or her views. Writing with purpose is a product of negotiations: How do I present a view on a given topic in a way that makes it useful for the audience and likely to be seriously heard?

What we say or write, then, along with how we say or write it, is affected by the conventions and values of those we address. That doesn't mean we have to speak or write only those arguments that have guaranteed approval or agreement, but it does mean that if we want to be listened to, we figure out how to approach an audience in ways that lessen the likelihood of our argument being dismissed. Stating the obvious in an academic argument, for example, is unlikely to give a reader a sense of real purpose in an essay, as we see in the following line from a student essay:

> *The Tempest* can be read from a postcolonial perspective.

Of course it can. The question is, why should we read it from that perspective? If the menu's author took a similar approach, the menu introduction would be something like "This restaurant employs a 'down home' theme." There's not much left for the essay writer to do but repetitively illustrate an obvious claim or for the menu writer to list the dishes the kitchen can prepare. Neither line offers a real argument or appeal to an audience from a persuasive authorial persona. Neither claim requires a progression of logical steps, and so the organization of the text that follows either line is likely to be repetitive, too. Some crucial rhetorical elements are missing from both lines. The reader is given no purpose for reading further.

An argument that requires explanation and support, however, and that offers readers a useful way of seeing some shared issue or text, can give real purpose to an essay (or menu, or any other text). In the composition class in which students were working on reading Shakespeare's *Tempest* from a postcolonial perspective, one of the students came up with the following argument:

> Like the island itself, Miranda is a colonized body.

Now that's a claim in which the writer actually establishes a context for the reader—the writer has expressed a purpose, and that's to explain how to interpret a character in Shakespeare's play as a body taken control of and made into a commodity by a particular historical and material process. The argument serves a purpose: it suggests a way of understanding an important concept; it offers a new way to read a familiar character; it promises to take the reader through a logical interpretive process, moving from a claim into a complex study of its implications. The writer has provided a reason, a purpose, for writing, and also has supplied a specific context for addressing a particular audience, one the writer has defined through rhetorical choices, which, in turn, gives the audience a purpose for reading.

Purpose—and the choices about organization and evidence that purpose informs—clearly connects with author and audience, since all these rhetorical elements work together when a writer/speaker is composing a text for a given rhetorical situation. That brings us to the question of where the actual arguments we might make can come from, and that's the realm of *invention*. In the following chapters, we move from the general notion of purpose, as it's discussed here, to examine how writers establish their purposes for specific topics in specific contexts. We ask you to work from theoretical critical frames, and we model how to use critical frames as an invention device—as a way to think about addressing a topic. In classical rhetoric, invention is the process through which we discover or create ideas—the ideas that you can work with to construct a thesis. Critical frames help you define a topic, since particular frames produce particular kinds of questions. They then provide an interpretive method—the theory itself works according to a set of logical procedures. And they sometimes suggest genres, or organizational schemes, and styles of writing or speaking as well. These critical frames are embedded with rhetorical tools, and your knowledge of both prepares you to address academic subjects and larger social issues from effective rhetorical and critical grounds.

Reading for Author, Audience, and Purpose

Reading for the rhetorical choices an author makes is not necessarily a dry matter of identifying author, purpose, and audience; instead, it can be a kind of adventure in detection, in which we attempt to identify an author's techniques for leading us into believing her or his text. An author who can lead us to believe an argument is valid—even if we don't ultimately agree with it and want to rebut or qualify it—has *agency*, has been successfully persuasive. Why? Because we've entered the conversation the author has created for us and invited us into.

In the opening paragraph that follows from Peter Gay's preface to his biographical work *Freud: A Life for Our Time*, for instance, we can use the rhetorical principles we've covered to offer an explanation for Gay's motives in opening his story as he does; we can detect some likely rhetorical goals laid bare by their own rhetorical workings.

First, we know the genre, a biography, a work of nonfiction that tells a life story built on historical evidence. We can expect that Gay sees evidence as a crucial factor for his credibility, and so, not surprisingly, his preface emphasizes the difficulties and limitations that he faced.

> In April 1885, in a much-quoted letter, Sigmund Freud announced to his fiancée that he had "almost completed an undertaking which a number of people, still unborn but fated to misfortune, will feel severely." He was referring to

his biographers. "I have destroyed all my notes of the last fourteen years, as well as letters, scientific extracts, and manuscripts of my works. Among letters, only family letters have been spared." With all the stuff he had scribbled piling up about him, he felt like a Sphinx drowning in drifting sands until only his nostrils, he wrote, were sticking up above the heaps of papers. He was pitiless about those who would be writing his life. "Let the biographers labor and toil, we won't make it too easy for them." He already looked forward to seeing how wrong they would be about him. Researching and writing this book, I have often visualized this scene: Freud the Sphinx freeing himself from mountains of paper that would have helped the biographer immeasurably. In later years, Freud repeated this destructive gesture more than once, and in the spring of 1938, preparing to leave Austria for England, he threw away materials that an alert Anna Freud, abetted by Princess Marie Bonaparte, rescued from the wastebasket.

As the opening of his book, the paragraph sets up a stance for the author: Gay is someone who faced an enormous challenge, who is to be pitied (*pathos*, or an appeal to emotion), but who soldiered on in the face of a resistant subject, Freud himself, a formidable enemy. The challenge is emphasized, arguing that any shortcomings in the text clearly are Freud's fault, not the writer's. Any ethical issue arising from Freud's clear desire to resist biographical inquiry is made defensible by a reference to Freud's own daughter's efforts (aided by a professional and friend) to supply the biographer needed materials. That the letter is "much quoted" suggests that other writers saw, and, we may guess, failed to meet the challenge of writing Freud's life story. Freud's voice enters into the text in its first line, with the interesting effect of giving the text his authority even as he himself is saying he does not wish to help any biographer—thus suggesting that this author has "mastered" Freud, adding greatly to his credibility. He has, after all, been able to quote from Freud's personal letter to his fiancée—a guarantee to the trusting (he hopes) reader that this biographer has gained access to Freud's personal life. That "[Freud] looked forward to seeing how wrong [his biographers] would be about him" is another kind of challenge, this time to Freud and any reader who might doubt the author's power: Gay offers an 810-page, densely footnoted text, trumping (at least apparently) Freud's confidence in the biographer's failure. The whole process is repeated when, near the paragraph's end, Gay reports that Freud destroyed documentation again near the end of his life. Through the author's carefully crafted rhetorical opening, we start the text with the impression of an author who is fully in control. His purpose is clear: he will present an authoritative biography, a claim he himself makes, if indirectly, through his rhetorical choices.

Even in this brief excerpt, several textual features tell us about Gay's intended audience as well. First, an 810-page text on Freud by itself limits its readership: it is likely to appeal to an educated reader who already knows something of Freud and his theories—it's not presented as an introduction to Freud's thought. So its subject and purpose help define its audience. Gay's language also limits the likely readership; his conversational style mixes in references that again suggest an educated reader, as can be seen in his phrase *a Sphinx drowning in drifting sands*. Gay expects readers to know what the Sphinx is and to pick up its connection to Oedipus, and then see it in relation to Freud's theory of the Oedipus complex. He sets himself up as someone who, like the mythic Greek character Oedipus, must solve the riddle of the menacing Sphinx, which Gay equates with Freud.

All of this is very sophisticated, effective rhetorical play. By developing skill in this kind of rhetorical analysis, you become better able to apply it to your own writing; when you're better able to understand what others are doing, you can avail yourself of similar strategies. This is what we mean by gaining rhetorical control, effectiveness, and sophistication—entering a variety of conversations as a valid voice.

● The Writer's Task

What Does Effective Persuasive Prose Look Like?

As carefully composed published work, the following excerpts from the opening paragraphs of essays and books embody conscious rhetorical choices on the authors' part. Read each and consider the subject, purpose, voice, stance, genre, and invoked audience. Below are some questions you might ask yourself as you go through each passage. You can develop others as you begin to detect what the writer has attempted to achieve rhetorically.

- Where is the author?
    - What identity/identities (or personas) do we see the author adopt, and why might the author have made such choices?
    - Is he or she openly employing a particular stance, thus assuming a particular value system?
    - Is he or she presenting ideas as "objective"—as simply existing "facts" that need no acknowledgment?
    - What voice(s) does the author create, and where and how do we see the author create it/them?
    - What does the author gain by the particular choices he or she makes?
- How does the author attempt to create an audience, a community of readers?
    - How does the author attempt to situate himself or herself in relation to the community in order to create a credible persona?
    - Is the author attempting to restrict his or her audience to a special group?
    - How does the audience the author addresses restrict the author's rhetorical choices?

- What argument(s) and assumptions does the author seem to challenge or promote?
  - Does the author assume the audience shares his or her views from the start?
  - How does the author create a sense of justification or need for a real purpose, for his or her argument?
- What formal choices—analytical essay, academic argument, personal narrative, historical narrative, journalistic reporting, for example—do you see the author employing?
  - What rhetorical benefits for his or her purpose might the author have seen in the particular choice(s) made?
  - Would some other form/genre be equally (or more) effective?

1. "The other day I was thinking of writing an essay on being a cripple. I was thinking hard in one of the stalls of the women's room in my office building, as I was shoving my shirt into my jeans and tugging up my zipper. Preoccupied, I flushed, picked up my book bag, took my cane down from the hook, and unlatched the door. So many movements unbalanced me, and as I pulled the door open I fell over backwards, landing fully clothed on the toilet seat with my legs splayed in front of me: the old beetle-on-its-back routine. Saturday afternoon, the building deserted, I was free to laugh aloud as I wriggled back to my feet, my voice bouncing off the yellowish tiles from all directions. Had anyone been there with me, I'd have been still and faint and hot with chagrin. I decided that it was high time to write the essay."

   —Nancy Mairs, "On Being a Cripple" (from *Plaintext*, a collection of her personal essays)

   - Does Mairs establish authority to speak on the topic of "being a cripple"? If so, how?
   - How does she give us a sense of her purpose—why for her is it "high time to write the essay"? She tells us that she'd have reacted with intense embarrassment if this incident had happened publicly; how is now making it public part of her possible writing purpose? How does her purpose lead her to write a personal narrative instead of an academic argument, for example?
   - Does Mairs invoke an audience of able-bodied readers, or a more diverse one? Does her choice relate to her purpose?
   - As someone with multiple sclerosis, Mairs has experienced frequent falls, yet she chose this particular incident from many to open her essay. What rhetorical goals might account for the selection?

2. "Hypertext reconfigures the way we conceive of texts. The facilities of manipulation, individual navigation, and freedom from given, authoritative structures provide us with new practices of writing and reading. However, the conduct of traditional print-age reading and writing has always been subject to complications and opposition. A brief examination of the way Ludwig Wittgenstein encountered severe problems with his own print-conditioned reading and

writing practices has much to offer anyone interested in the relations between hypertext and theory."

—Gunnar Liestol, "Wittgenstein, Genette, and the Reader's Narrative in Hypertext" (from the edited collection *Hyper/Text/Theory*)

- What means does the author use to invoke a specialized audience?
- How does the invoked audience help establish the author's persona and authority?
- Where do we see him attempt to create a purpose for his topic?
- We can read this opening paragraph as a traditional academic argument with a "funnel" introduction (general category narrowed to a specific topic and a particular thesis sentence). What might be the intended rhetorical effect of using this traditional form to introduce the topic of hypertext theory? Can you suggest other options?

3. "At a faculty meeting once, I raised several issues: racism among my students, my difficulty in dealing with it by myself, and my need for the support of colleagues. I was told by a white professor that 'we' should be able to 'break the anxiety by just laughing about it.' Another nodded in agreement and added that 'the key is not to take this sort of thing too seriously.'"

—Patricia J. Williams, "Mirrors and Windows" (from her collected essays *The Alchemy of Race and Rights*)

- Williams opens her essay by recounting an experience of rhetorical failure: she was unable to get her colleagues to respond to her concerns in her terms. In your eyes, does the exchange she describes damage her credibility as an author?
- In the second line, what is the effect of identifying the professor as white? Why is the "we" in quotation marks? What rhetorical problem(s) is Williams addressing? What voice and stance is she creating for herself?
- How can you see this brief paragraph establishing a strong purpose for the rest of Williams's essay?

4. "This essay—a meditation on the state of our souls, particularly those of the young, and their education—is written from the perspective of a teacher. Such a perspective, although it has grave limitations and is accompanied by dangerous temptations, is a privileged one. The teacher, particularly the teacher dedicated to liberal education, must constantly try to look toward the goal of human completeness and back at the natures of his students here and now, ever seeking to understand the former and to assess the capacities of the latter to approach it. Attention to the young, knowing what their hungers are and what they can digest, is the essence of the craft. One must spy out and elicit those hungers. For there is no real education that does not respond to felt need; anything else acquired is trifling display. What each generation is can best be discovered in its relation to the permanent concerns of mankind. This in turn can best be discovered in each generation's tastes, amusements, and especially

angers (this is above all true in an age that prides itself on calm self-awareness). Particularly revealing are the various impostors whose business it is to appeal to the young. These culture peddlers have the strongest of motives for finding out the appetites of the young—so they are useful guides into the labyrinths of the spirit of the times."

—Allan Bloom, Preface to *The Closing of the American Mind*

- Where does the author establish his claims for authority on his topic? How great an authority does he claim?

- Why might the author have chosen not to speak in the first-person "I" voice? What would have been the rhetorical difficulties and drawbacks of doing so?

- You as a student are the object of Bloom's discourse, but you are not addressed directly. How does Bloom represent you, your needs and interests? What image of the student emerges from his rhetorical choices?

5. "Americans are witnessing a resurgence of interest in the classics. Garry Wills discussed this phenomenon in an article in the *New York Times Magazine* (February 16, 1997), calling attention to the ancient Greeks and Romans. We have seen the success of a television series on the deeds of the mythological Greek hero Hercules, and a miniseries version of Homer's *Odyssey*. The television program *Xena, Warrior Princess* features a heroine modeled on the ancient myth of the Amazons, like Wonder Woman before her. Disney has released an animated feature film on Hercules, and followed it with stage shows and spectacles at various Disneylands and -worlds. Best-sellers recount the myths and legends of classical antiquity. Self-help books point to the ancient gods and goddesses as timeless paradigms of human character. At the beginning of the twenty-first century, people continue to be fascinated by the remnants of the cultures of ancient Greece and Rome, two millennia distant in time."

—Page duBois (from *Trojan Horses: Saving the Classics from Conservatives*)

- What is duBois's stance toward the topic of contemporary cultural uses of classical figures? Is hers a condescending view of pop culture? What does she gain by not speaking from the persona of an academic authority here?

- How do the specific details duBois lists help establish both her claim and her connection to her audience? Can she successfully appeal to both an academic and a more general audience?

- Page duBois draws her examples from a catalog of genres: newspaper articles, television series, miniseries, television programs, animated feature films, stage shows and spectacles, best-sellers, self-help books. How does actually listing these different genres help her support her opening-line claim?

6. "It is curious, I think, that with all the current interest in 'Basic Writing,' little attention has been paid to the most basic question: What is it? What is 'basic writing,' that is, if the term is to refer to a phenomenon, an activity, something a writer does or has done, rather than to a course of instruction? We know that

across the country students take tests of one sort or another and are placed in courses that bear the title, 'Basic Writing.' But all we know is that there are students taking courses. We know little about their performance as writers, beyond the bald fact that they fail to do what other, conventionally successful, writers do. We don't, then, have an adequate description of the variety of writing we call 'basic.' "

—David Bartholomae, "The Study of Error"

- Where do we see Bartholomae establishing a purpose for his essay?

- How does the opening problem he identifies—the lack of a definition of "basic" writing—create a role for the author and a possible means of organizing his essay?

- Bartholomae writes for a specialized academic audience of composition instructors, especially those who teach basic writing. How does he establish a connection with this group? Employing a "lecturing" voice, a stance of an instructor teaching instructors, would likely alienate his audience; how does he avoid this effect?

- Does his handling of the speaker-audience relationship in this instance offer rhetorical insights to others who face a similar challenge of speaking as an expert among experts, a knowledgeable person seeking to change the views of other knowledgeable persons?

7. "Despite its very evident prosperity, much of America's black middle class is in excruciating pain. And that distress—although most of the country does not see it—illuminates a serious American problem: the problem of the broken covenant, of the pact ensuring that if you work hard, get a good education, and play by the rules, you will be allowed to advance and achieve to the limits of your ability.

   Again and again, as I spoke with people who had every accouterment of success, I heard the same plaintive declaration—always followed by various versions of an unchanging and urgently put question: I have done everything I was supposed to do. I have stayed out of trouble with the law, gone to the right schools, and worked myself nearly to death. *What more do they want?* Why in God's name won't they accept me as a full human being? Why am I pigeonholed in a 'black job'? Why am I constantly treated as if I were a drug addict, a thief, or a thug? Why am I still not allowed to aspire to the same things every white person in America takes as a birthright? Why, when I most want to be seen, am I suddenly rendered invisible?

   What exactly do such questions mean? Could their underlying premise conceivably be correct? Why, a full generation after the most celebrated civil rights battles were fought and won, are Americans still struggling with basic issues of racial fairness? This book attempts to provide some possible answers. And in exploring why so many of those who have invested most deeply in the American dream are consumed with anger and pain, I hope to show how certain widespread and amiable assumptions held by whites—specifically about the black middle class but also about race relations in general—are utterly at odds with the reality many Americans confront daily."

—Ellis Cose (from *The Rage of a Privileged Class*)

- Cose uses the technique of posing rhetorical questions. What rhetorical benefits do you see him achieving from their repeated use?
- Whom does Cose seem to be addressing, a broad range of Americans or a middle-class African American readership?
- Cose uses a direct purpose statement—the final line of this excerpt. How does the line help generate a plan for organizing his text?

topics for writing

1. Compose an e-mail message to one or more of the following, and consider the persona, voice, and stance you'll use for each particular audience:
   - an instructor, asking for a conference, an advising appointment, or a meeting for some other purpose
   - a classmate, asking to copy notes from a class you missed
   - a classmate, asking her to complete her unfinished part of a collaborative project
   - a supervisor, informing him that you'll need to take time off from work

2. At some point in your academic career, you're likely to apply for a scholarship, research program, internship, professional/graduate school admission, or professional position. Consider the hypothetical announcements below, choose one, and draft the opening paragraph of an application letter, taking into account the rhetorical issues of purpose, audience, authorial persona/voice/stance.
   - *Scholarship*: The Merit Fund announces the availability of scholarship support for outstanding undergraduates. Applicants must be full-time students with demonstrated academic potential. The awards will be based on academic merit, including GPA, courses taken, and special projects completed. University and community service will also be considered. Send letter of application to Terry Jones, Merit Fund, Orange, CA 92866.
   - *Student Mentor Program*: The Office of the Provost is seeking applicants for its Student Mentor Program. Student Mentors work with incoming freshmen to provide them academic support, guidance in selecting a major field of interest, and an introduction to campus life. Mentors must be responsible, successful students with a desire to help other students succeed. Other important criteria include community service, tutoring and/or research experience. Stipend: $2000 per term. The Student Mentor Program actively seeks students from diverse backgrounds. Send detailed letter of application to the Student Mentor Program, Office of the Provost, Wilkinson Hall.

- *Research Internship*: Research Laboratories has openings for student interns. Internships are available in the following areas: biological sciences, engineering, communications, and business management. Qualifications include academic and professional interest in the area applied for; good work record; and the ability to work independently with minimal supervision. Responsibilities include helping senior employees with research activities and report preparation. Women and ethnic minorities are encouraged to apply. The six-month internships begin in September. Send letter of application to Research Laboratories, 800 Tech Road, Orange, CA 92866.

The Rhetorical Uses
of Critical Frames

**This Chapter's
Rhetorical Concepts**

● Understanding a critical frame
● How critical frames shape
  meaning
● How critical frames support
  rhetorical credibility
● How to read for an author's
  rhetorical and critical choices

Now you have a grasp of the concepts of author, audience, and purpose. The writer develops each of these rhetorical elements for each specific writing occasion. By understanding how to work with these concepts, you've developed a *heuristic* for *invention*—in other words, a model for generating, developing, and presenting your ideas on a topic. Invention is the process through which you discover and form thoughts about an issue you plan to address, in writing or speech, considering how best to organize and support the view you want to persuade an audience to consider. Thinking about author, audience, and purpose therefore helps to set up a method of generating ideas about the whole social interaction that the essay or speech will become. This chapter, adding another dimension to this rhetorical model, explains the use of *critical frames*.

Frames, Lenses, Perspectives

What we mean by "critical frames" might best be defined through the use of another concept: American philosopher and rhetorician Kenneth Burke's concept of *terministic screens* (as you may remember, Part One opens with a passage from his work). Burke used this term to point out that our often unrecognized cultural values shape our perceptions. In *Language as Symbolic Action* (1966), Burke describes how he once visited a photographer's studio and saw several photographs taken with different lens filters. The subject of the photos was always the same, but the lenses used to take the shots were all different. Burke expressed his amazement that, when seen through different lenses, the objects themselves looked different. Different lenses brought out different qualities of the object, made different characteristics visible, had different focuses. Think of your own critical perspectives as those lenses, and your rhetorical skills as the means by which you describe what you see to others.

Perhaps a good way to think about this relationship of rhetoric and frame would be to remember when you first entered high school. In most towns, high schools "consolidate" students from any number of different middle schools or junior highs, and each of these could send students to high school with different experiences of what it meant to be "popular," or "successful," or even "competent." At the new high school, however, students have to adapt to patterns of behavior and thinking and working that are common to that school. Students bring their experiences from different places—they don't lose them—but they're expected to focus on new goals, new procedures, new patterns. To say that one had "school spirit" could mean something entirely different from middle school to high school, or from one high school to another—the behaviors or attitudes that exemplified school spirit for one locale are not necessarily those of another. We could say that contexts here (the schools) help determine student perspectives (how they think of themselves in relation to others). In many ways, that's what learning or growing means: gaining experience in operating from an array of contexts and value systems. We do the same kind of learning and growing intellectually, acquiring different ways of understanding and explaining the experiences we have.

These experiences can be communicated, but communication is always also mediated. That is to say, language is never purely neutral—all communicated experiences come to us framed in some way. Try thinking about the concept of pleasure, for instance. What does it mean? See if you can describe it without talking about anything that's pleasurable. Aren't you in some ways forced to describe something *being* pleasurable in order to get across much about the concept itself? When someone tells you about a particular pleasure, they don't inject you with a serum to give you the same feelings they had; you're not really living their experience—you're living the *telling* of the experience, in writing or in speech. We don't share the experience itself but a representation of it, through the words of another, filtered through our own senses of these words. We interpret, or frame, the concept. Pleasure—the idea of pleasure—can be both the greatest concept of good (if you're a hedonist) *and* it can just as forcefully be considered a basic state of sin (if you're a Calvinist). A hedonist pursues pleasure for its own sake—for the experience of "feeling" it—while a Calvinist avoids pleasure because the very idea of it smacks of self-absorption, a sin. *Pleasure*: one word, one concept? Not exactly. The concept of pleasure being discussed at any moment would depend greatly upon whether the conversationalists were hedonists or Calvinists (or any other kind of "-ists," for that matter). How pleasure got defined would depend on which "lens" a writer or speaker applied. That's how we're defining a critical frame.

The more we are able to see how a critical frame we're using shapes how we see the world, the more able we become to consider and reconsider, reshape or replace, the frames we adopt. Without some explicit analysis of our own or another speaker's/writer's frame or lens, we're less able to fully understand what we or others are saying and why we/they are saying it. All of us operate as thinking beings with many unexamined assumptions, and often we judge intellectually from unrecognized biases that, if we consciously look at them, we might choose to drop. But most of us don't have direct and continual awareness of all the influences that have helped mold our perspectives, and we have much less knowledge of the influences that have helped mold the viewpoints, attitudes, or stances of others. To complicate this potential communication dilemma even more, as rational and feeling beings we have more than one belief about even a single topic; we have many prejudices, goals, or fears, and all of them have some part to play in determining how we see the world around us. We all look through lenses or frames. In this sense, objectivity is a logical impossibility; we are all biased in some way. We can choose a particular stance, but we can't choose not to have one. We can move from one context to another, or provide an effective or confusing context, but we can never be/speak/ write out of context altogether.

Even someone supposedly "disinterested," such as a researcher, also has to be someone, has to stand somewhere, has belief systems, preferences, and intentions that stimulate and guide the research work and interpretation of data. When a scientist writes up findings so others might learn, those others are not present in the laboratory, making decisions, drawing conclusions. The readers are presented with the scientist's "telling" about the experiment. And in these "telling" moments, the scientist—like everyone else—is motivated by many factors, is biased in particular ways, chooses one method or experimental design over others. We have come to see "bias" as a negative term rather than acknowledging that it's just how individual consciousness is expressed—some "one" is doing the telling, some "one" is writing or speaking, and that person is already positioned in the world. In fact, the very question of who we are includes questions of our gender, race, ethnicity, political views, education, social experience, and so on. Our identities are therefore neither absolute nor limitless. As writers and speakers, we can choose, however, to highlight particular contexts, personas, stances, and voices for the particular writing or speaking occasion. Making these choices of perspective entails a process of critical framing; we select from a wide range of possibilities particular ways of representing our selves and our subjects. Consciously or not, we necessarily see the world through the different frames we have at our disposal.

● The Writer's Task

Using Frames to Shape Meaning

1. The concepts and objects below are followed by various frames that shift how we see each one. Try adding other frames or "lenses" that produce a new view of each.

    • Pain
        • physician
        • economist
        • coach

- Family
  - court system
  - first-grader
  - college student
- Pride
  - parent
  - community activist
  - Christian
- Cell phone
  - engineer
  - marketing manager
  - theater manager

2. By framing a topic, you are selecting certain issues and elements to high-light, and certain values to apply. To see how consciously applying a frame can help you "invent," or identify, your topic and your rhetorical position in relation to it, try writing about an event or experience from two different frames.

   - Describe a concert or film you recently attended, using two different experiential frames. For example, describe a concert from the frame of a sense experience first (the space, sound, visual, experience, and so on) and then as an emotional experience (the sense of engagement, enjoyment, community you did or did not feel).

   - Describe a job you've had or a trip you've taken, first from an educational perspective, and then again from an economic perspective.

Rhetorical Uses of Critical Frames

Academic disciplines, whether classified as humanities, social sciences, or natural sciences, use varied critical frames to study or model the world and human experience. The framing systems employed in humanities and social sciences can seem less "real" than empirical (observation-based) study, because they are not based on sense data and do not make claims of a one-to-one correspondence with the natural world, and results are not typically tested by duplication, as in scientific studies. But such methods nonetheless provide specific organizing schemes for understanding and representing the self and the world, and the self *in relation to* the world.

The same can be said of any writing process: its implicit values are expressed in rhetorical form by the authorial choices made about structure, style, and voice; writers make choices among many competing and possible ways of communicating, depending upon where the writing is coming from, whom it's addressing, and what its task is. A given frame may stress one set of attitudes at the expense of others, determining what a valid subject is, what questions will be asked about it, how claims about it will be reasoned and supported, and in what form the overall argument will be presented. Scientific method, for example, first determines what kinds of phenomena you can study, and your resulting hypothesis, materials, procedure, and report of findings all signal to the audience that you have followed this recognized empirical, or scientific, method, which in turn gives authority to your work. Your results gain credibility because of your rhetorical stance as a scientist, which is demonstrated when you use the genre of lab report with all its associated rhetorical values of "neutral" knowledge and "objective" approaches.

Critical frames perform similarly useful rhetorical service. When we identify our work with a particular critical perspective, we are providing an orientation that signals others to see our points through this same particular frame or lens. The lens favors certain kinds of issues and problems; it's designed, in a sense, as a tool for investigating parts of experience, and certain of these tools are more useful than others for a given task. If we want to examine some particular problem related to social inequality, for example, we might go to gender theory, postcolonial theory, or other cultural theory that has power relations as a central frame. We'd be consciously using a special "camera lens" as a way of thinking about the topic.

The frame itself provides a good deal of context, and so it helps establish a strong authorial stance. Think about how hard it would be to describe different shades of blue to a sightless person, or, conversely, as a sightless person to convey to the sighted how perception works; think about trying to explain the great taste of a hamburger to a vegetarian. In these examples, you can see that where the author is "coming from," and where the audience is "coming from" will have a great impact on one's ability to communicate effectively. In many academic arguments, writers situate themselves critically in order to provide their audience with a context of shared knowledge "coming from" acknowledged and understood perspectives. Invoking a particular critical frame provides both you as author and your reader with a set of contextualizing values, issues, and concepts.

Invoking a critical frame also invites an audience to critically examine why you've chosen that frame along with how you support your claim—to consider, agree with, or resist the precepts and values associated with the frame. A writer's perspective, stance, or lens makes a claim about how the world works, in a sense, and so readers are being asked to accept the frame as a valid way of seeing reality, and most informed, critically sophisticated readers will consider your argument from the critical ground up, possibly reinterpreting your claims along the way. If, for example, we analyze a legend or fairy tale from a psychoanalytic perspective (a task you'll be asked to do in Chapter 5), we're asking our audience to accept, if only provisionally and temporarily, a set of theoretical concepts formulated by Sigmund Freud. We've provided the audience with the means to examine our interpretation for themselves using the critical frame of psychoanalytic principles.

At the same time, critical frames can help strengthen an author's credibility. Critical frames such as psychoanalytic theory, materialist critique, postcolonialism, and semiotics (all of them frames introduced in the following chapters) are built on recognized texts that are taken as authoritative. They also have a recognized analytical or interpretive method—steps in a process for examining and coming to some understanding and statement about a chosen topic. Thus when an author invokes a frame and its methods, they help establish authorial credibility. We've argued that the purpose of becoming rhetorically aware and skillful is to persuade an audience, and what works as persuasion changes as our rhetorical situations change. The kind of stance, voice, and invoked audience we use to attain our goal of being persuasive about a chosen topic depends on *context*, and critical frames provide that context.

Critical frames help an author determine which *means of persuasion* is most appropriate—meaning most likely to be effective in persuading an audience to see the author as credible and therefore the claim he or she makes as worthy of consideration. Ancient rhetoricians developed a theory about the means of persuasion: What kinds of appeals are likely to be effective in various writing/speaking situations? The classical rhetorician Aristotle defined three categories of "artistic" appeals as means of persuasion: *ethos, logos,* and *pathos.* Ethos connects with the speaker's character or authority in a given speaking or writing situation; logos refers to a "selfless" reason, an "objective" logical reasoning process; and pathos involves arousing an emotional response in an audience or appealing to the "common sense" of shared values. If we look at the Red Tractor Café menu example in Chapter 1, page 14, we can see that the author's primary means of persuasion is pathos, though ethos is important, too, since we're expected to accept the authorial persona as a sincere authority on idyllic farm life. Reason, however, certainly doesn't enter in, and an appeal to reason would in fact seriously undermine the author's claim. An author who decides to employ a Marxist critical frame for discussing a given subject, for example, should recognize that pathos is a problematic form of appeal: Marx argued that individual consciousness is the product of material conditions, not some authentic "self." Therefore, what we feel, what we experience as truth, is the result of larger social and economic forces that have shaped us, and so personal experience often produces "false consciousness." For a Marxist, truth doesn't reside in individual feeling—and so pathos is probably going to be a suspect, ineffective form of appeal in an argument framed this way.

Emotional appeals are frequently seen as suspect in argument, as unfair attempts to sway rational decisions by strong feeling, a technique that is common in marketing materials (and, in visual form, was the basis of prosecutor objections in the O. J. Simpson murder trial when housekeepers set out fresh flowers and lit fires in all the fireplaces in preparation for the jury's visit to the Simpson home). But pathos is also employed in academic persuasion, though rarely as the primary means. Academic arguments traditionally tend to favor ethos and logos, leading to the construction of a reliable speaker/author who uses a recognized method of reasoning. This makes sense because academic discourse has traditionally been shaped by rules of scientific inquiry. Pathos or logos or ethos by itself may not be sufficiently persuasive, and so part of the author's job is to consider the likely effect and effectiveness of each persuasive means for each particular writing/speaking occasion.

A critical frame helps a writer determine which means of persuasion are appropriate in a given writing situation, which in turn helps the author figure out what kinds of evidence will be persuasive. The same is true for the critical reader: analyzing the critical frame and means of persuasion an author is using can lead the reader to critically consider the evidence used as well. Critical frames are very effective in getting us as authors and readers to question appeals based in "objective" forms of evidence—forms of evidence that we have likely been conditioned to accept uncritically, such as facts, statistics, quotations from experts, textbooks, Web sites. What do we have to accept to see a "fact" as simply true, existing in the world in isolation from values, influences, interests? Think of some beliefs that have operated as "facts" in the past: women are more emotional and therefore less intellectually able than men; blacks are inferior to whites; the earth is flat; you'll get sick if you go outside in the cold with wet hair, and so on. Contextualizing each of these "facts" is a set of values and interests. Much of contemporary critical and rhetorical analysis is about "interrogating," or subjecting to questioning, such constructs and the reasoning and values behind them.

You'll find that it's not that difficult to develop a set of basic critical questions from a set of the different critical frames we'll cover. Our major goal is to develop these ideas as part of every writer's *rhetorical* ability.

● The Writer's Task

Reading for Persuasive Strategies

1. The following paragraphs form the opening of James Gee's introduction to his book *What Video Games Have to Teach Us about Learning and Literacy.*

   I want to talk about video games—yes, even violent video games—and say some positive things about them. By "video games" I mean both games played on game platforms (such as the Sony PlayStation 2, the Nintendo GameCube, or Microsoft's Xbox) and games played on computers. So as not to keep saying "video and computer games" all the time, I will just say "video games." I am mainly concerned with the sorts of video games in which the player takes on the role of a fantasy character moving through an elaborate world, solving various problems (violently or not), or in which the player builds and maintains some complex entity, like an army, a city, or even a whole civilization. There are, of course, lots of other types of video games.

But, first, I need to say something about my previous work and how and why I arrived here to discuss video games. In two earlier books, *Social Linguistics and Literacies* and *The Social Mind*, I argued that two things that, at first sight, look to be "mental" achievements, named literacy and thinking, are, in reality, also and primarily social achievements. (See the Bibliographic Note at the end of this chapter for references to the literature relevant to this chapter.) When you read, you are always reading something in some way. You are never just reading "in general" but not reading anything in particular. For example, you can read the Bible as history or literature or as a self-help guide or in many other ways. So, too, with any other text, whether legal tract, comic book, essay, or novel. Different people can interpret each type of text differently.

- How does Gee signal that he's trying to counter likely reader resistance to his opening statement, an apparent defense of violent video games?

- What rhetorical purpose(s) can you see in his choice to outline his theory of reading? What is his theory of reading?

- How broad an audience do you see Gee addressing? Is he writing for academics? Why do you think he refers to "self-help guides"?

- In how many ways does he spotlight his authority to readers?

2. *Women Who Run with the Wolves* is a hybrid text—a text that mixes essay, myth, storytelling, different voices—to capture the "Wild Woman," as author Clarissa Pinkola Estes refers to the "instinctual nature of women." In the passage below, she describes a "leg trap," a way in which women lose their psychic freedom through cultural pressure.

The Gilded Carriage, the Devalued Life

In archetypal symbolism, the carriage is a literal image, a conveyance that carries something from one place to another. In modern dream material and contemporary folklore it has been mostly supplanted by the automobile, which has the same archetypal "feel" to it. Classically, this sort of "carrying" conveyance is understood as the central mood of the psyche that transports us from one place in the psyche to another, from one idea to another.

Climbing into the old woman's gilded carriage here is very similar to entering the gilded cage; it supposedly offers something more comfortable, less stressful, but in effect it captures instead. It entraps in a way that is not immediately perceivable, since gilt tends to be so dazzling at first. So imagine we are going down the road of our own lives, in our handmade shoes, and a mood comes over us, something like this: "Maybe something else would be better, something that isn't so difficult, something that takes less time, energy, and striving."

It often happens in women's lives. We are in the midst of an endeavor, and feeling anywhere from bad to good about it. We are just making up our lives as we go along and doing the best we can. But soon something washes over us, something that says, This is pretty hard. But look at that beautiful something-or-other over there. That gussied-up thing looks easier, finer, more compelling. All of a sudden the gilded carriage rolls up, the door opens, the little stairs drop down, and we step in. We have been seduced. This temptation occurs on a regular and sometimes daily basis. Sometimes it's hard to say no.

So we marry the wrong person because it makes our economic lives easier. We give up on the new piece we're working on and go back to using the easier but old tired-out one we've been pushing around the floor for the last ten years. We don't take that good poem into the finer-than-fine range but leave it in its third draft instead of raking through it one more time.

The gilded carriage scenario overwhelms the simple joy of red shoes. 5 While we could interpret this as a woman's quest for material goods and comforts, more often it expresses a simple psychological desire to not have to toil so at the basic matters of creative life. The desire to have it easier is not the trap; that is something the ego naturally desires. Ah, but the price. The price is the trap. The trap is sprung when the child goes to live with the rich old woman. There she must remain proper and silent . . . no overt yearning allowed, and more specifically, no fulfillment of that yearning. This is the beginning of soul famine for the creative spirit.

Classical Jungian psychology emphasizes that the loss of soul occurs particularly at midlife, somewhere at, or after, age thirty-five. But for women in modern culture, soul loss is a danger every single day, whether you are eighteen or eighty, married or not, regardless of your bloodline, education, or economics. Many "educated" people smile indulgently when they hear that "primitive" people have endless lists of experiences and events they feel can steal their souls away from them—from sighting a bear at the wrong time of year to entering a house that has not yet been blessed after a death occurred there.

Though much in modern culture is wondrous and life-giving, it also has more wrong-time bears and unblessed places of the dead in a square block than throughout a thousand miles of outback. The central psychic fact remains that our connection to meaning, passion, soulfullness, and the deep nature is something we have to keep watch over. There are many things that try to force, sweep, seduce away those handmade shoes, seeming simple, things like saying, "Later, I'll do that dance, planting, hugging, finding, planning, learning, peace-making, cleansing . . . later." Traps all.

- What authoritative critical frames do you see Estes invoking in her analysis of how women lose their "souls"? What rhetorical effect do these have, given her informal, pathos-laden voice?

- How do the many references to fairy tale and folk imagery function as a kind of evidence? In what sense can you say Estes is writing from an anthropological frame? Do these images alter your sense of her "bias"?

- Do logos and ethos play a role in establishing a credible voice in the passage?

3. Charles Clements is a physician. In his book *Witness to War: An American Doctor in El Salvador* (1984), he recounts his experience treating the rural people living within guerrilla territory during the long and bloody Salvadoran civil war in the 1980s. Clements's goal was humanitarian: he strove to remain politically neutral as he worked among the impoverished *campesino* (peasant) population.

We had little time left.   1

Copapayo and its peninsula jutting north into Lake Suchitlan were cut off. Escape was blocked by a government garrison visible to the northwest on the opposite shore. To the south, the elite Ramon Belloso Battalion was advancing steadily upon us, pushing our few defenders back toward the village.

The soldiers had been trucked thirty miles north from the capital, San Salvador, and then deployed to sweep the hills and ravines of "subversives." With little resistance, they had ground their way to a ridge overlooking the neck of the peninsula. Around five o'clock that afternoon, the battalion set up its 81s and began firing down upon us.

Whump! whump! whump! We listened as the mortar rounds left their canisters. For a moment we heard nothing as the shells sped to the top of their arc. Then they came whistling down and exploded with concussions that shook the earth and sent shattered adobe in every direction.

The young children of Copapayo—several of whom I'd delivered—   5
were my gravest concern. They were hysterical with fright. They screamed each time the mortar clusters began their descent. They clawed and tore at their mothers, desperate to escape the explosions.

There was no choice but to quiet them.

I crushed my store of tranquilizer tablets and mixed them with orange juice and brown sugar. Then, as each three-*whump!* salvo was over, I began zigzagging my way from trench to trench.

Sitting still in the trenches, the women were as impassive during the bombardment as stone figures from a Mayan relief. None of the mothers questioned what I was doing; they knew death too well. Each cooed, "*Dulce, dulce*" (candy, candy), as I dosed their terrorized infants according to my best guess of individual weight. By dark, there wasn't a conscious child under three years old in Copapayo.

Then the *guinda* (evacuation) began. A single-file column of three hundred Salvadoran *campesinos* and a few lightly armed rebel militiamen snaked its way up out of the trenches and wound along the peninsula toward the government lines. In the ribbons of moonlight that broke through the cloud cover, I could see the stooped *campesinos* carrying their few belongings and comatose infants up a narrow trail leading them straight through a mile-wide zone held by the government troops.

There were still the stretcher cases to see to, as well as the women who   10
were too old, too sick, or too many months pregnant to risk an all-night march past the Belloso Battalion. In the dark, they would leave by boat. My assistant was Miguel, seventy-five, by far the oldest man in Copapayo, a *campesino* gnarled

by arthritis. Miguel was no stranger to fright and flight; his memory stretched back to the great *matanza* (slaughter) of the 1930s when 30,000 Salvadoran Indians and peasants were killed by the government. He had endured at least a dozen nights such as this and had declared he would flee no more.

"I'm tired," he told me, "and the enemy doesn't care about toothless old men."

- How is Clements's status as a physician a means of claiming neutrality? How does he rely on ethos to displace political affiliation, in a sense? How does he expect you to feel when he reports administering tranquilizers to the infants?

- Does he expect you as a reader to assume neutrality? How does he try to evoke a sense of pathos in you, and what effect do the details he includes have?

- How does the author's word choice—*rebel militiamen* instead of *guerrillas*, for instance—create bias? How does his depiction of the *campesinos* differ from that of the soldiers, and what rhetorical effects does it have on you?

- Almost half of the Copapayo population would soon be massacred in a massive government attack on the village (today, the area is called "New Copapayo," and the surviving old Copapayo villagers have formed new communities, one of them called "El Sitio Cenicero"—the place of ashes). Does that historical information reframe your reading of the passage and/or alter your sense of the author?

Reading for Critical Frames and Rhetorical Choices

As a reader, awareness of a writer's/speaker's critical frame helps you critically examine his or her statements. You probably already have experience in evaluating sources when you engage in research. Usually, sources are divided into popular and academic; you may have used the *Readers' Guide* for the former and *Humanities* or *Social Science Index* for the latter (or, at most schools, you can learn about these through self-directed library introduction courses). Being alert to an article's or book's critical frame is part of this evaluation process, as a reader and researcher. If you know or can surmise the critical orientation an author uses in a given text, you can more effectively judge its usefulness for your own writing purpose. Detecting a text's critical orientation is an important rhetorical analytic skill.

The author of the following excerpt—again, the opening paragraph, our first sustained contact with the writer—clearly frames the work in a psychoanalytic perspective. We can see it in the author's subject, voice, invoked audience, and use of specialized terminology:

All our stories are about what happens to our wishes. About the world as we would like it to be, and the world as it happens to be, irrespective of our wishes and despite our hopes. Our needs thwarted by the needs of others, our romances always threatened by tragedy, our jokes ruined by the people who don't get them. The usual antagonisms of daydream and reality. Freud redescribed this old story, at first, as a conflict between what he called the pleasure principle and the reality principle, between the satisfaction we are wanting and whatever frustrates or tempers our desire. And then, rather differently, as a war between the life instinct and the death instinct, a mythic war between nurture, growth, and delight and whatever it is inside us that seeks to destroy our love of life.

—Adam Phillips, Introduction to *The Beast in the Nursery*

Phillips begins with the idea that the foundational motives in our lives are our wishes, our desires—a Freudian premise called "wish fulfillment." He then follows up with the idea of reality and conflict, again echoing a basic Freudian theory, that life is a conflict between desire and duty, the pleasure principle and the reality principle. He then names Freud and uses Freud's technical terms of the two principles; rhetorically, he has both invoked Freud's authority but also established his own voice (Freud is not directly named until the fifth sentence, and Freud's theory is described as itself a redescribing of "an old story"). Phillips continues using Freudian concepts with the reference to the life instinct and the death instinct. He has told the reader that he will speak from this perspective, that it is a valid context for his subject, and that he assumes the reader will accept it as such. He also subtly diminishes Freud, creating a need, a purpose, for his own text, which is an exploration of the concept of appetite. His frame gives him a subject, a way to think about it, and a way to make his argument persuasive.

In the subsequent excerpts from academic texts, the authors clearly establish their critical frames through their rhetorical choices: the frames affect each author's stance, voice, and context; audience; and purpose/means of persuasion. Because you may be unfamiliar with the critical frames used (all of them presented in later chapters of this textbook), we've identified them, but you can by now identify the rhetorical effects of the frame.

The following paragraph comes from literary theorist Raymond Williams's introduction to his book *Culture and Society 1780–1950* (1958). He writes from a materialist critical frame (presented in Part Three), which can be identified from several common rhetorical markers. First, examine the diction: Williams uses material references—connecting words and specific historical periods— reflecting the materialist foundational claim that material conditions create cultural and individual consciousness. In this passage, he argues that language works the same way: the meanings of words, especially "key" words, change as economic values and practices change; language is materially determined. That gives history an especially important role, and we see Williams open by grounding his ideas in a particular historical era.

In the last decades of the eighteenth century, and in the first half of the nineteenth century, a number of words, which are now of capital importance, came for the first time into common English use, or, where they had already been generally used in the language, acquired new and important meanings. There is in fact a general pattern of change in these words, and this can be used as a special kind of map by which it is possible to look again at those wider changes in life and thought to which the changes in language evidently refer.

Five words are the key points from which this map can be drawn. They are *industry, democracy, class, art* and *culture*. The importance of these words, in our modern structure of meanings, is obvious. The changes in their use, at this critical period, bear witness to a general change in our characteristic ways of thinking about our common life: about our social, political and economic institutions; about the purposes which these institutions are designed to embody; and about the relations to these institutions and purposes of our activities in learning, education and the arts.

This next excerpt opens Ronald Takaki's *A Different Mirror: A History of Multicultural America* (1993). Takaki's paragraphs employ a postcolonialist perspective: he depicts an ordinary experience that quickly reveals a sense of center and margin, a native and "other," in which a member of the dominant group assumes a kind of national ownership that ignores a history of usurpation, exploitation, and cultural, sometimes also physical, oppression. Language itself becomes the grounds for a power struggle; here, the ownership of English is at issue. Identity becomes a related problem: despite being born in the United States, Takaki is reconstructed as a "foreigner." Rhetorical issues thus become an important focus—the right to name, claim, represent are all shown as forms of power.

I had flown from San Francisco to Norfolk and was riding in a taxi to my hotel to attend a conference on multiculturalism. Hundreds of educators from across the country were meeting to discuss the need for greater cultural diversity in the curriculum. My driver and I chatted about the weather and the tourists. The sky was cloudy, and Virginia Beach was twenty minutes away. The rearview mirror reflected a white man in his forties. "How long have you been in this country?" he asked. "All my life," I replied, wincing. "I was born in the United States." With a strong southern drawl, he remarked, "I was wondering because your English is excellent!" Then, as I had many times before, I explained, "My grandfather came here from Japan in the 1880s. My family has been here, in America, for over a hundred years." He glanced at me in the mirror. Somehow I did not look "American" to him; my eyes and complexion looked foreign.

Suddenly, we both became uncomfortably conscious of a racial divide separating us. An awkward silence turned my gaze from the mirror to the passing landscape, the shore where the English and the Powhatan Indians first encountered each other. Our highway was on land that Sir Walter Raleigh had renamed "Virginia" in honor of Elizabeth I, the Virgin Queen. In the English cultural appropriation of America, the indigenous peoples themselves would become outsiders in their native land. Here, at the eastern edge of the continent, I mused, was the site of the beginning of multicultural America. Jamestown, the English settlement founded in 1607, was nearby; the first twenty Africans were brought here a year before the Pilgrims arrived at Plymouth Rock. Several hundred miles offshore was Bermuda, the "Bermoothes" where William Shakespeare's Prospero had landed and met the native Caliban in *The Tempest*. Earlier, another voyager had made an Atlantic crossing and unexpectedly bumped into some islands to the south. Thinking he had reached Asia, Christopher Columbus mistakenly identified one of the islands as "Cipango" (Japan). In the wake of the admiral, many peoples would come to America from different shores, not only from Europe but also from Africa and Asia. One of them would be my grandfather. My mental wandering across terrain and time ended abruptly as we arrived at my destination. I said good-bye to my driver and went into the hotel, carrying a vivid reminder of why I was attending this conference.

Sometimes an author identifies her or his critical frame explicitly in order to establish a shared context or set of definitions with readers, as we see in the following paragraph from *Queer Theory: An Introduction* (1997) by Annamarie Jagose:

Once the term "queer" was, at best, slang for homosexual, at worst, a term of homophobic abuse. In recent years "queer" has come to be used differently, sometimes as an umbrella term for a coalition of culturally marginal sexual self-identifications and at other times to describe a nascent theoretical model which has developed out of more traditional lesbian and gay studies. What is clear, even from this brief and partial account of its contemporary deployment, is that queer is very much a category in the process of formation. It is not simply that queer has yet to solidify and take on a more consistent profile, but rather that its definitional indeterminacy, its elasticity, is one of its constituent characteristics.

Jagose's purpose is to define the many meanings of *queer*, and that term appears in each of her sentences, reflecting her purpose. *Queer* is a term of resistance to the conventional, the norms; it's not a constant concept—its meaning is "elastic," to use her image. Because it indicates some resistant stance, a queer-oriented text is likely to call attention to its theoretical grounds; the goal is to gain recognition of queer views and values.

As you work through the following chapters, you'll gain familiarity with particular critical frames and will be able to perform analyses such as those above on your own. You'll also be able to draw on such frames to help make rhetorical decisions about author, audience, purpose, and evidence. In each section, you'll use the critical frame to inform your thinking—to invent topics and arguments—and to engage, critically, with the ideas of others.

topics for writing

The following projects ask you to work with the material presented in the first two chapters as a way to gain fluency with rhetorical and critical framing concepts. You might work collaboratively to generate ideas on the topics. Frame your response rhetorically: decide on an audience to address, a persona/stance and critical frame to adopt in relation to it and to your topic, and the kind of appeal that the audience is likely to find persuasive.

1. Gather some texts that are part of daily experience. These can be magazine ads (for health or beauty products, for example), product containers (such as cereal boxes, CD covers, sports drinks), college/university home pages, events fliers, donation requests, or other objects you think of. Analyze their rhetorical content: What is the purpose? How does the object invoke you as an audience— how does it attempt to define your interests and values, your identity? Who is speaking in the text, and how does the text construct an authorial voice/identity? What means of persuasion are employed?

   Is any one of the texts offensive to you in some way? If so, what about it turns you off? What works—what appeals to you? Could it be altered to make it more effective for you and, if so, what does that tell you about your own rhetorical expectations?

2. Think of a product whose promotion is frequently disputed. For example, many people would like to see further restrictions placed on ads for tobacco products; people argue for and against ads that promote condom use. Develop an argument in advertisement form *for* the product/practice. Then develop another one that is *against* this product/practice.

   • How do the "for" and "against" arguments work? How do they differ in the appeal made to the audience, in the authorial voices created, and other rhetorical features?

   • What is your ethical role in composing these opposite appeals? If you have strong positive or negative feelings, have these influenced your work? Are there arguments you're unwilling to develop?

3. Kenneth Burke's image of the changing lens is one way to understand a critical frame. Use his image to chart the shifting meaning of an object, location, or practice. We've suggested some "lenses" that are likely to be familiar to you; apply those critical frames that you already know from your other classes and readings as well. How does what constitutes the important elements change?

   • Las Vegas
     • an economic lens (such as a marketing or urban development perspective)
     • a feminist lens (consider labor issues, nature of entertainment)
     • a fundamentalist Christian perspective

- The Greek system
  - a feminist lens
  - a labor or union perspective
  - a civic group/philanthropic perspective
- Psychics
  - a scientific lens
  - a psychoanalytic/psychological lens
  - an entertainment executive's perspective
- A film, object, or social event of your choice
  - a skinhead lens
  - a management perspective
  - a multicultural lens

4. Choose a figure from personal or public life (a friend, for example, or a celebrity) and compose a profile of this person from a critical lens of your choice. Your audience is an academic one—your classmates and instructor—and your purpose is to help your readers see this person from your chosen frame and to accept your assessment of him or her as credible.

The Rhetorical Uses
of Conventions

"I don't know what the teacher wants."

This statement of student frustration with a writing assignment is often equally frustrating for instructors, since both likely want the same thing—a good paper. But a student's and instructor's assumptions about what good writing looks like may not be shared, and, more confusing, the assumptions one instructor makes may differ from those of another. It's not surprising, then, that students come to regard "good" writing as a set of individual standards and preferences established arbitrarily by each instructor they encounter, and therefore they see their job as guessing "what the teacher wants." There is a better way, and that's why this chapter is devoted to

- the *conventions* of academic writing (the traditional and expected elements of a given piece of academic writing) in relation to academic *genres* (the "given pieces"—a lab report, research essay, summary, proposal, journal entry, and so on);
- *rhetorical* approaches to both; and
- a brief history of *rhetorical theories* that helps explain where writing conventions come from and how they (slowly) change over time.

Conventions are not fixed forms, or at least they become less fixed as you develop as a writer and write more complex papers in college courses. The thesis formula you may have found useful in high school writing (or the whole genre formula of a five-paragraph essay) is too basic to enable you to write effectively at a more advanced level. What develops as you progress as a writer is the rhetorical approach you take to conventions and genres. You still use the conventions of academic writing, but you need to do so with increased attention to purpose, audience, and all the rhetorical issues discussed in the prior chapters.

As you make decisions about how to approach writing tasks in your different classes, you can use your knowledge of rhetorical theory and history to help figure out the instructors' expectations and at least some of the assumptions implicit in those expectations. Most instructors, especially those outside the English department, will not articulate the theory of composing they operate with, largely because the traditional view is that writing is a *transparent* activity—a seamless transfer of ideas to written form or a mechanical matter of imitating models. Knowing that there is more than one set of assumptions about how to write can help you understand better "what the teacher wants" in the writing you do in your courses.

A Rhetorical Approach to Writing Conventions

It's very likely that many of you reading this book were trained as New Critics and current-traditional writers, whether these terms are familiar to you or not. If you've read a work of literature for theme, plot, and character, or symbol, metaphor, and poetic form, you've used a New Critical frame. And it's also likely that you've brought into your college courses a sense of the traditional academic essay and writing process. These are valid frames (although some instructors might find that an arguable claim), and certainly still common ones. What's important is to *see* them as frames, as *choices* you can make for how to read and write in given situations. Instead of seeing the five-paragraph theme as "the" form of academic writing, you can identify it as one among many others. Your knowledge of rhetorical theory will help you do that, and help you decide when other frames and choices might be more appropriate and effective. Appropriateness and effectiveness are two useful rhetorical values to use as you approach writing in any situation.

We can begin a rhetorical approach to conventions by first considering the characteristics of a "good" essay from a traditional composing model.

- It has a linear structure beginning with a thesis, which is typically in a one-sentence format at the end of an introductory paragraph.
- It has an "objective" voice throughout.
- It uses rhetorical modes such as comparison/contrast, classification and division, and definition as forms of arrangement, or organization.
- Its paragraphs begin with topic sentences directly tied to (or actually repeating part of) the thesis statement.
- It starts with a general introduction and ends with a concluding paragraph restating the thesis.
- It includes a concrete example and/or quotation from an expert as evidence in each body paragraph.
- It is correct in grammar, mechanics, and spelling.

Most writers use some of these conventions because most readers depend on familiar elements as part of their meaning-making. But accomplished writers choose to present them, adapt them, change them, or ignore them according to their purpose, their audience, and/or their authorial voice, persona, and stance. And such writers also approach writing not as a list of separate elements—as in the above list—that get pasted together to form a final product. Instead, they work with writing as first and always a social situation, adopting a *rhetorical* approach. You can be more effective rhetorically if you start with your identity, your purpose, and your audience as a whole writing environment rather than struggling to fill in sections of a predetermined form.

What happens if we revise the conventional traits of academic writing from a rhetorical perspective, incorporating consideration of author, audience, and purpose?

To begin to answer this question, imagine how you would approach the following assignment:

> Have a conversation about the electoral college system. Address its historical origins, effect on the election process, and major arguments for changes to it, and formulate your own position. Include evidence supporting your point of view.

How would you start a conversation? By drafting a thesis? Outlining major points? Finding quotations from experts on the electoral college system? While these conventional approaches may be useful at some point in the whole process of completing an assignment, they ignore the primary concern of *context*, of an implied and necessarily social environment. Thinking about your written assignments as types of conversations can help you see the rhetorical issues. Assignment prompts are often very topic-focused, omitting reference to the audience appropriate to the topic. In the case of the above assignment, you have to do the rhetorical thinking to address the social context of the paper/conversation. You have to have a conversation *with* someone, which means you have to have some idea of

- who would want to engage in a conversation on this topic, and why it might matter to them;
- what degree of familiarity with the topic you can assume they have, and what background information they would need;
- how you would address this audience, or what voice(s) and role(s) you can adopt in this situation, and in what tone(s);
- what you know about the electoral college system, and what research you would need to do to be seen as an informed speaker by the chosen audience;

- how you can best frame your views so that they are perceived as accessible and credible;
- what some likely questions and counterarguments might be from your audience; and
- what "shape" the conversation might take, including forms you think would not be appropriate.

The traditional approach to writing as a set model or predetermined structure favors *form* over *rhetorical situation*. To get at the rhetorical nature of the different types of academic papers you write, we can rename "form" as "genre." The term *genre* refers to a common writing situation, one that is familiar to readers in general or specifically to readers in a specialized field (editorials in a newspaper, for instance, or the literature review in a research paper, or a business memo).

A writer chooses a specific genre because it's appropriate to her or his purpose and to the social environment the readers have in common. You wouldn't communicate with a friend by writing a lab report, for instance; your friend wouldn't recognize that piece of writing as a personal note or its contents as having to do with friendship, personal news, shared feelings, invitations to entertainment, or other social connections typical for and appropriate between friends. And the genre of the lab report wouldn't let you write about such topics, anyway.

What that last point suggests is that genres not only "cue" readers about what to expect, they help direct writers in the writing process, too, from invention of ideas through revision of their presentation. The genre of the summary, for example, helps the writer focus, excluding some issues (biographical details about the author of the piece to be summarized, possible critical responses to the argument, and so on), suggesting appropriate style and voice (probably a more simple sentence style, probably not a personal voice), limiting relative length (in a brief analytic essay of five pages, for instance, a two-page summary would distort the purpose of the writer's primary genre, the analysis).

"Genres" are connected, in other words, not just to forms of writing but to the purposes of writers and to the values and knowledge set of groups of readers. This knowledge set can be broad or very specialized (or somewhere in between). A book review for two different audiences may follow fairly similar form—a summary of the book's central argument and topics, a critique comparing these to other major books in the area, the reviewer's impression of the text and recommendation to readers. But rhetorically, purpose, reader, and author are still the concerns that the writer has to consider, and imitating or filling in set sections won't help you write a rhetorically effective review. The review you write will have to take into consideration what you're trying to accomplish, what you know about your readership, and what your relationship to this readership is.

● The Writer's Task

Writing as a Social Situation

1. Provide the questions you think the writer should ask to treat each of the following assignments as a rhetorical situation:

   - Graphic novels have become a major new media form. Discuss reasons for their appeal.

   - Does Arendt's term *the banality of evil* apply to contemporary terrorist groups?

   - Describe your memory of a favorite childhood space. Explain its emotional effects in relation to its physical characteristics; whether its appeal depended on external factors such as time, company, prior events; how you discovered it; and when and why its appeal faded (if it did).

   - Explain the strengths you would bring to the MBA program and how the program fits into your professional aspirations.

2. In the following excerpts from readings in this book, analyze the genre you're being "cued" to expect. What knowledge base does the writer assume you bring to it?

   - Karl Marx, *Critique of Political Economy*

     I was led by my studies to the conclusion that legal relations as well as forms of state could neither be understood by themselves, or explained by the so-called general progress of the human mind, but that they are rooted in the material conditions of life, which are summed up . . . under the name "civil society"; the anatomy of that civil society is to be sought in political economy. . . .

   - Victor Villanueva, "An American of Color"

     A party, a bloody knife hanging from a hanging arm, eye level, Mom and Dad by the hand, running. Maybe three years old. Brooklyn. The picture remains, forty years later.

   - A syllabus

     This course surveys and compares the immigration of Europeans, Asians, and Latin Americans to the United States since the late nineteenth century. To a large extent, this comparison focuses on European immigration of the period 1880–1920 in comparison with the Mexican, Central American, Middle Eastern, and Asian immigration since 1965, hoping thereby to command the major issues. However, the course also offers some comparative coverage of current immigration to Europe as well. The purpose of this course is to provide a factually grounded survey of immigration experience of ethno-racial groups that migrated voluntarily to this country with some comparison to contemporary immigration to Europe. The criterion of voluntary migration distinguishes whites, Asians, and Latin Americans from African Americans, whose "immigration" was involuntary. However, the course will pay some attention to the relationship of African Americans to various immigrant groups.

Genre, Thesis, Voice

In the excerpts above, we can see that the authors made decisions about genre, which in turn helped them decide how best to present their arguments—the thesis "form" they chose was really also about the genre choice the authors made. And in each thesis choice we also see the author's choice of voice(s).

- The **narrative** piece by Villanueva opens with an **implied argument**, his credibility strengthened by the specialized, concretely detailed experience reflected in it. Villanueva's book is a kind of **academic memoir**, and he re-calls a personal scene that he will then go on to analyze from critical per-spectives, creating a voice that is at once **academic** and **emotional**.

- Marx writes a **theoretical**, **academic argument** with a closely reasoned claim that social institutions arise from a material economic base—a genre that leads to a **traditional thesis** in an **"objective" voice**, even as he begins with "I."

- The syllabus is also an **academic argument** in that it provides a **rationale** for the course's scope in relation to its purpose, but the author approaches his audience differently—he knows that he's writing to students who have not yet studied the topic, leading to his inclusion of more background information than Marx needs to supply for his more specialized audience. The voice here is **impersonal**, not surprising for a genre that convention-ally presents knowledge as measurable and therefore easily graded, free of any personal bias on the instructor's part.

First genre, then thesis and voice. In most academic genres, readers expect the writer to lay out in explicit terms the argument being made. The thesis is the purpose of the paper: What do I want my readers to understand as my pur-pose for writing? Rhetorically, then, the thesis is defined less by choices of form and more by a writer's intended effect on the reader. The *rhetorical* convention is to explain your purpose, not to observe a specific form of presenting it.

A writer's rhetorical options for formally presenting a thesis are thus broad, as you can see in the following variations on an argument about the psychoana-lytic content of the fairy tale "Little Red Riding Hood" (on p. 115).

- A writer can choose the conventional form of claim and reason.

  In "Little Red Riding Hood," we see how young girls are taught that virginity is a cultural requirement: if they "leave the path" and disobey the cultural demand of purity, they will be "overtaken" and ultimately "eaten up" by violent desires.

- A writer can pose the thesis idea as a rhetorical question.

  What lessons are being taught to and about young girls in this tale? Why is "staying on the path" so important, and why should "leaving the path" to "pick flowers" be fatal?

- A writer can formulate the thesis as a hypothesis.

  According to Freud, young children must learn to repress aggressive and libidinal desires. Following this theory, we should see that "Little Red Riding Hood" teaches its juvenile listeners to banish such feelings into the unconscious.

- A writer can lead readers to the thesis idea in a concluding "results statement" at the essay's end.

  We have seen that Little Red Riding Hood is given a "basket of goodies" that she must deliver intact to help ease the suffering of her sick grandmother—and to fail would be to suffer great guilt and to deserve punishment. By giving in to the wolf's temptations, Red Riding Hood causes the destruction of her grandmother and herself, signifying that all of womanhood has been betrayed. We witness these consequences of the wolf's triumph. And as children we learn through the happy ending that we can avoid Red Riding Hood's fate by obeying the demand to reject the pleasure principle and repress libidinal desire. Through one simple fairy tale, all children learn a serious psychological lesson.

- A writer can imply the thesis through a series of opening quotations.

  "[I]t is impossible to overlook the extent to which civilization is built upon a renunciation of instinct."

  "The tension between the harsh super-ego and the ego that is subjected to it is called by us the sense of guilt; it expresses itself as a need for punishment."

  —Sigmund Freud, from *Civilization and Its Discontents*

  "Little Red Riding Hood said to herself that she would never more stray about in the wood alone, but would mind what her mother told her."

  —The Brothers Grimm, "Little Red Riding Hood"

The author is asserting or implying an argument in each case, and in each case readers are given a clear sense of what logical proposition the author is asking them to consider. The form changes in each, but the rhetorical purpose remains the same: "Here is my logical claim, which I want you, my readers, to see as credible." The writer decides on the best presentation according to what he or she thinks will work for readers.

Some other approaches to presenting a thesis include any of the following (and you can probably generate other approaches as well). The important rhetorical question for the writer to consider is which form(s) will likely work well in helping readers both understand the argument and be open to it as a credible claim.

- A writer can make an implied claim (which may take a narrative form, as in a creative nonfiction essay or a literary work).
- A writer can present a polemical (extreme) assertion (perhaps appropriate for an opinion or editorial essay).

- A writer can start with an equation (in a natural or social science research paper, for example).
- A writer can open the paper with an epigraph (a short saying or excerpt from a text that sets up a main topic; this chapter opens with an epigraph of sorts).
- A writer can develop the thesis through a dialogue (differing voices and perspectives that frame for readers the critical issues in an analytic argument; not just a "pro" and "con" approach but two or more views out of which the author might make some synthesizing point or establish the point of irresolvable difference).

If you're working within a specific genre, such as a research report, an application letter, or a project proposal, you still have rhetorical options for how to present your thesis. In a research report, the writer can pose the topic studied through a rhetorical question, inviting readers to consider it along with the researcher from the first step in the process through its conclusion. A proposal can begin with a concise quotation from a relevant expert that succinctly formulates the project, contextualizing for readers the writer's purpose statement, or thesis.

Remember that the first audience for the thesis is the writer—you, yourself. That's why revising is critical; you'll have a better sense of your own argument the more you work on your paper, so you should be refining it and rethinking its presentation as part of the whole writing process. It's appealing to think that we compose the thesis first and then just let the rest of the paper unfold from it, but writing is more recursive than that—we return to earlier ideas and sections to revise them in light of later ideas and rhetorical choices.

And so back to voice. The traditional "objective" voice is one of many possible rhetorical choices that a writer makes, once again guided by rhetorical purpose. Effective writers are able to write from a range of voices, personas, and stances (as discussed in Chapter 1). A rhetorical approach to voice, then, is another aspect of the writing situation, and the choices you make about voice are again a part of the genre.

In any specific writing situation, what are your options for authorial voice, persona, and stance? What questions can you ask to figure out your options? Think about your role in the situation.

- You can speak as an informed, knowledgeable commentator.
- You can adopt the persona of an inquirer, asking questions, discovering possibilities, making judgments.
- You can be an advocate for a particular view, and you can choose the degree of advocacy you think is appropriate and effective, from "reasonable" to polemical.

- You can adopt a range of social roles—student, citizen/community member, witness, content expert, professional, family member, critic, supporter, group representative, or any other role you can credibly occupy—all from an ethnic, gender, or other identity position, such as political affiliation.

- You can be close to the topic, speaking from experience or other personal connection; distanced from it, the observer adopting a clinical, analytical stance; or you can shift positions, speaking from "within" and moving to "outside."

You can shift voices, personas, and stances in most genres, though clearly you have to think carefully about which are most appropriate and effective in any specific writing situation.

● The Writer's Task

Working with Thesis and Voice Through Genre

The following writing situations provide a topic and genre. What are some of your options for the presentation of a thesis and the voice(s), persona(s), and stance(s) you can adopt?

1. Review the latest release from a major musical group for your campus newspaper.

2. Compose an e-mail message to a professor who is seeking a research assistant to ask for more information.

3. In letter form, report to the sponsoring group of your scholarship aid on the progress you've made thus far toward your degree.

4. Using a narrative-based essay, describe on a college application form two people who were major educational influences on you.

5. In your composition class, compose
   - a summary of Chapters 1 and 2
   - an essay discussing a proposal to end free access to the Internet.

Genre and Organization

Remember that genre cues reader expectations. The author develops the topic in relation to the genre, or writing situation, with the reader's expectations in mind. (This is the invention process, or genre as *heuristic*.) Organization—also called arrangement, logical order, or structure—is part of this whole dynamic of authorial purpose and reader expectations. Conventional outlines usually don't help you consider the arrangement of your ideas in relation to your audience. Outlining tends not to be rhetorical, especially if it leads you to adopt a plan not directly related to genre, purpose, or audience, such as "most to least important" schemes or other isolated organizational systems. Instead, try using the genre and thesis to help you consider how you might organize the paper so it guides your reader through the discussion of your argument. Your goal, after all, is that others see how you're thinking, and why.

In a biographical sketch, for example, the "best" organization is the one that lets the writer create an impact on the reader's perception and judgment. If you were to write about Michael Jackson, decisions about which biographical elements you would highlight and the order in which you'd present them would be affected by how you wanted the audience to see him. The genre of biographical sketch or profile cues readers to expect certain information: dates, place of origin, family background, education and career information, major accomplishments, problems or challenges, personality traits, historical importance, all in the context of relevance to context and purpose (why you're writing about this subject for the audience you're addressing). If you decided to write a biographical profile of Michael Jackson in a course on pop culture, with your audience an academic one, you'd have to think about what, within this genre, your purpose would be: perhaps to clarify the contributions this controversial figure has made to the fusion of music and visual art.

You have a sense of the genre's typical moves, and you can arrange these elements to enhance your argument. Deciding to work chronologically just because that's an available organizing pattern is not the most effective rhetorical choice. You should consider instead how you want readers to perceive the subject and argument. You might decide to start with a hyperlink clip (if your paper will be in electronic form) of stills from Jackson's influential music video "Thriller." That works to contextualize your subject as you want him seen and provides context on him for readers who may not be familiar with his 1980s video. You can establish your thesis and make choices about how to tell Jackson's biographical story in ways that help explain and support your argument, organizing and developing the expected biographical elements to enable readers to follow your reasoning and accept it as credible. That's a rhetorical approach to organization.

You can also use visual rhetorical elements to organize the paper and to help readers see the sections and their logical relationship. You can use headings and subheadings; boldfacing of key points; an opening abstract (a condensed summary of the whole); images that represent the section topic. Imagine how an approach like this might work for the Jackson biographical sketch. A conceptual outline of the paper using only headings and subheadings can illustrate the rhetorical choice to highlight Jackson's musical influence as the primary biographical view.

Michael Jackson, the Music (and Video) Man

- "Thriller" and the Rise of Music Videos

- Jackson's Visual Theory of Performance

- Early Media Experience: Jackson on the Small Screen

- Heritage: Musical Influences on the Jackson Five

- Michael Solo

- Post-"Thriller" Media Problems

- The Music Left Behind

What you can detect through the subheadings is an argument that Jackson should be known through his contributions to music history, with "Thriller" as the ultimate example. The author will explain the historical importance of the video in the first section; analyze how Jackson developed so powerful a blend of music and image in the second, tracing his musical origins in the third; how he differentiated himself in his solo career after that, with the commonly known personal quirks and legal problems covered but made secondary to the central argument; and a final section playing off the artistic possibilities not pursued and the one that he left as what we should consider his defining legacy. Jackson is profiled not in a simple chronological way but in a way that supports the author's view of him as an important media pioneer.

What you may notice in this conceptual outline is that there is no section heading named "Introduction" or "Conclusion." A writer could certainly use these headings, but they're likely to be rhetorically redundant. Readers expect the opening section of a document to do introductory, or contextual, work, and they expect the ending to bring some logical result, judgment, comment, or other final point; using the introduction/conclusion labels simply repeats formally what the writing is already doing rhetorically. The traditional approach to writing introductions, the "funnel" model, often ends up having a formulaic, nonrhetorical effect. In a "funnel" introduction, the writer starts with a broad statement and narrows it down to the actual thesis by the end of the opening paragraph. In the opening of the following essay, written by a first-year college student in a composition class, we see how irrelevant such an introduction can be. The assignment was to use philosopher Michel Foucault's concept of "truth regime" to analyze a historical event.

For thousands of years, some of the world's most accomplished intellectuals have wrestled with the definition of truth. Many approaches have been taken to examine this concept of truth, but no single description seems to be widely accepted; some see truth as the proving of a subject with factual evidence while others see it as an unattainable state of all-knowing; some believe in the concept of altruism, while others believe truth to be relative. Philosopher Michel Foucault supports the concept of relative truth. Foucault says, " 'Truth' is linked in a circular relation with systems of power which produce and sustain it, and to effects of power which it induces and which extend it. A 'regime' of truth" (74). Truth thus is connected to power, and what maintains a regime—a government, an elite group, a dominant religious organization—is what is true in that regime. Foucault's theory can help make sense of the phenomenon of genocide, which otherwise seems a completely irrational evil that is beyond our ability to comprehend, and to prevent. In the Rwandan genocide, common people were transformed into murderers. The leaders of the Hutu Power movement, supported by the government, were able to increase and maintain their power by making a majority of Hutus believe that their Tutsi friends and neighbors were evil "cockroaches" who had committed crimes against all Hutus. They succeeded in tying power and truth in Foucault's "circular relation." The genocide was evil, but it was not irrational or beyond our comprehension. That means it might be possible to prevent such evil truth regimes in the future.

This author has formulated an impressive and complex argument about the nature of genocide. The reader needs to understand a very dense concept drawn from the theoretical work of Michel Foucault, and to connect it to a historical atrocity that an academic audience is likely to know about. To revise the opening for the best rhetorical effect, then, the writer should delete the overly general, unhelpful, formulaic lines:

> For thousands of years, some of the world's most accomplished intellectuals have wrestled with the definition of truth. Many approaches have been taken to examine this concept of truth, but no single description seems to be widely accepted; some see truth as the proving of a subject with factual evidence while others see it as an unattainable state of all-knowing; some believe in the concept of altruism, while others believe truth to be relative. Philosopher Michel Foucault supports the concept of relative truth. Foucault says, " 'Truth' is linked in a circular relation. . . ."

The writer can then reorganize the opening according to the specific audience, which means starting with the familiar historical event, then introducing Foucault's concept as a critical lens, and naming the result:

> For one hundred days in the spring of 1994, the African nation of Rwanda was the site of a horrific genocidal massacre. This kind of mass killing seems a completely irrational evil that is beyond our ability to comprehend, and to prevent. But we can both understand and perhaps prevent other genocides through

philosopher Michel Foucault's concept of "truth regimes." Truth, Foucault argues, is connected to power, and what maintains a regime—a government, an elite group, a dominant religious organization—becomes what is true in that regime: "'Truth' is linked in a circular relation with systems of power which produce and sustain it, and to effects of power which it induces and which extend it. A 'regime' of truth" (74). In the Rwandan genocide, the leaders of the Hutu Power movement, supported by the government, were able to increase and maintain their power by making a majority of Hutus believe that their Tutsi friends and neighbors were evil "cockroaches" who had committed crimes against all Hutus. Common people were transformed into murderers when the leaders succeeded in tying power and truth in a "circular relation."

As with introductions, the traditional approach to conclusions, a repetition of the thesis, is again redundant rather than rhetorical. If you've addressed your audience effectively and have provided a clear argument and persuasive evidence in a form that joins purpose and expectations, you probably don't need to remind readers what your purpose has been. Instead, think about the rhetorical options open to a writer who has amply demonstrated her or his credibility. You have earned the authority to end your paper by

- adding a comment about the topic;
- suggesting a next step or needed further work;
- emphasizing the importance or relevance of the major finding; or
- using a stylistic ending—a relevant quotation, a reference to the paper's title, a rhetorical question.

In the list of the traits of "good" writing as they are traditionally defined, two remain to reconsider from a rhetorical perspective: evidence and correctness. You should be well prepared by this point to figure out what a rhetorical approach to using evidence would be. It's going to be something other than adding a quotation or a concrete detail to every paragraph. First, evidence comes in a much wider variety than only quotation or detail. Evidence certainly includes citation of scholarly or professional experts, but it can also take the form of witness, textual examples, interview subjects, experience, community members, statistical data, journalistic accounts, media clips, or other sources whose inclusion can add to a rhetorical effect of credibility. What sort of evidence will the reader be expecting in your paper? And what types of evidence will your specific audience likely find most compelling? In the pop culture paper on Michael Jackson, visual and aural evidence—the music video excerpt—will likely have an informative, persuasive effect on an audience attuned to the role of media in pop culture. Meeting the conventional expectation is part of persuading readers that you're presenting a credible view.

The issue of correctness in grammar, mechanics, and spelling is one of the most problematic of all issues in the teaching of writing. Rhetorically, the matter is fairly clear: repeated or multiple errors distract readers from the author's purpose and may undermine the writer's credibility as an authoritative voice, and so correctness is a lapse in rhetorical effectiveness. That's ducking the political issues surrounding correctness, though, and writers have a right, we believe, to consider the political implications of "standard" language use, and to make their rhetorical choices in that context.

"Correctness" traditionally means that a writer adheres to the rules of what's called standard edited English, consisting of syntax, punctuation, capitalization, spelling, and other conventions of written language use. In traditional practice, instructors are likely to note and take off points for sentence fragments, run-on sentences, subject-verb agreement errors, nonstandard or "awkward" constructions, word choice errors, misspellings, and other infractions.

There are at least two schools of thought that argue against treating correctness as an isolated trait of "good" writing. Politically, some rhetoric-composition scholars have argued that "standard" English really means the usage conventions of middle-class society, and that correctness as a grading value is necessarily biased against minority, immigrant, and working-class students. Some instructors argue that grading for correctness makes them "gatekeepers," forcing them to assign lower grades to students who differ from the middle-class profile, making it harder for them to succeed in college. But others have argued that *not* teaching the language of social access works against the interests of students who seek to enter the mainstream.

Pedagogically, some scholars argue that overattention to matters of correctness interferes with students' composing ability, making them shift attention from invention, or ideas, to surface matters that can be addressed later in the writing process, in final steps of proofreading and editing. If you've ever tried "freewriting," you've worked out of this view of correctness, since in freewriting the writer is to write down all his or her thoughts on a topic, not stopping to connect ideas, organize paragraphs, correct grammatical usage, or edit the text at any level. The writer writes continuously, not stopping, letting the internal flow of ideas take shape on the paper. The goal is to separate editing and proofreading from drafting and revising, on the theory that better writing emerges when the writer is free to focus on ideas rather than sentence-level issues.

In Part Four, you'll work within a postcolonial frame and the politics of language. You'll read and experiment with what's called "alternative discourses." We'll raise this issue of correctness again there. What you should consider at this point is the rhetorical effect of correctness: readers, academic and professional readers especially, expect writers to observe the conventions of standard edited English. As a student and as an applicant (for a job, scholarship, or academic program), you probably will find that your written work is looked at closely for its level of correctness, possibly because readers expect that the genre of student writing will have errors in it. In contrast, readers expect published professional writing to be error-free.

One area in which correctness increasingly matters for all writers is documentation—the citation of sources. As knowledge becomes "property," copyright laws become more stringently enforced, and documenting sources is the way to avoid plagiarism charges. You should have and use a handbook that gives details on the major documentation styles such as the Modern Language Association (MLA), the American Psychological Association (APA), and so on. Such guides are also available in electronic form.

Almost every school has physical and/or online academic centers, such as a writing lab, where you can work on all facets of composing a paper, including proofreading and editing it, with a peer or writing center professional. Many writing classes use peer response workshops, another way you can get feedback on how readers are receiving your work, including whether or not they are reacting to errors. Academic writers seek out peer response as a critical part of the writing process. That only makes sense, given the rhetorical nature of writing.

Rhetorical Values over Time

The conventions of academic writing are the products of a long history of rhetorical theory and writing instruction. They reflect the values of their particular locations, whether academic, professional, or personal. This section covers the major historical views that you may see still at work in your various classrooms. Having a basic sense of the views behind different writing values can help you understand the different approaches to writing that you may encounter.

In classical rhetoric, composition was orally based—rhetoricians composed speeches. Writing was a secondhand task for the scribe. As cultures became literate, composing was no longer restricted to the trained, acknowledged experts, and speechmaking was no longer the principle means of public or private persuasion. People could read the texts of others. But to respond, to engage in the conversation, they had to be able to write back. Classical rhetorical theory was used as a basis for teaching people to become proficient in written communication. Composition, therefore, inherited most of classical rhetoric's forms, rules, and conventions. Teachers of composition typically emphasized those traits of classical rhetorical theory that they thought were most relevant and easily adapted to written composing.

By the eighteenth century, composition classes concentrated on arrangement, style, and form. Invention continued as a matter of "finding" premade arguments. Although in ancient times Aristotle believed that invention could also be a means of *creating* persuasive arguments, these theories later came to be seen as polar opposites, and a rule-bound, mechanistic approach to composition prevailed. This division spawned two common approaches to modern composing:

the formulaic (what is commonly termed current-traditional, the rule-bound) and the expressivist (sometimes also called personal writing).

Jumping to the 1960s, we see the start of a different era in writing instruction. Students were organizing, marching, sitting in, and otherwise exercising forms of social protest. They were not only resisting the draft and the Vietnam War; they were also demanding more freedom and representation in the college curriculum. The way college study was organized and college courses taught underwent enormous change along with other social conventions. The fact that you most likely have the chance to evaluate your class at the end of the term is a direct result of this enormous change. As always, writing classes came to reflect the social polarization of the day. We see this split in mechanistic and expressivist composing and teaching theories. Some writing teachers chose to stick with a rules-and-error approach, in which students concentrated on grammar, paragraph structure, and logical development. Other teachers, attempting to make the classroom "relevant," encouraged a personal voice in writing and rewarded more feelings-based responses.

The frame of New Criticism held sway in the humanities up to this period. Its name rightly suggests that its primary theorists were reacting against earlier traditions—in their case, against interpreting literary texts in relation to the author's biographical and historical/national background. In this scheme, great literature was an art; other writing was simply craft, a use of language for practical purposes and so not valued as highly as poetry, drama, or fiction. Writing classes usually consisted of students studying literary texts and writing interpretive essays about them. The theory was that students should be exposed to and taught to imitate the "best" writers of the language. (We should note that this modeling approach was also a major feature of rhetorical instruction in ancient Rome and has been repeated in Western culture throughout the centuries.) At the same time, the rhetorical values applied to student essays in such classes were clarity and concision—a kind of efficiency model of writing. Organization thus came to be a primary grading criterion, and organizational "schemes," or plans, became prescriptive. Since an essay's purpose was to show how a literary work "worked," the authorial voice was objective—personal feelings or connections were considered irrelevant or digressive. This rhetorical theory assumes that knowledge is separate from the individual, that writers "find" ideas (or rely on experts for them) and then recast them in formal academic prose, following the conventions of the academic essay. But with the social protests of the era came a new emphasis on individual expression. The result was that many writing classes began to value student voices as the major texts of the class, dropping the traditional approach to writing.

Expressivist writing is still a popular composing theory with its own rhetorical values. It emphasizes *motive* as a version of the classical notion of purpose, and the writer writes out of his or her own beliefs, feelings, and desire to write, to express ideas. The assumption is that an *author* writes best from an *authentic self*, or voice, and that the writer discovers meaning by freewriting. Some expressivist composing theorists argued for ignoring audience in the early stages of the writing process. Some claimed the writer is his or her own best audience, and connecting with an audience should come as a later revision issue.

Not surprisingly, the intense social upheaval of the 1960s affected the common critical frames and rhetorical practices in English studies, too. Critical theory, particularly forms of it developed in 1960s France, came into the English curriculum, challenging New Criticism and radically changing how we see writers, texts, and their relations to social reality. Critical frames began to reflect what theorists call the social, cultural, or linguistic turn. Language, rather than being simply a means of expressing some objective reality or individual perception, came to be understood as the site and cause of our experience. That's a radical philosophical shift: we are who we are and have the values we have because of our immersion in the language of a particular place and time. That's a doctrine of *relativism*, one that challenges *universalism* or *absolutism*. From a relativist point of view, we can never know precisely and unarguably what a word means, since words are steeped in a value system that far exceeds our individual experience. Language, and therefore texts, can have no final, unquestionable meaning, since language is unstable.

As critical frames such as deconstruction (a philosophical approach to language and meaning as unstable popularized by the late French philosopher Jacques Derrida) came into the U.S. curriculum, the composition course also changed and came to reflect a more relativist perspective. Social construction-ism—the idea that reality is "made" by the words used to represent it—joined with a revival of interest in classical rhetoric to move composition classes away from a focus on imitative models and to a new interest in students as authors, as themselves meaning-makers, rather than just as arrangers of meaning that is "found" elsewhere.

This change has not taken place as a seamless set of steps. As we've seen, many of the conventions associated with current-traditional rhetoric remain central parts of academic writing. But increasingly, composition classes tie these practices to rhetorical understanding of author, purpose, audience, context, and the other rhetorical concepts discussed in this and the preceding chapters. And students are increasingly likely to find themselves in decentered classrooms, working collaboratively on topics they frame themselves, rather than being passive scribes listening to an instructor lecture. Alternative forms/alternative discourses are entering the usual curriculum, and you may be asked to write personal reflections, ethnographic reports, electronic text, visual argument, and other departures from traditional essay form.

The texts you work with have also changed, in all likelihood. Instead of or in addition to canonical literary works, you'll read, for example, memoirs, histories, scientific papers, popular (meaning nonacademic) cultural pieces, song lyrics, advertisements, political treatises, and visual texts. These changes reflect the critical shift to language use as a social activity, as a behavior that happens in changing social contexts.

Chronology of Rhetoric Instruction

Ancient World

- **Who taught it:** Before the Common Era (BCE; formerly BC), both Greek and Roman cultures placed great value on studying rhetoric. In Greece, the most recognizable figures associated with the discipline were Aristotle, Isocrates, and Plato. Early Roman rhetoricians include Quintilian, Seneca, and Cicero. In both of these cultures, knowledge of rhetoric was indispensable if one wanted to be considered an educated citizen. After the advent of Christianity, St. Augustine, a rhetorician by training, wrote several texts incorporating Christian doctrine into classical rhetorical theory.

- **What subjects were taught:** Logic, grammar, argument.

- **Who studied it and why:** Rhetoric was the foundational field of study for lawyers, politicians, and most wealthy young men, so success in public oratory or orally arguing law was a motivation for students. "Public" in these cultures really meant the wealthy elite, not the great majority of the population, and certainly not slaves. Women in the ancient world were either not allowed or not encouraged to study rhetoric, or any other subject, for that matter.

Medieval World

- **Who taught it:** European scholars, almost always affiliated with the Catholic Church in some way, offered instruction in rhetoric at monastery and cathedral schools. The earliest universities appeared in Italy, Germany, France, and England. Some thinkers of the period still studied extensively are St. Thomas Aquinas, John Duns Scotus, St. Anselm, and St. Jerome. Muslim scholars such as Averroes studied ancient rhetoric written by pagan Greeks and Romans, but European rhetoric limited its use of pagan writers to essentially Aristotle and Plato.

- **What subjects were taught:** Preaching, teaching, notarizing, letter writing, church law.

- **Who studied it:** Most of the young men studying rhetoric during this time were in some way employed by or in the service of the "church," which meant the Roman Catholic Church. When cathedral schools were superseded by the early universities, wealthy or "sponsored" young men could take rhetoric courses to prepare for civil law. Mostly, however, the rhetorical arts were necessary for advancement in church society. Since most European countries were governed by monarchs, opportunities in government were restricted to a ruling elite. "Public" persuasion in the medieval era usually meant the public of the church's congregation, hierarchy, or clergy. Scholastics used writing extensively, but common people still relied on oral persuasion.

Renaissance World

- **Who taught it:** Priests, philosophers, poets, courtiers (educated gentlemen), and scholars all taught rhetoric in the Renaissance. A revival of the arts and an increasing number of universities in Europe (especially in Italy) restored the teaching of rhetoric to a prominent position. The arrival of the printing press meant that written language could be disseminated much more easily and cheaply than ever before, although the percentages of literacy in any particular society were still miniscule.

- *What subjects were taught:* Philology (study of origins and histories of language), poetics, philosophy, law, and Greek and Latin rhetorical history.
- *Who studied it:* Private schools and universities took on male students who could pay for training in teaching, the law, politics, even business communication. Church-affiliated schools still taught preaching, but the so-called liberal arts (jurisprudence, natural philosophy, writing, and so on) were taking on a larger role in institutionalized education. Higher education, however, was still almost exclusively the privilege of men.

Enlightenment World

- *Who taught it:* With the swift rise of the empirical sciences, rhetoric falls out of favor. The *philosophes* (Voltaire, Condillac, Condorcet) and scientists like Descartes in France considered classical rhetoric a holdover from the days of superstition and so condemned its study. The British empiricist John Locke and the Scottish philosopher David Hume likewise criticized the teaching of persuasion as unscientific. Since universities no longer needed affiliation with the Catholic Church to ensure their existence, Protestants could also fill faculty ranks.
- *What subjects were taught:* Since science and scientific thinking were now the standard against which any education was measured, the courses previously taught as part of a rhetorical education were for the most part either dispensed with or reframed to fit into a philosophy curriculum. A scientific perspective meant that words were thought of as transparent, or neutral—only carriers of meaning that science found. Objectivity was most sought after, and plain language was believed to carry "truth" without affecting its content.
- *Who studied it:* Law students still studied rhetoric for oral persuasion, but a majority of rhetoric courses (those that were left) focused on correctness and logical argumentation. Persuasion itself was generally believed to be a form of deceit (just as Plato had taught) so rhetoric became a "negative" field of study, providing examples of how *not* to use language.

Modern/Postmodern World

- *Who teaches it:* Until the second half of the twentieth century, rhetoric was essentially a dead discipline—especially at the university level. Courses in rhetoric that did exist were still wedded to the Enlightenment standards of an emphasis on correctness and argumentation. In the 1970s, rhetoric experienced a resurgence in popularity as a separate field of study, one with a long historical tradition. Courses today are often titled Composition and Rhetoric, reflecting rhetoric's return to established curricula.
- *What subjects are taught:* Someone studying rhetoric today might take courses in philosophy, psychology, cultural studies, critical theory, literature, or a whole range of writing courses.
- *Who studies it:* In most U.S. universities, every student has some contact with the study of persuasion, either in communication or English departments. Worldwide, rhetoric is a common field of study for lawyers, teachers, those interested in careers in business (advertising, marketing, and so on), people looking to join NGOs or government agencies, and any other subject involving communication.

topics   for   writing

1. The first of the following student essays reflects traditional writing values; the second works from a more consciously rhetorical perspective. The first was written by a junior high school student, the second by a first-year college student. How do the differences you'll see relate to different cultural assumptions about these two student populations? What is expected of the younger student, and how do you see expectations changed for the college student? Consider the rhetorical and cultural issues implicit in the topics assigned and the writing values their work displays.

   What genres might be appropriate for this assignment? For example, you could approach the task as a report, using headings for the major rhetorical and cultural issues you identify; or you could write an analytic essay that mixes in experiential commentary, if you identify with the shifts in writing expectations evident in the essays; or you could write from your own responses as a reader, organizing the issues rhetorical and cultural issues as you perceive the two different authors. Try developing a conceptual outline for whichever approach you choose.

To Smoke or Not to Smoke

Katherine Muller

April 2, 2005

English Honors

Smoking is the cause of some of the most common preventable illnesses in the United States, and kills almost four million people each year. As the Bible says, "the body is a temple," but all these people defile their temples with smoking and tobacco. One million stop smoking, but do you want to gamble your life on four-to-one odds? The physical addiction to nicotine is one of the strongest reasons people keep smoking, but it is the easiest to stop. Peer pressure and social reasons often are causes when kids start to smoke. Emotional problems like depression also convince some adults to smoke. Sometimes smokers live long and healthy lives, but more often smokers live up to ten years less than the average. Even quitting does not help immediately, for the lung damage can take fifteen years to reverse. Sometimes the damage is bad enough to be irreversible. Unless you want to suffer the consequences of smoking, I suggest you quit.

The physical addiction to nicotine is one of the strongest reasons people keep smoking, but it is the easiest to stop. Modern doctors have invented ways to stop the craving, so none must suffer the nicotine need. Nicotine patches are most common though expensive, but other methods are also available. Relapses of smoking from the physical addiction happen within the first few months sometimes, but distracting activities like exercising can keep

---

you busy. Even if you fail to keep smoke-free during a relapse, statistics show that every time you try to quit, you can last longer next time, if not quit forever. However, there are other things to keep you from quitting.

Peer pressure and social reasons often are causes when kids start to smoke. Young people are not easily able to follow the advice, "to thine own self be true," and few can resist the pressure. Boyfriends or girlfriends who smoke can induce their dates to smoke, but smoking people have a difficult time marrying or dating anyone who does not smoke. Being cool when you smoke is being cool because you have bad breath and brown teeth. Thinking smoking makes you tough is also wrong, because the smoke in your lungs limits your ability to take in oxygen, consequently making it harder for you to breathe. Some think it makes you seem older, but your age is not decided by how bad your lungs are. These things may lead to depression, a common cause of smoking.

Emotional reasons often hook people deeply into smoking. Since smoking when you're depressed makes you feel much better almost instantly, it is tempting to try. Sadly, this is only temporary. One cigarette turns to ten, and suddenly you are smoking a pack a day to keep from being depressed, and feeling worse than ever. Shy or nervous people take it to calm their nerves or make them feel stronger. Teens feel they are stronger when they disobey their parents and start smoking. People believe all those untrue things, and turn their nails yellow, make their skin wrinkle, diminish their taste and smell, kill their lungs, hurt others with secondhand smoke, make themselves ill, and die ten to twelve years younger because they don't quit.

However preventable and stoppable smoking is, it kills thousands of people a year and hooks about 3000 young people a day. Women especially are affected, because smoking is more likely to give them blood clots and heart attacks as well as causing birth defects and lowering children's immune systems. The message is clear: Stop Smoking or Smoking Will Stop You.

5

Control, Status, and the Library
Andrew Merrill
November 1, 2006
English 103: Seminar in Rhetoric and Writing
Our world is influenced, and to a certain extent controlled, by cultural myths that were created perhaps centuries ago. Semiotics is the study of

these cultural myths, or the study of how society imposes these cultural myths and who benefits from the ideological beliefs they promote. Jack Solomon, in the book <u>Semiotics: The Science of the Sign</u>, states that "[c]ultures tend to cover up their ideological investments by making them appear to be the only ones that conform to nature" (11), naturalizing beliefs that are, in fact, only social and conventional. What he is saying is that the myths society tries to make people believe are not necessarily the only way to view things; in other words, what some may consider unnatural just because society says so may not be all that unnatural—it's only considered unnatural by society because of cultural interests dating way back in history. The role of semiotics is not to determine what is right or wrong, which myths are correct and which are illogical, but merely to reveal the myths for what they are: hidden cultural agendas. These hidden agendas can be found everywhere in the world: in clothes, books, magazines, television, music, ordinary objects, and normal, everyday places. One would think that these hidden signs might be absent from certain places, such as churches or libraries, but myths can be found in those places as well—and probably to a greater extent. For example, a university library is ripe with cultural myths and signs, but in order to see these hidden symbols one must delve below the surface of what a library appears to be, to see the myths hiding between bookshelves and study tables: cultural myths are everywhere. How could one find hidden semiotic myths in a library, a place for study and research? To understand, one must look deeply into the structure of a library.

First of all, what do libraries look like? The setup of a place can reveal cultural agendas, for it is not the object alone that has cultural myths, it is sometimes just the concept of a place, object, or idea that can reflect society's myths. A library is a building full of books, with people coming to check out books or conduct research for projects, only to return the checked out books before the deadline, or else they are fined. All libraries are designed, more or less, the same: books on shelves, study tables off to the side, and for the more advanced libraries, a computer area for researching on the Internet and typing up school papers. Some libraries have food areas off to the side where people can read and eat at the same time, but the rest of the library is a strictly no-eating zone. Libraries are practically sterile, with everything clean, neat, and nothing out of place.

A library's setup is connected to a social purpose, for there are myths about libraries that encourage an intellectual ranking system, where the intellects are at the top, and the general public is at the bottom. It is a commonly held belief that libraries are only used by intellectuals, people who want to study and expand their minds to improve themselves intellectually. While libraries are all set up the same, there is a difference between a public library and university library. A public library is considered less prestigious than a university library—only the elite intellects are able to enter a university library, whereas the lowly general public is not allowed to check out books or sometimes even enter a university library. A public library also has less research material and more novels and media that appeal to the general public; a university library, on the other hand, is filled with more research books than leisure reading books. The social value of the library has stayed more or less the same over time, continually reproducing long accepted cultural "truths" about the people who are in it.

Whenever people talk about librarians, it is assumed that the librarian is female, unless the library is full of books that are of some importance, which then it is guarded by men. But why are librarians thought of as women—is it because women are considered more studious? Apparently not, for librarians do not seem to need some higher intelligence in order to do their job, but rather, librarians need to be organized. Librarians file, organize, sort, and take care of books; thinking about them like this, it becomes obvious that the closest jobs to a librarian are motherhood and maids. In fact, another cultural myth is that librarians are strict, which adds further to the sense of motherly skills that they need to possess in order to be successful librarians. They are there to control the environment, to make sure that people are quiet and respectful, and that people don't harm the books in any way. While males could easily do this job as well, society holds that women are better at taking care of things, better at cleaning things, and better at organizing things—this is a position that society likes women to be in, because the conventional view of librarians reinforces myths of gender.

The central feature of libraries, however, is the books. In libraries, books are considered more important than people, and there are many ways to see this privileging. First of all, right at the doors there are bar code readers to ensure that books are not stolen. The librarian's desk is there, too, set up in circular sections, like a fortress tower, so that the librarians can look in all directions. In the book sections, the books are all on shelves in the middle of the room, with study tables pushed to the outside—the books are placed at the center of attention, with students shoved off to the side. Also, librarians are always on the lookout for people who are abusing books. If books are damaged, or not returned on time, the student is fined to help pay to repair

5

the book, or fined for keeping the book too long. There are even books that people cannot read, are not allowed to read, unless they have special permission—these books are sectioned off from the other books, hidden in the back until they are requested. Libraries, traditionally, have been set up this way in the modern world, where books are held in high regard and the people checking out the books are regarded as less than worthy.

Libraries are thus about control, and when a person is in the library he or she is forced to comply with the rules that a library has laid down. Besides the rules such as books being checked out and returned on time, there are also behavioral rules to be followed. The main rule above all is "Silence is golden," and the library is designed accordingly, with work stations secluded from one another, and librarians ready to pounce on those who speak above a whisper. This emphasis on silence is another myth held by society that in order to be able to research, a person needs complete silence, and must study by themselves. Even though not everybody can concentrate this way, the library makes solitude seem the best way. Some people need study groups to help them understand problems, and some projects depend on collaborating. Libraries, conversely, do not encourage this type of studying. They continue the tradition of individual work because society says that is how we are supposed to learn—on our own.

Every once in a while, it is helpful to stop and consider why some aspects of life are the way they are, and whether what society tells people is natural or unnatural. At first, it may seem only natural to say that libraries are quiet places to read and study, with books being held in high regard over people, governed by female librarians—this is how a library should be, right? On the other hand, looking deeper into the concept of libraries and how they're designed, people should ask themselves if libraries are cultural influence systems. Do they help create differences in social status? Do they help keep class and gender stereotypes going? Semiotics isn't a study to find out which answer is right, but merely the study of why the cultural system is set up the way it is, and who benefits from this "natural" way. Libraries encourage people to learn and expand their minds, but by the rules laid down by the library.

2. A literacy narrative is a reflective essay in which a writer recounts his or her experiences with language. Such narratives include the individual's experiences with reading (or being read to); early school experiences with literacy (spoken

and written); development as a writer, academic as well as creative or personal; changes in the relationship of self/writing/audience (or public sphere—the places in which one occupies a writerly role, such as a classroom); any individual language issues (being bilingual, for example). Do you consider yourself to have various forms of literacy—print literacy, computer literacy, symbolic literacy, music literacy, something else? Think about your own development as a literate individual to this point.

- What are some primary rhetorical concerns in this assignment?
- How does this genre affect your options for presenting your thesis? Will it be open-ended? Do you want some definitive statement about your own experiences of coming to literacy?
- What voice(s) will you use? What persona(s) and stance(s)? Will you use multiple languages?
- Conceptually, imagine different ways of framing the narrative. Will your narrative have visual elements, such as images or headings? How will the frame you choose reflect your argument in the narrative?
- What will constitute persuasive evidence in this kind of paper?

3. Compose a biographical sketch of the sort discussed in the "Genre and Organization" section of this chapter. Include the conventional elements of the genre in a way that supports your argument about this figure—tie the form to the purpose of the sketch. Think about the possible uses of visual elements, from document design to illustrations, pictorial/video/audio links, or other media.

The Psychoanalytic Frame

Introduction and Historical Origins

Most of us have some acquaintance with Freudian psychoanalytic theory, the foundational set of teachings about the human mind and motivation, whether or not we have formally studied Sigmund Freud's writings. We frequently use terms such as *ego, anxiety, neurotic, Freudian slip*, and *death wish* in everyday conversations or see them used in the media. These are all terms coined by Freud or derived from Freudian theory. Such terms routinely come up in academic discussions; in specialized articles and textbooks, we're likely to encounter references to the concepts of *Eros, repression, guilt*, the *Oedipus complex*, and may even come across *oceanic feeling* and *castration anxiety* (the former being a very satisfying way of denying fear of the latter). Far more than other theoretical methods, Freudian, or psychoanalytic, theory has become a familiar part of social exchange.

This familiarity reflects Freud's very important cultural influence. The appearance of his psychological theory of human behavior in the late nineteenth and early twentieth centuries resulted in a fundamental reshaping of how Western philosophy and science conceived of human nature and experience. The various models of the human mind that scientists and moral philosophers had assumed or consciously constructed over the centuries were replaced by a theory that challenged the rational basis of human nature and tied it to an animalistic biological foundation. Predictably, Freud's ideas met with little professional and even less popular acceptance in their time. Nevertheless, his work would ultimately have enormous intellectual influence in the emerging field of psychology and in other disciplines that adopted and adapted a Freudian frame to their own topics of inquiry. The psychologists who took up Freud's theories altered them in various ways, in many cases taking issue with the sexual foundation of his system, critiquing it as a product of the time and place of Freud's subjects. Since Freud's time (he lived from 1856 to 1939), many psychologists, especially female psychologists, have expanded and amended his theories on psychic development and femininity.

Freudian theory, although originally received as a scandalous challenge to idealized notions of human nature, has come into our culture as a useful lens for viewing or talking about our "invisible" experience—our feelings, conflicts, and desires. We can suggest two reasons for the popular acceptance of at least parts of this theory. First, it seems to help explain much of human behavior that is apparently irrational, behavior we cannot otherwise account for, and which therefore becomes perplexing, frightening, even threatening. The theory of *parapraxes* (the technical term for Freudian slips), for instance, can help us understand our own peculiar behavior on occasions. Whether in individual psychoanalytic sessions or in applying psychoanalytic theories to social situations, we can gain through the theory a sense of our own power to understand that which is not visible, representing the formerly "unknown" in language. A systematic theory of psychosis, for example, comfortingly transforms "mad" people into patients, people who are ill and in need of medical intervention. The theory helps us explain disturbing phenomena and gives us a sense of (potential) control over them and defense against them, and so it has found acceptance in the popular as well as academic realm.

A second appeal of psychoanalytic theory is its comprehensiveness: it claims to give us a key to exploring and, to a degree, understanding human life and actions as a closed system of cause and effect. If all experience and social history is a product of our psychological situation, and if psychoanalytic theory offers the possibility of a complete description of the human mind, including reasons for its disturbances, then we have a powerful interpretive and prescriptive tool. We can explain and develop antidotes for such issues as urban problems along with individual neuroses. We can understand the origins, or motives, of war, art, or simply chronic lateness. It promises us a kind of universal key. It seems to say that we can understand our own psyches and so free ourselves from our conflicts, as individuals and as members of a collective society. It seems, in its popular version anyhow, to offer us what Freud says we seek in all our dreams and fantasies—complete wish fulfillment, the satisfaction of all desires for personal power and pleasure.

There's always a catch—that's the reality principle. We're born into a world where our first, or primal, desires are fairly easily met: our mothers (or mother figures) feed us, keep us warm, and cuddle us. Life is good; the pleasure principle has been fulfilled. But then our stomachs grow empty, or Mother goes away. We scream. If Mother doesn't appear immediately, we grow increasingly upset and demanding: it simply cannot be that we do not have what we want. Life, according to Freud, is a series of such learning incidents—a kind of painful progress to the recognition that we are not all-powerful figures, that in fact we must continually compromise and accommodate our desires to others outside us over whom we have little or no control, that some vast proportion of our own psychic life happens at the unconscious level, a realm almost completely closed to us, making us radical strangers even to ourselves. Maturity is a hard state to reach precisely because it begins with accepting this principle of necessary renunciation and inevitable alienation.

This very principle that suggests the impossibility of attaining total satisfaction applies, unfortunately, to our desires about theory and method as well. We seek the "key to all mythologies," but the human experience seems to resist closed systems of absolute certainty. And so psychoanalytic theory is itself undermined by theories that come later and illustrate its limits, exposing its own wishful thinking. We continually seek keys to understanding, only to find that more than one lock separates us from this ideal, ultimately leading us to question the concept of an ideal itself.

Growing out of Freud's medical study, psychoanalytic theory was originally intended to have therapeutic use—that is, it was developed as a means to diagnose and then help heal or at least lessen the effects of mental disturbances. Freud believed that a patient's conscious investigation of the conflicts hidden within his or her symbolic images (dreams, for example) and behaviors can lead to a "cure," defined as the patient's conscious understanding of the conflict and enhanced ability to adapt in daily life. Thus a psychoanalytic frame requires that we gather data from a particular case or social situation, consider it in relation to the mental structures and systems defined by Freud, and reach some conclusion about the nature of disturbances and needed adjustments. *Rhetorically*, it guides the writer in the type of questions to ask, in the way to interpret, or analyze, the information gathered, and in the way to demonstrate the logic of the analysis by placing it in the context of specific psychoanalytic principles.

In this section, we ask you not to undertake do-it-yourself therapy sessions but a more socially based exploration of how the individual becomes a social being, one who has learned (or failed to learn) how to balance instincts and drives with repressive societal demands and social practices designed to "civilize" us. To engage in this psychosocial critique, we need a set of principles that lay out the hypotheses of psychoanalytic thought, and then data, or material, on which to test them—the purpose of the readings in this part.

As you work with this material, you will be adding the analyst's role to your rhetorical abilities, for built into the psychoanalytic frame is an invention model for how to go about analyzing and interpreting a text and how to construct one's own text communicating the discoveries one makes. The steps in psychoanalysis include collecting experiential data—the details of a text or event—followed by analysis of them in relation to major psychoanalytic tenets. The "argument" one can build relates to the individual text and also to a broader reality: it can help explain how the unconscious mind works, how it finds expression in conscious reality, and how desires and conflicts can or cannot be resolved. As we move through the chapters, you'll be invited to use your own experience as data, along with written and cultural texts—the objects, locations, practices, and visual displays we encounter in daily life.

● Adding to the Conversation

In a notebook or journal, reflect on the above material, perhaps considering the following questions:

1. What do you already know about Freudian theory and Freudian terms?

2. What is your impression of Freud's importance today? In what contexts have you heard (or used) references to his ideas?

3. What parts of his theory as outlined above do you find interesting, what parts alienating, and why?

4. Where do you see the influence or applicability of psychoanalytic thought in the media, such as films, advertising, or music?

5. Pick a line from the above introduction—something that you didn't fully understand, or reacted against, or found engaging—and explore it further in your own words.

Rhetorical Issues in the Psychoanalytic Frame

One of the fundamental genres of academic writing is analysis. According to the dictionary definition of the term, *analysis* consists of breaking down some concept or object into its component parts. As a rhetorical act, analysis takes into account purpose and audience: we analyze the parts of some event or concept to explain it, presenting an argument about how this event or concept works. Analysis explains and supports a thesis about a topic.

Using a psychoanalytic perspective, a writer sets up a specific context—the Freudian framework of human desires in conflict with the laws of society—as the foundation for analyzing the phenomena of human reality, in texts or actual social experience. The writer becomes the analyst who considers the data of a given situation, compares it to the theoretical model provided by Freud (or other theorists after him), explains what the wishes and conflicts in the situation are, and perhaps offers a solution that will enable a more balanced situation to prevail—the purpose of the analysis. The perspective thus provides a stance for the writer in relation to the topic; a body of knowledge that forms the topic's, and writer's, intellectual context; and ways to structure the writer's topic. And since the approach enables the writer to study all things human, it also allows the writer to address a wide variety of audiences—academic readers, public policy makers, concerned citizens, or even oneself. Writing from a psychoanalytic frame, you enter into an already ongoing conversation, one that's likely to be familiar to other academic writers.

How does a psychoanalytic frame interact with *rhetorical* issues? Like most critical frames, it offers some fundamental operating guidelines.

- **It helps shape and limit the universe of topics.**

Psychoanalytic theory is humanistic—it places human concerns at the center, particularly concerns about behavior in relation to social control. It focuses us on human desires, the resulting conflicts with social rules, and the accommodations we must make to be accepted in society. A psychoanalytic frame thus directs us to arguments about motives—how desire and aggression affect behavior; why conflicts arise; how social controls interfere with satisfying our desires; and how and why we succeed or fail in adapting to society. You can use this frame to begin exploring text-based, personal, and social issues you consider important, and consider how far psychoanalytic theory can take us toward understanding or even solutions.

- **It provides a system of logical reasoning.**

Psychoanalysis is a **structuralist** approach. That means it sees all human experience as a whole piece, a closed system with discoverable laws. In such a system, logical reasoning happens in a linear way: we can explain data in relation to objective "rules." We can move from observing a child who persistently bites other children for no apparent reason to the psychoanalytic given that children experience erotic and aggressive desires, for example, and biting allows pleasurable bodily contact and the thrill of power. This reasoning works on larger levels, too, since society, in this approach, is a collection of individuals, and the "rules" hold for the group. (However, Freud argues that Eros, the desire to preserve and expand life, dominates the collective entity of society, although it may not dominate any one individual.) If you formulate and approach a topic psychoanalytically, you generate ways of building your argument and options for organizing it logically.

- ### It supports specific genres, or ways of organizing a text.

A psychoanalytic frame conventionally generates certain genres. Freud wrote case studies—presentations of extensive data about a particular individual or condition, which can then be synthesized to derive specific "rules" about how the mind works, or how people behave socially. The genre of the case study can be organized as a cause-and-effect argument in reverse—the effects, or symptoms, and then the causes, or psychoanalytic hypotheses. The case study genre also suggests a problem-solving organizational plan, in which the writer describes a particular problem and then analyzes its causes and possible solution(s). It also commonly generates a profile, which is either a real-life or composite depiction of a particular individual who best illustrates a given psychological condition. It thus provides the writer with a way of framing an essay: the writer can examine a given event as a case study, a profile, and then use the genre to help organize an analytic treatment of it.

- ### It positions the writer as an authoritative voice.

Because it claims a *scientific* grounding (though this claim has been much disputed), the psychoanalytic frame offers its users a rhetorical stance of authority. By grounding an argument in the theory, you are invoking a recognized (if not always accepted) body of knowledge as your logical foundation. Using the frame, you create a credible voice—though others are free to challenge your theory, your reasoning can be challenged only where you depart from the theoretical doctrine or use the theoretical concepts incorrectly or unfairly—for example, employing it to explain animal behavior, or extraterrestrial existence, applications which the scientific data Freud collected can't logically support.

- ### It employs a specialized vocabulary for its central theories.

Having this specialized vocabulary (which, taken to an extreme or used for nontechnical purposes, can become **jargon**, an effect to avoid) focuses our attention on the central concepts and values of the theory. "Oedipus complex," "id," "sublimation," "repression," "superego": these all encapsulate a set of ideas and make these sets the focus of interest and meaning. Note that this narrowing of focus, however, also tends to exclude certain topics and issues (such as race) from attention or fosters unexamined assumptions about them. ("Penis envy," for example, is a specialized psychoanalytic term that brings with it a judgment about women's inherently lesser status and perpetuates a view of the female as incomplete and inferior.) The kind of *discourse*, or specialized language use, that follows from a particular critical frame enforces certain *values*.

- **It can be used rhetorically as a means of persuasion, invoking ethos, logos, and/or pathos.**

If your readers accept the plausibility of the theory, or are willing to consider its validity, then you as a writer can apply the frame's principles in particular arguments to sway readers' views on your subject. If we agree that aggression is a powerful instinct we all possess, we might agree to a social policy you propose to limit access to weapons, for example, or to provide anger management therapy to those with a history of spousal abuse, moving the discussion away from strictly punitive terms and into potentially therapeutic contexts. Using the frame, you can develop a line of reasoning for your argument that may help gain an audience's agreement. You also can write from this frame using ethos to be persuasive, since the theory assumes that all humans have the same instincts and face the same restrictions; you become a typical representative of the conflicts and desires that characterize human motivation. And, as you read Freud, you'll come to see the many possibilities of appeals to pathos, since Freud focuses on the unbounded human desire for joy as it struggles with the many unavoidable sources of human pain.

You can draw on this frame to investigate the psychological dimensions of a topic. To understand social phenomena such as gang culture, for example, you might want to consider how gang membership meets fundamental psychological needs for social membership; next, to see how, for individuals in privileged social environments, fraternities and sororities may have a very similar function. Your purpose can be more than providing a simple analysis: by getting at the root needs, you can develop a powerful argument about the human and social costs of excluding certain groups from meaningful membership in society—membership in organizations that lead to power defined in ways beyond turf and guns. Working logically from the principles of the frame, you can structure detailed analyses of real-world issues and problems, and engage in creating real understanding that leads, possibly, to real solutions, using the theory as grounds for a persuasive argument.

chapter 4

Exploring
Psychoanalytic Frames

- Understanding the logical
  system of the psychoanalytic
  frame
- Using the frame to invent and
  shape arguments
- Experimenting with the genres
  that the frame generates

Introduction to Psychoanalysis

JEROME KAGAN and ERNEST HAVEMANN

This excerpt from Psychology: An Introduction, *a college psychology textbook first published in 1968, provides a sketch of the major principles of Freudian theory, focusing particularly on Freud's three-part model of the mind. According to this model, our psyches consist of the id, the ego, and the superego, leading us into a system of desire, repression, and sublimation. A strong ego is necessary to balance the demands of the primal id and the recriminations of the socially induced superego, the product of the Oedipus complex. Note that the authors present their material in the form of a narrative: this frame has a unified logic to it, with all the pieces fitting together to tell the story of how powerful human desires meet up with the even more powerful rules of civilized life. Note: We've highlighted the key terms that you'll need to use the frame for your own rhetorical ends.*

The most influential personality theory during the past half century has been "psychoanalytic theory," originally formulated by Sigmund Freud. Freud began his career in Vienna in the 1880s as a physician and neurologist. He became interested in psychological processes as the result of his experiences with patients who were suffering from hysteria—that is, from paralysis of the legs or arms that seemed to have no physical cause. His final theories represent a lifetime of treating and observing many kinds of neurotic patients and also of attempting to analyze the unconscious aspects of his own personality.

When Freud introduced his ideas around the turn of the century, they were bitterly attacked. Many people were repelled by his notion that man, far from being a rational animal, is largely at the mercy of his irrational unconscious thoughts. Many were shocked by Freud's emphasis on the role of sexual impulses and particularly by his insistence that young children have intense sexual motives. Over the years, however, the furor has died down. There is considerable controversy over the value of psychoanalytic methods in treating neurotic patients, but even those who criticize psychoanalysis as a form of therapy accept some of Freud's basic notions about personality and its formation.

Freud's most influential ideas concerned concepts central to the study of psychology. One of them was the role of anxiety. Freud was a pioneer in emphasizing the importance of anxiety, which he believed to be the central problem in mental disturbance. Another was **repression** and the other **defense mechanisms**. Freud believed that these mechanisms, and especially the process of repression, are frequently used to eliminate from conscious awareness any motive or thought that threatens to cause anxiety. Another influential idea was his concept of the **unconscious** mind, composed in part of repressed motives and thoughts. Freud was the first to suggest the now widely held theory that the human mind and personality are like an iceberg, with only a small part visible and the great bulk submerged and concealed. All of us, he maintained, have many unconscious motives of which we are never aware but which nonetheless influence our behavior. An example is the case of a man who sincerely believes that he has no hostile motives, yet who in subtle ways performs many acts of aggression against his wife, his children, and his business associates.

The core of the unconscious mind, according to Freud, is the "**id**," composed of raw, primitive, inborn forces that constantly struggle for gratification. Even the baby in his crib, Freud said, is swayed by two powerful drives. One is what he called the "**libido**," embracing sexual urges and such related desires as to be kept warm, well fed, and comfortable. The other is **aggression**—the urge to fight, dominate, and, where necessary, destroy.

The id operates on what Freud called the "**pleasure principle**," insisting on   5
immediate and total gratification of all its demands. Freud felt, for example, that the baby—though unable to think as yet like a human being and thus more like a little animal—wants to satisfy his libido by possessing everything he desires and loves and to satisfy his aggressive urges by destroying everything that gets in his way. As the child grows up, he learns to control the demands of the id, at least in part. But the id remains active and powerful throughout life; it is indeed the sole source of all the psychic energy put to use in behaving and thinking. It is unconscious and we are not aware of its workings, but it continues to struggle for the relief of all its tensions.

The conscious, logical part of the mind that develops as the child grows up was called by Freud the **ego**—the "real" us, as we like to think of ourselves. In contrast to the id, the ego operates on the "**reality principle**"; it tries to mediate between the demands of the id and the realities of the environment. Deriving its energies from the id, the ego perceives what is going on in the environment and develops the operational responses (such as finding food) necessary to satisfy the demands of the id. The ego does our logical thinking; it does the best it can to help us lead sane and satisfactory lives. To the extent that the primitive drives of the id can be satisfied without getting us into danger or harm, the ego permits them satisfaction. But when the drives threaten to get us jailed as a thief or rejected by society as a brawler and a rake, the ego represses them or attempts to satisfy them with substitutes that are socially acceptable.

In the ego's constant struggle to satisfy the demands of the id without permitting the demands to destroy us, it has a strong but troublesome ally in the third part of the mind as conceived by Freud—the "**superego.**" In a sense the superego is our conscience, our sense of right and wrong. It is partly acquired by adopting the notions of right and wrong that we are taught by society from the earliest years. However, Freud's concept of the superego represents a much stronger and more dynamic notion than the word "conscience" implies. Much like the id, the superego is mostly unconscious, maintaining a far greater influence over our behavior than we realize. It is largely acquired as a result of that famous process that Freud called the "**Oedipus complex,**" which can be summarized as follows.

According to Freud, every child between the ages of about two and a half through six is embroiled in a conflict of mingled affection and resentment for his parents. The child has learned that the outer world exists and that there are other people in it, and the id's demands for love and affection reach out insatiably toward the person he has been closest to—the mother. Although the child has only the haziest notion of sexual feelings, he wants to possess his mother totally and to take the place of his father with her. But his anger against his father, the rival with whom he must share her, makes him fearful that his father will somehow retaliate against his mother—so that he becomes overwhelmed with strong feelings of mingled love, anger, and fear toward both parents at once.

The Oedipus conflict must somehow be resolved; the way this is done, according to Freud, is through identification with the parents. The child ends his mingled love and hate of his parents by becoming like them, by convincing himself that he shares their strength and authority and the affection they have for each other. The parents' moral judgments, or what the child conceives to be their moral judgments, become his superego. This helps him hold down the drives of the id, which have caused him such intense discomfort during the Oedipal period. But, forever after, the superego tends to oppose the ego. As his parents once did, the superego punishes him or threatens to punish him for his transgressions. And, since its standards were rigidly set in childhood, its notions of crime and **guilt** are likely to be completely illogical and unduly harsh.

In their own way the demands of the superego are just as insatiable as the id's blind drives. Its standards of right and wrong and its rules for punishment are far more rigid, relentless, and vengeful than anything in our conscious minds. Formed at a time when the child was unable to distinguish between a "bad" wish and a "bad" deed, the superego may sternly disapprove of the merest thought of some transgression—the explanation, according to Freud, of the fact that some people who have never actually committed a "bad" deed nonetheless feel guilty all their lives.

The three parts of the human personality are in frequent conflict. One of the important results of the conflict is **anxiety**, which is produced in the ego whenever the demands of the id threaten danger or when the superego threatens disapproval or punishment. Anxiety, though unpleasant, is a tool that the ego uses to fight the impulses or thoughts that have aroused it. In one way or another—by using repression and the other defense mechanisms, by turning the mind's attention elsewhere, by gratifying some other impulse of the id—the ego defends itself against the threat from the id or superego and gets rid of the anxiety.

In a sense the conscious ego is engaged in a constant struggle to satisfy the insatiable demands of the unconscious id without incurring the wrath and vengeance of the largely unconscious superego. To the extent that a person's behavior is controlled by the ego, it is sensible and generally satisfying. To the extent that it is governed by the childish passions of the id and the unrelenting demands of the superego, it tends to be foolish, unrewarding, painful, and neurotic.

If the ego is not strong enough to check the id's drives, a person is likely to be a selfish and hot-headed menace to society. But if the id is checked too severely, other problems may arise. Too much repression of the libido can make a person unable to enjoy a normal sex life or to give and take competition. Too strong a superego may result in vague and unwarranted feelings of guilt and unworthiness, and sometimes in an unconscious need for self-punishment.

There can be little question that Freud was an important innovator who had a number of most useful insights into the human personality. He was the first to recognize the role of the unconscious and the importance of anxiety and defenses as a factor in personality. He also dispelled the myth, widely accepted before his time, that children do not have the sexual urges and hostile impulses that characterize adults.

One criticism of Freud is that he may have overemphasized the role of   15
sexual motivation in personality. In Freud's nineteenth and early twentieth century Vienna, with its strict sexual standards, it is perhaps only natural that many of his neurotic patients should have had conflicts and guilt feelings centering around their sexual desire. In today's Western world, with its more permissive attitudes toward sexual behavior, this kind of conflict and guilt seems to be less frequent. Yet people continue to have personality problems and the incidence of serious mental disturbance seems to remain about the same as ever. This would indicate that conflicts over sexuality cannot be the sole or perhaps even the most important cause of personality disturbances. Another frequent criticism of Freud is that many of his ideas about the dynamics of human behavior can be explained more economically without using his concepts of the id, ego, and superego.

● Building the Frame Through Writing

The following questions and cultural examples help you work out psychoanalytic theories in your own words. By writing about the above passage, you get to work through its abstract ideas, explain them to yourself, and "translate" them into concepts you can use in your own critical thinking. You're building a critical frame for your own critical and rhetorical use.

1. Work out your own definition of the following concepts by providing an illustrating scenario—an extended example of the concept in your own experience or in hypothetical form. You can share several of these examples in group discussion to refine your understanding of the concept and to reach consensus on it.

   • id

   • ego

   • superego

   • pleasure principle and reality principle

   • libido and aggression

   • Oedipal feelings

   • anxiety

2. Identify a situation, either real or hypothetical, in which you can see the role the ego plays in finding an alternative, "safe" means of satisfying an idic urge. How do you think the superego might influence this redirection, or sublimation, of desire?

3. What are some contemporary, adult means to anger-venting? Consider the hobbies and interests that attract a wide following. In what ways might these activities channel desires and frustrations into socially acceptable forms?

4. What is the "story" of human life as this theory constructs it? What path are we all destined to travel, from birth, through childhood, to adulthood? Do you see it as a happy story? a tragic story? Does the story you think it tells affect your feelings about the theory?

5. The authors frequently use the first-person plural pronoun "we," and they speak of "our" psychological experience. How might the nature of their task—the presentation of material that has historically created great resistance on the part of its audience—have affected their choice of authorial stance and voice? Do you see them make other rhetorical choices to help minimize their readers' possibly negative reactions against Freudian theory?

6. A major criticism of Freudian theory is its inattention to or misrepresentation of women's experience. Does the excerpt summarizing Freud's theories represent both male and female experience? Do you feel it is slanted toward a male perception of reality? Look at the gender roles implicit in the Oedipus complex, for instance; look at the language use itself—pronoun choice, for example.

Civilization and Its Discontents

SIGMUND FREUD

Civilization and Its Discontents, *one of Freud's final works, first published in 1930, sets out the apparently unresolvable conflict between human nature and human civilization. In the book's brief chapters, Freud outlines our instinctual desires, which are themselves in conflict, making us choose between survival and pleasure. Freud's characterization of human nature in this text led to a collection of philosophical charges against him, with misanthropy and immorality being two of the most common. Both represent a distortion of Freud's thought. He attempts in the text to outline the conflicts we inevitably face in civilization, not to judge the worth of particular social practices or cultures. And he does not endorse an unrestricted pursuit of pleasure, pointing out that uncontrolled indulgence of desire is likely to lead to much suffering and early death. So, at base, humans are sentenced to live compromised lives. Their desires can be attained, but in weak forms; their duties can be fulfilled, but at the price of their desires. Freud's apparent pessimism about the human condition finds expression in his theory of the death instinct, which opposes the life principle, Eros. Freud ends the text with a question that challenges the results of civilization and opens up his work for social critique. Note: We've highlighted key lines to help you focus on the fundamental claims of Freud's argument.*

I

. . . **I had sent [a friend] my small book that treats religion as an illusion** [*The Future of an Illusion*, 1927], and he answered that he entirely agreed with my judgment upon religion, but that he was sorry I had not properly appreciated the true source of religious sentiments. This, he says, consists in a peculiar feeling, which he himself is never without, which he finds confirmed by many others, and which he may suppose is present in millions of people. It is a feeling which he would like to call **a sensation of "eternity," a feeling as of something limitless, unbounded—as it were, "oceanic."** This feeling, he adds, is a purely subjective fact, not an article of faith; it brings with it no assurance of personal immortality. . . . One may, he thinks, rightly call oneself religious on the ground of this oceanic feeling alone, even if one rejects every belief and every illusion.

The views expressed by the friend whom I so much honor, and who himself once praised the magic of illusion in a poem, caused me no small difficulty. I cannot discover this "oceanic" feeling in myself. . . . If I have understood my friend rightly, he means the same thing by it as the consolation offered by an original and somewhat eccentric dramatist to his hero who is facing self-inflicted death. "We cannot fall out of this world." That is to say, it is **a feeling of an indissoluble bond, of being one with the external world as a whole**. . . . From my own experience I could not convince myself of the primary nature of such a feeling. But this gives me no right to deny that it does in fact occur in other people. The only question is whether it is being correctly interpreted and whether it ought to be regarded as the *fons et origo* of the whole need for religion.

I have nothing to suggest which could have a decisive influence on the solution of this problem. The idea of men's receiving an intimation of their connection with the world around them through an immediate feeling which is from the outset directed to that purpose sounds so strange and fits in so badly with the fabric of our psychology that one is justified in attempting to discover a psycho-analytic—that is, genetic—explanation of such a feeling. The following line of thought suggests itself. Normally, there is nothing of which we are more certain than the feeling of our self, of our own ego. **This ego appears to us as something autonomous and unitary, marked off distinctly from everything else. That such an appearance is deceptive, and that on the contrary the ego is continued inwards, without any sharp delimitation, into an unconscious mental entity which we designate as the id and for which it serves as a kind of facade—this was a discovery first made by psycho-analytic research,** which should still have much more to tell us about the relation of the ego to the id. But towards the outside, at any rate, the ego seems to maintain clear and sharp lines of demarcation. There is only one state—admittedly an unusual state, but not one that can be stigmatized as pathological—in which it does not do this. At the height of being in love the boundary between the ego and object threatens to melt away. Against all the evidence of his senses, a man who is in love declares that "I" and "you" are one, and is prepared to behave as if it were a fact. What can be temporarily done away with by a physiological [i.e., normal] function must also, of course, be liable to be disturbed by pathological processes. Pathology has made us acquainted with a great number of states in which the boundary lines between the ego and the external world become uncertain or in which they are actually drawn incorrectly. There are cases in which parts of a person's own body, even portions of his own mental life—his perceptions, thoughts, and feelings—appear alien to him and as not belonging to his ego; there are other cases in which he ascribes to the external world things that clearly originate in his own ego and that ought to be acknowledged by it. Thus even the feeling of our own ego is subject to disturbances and the boundaries of the ego are not constant.

Further reflection tells us that **the adult's ego-feeling cannot have been the same from the beginning. It must have gone through a process of development**, which cannot, of course, be demonstrated but which admits of being constructed with a fair degree of probability. An infant at the breast does not as yet distinguish his ego from the external world as the source of the sensations flowing in upon him. He gradually learns to do so, in response to various promptings. He must be very strongly impressed by the fact that some sources of excitation, which he will later recognize as his own bodily organs, can provide him with sensations at any moment, whereas other sources evade him from time to time—among them what he desires most of all, his mother's breast—and only reappear as a result of his screaming for help. In this way there is for the first time set over against the ego an "object," in the form of something which exists "outside" and which is only forced to appear by a special action. A further incentive to a disengagement of the ego from the general mass of sensations—that is, to the recognition of an "outside," an external world—is provided by the frequent, manifold and unavoidable sensations of pain and unpleasure the removal and avoidance of which is enjoined by the pleasure principle, in the exercise of its unrestricted domination. A tendency arises to separate from the ego everything that can become a source of such unpleasure, to throw it outside and to create a pure pleasure-ego which is confronted by a strange and alien "outside." **The boundaries of this primitive pleasure-ego cannot escape rectification through experience. . . . In this way one makes the first step towards the introduction of the reality principle which is to dominate future development. . . .**

In this way, then, the ego detaches itself from the external world. Or, to put it more correctly, originally the ego includes everything, later it separates off an external world from itself. Our present ego-feeling is, therefore, only a shrunken residue of a much more inclusive—indeed, an all-embracing—feeling which corresponded to a more intimate bond between the ego and the world about it. . . .

[W]hat is past in mental life *may* be preserved and is not *necessarily* destroyed. . . . [I]t is rather the rule than the exception for the past to be preserved in mental life.

Thus we are perfectly willing to acknowledge that the "oceanic" feeling exists in many people, and we are inclined to trace it back to an early phase of ego feeling. The further question then arises, what claim this feeling has to be regarded as the source of religious needs.

To me the claim does not seem compelling. After all, a feeling can only be a source of energy if it is itself the expression of a strong need. **The derivation of religious needs from the infant's helplessness and the longing for the father aroused by it seems to me incontrovertible, especially since the feeling is not simply prolonged from childhood days, but is permanently sustained by fear of the superior power of Fate.** I cannot think of any need in childhood as strong as the need for a father's protection. Thus the part played by the oceanic feeling, which might seek something like the restoration of limitless narcissism, is ousted from a place in the foreground. The origin of the religious attitude can be traced back in clear outlines as far as the feeling of infantile helplessness.

II

Life, as we find it, is too hard for us; it brings us too many pains, disappointments and impossible tasks. In order to bear it we cannot dispense with palliative measures. . . . There are perhaps three such measures: powerful **deflections**, which cause us to make light of our misery; **substitutive satisfactions**, which diminish it; and **intoxicating substances**, which make us insensitive to it. Something of the kind is indispensable. Voltaire has deflections in mind when he ends *Candide* with the advice to cultivate one's garden; and scientific activity is a deflection of this kind, too. The substitutive satisfactions, as offered by art, are illusions in contrast with reality, but they are none the less psychically effective, thanks to the role which fantasy has assumed in mental life. The intoxicating substances influence our body and alter its chemistry. . . .

What do [men] demand of life and wish to achieve in it? The answer to this   10
can hardly be in doubt. They strive after happiness; they want to become happy and to remain so. This endeavor has two sides, a positive and a negative aim. It aims, on the one hand, at **an absence of pain and unpleasure, and, on the other, at the experiencing of strong feelings of pleasure**. . . .

As we see, what decides the purpose of life is simply the program of **the pleasure principle**. This principle dominates the operation of the mental apparatus from the start. There can be no doubt about its efficacy, and yet its program is at loggerheads with the whole world, with the macrocosm as much as with the microcosm. There is no possibility at all of its being carried through; all the regulations of the universe run counter to it. . . .When any situation that is desired by the pleasure principle is prolonged, it only produces a feeling of mild contentment. We are so made that we can derive intense enjoyment only from a contrast and very little from a state of things. Thus our possibilities of happiness are already restricted by our constitution. Unhappiness is much less difficult to experience. We are threatened with suffering from three directions: from our own body, which is doomed to decay and dissolution and which cannot even do without pain and anxiety as warning signals; from the external world, which may rage against us with overwhelming and merciless forces of destruction; and finally from our relations to other men. The suffering which comes from this last source is perhaps more painful to us than any other. . . .

It is no wonder if, under the pressure of these possibilities of suffering, **men are accustomed to moderate their claims to happiness—just as the pleasure principle itself, indeed, under the influence of the external world, changed into the more modest reality principle**—if a man thinks himself happy merely to have escaped unhappiness or to have survived his suffering, and if in general the task of avoiding suffering pushes that of obtaining pleasure into the background. Reflection shows that the accomplishment of this task can be attempted along very different paths; and all these paths have been recommended by the various schools of worldly wisdom and put into practice by men. An unrestricted satisfaction of every need presents itself as the most enticing method of conducting one's life, but it means putting enjoyment before caution, and soon brings its own punishment. The other methods, in which avoidance of unpleasure is the main purpose, are differentiated according to the source of unpleasure to which their attention is chiefly turned. . . .

The crudest, but also the most effective among these methods of influence is the chemical one—**intoxication**. I do not think that anyone completely understands its mechanism, but it is a fact that there are foreign substances which, when present in the blood or tissues, directly cause us pleasurable sensations; and they also so alter the conditions governing our sensibility that we become incapable of receiving unpleasurable impulses. . . . [W]ith the help of this "drowner of cares" one can at any time withdraw from the pressure of reality and find refuge in a world of one's own with better conditions of sensibility. As is well known, it is precisely this property of intoxicants which also determines their danger and their injuriousness. They are responsible, in certain circumstances, for the useless waste of a large quota of energy which might have been employed for the improvement of the human lot. . . .

Another technique for fending off suffering is the employment of the displacements of libido which our mental apparatus permits of and through which its function gains so much in flexibility. The task here is that of shifting the instinctual aims in such a way that they cannot come up against frustration from the external world. In this, **sublimation of the instincts** lends its assistance. . . . A satisfaction of this kind, such as an artist's joy in creating, in giving his fantasies body, or a scientist's in solving problems or discovering truths, has a special quality which we shall certainly one day be able to characterize in metapsychological terms. At present we can only say figuratively that such satisfactions seem "finer and higher." But their intensity is mild compared with that derived from the sating of crude and primary instinctual impulses; it does not convulse our physical being. And the weak point of this method is that it is not applicable generally: it is accessible to only a few people. It presupposes the possession of special dispositions and gifts which are far from being common to any practical degree. . . .

In [the next procedure], the connection with reality is still further loosened; | 15 | satisfaction is obtained from illusions, which are recognized as such without the discrepancy between them and reality being allowed to interfere with enjoyment. The region from which these illusions arise is the life of the imagination . . . . At the head of these satisfactions through fantasy stands the enjoyment of works of art—an enjoyment which, by the agency of the artist, is made accessible even to those who are not themselves creative. People who are receptive to the influence of art cannot set too high a value on it as a source of pleasure and consolation in life. Nevertheless the mild narcosis induced in us by art can do no more than bring about a transient withdrawal from the pressure of vital needs, and it is not strong enough to make us forget real misery.

Another procedure operates more energetically and more thoroughly. It regards reality as the sole enemy and as the source of all suffering, with which it is impossible to live, so that one must break off all relations with it if one is to be in any way happy. The hermit turns his back on the world and will have no truck with it. But one can do more than that; one can try to re-create the world, to build up in its stead another world in which its most unbearable features are eliminated and replaced by others that are in conformity with one's own wishes. But whoever, in desperate defiance, sets out upon this path to happiness will as a rule attain nothing. Reality is too strong for him. He becomes a madman, who for the most part finds no one to help him in carrying through his delusion. It is asserted, however, that each one of us behaves in some one respect like a paranoic, corrects some aspect of the world which is unbearable to him by the construction of a wish and introduces this delusion into reality. A special importance attaches to the case in which this attempt to procure a certainty of happiness and a protection against suffering through a delusional remolding of reality is made by a considerable number of people in common. **The religions of mankind must be classed among the mass-delusions** of this kind. No one, needless to say, who shares a delusion ever recognizes it as such.

III

. . . Human life in common is only made possible when a majority comes together which is stronger than any separate individual and which remains united against all separate individuals. The power of this community is then set up as "right" in opposition to the power of the individual, which is condemned as "brute force." **This replacement of the power of the individual by the power of a community constitutes the decisive step of civilization**. The essence of it lies in the fact that the members of the community restrict themselves in their possibilities of satisfaction, whereas the individual knew no such restrictions. The first requisite of civilization, therefore, is that of justice—that is, the assurance that a law once made will not be broken in favor of an individual. . . .

The liberty of the individual is not a gift of civilization. It was greatest before there was any civilization, though then, it is true, it had for the most part no value, since the individual was scarcely in a position to defend it. The development of civilization imposes restrictions on it, and justice demands that no one shall escape those restrictions. . . . A good part of the struggles of mankind center round the single task of finding an expedient accommodation—one, that is, that will bring happiness—between this claim of the individual and the cultural claims of the group; and one of the problems that touches the fate of humanity is whether such an accommodation can be reached by means of some particular form of civilization or whether this conflict is irreconcilable. . . .

[I]t is impossible to overlook the extent to which **civilization is built upon a renunciation of instinct,** how much it presupposes precisely the non-satisfaction (by suppression, repression or some other means?) of powerful instincts. This "cultural frustration" dominates the large field of social relationships between human beings. As we already know, it is the cause of the hostility against which all civilizations have to struggle. . . .

IV

After primal man had discovered that it lay in his own hands, literally, to improve his lot on earth by working, it cannot have been a matter of indifference to him whether another man worked with or against him. The other man acquired the value for him of a fellow-worker, with whom it was useful to live together. Even earlier, in his ape-like prehistory, man had adopted the habit of forming families, and the members of his family were probably his first helpers. . . . [T]he male acquired a motive for

20

keeping the female, or, speaking more generally, his sexual objects, near him; while the female, who did not want to be separated from her helpless young, was obliged, in their interests, to remain with the stronger male. . . . **The communal life of human beings had, therefore, a two-fold foundation: the compulsion to work, which was created by external necessity, and the power of love**, which made the man unwilling to be deprived of his sexual object—the woman—and made the woman unwilling to be deprived of the part of herself which had been separated off from her—her child. . . .

As regards the sexually mature individual [in civilization], the choice of an object is restricted to the opposite sex, and most extra-genital satisfactions are forbidden as perversions. The requirement, demonstrated in these prohibitions, that there shall be a single kind of sexual life for everyone, disregards the dissimilarities, whether innate or acquired, in the sexual constitution of human beings; it cuts off a fair number of them from sexual enjoyment, and so becomes the source of serious injustice. . . . **[H]eterosexual genital love, which has remained exempt from outlawry, is itself restricted by further limitations, in the shape of insistence upon legitimacy and monogamy**. Present-day civilization makes it plain that it will only permit sexual relationships on the basis of a solitary, indissoluble bond between one man and one woman, and that it does not like sexuality as a source of pleasure in its own right and is only prepared to tolerate it because there is so far no substitute for it as a means of propagating the human race.

V

. . . Reality shows us that civilization is not content with the ties that we have so far allowed it. It aims at binding the members of the community together in a libidinal way as well and employs every means to that end. It favors every path by which strong identification can be established between the members of the community, and it summons up aim-inhibited libido on the largest scale so as to strengthen the communal bond by relations of friendship. In order for these aims to be fulfilled, a restriction upon sexual life is unavoidable. But we are unable to understand what the necessity is which forces civilization along this path and which causes its antagonism to sexuality. There must be some more disturbing factor which we have not yet discovered.

The clue may be supplied by one of the ideal demands, as we have called them, of civilized society. It runs: "Thou shalt love thy neighbor as thyself." It is known throughout the world and is undoubtedly older than Christianity, which puts it forward as its proudest claim. . . .

The element of truth behind all this, which people are so ready to disavow, is that **men are not gentle creatures who want to be loved, and at most can defend themselves if they are attacked; they are, on the contrary, creatures among whose instinctual endowments is to be reckoned a powerful share of aggressiveness**. As a result, their neighbor is for them not only a potential helper or sexual object, but also someone who tempts them to satisfy their aggressiveness on him, to exploit his capacity for work without compensation, to use him sexually without his consent, to seize his possessions, to humiliate him, to cause him pain, to torture and to kill him. . . . Anyone who calls to mind the atrocities committed during the racial migration or the invasions of the Huns, or by the people known as Mongols under Jenghiz Khan and Tamerlane, or at the capture of Jerusalem by the pious Crusaders, or even, indeed, the horrors of the recent World War—anyone who calls these things to mind will have to bow humbly before the truth of this view.

The existence of this inclination to aggression, which we can detect in ourselves and justly assume to be present in others, is the factor which disturbs our relations with our neighbor and which forces civilization into such a high expenditure [of energy]. In consequence of this primary mutual hostility of human beings, civilized society is perpetually threatened with disintegration. The interests of work in common would not hold it together; instinctual passions are stronger than reasonable interests. **Civilization has to use its utmost efforts in order to set limits on man's aggressive instincts** and to hold the manifestations of them in check by psychical reaction-formations. Hence, therefore, the use of methods intended to incite people into identifications and aim-inhibited relationships of love, hence the restriction upon sexual life, and hence too the ideal's commandment to love one's neighbor as oneself— a commandment which is really justified by the fact that nothing else runs so strongly counter to the original nature of man. . . .

If civilization imposes such great sacrifices not only on man's sexuality but on his aggressivity, we can understand better why it is hard for him to be happy in civilization. In fact, primitive man was better off in knowing no restrictions of instinct. To counterbalance this, his prospects of enjoying this happiness for any length of time were very slender. **Civilized man has exchanged a portion of his possibilities of happiness for a portion of security**.

VI

. . . Starting from speculations on the beginning of life and from biological parallels, I drew the conclusion that, **besides the instinct to preserve living substance and to join it into ever larger units, there must exist another, contrary instinct seeking to dissolve those units and to bring them back to their primeval, inorganic state. That is to say, as well as Eros there was an instinct of death**. The phenomena of life could be explained from the concurrent or mutually opposing action of these two instincts. It was not easy, however, to demonstrate the activities of this supposed death instinct. The manifestations of Eros were conspicuous and noisy enough. It might be assumed that the death instinct operated silently within the organism towards its dissolution, but that, of course, was no proof. A more fruitful idea was that **a portion of the instinct is diverted towards the external world and comes to light as an instinct of aggressiveness and**

destructiveness. In this way the instinct itself could be pressed into the service of Eros, in that the organism was destroying some other thing, whether animate or inanimate, instead of destroying its own self. Conversely, any restriction of this aggressiveness directed outwards would be bound to increase the self-destruction, which is in any case proceeding. At the same time one can suspect from this example that the two kinds of instinct seldom—perhaps never—appear in isolation from each other, but are alloyed with each other in varying and very different proportions and so become unrecognizable to our judgement. . . .

The name "libido" can once more be used to denote the manifestations of the power of Eros in order to distinguish them from the energy of the death instinct. It must be confessed that we have much greater difficulty in grasping that instinct; we can only suspect it, as it were, as something in the background behind Eros, and it escapes detection unless its presence is betrayed by its being alloyed with Eros. It is in sadism, where the death instinct twists the erotic aim in its own sense and yet at the same time fully satisfies the erotic urge, that we succeed in obtaining the clearest insight into its nature and its relation to Eros. But even where it emerges without any sexual purpose, in the blindest fury of destructiveness, we cannot fail to recognize that the satisfaction of the instinct is accompanied by an extraordinarily high degree of narcissistic enjoyment, owing to its presenting the ego with a fulfillment of the latter's old wishes for omnipotence. . . .

In all that follows I adopt the standpoint, therefore, that the inclination to aggression is an original, self-subsisting instinctual disposition in man, and I return to my view that it constitutes the greatest impediment to civilization. At one point in the course of this inquiry I was led to the idea that civilization was a special process which mankind undergoes, and I am still under the influence of that idea. I may now add that **civilization is a process in the service of Eros, whose purpose is to combine single human individuals, and after that families, then races, peoples and nations, into one great unity, the unity of mankind**. Why this has to happen, we do not know; the work of Eros is this precisely this. . . . But man's natural aggressive instinct, the hostility of each against all and of all against each, opposes this program of civilization. This aggressive instinct is the derivative and the main representative of the death instinct which we have found alongside of Eros and which shares world-dominion with it. And now, I think, **the meaning of the evolution of civilization is no longer obscure to us. It must present the struggle between Eros and Death, between the instinct of life and the instinct of destruction, as it works itself out in the human species.** This struggle is what all life essentially consists of, and the evolution of civilization may therefore be simply described as the struggle for life of the human species.

VII

. . . What means does civilization employ in order to inhibit the aggressiveness 30
which opposes it, to make it harmless, to get rid of it, perhaps? We have already become acquainted with a few of these methods, but not yet with the one that appears

to be the most important. This we can study in the history of the development of the individual. What happens in him to render his desire for aggression innocuous? Something very remarkable, which we should never have guessed and which nevertheless is quite obvious. His aggressiveness is introjected, internalized; it is, in point of fact, sent back to where it came from—that is, it is directed towards his own ego. There it is taken over by a portion of the ego, which sets itself over against the rest of the ego as super-ego, and which now, in the form of "conscience," is ready to put into action against the ego the same harsh aggressiveness that the ego would have liked to satisfy upon other, extraneous individuals. **The tension between the harsh super-ego and the ego that is subjected to it, is called by us the sense of guilt; it expresses itself as a need for punishment. Civilization, therefore, obtains mastery over the individual's dangerous desire for aggression by weakening and disarming it and by setting up an agency within him to watch over it**, like a garrison in a conquered city. . . .

VIII

. . . **The fateful question for the human species seems to me to be whether and to what extent their cultural development will succeed in mastering the disturbance of their communal life by the human instinct of aggression and self-destruction.** It may be that in this respect precisely the present time deserves a special interest. Men have gained control over the forces of nature to such an extent that with their help they would have no difficulty in exterminating one another to the last man. They know this, and hence comes a large part of their current unrest, their unhappiness and their mood of anxiety. And now it is to be expected that the other of the two "Heavenly Powers," eternal Eros, will make an effort to assert himself in the struggle with his equally immortal adversary. But who can foresee with what success and with what results?

● Building the Frame Through Writing

1. Freud's main argument is that we are caught between our basic animal nature and our need for civilization. Explain why and how these two impulses come into conflict.
   - What is Freud's view of human nature outside of any social control?
   - What "price" does the individual pay to be part of civilized society, and what benefit(s) does he or she receive?

2. The pain of the reality principle creates a need for relief, three forms of which Freud identifies. Illustrate how these forms operate in daily life—in your own, perhaps. How effective do you think each is in the twin human goals of avoiding pain and experiencing pleasure? Why are they all fleeting forms of relief?

Think about how this aspect of the theory informs social issues such as physician-assisted suicide, or the use of drugs for medicinal or recreational purposes. How might you use the theory to argue for or against them as social policies?

3. The pleasure principle gives way to the reality principle in small stages; humans, Freud argues, come to accept the reality principle developmentally. Where are adolescents in this process, in your opinion? Are most adolescents dominated by the reality principle? What are some examples you can draw from your own experience to support your view?

4. Freud argues that the ego is not a single, stable "self" but in fact has changeable boundaries—our "selves" can contract or expand, in a sense, to include less or more of the external world, depending on our perceptions. Freud cites the experience of falling in love as proof. Explain his reasoning about how being in love affects ego boundaries.

   • Try using this reasoning to explain other forms of social connection: in what other experiences or situations are ego boundaries likely to be experienced as shrinking or expanding? In what circumstances might we feel alienated from others, and what situations make us feel united?

   • How might this concept of fluid ego boundaries be a potentially useful insight for social purposes—from organizing a group project, for example, to negotiating a peace agreement?

5. In one of his more resisted claims, Freud argues that religious feelings are actually generated by the infantile ego. What kind of reader reaction would you expect this part of his argument to generate? How does his argument depict the individual who is a religious believer?

6. Freud's thesis states that we have two opposing instincts—life and death. How does Eros, the life instinct, use the energy of the death instinct to support community and civilization? How can the aggression of the death instinct be used to enhance Eros/life?

   Identify specific illustrations from historical and/or contemporary social practices. What are some campus-based practices you know of that help illustrate this part of Freudian theory?

7. Although the passage is a translation from the original German, we still can see Freud's rhetorical choices and common patterns in the nature of the appeals he uses and the stances he adopts.

   • Look at the range of appeals used—logos, ethos, pathos. Do you see him consistently using all three, or does he favor a particular kind?

   • Does he speak primarily as a man of science? Is his invoked audience other members of the scientific community?

   • What types of evidence does he use for what are very broad claims about human nature and civilization?

- Given his purpose—to explain the inevitable conflict of nature and civilization, and the inevitable human pain that results—what do you see as the rhetorical challenges of presenting his argument?
- Freud ends the text with a rhetorical question. How do you think the historical context of this work—published in 1930 Vienna, Austria, in the period between two world wars—may have influenced him to choose this stylistic conclusion?

Psychoanalysis

TERRY EAGLETON

In the first part of this reading (an excerpted chapter from Literary Theory: An Introduction, *1983), Terry Eagleton, a Marxist literary theorist, provides a detailed overview of the major Freudian theories, extending the explanation of such fundamental concepts as the Oedipus complex, the emergence of the self, and the coping mechanisms of the mind, and ending with a summary of Freud's philosophical attitudes. This excerpt complements the Kagan and Havemann overview (p. 75), providing more specific explanations of Freud's fundamental concepts and making a more explicit connection to social critique. Like the Kagan and Havemann textbook excerpt, Eagleton's chapter is a narrative, a story. As you read, watch for the different ways in which Eagleton shapes the story, the different parts that he emphasizes.*

. . . "The motive of human society is in the last resort an economic one." It was Freud, not Karl Marx, who made this statement, in his *Introductory Lectures on Psychoanalysis.* What has dominated human history to date is the need to labour; and for Freud that harsh necessity means that we must repress some of our tendencies to pleasure and gratification. If we were not called upon to work in order to survive, we might simply lie around all day doing nothing. Every human being has to undergo this repression of what Freud named the "pleasure principle" by the "reality principle," but for some of us, and arguably for whole societies, the repression may become excessive and make us ill. We are sometimes willing to forego gratification to an heroic extent, but usually in the canny trust that by deferring an immediate pleasure we will recoup it in the end, perhaps in richer form. We are prepared to put up with **repression** as long as we see that there is something in it for us; if too much is demanded of us, however, we are likely to fall sick. This form of sickness is known as **neurosis**; and since, as I have said, all human beings must be repressed to some degree, it is possible to speak of the human race, in the words of one of Freud's commentators, as the "neurotic animal." It is important to see that such neurosis is involved with what is creative about us as a race, as well as with the causes of our unhappiness. One way in which we cope with desires we cannot fulfil is by **"sublimating"** them, by which Freud means directing them towards a more socially valued end. We might find an unconscious outlet for sexual frustration in building bridges or cathedrals. For Freud, it is by virtue of such sublimation that civilization itself comes about: by switching and harnessing our instincts to these higher goals, cultural history itself is created.

If Marx looked at the consequences of our need to labour in terms of the social relations, social classes and forms of politics which it entailed, Freud looks at its implications for the psychical life. The paradox or contradiction on which his work rests is that we come to be what we are only by a massive repression of the elements which have gone into our making. We are not of course conscious of this, any more than for Marx men and women are generally conscious of the social processes which determine their lives. Indeed we could not be by definition conscious of this fact, since the place to which we relegate the desires we are unable to fulfil is known as the unconscious. One question which immediately arises, however, is why it is human beings who should be the neurotic animal, rather than snails or tortoises. It is possible that this is merely a Romantic idealization of such creatures and that they are secretly a good deal more neurotic than we think; but they seem well-adjusted enough to an outsider, even though there may be one or two cases of hysterical paralysis on record.

One feature which distinguishes human beings from the other animals is that for evolutionary reasons we are born almost entirely helpless and are wholly reliant for our survival on the care of the more mature members of the species, usually our parents. We are all born "prematurely." Without such immediate, unceasing care we would die very quickly. This unusually prolonged dependence on our parents is first of all a purely material matter, a question of being fed and kept from harm: it is a matter of the satisfaction of what may be called our "instincts," by which is meant the biologically fixed needs human beings have for nourishment, warmth and so on. (Such self-preservative instincts are, as we shall see, a good deal more immutable than "drives," which very often alter their nature.) But our dependence on our parents for these services does not stop at the biological. The small baby will suck its mother's breast for milk, but will discover in doing so that this biologically essential activity is also pleasurable; and this, for Freud, is the first dawning of **sexuality**. The baby's mouth becomes not only an organ of its physical survival but an "erotogenic zone," which the child might reactivate a few years later by sucking its thumb, and a few years later than that by kissing. The relation to the mother has taken on a new, libidinal dimension: sexuality has been born, as a kind of drive which was at first inseparable from biological instinct but which has now separated itself out from it and attained a certain autonomy. Sexuality for Freud is itself a "perversion"—a "swerving away" of a natural self-preservative instinct towards another goal.

As the infant grows, other erotogenic zones come into play. The **oral stage**, as Freud calls it, is the first phase of sexual life, and is associated with the drive to incorporate objects. In the **anal stage**, the anus becomes an erotogenic zone, and with the child's pleasure in defecation a new contrast between activity and passivity, unknown in the oral stage, comes to light. The anal stage is sadistic, in that the child derives erotic pleasure from expulsion and destruction; but it is also connected with the desire for retention and possessive control, as the child learns a new form of mastery and a manipulation of the wishes of others through the "granting" or withholding of the faeces. The ensuing "**phallic**" **stage** begins to focus the child's libido (or sexual drive) on the genitals, but is called "phallic" rather than "genital" because according to Freud only the male organ is recognized at this point. The little girl in Freud's view has to be content with the clitoris, the "equivalent" of the penis, rather than with the vagina.

What is happening in this process—though the stages overlap, and should not be seen as a strict sequence—is a gradual organization of the libidinal drives, but one still centred on the child's own body. The drives themselves are extremely flexible, in no sense fixed like biological instinct: their objects are contingent and replaceable, and one sexual drive can substitute itself for another. What we can imagine in the early years of the child's life, then, is not a unified subject confronting and desiring a stable object, but a complex, shifting field of force in which the subject (the child itself) is caught up and dispersed, in which it has as yet no centre of identity and in which the boundaries between itself and the external world are indeterminate. Within this field of libidinal force, objects and part-objects emerge and disappear again, shift places kaleidoscopically, and prominent among such objects is the child's body as the play of drives laps across it. One can speak of this also as an "**auto-eroticism**," within which Freud sometimes includes the whole of infantile sexuality: the child takes erotic delight in its own body, but without as yet being able to view its body as a complete object. Auto-eroticism must thus be distinguished from what Freud will call "narcissism," a state in which one's body or ego as a whole is "cathected," or taken as an object of desire.

It is clear that the child in this state is not even prospectively a citizen who could be relied upon to do a hard day's work. It is anarchic, sadistic, aggressive, self-involved and remorselessly pleasure-seeking, under the sway of what Freud calls the pleasure principle; nor does it have any respect for differences of gender. It is not yet what we might call a "**gendered subject**": it surges with sexual drives, but this libidinal energy recognizes no distinction between masculine and feminine. If the child is to succeed in life at all, it obviously has to be taken in hand; and the mechanism by which this happens is what Freud famously terms the **Oedipus complex**. The child who emerges from the pre-Oedipal stages we have been following is not only anarchic and sadistic but incestuous to boot: the boy's close involvement with his mother's body leads him to an unconscious desire for sexual union with her, whereas the girl, who has been similarly bound up with the mother and whose first desire is therefore always homosexual, begins to turn her libido towards the father. The early "dyadic" or two-term relationship between infant and mother, that is to say, has now opened up into a triangle consisting of child and both parents; and for the child, the parent of the same sex will come to figure as a rival in its affections for the parent of the opposite sex.

What persuades the boy-child to abandon his incestuous desire for the mother is the father's threat of **castration**. This threat need not necessarily be spoken; but the boy, in perceiving that the girl is herself "castrated," begins to imagine this as a punishment which might be visited upon himself. He thus represses his incestuous desire in anxious resignation, adjusts himself to the "reality principle," submits to the father, detaches himself from the mother, and comforts himself with the unconscious consolation that though he cannot *now* hope to oust his father and possess his mother, his father symbolizes a place, a possibility, which he himself will be able to take up and realize in the future. If he is not a patriarch now, he will be later. The boy makes peace with his father, identifies with him, and is thus introduced into the symbolic role of manhood. He has become a gendered subject, surmounting his Oedipus complex; but in doing so he has, so to speak, driven his forbidden desire underground, repressed it into the place we call the unconscious. This is not a place that was ready and waiting to receive such a desire: it is produced, opened up, by this act of primary repression. As a man in the making, the boy will now grow up within those images and practices which his society happens to define as "masculine." He will one day become a father himself, thus sustaining this society by contributing to the business of sexual reproduction. His earlier diffuse libido has become organized through the Oedipus complex in a way which centres it upon genital sexuality. If the boy is unable successfully to overcome the Oedipus complex, he may be sexually incapacitated for such a role: he may privilege the image of his mother above all other women, which for Freud may lead to homosexuality; or the recognition that women are "castrated" may have traumatized him so deeply that he is unable to enjoy satisfying sexual relationships with them.

The story of the little girl's passage through the Oedipus complex is a good deal less straightforward. It should be said right away that Freud was nowhere more typical of his own male-dominated society than in his bafflement in the face of female sexuality—the "dark continent," as he once called it. We shall have occasion to comment later on the demeaning, prejudiced attitudes towards women which disfigure his work, and his account of the girl's process of oedipalization is by no means easily separable from this sexism. The little girl, perceiving that she is inferior because "castrated," turns in disillusionment from her similarly "castrated" mother to the project of seducing her father; but since this project is doomed, she must finally turn back reluctantly to the mother, effect an identification with her, assume her feminine gender role, and unconsciously substitute for the penis which she envies but can never possess a baby, which she desires to receive from the father. There is no obvious reason why the girl should abandon this desire, since being "castrated" already she cannot be threatened with castration; and it is therefore difficult to see by what mechanism her Oedipus complex is dissolved. "Castration," far from prohibiting her incestuous desire as with the boy, is what makes it possible in the first place. Moreover the girl, to enter into the Oedipus complex, must change her "love-object" from mother to father, whereas the boy has merely to carry on loving the mother; and since a change of love-objects is a more complex, difficult affair, this too raises a problem about female oedipalization.

Before leaving the question of the Oedipus complex, its utter centrality to Freud's work should be emphasized. It is not just another complex: it is the structure of relations by which we come to be the men and women that we are. It is the point at which we are produced and constituted as subjects; and one problem for us is that it is always in some sense a partial, defective mechanism. It signals the transition from the pleasure principle to the reality principle; from the enclosure of the family to society at large, since we turn from incest to extra-familial relations; and from Nature to Culture, since we can see the infant's relation to the mother as somehow "natural," and the post-Oedipal child as one who is in the process of assuming a position within the cultural order as a whole. (To see the mother–child relationship as "natural," however, is in one sense highly dubious: it does not matter in the least to the infant who the provider actually is.) Moreover, the Oedipus complex is for Freud the beginnings of morality, conscience, law and all forms of social and religious authority. The father's real or imagined prohibition of incest is symbolic of all the higher authority to be later encountered; and in "introjecting" (making its own) this patriarchal law, the child begins to form what Freud calls its "superego," the awesome, punitive voice of conscience within it.

All, then, would now seem in place for gender roles to be reinforced, satis-   10
factions to be postponed, authority to be accepted and the family and society to be reproduced. But we have forgotten about the unruly, insubordinate unconscious. The child has now developed an ego or individual identity, a particular place in the sexual, familial and social networks; but it can do this only by, so to speak, splitting off its guilty desires, repressing them into the unconscious. The human subject who emerges from the Oedipal process is a *split* subject, torn precariously between conscious and unconscious; and the unconscious can always return to plague it. In popular English speech, the word "subconscious" rather than "unconscious" is often used; but this is to underestimate the radical *otherness* of the unconscious, imagining it as a place just within reach below the surface. It underestimates the extreme strangeness of the unconscious, which is a place and a non-place, which is completely indifferent to reality, which knows no logic or negation or causality or contradiction, wholly given over as it is to the instinctual play of the drives and the search for pleasure.

The "royal road" to the unconscious is dreams. Dreams allow us one of our few privileged glimpses of it at work. Dreams for Freud are essentially **symbolic fulfilments of unconscious wishes**; and they are cast in symbolic form because if this material were expressed directly then it might be shocking and disturbing enough to wake us up. In order that we should get some sleep, the unconscious charitably conceals, softens and distorts its meanings, so that our dreams become symbolic texts which need to be deciphered. The watchful ego is still at work even within our dreaming, censoring an image here or scrambling a message there; and the unconscious itself adds to this obscurity by its peculiar modes of functioning. With the economy of the indolent, it will condense together a whole set of images into a single "statement"; or it will "displace" the meaning of one object on to another somehow associated with it, so that in my dream I am venting on a crab an aggression I feel towards somebody with that surname. This constant condensation and displacement of meaning corresponds to what Roman Jakobson identified as the two primary operations of human language: metaphor (condensing meanings together), and metonymy (displacing one on to another). It was this which moved the French psychoanalyst Jacques Lacan to comment that "the unconscious is structured like a language." Dream-texts are also cryptic because the unconscious is rather poor in techniques for representing what it has to say, being largely confined to visual images, and so must often craftily translate a verbal significance into a visual one: it might seize upon the image of a tennis *racket* to make a point about some shady dealing. At any rate, dreams are enough to demonstrate that the unconscious has the admirable resourcefulness of a lazy, ill-supplied chef, who slings together the most diverse ingredients into a cobbled-together stew, substituting one spice for another which he is out of, making do with whatever has arrived in the market that morning as a dream will draw opportunistically on the "day's residues," mixing in events which took place during the day or sensations felt during sleep with images drawn deep from our childhood.

Dreams provide our main, but not our only, access to the unconscious. There are also what Freud calls "**parapraxes**," unaccountable slips of the tongue, failures of memory, bunglings, misreadings and mislayings which can be traced to unconscious wishes and intentions. The presence of the unconscious is also betrayed in jokes, which for Freud have a largely libidinal, anxious or aggressive content. Where the unconscious is most damagingly at work, however, is in psychological disturbance of one form or another. We may have certain unconscious desires which will not be denied, but which dare not find practical outlet either; in this situation, the desire forces its way in from the unconscious, the ego blocks it off defensively, and the result of this internal conflict is what we call neurosis. The patient begins to develop symptoms which, in compromising fashion, at once protect against the unconscious desire and covertly express it. Such neuroses may be obsessional (having to touch every lamp-post in the street), hysterical (developing a paralyzed arm for no good organic reason), or phobic (being unreasonably afraid of open spaces or certain animals). Behind these neuroses, psychoanalysis discerns unresolved conflicts whose roots run back to the individual's early development, and which are likely to be focused in the Oedipal moment; indeed Freud calls the Oedipus complex the "nucleus of the neuroses." There will usually be a relation between the kind of neurosis a patient displays, and the point in the pre-Oedipal stage at which his or her psychical development became arrested or "fixated." The aim of psychoanalysis is to uncover the hidden causes of the neurosis in order to relieve the patient of his or her conflicts, so dissolving the distressing symptoms.

Much more difficult to cope with, however, is the condition of **psychosis**, in which the ego, unable as in neurosis partly to repress the unconscious desire, actually comes under its sway. If this happens, the link between the ego and the external world is ruptured, and the unconscious begins to build up an alternative, delusional reality. The psychotic, in other words, has lost contact with reality at key points, as in paranoia and schizophrenia: if the neurotic may develop a paralyzed arm, the psychotic may believe that his arm has turned into an elephant's trunk. "Paranoia" refers to a more or less systematized state of delusion, under which Freud includes not only delusions of persecution but delusional jealousy and delusions of grandeur. The root of such paranoia he locates in an unconscious defence against homosexuality: the mind denies this desire by converting the love-object into a rival or persecutor, systematically reorganizing and reinterpreting reality to confirm this suspicion. Schizophrenia involves a detachment from reality and a turning in on the self, with an excessive but loosely systematized production of fantasies: it is as though the "id," or unconscious desire, has surged up and flooded the conscious mind with its illogicality, riddling associations and affective rather than conceptual links between ideas. Schizophrenic language has in this sense an interesting resemblance to poetry.

Psychoanalysis is not only a theory of the human mind, but a practice for curing those who are considered mentally ill or disturbed. Such cures, for Freud, are not achieved just by explaining to the patient what is wrong with him, revealing to him his unconscious motivations. This is a part of psychoanalytical practice, but it will not cure anybody in itself. Freud is not in this sense a rationalist, believing that if only we understand ourselves or the world we can take appropriate action. The nub of the cure for Freudian theory is what is known as "transference," a concept sometimes popularly confused with what Freud calls "projection," or the ascribing to others of feelings and wishes which are actually our own. In the course of treatment, the analysand (or patient) may begin unconsciously to "transfer" on to the figure of the analyst the psychical conflicts from which he or she suffers. If he has had difficulties with his father, for example, he may unconsciously cast the analyst in that role. This poses a problem for the analyst, since such "repetition" or ritual re-enactment of the original conflict is one of the patient's unconscious ways of avoiding having to come to terms with it. We repeat, sometimes compulsively, what we cannot properly remember, and we cannot remember it because it is unpleasant. But transference also provides the analyst with a peculiarly privileged insight into the patient's psychical life, in a controlled situation in which he or she can intervene. (One of the several reasons why psychoanalysts must themselves undergo analysis in training is so that they can become reasonably aware of their own unconscious processes, thus resisting as far as possible the danger of "counter-transferring" their own problems to their patients.) By virtue of this drama of transference, and the insights and interventions which it permits the analyst, the patient's problems are gradually redefined in terms of the analytic situation itself. In this sense, paradoxically, the problems which are handled in the consulting room are never quite at one with the real-life problems of the patient: they have, perhaps, something of the "fictional" relation to those real-life problems which a literary text has to the real-life materials it transforms. Nobody leaves the consulting room cured of exactly the problems with which he walked in. The patient is likely to resist the analyst's access to her unconscious by a number of familiar techniques, but if all goes well the transferential process will allow her problems to be "worked through" into consciousness, and by dissolving the transference relation at the right moment the analyst will hope to relieve her of them. Another way of describing this process is to say that the patient becomes able to recollect portions of her life which she has repressed: she is able to recount a new, more complete narrative about herself, one which will interpret and make sense of the disturbances from which she suffers. The "talking cure," as it is called, will have taken effect.

The work of psychoanalysis can perhaps best be summarized in one of Freud's own slogans: "Where id was, there shall ego be." Where men and women were in the paralyzing grip of forces which they could not comprehend, there reason and self-mastery shall reign. Such a slogan makes Freud sound rather more of a rationalist than he actually was. Though he once commented that nothing in the end could withstand reason and experience, he was about as far from underestimating the cunning and obstinacy of the mind as it is possible to be. His estimate of human capacities is on the whole conservative and pessimistic: we are dominated by a desire for gratification and an aversion to anything which might frustrate it. In his later work, he comes to see the human race as languishing in the grip of a terrifying **death drive**, a primary masochism which the ego unleashes on itself. The final goal of life is death, a return to that blissful inanimate state where the ego cannot be injured. **Eros**, or sexual energy, is the force which builds up history, but it is locked in tragic contradiction with Thanatos or the death drive. We strive onwards only to be constantly driven backwards, struggling to return to a state before we were even conscious. The ego is a pitiable, precarious entity, battered by the external world, scourged by the cruel upbraidings of the superego, plagued by the greedy, insatiable demands of the id. Freud's compassion for the ego is a compassion for the human race, labouring under the almost intolerable demands placed upon it by a civilization built upon the repression of desire and the deferment of gratification. He was scornful of all utopian proposals for changing this condition; but though many of his social views were conventional and authoritarian, he nevertheless looked with a certain favour upon attempts to abolish or at least reform the institutions of private property and the nation state. He did so because he was deeply convinced that modern society had become tyrannical in its repressiveness. As he argued in *The Future of an Illusion*, if a society has not developed beyond a point at which the satisfaction of one group of its members depends upon the suppression of another, it is understandable that those suppressed should develop an intense hostility towards a culture whose existence their labour has made possible, but in whose riches they have too small a share. "It goes without saying," Freud declares, "that a civilization which leaves so large a number of its participants unsatisfied and drives them into revolt neither has nor deserves the prospect of a lasting existence." . . .

● Building the Frame Through Writing

1. You have already defined some of the following concepts in your own words. Use Eagleton's chapter to refine and expand your definitions, building a stronger understanding of the psychoanalytic frame.

   - Structure and Function of the Psyche:
     - id, ego, superego
     - pleasure principle and reality principle
   - Coping Mechanisms and Disturbances:
     - repression and sublimation
     - neurosis
     - dream work
     - parapraxes
     - psychosis
   - Individual Development and Adaptation to Civilization:
     - psychosexual stages
     - auto-eroticism
     - Oedipus complex
     - Eros
     - death instinct

2. We often use terms such as *oral fixation* and *anal compulsive* conversationally to refer to certain types of behavior. Use Eagleton's discussion of psychosexual stages to explain what such terms mean in popular culture. Why do you think they have come to have negative connotations? Why is social disapproval attached?

3. Trace the path the child follows as "it" becomes a gendered subject—a "he" or a "she."

   - What difference does identification with a gender make in the child's experience of the world and in his or her sense of self?
   - Do you think it's possible, according to psychoanalytic theory, for us to resist becoming gendered subjects? What inducements to become gendered exist, especially for the male?
   - How is Freud's understanding of the process for the female problematic?
   - How do we end up as "split subjects"?

4. Eros, the life instinct, is opposed by Thanatos, the death instinct (or "death wish"). Eros directs us to join in communities, supporting a larger organization of life; Thanatos directs us to seek simplicity, to break down connections. Ideally, Eros can use the energy of the death instinct to some productive ends.

Without such redirection, we act against society's interests or against our own. Consider how these opposing forces are acted out in the social world.

- Where can we see Eros at work?
- Where can we see Eros successfully redirecting the death instinct to serve Eros?
- Where can we see the death instinct operating on its own?
- Have you activated/been activated by both instincts in the course of your day so far?

Writing from a Psychoanalytic Frame

a   sample   drafting   process

Most of you probably have seen the film *Jurassic Park*, one of the most successful films of all time in terms of ticket sales, in the United States and abroad. The film has had mass appeal, which makes it an interesting text to examine psychoanalytically: critically, we can assume that its appeal lies in its embodiment of forbidden, perhaps repressed, desires, fulfilling our wishes but also protecting us from "punishment" for having them. Our chosen purpose, therefore, is to lay out for an audience how the film works to arouse desire yet prevents desire from becoming threatening, ensuring that the overall experience will be pleasurable. As writers, we can draw on the authority of psychoanalytic theory, invite the reader to accompany us through the analysis, and offer insight into the film's appeal. Below we take you through one possible version of this planned essay. You may first want to view the film even if you've seen it before, since you now have rhetorical and critical frames to use actively. And we use *Jurassic Park* throughout this book as a shared text, asking you to reread it with all the critical frames in the following chapters.

Inventing Through Key Concepts

Our purpose in this invention/drafting process is to offer one possible interpretation, or one frame for understanding, the appeal of this now-classic film. We'll use the psychoanalytic frame to develop ideas—to "invent" our argument and means of persuasion. We can work from the data *or* the frame: we can look at the conflicts represented in the film and analyze them, or we can consider the major theoretical concepts and examine how they are embodied in the film. Doing both might lead to the most detailed close reading.

Let's start with the major concepts: in what ways do the concepts of id, ego, and superego get represented in the movie, and, once we've identified these, what view of human potential emerges? One can clearly see the basic instincts and power of the dinosaurs as symbols of the id; one can thus see the human interest in but also the controls placed on them as symbols of our civilization's demands that we repress these powerful animal instincts and desires. Dr. Ian Malcolm, the scientist who is a "chaos theorist," becomes a kind of ego figure: he repeats the prediction that we cannot control nature, that we should not be trying to tamper with the rules, that we must accept the conditions under which we can best live, and so on—like the ego, he attempts to mediate between desire and reason, at one point illustrating the superego function by making a distinction between what the park developer "could have" and "should have" done with his technological knowledge. Thus we might read the film as a working out of the ego's mission: to allow satisfaction of our desires to the extent that these do not interfere with our survival or evoke severe criticism from our superego, saddling us with paralyzing guilt. The very idea of a "chaos theorist" reflects Freud's sense that we're caught in a bind between polymorphous (many-shaped) desires and an external structure for containing and ordering them (society as a construct, or theory of living). (A side point we might want to return to: Dr. Malcolm acts seductively toward Dr. Ellie Sadler, and at one point he mentions to Dr. Alan Grant that he's had three wives; how do these details affect our sense of him as ego? Is it to remind viewers that ego can't rule over desire?)

Another major theme of the film seems to be the desire to enjoy our basic urges without consequence, as the id/dinosaurs do, a fantasy that the ego (and superego, in the voice of the disapproving traditional scientist) must deny. The film also offers a warning against this desire. In this apparently dual message, the film expresses the desire in a way that allows us to fulfill it indirectly—it is a form of redirected pleasure, a sublimated experience of it. We get the thrill of unrestrained aggression by watching the carnivorous dinosaurs break out of their pens and attack their prey (especially the lawyer, the representative of law, of restrictions, who is positioned in relation to a toilet, another id-pleasing aggressive image). These urges are assigned in the film to "dinosaurs," which are archaic, extinct phenomena—just like our infantile desires for pure power and pleasure. We are thus free to identify with these desires even as we avoid the guilt that our civilized adult selves would feel.

Where the individual dares to have these desires, the message is different. At first, we're led to see Jurassic Park's location as a lush, fertile, isolated island—a place that suggests a new Eden, where the all-female dinosaurs are controlled by us and exist for our pleasure. The masculine world of research, technology, and marketing have provided us with this infantile playland inhabited by powerful mother figures, but these figures are under *our* control—just as the infant wishes are: we feed them, and they exist for us. The scenario seems to promise us that we can reenter the infantile, sin-free state. But the wish is, alas, ultimately shown to be unacceptable; the enterprise ends in failure and death. We can never make the flea circus real or possess the dinosaurs (as the park founder wishes to do). We are exiled into reality once again (though a sequel will take us through this primal scene again, just as we individually reenact it in all our endeavors).

Is the conflict of Eros, the life instinct, and Thanatos, the death instinct, evident in the film? We see a recurrent conflict related to the idea of propagation of the species. First, the two paleontologists, Dr. Grant and Dr. Sadler, engage in banter about children, with the female suggesting the desirability of having children, the male resisting the idea (and in one early scene actively [aggressively] seeking to scare a young boy, who is depicted as a less-than-desirable being in the first place). Dr. Grant prefers a simple life dedicated to his own field of interest—a preference that suggests the death wish, the desire to exist apart from a community. At first he is willing to socialize only to get what he wants—grant money; he enters society through self-interest alone. His female companion gently urges him to cooperate with Eros, as she does; we see her tend to a sick triceratops and later risk her life for the imperiled children and love object (Dr. Grant). Over the course of the action, the male scientist discovers his "maternal" side when he becomes the caretaker of the two children, protecting and comforting them. He embraces Eros and rejects his earlier urge to be separate and single, as we see in the final scene, where he is embracing the children and smiling at his female companion as they fly back to civilization. The failure of the cloning-based Jurassic Park enterprise, one can argue, is a victory for the traditional social organization of male–female reproduction, family, and community.

We can also see the struggle to direct the energy of the death instinct into the service of Eros in the creation of the "park" itself. Primal, seemingly defunct creatures of enormous destructive potential are reactivated—the conscious manifestation of the formerly repressed death instinct—and then are used as the centerpiece of an enterprise that will draw people together—the scientists working on the technology of the enterprise; the generations, represented in the grandfather–grandchildren reunion; the masses who will come to the park on vacation. We will be able to enjoy our raw nature at a safe remove, and we will do so as a collective experience, one that will strengthen our bonds of community. That the "creatures" overwhelm the creators can be read as evidence of contemporary cultural anxiety, however; we seem not quite able to renounce our animal selves, and have some divided reaction to such primal elements, perhaps not ever being capable of "harnessing" them. Our socially sophisticated selves may not be as well established as we had hoped.

Inventing from Textual Data

We can think about the film in a different way, by selecting some scene, event, figure, or image that has caught our attention (a kind of psychoanalytic free association). Which scenes/lines/people come to mind? Take the young girl, Lex, as one possible focus. What background data do we have on her? She has a younger brother; she's sophisticated in her knowledge of computers; we see her in loving relation to her grandfather; her parents are absent and, we're told, in the process of divorcing. During the first attack of the tyrannosaurus rex, she is immobilized by fear. When Dr. Grant comes into the jeep, she repeats hysterically, "He left us! He left us!"—referring to the lawyer (the father), who left the children in the Jeep as he ran into the restroom to hide and save himself. Dr. Grant must coax her out of the car, must guide her to a place of safety, must comfort her and reassure her when she wakes to see a large, plant-eating dinosaur next to her. At his coaxing, she touches the dinosaur, only to be covered in its mucus when it sneezes on her. Back at the resort, she feasts happily on ice cream and Jell-O until the vibrations reveal the approach of the t. rex. In the scenes that follow, she conquers her fear and helps save herself and her brother from the raptors. She also saves the others by figuring out the computer system, which she finally gets online, reactivating the security gates and communications system (check the root meaning of her nickname; "Lex" has an interesting word association). How can her depiction, conflicts, and the resolutions of these conflicts be explained? Using the relevant central psychoanalytic concepts, we can identify:

- her desires (evidence of erotic attachment to/dependence on males; her physical pleasures)
- her sense of right and wrong/presence of the superego (evidence of socialization)
- her neurotic, "hysterical" responses (immobilization, repetition)
- her use of the Eros instinct to sublimate fear/anxiety, to preserve and expand connections
- her use of computer code (a "masculine" language form)

Framing an Analytic Argument

One argument that emerges from our above reading of Lex is that we have a replication of the female psyche as Freud saw it: a dependent, emotionally weak being in need of protection and erotic satisfaction from male figures, desires which must be transferred from a father figure to an appropriate male, a struggle which is seen as the central issue of the girl's experience. She adopts the laws of the father and uses this knowledge to save/reproduce life, voluntarily containing/repressing the unbridled power of the aggressive, reproductively self-sufficient female "monsters." We can claim that the film thus promotes a very traditional, conservative view of the female and resolves all conflicts by reasserting a patriarchal psychosocial structure. The film fits in well with and helps perpetuate dominant cultural values, explaining its appeal, but also letting us question its social value—is this a film we should see as problematic?

If we use our earlier topic as the essay's thesis, we can frame an argument that represents the film as an attempt to let us as viewers enjoy aggression but safely remove ourselves from its consequences. It provides wish fulfillment in escapist form—aggression without punishment, pleasure without pain. What more could a body want? The film acts as a kind of social safety valve, letting us express dangerous feelings in a completely controlled way, providing an outlet for our aggression but maintaining the codes and laws of civilized life.

These arguments are two of many possible readings of the film; you may or may not agree with all their interpretive premises. You can "correct" the reading by following a similar interpretive process, however; the frame allows for a multiplicity of results. The goal is not to produce a psychoanalytic reading only. Such a reading lets you then take the more important next step: what can the interpretation you've constructed tell us about our social situation? How can you use it to gain insight on the conflicts of modern society, or the frustrations of the individual within society—your own or those of some hypothetical individual? And how best to present such a view to your audience?

Connecting with the Audience

We're writing for an academic audience—for a group of people like you who are likely to be familiar with basic psychoanalytic premises (though we'll continually present and define technical psychoanalytic terms, both to provide shared context and clarity and to establish ourselves as credible, knowledgeable speakers).

We need to create shared context with the reader, and so we will write a summary of the film's basic plot. That's a real rhetorical challenge: a summary usually means a brief overview of a text highlighting its salient, or most important, details and ideas. But, as Kenneth Burke's concept of the lens shows, "important" is a value defined by a viewer's (or reader's) critical perspective. Any summary therefore exists as already framed, interpreted reading. We'll open with a summary that provides the observable data, the film's sequence of main events (though again what we provide is a particular reading; we can't *not* interpret when we use language). Our opening in draft form:

> In simple terms, *Jurassic Park* is the story of what happens one weekend when an entrepreneur, John Hammond, brings in three scientists and a lawyer to visit a theme park he is developing on a remote island off Central America. Hammond is hoping to get the scientists' and lawyer's endorsement of his project, which will pave the way for its public opening. The "theme" of his park is live dinosaurs—clones produced by the team of scientists Hammond employs. Hammond has hired a computer contractor to design and implement the park's security system; this man, Dennis, is disgruntled about his fee and has secretly agreed to sell dinosaur embryos to a rival firm, a transaction set to take place the same weekend as the scientists and lawyer visit. Also arriving for the demo tour are Hammond's grandchildren, Lex and Tim. When Dennis shuts down the safety system so he can steal the embryos, the dinosaurs escape their enclosures and attack the visitors. The lawyer and Dennis are killed; one of the scientists,

Dr. Grant, saves the children and brings them back to the main building. The dinosaurs, cloned as all one gender—female—to prevent uncontrolled reproduction, are found to be reproducing through frog DNA used in the cloning process. With the island overrun by dinosaurs, Hammond, the three scientists, and the children escape by helicopter.

If you've seen the film, you probably have some objections to our summary. Try adding in the important details you think are missing. How does your revision change the sense of the film as represented here?

Developing the essay, you have a purpose, an argument; using the psychoanalytic frame, you have an audience—an academic reader who will likely be open to a psychoanalytic interpretive process and to seeing the social purpose of such a critique as a valid topic. With its humanistic orientation, psychoanalytic theory provides a structuring device: you are telling a developmental story, starting with individual experience—here, Lex's conflict and resolution. In the next section of the draft, we move toward establishing the problem posed by the plot and a psychoanalytic explanation of the solution it offers:

Much of the dialogue in the film calls attention to the ethical use of technology. Characters such as Dr. Malcolm question the human right to interfere with the natural order; the subplot involving Dennis and John Hammond's desire for personal glory suggests that human greed and self-interest lead to inevitably irresponsible uses of technology. The film presents a problem: our humanity is at risk, and we must find some way to remain civilized. The basis of civilization, as Sigmund Freud has theorized, is repression of individual desires in service to Eros, or the life of the community. And so we see in the film an idealization of the nuclear family and a process of channeling one's instincts to satisfy Eros and to observe the laws of civilization. The young girl in the film, Lex, embodies this process. Her ultimate ability to control her desires and fears and to use her reason to preserve life provides viewers with a reassuring message about all of us: if even a young girl can overcome the powers of nature, we have reason to believe in the power and worth of civilization. The film thus satisfies a basic desire of our own, as its phenomenal popularity attests.

We've given the reader an argument and a logical claim to support it: a basic psychoanalytic premise that will be illustrated through analysis of the girl. And we've stated a purpose: we're claiming the film's popularity can be explained by its flattering, wish-fulfilling message that our civilized selves can rise above our base instincts—that we are different from the destructive beasts that consume each other.

To develop the analysis and support the argument, you can use logos as you reason from psychoanalytic principles, and pathos as you help the reader see Lex's experiences empathetically, since they are, ultimately, at least according to the theory, common to all of us. In outline form, the discussion might proceed in the following way:

- Lex as a model of "civilized" psychic life
  - her love of the (grand)father
  - her redirection of libidinal feelings to the unrelated male, Dr. Grant
  - her obedience to the lawyer, the symbol of law
  - her horror at the feeding of a live goat to a dinosaur
- Lex's primal fears when the rules of civilization break down
  - her immediate concern when the car stops on the tour through the park
  - her horror at the unrestrained aggression of the t. rex
  - her terror at being abandoned by the lawyer
  - her survival-threatening reactions to the dinosaur when she disregards the directions of Dr. Grant and her brother
- Lex's return to civilized behavior
  - her acceptance of Dr. Grant's authority and protection/repression of libidinal feelings
  - her use of her technological literacy to restore order/security
  - her final peaceful repose in a return to the "normal" family setting in the helicopter en route back to civilization
- Conclusion: Lex embodies the necessary sublimation of basic instincts to the larger good of society, creating an appeal to our desire for coexisting happiness and order

You have a set of concepts and specialized vocabulary that announce your frame and give you a credible voice from within it. You can thus invent (develop a topic and argument) and arrange (organize the form and logical parts) your essay, and do so in an authoritative voice. You've joined the critical and the rhetorical in the composing process.

topics for writing

The following topics ask for a formal essay response, though how you approach each is a matter of your own rhetorical choices. You might want to review Chapters 1 through 3 to remind yourself of the many rhetorical and critical framing choices a writer makes in the writing process.

1. Freud describes the role of deflections and substitutive satisfactions in helping us adjust to the restrictions social membership places on us. Choose one such activity/interest (he suggests several) and examine how it works.
   - How does it allow us to redirect idic energy in a way that offers pleasure or reduces "unpleasure"? What are the means to pleasure (or avoidance of pain) that it offers?

- Does society encourage it, and, if so, how? Are some deflections/substitutions more socially valued than others, or particularly valued by specific social groups? Why?

- How should we see the activity/interest and the process of deflection itself—as useful, numbing, passively aggressive, contributing to Eros, or some other way?

- Clarify your purpose and argument; decide on and evoke an audience in the opening, consider your possible stances (you can occupy more than one, remember, especially if you speak not only as an authority but as someone who engages in the activity/interest).

2. Consider the role of sports in contemporary American culture from a psychoanalytic perspective.

- What are some psychological causes for their immense popularity?

- Apply the concepts of id and ego: how are sports a redirection of unacceptable aggression into socially permissible form?

- What sorts of libidinal satisfaction are indirectly enabled via sports? How can you account for such phenomena as fan loyalty, superstars, the increased interest in women's teams?

- As always, clarify your purpose and argument; decide on and evoke an audience in the opening; consider your possible stances (and you can occupy more than one, especially if you can speak from direct experience with sports).

3. Select a film that has attracted a large audience—perhaps a classic film, such as *Casablanca*, or a popular film, like one of the *Harry Potter* or *Lord of the Rings* series, or a particular genre, such as action or comedy, or a text of your choice—a popular children's classic, a science fiction story, a music video—to trace its psychoanalytic content and social purpose(s).

- Analyze the plot of the film: what is the conflict, and how is it resolved?

- How can you explain the film's mass appeal? How is it structured to appeal to basic instincts?

- Does the film serve a valid social purpose, as psychoanalytic theory would define it?

- Clarify your purpose; decide on and evoke an audience in the opening; consider your possible stances (you can move between the role of authority and the individual reacting to the film/text, for instance, using your own reactions as data).

4. Desire and aggression frequently, and often dangerously, become intertwined forces. Why are these two forces so easily conjoined?

- Where in our cultural practices and traditions do we see this powerful connection made? Think of religious doctrine and imagery; romantic relations; competition, at school or at work, or in friendships or family settings; aggressive forms of humor.

- How are such experiences both pleasurable and painful?
- Your voice should reflect your view of this phenomenon: do you see it simply as a psychoanalytic reality, a moral issue, an inevitable human frailty?

5. The *talking cure*, a term used to describe Freud's psychoanalytic clinical method, involves significant attention to the interpretation of dreams. Dreams are a form of visual text—of argument, in a sense, in that they work out some conflict or express some desire the dreamer is experiencing. To explain a portion of psychoanalytic theory, compose a visual text that embodies Freud's theoretical points.

   - Visual texts can include print as well. Consider various ways of representing Freud's three-part structure of the mind—id, ego, and superego. How can you visually represent the different and often unequal influences Freud sees them as having on our desires and/or behavior? How might print be put in relation to images to capture the ideal balance of these elements, or the causes of anxiety or neurosis, or the id-dominated personality?

   - Construct a visual narrative of one imagined life, told psychoanalytically. Use images to show the stages of psychoanalytic development; the conflicts this imagined individual may have faced and been shaped by; the social environments that provide him or her satisfaction through sublimation.

   - Treat any of the topics outlined above in a visually based composition.

Reading Case Studies

- Reading critically from a psychoanalytic frame
- Connecting argument and data
- Writing with an authoritative voice

Shane

JACK SCHAEFER

In this classic 1949 western novel depicting the late-nineteenth-century frontier, the story is told from the perspective of a young boy, Bob Starrett. His encounter with the mysterious loner Shane makes him see himself and his family, members of a homesteading community, in a new, more complicated light; it's a tale of growing up, complete with the conflicts of id and Eros. The novel is typically considered "youth literature," for the cultural work it does: it teaches preadolescents a certain lesson about life in civilization, doing so in a moral tale that operates below surface level, or unconsciously. As you read, use the details of Bob's encounter with Shane to begin to frame his story psychoanalytically: how can you relate the details of the story to Freud's argument that life in civilization demands repression of powerful natural desires?

He rode into our valley in the summer of '89. I was a kid then, barely topping the backboard of father's old chuck-wagon. I was on the upper rail of our small corral, soaking in the late afternoon sun, when I saw him far down the road where it swung into the valley from the open plain beyond.

In that clear Wyoming air I could see him plainly, though he was still several miles away. There seemed nothing remarkable about him, just another stray horseman riding up the road toward the cluster of frame buildings that was our town. Then I saw a pair of cowhands, loping past him, stop and stare after him with a curious intentness.

He came steadily on, straight through the town without slackening pace, until he reached the fork a half-mile below our place. One branch turned left across the river ford and on to Luke Fletcher's big spread. The other bore ahead along the right bank where we homesteaders had pegged our claims in a row up the valley. He hesitated briefly, studying the choice, and moved again steadily on our side.

As he came near, what impressed me first was his clothes. He wore dark trousers of some serge material tucked into tall boots and held at the waist by a wide belt, both of a soft black leather tooled in intricate design. A coat of the same dark material as the trousers was neatly folded and strapped to his saddle-roll. His shirt was finespun linen, rich brown in color. The handkerchief knotted loosely around his throat was black silk. His hat was not the familiar Stetson, not the familiar gray or muddy tan. It was a plain black, soft in texture, unlike any hat I had ever seen, with a creased crown and a wide curling brim swept down in front to shield the face.

All trace of newness was long since gone from these things. The dust of   5
distance was beaten into them. They were worn and stained and several neat patches showed on the shirt. Yet a kind of magnificence remained and with it a hint of men and manners alien to my limited boy's experience.

Then I forgot the clothes in the impact of the man himself. He was not much above medium height, almost slight in build. He would have looked frail alongside father's square, solid bulk. But even I could read the endurance in the lines of that dark figure and the quiet power in its effortless, unthinking adjustment to every movement of the tired horse.

He was clean-shaven and his face was lean and hard and burned from high forehead to firm, tapering chin. His eyes seemed hooded in the shadow of the hat's brim. He came closer, and I could see that this was because the brows were drawn in a frown of fixed and habitual alertness. Beneath them the eyes were endlessly searching from side to side and forward, checking off every item in view, missing nothing. As I noticed this, a sudden chill, I could not have told why, struck through me there in the warm and open sun.

He rode easily, relaxed in the saddle, leaning his weight lazily into the stirrups. Yet even in this easiness was a suggestion of tension. It was the easiness of a coiled spring, of a trap set.

He drew rein not twenty feet from me. His glance hit me, dismissed me, flicked over our place. This was not much, if you were thinking in terms of size and scope. But what there was was good. You could trust father for that. The corral, big enough for about thirty head if you crowded them in, was railed right to true sunk posts. The pasture behind, taking in nearly half of our claim, was fenced tight. The barn was small, but it was solid, and we were raising a loft at one end for the alfalfa growing green in the north forty. We had a fair-sized field in potatoes that year and father was trying a new corn he had sent all the way to Washington for and they were showing properly in weedless rows.

Behind the house mother's kitchen garden was a brave sight. The house   10
itself was three rooms—two really, the big kitchen where we spent most of our time indoors and the bedroom beside it. My little lean-to room was added back of the kitchen. Father was planning, when he could get around to it, to build mother the parlor she wanted.

We had wooden floors and a nice porch across the front. The house was painted too, white with green trim, rare thing in all that region, to remind her, mother said when she made father do it, of her native New England. Even rarer, the roof was shingled. I knew what that meant. I had helped father split those shingles. Few places so spruce and well worked could be found so deep in the Territory in those days.

The stranger took it all in, sitting there easily in the saddle. I saw his eyes slow on the flowers mother had planted by the porch steps, then come to rest on our shiny new pump and the trough beside it. They shifted back to me, and again, without knowing why, I felt that sudden chill. But his voice was gentle and he spoke like a man schooled to patience.

"I'd appreciate a chance at the pump for myself and the horse."

I was trying to frame a reply and choking on it, when I realized that he was not speaking to me but past me. Father had come up behind me and was leaning against the gate to the corral.

"Use all the water you want, stranger."   15

Father and I watched him dismount in a single flowing tilt of his body and lead the horse over to the trough. He pumped it almost full and let the horse sink its nose in the cool water before he picked up the dipper for himself.

He took off his hat and slapped the dust out of it and hung it on a corner of the trough. With his hands he brushed the dust from his clothes. With a piece of rag pulled from his saddle-roll he carefully wiped his boots. He untied the handkerchief from around his neck and rolled his sleeves and dipped his arms in the trough, rubbing thoroughly and splashing water over his face. He shook his hands dry and used the handkerchief to remove the last drops from his face. Taking a comb from his shirt pocket, he smoothed back his long dark hair. All his movements were deft and sure, and with a quick precision he flipped down his sleeves, reknotted the handkerchief, and picked up his hat.

Then, holding it in his hand, he spun about and strode directly toward the house. He bent low and snapped the stem of one of mother's petunias and tucked this into the hatband. In another moment the hat was on his head, brim swept down in swift, unconscious gesture, and he was swinging gracefully into the saddle and starting toward the road.

I was fascinated. None of the men I knew were proud like that about their appearance. In that short time the kind of magnificence I had noticed had emerged into plainer view. It was in the very air of him. Everything about him showed the effects of long use and hard use, but showed too the strength of quality and competence. There was no chill on me now. Already I was imagining myself in hat and belt and boots like those.

He stopped the horse and looked down at us. He was refreshed and I would   20 have sworn the tiny wrinkles around his eyes were what with him would be a smile. His eyes were not restless when he looked at you like this. They were still and steady and you knew the man's whole attention was concentrated on you even in the casual glance.

"Thank you," he said in his gentle voice and was turning into the road, back to us, before father spoke in his slow, deliberate way.

"Don't be in such a hurry, stranger."

I had to hold tight to the rail or I would have fallen backwards into the corral. At the first sound of father's voice, the man and the horse, like a single being, had wheeled to face us, the man's eyes boring at father, bright and deep in the shadow of the hat's brim. I was shivering, struck through once more. Something intangible and cold and terrifying was there in the air between us.

I stared in wonder as father and the stranger looked at each other a long moment, measuring each other in an unspoken fraternity of adult knowledge beyond my reach. Then the warm sunlight was flooding over us, for father was smiling and he was speaking with the drawling emphasis that meant he had made up his mind.

"I said don't be in such a hurry, stranger. Food will be on the table soon and   25
you can bed down here tonight."

The stranger nodded quietly as if he too had made up his mind. "That's mighty thoughtful of you," he said and swung down and came toward us, leading his horse. Father slipped into step beside him and we all headed for the barn.

"My name's Starrett," said father. "Joe Starrett. This here," waving at me, "is Robert MacPherson Starrett. Too much name for a boy. I make it Bob."

The stranger nodded again. "Call me Shane," he said. Then to me: "Bob it is. You were watching me for quite a spell coming up the road."

It was not a question. It was a simple statement. "Yes . . ." I stammered. "Yes. I was."

"Right," he said. "I like that. A man who watches what's going on around   30
him will make his mark."

A man who watches . . . For all his dark appearance and lean, hard look, this Shane knew what would please a boy. The glow of it held me as he took care of his horse, and I fussed around, hanging up his saddle, forking over some hay, getting in his way and my own in my eagerness. He let me slip the bridle off and the horse, bigger and more powerful than I had thought now that I was close beside it, put its head down patiently for me and stood quietly while I helped him curry away the caked dust. Only once did he stop me. That was when I reached for his saddle-roll to put it to one side. In the instant my fingers touched it, he was taking it from me and he put it on a shelf with a finality that indicated no interference.

When the three of us went up to the house, mother was waiting and four places were set at the table. "I saw you through the window," she said and came to shake our visitor's hand. She was a slender, lively woman with a fair complexion even our weather never seemed to affect and a mass of light brown hair she wore piled high to bring her, she used to say, closer to father's size.

"Marian," father said, "I'd like you to meet Mr. Shane."

"Good evening, ma'am," said our visitor. He took her hand and bowed over it. Mother stepped back and, to my surprise, dropped in a dainty curtsy. I had never seen her do that before. She was an unpredictable woman. Father and I would have painted the house three times over and in rainbow colors to please her.

"And a good evening to you, Mr. Shane. If Joe hadn't called you back, I would have done it myself. You'd never find a decent meal up the valley." 35

She was proud of her cooking, was mother. That was one thing she learned back home, she would often say, that was of some use out in this raw land. As long as she could still prepare a proper dinner, she would tell father when things were not going right, she knew she was still civilized and there was hope of getting ahead. Then she would tighten her lips and whisk together her special most delicious biscuits and father would watch her bustling about and eat them to the last little crumb and stand up and wipe his eyes and stretch his big frame and stomp out to his always unfinished work like daring anything to stop him now.

We sat down to supper and a good one. Mother's eyes sparkled as our visitor kept pace with father and me. Then we all leaned back and while I listened the talk ran on almost like old friends around a familiar table. But I could sense that it was following a pattern. Father was trying, with mother helping and both of them avoiding direct questions, to get hold of facts about this Shane and he was dodging at every turn. He was aware of their purpose and not in the least annoyed by it. He was mild and courteous and spoke readily enough. But always he put them off with words that gave no real information.

He must have been riding many days, for he was full of news from towns along his back trail as far as Cheyenne and even Dodge City and others beyond I had never heard of before. But he had no news about himself. His past was fenced as tightly as our pasture. All they could learn was that he was riding through, taking each day as it came, with nothing particular in mind except maybe seeing a part of the country he had not been in before.

Afterwards mother washed the dishes and I dried and the two men sat on the porch, their voices carrying through the open door. Our visitor was guiding the conversation now and in no time at all he had father talking about his own plans. That was no trick. Father was ever one to argue his ideas whenever he could find a listener. This time he was going strong.

"Yes, Shane, the boys I used to ride with don't see it yet. They will some day. The open range can't last forever. The fence lines are closing in. Running cattle in big lots is good business only for the top ranchers and it's really a poor business at that. Poor in terms of the resources going into it. Too much space for too little results. It's certain to be crowded out." 40

"Well, now," said Shane, "that's mighty interesting. I've been hearing the same quite a lot lately and from men with pretty clear heads. Maybe there's something to it."

"By Godfrey, there's plenty to it. Listen to me, Shane. The thing to do is pick your spot, get your land, your own land. Put in enough crops to carry you and make your money play with a small herd, not all horns and bone, but bred for meat and fenced in and fed right. I haven't been at it long, but already I've raised stock that averages three hundred pounds more than that long-legged stuff Fletcher runs on the other side of the river and it's better beef, and that's only a beginning.

"Sure, his outfit sprawls over most of this valley and it looks big. But he's got range rights on a lot more acres than he has cows and he won't even have those acres as more homesteaders move in. His way is wasteful. Too much land for what he gets out of it. He can't see that. He thinks we small fellows are nothing but nuisances."

"You are," said Shane mildly. "From his point of view, you are."

"Yes, I guess you're right. I'll have to admit that. Those of us here now   45 would make it tough for him if he wanted to use the range behind us on this side of the river as he used to. Altogether we cut some pretty good slices out of it. Worse still, we block off part of the river, shut the range off from the water. He's been grumbling about that off and on ever since we've been here. He's worried that more of us will keep coming and settle on the other side too, and then he will be in a fix."

The dishes were done and I was edging to the door. Mother nailed me as she usually did and shunted me off to bed. After she had left me in my little back room and went to join the men on the porch, I tried to catch more of the words. The voices were too low. Then I must have dozed, for with a start I realized that father and mother were again in the kitchen. By now, I gathered, our visitor was out in the barn in the bunk father had built there for the hired man who had been with us for a few weeks in the spring.

"Wasn't it peculiar," I heard mother say, "how he wouldn't talk about himself?"

"Peculiar?" said father. "Well, yes. In a way."

"Everything about him is peculiar." Mother sounded as if she was stirred up and interested. "I never saw a man quite like him before."

"You wouldn't have. Not where you come from. He's a special brand we   50 sometimes get out here in the grass country. I've come across a few. A bad one's poison. A good one's straight grain clear through."

"How can you be so sure about him? Why, he wouldn't even tell where he was raised."

"Born back east a ways would be my guess. And pretty far south. Tennessee maybe. But he's been around plenty."

"I like him." Mother's voice was serious. "He's so nice and polite and sort of gentle. Not like most men I've met out here. But there's something about him. Something underneath the gentleness . . . Something . . ." Her voice trailed away.

"Mysterious?" suggested father.

"Yes, of course. Mysterious. But more than that. Dangerous."   55

"He's dangerous all right." Father said it in a musing way. Then he chuckled. "But not to us, my dear." And then he said what seemed to me a curious thing. "In fact, I don't think you ever had a safer man in your house."

● Applying a Psychoanalytic Frame

1. How do you think using a young boy as the narrator helped the author achieve his rhetorical purpose(s) in the story?

2. A common question students ask about this and other works that seem open to psychoanalytic interpretation is whether the author consciously wrote from a psychoanalytic perspective. Do you see any evidence that Schaefer did so? For example, did he use Freudian terminology? Why might his text seem consistent with psychoanalytic thought?

3. Do you see the descriptions of the homestead and family as symbols of Eros? Do these and other social practices, places, and groups function for us today as signs of Eros?

4. In your view of him, is Shane the opposite of Eros, the embodiment of id and/or the death instinct? Does Bob (and do you) see Shane and Fletcher as equal threats to Eros?

5. Both Bob and his mother are attracted to Shane, even as they find him "dangerous." Explain this split reaction of attraction and repulsion, excitement and fear. What contemporary examples might serve as support for your analysis?

6. The events of the day form a mystery that absorbs Bob. From a psychoanalytic perspective, explain the psychic issues he is confronting—treat Bob as a kind of psychoanalytic case study. What feelings and conflicts do you see him trying to figure out?

Little Red Riding Hood
THE BROTHERS GRIMM

You may find that reading the following text from a psychoanalytic frame generates a very different understanding of its purpose than we typically assign to fairy tales. This popular tale involves a child, a parent who warns her to resist temptation, and fatal consequences for straying from the path. Try using the frame to explain the story and its continuing popularity. Is this a story for children only?

There was once a sweet little maid, much beloved by everybody, but most of all by her grandmother, who never knew how to make enough of her. Once she sent her a little riding hood of red velvet, and as it was very becoming to her, and she never wore anything else, people called her Little Red Riding Hood.

One day her mother said to her, "Come, Little Red Riding Hood, here are some cakes and a flask of wine for you to take to grandmother; she is weak and ill, and they will do her good. Make haste and start before it grows hot, and walk properly and nicely, and don't run, or you might fall and break the flask of wine, and there would be none left for grandmother. And when you go into her room, don't forget to say good morning, instead of staring about." "I will be sure to take care," said Little Red Riding Hood to her mother, and gave her hand upon it.

Now the grandmother lived away in the wood, half an hour's walk from the village; and when Little Red Riding Hood had reached the wood, she met the wolf; but as she did not know what a bad sort of animal he was, she did not feel frightened.

"Good day, Little Red Riding Hood," said he. "Thank you kindly, wolf," answered she. "Where are you going so early, Little Red Riding Hood?" "To my grandmother's." "What are you carrying under your apron?" "Cakes and wine; we baked yesterday; and my grandmother is very weak and ill, so they will do her good, and strengthen her."

"Where does your grandmother live, Little Red Riding Hood?" "A quarter   5 of an hour's walk from here; her house stands beneath the three oak trees, and you may know it by the hazel bushes," said Little Red Riding Hood.

The wolf thought to himself, "That tender young thing would be a delicious morsel, and would taste better than the old one; I must manage somehow to get both of them."

Then he walked by Little Red Riding Hood a little while, and said, "Little Red Riding Hood, just look at the pretty flowers that are growing all round you; and I don't think you are listening to the song of the birds; you are posting along just as if you were going to school, and it is so delightful out here in the wood."

Little Red Riding Hood glanced round her, and when she saw the sun-beams darting here and there through the trees, and lovely flowers everywhere, she thought to herself, "If I were to take a fresh nosegay to my grandmother she would be very pleased, and it is so early in the day that I shall reach her in plenty of time"; and so she ran about in the wood, looking for flowers. And as she picked one she saw a still prettier one a little farther off, and so she went farther and farther into the wood.

But the wolf went straight to the grandmother's house and knocked at the door. "Who is there?" cried the grandmother. "Little Red Riding Hood," he an-swered, "and I have brought you some cake and wine. Please open the door." "Lift the latch," cried the grandmother; "I am too feeble to get up."

So the wolf lifted the latch, and the door flew open, and he fell on the   10 grandmother and ate her up without saying one word. Then he drew on her clothes, put on her cap, lay down in her bed, and drew the curtains.

Little Red Riding Hood was all this time running about among the flowers, and when she had gathered as many as she could hold, she remembered her grandmother, and set off to go to her. She was surprised to find the door stand-ing open, and when she came inside she felt very strange, and thought to herself, "Oh dear, how uncomfortable I feel, and I was so glad this morning to go to my grandmother's."

And when she said, "Good morning," there was no answer. Then she went up to the bed and drew back the curtains; there lay the grandmother with her cap pulled over her eyes, so that she looked very odd.

"O grandmother, what large ears you have!" "The better to hear with."

"O grandmother, what great eyes you have!" "The better to see with."

"O grandmother, what large hands you have!" "The better to take hold of   15 you with."

"But, grandmother, what a terrible large mouth you have!" "The better to devour you!" And no sooner had the wolf said it than he made one bound from the bed, and swallowed up poor Little Red Riding Hood.

Then the wolf, having satisfied his hunger, lay down again in the bed, went to sleep, and began to snore loudly. The huntsman heard him as he was passing by the house, and thought, "How the old woman snores—I had better see if there is anything the matter with her."

Then he went into the room, and walked up to the bed, and saw the wolf lying there. "At last I find you, you old sinner!" said he; "I have been looking for you a long time."

And he made up his mind that the wolf had swallowed the grandmother whole, and that she might yet be saved. So he did not fire, but took a pair of shears and began to slit up the wolf's body. When he made a few snips Little Red Riding Hood appeared, and after a few more snips she jumped out and cried, "Oh dear, how frightened I have been! It is so dark inside the wolf." And then out came the old grandmother, still living and breathing. But Little Red Riding Hood went and quickly fetched some large stones, with which she filled the wolf's body, so that when he waked up, and was going to rush away, the stones were so heavy that he sank down and fell dead.

They were all three very pleased. The huntsman took off the wolf's skin, and   20 carried it home. The grandmother ate the cakes, and drank the wine, and held up her head again, and Little Red Riding Hood said to herself that she would never more stray about in the wood alone, but would mind what her mother told her.

It must also be related how a few days afterwards, when Little Red Riding Hood was again taking cakes to her grandmother, another wolf spoke to her, and wanted to tempt her to leave the path; but she was on her guard, and went straight on her way, and told her grandmother how that the wolf had met her, and wished her good day, but had looked so wicked about the eyes that she thought if it had not been on the high road he would have devoured her.

"Come," said the grandmother, "we will shut the door, so that he may not get in."

Soon after came the wolf knocking at the door, and calling out, "Open the door, grandmother, I am Little Red Riding Hood, bringing you cakes." But they remained still, and did not open the door. After that the wolf slunk by the house, and got at last upon the roof to wait until Little Red Riding Hood should return home in the evening; then he meant to spring down upon her, and devour her in the darkness. But the grandmother discovered his plot. Now there stood before the house a great stone trough, and the grandmother said to the child, "Little Red Riding Hood, I was boiling sausages yesterday, so take the bucket, and carry away the water they were boiled in, and pour it into the trough."

And Little Red Riding Hood did so until the great trough was quite full. When the smell of the sausages reached the nose of the wolf he snuffed it up, and looked round, and stretched out his neck so far that he lost his balance and began to slip, and he slipped down off the roof straight into the great trough, and was drowned.

Then Little Red Riding Hood went cheerfully home, and came to no harm.   25

● Applying a Psychoanalytic Frame

1. Try retelling the tale in academic form as a process of psychic education, a process in which Red Riding Hood learns to recognize and disapprove of her own animal instincts.

   - What external forces become internalized in Red Riding Hood's effort to be a "good" girl? Look carefully at the role of the woodcutter and at Red Riding Hood's action after she is freed from the wolf's stomach.
   - Why do you think she loads the wolf with stones?
   - Are we to believe that she has learned her lesson?

2. The story can be read again as a moral tale intended to teach young children, particularly girls, about the limits society places on sexuality. Analyze the text for its sexual message. Look at images of virginity and defloration; lust and repression; acceptable pleasure and forbidden experience. What attitudes and standards related to sexuality do you think are communicated to the tale's young audience?

3. Once again drawing on the psychoanalytic frame, explain how the tale "Little Red Riding Hood" becomes the tale of Eros struggling with the death instinct. Trace the images of Eros in the text, and then the images of destructive energy. Would you argue that the two come together in the end to serve Eros?

4. What attitude(s) toward violence do we see in the fairy tale?

   - Do you see it encouraging its intended young audience to accept violence as part of human nature?
   - In the tale, who uses violence in a way that is treated as acceptable? Are only certain people or groups "allowed" to engage in it? How might such depictions shape a child's social values?
   - Consider other texts intended for young children—other fairy tales, Disney movies, simplified Bible stories. Do these support the Freudian view of innate aggression, in your assessment, or do they offer an alternative view of the role of violence in individual and social life?

5. What forms of social control are reinforced by the tale? How is the reader directed to "pervert" the instinct for pleasure—how is desire redirected to acceptable social ends?

Pygmalion and Galatea

The following ancient Greek myth tells a story of desire and wish fulfillment. Its appeal has continued over the ages: it is the basis for George Bernard Shaw's play Pygmalion, *which in turn became the musical and later the film* My Fair Lady. *You may also recognize the myth as the outline for many popular contemporary films, such as* Pretty Woman, Dirty Dancing, Maid in Manhattan, Never Been Kissed, Ever After, She's All That, Miss Congeniality, Sabrina, *and* Dreamgirls, *among many others. As you read, consider this myth's continuing cultural appeal, and try constructing an explanation for it, perhaps with parallels to contemporary examples of similar desires.*

A gifted young sculptor of Cyprus, named Pygmalion, was a woman-hater. Detesting the faults beyond measure which nature has given to women, he resolved never to marry. His art, he told himself, was enough for him. Nevertheless, the statue he made and devoted all his genius to was that of a woman. Either he could not dismiss what he so disapproved of from his mind as easily as from his life, or else he was bent on forming a perfect woman and showing men the deficiencies of the kind they had to put up with.

However that was, he labored long and devotedly on the statue and produced a most exquisite work of art. But lovely as it was he could not rest content. He kept on working at it and daily under his skillful fingers it grew more beautiful. No woman ever born, no statue ever made, could approach it. When nothing could be added to its perfection, a strange fate had befallen its creator: he had fallen in love, deeply, passionately in love, with the thing he had made. It must be said in explanation that the statue did not look like a statue; no one would have thought it was ivory or stone, but warm human flesh, motionless for a moment only. Such was the wondrous power of this disdainful young man. The supreme achievement of art was his, the art of concealing art.

But from that time on, the sex he scorned had their revenge. No hopeless lover of a living maiden was ever so desperately unhappy as Pygmalion. He kissed those enticing lips—they could not kiss him back; he caressed her hands, her face—they were unresponsive; he took her in his arms—she remained a cold and passive form. For a time he tried to pretend, as children do with their toys. He would dress her in rich robes, trying the effect of one delicate or glowing color after another, and imagine she was pleased. He would bring her the gifts real maidens love, little birds and gay flowers and the shining tears of amber Phaethon's sisters weep, and then dreamed that she thanked him with eager affection. He put her to bed at night, and tucked her in all soft and warm, as little girls do their dolls. But he was not a child; he could not keep on pretending. In the end he gave up. He loved a lifeless thing and he was utterly and hopelessly wretched.

This singular passion did not long remain concealed from the Goddess of Passionate Love. Venus was interested in something that seldom came her way, a new kind of lover, and she determined to help a young man who could be enamored and yet original.

The feast day of Venus was, of course, especially honored in Cyprus, the island which first received the goddess after she rose from the foam. Snow-white heifers whose horns had been gilded were offered in numbers to her; the heavenly odor of incense was spread through the island from her many altars; crowds thronged her temples; not an unhappy lover but was there with his gift, praying that his love might turn kind. There too, of course, was Pygmalion. He dared to ask the goddess only that he might find a maiden like his statue, but Venus knew what he really wanted and as a sign that she favored his prayer the flame on the altar he stood before leaped up three times, blazing into the air.

Very thoughtful at this good omen Pygmalion sought his house and his love, the thing he had created and given his heart to. There she stood on her pedestal, entrancingly beautiful. He caressed her and then he started back. Was it self-deception or did she really feel warm to his touch? He kissed her lips, a long lingering kiss, and felt them grow soft beneath his. He touched her arms, her shoulders; their hardness vanished. It was like watching wax soften in the sun. He clasped her wrist; blood was pulsing there. Venus, he thought. This is the goddess's doing. And with unutterable gratitude and joy he put his arms around his love and saw her smile into his eyes and blush.

Venus herself graced their marriage with her presence, but what happened after that we do not know, except that Pygmalion named the maiden Galatea, and that their son, Paphos, gave his name to Venus' favorite city.

● Applying a Psychoanalytic Frame

1. Explain the myth as a story of wish fulfillment: what fundamental desire does Pygmalion act on in constructing an ideal female figure he can shape and control? We're told that he realizes "he [is] not a child; he [cannot] keep on pretending." What conflict has he encountered? How does the narrative resolve this conflict in an idealized way?

2. How might we see the myth as an adolescent fantasy? What anxieties does it acknowledge and then imagine out of existence?

3. How might you frame the myth as a male fantasy?

   • What power relation between the genders is established? If you've seen the film *Pretty Woman*, do you consider it as a repetition of the Pygmalion fantasy?

   • What potential implications for real-world gender relations do you see reflected in, and perhaps encouraged by, this myth? How does it imagine the ideal "rules" for dating? How do you think it frames how we might see such social problems as dominating or abusive relationships, date rape, or other forms of violence?

   • Does the myth create an illusion of male sufficiency—a sense of mastery and completeness? Do you see equivalent "Pygmalion" illusions in contemporary narratives and images, in videos, ads, and films?

4. The contemporary films that retell the myth are almost all "chick flicks," films that attract a predominantly female audience. How can you explain the appeal of these films to women, if the foundational story is one of innate female inferiority?

5. Rhetorically, the myth has an open ending, rather than the "happily ever after" resolution conventionally found in fairy tales. What do you think the psycho-analytic implications might be of this uncertainty?

Pygmalion

ROY RICHARD GRINKER

This essay forms the opening of Grinker's biographical work In the Arms of Africa: The Life of Colin M. Turnbull *(2000). Turnbull gained fame as an anthropologist through two major published studies that became popular successes—*The Mountain People *(1973) and* The Forest People *(1961). He provided two very different descriptions of these cultural groups, the former the Ik tribe, a marginalized and, as Turnbull saw them, dehumanized group of nomadic hunters restricted to a mountainous region of Uganda by the government, and the Pygmies, of central Africa, whom Turnbull represented as a cooperative, peace-loving, idyllic community on the fringes of the organized village social system. In the following essay, Grinker sets up Turnbull himself as a man defined by conflicts and desires at odds with his social group, and suggests that in Turnbull's life and writing we see powerful desire for fulfillment of our deepest wishes—hence the chapter title.*

On most mornings in 1957, the Scottish anthropologist Colin Macmillan Turnbull would wake up in his hut next to his young Mbuti assistant, Kenge, their legs and arms intertwined in the way that Mbuti men like to sleep with each other to stay warm. At four foot eight, Kenge was more than a foot and a half shorter than Colin, so Colin could hold him easily with his long legs, arms, and wide hands, keeping them both warm in the damp forest nights.

By daybreak in the Ituri forest of central Africa the temperature often falls below sixty-five degrees, but it feels colder because dew drips incessantly from the forest canopy. Even if you are lucky enough to have a blanket, as Colin and Kenge did, the wool feels heavy and wet. The camp quickly comes alive with the pungent odor of small campfires and the sounds of children singing to welcome the new day. Light enters gently into the small hemispherical huts, made out of thin trees and thatched with *mongongo* leaves, overlapped like tiles. Kenge would emerge first to rekindle the campfire logs, with any luck still smoldering from the night before, for the Mbuti Pygmies do not know how to make fire.

In the afternoons, as thunder rumbled in the distance, Colin and Kenge would rush to the river to bathe. The skies in the Ituri open up, usually within an hour before sunset, releasing a hard and fast rain. When it stops, a few minutes later, the air feels cool and fresh, and black and white magpies and other birds can be seen flying out of their nests to wade in the new streams of rain water. By nightfall, Colin and Kenge had begun to warm themselves by the fire, perhaps eating the smoked meat of a small antelope or water chevrotain, or cassava leaves cooked in palm oil.

Colin spent most of his time with Kenge, who was unusually free to work for him. Kenge had only one blood relative in the area, a half sister, and so he was far less constrained by family obligations than others; because he was an outsider, he had license to be sexually playful with a wide range of people, and he used that freedom in excess. There were also few other Pygmy men willing to be so familiar with a European. Colin relished the nights they spent together, Kenge's sweet body odor, so distinctive to Pygmy men, and the hardness and compactness of Kenge's body, since Mbuti men have virtually no body fat. He would always remember the feeling of Kenge's callused feet rubbing against the soft skin on his legs and feet, protected from the elements by long pants, socks and shoes. Had Kenge commented on Colin, he would likely have talked about the ever-present smell of soap that the Mbuti associate with European bodies, the stark whiteness of his skin, and the enormity of Colin's body as he towered over him during the day, and enveloped and insulated him in the night.

Colin learned quickly that Mbuti men enjoy holding hands and embracing   5
each other at night. The Mbuti have no concept, no word, for sexuality or homosexuality, so physical affection between men does not denote a sexual identity and carries no stigma. Mbuti men can therefore freely express their love for each other. When Colin touched Kenge, he was loving him and making love to him. For Colin also believed that one could make love without sex. One could make love with the rain forest, with music, and with other spiritual phenomena. The Pygmies knew this. They even used the same word for dancing that they used for sexual intercourse. For both Kenge and Colin, love was much more about spiritual ecstasy than about orgasm, more about beholding a universe in the reciprocal gaze and embrace of two men than about mere physical pleasure.

To Colin, Kenge represented the sensuality of the rain forest, and in his 1961 best-selling book, *The Forest People*, he wrote about one evening in particular, when the Pygmies with whom he lived were rejoicing in the forest. Alone in his hut, Colin tried to fall asleep, but the moon was full and shone through. Outside the hut, he heard the Mbuti Pygmies dancing. It was late at night but eventually he felt compelled to get out of his bed, a small black rubber pad and a gray blanket. Anthropologists are, at least at the beginning of their fieldwork, like dogs in a family fight, responding to every stimulus, moving rapidly here and there, but seldom knowing what is really happening around them. They imagine themselves to be human tape recorders, regretting every missed observation or interview for fear it may have contained a revelation. So Colin fought against his fatigue, wrapped the blanket around his back and crawled through the entrance of the hut to watch the festivities. And as he stood up outside the hut, he noticed Kenge.

"There in the tiny clearing," he wrote, "splashed with silver, was the sophisticated Kenge, clad in bark cloth, adorned with leaves, with a flower stuck in his hair. He was all alone, dancing around and singing softly to himself as he gazed up at the treetops.

"Now Kenge was the biggest flirt for miles, so, after watching a while, I came into the clearing and asked, jokingly, why he was dancing alone. He stopped, turned slowly around and looked at me as though I was the biggest fool he had ever seen; and he was plainly surprised by my stupidity.

"'But I'm not dancing alone,' he said. 'I'm dancing with the forest, dancing with the moon.' Then, with the utmost unconcern, he ignored me and continued his dance of love and life."

Turnbull dedicated *The Forest People* to Kenge, for whom, he wrote, the forest was many things, including his lover. Through Kenge, Colin realized a total and consuming passion for both the forest and the Pygmies who lived there, and he would remember the night of that dance as a revelation. For it was on that night, amidst the music and the effervescence, in a momentary vision and a brief conversation, that he became convinced of the human capacity for love and for goodness, which he believed was embodied in the Pygmies. His life and his anthropology were pilgrimages to a beautiful dream world that, in the African rain forest, was inexplicably real. His greatest challenge was to find that same humanity, that same dream, outside the rain forest.

Turnbull looked for it everywhere, and thought he found it in Joseph A. Towles, a young African American man the same age as Kenge, whom he met in New York City two years after he left the Pygmies, in 1959. When Turnbull first laid eyes on him, he thought to himself, "I am back in Africa." Turnbull was thirty-four years old and he would live with Joseph for the next thirty years. In 1959, Towles was an aspiring actor and model but he would soon become an anthropologist. While the Pygmies could be romanticized in writing in words that Colin shaped to fit his own vision, Towles, however, was not so easily fixed.

With the evocative and magical words of *The Forest People*, Colin Turnbull conjured an image of the Pygmies and their world that seized the public imagination and brought him both fame and wealth. Next to Margaret Mead and Louis Leakey, he is perhaps the most well-known anthropologist of the twentieth century. A gifted and persuasive writer, Turnbull used the power of his words and personality to project onto the Pygmies a reflection of his own ideals, altering forever the way that most European and American readers would see the African rain forest and its peoples. Though many anthropologists have disdained the romance and idealism of *The Forest People* as failed science, almost every anthropologist who has ever written about hunter-gatherers anywhere in the world has made use of his work, and what we know about the Pygmies today is derived almost entirely from his work. Many professional anthropologists trace their career decisions to a single reading of *The Forest People*, and the book remains required reading in many high schools and colleges.

If *The Forest People* made his reputation, Turnbull's next major publication, *The Mountain People* (1973), made him controversial. His book told the story of the starving Ik of Uganda, a people on the brink of extinction whose depravity he described in stark detail. In *The Forest People*, he had thanked the Indian guru, Sri Anandamayi Ma, with whom he lived just before he left for central Africa, for giving him his mantra, *Satyam, sivam, sundarm* (truth, goodness, beauty), and for convincing him that those qualities could be found if he looked hard enough; they were the same qualities he had found among the Pygmies and that he believed the Ik had cast aside. If, for Turnbull, the Pygmies showed us the "noble savage" we once were, the Ik, dislocated from their villages to a drought-stricken wasteland, showed us what we might one day become. He portrayed the Ik as a materially and morally impoverished collection of selfish individuals, a people who had abandoned the values of family, love, and altruism for a cutthroat individualism matched only by what he had seen in World War II while serving as a gunnery officer. He watched with horror as Ik men and women attacked each other, even within their own families, to induce vomiting and then eat the vomit; people defecated on each other's doorsteps; expressed joy at the tragedies of others; and having abandoned any effort to cooperate or share, the stronger left the weaker, usually children and the elderly, to die of starvation. "That is the point," he wrote in *The Mountain People*, "at which there is an end to truth, to goodness, and to beauty. . . . The Ik have relinquished all luxury in the name of individual survival, and the result is that they live on as a people without life, without passion, beyond humanity."

He proposed to the Ugandan government that the Ik society should be eliminated, that individuals should be rounded up and dispersed over an area wide enough to make sure they never found each other again. The Ugandan government and the anthropological community were outraged. Angered by Turnbull's proposal and what was called a complete lack of objectivity, Fredrik Barth, the anthropologist who led the international attack against him, wrote that *The Mountain People* "deserves both to be sanctioned and to be held up as a warning to us all," that the book was "dishonest," "grossly irresponsible and harmful," threatening to the "hygiene" of the discipline. Turnbull, who had never shared science's devotion to objectivity and had never thought of himself as a conventional scholar, was unmoved.

His life was marked by a heroic piety to such lofty concepts as goodness, perfection, and love—words many people might find sentimental or vague, but which Colin Turnbull elevated to the sacred. For this reason, he decided to write more about experiences and feelings than about scientific facts. He wanted to show the world the goodness he had found among the Pygmies and the evils he had found among the Ik. The truth of the Zairean rain forest or the tragedy of the Ugandan mountains could not be conveyed in an academic publication to be read by a few hundred scholars. It had to reach millions of people and to come from the heart, not through science but through the emotional and spiritual paths for which his anthropology was an ongoing quest.

Despite his popularity, much about Colin Turnbull has remained a mystery, especially the relationship between his own, often tragic life, and the kinds of work he produced. Few people know that he devoted most of his adult life to one partner, with whom he lived openly as a gay, interracial couple in one of the smallest and most conservative rural towns in Virginia, or that despite Turnbull's refined public demeanor and even temper, his relationship with Towles was often cruel and violent. Few know that, in India, Turnbull was one of only a few Europeans ever permitted to live in the ashram of an Indian saint, Sri Anandamayi Ma, that he was fully ordained as a Buddhist monk by the Dalai Lama, that he helped build one of the most famous boats of the twentieth century, *The African Queen*, that he rejected university tenure (lifetime job security) when it was granted to him, or that he had a major influence on anti–death penalty advocacy. Even fewer know of Turnbull's bizarre reaction to Towles's death from AIDS in 1988.

This is a book about Colin Turnbull's public and private lives, and because it is an intimate study it explores some dimensions of experience that biographical subjects or their estates sometimes want to keep confidential. But Turnbull wanted to disclose the full details of his life with Towles, if only because he wanted Towles's life to be widely known. Turnbull believed that Towles was an African American hero, a gay hero, who could model for a younger generation the capacity to overcome oppression. To that end, Turnbull arranged all of his and Joe's papers for Joe Towles's future biographer, and wrote a rambling, unedited, one-thousand-page manuscript he called "Lover and Beloved." Ostensibly a history of his relationship with Towles, it is primarily a transcription of Joe's diaries and a record of Joe's efforts to become a professional anthropologist.

Colin Turnbull donated his private collection of hundreds of African artifacts, ten thousand slides and photographs, tape recordings, videos, and all his field notes to the Avery Center for Research on African American History and Culture at the College of Charleston, South Carolina. He called it the "Joseph A. Towles Collection." Turnbull also gave the Avery the hundreds of greeting cards he and Towles exchanged on holidays over the years, even empty boxes of Valentine's candy. He made sure that if anyone went to the Avery to look through the collections, that person would also find the name of Joseph A. Towles. And any future biographer would have access to everything, from insurance forms and tax returns to sexually playful notes written on scrap paper. The collection had another purpose, to make sure that no one could learn about Turnbull without also learning about Towles, that the life of Colin Turnbull would be visible as a transparency lit only by Joe.

The archive shows Turnbull's extraordinary commitment to Towles. Shortly after they met in 1959, they took wedding vows and considered themselves to be married as husband and wife. Colin called Joe "Josephine" and his love for his wife became a sacred object of worship and devotion. Thirty-five years later, he would pray daily to a shrine consisting of Buddhist and Hindu relics and three photographs, one of his former guru, Sri Anandamayi Ma, who Colin believed was an embodiment of God, the other two of Joe.

The archive and the history Turnbull wrote of his relationship with Towles are both expressions of the way in which Colin sought to merge his life with Joe's. Each took on parts of the other. Towles played out Turnbull's rage and recklessness so that Turnbull appeared to the world as a modest, unassuming and even-tempered man. Towles even fully realized Turnbull's deep-seated wish to be imprisoned, a wish that can be traced to Turnbull's early childhood. On the other side, Towles's imperfections satisfied Turnbull's need to fashion someone born without privilege, wealth or pedigree, and in showing Towles's worth, to prove, by comparison, his sense of his own mediocrity. Turnbull adapted to Towles's own sense of worthlessness—indeed, the very worst of his idea of his blackness—by becoming a stable father figure, one who could give Towles unconditional approval. Turnbull spent much of his life attempting to shape Towles into a world-class scholar. He became convinced that he could single-handedly bring to life the brilliance of Towles's undiscovered and unpolished mind.

Colin Turnbull struggled to create Joseph Towles, but he did so without the arrogance and whimsy of George Bernard Shaw's Pygmalion, Professor Henry Higgins, and he remained largely oblivious to the reasons behind his actions. He was perhaps more like the original Pygmalion, the ancient King of Cyprus, the noble bachelor and sculptor who crafted and fell in love with an ivory statue of a maiden so beautiful she looked as if she must be a work of nature. The tragedy of Towles was that he tried to comply with Turnbull's need to create him. Turnbull helped make Towles an unsuccessful professor who would never publish or find continuous academic employment and who would continually threaten his ideals with affairs and alcoholism, and later with the psychiatric complications that accompany AIDS. His hope for Joe was a heavy burden for both of them, a burden that no intellectual vigor could lay down.

Both Joseph Towles and the Pygmies were the creations of Colin Turnbull, who was motivated by a deep-seated wish to find goodness, beauty, and power in the oppressed or ridiculed and, by making those qualities known, reveal the evils of western civilization. The vision of the world he summoned was so perfect, so true, so right for him, that it gave all the appearances of being real.

● Applying a Psychoanalytic Frame

1. Consider Grinker's chapter title: how has the author used the myth of Pygmalion to structure his view of Turnbull? What psychological parallels can you draw from the biographical information he provides?

2. Grinker writes that "Turnbull used the power of his words and personality to project onto the Pygmies a reflection of his own ideals." How do you see Grinker using both psychoanalytic and rhetorical framing to shape this view and give it credibility? Does the same pattern appear in Turnbull's sense of Joseph Towles, as Grinker presents it?

3. Reading Grinker's description of Turnbull, we might consider the anthropologist a heroic idealist committed to goodness and beauty. How can his search for these ideals also be seen as self-serving, perhaps even violent in nature?

4. Analyze Grinker's essay for the rhetorical techniques he uses to form a cohesive story out of selected details from Turnbull's life. On the surface, Turnbull's life

is a "mystery," Grinker claims; how does he link together parts of Turnbull's experience to suggest a unified set of values and desires?

5. Think of various public figures whose unified personas, or public masks, have been shattered: O. J. Simpson, Rock Hudson, Richard Nixon, Michael Jackson, Martha Stewart, or other recent examples.

   • Why do you think the public often reacts with a sense of shock, outrage, betrayal, anger?

   • Is this reaction itself split—do we feel both satisfaction and also relief from guilt by witnessing the downfall of others?

   • What might the psychoanalytic logic be for such a reaction? (This reaction is also called "Schadenfreude." The German word refers to a hidden malicious pleasure at another's misfortune.)

topics for writing

1. Develop a profile, either individual or composite (a description drawn from multiple examples), of one of the figures in this chapter's readings using a psychoanalytic frame. Your argument might be the dominant motivation that defines this figure's relation to the world—aggression, libidinal desire, Eros— and how you see the effect of it. Is this figure able to meet Freud's challenge of finding enough satisfaction to make life bearable?

   • A profile focuses on a single individual and tells her or his story—what her or his defining trait is, and what events or experiences best illustrate this figure's personality. You may have composed your own profile for an online community such as MySpace, for example.

   • Think about what your readers need: an overview of the figure's situation; specific textual evidence to support your argument that she or he is dominated by a particular instinct, and explanation of what that instinct is/how it works, according to psychoanalytic theory; the logic for your sense of her or his possibilities for satisfaction.

   • Consider your options in terms of stance: will you offer some judgment of the figure, leave any judgment to readers, actively discourage judgment by focusing on the psychoanalytic concept instead of the figure?

2. Two of the readings in this chapter, the *Shane* excerpt and "Little Red Riding Hood," focus on a child's experience. Use the psychoanalytic frame to develop a topic that helps explain some aspect of children's psychological development; the conflicts inherent in that process; social expectations and how they conflict with childish desires; or some other issue about children or childhood suggested by the frame.

- You're being asked to *invent* a valid topic here using the psychoanalytic frame you've built. Approach the invention process from multiple ways and techniques: move from the theory to the two readings; consider problems that the readings present and go back to the theory; think about contemporary conversations about children and violence, families, rebelliousness, gender roles, and other topics you can name/brainstorm.

- You might work collaboratively to invent and frame possible topics. Some possible topics to start with: children's relationship to aggression/violence; how children begin to identify as a gendered self; the role of the reality principle in developing maturity.

- As you articulate a topic, use the frame to develop your argument and how you wish your audience to see it. Connect details of the stories to the steps of the theoretical reasoning, both as you plan the essay and as logical evidence as you write—use the stories rhetorically to organize and develop your argument.

3. Two of the readings, the two versions of the Pygmalion myth, represent figures whose experience is dominated by fantasy. The mythic account ends happily; Colin Turnbull's story is not so ideal. Think about examples of the two—the imaginary and the real—and choose one to analyze in depth. Use the psychoanalytic frame to explore and explain either

   - how fantasy works on the purely wish fulfillment level, where the "dreamer" controls the outcome. Consider films (*It Could Happen to You, Finding Nemo, The Player, The Girl Next Door, Sleepless in Seattle, Big*) or written texts, including fairy tales ("Cinderella") or fantasy novels (the *Lord of the Rings* trilogy, *The Bridge to Terabithia*). Some questions to pose as part of your inquiry:
     - How are the needs of the ego addressed?
     - How is the figure insulated from feeling guilt for his or her desires?
     - What idic outlets are provided?
     - How does the figure enjoy Eros and self-centered satisfaction as well?

     OR

   - how fantasy in lived experience seems to break down, destroy, or disappoint. Consider the cases of celebrities (Elvis, Marilyn Monroe, Kurt Cobain), cult figures (Jim Jones/Jonestown, David Koresh/Branch Davidians), or fads (diets, get-rich-quick schemes). The questions listed above apply here as well.

Reading for Rhetorical Techniques

● Reading critically from a
  psychoanalytic frame
● Synthesizing sources
● Moving an audience

On Touching by Accident

NANCY MAIRS

The titles of Nancy Mairs's books tell us a great deal about her rhetorical values. Waist-High in the World *reflects a common stance she adopts: living with advanced multiple sclerosis, she now uses a wheelchair and calls attention to her new perspective on the mainstream "abled" world.* Remembering the Bone House—*the bone house being a metaphor for the body—suggests how her writing connects memory, place, and sense of self (a connection she makes again in* Carnal Acts*). The following essay is from her first collection,* Plaintext *(1986), a title that highlights her stylistic choices in relation to her view of life (and death) issues. In it she recounts her experiences with depression and attempted suicide, two topics that might easily alienate an audience. Does she succeed in moving you instead?*

Those of us who would be suicides come at odd bits of knowledge about the failings of the human heart. Not necessarily literal heart failure, of course: A good many of us stop short of that point, for one reason or another. Virginia Woolf, for instance, who swallowed a lethal dose of veronal in 1913, did not take her final walk, into the River Ouse with her pockets full of stones, until 1941. We may survive. We often do. The failings I'm talking about have to do not with death, which is another matter altogether ("the one experience," Woolf noted, "I shall never describe"), but with life—with lives. The last time I tried to kill myself, a number of things happened to me, most of them predictable and some of them not very pleasant. But one of them was odd enough that still, months later, I return to the thought of it, amused and puzzled and more than a little anxious about its significance.

I am a depressive. Researchers know surprisingly little about my condition, which is called "unipolar" depression to distinguish it from "bipolar" or manic depression. It may be caused by a chemical imbalance in the brain. It occurs cyclically, and each person has his own cycle—or, more likely, her own cycle, since far more women suffer from depression than men. No one knows why, though some very good reasons have been proposed. (A thorough review of depression in women is Maggie Scarf's *Unfinished Business: Pressure Points in the Lives of Women* [New York: Ballentine Books, 1980].) Depression is characterized by disturbances in normal physiological functions like eating and sleeping and by suicidal thoughts or acts arising from a sense of personal worthlessness and despair. As a rule, a depressive does not attempt suicide until she begins to feel better, probably because, in the depths of depression, she has felt too powerless even to kill herself. Several doctors have told me, with a good deal of satisfaction, that I am a textbook case. I do not like being a textbook case. I feel dull. Nonetheless, every so often I fall off the edge of the world into a void even blacker than the one that kept medieval sailors in charted waters; and as soon as I begin to emerge, I grab for the bottle of pills.

Just so the last time. Gradually my consciousness filled with the image of a thin sharp blade drawing again and again across the blue veins in my wrist. This image is symbolic only—except for one youthful attempt, I have never tried to slash my wrists and would not now choose to do so—and I am never entirely free from it. But when it becomes so repetitive that it screens out the faces and voices of people around me, even my own face in the mirror, then I know I am in mortal danger. (Wonderful how such clichés take on their original purity and force in a literal context.) I kept checking myself for signs of survival: I polished my fingernails and had a permanent; I bought a director's chair in which to sit in the sun and a soft plum-colored velveteen blazer; I sent a short story to *The New Yorker*. People who do such things, I reasoned, do not commit suicide. Finally, however, exhausted by the moment-to-moment decisions to stay alive, I decided on a Tuesday that I would kill myself on Friday night.

From then on, I was frantically busy. I had to sort through the tottering piles on my desks at home and in my office. I had to catch up on the teaching duties I had neglected and plan activities for the rest of the semester, so that whoever took over could do so with the least possible disruption of my students' learning. I had to write a long letter to George, listing the names and numbers of people to notify, reminding him that my body was to be donated for research into multiple sclerosis, detailing the distribution of my personal effects. During that time I also did a couple of interviews for a television program about the disabled that I was hosting. I had a drink with a friend. I invited my daughter to spend a night with me in the apartment to which I'd moved a few weeks before and bought her a pink striped shirt and a pair of purple jeans at the same time I bought my blazer.

By Friday night I was tired. I thought about staying home from the Hallowe'en party I'd said I'd go to, but finally I put on my new blazer and went (and all evening harlequins and witches and men with gigantic bosoms and miniskirts asked me, "Where's your costume?" and I said, carefully, each time, "You're looking at it"). I had a pretty good time. To be sure, the man with whom I was in

5

love, who had recently thrown me over (another pure and forceful cliché), was there, annihilating me; but then, a well-known novelist flirted with me, so I must have had some substance. I was kissed by a pirate and possibly also by a devil. I didn't drink much. I left early.

When I got home, the back yard of my little apartment building, where I parked my car, was dark; but there was a moon, and I'd left my porch light on, so I could find my door. As I stuck the key into the lock, a figure danced out of the darkness—a clown, I think, in a pink ruffled suit—and pleaded, "Oh, can I use your bathroom? I'm at this party over there"—vague gesture—"and the line to the bathroom is *miles* long and I've been drinking all this *beer* and I'm about to *burst* and . . ." "Sure," I said, swinging the door in. "It's in there." While she peed torrentially, I turned on the radio, opened a beer, and put down fresh food for Bête Noire, who was twisting around my ankles like a dervish. The clown flushed and came out, yanking at her ruffles. "This is so *hard* to get in and out of," she moaned. "Oh, thank you. You saved my *life*. I just couldn't have waited any longer." She was pink and plump. I didn't think she was old enough for the beer. "Oh, *there* you are," she called to a shadow that loomed on the doorstep, and off she bounded, recounting my heroic rescue of her in her moment of greatest need.

I closed the door behind her. I went into the bathroom and started taking Elavil while I washed my face and undressed. I went back into the tidy white bedroom/living room/kitchen/study and sat down at my desk. Still taking the Elavil, three by three, I finished my letter to George and tried to write in my journal, but my vision was too badly blurred. I dropped the bottle of Elavil and couldn't see to pick up the small yellow tablets. That clumsiness probably saved my life. That, and Bête Noire. I had at first thought I would turn on my stove and heater, which had no pilot lights, and thus hasten the work of the drug. But Bête was so tiny that I knew that the gas would kill her long before me, and I couldn't bear the thought of her black body still and lifeless. By this time I had no sense of myself or anyone else as a living creature; and when, later, a psychiatrist asked if I hadn't tried to call for help after taking all those pills, I had to say that I didn't know there was anyone to call; yet I couldn't kill the kitten.

George found me eighteen hours later and took me to the emergency room, where, after a few hours on a heart monitor and the obligatory psychiatric interview, I was pronounced a survivor and sent home. I had at some point roused having to go to the bathroom and, unable to get even to my hands and knees, had dragged myself around my apartment, battering my body and smearing the floor with blood and urine; but I heal quickly. Before long the bruises faded and the scabs fell off. I was still shaky but no longer suicidal. I had let a lot of my responsibilities slide, so I threw myself into activity and forgot the whole mess as much and as quickly as possible.

Then one day, six weeks or so later, when I was having lunch with a friend and we were swapping stories of failed love and suicide, I saw suddenly the round pink ruffled form of the little clown dancing through my door and into my bathroom. I had wholly forgotten her and the young man waiting for her in the shadows under my cedar trees. I was startled by the memory—so quick, so complete—startled and amused, and I began to describe it to my friend. Just then, though, the man who had thrown me over, with whom I was still in love, asked if he might join us, and naturally we had to speak of other things. I never finished my story about the clown.

I have thought of her often since then, however. She entered my life so   10
lightly, this child, needing only a place to empty her bladder so that she wouldn't disgrace herself, at just the moment when I was planning to leave, though she couldn't have known that. And I wonder whether I have done just the same thing myself, wandering through some other's desolation in my costume—tight jeans, soft shirt, dusky velveteen blazer, cane—needing some quick favor on my way. How many times? And when?

● Applying a Psychoanalytic Frame

1. Mairs grounds her story in physical details, such as discussing the chemical basis for depression; she does not write from a psychoanalytic perspective. Can you reread her story as a psychoanalytic text? How do the personal experiences get reframed in such an approach—the romantic break-up, the suicidal despair and self-violence, the detached decision about timing, the directions about her body and possessions?

2. Some readers react with hostility to Mairs's dispassionate account of her attempted suicide. Why do you think talk of suicide so often evokes angry responses, charges of selfishness, cowardice, or insanity? How can the psychoanalytic frame help explain such responses?

3. Why might the image of and encounter with the clown-costumed young woman have stayed so forcefully with Mairs after her recovery from the suicide attempt? How might Freud "read" the incident?

4. If work and love are the essential elements of a happy life (however limited that happiness is), according to Freud, then where do we see these experiences affecting Mairs's sense of a bearable life? Can you suggest why work and love may offer hope and yet also threaten deep pain?

5. Mairs's essay is confessional, in a sense, but one could also argue that it's aggressive as well—it's a largely unapologetic revelation of an attempted act that the community usually sees as taboo. Rhetorically, how does she keep her readers from rejecting her? Consider your own reactions as you first read the essay. Is pathos effectively at work here?

Life in the Gang

SCOTT H. DECKER and BARRIK VAN WINKLE

The following is an excerpt from a research report (published in 1996) on the phenomenon of gangs. Read the piece from a psychoanalytic perspective to see how the gang fills the role of "civilization" as Freud discusses it. Look also at the report's organizational design: its subheadings, their order, its use of testimony from gang members. What is the effect of the genre on the stance(s) of the authors? And what effect does the genre have on how you as a reader react to the topic?

Pushed or Pulled into Membership   We now move to consider the reasons offered by gang members for their decision to join the gang. In every instance, joining the gang was the result of a process that evolved over a period of time, typically less than a year. In some cases, the process more closely resembled recruitment, whereby members of a gang would identity a particular individual and convince them to join the gang. This, however, accounted for very few of the individuals in our sample, fourteen out of ninety-nine. For the most part, the process of joining the gang was consistent with the formation of neighborhood friendship groups. Twenty of our respondents specifically mentioned that they had grown up in the same neighborhood as other gang members and had done things with them over a lengthy period of time. For these individuals, their gang evolved from these playgroups into a more formal association, in much the same way Thrasher (1927) described gangs in Chicago.

The process of joining the gang has two elements; the first is a series of "pulls" that attract individuals to the gang, the second are the "pushes" that compel individuals to join the gang. The pull or lure of gangs was an opportunity to make money selling drugs (a response offered by 84 percent of our subjects), to increase one's status in the neighborhood (indicated by 60 percent), or both. The primary factor that pushes individuals into gangs is their perceived need for protection. Again and again, our subjects described in considerable detail the threat they were under from rival gangs in nearby neighborhoods. A number of gang members (84 percent) found it impossible to live without some form of protection, typically finding such protection through their association with a gang. It is our argument that, for most members, both pushes and pulls play a role in the decision to join the gang. Four specific reasons were cited for joining the gang. In declining order of importance, they were: (1) protection, (2) the prompting of friends and/or relatives, (3) the desire to make money through drug sales, and (4) the status associated with being a gang member. The desire for protection is an example of a "push"—an external force compelling gang membership. The efforts of friends or relatives to encourage gang membership also represent a push toward gang membership. The other two reasons, desire for money and status, are clearly "pulls," or forces that attract individuals to gangs.

As noted above, most of the individuals we interviewed felt their physical safety was in jeopardy in their neighborhood; for the majority, moving to a safer neighborhood was simply not a viable option as few had the resources to effect such a move. Given these circumstances, most gang members (eighty-three) chose to align themselves with a gang for "protection."

> That is the advantage, protection. There wouldn't be all this stuff if certain people wouldn't try to be tough. So they try to be tough, so now we be Crips. They stay out of our business. Some cats from the city came over, that's how it all started. Jumped my friend. (Male #022, "8 Ball," fifteen-year-old 107 Hoover Gangster Crip)

> I thought about it [protection]; every time I walked somewhere people would try to start stuff. Yeah, like one time I got off my bus and these two dudes tried to double pin me. (Male #010, "Jason C.," fifteen-year-old Compton Gangster)

Few gang members acknowledged the fact that affiliating with a gang increased their risk of victimization. Indeed, some went so far as to state that being in a gang insulated them from fighting.

> It keeps people from fucking with me. So I don't have no trouble, no fights out on the street and all that. (Female #011, "Lisa," fifteen-year-old Compton Gangster)

And other gang members recognized the dilemma of not being in a gang yet having friends who lived in a neighborhood identified with a particular gang. "Bullet" decided to join his gang since he was seen as a gang member anyway.

> Yeah, all your friends Bloods so you don't want to be the odd ball. Say I didn't become a Blood but I was always down with them and when dudes shot at us they was shooting at me too. Any way it goes, I was going to be a gang member. If dudes ride by shooting or whatever they will see me with them. (Male #060, twenty-year-old Inglewood Family Gangster Blood)

Similarly, "Smith & Wesson" reported that already being identified as a rival gang member also played a role in the decision to join.

> I got tired of these Crabs saying what's up Fuz and I'm telling them I ain't in no gang. So I got in the gang. See what they do? (Male #057, fifteen-year-old Neighborhood Posse Blood)

Nearly a third (29 percent) of gang members reported that they joined because of the presence of a relative or friend in the gang. The process of recruiting friends and family members into the gang was seldom coercive; indeed most needed only minor forms of encouragement. Many gang members found their way into the gang through emulating a relative (#036) or friend (#054). One reported that he had joined, "Cause my brother was in it mostly" (#031). And another said, "Cause all my friends become one" (#010). Others indicated that it was a natural part of hanging out with friends in the neighborhood.

> I ain't going to say it's going to be my life but it was just something that came up to me where I was staying. I was with the fellas and it just happened that I became one of them. I just got in the same stuff they was in. To me I see it as something to do. I can't put it a more better way than that. (Male #020, "Lil Thug," sixteen-year-old Gangster Disciple)

We have identified drug money and status as two of the factors cited most often as attractive features that "pulled" young men and women into gangs. As we document below, drug sales grew in importance once individuals joined their gang. However, only a small fraction (6 percent) were influenced by the opportunity to sell drugs in making the decision to join their gang. Others were more direct, stating that they found the money attractive or that money had initially attracted them to the gang.

> My interest was in getting paid, man, strictly getting paid. I had a job at 13. I sold dope, cocaine, but it wasn't a career thing, it was like for extra money. (Male #040, "Knowledge," twenty-one-year-old Compton Gangster)

Girls are a frequent topic among adolescent males, and the opportunity to impress girls through increased status was cited by 40 percent of our subjects as the reason why they joined the gang. In this sense, their motivations closely resemble those of their adolescent peers who were not involved in gangs.

> Yeah, you get respect, girls, money, drive around with your friends in fancy cars, saying stuff that nobody else know about. I wanted to be in cause they had the pretty girls and everything. (Male #015, "Karry," fifteen-year-old Crenshaw Gangster Blood)

But status concerns were not confined solely to the pursuit of women.

> It make me big, it make me carry guns, it made me like if somebody called and I tell them to come over and they don't come over I get mad cause I'm the big man, he supposed to come to me. I might pop them upside they head or I might pistol whoop them or I just sit back and just dog them out. Many things I can do to a person that they don't ask. (Male #018, "Maurice," twenty-year-old 107 Hoover Gangster Crip)

Process of Entry   Typically, the process of joining the gang was gradual and evolved out of the normal features of street life in the neighborhood. Indeed, the imitative aspects of adolescent life are strong enough to suggest that most gang members affiliated themselves with friends from the neighborhood already involved in the gang. In describing how they came to join their gang, twenty-nine of the fifty-four who offered an answer to this question indicated they joined as a consequence of neighborhood friendships. On average, members of our sample heard about their gang while they were twelve, started hanging out with gang members at thirteen, and had joined before their fourteenth birthday. This suggests a gradual process of affiliation rather than one of active recruitment.

Eleven percent of our respondents began the process of affiliating with their gang by being involved in fights. In these instances, they joined with friends in the neighborhood to fight rival groups in other neighborhoods before formally accepting membership. Violence is a hallmark activity for gangs and serves a variety of latent functions. It strengthens the bonds between existing members, increases the stake of prospective or fringe members in the gang, and serves as a means by which nongang youth come to join the gang.

> It was just when I was being around them they was cool with me and stuff so they just asked them to join in one time. They helped me in a lot of fights and stuff like that. (Male #093, "Lil-P," sixteen-year-old Crenshaw Mob Gangster Bloods)

> I just went on a few posses, I just started hanging around a little bit with them but I was seeing the way things was going and I wanted to join in so I initiated it by the hand signs. (Male #017, "Billy," twenty-one-year-old North Side Crip)

Another route to entering the gang stemmed from normal activities in the neighborhood. As such, becoming part of the gang is a gradual process, often the logical outgrowth of having gang-involved friends in a particular neighborhood.

> The people I hang with are all in it. You know like how you find yourself in a situation. (Female #047, "Baby," fifteen-year-old Rolling 60's Crip)

> I was hanging with them, it was just the area I was in was claimed by them so I just started claiming with them. (Male #025, "Tony," seventeen-year-old 107 Hoover Gangster Crip)

For others, school was the place where entry into the gang occurred. After all, it is not uncommon for friends at school to self-select into the same activities. Viewed in this light, the gang represents a "normal" feature of adolescent life.

Initiation   Becoming a gang member requires more than a decision. Most gangs require prospective members to undergo some sort of an initiation process. Over 90 percent of our sample indicated that they participated in such a ritual.

The initiation ritual fulfills a number of important functions. The first is to determine whether a prospective gang member is indeed tough enough to endure the rigors of violence they will undoubtedly face. After all, members of the gang may have to count on this individual for back up, and someone who turns tail at the first sign of violence is not an effective defender. But the initiation serves other purposes as well. In particular, the initiation increases solidarity among gang members by engaging them in a collective ritual. The initiation reminds active members of their earlier status as a nonmember and gives the new member something in common with individuals who have been with their gang for a longer period of time. Because of these common experiences, the initiation ritual—especially to the extent that it involves violence—creates aspects of what Klein (1971) has called "mythic violence," the legends and stories shared by gang members about their participation in violence. The telling of these stories increases cohesiveness among gang members. Further, mythic violence enables gang members to engage in acts they may otherwise regard as irrational, risky, or both.

Padilla (1992) reports the most common initiation ritual is being beaten in 10 or "V-ed" in, a finding similar to those of Moore (1978), Hagedorn (1988), and Vigil (1988). Gangs in St. Louis also employ this method of initiation. This form of initiation included seventy of the ninety-two gang members who offered an answer to this question. While it took many forms, in its most common version a prospective gang member walked between a line of gang members or stood in the middle of a circle of gang members who beat the initiate with their fists. Falling down, crying out, failing to fight back, or running away sounded the death knell for membership.

> I had to stand in a circle and there was about ten of them. Out of these ten there was just me standing in the circle. I had to take six to the chest by all ten of them. Or I can try to go to the weakest one and get out. If you don't get out they are going to keep beating you. I said I will take the circle. (Male #020, "Lil Thug," sixteen-year-old Gangster Disciple)

Taking six to the chest was commonly reported as a means of initiation, especially by gangs who use the six-pointed star as one of their symbols, such as the Disciples.

> Well it's like this, if you around us and we recommend you to G, we just make up our minds and then somebody look at they watch we'll yell it's on, we'll initiate you. Then after you initiated you on the ground we pick you up hug you and say what's up G, just showing him that it's love. It wasn't that we wanted to rush you or hurt you nothing like that. It's meant because we want you to be around us, we want you to be a part of us too. (Male #036, "NA," eighteen-year-old Compton Gangster BIC)

The initiation fulfills other purposes, such as communicating information about the gang, its rules, and activities.

> INT: So that was your initiation?
>
> MALE: #099, "Joe L.," eighteen-year-old Insane Gangster Disciple: Yeah. And then they sat down and blessed me and told me the 16 laws and all that. But now in the new process there is a 17th and 18th law.

Other gang members reported that they had the choice of either being beaten in or going on a "mission" or a "posse." A mission required a prospective gang member to engage in an act of violence, usually against a rival gang member on rival turf. Nearly a fifth of our respondents were required to confront a rival gang member face to face.

> You have to fly your colors through enemy territory. Some step to you, you have to take care of them by yourself, you don't get no help. (Male #041, "C. K.," twenty-two-year-old Blood)

> To be a Crip you have to put your blue rag on your head and wear all blue and go in a Blood neighborhood that is the hardest of all of them and walk through the Blood neighborhood and fight Bloods. If you come out without getting killed that's the way you get initiated. (Male #084, "Rolo," fifteen-year-old Rolling 60's Crip)

The requirements of going on a mission also may include shooting someone. Often the intended victim is known to the gang before the prospective member sets out on the mission.

> Something has got to be done to somebody. You have to do it. Part of you coming in is seeing if you for real and be right on. The last person came in, we took him over to a store. That person identified somebody out of our gang members that shot somebody. We told him that in order to be in the gang he had to shoot him. So he did. (Male #013, "Darryl," twenty nine-year-old Blood)

> INT: How was he brought in?
>
> MALE: #069, "X-Men," fourteen-year-old Inglewood Family Gangster: We asked him how he wanted to get in and he said he wanted to do a ride-by and shoot the person who killed his brother. So he did a ride-by shooting and killed him.
>
> INT: Was his brother a gang member?
>
> 069: A Neighborhood Piru Blood.
>
> INT: His brother was killed?
>
> 069: Yeah, that's why he wanted to be in. He wasn't gonna get in anyway but his brother got killed.

Gang members and their victims in such encounters are not always strangers, as seen in the case of a gang member who shot his brother, a member of a rival gang.

> INT: What did you have to do to be accepted as a member of the Rolling 60's?
>
> MALE: #087, "Blue Jay," eighteen-year-old-Rolling 60's Grip: Either kill somebody close to you or just shoot somebody, do harm to somebody close to you like family or something.
>
> INT: Which one did you take?
>
> 087: I shot my brother. He didn't know I did it.

Others told us that shooting someone, especially a rival gang member, as part of the initiation gave them "rank," higher status, and responsibility in the gang.

Six gang members reported an alternative means of initiation. Two members told us that they got "tagged" (tattooed) with India Ink and a needle or with a white hot coat hanger as part of the initiation process. Another gang member told us he was expected to sell a certain amount of crack cocaine in order to be accepted. Three gang members told us that as relatives of influential gang members, they were able to avoid the initiation ritual that characterized entry into their gang. These examples illustrate the adaptive nature of most of the gangs we studied; after all, for the most part, they were organized and run by adolescents. As such, we would not expect to find a rigid set of procedures to govern the initiation process.

In late 1991, we received a fax from city hall, advising the public of a new form of gang initiation taking place across the country. The fax described a process by which gang members drove a car at night with their lights out and followed anyone who flashed their lights at them. It was reputed that the gang members would then kill those individuals. We were skeptical about the validity of such claims, a skepticism shared by local law enforcement officials. At scores of local and national conferences, we have been unable to verify a single instance in which this process occurred. This incident illustrates the symbolic threat represented by gang members and how effectively the process of cultural transmission of gang images can work. The creation of images such as this leads to further isolation of gang members from social institutions and interactions.

The steps by which women were initiated into the gang varied considerably from those reported by men. While one, a leader of the C Queens, reported that fighting was the primary means of being initiated, other women said female members of her gang had the option of engaging in property crimes such as burglary or shoplifting. We did hear stories, exclusively from male gang members, that prospective female gang members were required to have sex with male gang members. Two male gang members illustrate that contention.

Yes, they with it. For them [the Crippettes] to be down they got to have sex with us. One night one little gal and her friends were out saggin, she was a fine little gal, and she said she wanted to be down with us. She had to fuck everybody but I felt sorry for the little gal. (Male #033, "Larry," eighteen-year-old Thundercat)

INT: Did she have to be beat in?

MALE: #084, "Rolo," fifteen-year-old Rolling 60's Crip: No, she got to poke everybody in the crew to get in. There was about 30 or 40 of us.

Female gang members, however, disputed this notion. Not one woman indicated she chose this means of initiation; indeed none could recall a woman who had. One woman's response, when asked about being required to have sex with members of the gang to be initiated, was laughter. This discrepancy illustrates the belief systems and bravado of adolescent males about their sexuality and control over females.

Reasons to Be in a Gang We now consider what gang members regard as the   15
positive features or advantages of gang membership. We presented subjects with twelve features of gang life, asking them to specify whether they represented a good reason to be in their gang. The responses to this question are found in Figure 1, where we list, in rank order, the percent of gang members who indicated that each category was a good reason to be in their gang.

Protection was identified as a positive feature of gang membership by 86 percent of the subjects, more than any other category. However, selling drugs

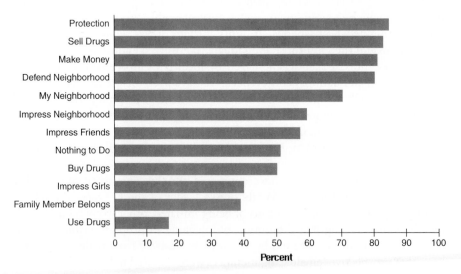

Figure 1 Reasons to Belong to the Gang

and opportunities to make money were seen as advantages of gang membership by 84 percent and 82 percent of subjects respectively. Defending the neighborhood also was viewed as an important reason to belong, as 81 percent of gang members responded in the affirmative when asked if this activity was a positive feature of gang membership. Interestingly, impressing people in the neighborhood, impressing friends, and impressing girls, all measures of status, received lower levels of support from gang members than did the categories just reviewed. In general, status concerns were endorsed as advantages to being in the gang by fewer members (thirty-eight) than were more instrumental aspects of gang life such as protection (eighty-three) or making money (seventy-nine). These responses reflect a preference for instrumental benefits of a more tangible nature than status concerns.

It is interesting to compare the responses to this series of questions to the answers gang members gave us about their reasons to join the gang. The desire for protection was the overwhelming motivation cited by gang members in their decision to join the gang. Their experiences in the gang had done little to change this. However, two notable differences can be observed between the reasons to join the gang and, once having joined, the advantages of membership. The second and third most frequent responses to the question Why did you join your gang? were the chance to sell drugs and make money. However, these categories received far stronger endorsements from currently active gang members as reasons to belong to their gang. At the same time, status concerns (ranked as the fourth most important reason to join) fell farther down the list as advantages to membership. This pattern suggests that once in the gang, instrumental concerns like protection and money assume even greater importance. In addition, it is no surprise that drug sales and defending the neighborhood received similar high levels of support. In a sense, these are mutually reinforcing categories, since successful drug sales require a secure turf or neighborhood base from which to operate. Thus, one way to enhance the profitability of drug sales is to protect the neighborhood, particularly against rival gangs that would seek to use a gang member's neighborhood as a location for selling drugs.

Many gang members who cited protection as a positive feature of gang membership echoed sentiments similar to those who cited this as a reason to join. There is a very utilitarian tone to these comments.

> It's like a comfortable feeling, you got someone to back you up and protect you. (Male #017, "Billy," twenty-one-year-old North Side Crip)

Those who noted the importance of the gang for making money have a similarly utilitarian perspective toward drug sales.

> There's money in a gang. I want to be in it, you see a lot of money in it man. That's why I really got in the gang, money and all. (Male #033, "Larry," eighteen-year-old Thundercat)

> You live in a neighborhood that's run by a gang you just can't up and start sell-
> ing drugs getting they profit. They'll tell you. You either got to be in their gang
> or give them half of what you make or don't sell at all. (Male #038, "G.O.D.,"
> nineteen-year-old Compton Gangster)

Gangs can "organize" drug sales in two important ways. First, some gang members have the economic capacity to "front" drugs that would allow an individual
gang member to begin selling drugs or to make more profit than they could if
they were independent of the gang. Second, and more importantly, gangs have
both the will and the mechanism to use violence in order to control a particular
turf and keep competing drug sales from interfering with their profits. The ability to accomplish these goals contributed to the large number of gang members
who responded that making money or selling drugs was a good reason to be in
the gang.

Despite these instrumental concerns (protection and making money),
a number of members indicated that their gang fulfilled a variety of more typical
adolescent needs—especially companionship and support. While we maintain
that violence or its threat is central to understanding gangs, street gangs of the
1990s meet a number of the emotional needs of adolescents that do not differ
much from those of nongang adolescents.

> One thing I like about gangs it's more people to be around, more partners to go
> places with. Like certain days we do, like Saturday and Sunday we go up to
> Skate King. Like next weekend we might go out to Northwest Plaza (a large
> shopping mall) and wear all blue colors. (Male #003, "Jerry," eighteen-year-old
> Thundercat)
>
> Social stuff and if somebody mess with you. You know you grow up into this shit.
> Mostly social. (Male #012, "Lance," twenty-year-old West Side Mob member)

Each of these quotes illustrates typical adolescent activities—hanging out at the
mall, being in the company of friends, and engaging in "social stuff"—behaviors
that resemble those of other adolescents.

● Applying a Psychoanalytic Frame

1. Freud saw work and love as the two major needs in civilized life. Does gang
   membership as these researchers discuss it meet these needs? Look at the
   words of the young people who discuss the "work" aspect of gang membership.

   • Do you see gangs serving the purposes of Eros? Would Freud see them as
     doing so?

   • How do gangs use the energy of the death instinct—is it successfully made to
     serve Eros?

2. Compare the initiation rites and social connections created by gang membership and fraternity/sorority membership. Would you accept the argument that they are equivalent social organizations for different social classes?

3. Reread the final lines of the excerpt from Freud's *Civilization and Its Discontents* (p. 80) as context for framing the following questions:

   • In your view, is the social phenomenon of gangs a sign that society has reached a point at which it cannot justly lay claim to the loyalties of its members?

   • Do you see society as having failed to meet the needs of such members?

   • Do gang members differ from individual adolescents who become alienated from society, like the students responsible for the Columbine or Virginia Tech school killings?

4. Gang-"infested" neighborhoods clearly threaten the people who live in them, and the common perception is that gangs threaten society as a whole as well.

   • What emotional effect does the term *infested* have?

   • Why do you think the gang phenomenon has received so much social attention? Is the criminal activity associated with gangs the primary source of social fear and disapproval?

   • Is the violence associated with gangs a threat to mainstream society, or can you argue that it is in some way useful?

   • Can we see the kind of violence we see in gang life as possible evidence of the death wish expressed on a broad social scale?

Into the Wild

JON KRAKAUER

In this nonfiction account of Emory University graduate Christopher McCandless, aka Alexander Supertramp, Krakauer traces Alex's wanderings throughout the southwest, Pacific northwest, and ultimately to Alaska. Seeking a life free of social controls and human bonds, Alex walked "into the wild" just outside of Denali National Park, with plans to live off the land. He was found dead from illness and starvation four months later. In this chapter, Krakauer profiles Ron Franz, an eighty-year-old loner who not only befriended Alex, but came to love him deeply—not a form of Eros that freedom-and-nature-loving Alex could tolerate. Franz relates his story, and Krakauer stays in the background, a subtle rhetorical plan to enhance the emotional impact of Franz's experience.

No man ever followed his genius till it misled him. Though the result were bodily weakness, yet perhaps no one can say that the consequences were to be regretted, for these were a life in conformity to higher principles. If the day and the night are such that you greet them with joy, and life emits a fragrance like flowers and sweet-scented herbs, is more elastic, more starry, more immortal,—that is your success. All nature is your congratulation, and you have cause momentarily to bless yourself. The greatest gains and values are farthest from being appreciated. We easily come to doubt if they exist. We soon forget them. They are the highest reality. . . . The true harvest of my daily life is somewhat as intangible and indescribable as the tints of morning or evening. It is a little star-dust caught, a segment of the rainbow which I have clutched.

—Henry David Thoreau, *Walden, or Life in the Woods*
(Passage highlighted in one of the books found with Chris McCandless's remains)

On **January 4, 1993,** this writer received an unusual letter, penned in a shaky, anachronistic script that suggested an elderly author. "To Whom It May Concern," the letter began.

> I would like to get a copy of the magazine that carried the story of the young man (Alex McCandless) dying in Alaska. I would like to write the one that investigated the incident. I drove him from Salton City Calif. . . . in March 1992. . . to Grand Junction Co. . . . I left Alex there to hitch-hike to S.D. He said he would keep in touch. The last I heard from him was a letter the first week in April, 1992. On our trip we took pictures, me with the camcorder + Alex with his camera.
>
> If you have a copy of that magazine please send me the cost of that magazine. . . .
>
> I understand he was hurt. If so I would like to know how he was injured, for he always carried enough rice in his backpack + he had arctic clothes + plenty of money.
>
> SINCERELY,
> RONALD A. FRANZ
>
> Please do not make these facts available to anybody till I know more about his death for he was not just the common wayfarer. Please believe me.

The magazine that Franz requested was the January 1993 issue of *Outside*, which featured a cover story about the death of Chris McCandless. His letter had been addressed to the offices of *Outside* in Chicago; because I had written the McCandless piece, it was forwarded to me.

McCandless made an indelible impression on a number of people during the course of his *hegira*, most of whom spent only a few days in his company, a week or two at most. Nobody, however, was affected more powerfully by his or her brief contact with the boy than Ronald Franz, who was eighty years old when their paths intersected in January 1992.

After McCandless bid farewell to Jan Burres at the Salton City Post Office, he hiked into the desert and set up camp in a brake of creosote at the edge of Anza-Borrego Desert State Park. Hard to the east is the Salton Sea, a placid ocean in miniature, its surface more than two hundred feet below sea level, created in 1905 by a monumental engineering snafu: Not long after a canal was dug from the Colorado River to irrigate rich farmland in the Imperial Valley, the river breached its banks during a series of major floods, carved a new channel, and began to gush unabated into the Imperial Valley Canal. For more than two years the canal inadvertently diverted virtually all of the river's prodigious flow into the Salton sink. Water surged across the once-dry floor of the sink, inundating farms and settlements, eventually drowning four hundred square miles of desert and giving birth to a landlocked ocean.

Only fifty miles from the limousines and exclusive tennis clubs and lush green fairways of Palm Springs, the west shore of the Salton Sea had once been the site of intense real estate speculation. Lavish resorts were planned, grand subdivisions platted. But little of the promised development ever came to pass. These days most of the lots remain vacant and are gradually being reclaimed by the desert. Tumbleweeds scuttle down Salton City's broad, desolate boulevards. Sun-bleached FOR SALE signs line the curbs, and paint peels from uninhabited buildings. A placard in the window of the Salton Sea Realty and Development Company declares CLOSED/CERRADO. Only the rattle of the wind interrupts the spectral quiet.

Away from the lakeshore the land rises gently and then abruptly to form the desiccated, phantasmal badlands of Anza-Borrego. The *bajada* beneath the badlands is open country cut by steep-walled arroyos. Here, on a low, sun-scorched rise dotted with chollas and indigobushes and twelve-foot ocotillo stems, McCandless slept on the sand under a tarp hung from a creosote branch.

When he needed provisions, he would hitch or walk the four miles into town, where he bought rice and filled his plastic water jug at the market–liquor store–post office, a beige stucco building that serves as the cultural nexus of greater Salton City. One Thursday in mid-January, McCandless was hitching back out to the *bajada* after filling his jug when an old man, name of Ron Franz, stopped to give him a ride.

"Where's your camp?" Franz inquired.

"Out past Oh-My-God Hot Springs," McCandless replied.

"I've lived in these parts six years now, and I've never heard of any place goes by that name. Show me how to get there."

They drove for a few minutes down the Borrego-Salton Seaway, and then McCandless told him to turn left into the desert, where a rough 4-x-4 track twisted down a narrow wash. After a mile or so they arrived at a bizarre encampment, where some two hundred people had gathered to spend the winter living out of their vehicles. The community was beyond the fringe, a vision of post-apocalypse America. There were families sheltered in cheap tent trailers, aging hippies in Day-Glo vans, Charles Manson look-alikes sleeping in rusted-out Studebakers that hadn't turned over since Eisenhower was in the White House. A substantial number of those present were walking around buck naked. At the center of the camp, water from a geothermal well had been piped into a pair of shallow, steaming pools lined with rocks and shaded by palm trees: Oh-My-God Hot Springs.

McCandless, however, wasn't living right at the springs; he was camped by himself another half mile out on the *bajada*. Franz drove Alex the rest of the way, chatted with him there for a while, and then returned to town, where he lived alone, rent free, in return for managing a ramshackle apartment building.

Franz, a devout Christian, had spent most of his adult life in the army, stationed in Shanghai and Okinawa. On New Year's Eve 1957, while he was overseas, his wife and only child were killed by a drunk driver in an automobile accident. Franz's son had been due to graduate from medical school the following June. Franz started hitting the whiskey, hard.

Six months later he managed to pull himself together and quit drinking, cold turkey, but he never really got over the loss. To salve his loneliness in the years after the accident, he started unofficially "adopting" indigent Okinawan boys and girls, eventually taking fourteen of them under his wing, paying for the oldest to attend medical school in Philadelphia and another to study medicine in Japan.

When Franz met McCandless, his long-dormant paternal impulses were   15
kindled anew. He couldn't get the young man out of his mind. The boy had said his name was Alex—he'd declined to give a surname—and that he came from West Virginia. He was polite, friendly, well-groomed.

"He seemed extremely intelligent," Franz states in an exotic brogue that sounds like a blend of Scottish, Pennsylvania Dutch, and Carolina drawl. "I thought he was too nice a kid to be living by that hot springs with those nudists and drunks and dope smokers." After attending church that Sunday, Franz decided to talk to Alex "about how he was living. Somebody needed to convince him to get an education and a job and make something of his life."

When he returned to McCandless's camp and launched into the self-improvement pitch, though, McCandless cut him off abruptly. "Look, Mr. Franz," he declared, "you don't need to worry about me. I have a college education. I'm not destitute. I'm living like this by choice." And then, despite his initial prickliness, the young man warmed to the old-timer, and the two engaged in a long conversation. Before the day was out, they had driven into Palm Springs in Franz's truck, had a meal at a nice restaurant, and taken a ride on the tramway to the top of San Jacinto Peak, at the bottom of which McCandless stopped to unearth a Mexican serape and some other possessions he'd buried for safekeeping a year earlier.

Over the next few weeks McCandless and Franz spent a lot of time together. The younger man would regularly hitch into Salton City to do his laundry and barbecue steaks at Franz's apartment. He confided that he was biding his time until spring, when he intended to go to Alaska and embark on an "ultimate adventure." He also turned the tables and started lecturing the grandfatherly figure about the shortcomings of his sedentary existence, urging the eighty-year-old to sell most of his belongings, move out of the apartment, and live on the road. Franz took these harangues in stride and in fact delighted in the boy's company.

An accomplished leatherworker, Franz taught Alex the secrets of his craft; for his first project McCandless produced a tooled leather belt, on which he created an artful pictorial record of his wanderings. *ALEX* is inscribed at the belt's left end; then the initials *C.J.M.* (for Christopher Johnson McCandless) frame a skull and crossbones. Across the strip of cowhide one sees a rendering of a two-lane blacktop, a NO U-TURN sign, a thunderstorm producing a flash flood that engulfs a car, a hitchhiker's thumb, an eagle, the Sierra Nevada, salmon cavorting in the Pacific Ocean, the Pacific Coast Highway from Oregon to Washington, the Rocky Mountains, Montana wheat fields, a South Dakota rattlesnake, Westerberg's house in Carthage, the Colorado River, a gale in the Gulf of California, a canoe beached beside a tent, Las Vegas, the initials *T.C.D.*, Morro Bay, Astoria, and at the buckle end, finally, the letter *N* (presumably representing north). Executed with remarkable skill and creativity, this belt is as astonishing as any artifact Chris McCandless left behind.

Franz grew increasingly fond of McCandless. "God, he was a smart kid,"   20
the old man rasps in a barely audible voice. He directs his gaze at a patch of sand between his feet as he makes this declaration; then he stops talking. Bending stiffly from the waist, he wipes some imaginary dirt from his pant leg. His ancient joints crack loudly in the awkward silence.

More than a minute passes before Franz speaks again; squinting at the sky, he begins to reminisce further about the time he spent in the youngster's company. Not infrequently during their visits, Franz recalls, McCandless's face would darken with anger and he'd fulminate about his parents or politicians or the endemic idiocy of mainstream American life. Worried about alienating the boy, Franz said little during such outbursts and let him rant.

One day in early February, McCandless announced that he was splitting for San Diego to earn more money for his Alaska trip.

"You don't need to go to San Diego," Franz protested. "I'll give you money if you need some."

"No. You don't get it. I'm *going* to San Diego. And I'm leaving on Monday."

"OK. I'll drive you there."   25

"Don't be ridiculous," McCandless scoffed.

"I need to go anyway," Franz lied, "to pick up some leather supplies."

McCandless relented. He struck his camp, stored most of his belongings in Franz's apartment—the boy didn't want to schlepp his sleeping bag or backpack around the city—and then rode with the old man across the mountains to the coast. It was raining when Franz dropped McCandless at the San Diego waterfront. "It was a very hard thing for me to do," Franz says. "I was sad to be leaving him."

On February 19, McCandless called Franz, collect, to wish him a happy eighty-first birthday; McCandless remembered the date because his own birthday had been seven days earlier: He had turned twenty-four on February 12. During this phone call he also confessed to Franz that he was having trouble finding work.

On February 28, he mailed a postcard to Jan Burres. "Hello!" it reads,   30

Have been living on streets of San Diego for the past week. First day I got here it rained like hell. The missions here suck and I'm getting preached to death. Not much happening in terms of jobs so I'm heading north tomorrow.

I've decided to head for Alaska no later than May 1st, but I've got to raise a little cash to outfit myself. May go back and work for a friend I have in South Dakota if he can use me. Don't know where I'm headed now but I'll write when I get there. Hope all's well with you.

TAKE CARE, ALEX

On March 5, McCandless sent another card to Burres and a card to Franz as well. The missive to Burres says,

Greetings from Seattle! I'm a hobo now! That's right, I'm riding the rails now. What fun, I wish I had jumped trains earlier. The rails have some drawbacks, however. First is that one becomes absolutely filthy. Second is that one must tangle with these crazy bulls. I was sitting in a hotshot in L.A. when a bull found me with his flashlight about 10 P.M. "Get outta there before I <u>KILL</u> ya!" screamed the bull. I got out and saw he had drawn his revolver. He interrogated me at gunpoint, then growled, "If I ever see you around this train again I'll kill ya! Hit the road!" What a lunatic! I got the last laugh when I caught the same train 5 minutes later and rode it all the way to Oakland. I'll be in touch,

ALEX

A week later Franz's phone rang. "It was the operator," he says, "asking if I would accept a collect call from someone named Alex. When I heard his voice, it was like sunshine after a month of rain."

"Will you come pick me up?" McCandless asked.

"Yes. Where in Seattle are you?"

"Ron," McCandless laughed, "I'm not in Seattle. I'm in California, just up the road from you, in Coachella." Unable to find work in the rainy Northwest, McCandless had hopped a series of freight trains back to the desert. In Colton, California, he was discovered by another bull and thrown in jail. Upon his release he had hitchhiked to Coachella, just southeast of Palm Springs, and called Franz. As soon as he hung up the phone, Franz rushed off to pick McCandless up.

"We went to a Sizzler, where I filled him up with steak and lobster," Franz recalls, "and then we drove back to Salton City."

McCandless said that he would be staying only a day, just long enough to wash his clothes and load his backpack. He'd heard from Wayne Westerberg that a job was waiting for him at the grain elevator in Carthage, and he was eager to get there. The date was March 11, a Wednesday. Franz offered to take McCandless to Grand Junction, Colorado, which was the farthest he could drive without missing an appointment in Salton City the following Monday. To Franz's surprise and great relief, McCandless accepted the offer without argument.

Before departing, Franz gave McCandless a machete, an arctic parka, a collapsible fishing pole, and some other gear for his Alaska undertaking. Thursday at daybreak they drove out of Salton City in Franz's truck. In Bullhead City they stopped to close out McCandless's bank account and to visit Charlie's trailer,

35

where McCandless had stashed some books and other belongings, including the journal-photo album from his canoe trip down the Colorado. McCandless then insisted on buying Franz lunch at the Golden Nugget Casino, across the river in Laughlin. Recognizing McCandless, a waitress at the Nugget gushed, "Alex! Alex! You're back!"

Franz had purchased a video camera before the trip, and he paused now and then along the way to record the sights. Although McCandless usually ducked away whenever Franz pointed the lens in his direction, some brief footage exists of him standing impatiently in the snow above Bryce Canyon. "OK, let's go," he protests to the camcorder after a few moments. "There's a lot more ahead, Ron." Wearing jeans and a wool sweater, McCandless looks tan, strong, healthy.

Franz reports that it was a pleasant, if hurried trip. "Sometimes we'd drive 40 for hours without saying a word," he recalls. "Even when he was sleeping, I was happy just knowing he was there." At one point Franz dared to make a special request of McCandless. "My mother was an only child," he explains. "So was my father. And I was their only child. Now that my own boy's dead, I'm the end of the line. When I'm gone, my family will be finished, gone forever. So I asked Alex if I could adopt him, if he would be my grandson."

McCandless, uncomfortable with the request, dodged the question: "We'll talk about it when I get back from Alaska, Ron."

On March 14, Franz left McCandless on the shoulder of Interstate 70 outside Grand Junction and returned to southern California. McCandless was thrilled to be on his way north, and he was relieved as well—relieved that he had again evaded the impending threat of human intimacy, of friendship, and all the messy emotional baggage that comes with it. He had fled the claustrophobic confines of his family. He'd successfully kept Jan Burres and Wayne Westerberg at arm's length, flitting out of their lives before anything was expected of him. And now he'd slipped painlessly out of Ron Franz's life as well.

Painlessly, that is, from McCandless's perspective—although not from the old man's. One can only speculate about why Franz became so attached to McCandless so quickly, but the affection he felt was genuine, intense, and unalloyed. Franz had been living a solitary existence for many years. He had no family and few friends. A disciplined, self-reliant man, he got along remarkably well despite his age and solitude. When McCandless came into his world, however, the boy undermined the old man's meticulously constructed defenses. Franz relished being with McCandless, but their burgeoning friendship also reminded him how lonely he'd been. The boy unmasked the gaping void in Franz's life even as he helped fill it. When McCandless departed as suddenly as he'd arrived, Franz found himself deeply and unexpectedly hurt.

In early April a long letter arrived in Franz's post-office box bearing a South Dakota postmark. "Hello Ron," it says,

Alex here. I have been working up here in Carthage South Dakota for nearly 45 two weeks now. I arrived up here three days after we parted in Grand Junction,

Colorado. I hope that you made it back to Salton City without too many problems. I enjoy working here and things are going well. The weather is not very bad and many days are surprisingly mild. Some of the farmers are even already going out into their fields. It must be getting rather hot down there in Southern California by now. I wonder if you ever got a chance to get out and see how many people showed up for the March 20 Rainbow gathering there at the hotsprings. It sounds like it might have been a lot of fun, but I don't think you really understand these kind of people very well.

I will not be here in South Dakota very much longer. My friend, Wayne, wants me to stay working at the grain elevator through May and then go combining with him the entire summer, but I have my soul set entirely on my Alaskan Odyssey and hope to be on my way no later than April 15. That means I will be leaving here before very long, so I need you to send any more mail I may have received to the return address listed below.

Ron, I really enjoy all the help you have given me and the times that we spent together. I hope that you will not be too depressed by our parting. It may be a very long time before we see each other again. But providing that I get through this Alaskan Deal in one piece you will be hearing from me again in the future. I'd like to repeat the advice I gave you before, in that I think you really should make a radical change in your lifestyle and begin to boldly do things which you may previously never have thought of doing, or been too hesitant to attempt. So many people live within unhappy circumstances and yet will not take the initiative to change their situation because they are conditioned to a life of security, conformity, and conservatism, all of which may appear to give one peace of mind, but in reality nothing is more damaging to the adventurous spirit within a man than a secure future. The very basic core of a man's living spirit is his passion for adventure. The joy of life comes from our encounters with new experiences, and hence there is no greater joy than to have an endlessly changing horizon, for each day to have a new and different sun. If you want to get more out of life, Ron, you must lose your inclination for monotonous security and adopt a helter-skelter style of life that will at first appear to you to be crazy. But once you become accustomed to such a life you will see its full meaning and its incredible beauty. And so, Ron, in short, get out of Salton City and hit the Road. I guarantee you will be very glad you did. But I fear that you will ignore my advice. You think that I am stubborn, but you are even more stubborn than me. You had a wonderful chance on your drive back to see one of the greatest sights on earth, the Grand Canyon, something every American should see at least once in his life. But for some reason incomprehensible to me you wanted nothing but to bolt for home as quickly as possible, right back to the same situation which you see day after day after day. I fear you will follow this same inclination in the future and thus fail to discover all the wonderful things that God has placed around us to discover. Don't settle down and sit in one place. Move around, be nomadic, make each day a new horizon. You are still going to live a long time, Ron, and it would be a shame if you did not take the opportunity to revolutionize your life and move into an entirely new realm of experience.

You are wrong if you think Joy emanates only or principally from human relationships. God has placed it all around us. It is in everything and anything we might experience. We just have to have the courage to turn against our habitual lifestyle and engage in unconventional living.

My point is that you do not need me or anyone else around to bring this new kind of light in your life. It is simply waiting out there for you to grasp it, and all you have to do is reach for it. The only person you are fighting is yourself and your stubbornness to engage in new circumstances.

Ron, I really hope that as soon as you can you will get out of Salton City, put a little camper on the back of your pickup, and start seeing some of the great work that God has done here in the American West. You will see things and meet people and there is much to learn from them. And you must do it economy style, no motels, do your own cooking, as a general rule spend as little as possible and you will enjoy it much more immensely. I hope that the next time I see you, you will be a new man with a vast array of new adventures and experiences behind you. Don't hesitate or allow yourself to make excuses. Just get out and do it. Just get out and do it. You will be very, very glad that you did.

Take Care Ron,
Alex

Please write back to:
Alex McCandless
Madison, SD 57042

Astoundingly, the eighty-one-year-old man took the brash twenty-four-year-old vagabond's advice to heart. Franz placed his furniture and most of his other possessions in a storage locker, bought a GMC Duravan, and outfitted it with bunks and camping gear. Then he moved out of his apartment and set up camp on the *bajada*.

Franz occupied McCandless's old campsite, just past the hot springs. He arranged some rocks to create a parking area for the van, transplanted prickly pears and indigobushes for "landscaping." And then he sat out in the desert, day after day after day, awaiting his young friend's return.

Ronald Franz (this is not his real name; at his request I have given him a pseudonym) looks remarkably sturdy for a man in his ninth decade who has survived two heart attacks. Nearly six feet tall, with thick arms and a barrel chest, he stands erect, his shoulders unbowed. His ears are large beyond the proportions of his other features, as are his gnarled, meaty hands. When I walk into his camp in the desert and introduce myself, he is wearing old jeans and an immaculate white T-shirt, a decorative tooled-leather belt of his own creation, white socks, scuffed black loafers. His age is betrayed only by the creases across his brow and a proud, deeply pitted nose, over which a purple filigree of veins unfolds like a finely wrought tattoo. A little more than a year after McCandless's death he regards the world through wary blue eyes.

To dispel Franz's suspicion, I hand him an assortment of photographs I'd taken on a trip to Alaska the previous summer, during which I'd retraced McCandless's terminal journey on the Stampede Trail. The first several images in the stack are landscapes—shots of the surrounding bush, the overgrown trail, distant mountains, the Sushana River. Franz studies them in silence, occasionally nodding when I explain what they depict; he seems grateful to see them.

When he comes to the pictures of the bus in which the boy died, however, 55 he stiffens abruptly. Several of these images show McCandless's belongings inside the derelict vehicle; as soon as Franz realizes what he's seeing, his eyes mist over, he thrusts the photos back at me without examining the rest, and the old man walks away to compose himself as I mumble a lame apology.

Franz no longer lives at McCandless's campsite. A flash flood washed the makeshift road away, so he moved twenty miles out, toward the Borrego badlands, where he camps beside an isolated stand of cottonwoods. Oh-My-God Hot Springs is gone now, too, bulldozed and plugged with concrete by order of the Imperial Valley Health Commission. County officials say they eliminated the springs out of concern that bathers might become gravely ill from virulent microbes thought to flourish in the thermal pools.

"That sure could of been true," says the clerk at the Salton City store, "but most people think they bulldozed 'em 'cause the springs was starting to attract too many hippies and drifters and scum like that. Good riddance, you ask me."

For more than eight months after he said good-bye to McCandless, Franz remained at his campsite, scanning the road for the approach of a young man with a large pack, waiting patiently for Alex to return. During the last week of 1992, the day after Christmas, he picked up two hitchhikers on his way back from a trip into Salton City to check his mail. "One fella was from Mississippi, I think; the other was a Native American," Franz remembers. "On the way out to the hot springs, I started telling them about my friend Alex, and the adventure he'd set out to have in Alaska."

Suddenly, the Indian youth interrupted: "Was his name Alex McCandless?" 60 "Yes, that's right. So you've met him, then—"

"I hate to tell you this, mister, but your friend is dead. Froze to death up on the tundra. Just read about it in *Outdoor* magazine."

In shock, Franz interrogated the hitchhiker at length. The details rang true; his story added up. Something had gone horribly wrong. McCandless would never be coming back.

"When Alex left for Alaska," Franz remembers, "I prayed. I asked God to keep his finger on the shoulder of that one; I told him that boy was special. But he let Alex die. So on December 26, when I learned what happened, I renounced the Lord. I withdrew my church membership and became an atheist. I decided I couldn't believe in a God who would let something that terrible happen to a boy like Alex.

"After I dropped off the hitchhikers," Franz continues, "I turned my van around, drove back to the store, and bought a bottle of whiskey. And then I went out into the desert and drank it. I wasn't used to drinking, so it made me sick. Hoped it'd kill me, but it didn't. Just made me real, real sick."

● Applying a Psychoanalytic Frame

1. Reread the opening passage from Thoreau's *Walden* (p. 143), which, we're told, Alex had highlighted in his copy of the book, and which was found with his body. Does the passage contextualize for you how Alex may have seen his approaching death?

2. Krakauer could have depicted Franz as a crank, or as emotionally needy or unbalanced, or as the wise, all-knowing father. Instead, he offers physical descriptions and leaves our impressions to be formed by his selection of Franz's own words. What do you see as his possible rhetorical purpose(s) in these choices? Are we able to see Franz according to our own values, or do you see Krakauer exercising rhetorical influence on his readers, shaping our perception of him?

3. Knowing Alex for a few short weeks, Franz nonetheless developed deep affection, even love, for him. When Alex calls after a brief absence, Franz says, "When I heard his voice, it was like sunshine after a month of rain." How can you account psychoanalytically for so sudden and so strong a bond? How many forms of Eros do you see enacted in their relationship? Are they initiated by Franz or does Alex participate? Does Franz go through a kind of rebirth?

4. "Astoundingly, the eighty-one-year-old man took the brash twenty-four-year-old vagabond's advice to heart." What in Alex's letter to Franz (p. 149) do you see as rhetorically powerful enough to move a man in his eighties to uproot his conventional life? Do you see Alex making use of the emotional context of their relationship to strengthen his argument's appeal? How, in other words, has Alex so effectively addressed his audience?

5. The final two paragraphs are in Franz's words. Why do you think Krakauer chooses to end the chapter with Franz's voice? In what ways is it intended to intensify the emotional impact of what he says? And what do you think Freud's diagnosis of Franz's emotional reaction to Alex might have been?

A Problem from Hell: America and the Age of Genocide

SAMANTHA POWER

From April through June, 1994, Rwandan Hutus, under the sway of a powerful political movement called Hutu Power, systematically murdered their Tutsi neighbors, family members, random strangers, children, and elderly, until Tutsi-led rebels brought the genocide to a halt. Aided by the government, Hutu Power leaders used the media to incite and continue the genocidal attacks. (Genocide is the systematic extermination of an ethnic, racial, or national group; the Hutu géno-cidaires, or genocidal killers, called for extermination of Tutsi "cockroaches.") The United Nations, aware of the mounting tensions in the country prior to the one hundred days of slaughter, had sent a small peacekeeping force to Rwanda. But when the genocide began and nine Belgian soldiers were murdered as they tried to protect a Tutsi political figure, the Belgians pulled out of their former colony, and Canadian General Roméo Dallaire was left in charge of the few remaining troops, with orders not to use force of any kind for any reason. Almost one million Rwandans, Tutsis and Hutu resisters, were killed by machetes, guns, and beatings. Houses were pillaged, families dragged out and killed. Thousands of women and young girls were raped. Churches were burned along with the people seeking sanctuary inside them. You may know the film Hotel Rwanda, *the true story of hotel manager Paul Rusesabagina, who saved 1200 people in one of the few instances of successful protection. Samantha Power's critique here takes up two perspectives: her analysis of the motives and rhetorical stances adopted by Western nations, especially the United States, in their failure to intervene, and her profile of General Dallaire, a witness to this failure. Almost destroyed by the experience, he has become an internationally acclaimed speaker on the Rwandan genocide and the causes for the Western nations' choice to be bystanders as the horrors played out.*

The Stories We Tell

It is not hard to conceive of how the United States might have done things differently. Ahead of the April killing, as violence escalated, it could have agreed to Belgian pleas for UN reinforcements. Once the killing of thousands of Rwandans a day had begun, the president could have deployed U.S. troops to Rwanda. The United States could have joined Dallaire's beleaguered UNAMIR forces, or, if it feared associating with shoddy UN peacekeeping, it could have intervened unilaterally with the Security Council's backing, as France did in June. The United States could also have acted without the UN's blessing, as it would do five years later in Kosovo. Securing congressional support for U.S. intervention would have been extremely difficult, but by the second week of the killing, Clinton, one of the most eloquent presidents of the twentieth century, could have made the case that something approximating genocide was under way, that an inviolable American value was imperiled by its occurrence, and that U.S. contingents at relatively low risk could stop the extermination of a people.

Even if the White House could not have overcome congressional opposition to sending U.S. troops to Africa, the United States still had a variety of options. Instead of leaving it to midlevel officials to communicate with the Rwandan leadership behind the scenes, senior officials in the administration could have taken control of the process. They could have publicly and frequently denounced the slaughter. They could have branded the crimes "genocide" at a far earlier stage. They could have called for the expulsion of the Rwandan delegation from the Security Council. On the telephone, at the UN, and over the Voice of America, they could have threatened to prosecute those complicit in the genocide, naming names when possible. They could have deployed Pentagon assets to jam—even temporarily—the crucial, deadly radio broadcasts.

Instead of demanding a UN withdrawal, quibbling over costs, and coming forward (belatedly) with a plan better suited to caring for refugees than to stopping massacres, U.S. officials could have worked to make UNAMIR a force to contend with. They could have urged their Belgian allies to stay and protect Rwandan civilians. If the Belgians insisted on withdrawing, the United States could have done everything within its power to make sure that Dallaire was immediately reinforced. Senior officials could have spent U.S. political capital rallying troops from other nations and could have supplied strategic airlift and logistic support to a coalition that it had helped to create. In short, the United States could have led the world.

It is striking that most officials involved in shaping U.S. policy were able to define the decision not to stop genocide as ethical and moral. The administration employed several devices to dampen enthusiasm for action and to preserve the public's sense—and more important, its own—that U.S. policy choices were not merely politically astute but also morally acceptable. First, administration officials exaggerated the extremity of the possible responses. Time and again U.S. leaders posed the choice as between staying out of Rwanda and "getting involved everywhere." In addition, they often presented the choice as one between doing nothing and sending in hundreds of thousands of marines.

Second, administration policymakers appealed to notions of the greater good. They did not simply frame U.S. policy as one contrived in order to advance the national interest or avoid U.S. casualties. Rather, they often argued against intervention from the standpoint of people committed to protecting human life. Owing to recent failures in UN peacekeeping, many humanitarian interventionists in the U.S. government were concerned about the future of America's relationship with the United Nations generally and peacekeeping specifically. They believed that the UN and humanitarianism could not afford another Somalia. Many internalized the belief that the UN had more to lose by sending reinforcements and failing than by allowing the killings to proceed. Their chief priority, after the evacuation of the Americans, was looking after UN peacekeepers, and they justified the withdrawal of the peacekeepers on the grounds that it would ensure a future for humanitarian intervention. In other words, Dallaire's peacekeeping mission in Rwanda had to be destroyed so that peacekeeping might be saved for use elsewhere.

A third feature of the response that helped to console U.S. officials at the time was the sheer flurry of Rwanda-related activity. U.S. officials with a special concern for Rwanda took their solace from minivictories, working on behalf of specific individuals such as Monique Mujawamariya or groups like the Rwandans gathered at the hotel and the stadium. "We were like the child in the ghetto who focuses all of her energy on protecting her doll," says one senior official. "As the world collapses around her, she can't bear it, but she takes solace in the doll, the only thing she can control." Government officials involved in policy met constantly and remained, in bureaucratic lingo, "seized of the matter"; they neither appeared nor felt indifferent. Although little in the way of effective intervention emerged from midlevel meetings in Washington or New York, an abundance of memoranda and other documents did.

Finally, the almost willful delusion that what was happening in Rwanda did not amount to genocide created a nurturing ethical framework for inaction. "War" was "tragic" but created no moral imperative.

One U.S. official kept a journal during the crisis. In late May, exasperated by the obstructionism pervading the bureaucracy, the official dashed off this lament:

> A military that wants to go nowhere to do anything—or let go of their toys so someone else can do it. A White House cowed by the brass (and we are to give lessons on how the armed forces take orders from civilians?). An NSC that does peacekeeping by the book—the accounting book, that is. And an assistance program that prefers whites (Europe) to blacks. When it comes to human rights we have no problem drawing the line in the sand of the dark continent (just don't ask us to do anything—agonizing is our specialty), but not China or any place else business looks good.
>
> We have a foreign policy based on our amoral economic interests run by amateurs who want to stand for something—hence the agony—but ultimately don't want to exercise any leadership that has a cost.
>
> They say there may be as many as a million massacred in Rwanda. The militias continue to slay the innocent and the educated. . . . Has it really cost the United States nothing?

Aftermath

Guilt

The genocide in Rwanda cost Romeo Dallaire a great deal. It is both paradoxical and natural that the man who probably did the most to save Rwandans feels the worst. By August 1994 Dallaire had a death wish. "At the end of my command, I drove around in my vehicle with no escort practically looking for ambushes," Dallaire recalls. "I was trying to get myself destroyed and looking to get released from the guilt."

Upon his return to Canada, he behaved initially as if he had just completed a routine mission. As the days passed, though, he began to show signs of distress. In late 1994 the UN Security Council established a war crimes tribunal for Rwanda modeled after one just set up to punish crimes committed in the former Yugoslavia. When the UN tribunal called Dallaire to take the stand in February 1998, four years after the genocide, he plunged back into his memories. Pierre Prosper, the UN prosecutor, remembers the scene: "He carried himself so proudly and so commanding. Just like a soldier. He saluted the president of the tribunal. All of his answers were 'Yes, sir,' 'No, sir.' He was very stoic. And then, as the questioning progressed, you could just see it unraveling. It was as though he was just reliving it right there in front of us." As Dallaire spoke, it became clear how omnipresent the genocide was in his life. On one occasion, as he described his operational capacity, he said, "I had a number of bodies on the ground"—but then paused and corrected himself: "Forgive me—a number of troops on the ground." His voice cracked as he struggled to find words to match his shock and disappointment: "It seems . . . inconceivable that one can watch . . . thousands of people being . . . massacred . . . every day in the media . . . and remain passive."

Dallaire seemed to be searching the courtroom for answers. He still could not understand how the major powers could have sent troops to the region with a genocide under way, extracted their civilian personnel and soldiers, and stranded the people of Rwanda and the UN peacekeepers. Dallaire stared straight ahead and said stiffly that the departure of those military units "with full knowledge of the danger confronting the emasculated UN force, is inexcusable by any human criteria."

The defense attorney at the tribunal interjected at this point: "It seems as though you regret that, Major General." Dallaire glanced up as if the trance had been broken, fixed his gaze on the interrogator, and responded, "You cannot even imagine."

At a news conference after his testimony, Dallaire said, "I found it very difficult to return to the details. . . . In fact, at one point yesterday, I had the sense of the smell of the slaughter in my nose and I don't know how it appeared, but there was all of a sudden this enormous rush to my brain and to my senses. . . . Maybe with time, it will hurt less." He hoped to visit Rwanda after testifying. "Until I can see many of those places, until I can see some of the graves, until I can see those hills and those mountains and those villages," he said. "I don't think I'll ever have closure." He hoped to bring his wife.

President Clinton visited Rwanda a month after Dallaire testified. With the grace of one grown practiced at public remorse, he issued something of an apology. "We in the United States and the world community did not do as much as we could have and should have done to try to limit what occurred," Clinton said. "It may seem strange to you here," he continued, "but all over the world there were people like me sitting in offices, day after day after day, who did not fully appreciate the depth and the speed with which you were being engulfed by this unimaginable terror." But Clinton's remorse came too late for the 800,000 Rwandans who died, and for Dallaire, who often feels sorry he lived.

Some of Dallaire's colleagues speculated that he was reacting emotionally to his experience in Rwanda because the Belgian press and the families of the deceased Belgian soldiers had vilified him. He claims to be reconciled to his decisions. "I've been criticized by the Belgians for sending their troops to a 'certain death' by directing them to protect Prime Minister Agathe," he notes. "I'll take that heat, but I could not take the heat of having hunkered down and not having tried to give Agathe the chance to call to the nation to avert violence. You couldn't let this thing go by and watch it happen."

His bigger problem is his guilt over the Rwandans. They entrusted their fate to the UN and were murdered: "I failed my mission," he says. "I simply cannot say these deaths are not mine when they happened on my mission. I cannot erase the thousands and thousands of eyes that I see, looking at me, bewildered. I argued, but I didn't convince, so I failed."

In an effort to help Canadians deal with the stress of their military experiences, Dallaire agreed to produce a thirty-minute video, "Witness the Evil." In the video he says it took two years for the experiences to hit him but that eventually he reached a point where he couldn't "keep it in the drawer" any longer:

> I became suicidal because . . . there was no other solution. I couldn't live with the pain and the sounds and the smell. Sometimes, I wish I'd lost a leg instead of having all those grey cells screwed up. You lose a leg, it's obvious and you've got therapy and all kinds of stuff. You lose your marbles, very, very difficult to explain, very difficult to gain that support that you need.

As the passage of time distanced Dallaire from Rwanda, the nights brought him closer to his inner agony. He carried a machete around and lectured cadets on post-traumatic stress disorder, he slept sparingly, and he found himself nearly retching in the supermarket, transported back to Rwandan markets and the bodies strewn within them. In October 1998 Canada's chief of defense staff, General Maurice Baril, asked Dallaire to take a month of stress-related leave. Dallaire was shattered. After hanging up the phone, he says, "I cried for days and days." He tried to keep up a brave public front, sending a parting e-mail to his subordinates that read: "It has been assessed essential that I recharge my batteries due to a number of factors, not the least being the impact of my operational experience on my health. . . . Don't withdraw, don't surrender, don't give up."

Dallaire returned from leave, but in December 1999 Baril called again. He had spoken with Dallaire's doctors and decided to force a change with an ultimatum: Either Dallaire had to abandon the "Rwanda business" and stop testifying at the tribunal and publicly faulting the international community for not doing more, or he would have to leave his beloved armed forces. For Dallaire, only one answer was possible: "I told them I would never give up Rwanda," he says. "I was the force commander and I would complete my duty, testifying and doing whatever it takes to bring these guys to justice." In April 2000 Dallaire was forced out of the Canadian armed services and given a medical discharge.

Dallaire had always said, "The day I take my uniform off will be the day that I will also respond to my soul." But since becoming a civilian he has realized that his soul is not readily retrievable. "My soul is in Rwanda," he says. "It has never, ever come back, and I'm not sure it ever will." He feels that the eyes and the spirits of those killed continue to watch him.

In June 2000 a brief Canadian news wire story reported that Dallaire   20
had been found unconscious on a park bench in Hull, Quebec, drunk and alone. He had consumed a bottle of scotch on top of his daily dose of pills for post-traumatic stress disorder. He was on another suicide mission. After recovering, Dallaire sent a letter to the Canadian Broadcast Corporation thanking them for their sensitive coverage of this episode. His letter was read on the air:

Thank you for the very kind thoughts and wishes.

There are times when the best medication and therapist simply can't help a soldier suffering from this new generation of peacekeeping injury. The anger, the rage, the hurt, and the cold loneliness that separates you from your family, friends, and society's normal daily routine are so powerful that the option of destroying yourself is both real and attractive. That is what happened last Monday night. It appears, it grows, it invades, and it overpowers you.

In my current state of therapy, which continues to show very positive results, control mechanisms have not yet matured to always be on top of this battle. My doctors and I are still [working to] establish the level of serenity and productivity that I yearn so much for. The therapists agree that the battle I waged that night was a solid example of the human trying to come out from behind the military leader's ethos of "My mission first, my personnel, then myself." Obviously the venue I used last Monday night left a lot to be desired and will be the subject of a lot of work over the next while.

Dallaire remained a true believer in Canada, in peacekeeping, in human rights. The letter went on:

This nation, without any hesitation nor doubt, is capable and even expected by the less fortunate of this globe to lead the developed countries beyond self-interest, strategic advantages, and isolationism, and raise their sights to the realm of the pre-eminence of humanism and freedom. . . . Where humanitarianism is being destroyed and the innocent are being literally trampled into the ground . . . the soldiers, sailors, and airpersons . . . supported by fellow countrymen who recognize the cost in human sacrifice and in resources will forge in concert with our politicians . . . a most unique and exemplary place for Canada in the league of nations, united under the United Nations Charter.

I hope this is okay.

Thanks for the opportunity.

Warmest regards,

Dallaire

● Applying a Psychoanalytic Frame

1. What do you take Power's dominant tone in the first section to be? What stylistic choices do you see her make to create it?

2. Power argues that the U.S. motives for not intervening to prevent or later to stop the genocide were carefully shaped rhetorically. She identifies four "devices" the U.S. administration employed to "dampen enthusiasm for action." Identify these rhetorical devices. Then look at the statement former President Clinton made when he visited Rwanda after the genocide: "It may seem strange to you here, but all over the world there were people like me sitting in offices, day after day

after day, who did not fully appreciate the depth and the speed with which you were being engulfed by this unimaginable terror." What logical results can you draw from a rhetorical and psychoanalytic analysis of these two data sets?

- Does Power lead us to see the administration's policies as consistent with Clinton's explanation?
- In what way(s) did U.S. policy makers frame false choices, as Power suggests?
- How might you explain the desire to remain uninvolved, from a psychoanalytic perspective? Is there room in the frame for the idea of what Power calls a "moral imperative"?

3. Like Krakauer, Power ends her chapter with her subject's words. Consider General Dallaire's ethos as a speaker: why might Power have decided he'd be more persuasive than she could be in evoking for readers the guilt of the bystander, the one who sees evil but does nothing to stop it?

4. We talk of nervous "breakdowns," the "disintegration" of the self, or "losing one's grip" on reality; here, the author describes Dallaire as "shattered." How did Dallaire's experience in Rwanda lead to this sense of a broken self whose tie to reality "snapped"?

- What social roles do you see him relying on for a sense of a unified, stable self? How did they function to provide this illusion?
- What relation between this self and the social world did he depend on? For him to be General Dallaire, in other words, what did the world have to be like?
- How did the genocide destroy his sense of the self–world relation?

5. Genocide seems an illogical act, given the theory of Eros, which states that we are motivated to organize ourselves into ever-greater communities, placing the good of the whole over the desires of the individual. Think through this apparent logical contradiction: how could Eros, the life force, allow the majority to participate in or ignore the destruction of a unified community of millions? Logically, how do you think the majority would have to frame the targeted group? What historical evidence can you think of to support your view? To what extent does this reasoning apply to the U.S. decision not to intervene in Rwanda?

topics for writing

1. Many religions, including Christianity, consider suicide a sinful act of despair, a rejection of God's grace and power, and as damning as rejection of belief itself. From a psychoanalytic perspective, explain why Nancy Mairs's attempted suicide is a violation equal to Ron Franz's repudiation of God when he learns that Alex is dead. Using the details of the two cases, consider the following:

- How would Freud explain the psychological purposes of religious community?
- Do you see religious belief as inconsistent with acceptance of the theory of the death instinct?

- Mairs is a Catholic; how might Freud see her act in relation to her faith? Does her attempt help support Freud's theories?

- How might a Christian explain her recovery? How might Freud counter or reinterpret any reading of it that suggests a divine intervention or plan?

2. In all of this chapter's readings, we learn of immense pain of an order that threatens the individual will to survive or a shared sense of humanity. Amazingly, most of the individuals we read about did find a way to cope and continue. Consider several of these cases using Freud's analysis of coping mechanisms, as he outlines these in Chapter II of *Civilization and Its Discontents*. Where do you see these individuals turn to some form of intoxication, sublimation, and/or illusion to help them bear what Freud says is the inevitable pain of life? Do you see certain of these "palliative measures," or coping mechanisms, as being more effective or more socially useful than others? Draw on the experiences and choices of the figures in the chapter readings to build your argument, synthesizing the data to give credibility to your thesis. What rhetorical role will quotation play, especially quotation of the voices of these individuals?

3. Each of the essays could produce anxiety in a reader, and yet most are by authors who have found a fairly broad audience. Work out a psychoanalytic theory of reading from these essays.

- Why might we welcome what makes us anxious? Why might we be motivated to read the essays?

- What desires are satisfied by reading the authors' treatment of threatening topics?

- Do you find that the conclusions of all the essays reassure us in some way?

- What rhetorical choices are important in making the topics appealing, despite their content?

4. Both Nancy Mairs and Roméo Dallaire have chosen to revisit in public forums their near-destruction, by writing books, giving lectures, and, in Dallaire's case, being featured in a documentary (*Shake Hands with the Devil*). Consider whether their public recountings of their experiences might be considered a type of Freud's "talking cure": do you see ways in which it might be therapeutic, for them and for their audiences? How might reliving the traumatic events put them in touch with a sense of shared humanity? Consider the following:

- What will readers need to understand this topic? Think about specialized terms (the "talking cure," for instance); key ideas ("trauma"); genre expectations (what role does the genre of a public lecture put them in, for example?).

- Think of which psychoanalytic frames might help you develop ideas on the topic: Eros, certainly, but consider how the concepts of guilt, sublimation, ego, superego, id, anxiety, neurosis, death instinct, or other key concepts might help you generate ideas.

- How will you incorporate their voices as evidence?

Framing and Composing
from a Psychoanalytic Perspective

The following writing projects draw on the critical and rhetorical frames covered in Parts One and Two, but their topics ask you to use contemporary social issues as your "texts," or focus of study. Some ask you to look at print texts and to explain their use in the larger culture; some require further library-based and/or field-based (observational) research. All require you to consider the rhetorical options you have as a writer who seeks to influence readers. They also invite response in conventional essay form. But you can choose to vary the form by changing the genre (i.e., report, personal essay, profile); by adding visual elements (i.e., graphs, images); or by choosing a mode of presentation (i.e., oral report, PowerPoint presentation).

1. Many schools today require extra- or cocurricular social involvement, in the form of volunteer service or community service–based courses. If you've participated in such activities, reflect on the experience using the psychoanalytic frame.

   - Was it an engagement in Eros?
   - Did it disrupt your sense of an established social self in any way?
   - How has the experience affected your sense of your relationship to/place in the social world?
   - What view do you want your reader to adopt? What kind of evidence can you bring in that will influence the reader?
   - What genres can you draw on as you think of how to shape your ideas?

2. Read Maurice Sendak's *Where the Wild Things Are*, a children's story about Max, a boy who is sent to his room after acting like a "wild thing." Analyze the text from a Freudian perspective.

   - How is it a text of desire, aggression, and ultimately repression of the id?
   - What social realities does it teach?
   - How is Max "civilized"?
   - Is this a book that, if you are or plan to become a parent, you'd give to your children?
   - What do your readers need in order to follow your argument? They may not know or may have forgotten the book, they may need visual cues or actual illustrations, since the visual elements of the story are integral to its meaning; and they may need a summary of the psychoanalytic concepts of aggression and sublimation (or whichever concepts you find useful as means of invention for this topic).

3. Electronic communication—e-mail, blogs, and so on—is a major form of social connection, though the definition of "social" in this context is very complex. Examine a particular aspect of the Internet—visit personal Web pages, chat rooms, and so on, and then consider the attractions of virtual social exchange from a psychoanalytic perspective.

   • How do you think one's sense of identity is affected?

   • What about the nature of electronic communication encourages a sense of community, and what about it might tend to diminish connection?

   • What forms/genres might you imagine using for this argument, given that you're looking at different electronic genres/media?

4. Observe a social interaction in a particular community, such as a study group, a workplace, a club, or some other community you have access to, over the course of several meetings. Focus on two or three individuals in the group.

   • How do they interact with the others?

   • What role(s) do they play?

   • How is a sense of community established, and where and how do you see it get reinforced?

   • How do the "rules" of the group define and control the individuals you are observing?

   • Does the group dynamic operate as Freud would predict, to provide some indirect satisfactions at the cost of some self-repression?

   • What, finally, are the social purposes of the group, psychoanalytically?

5. Apply the psychoanalytic frame to a particular event or phenomenon that you think might be better understood through its use. Gather information on the event or phenomenon, engage in your own psychoanalytic rereading, and present your findings in written form. Add your own suggestions to the following list of possible topics. Decide on the audience you wish to appeal to, the forms of appeal that might be most effective, and the types of evidence that will let you realize that rhetorical effect.

   • a current film rated "R" for violent content or a popular computer game that features violent themes

   • denial of or indifference to global warming

   • a current sports or celebrity entertainer's appeal

6. Many classic texts assigned as adolescent reading treat conflicts of maturity in which a young person must confront choices in the "real," adult world. Some idealize the conflicts, promoting a view of perfectible human nature; some present the more Freudian view of a harsh human reality. Reread a text of this sort that you've previously studied and analyze it from a psychoanalytic perspective.

- Does it encourage the young reader to accept the demands of the reality principle? What incentives (or punishments) does it offer to encourage compliance?

- Does it promise a "happy ending" in which such conflicts are erased?

- Some common texts in this genre are Jack Schaefer's *Shane*, Charles Dickens's *Great Expectations*, *The Diary of Anne Frank*, John Steinbeck's *Of Mice and Men*, S. Hinton's *Rumblefish*, John Knowles's *A Separate Peace*, Lorraine Hansberry's *A Raisin in the Sun*, and Harper Lee's *To Kill a Mockingbird*. Add to the list of possibilities, and consider which seem particularly open to the psychoanalytic frame.

part three

The Materialist Critique

Introduction: Linking Language, Ideology, and the Real World

Of all the species flourishing on our planet, most of which have elaborate communicative systems, some of which are even organized into what we might call family units, humankind is the only group able to tell stories about itself, to write its own histories. As far as we generally know, no other species can even *think* about history. While most animals use sounds or behaviors to warn one another of danger, or to attract a mate, or to identify food sources, or perhaps even to communicate, only *Homo sapiens* is defined by a complex verbal language. What we *know* about ourselves, whether anthropological discoveries of early hominids or accounts of the Boston Tea Party, has been recorded and transmitted by language, through oral and written traditions. We tell stories *about* ourselves: who we are; how we came to be what we are; who we *ought* to be and why. In the relatively recent past, we've developed photographic, film, video, and now digital reproduction, but what any particular sight or scene *means* to us is still a function of language.

As a student in a college writing class, you may be concerned about your language use in terms of understanding grammar, improving your vocabulary, or learning to organize your points in a logical way. These are all important elements of academic writing, but we're suggesting here a different kind of thinking about language. We're asking you to consider the relationship between language and the real world, or material reality. A materialist critique begins at this intersection of language, stories, and events. The language we use shapes the stories we tell. That process is *ideological:* by using language, we are automatically applying a particular lens that tells us how to see events, how to understand and judge them. Our view of our lives and the world at large is thus *mediated* by language. How we see, act in, and are affected by the "real" world is determined by the language we use as we think, speak, and write. A materialist critique helps reveal the stories—the ideologies—we use, typically without being aware we're doing so, to shape and so understand our world.

All human social organization is mediated by language, which is to say that the ways we form our societies, our families, ourselves—the values, or principles or laws we accept as our own—are transmitted by and through language. Underlying social values that determine conduct, family codes that condition attitudes, or laws that directly control individuals—all these social understandings rely on language in order to be "passed along" to others (sometimes, it's called "passed down," as in from top to bottom, wise to naïve, teacher to student). The mere fact that any one of us can conceive of something called a *social understanding* implies that the concept has been circulated through culture by language.

You've no doubt completed several history courses by this point in your academic career. You may "know" the history of this country's colonial period, or the events of World War II. But what you know about these events has been shaped by a range of social material conditions—by where you went to school, by family memories and values, by various media, and by many other social factors. The way we organize data in our minds is conditioned by the kinds of stories we've already learned. These stories provide the value systems we use to interpret the world around us—our ideologies. We're not talking here about *idealism*, a term you're probably more familiar with. Idealism means to elevate an idea into a universal law, to believe that ideals govern motivation and behavior. *Ideology*, however, is a different conception entirely. You can think of ideology as the DOS (disc operating system) of consciousness, a necessary component of all intellectual activity because it provides a *context* for how we think about most everything that affects our lives, even how we think about language itself.

Ideologies aren't things that exist separate from the self. When you decide to act a certain way, adopt a particular attitude toward others, or tell someone else what he or she ought to do, you're also, in effect, making a claim that your advice or opinion makes sense in, for lack of a better word, the "real" world. In this context, ideology isn't simply one's looking into or thinking seriously about certain ideas; rather, and this is an important distinction, ideology is a "lived" experience—we're all ideological insofar as we have attitudes or beliefs or ideas. Kenneth Burke's passage about the "unending conversation" at the start of this book includes the line, "It is from this 'unending conversation' that the materials of your drama arise." Burke uses "drama" to mean *motivated action*, and he thinks of language as *symbolic action* (always motivated). We use words instead of pushing, whistling, or pointing: "Move the car, please. . . . Here's the answer. . . . Do what's right." In other words, language, ideology, and real life interconnect.

Consider what happens every time you enter a writing class. Questions of what specific readings are assigned, where the instructor places grading emphasis, even the style or *mode* of writing encouraged in any individual course—these basic assumptions about what you ought to do or be as a writer in a college classroom—are *ideologically informed*. School districts have policies that must be adhered to; individual teachers operate from ideas about teaching methods that make sense to them; you, as the writer, come to the classroom equipped with your previous experiences in writing classes, experiences which have done much to condition or form your attitude about the subject before you ever take your seat. Remember what Burke said (we've added italics):

> Imagine that you enter a parlor. You come late. When you arrive, others have long preceded you, and they are engaged in a heated discussion [that] had begun long before any of them got there. . . . You listen for a while, until you decide that you have caught the tenor of the argument; then you put in your oar. Someone answers; you answer him; another comes to your defense; another aligns himself against you. . . . It is from this "unending conversation" that the materials of your drama arise. Nor is verbal action all there is to it. For all these words are grounded in . . . "contexts of situation." *And very important among these "contexts of situation" are . . . the material interests (of private or class structure) that you symbolically defend or symbolically align yourself with in the course of your own assertions. These interests do not "cause" your discussion: its "cause" is in the genius of man himself. . . . But they greatly affect the* idiom *in which you speak, and so the* idiom *by which you think.*

Call them ideas, beliefs, or principles, but our lives filled with layers of such *idioms* or learned concepts, mostly transmitted by language. Your attitudes about race, religion, sexuality, or alcohol, drugs, and music, for example, are most likely either aligned with, tolerant of, resistant to, or carefully hidden from your parents—in other words, we all think *in relation to* the ways of thinking we've been exposed to, those which we grew up with—the ideologies of those who taught us language in the first place, or the ideologies they chose (actively or unconsciously) to teach.

Can we talk meaningfully about *education* as a concept without trying to understand who's teaching what to whom, and why? Is a teacher (or school, or school district, or school board, or state legislature, or federal law) dedicated to teaching evolution or creationism? To whom? Kindergarten toddlers or college sophomores? And who actually attends which schools? You know all schools are not equally endowed with teacher salaries, equipment, technology, or even a good paint job. To what degree do social stratifications, ethnicities, religions, political orientations, or genders determine school populations? Why did you study one set of facts, one explanation for why things are the way they are versus any others? Even if you were fortunate enough to have access to a plurality of opinions or lifestyles or belief-systems (in short, ideologies) directly through teaching content or styles, even those choices necessarily have excluded a great many other possibilities—possibilities you're *not* going to learn. Clearly, it does matter what lessons are being taught, who gets to learn these lessons or who decides what's teachable and important. These are ideological decisions that are not arrived at out of thin air—there are reasons that dictate and determine choice. And those reasons themselves are based on value judgments: Why think this way? Why believe this or that? Why base your decisions on this particular idea of love, or law, or life?

These are the very questions that we all grapple with as we try to define our lives, our purposes, our beliefs, as we try to make our way through a seemingly endless series of daily choices: who to like or dislike and, more important, why. How do you treat other people, and on what basis do you make distinctions among them: race? gender? nationality? sexual identity? athletic ability? physical appearance? material possessions? Every one of us has stances or positions or beliefs about these and infinitely more potentially distinguishing or defining characteristics. *What* stance, or *which* position, or *whose* belief we adopt—these very real elements of who we think we are and how we act—are described by language, by the stories we tell each other about ourselves, by the *ideologies* we live (even when the way we live is different from how we tell ourselves we're living).

Sometimes the term *narrative* is used as a synonym for ideology, as in the claim that the narrative of the United States in the nineteenth century was "progress"—that the country was growing, describing expansion as a "natural" process. Boundaries being stretched, great chunks of land incorporated into the Union, several wars fought, whole indigenous populations routed or decimated—all this could be explained from the narrative of progress. The whole concept of *Manifest Destiny* rested on a "natural" and "predestined" process by which the country would more than double in size. Most of the arguments supporting national expansion described a "wilderness" and the "savages" who lived there, both of which needed to be civilized. In this context, if someone were to raise questions about the government treatment of natives, or the place the railroad was being built, or who was qualified to be governor of the new territory, the answers might well just come back to the same premise: Progress. Progress pushed out the natives, but what else could be done? It was the "nature" of things. Progress meant the railroad had to go through one town while completely bypassing another: the law of supply and demand at work. Progress depended upon electing "so and so" to "such and such" an office because he (not she) was committed to growth, or owned a bank. No matter what particular detail one wants to pick, the answer can always be justified by a familiar narrative—the story of a steadily growing, inherently good, and inevitable progress.

Take a look at the introduction to a history book (pp. 169 and 170) written by Professor Allen Fowler for young children, published in 1898. It would be easy to poke fun at Professor Fowler's "history," but that is not our intention here. We're interested in how you can see his descriptions of "true and factual events" as accurate reflections of the ideological premises of American secondary education in his time.

Some definitions of ideology stress that it's a form of "false consciousness," of being mistaken. For example, you might fervently support a certain

Introduction.

NE cannot fail to notice that within the last few years a taste for the study of American History has been rapidly growing. A pleasing feature of this tendency is, that it has reached the home as well as the school.

As a usual thing, history is dry, so a book for young people ought, before all things else, be interesting. A fact pleasantly told remains fixed in the memory, while that which is learned listlessly is lost easily. There is a fundamental difference between simplicity of thought and simplicity of expression. This book is designed to meet this difference; it tells the Stories of American History as our father told them to us many years ago, in a simple and natural manner. The language makes it especially suitable for young people and even for children, while, on the other hand, it is also equally interesting to grown people.

It aims to teach the history of the country by bringing out the most illustrious actors and events in it. Young people are always interested in persons and things. Biography and story for them is the natural door into history. The order of dates is usually above their reach, but the course of events and the personal achievements of an individual are delightful. So in teaching by means of biography and story, we are teaching the very alphabet of history.

It gives interesting glimpses of life in early times by means of personal anecdote. The customs of foreign courts, the wigwams of the Indians, the struggles of pioneer life, the desolations of the early wars with the savages, the spinning industry, the cotton and tobacco raising, the Tea Party, the cause of negro slavery, etc., are suggested in unforgettable stories of real people.

In United States History there are also materials for moral instruction. The perseverance of Columbus, of De Soto and of

9

10   *INTRODUCTION.*

Field, the fortitude of John Smith, of William Penn and of Stonewall Jackson, cannot but excite the courage of those who read the stories of their lives. No one can follow the story of Franklin's pursuit after knowledge without a quickening of his own aspirations. What life could teach kindness, truth-telling, manly honor and public spirit better than the life of Washington? And where will a poor lad struggling with poverty find more encouragement in diligent study and simplicity of character than in the life of Lincoln? It would be a pity for a country with such examples in her history not to use them for the moral training of the young. The faults as well as the virtues of the persons whose lives are told here will afford both mother and teacher opportunities to encourage all that is best and noblest in the children.

Parents and teachers can here often select material for reading or recreation. Nothing can better aid in fixing a fact in the memory of a boy or girl than a stirring ballad or poem, pictured before him with all the charms of imagination. Take, for example, the story of Paul Revere and follow it up with a recitation of "Paul Revere's Ride;" or take, for example, the thought that prompted Francis Key to write "The Star Spangled Banner" and follow it up with the song; or take, for example, those immortal words of Charles Pinckney inspired by patriotism when he said, "Millions for defense, but not one cent for tribute."

Great care has been taken to secure accuracy in all the delineations of men and things, so that they may not convey false instruction.

So, dear people, I suggest, nay, I urge, that you place before the children books which will teach, by great examples, the way to honor, success and happiness. Hoping that this volume will, at least in a small measure, be instrumental in bringing good results, I am,   Most sincerely,

Allen E. Fowler.

government, the "false consciousness" argument would conclude, either because you actually believe (you've been taught) this government will protect you or your possessions, or, even though you know it's a lie, you *pretend* to believe in its policies because doing so provides some sense of security, provides a reason why you're prospering. An example of the first sort might be a country's dehumanizing of the enemy during times of war—the culture really *is* supposed to believe that the enemy is subhuman in some fundamental way, according to "our" definition of human values. This "our" could be any particular group, or country, or religion—the United States is not the only place where people think this way. Once the enemy is labeled as weak or corrupt, their systematic extermination or mistreatment is less likely to cause public outcry or foster war resistance movements. An example of the second kind of "false consciousness" (*pretending* to believe) might be our relation to politicians in general. They appear on television to say they have no interests that might conflict with the interests of their constituents. Their constituents know this isn't always true. The politician knows the constituents know. But everyone goes about the business of voting and acting as though politicians are somehow *above* their own self-interest. These are just two examples of what people mean when they talk about ideology—belief systems that determine our thinking about the world, our place in it, our relation to others.

All this is not to say that ideology ought to be looked at as good or bad in some blanket judgment like "I'm so glad I finally got rid of that horrible ideology." The point is that we all have ideologies, all the time, and those ideologies help shape the way we think about ourselves and the world around us, about our place in the world in relation to others. Typically, we can identify the ideologies of others much more easily than we can lay out the specifics of our own. Or, as some like to say, "*they* have ideological motives," seeming to imply that the speaker is above such a condition, that to have motives is to somehow be tainted, less reasonable, less valid. Language theorist V. N. Voloshinov writes: "An experience of which an individual is conscious is already ideological and, therefore, from a scientific point of view, can in no way be a primary and irreducible datum; rather, it is an entity that has already undergone ideological processing of some specific kind." Let's separate these ideas so they're a little easier to grasp.

If you're aware of yourself (a self separate from anyone else's), Voloshinov seems to be saying, then you've already become conscious of your relationships to those things that aren't you: your parents, a neighbor, anyone else. None of these are you and you're quite aware of that. But you have *relationships* with each of them. As a small child, you desire warmth and protection from parents, but might also be afraid of, or feel uncomfortable around, a certain neighbor. People either induce some reaction from you, or you don't notice their existence, or you don't care to notice. But in any of these cases, you're not viewing these "others" from any *neutral* perspective—it's *you* doing the viewing. In fact, Voloshinov suggests, the only way you know about them at all is due to your having a "position" about them; what you think *about* them comes from your relation *to* them. To put all this perhaps even more simply: Voloshinov is saying that once we are aware that we are thinking (being self-reflective), we've already undergone what he calls "ideological processing," because we know the "I" who is thinking has motives not necessarily identical at every moment with anyone else's. We recognize that, in order to meet our needs, however we define them, we must be able to use language to make our needs known; we must persuade people to pay attention to us, to understand us. We think in language, and language is a social activity, communicating attitudes, values, prejudices, biases—in short, already ideological when we learn it.

So, our experience of the material world can't be separated from language and ideology. "Materialism," as we're using it, is a method of thought that emphasizes the "material" effects of cultural values (as opposed to the more familiar term *materialistic*, meaning overly occupied with gaining wealth at the expense of most other goals). At the end of the story, say materialists, we'd like to know who ends up with the most toys, who is making the crucial decisions that affect everyone else, who runs the enterprise, who profits most from "the way things are." A materialist critique seeks to explain how philosophic opinions, political beliefs, or any ideology can be traced to specific social relationships of money, status, and power.

As is true of most "isms," there are probably as many interpretations of materialism as there are people to make them. We can identify some common, basic principles, however. No examination of how materialism can provide an economic explanation of ideology will get very far without taking into consideration the concepts of Karl Marx. In our post–cold war world, after the disintegration of the Eastern bloc, to mention Marx or Marxism may seem to be an antiquated idea. After all, isn't Marx the one who said communism could solve the problems inherent in social systems where small numbers of people essentially controlled the fortunes or possibilities of the many? And hasn't recent history shown us that every state which claims to be Marxist in principle has lapsed into totalitarian, authoritarian, freedom-limiting dictatorships of some kind? Don't we think of Marxism as being fundamentally antidemocratic? The answer, of course, is "yes" to these questions—these *are* the prevalent attitudes about Marx and Marxism, the common popular story or cultural narrative. But we can also construct the story, or history, of Marxist theory from the texts Marx and his close colleague Engels wrote, the concepts they articulated as a result of examining their material environment.

Karl Marx (1818–1883) was a social scientist—he studied how human societies were organized. Working with Friedrich Engels (1820–1895), Marx devoted much of his life to developing his theories of social organization. Both Marx and Engels were born in Germany, but they worked together in France, Belgium, and England. We'll concentrate here on the social theories associated with their work.

Marx and Engel's social theories can be said to consist of two major facets: a historical and theoretical analysis of the inequality of social classes, and a blueprint for solving those problems. We'll use the questions we asked above to begin working with these concepts.

- **Isn't Marx the one who said communism could solve the problems inherent in social systems where small numbers of people essentially controlled the fortunes or possibilities of the many?**

Marx and Engels published the *Manifesto of the Communist Party* in 1848, a year during which numerous attempts at social revolution or uprisings in Europe occurred. Coming on a swelling tide of industrialization in those countries wealthy enough to support such ventures, *The Communist Manifesto* (as it is commonly referred to) was written to appeal to laborers, who in those days were called the *proletariat*. "Proletarian conscience," for example, was meant to describe the generally shared ideologies of those who work for others, those who "sell" their labor. The basic assumption in this classification is that "owners" would undoubtedly have very different ideas about what might constitute good working conditions or fair wages than would workers who suffer the conditions or earn the wages.

- **Don't we think of Marxism as being fundamentally antidemocratic?**

Certainly, in the parlance of popular culture, Marxism is identified with dictatorships. The bestialities of Stalin's purges or Mao's Cultural Revolution are the most obvious cases. We know quite well from reference to so-called "Marxist" states such as North Korea that personal freedoms are all but nonexistent. But look at what Marx himself had to say about democracy in 1843:

> In all states distinct from democracy the *state*, the *law*, the *constitution* is what dominates without actually governing, i.e. materially permeating the content of the remaining non-political spheres. In democracy the constitution, the law, the state is itself . . . a self-determination of the people. . . . Furthermore, it is self-evident that all forms of state have democracy as their truth and for that reason are untrue to the extent that they are not democracy.

Marx always argued for "self-determination of the people" as a guiding principle of democracy. In the passage above, Marx points out that almost all forms of government promise some kind of democratic foundation for their citizens—it's the "truth" they claim to uphold. His objection is that most governments *do not* operate democratically, but instead privilege a powerful few at the expense of the many. Ideally, Marx might say, democracy is the appropriate goal of human social interaction, but realistically, this has never been the case.

Marx ties the social to the economic. We come into our various worlds without any innate concept of money or of social organization. But early in life, most of us become aware that money, particularly the possession of it, is the glue that cements what we know to be our social structure. Who we are in relation to other people, whether the potholes in our streets are ever filled, whether we have access to reliable health care, what kinds of clothes we wear—all these, in one way or another, are related to how much capital we have access to, own, or control. We're all probably going to have to work so that we can earn money, pay our bills, and survive in our society. The materialist critique offers us one system for examining how our society came to be structured as it is, for making sense of the relationships between people and the "capitals" they use to satisfy their needs, however needs have been defined, whoever has defined them.

Think for a moment about the extent to which each of us is entangled and entrenched in economic webs, often without much systematic thought about the parts we play, often without questioning our power to alter those roles. Focus in particular on what is frequently called "growing up" or "becoming responsible." Clearly, one of the basic premises of such statements hinges on acting/becoming/learning to be financially responsible. After all, you're probably not attending school under the impression that you'll retire immediately upon graduation; you're most likely seeking higher education essentially to be employable sometime in the future. For most of us, work *is* how we accumulate the money necessary to support ourselves and our families.

Virtually every element of our existence, from birth to burial, relies on the exchange of money, of capital. If you think about money (cash, check, or credit), you know it has relatively little "use value." That is, you can't live by eating it; you can't really build your shelter out of it; you can't wear it. In other words, money *in itself* is virtually worthless. But as an *exchange medium*, it's what we all work for. We can trade these symbolic tokens for things we can use, services we need, even for time. In order to have these symbolic exchange tokens, however, most of us have to sell our labor somewhere, somehow— unless, of course, we already have a large supply of the symbolic exchange tokens, in which case they can "grow" with interest.

Odds are good that most readers of this text are doing so in the relative comfort of a postindustrial society. No doubt you've heard of times when sons followed in their father's footsteps as merchant, farmer, or aristocrat, while daughters could only hope to marry "well." You've obviously gone to school for most of your life and may feel you've had little choice in that, but you know from your studies that a mere century or so ago the best that some children could hope for was to be apprenticed to some occupation. You are probably also aware that, in many places in the world, people currently still work long hours in hand labor for what amounts to a few dollars a day if the job is good. But why is this? Where do these particular structures for social organization come from? Is this a case of "that's just the way it is"? If so, how did you learn "how things worked"?

Cultures have often been organized according to belief systems, or ideologies, that explain their social structures as being "given by God," or as being just "naturally" what they are. In each of these cases, the actual social structure appears as something external to people: from God, from Nature, from experience of God and Nature. A materialist approach, however, would first ask you what relationship you have to capital, to what the English writer Charles Dickens called "portable property." How do you see the minutes, days, months, and years of your own life in relation to the money you can earn, the things you can buy, the work you must do to earn that money? Why do you live in those relationships, instead of others? How did you come to accept them as "natural"?

The materialist critique offers you a systematic way to understand the reality of your own social structures. It helps you examine the relationship between human possibilities for enrichment, for creating useful lives, and the economic systems that essentially determine those possibilities *for* us, without our being able to intervene personally in many meaningful ways. It lets you connect material reality with the ideologies we use to justify material conditions, and to understand how language participates in, or actually creates, this connection.

● Adding to the Conversation

You come to know other students in your class not just by names and the faces or voices that go with them. Through social exchanges with others, you learn something about the way ideology and language are intimately connected. Address the questions below using the following line as your guide: "[W]e think in language, and language is a social activity, communicating attitudes, values, prejudices, biases—in short, already ideological when we learn it."

1. Take a moment to explain to a peer what you think "death" means. Do you believe that once the body dies all consciousness is over, or that you have a soul which, in some way, lives past your last breath and can "travel," or that reincarnation is a possibility? Compare your response to those of others in class. See whether you can explain how different *ideologies* result in different stories being told.

2. Try unpacking Burke's discussion of "contexts of situation" ("unpack" means to find the basic points to see how they do or don't make sense together):

   And very important among these "contexts of situation" are . . . the material interests (of private or class structure) that you symbolically defend or symbolically align yourself with in the course of your own assertions. These interests do not "cause" your discussion: its "cause" is in the genius of man himself. . . . But they greatly affect the idiom in which you speak, and so the idiom by which you think.

- Burke argues we all "symbolically" align ourselves with or oppose specific "material interests." What do you think such material interests might be?

- When you express an attitude about any kind of political question, can you see ways in which the attitude you accept connects with broader, more deep-seated ways of seeing the world?

- Rather than asking just *what* you or other students believe about foreign policy, immigration laws, or any other political issue, try to get at *why* you think the way you do. Where did you get your ideas?

3. As a follow-up to what you've just been discussing, reread the excerpt below to see if it might help you as you try to place yourself in relation to others.

> All human social organization is mediated by language, which is to say that the ways we *form* our societies, our families, ourselves—the values, or principles or laws we accept as our own—are transmitted by and through language. Underlying social values that determine conduct, family codes that condition attitudes, or laws that directly control individuals—all these social *understandings* rely on language in order to be "passed along" to others. . . . The mere fact that any one of us can conceive of something called a *social understanding* implies that the concept has been circulated through culture by language.

- Identify some of the "underlying social values" that "directly control individuals," ones you've personally experienced as "handed down" or "passed along." Consider attitudes, beliefs, or convictions. What *did* you learn from your own family about the values of education, for example?

- What did you internalize from your own educational experiences as to why you were learning what you were learning, or whom it would benefit, or why it was important?

- Share your own experiences with others in your class to see if you can get a sense of how values are "passed down."

4. What can you learn about the ideological premises of Professor Allen Fowler from the pages of his history book (see pp. 169 and 170)?

- What assumptions can you reasonably make about the "we" who would be reading, and can you explain why you come to those assumptions?

- How does Fowler use language not just to try to pass along information, but also to persuade you how to "receive" the text?

- What kinds of implicit claims about who's in a position of authority are being made in this short introduction?

5. Survey your classmates about their relationships to credit.
   - Do they have loans to repay? How much credit card debt do they currently carry? Why?
   - What's their attitude about "putting it on plastic"? How do they justify those attitudes?
   - What conclusions about the importance of being able to "purchase" do you draw?

6. To see what kinds of popular attitudes you've inherited your own ideas from, ask a random group of students, relatives, friends, or teachers what it means to be a "Marxist." Share them with others in class. What ideological views of Marxism emerge?

7. Using the Norman Rockwell illustration, write a brief analysis of how you see it "telling stories about who we think we are." What are the ideological implications of the "narrative" being framed in this painting, which served as a cover for *The Saturday Evening Post*.

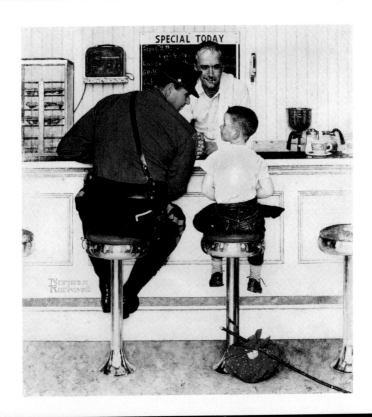

Rhetorical Issues in the Materialist Critique

A **materialist critique connects language and experience.** Several fundamental assumptions therefore define the focus or limit the boundaries of one's discussion.

- We live and die in a real, physical, material world; the underlying organizing principle for *all of social existence* is both material (physical) and economic.

- We can gain knowledge of who we are by examining what we actually do socially: what we do for work, how we worship, how we play, what we consider entertainment, what attitudes we have about others.

- How we worship or play is, in part, determined by our culture, which is controlled (or shaped) by a social elite, those who have the most of what's valued.

- The beliefs and attitudes of the social elite become the "natural" or "correct" beliefs and attitudes—those perpetuated in schools and in popular culture.

- We can better understand a "material phenomenon" (social practice, attitude, belief, bias) by contextualizing it, by understanding its historical context.

- Histories are written by those who are themselves *products* of certain ideologies, lenses, or frames, that shape the world we perceive.

These are all rhetorical positions, things you'd want to consider *before* you actually begin writing. You don't necessarily have to learn a whole new vocabulary or system of logic or book of rules to write from this critique; you only have to agree beforehand to focus on material and economic factors as you try to understand a political belief, a common cultural practice, a specific way of thinking. Doing so leads to some fundamental rhetorical approaches.

- **A materialist critique is an *inductive* process aimed at explaining how social systems work the way they do (who's in power; whose opinions count most) or why individuals behave or believe in specific ways.**

You wouldn't conduct a materialist analysis by beginning with an abstract law or statement like "people everywhere are basically good" and then look around for personal, idiosyncratic anecdotes that you think prove your statement—that's a *deductive* process. Working inductively, one begins by analyzing specific instances and then draws conclusions that tie them together or explain them persuasively.

- **A materialist critique therefore relies heavily on careful contextualizing of a topic and supporting detail.**

This is not to say that a writer doing a materialist analysis won't appeal to or refer to theoretical arguments—this section includes a number of them—but the rhetorical emphasis will most likely concentrate on providing your reader with data (historical, sociological, scientific) that leads inexorably to the general argument. Though you may indeed have a specific thesis or point to make, as a writer you'd want to explain the how's, what's, and why's of particular social relationships that lead to your main point. This approach is often particularly attractive to those who like to work from more scientific or "real life" stances.

- **In materialism, *logos* is likely to be the most persuasive form of appeal.**

If one is trying to "unmask" the structures or systems that control social behavior, then appeals to emotion (**pathos**) or appeals to credibility (**ethos**) would be less persuasive than what we consider facts, statistics, or historical evidence. This certainly doesn't mean that human emotional response, for instance, is ruled out by materialists as an element of persuasion. But materialists would want to examine that emotional response to see how it was generated, would want to look for the concrete, material circumstances that such an emotional response affirms, or reacts to, or ignores. Why, for instance, immediately after 9/11 did "spending" become a patriotic duty? That's the kind of question you might examine from a materialist perspective.

- **A materialist critique uses *dialectical* thinking.**

The obvious first questions are what is dialectical thinking, and how will it help you write for academic audiences? Simply put, to think dialectically is to focus on the relationships between and among people, things, and ideas. A magnifying glass provides a useful analogy. If you just look *at* it, you can identify what it is. You can describe it so others have a sense of what you are talking about. You can logically assume that if you said, "It makes things look larger," people will know what you mean. But what happens when you actually look *through* a magnifying glass? Describing what you're seeing then would have less to do with the details of the magnifying glass itself than with how things look through it. This is the difference between looking at and looking through. It's an entirely different matter to describe the essential points of psychoanalytic theory, for example, than it is to actually think analytically. In the previous section you saw that what was useful about psychological theory was not just knowing the terms *id*, *ego*, and *superego*, but understanding their relationships in forming human personality.

Thinking dialectically means to focus on how ideas relate to other ideas, or people, or things. Thinking dialectically also means to understand that human society and human psyches are constantly changing, adapting to new events, ideas, or things. The "you" who is reading right now is not necessarily the same "you" who was reading on page one. All the facts and theories and equations and hypotheses you grapple with day to day as a college student become part of who you "are." In significant ways, then, everything you come into contact with affects you in some way. Even if you reject a specific theory or person's opinion, or choose not to believe a certain point, you're still affected by them. If you think about it, those ideas you least agree with probably affect you the most in that you're consciously trying to find ways to counter them, to discredit them, to refute them. That's the nature of dialectical thinking—recognizing and examining the constant interactions between and among people, ideas, and things.

- **Language style is not separate from ideas; ideas can reflect material reality; language clearly is thus materially important.**

As writing professors, the authors encounter student writing on a near daily basis, over years of teaching. Given this experience, we think we can reliably comment on what we see when we collect writing assignments. You might recognize the style and language of the following example: "The values that he possessed allowed him to deal with most adverse situations." The line almost looks as if it's saying something meaningful. But the statement is vague, generalized, and actually says practically nothing. "*The values that he possessed . . .*" Which specific values might these be? And doesn't *possessing* mean to have, like *possessions*? Are a person's values really possessions, like cars or kites? Does "*allowed him to deal with*" correctly express what it means to make a decision? What exactly are "*adverse situations*"? A writer working dialectically would acknowledge that personal values are related to how people actually think—that, in fact, these values often explain or determine how people actually think, that the person and the person's values are not two separate "things" waiting to be connected somehow with language. A more persuasive and informative sentence might then look like this: "His reliance on God helped him overcome adversity." The next question, of course, would be how this reliance helped him and what adversities were overcome. Those explanations, in some detail, would be what writing instructors often call "development"—the writer would be providing useful information to the reader *and* persuasively making her or his point.

To think and write dialectically is to acknowledge that when you're writing about people in social relationships, or about the ideas inherent in such relationships, it doesn't make much sense to treat them (people or ideas) as isolated, ahistorical absolutes. Consider this example of undialectical thinking heard on a radio news story: "Unfortunately, he experienced an unexpected cardiac event which subsequently took his life." If we break this sentence down, we can see yet another instance of language that's grammatically correct but nonetheless confuses or contradicts the reality being described. What's at stake here is the thinking that's being communicated. In the above sentence, a man experiences an event—it sounds almost like he went to a movie or concert—the event existed somewhere separate from the man, and he experienced it as something he might turn the corner to see or bump into. But the event being experienced in this case is a heart attack. His heart quit working and he died. The way the sentence reads, however, makes it seem as though these are things that just happened to him. Thinking and writing this way creates scenarios where logically direct relationships appear unrelated, haphazard, completely by chance.

Here's another example of undialectical thinking.

I was setting up camp on a river late one summer day when a state policeman approached me, asking whether I'd seen anyone suspicious driving through the campground. I said I'd just arrived, and hadn't seen any cars at all.

"Well," he said, "some folks in a camper two sites over reported that while they were out fishing someone broke into their rig and stole a handgun."

I shook my head and remarked that this was disturbing news to get, that I wasn't comfortable thinking someone was running around in the campground with a pistol.

"I wouldn't worry," the policeman said. "I imagine whoever did it is pretty far away by now. We have a few of these kinds of incidents, and it seems that these are crimes of opportunity. It's pretty easy to just drive in and drive out and be gone. I wouldn't worry."

Later that evening, as I was returning from fishing myself, I walked past the camper where the theft had occurred. A middle-aged couple was sitting in lawn chairs at the campsite and I stopped to ask if they'd been the ones who'd been broken into.

"Yes," the wife said. "We left the window cracked so the cat could get fresh air and someone came in that way."

I muttered something about it being sad that this had happened, when the woman uttered the following: "Yes, it's unfortunate, but what we're really worried about is that the gun will end up in the wrong hands."

This is undialectical thinking—that the gun was stolen by someone, but the woman was worrying it might eventually end up in "the wrong hands." Wouldn't it be obvious that whoever broke into the camper to steal the gun would also be considered "the wrong hands"? To think dialectically, then, is to recognize what Burke refers to as the "contexts of situation" that determine how language creates meaning. In the case above, there wasn't a theft that somehow "occurred" without someone doing the stealing. The act of stealing had an agent, the thief, someone doing the stealing—they are one and the same: the theft and the thief stealing. To separate these two into distinct elements or features of a situation or occurrence is to severely disfigure the event itself by separating language and material reality.

Putting all these rhetorical approaches together, we can develop a statement one of our students suggested for a material critique: cultural changes are the result of changing economic conditions. As a writer, you're in the position of defining the scope or depth of your discussions. In this case, you would likely begin by *contextualizing* your inquiry. You're not going to discuss every conceivable kind of cultural change and you're not going to work from an amorphously general idea of "changing economic conditions." Not, that is, if you want to be persuasive. Let's say someone has suggested that American families have suffered irreparable damage because too many women have given up staying home with children in order to have careers. So, the cultural change you're going to talk about is the upsurge in the numbers of women working outside the home.

You could talk about this issue from a moral stance—"the family unit is being destroyed" or "These women are tearing apart our notion of the family by denying their maternal responsibilities in order to compete with men." Undertaking a materialist analysis of this question, however, means first showing that the main assumption of the statement is accurate. How many women have joined the workforce? When? In what capacities? We need historical detail to contextualize the discussion. The main point reflects a specific historical era—post–World War II. During that war, American women were enlisted in all facets of the economy. Filling jobs left vacant by men who were serving in the various branches of the military, women were afforded opportunities to learn skills and develop talents—in short, they were necessary to the country's functioning. These employment opportunities were not restricted to the familiar stories of "Rosie the Riveter"; women also took places in private enterprise, in government, in virtually all aspects of social life. With so many doctors, for instance, enlisted for the war effort, many women found positions in health care that were not previously available to them.

For our analysis, what's important here is that women filled a basic economic need created by the enormous drain of men from the labor markets. But when the war came to an end, and millions of men returned to take their places as "providers" for their families, women were essentially turned out of their jobs. Considering the social values of the 1950s in relation to the place and function of women in American society, we can say that homemaking was elevated to a near-saintly position. Advertisements in popular magazines of those times show continuing campaigns for labor-saving appliances in the home or for beauty aids—all accompanied by depictions of wives and mothers as being "queens" of their homes.

If we want to make a compelling argument here, we could collect data that demonstrates the actuality of what we've just said: labor statistics from during World War II and the 1950s, or samples of magazine or television advertising. From this basis, then, we could make a good case that notions of women's roles in American culture vary depending upon social needs. If large numbers of women are forced to leave the labor market to make way for men, then what roles are they supposed to play, where will they spend their time, what will they do? And how can we explain the large number of women reentering labor markets at the end of the twentieth century?

After presenting data or examples to explain what happened during and right after World War II, we could make the following claim: "Women work outside of the home because it's once again necessary for them to do so." Instead of being a moral or ethical argument about the nature of women's attitudes, this argument is fundamentally materialist. Our reasoning might go like this: if women were (as a group) encouraged to be consumers rather than producers, and if the objects of that increasingly hyped value of consumption—houses with appliances, cars, clothes, trendy items, even food—become more and more costly (which is certainly the case), then simple logic tells us that the mythical American family of mother, father, and 2.3 children will need more income than can be provided from only the father's labor. And if we add in the incredibly vast collection of goods that are marketed to and for children and adolescents in our culture, not to mention any kind of higher education, then we can readily see that a mass movement of women from the home to the office or factory likely has very little to do with "undermining the notion of the family" or "destroying family values." In fact, one could argue that "valuing" the family is exactly what caused the movement in the first place.

We've constructed this argument *inductively* so you can see how the process works. To be truly persuasive, we'd have to supply the data or examples that would support our case. Such proof is at the heart of any materialist critique. Our discussion could become even more focused and potentially persuasive if we were to consider such factors as age or race in our examination. To what extent are (or were) the assumptions about what American women should do or be limited to white women of a certain age? This analysis could conceivably tell you quite a lot about how dominant cultural values are formed to begin with—who they apply to and why. Once again, we're saying that, rather than arguing or writing from a vast or sweeping generalization based on some kind of idealist notion— "Women deny traditional family values when they work outside the home or strive to pursue a career"—we can write a persuasive materialist critique of the issues by offering evidence and following logical connections. Rhetorically, then, we've chosen to establish our authorial credibility or ethos in concrete, historical ways that are much harder to dismiss than someone simply saying, "Believe me because I'm telling the truth."

Materialist thought provides, in the most tangible of ways, a systematic and recoverable method for cultural analysis. By "recoverable" in this case we mean that you can examine events or behaviors or attitudes from the past by contextualizing your discussions, by examining historical data. You don't have to be an expert in economics to engage in this critique. And the critique need not be limited to wide-ranging social issues. You could easily and productively apply materialist principles to explain any number or kind of social circumstance, political ideology, or cultural artifact: Why are car ads targeted to young men? Why are current political campaigns tied so closely to "character issues"? Why have espresso shops sprung up all over the country? How has the Internet affected our methods of consumption? This method provides a common language and theoretical foundation by which anyone can examine his or her relation to any social event, principle, product, or arrangement. And its very premise provides the incentive to do so: as Marx and Engels argued, material conditions determine our consciousness. Understanding the role of language and ideology in this process helps us understand how we came to be where we are socially, and why we may never have questioned the social and economic processes that have shaped us. Writing from this materialist perspective makes us pay attention to language and our relationship to it.

**This Chapter's
Rhetorical Concepts**

- Focusing topics using a
  materialist frame
- Using "history" as argument
- How inductive argument
  works in a materialist critique

chapter 7

Exploring in the Materialist Critique

A Contribution to the Critique of Political Economy

KARL MARX

Engels published the book from which this excerpt is taken in 1888, after Marx's death. Found among Marx's papers, it is thought to be a fragment of an introduction to his main works written as early as 1859. As such, it provides an inroad to some of the basic social concepts of modern materialism.

I was led by my studies to the conclusion that legal relations as well as forms of state could neither be understood by themselves, or explained by the so-called general progress of the human mind, but that they are rooted in the material conditions of life, which are summed up . . . under the name "civil society"; the anatomy of that civil society is to be sought in political economy. . . . The general conclusion at which I arrived and which, once reached, continued to serve as the leading thread in my studies, may be briefly summed up as follows: In the social production which men carry on they enter into definite relations that are indispensable and independent of their will; these relations of production correspond to a definite stage of development of their material powers of production. The sum total of these relations of production constitutes the economic structure of society—the real foundation, on which rise legal and political superstructures and to which correspond definite forms of social consciousness. The mode of production in material life determines the general character of the social, political and spiritual processes of life. It is not the consciousness of men that determines their existence, but, on the contrary, their social existence determines their consciousness. At a certain stage of their development, the material forces of production in society come in conflict with the existing relations of production, or—what is but a legal expression for the same thing—with the property relations within which they had been at work before. From forms of development of the forces of production these relations turn into their fetters. Then comes the period of social revolution. With the change of the economic foundation the entire immense superstructure is more or less rapidly transformed. In considering such transformations the distinction should always be made between the material transformation of the economic conditions of production which can be determined with the precision of natural science, and the legal, political, religious, aesthetic, or philosophic—in short ideological forms in which men become conscious of this conflict and fight it out. Just as our opinion of an individual is not based on what he thinks of himself, so can we not judge of such a period of transformation by its own consciousness; on the contrary, this consciousness must rather be explained from the contradictions of material life, from the existing conflict between the social forces of production and the relations of production. No social order ever disappears before all the productive forces, for which there is room in it, have been developed; and new higher relations of production never appear before the material conditions of their existence have matured in the womb of the old society. Therefore, mankind always takes up only such problems as it can solve; since, looking at the matter more closely, we will always find that the problem itself arises only when the material conditions necessary for its solution already exist or are at least in the process of formation.

● Building the Frame Through Writing

1. In order to discuss materialism effectively, as with all critical frames, you'll need a common vocabulary or set of shared understanding of foundational points. Break into groups to address each of the seven statements below. As a class, you can come away from this reading with a coherent overall sense of what Marx is saying. See if you can put the specific quotation into words that help explain the quotation to everyone else. If each group reports back in order, by the time you're done everyone should have engaged in "making meaning," so that one translation sets the stage for the next.

   • In the social production which men carry on they enter into definite relations that are indispensable and independent of their will.

   What does "social production" mean in this context? Remember that, from a materialist perspective, "production" refers to the result of labor. "Mode of Production" refers to what one does for a living. How are these relations "indispensable"? Why are they "independent of their will"?

   • These relations of production correspond to a definite stage of development of their material powers of production.

   How do you think "these relations of production" can be said to "correspond" to some stage of development? What does "development of their material powers of production" mean? People work at jobs that are defined by economic possibilities. Explain this through examples that others can identify with.

- The sum total of these relations of production constitutes the economic structure of society—the real foundation, on which rise legal and political superstructures and to which correspond definite forms of social consciousness.

Why is the economic the "real" foundation of society? What are "superstructures" (legal and political) and how do they create different forms of "social consciousness"? Does this make sense to you—that money talks and laws, for instance, follow?

- The mode of production in material life determines the general character of the social, political, and spiritual processes of life.

Does this mean that accountants, for example, all agree on social, political, and spiritual processes? Is the "general character" of these processes somehow different from the way any particular person lives? Are we talking about specific occupations or specific relations to other professions? Do executives think, vote, and believe like the mailroom clerk? Is this a question anyone can answer?

- It is not the consciousness of men that determines their existence, but, on the contrary, their social existence determines their consciousness.

Do people learn lessons about life through ideas? Or do people have ideas based on their lived experiences? Try to explain how "social existence" might "determine consciousness." How do you arrive at the values you believe in?

- With the change of the economic foundation the entire immense superstructure is more or less rapidly transformed.

In what ways do laws, customs, beliefs—any cultural values—change depending upon whether an "economic foundation" is agrarian or industrial, individuals or corporations? Can you come up with examples from your own experience? technological change?

- In considering such transformations the distinction should always be made between the material transformation of the economic conditions of production which can be determined with the precision of natural science, and the legal, political, religious, aesthetic, or philosophic—in short ideological forms in which men become conscious of this conflict and fight it out.

How can "material transformations" (changes in what jobs are available to whom) be measured with the "precision of natural science"? How are "legal, political, religious, aesthetic, or philosophic" attitudes explained by ideology? What do you think it means to "fight it out" in ideological forms?

2. In *Critique of Political Economy*, Marx lays out the base/superstructure configuration that's long been identified with his thought. The basic argument is that all systems of beliefs about politics, religion, education, aesthetics, and so on are interconnected by being rooted or grounded in an economic base, such as in the figure. Write down two statements from the *Critique of Political Economy* that you think best exemplify this base (economic) superstructure argument. Explain how you interpret each statement and how you see it exemplifying

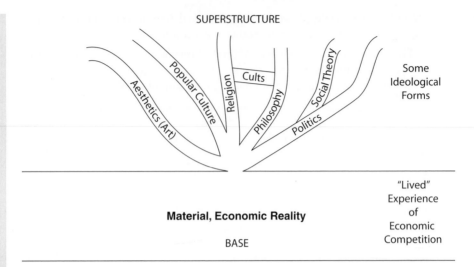

Marx's base/superstructure argument. Use examples that would be familiar to your audience—other students.

3. Everything about the Marx excerpt seems to rely on some notion of competition, or struggle, or conflict. Does this make sense to you? Is human existence in social units always a site of contest? The corollary to this question would be that the fundamental human organizing activity is competition. Does this seem accurate to you? Using your own experience, write in your journal or bring a brief response to class for discussion.

4. How does Marx position himself rhetorically? Can you get a feeling for whom the audience might have been? Can you make some assumptions about that audience based on the language, style, or content of the writing? Which rhetorical appeal seems most evident here—pathos, ethos, logos?

The Condition of the Working Class in England

FRIEDRICH ENGELS

This is the introduction written between September 1844 and March 1845. The text was first published in Leipzig, Germany, in 1845, but an English translation was not available until 1887. Engels's father was a German manufacturer, and Engels worked as an agent in his father's Manchester, England, factory. Engels dedicated this volume to the English "Working Man," telling him,

To you I dedicate a work, in which I have tried to lay before my German Countrymen a faithful picture of your condition, of your sufferings and struggles, of your hopes and prospects. I have lived long enough amidst you to know something about your circumstances; I have devoted to their knowledge my most serious attention, I have studied the various official and non-official documents as far as I was able to get hold of them—I have not been satisfied with this, I wanted more than a mere abstract knowledge of my subject, I wanted to see you in your own homes, to observe you in your everyday life, to chat with you on your condition and grievances, to witness your struggles against the social and political power of your oppressors. I have done so: I forsook the company and the dinner-parties, the port-wine and champagne of the middle-classes, and devoted my leisure-hours almost exclusively to the intercourse with plain Working-Men; I am both glad and proud of having done so.

The history of the proletariat in England begins with the second half of the last century, with the invention of the steam-engine and of machinery for working cotton. These inventions gave rise, as is well known, to an industrial revolution, a revolution which altered the whole civil society; one, the historical importance of which is only now beginning to be recognised. England is the classic soil of this transformation, which was all the mightier, the more silently it proceeded; and England is, therefore, the classic land of its chief product also, the proletariat. Only in England can the proletariat be studied in all its relations and from all sides.

We have not, here and now, to deal with the history of this revolution, nor with its vast importance for the present and the future. Such a delineation must be reserved for a future, more comprehensive work. For the moment, we must limit ourselves to the little that is necessary for understanding the facts that follow, for comprehending the present state of the English proletariat.

Before the introduction of machinery, the spinning and weaving of raw materials was carried on in the workingman's home. Wife and daughter spun the yarn that the father wove or that they sold, if he did not work it up himself. These weaver families lived in the country in the neighbourhood of the towns, and could get on fairly well with their wages, because the home market was almost the only one and the crushing power of competition that came later, with the conquest of foreign markets and the extension of trade, did not yet press upon wages. There was, further, a constant increase in the demand for the home market, keeping pace with the slow increase in population and employing all the workers; and there was also the impossibility of vigorous competition of the workers among themselves, consequent upon the rural dispersion of their homes. So it was that the weaver was usually in a position to lay by something, and rent a little piece of land, that he cultivated in his leisure hours, of which he had as many as he chose to take, since he could weave whenever and as long as he pleased. True, he was a bad farmer and managed his land inefficiently, often obtaining but poor crops; nevertheless, he was no proletarian, he had a stake in the country, he was permanently settled, and stood one step higher in society than the English workman of today.

So the workers vegetated throughout a passably comfortable existence, leading a righteous and peaceful life in all piety and probity; and their material position was far better than that of their successors. They did not need to over-work; they did no more than they chose to do, and yet earned what they needed. They had leisure for healthful work in garden or field, work which, in itself, was recreation for them, and they could take part besides in the recreations and games of their neighbours, and all these games—bowling, cricket, football, etc., contributed to their physical health and vigour. They were, for the most part, strong, well-built people, in whose physique little or no difference from that of their peasant neighbours was discoverable. Their children grew up in the fresh country air, and, if they could help their parents at work, it was only occasion-ally; while of eight or twelve hours work for them there was no question.

What the moral and intellectual character of this class was may be guessed.   5 Shut off from the towns, which they never entered, their yarn and woven stuff being delivered to travelling agents for payment of wages—so shut off that old people who lived quite in the neighborhood of the town never went thither until they were robbed of their trade by the introduction of machinery and obliged to look about them in the towns for work—the weavers stood upon the moral and intellectual plane of the yeomen with whom they were usually immediately con-nected through their little holdings. They regarded their squire, the greatest landholder of the region, as their natural superior; they asked advice of him, laid their small disputes before him for settlement, and gave him all honour, as this patriarchal relation involved. They were "respectable" people, good husbands and fathers, led moral lives because they had no temptation to be immoral, there being no groggeries or low houses in their vicinity, and because the host, at whose inn they now and then quenched their thirst, was also a respectable man, usually a large tenant-farmer who took pride in his good order, good beer, and early hours. They had their children the whole day at home, and brought them up in obedience and the fear of God; the patriarchal relationship remained undisturbed so long as the children were unmarried. The young people grew up in idyllic simplicity and intimacy with their playmates until they married; and even though sexual intercourse before marriage almost unfailingly took place, this happened only when the moral obligation of marriage was recognised on both sides, and a subsequent wedding made everything good. In short, the English industrial workers of those days lived and thought after the fashion still to be found here and there in Germany, in retirement and seclusion, without mental activity and without violent fluctuations in their position in life. They could rarely read and far more rarely write; went regularly to church, never talked politics, never conspired, never thought, delighted in physical exercises, listened with inherited reverence when the Bible was read, and were, in their unquestioning humility, exceedingly well-disposed towards the "superior" classes. But intellectually, they were dead; lived only for their petty, private interest, for their looms and gardens, and knew nothing of the mighty movement which, beyond their horizon, was sweeping through mankind. They were comfortable in their silent vegetation, and but for the industrial revolution they would never have emerged from this existence, which, cosily romantic as it was, was nevertheless not worthy of human beings. In truth, they were not human beings; they were merely toiling machines in the service of the few aristocrats who had guided history down to that time. The industrial revolution has simply carried this out to its logical end by making the workers machines pure and simple, taking from them the last trace of independent activity, and so forcing them to think and demand a position worthy of men. As in France politics, so in England manufacture and the movement of civil society in general drew into the whirl of history the last classes which had remained sunk in apathetic indifference to the universal interests of mankind.

The first invention which gave rise to a radical change in the state of the English workers was the jenny, invented in the year 1764 by a weaver, James Hargreaves, of Stanhill, near Blackburn, in North Lancashire. This machine was the rough beginning of the later invented mule, and was moved by hand. Instead of one spindle like the ordinary spinning-wheel, it carried sixteen or eighteen manipulated by a single workman. This invention made it possible to deliver more yarn than heretofore. Whereas, though one weaver had employed three spinners, there had never been enough yarn, and the weaver had often been obliged to wait for it, there was now more yarn to be had than could be woven by the available workers. The demand for woven goods, already increasing, rose yet more in consequence of the cheapness of these goods, which cheapness, in turn, was the outcome of the diminished cost of producing the yarn. More weavers were needed, and weavers' wages rose. Now that the weaver could earn more at his loom, he gradually abandoned his farming, and gave his whole time to weaving. At that time a family of four grown persons and two children (who were set to spooling) could earn, with eight hours' daily work, four pounds sterling in a week, and often more if trade was good and work pressed. It happened often enough that a single weaver earned two pounds a week at his loom. By degrees the class of farming weavers wholly disappeared, and was merged in the newly arising class of weavers who lived wholly upon wages, had no property whatever, not even the pretended property of a holding, and so became workingmen, proletarians. Moreover, the old relation between spinner and weaver was destroyed. Hitherto, so far as this had been possible, yarn had been spun and woven under one roof. Now that the jenny as well as the loom required a strong hand, men began to spin, and whole families lived by spinning, while others laid the antiquated, superseded spinning-wheel aside; and, if they had not means of purchasing a jenny, were forced to live upon the wages of the father alone. Thus beg`an with spinning and weaving that division of labour which has since been so infinitely perfected.

While the industrial proletariat was thus developing with the first still very imperfect machine, the same machine gave rise to the agricultural proletariat.

There had, hitherto, been a vast number of small landowners, yeomen, who had vegetated in the same unthinking quiet as their neighbours, the farming weavers. They cultivated their scraps of land quite after the ancient and inefficient fashion of their ancestors, and opposed every change with the obstinacy peculiar to such creatures of habit, after remaining stationary from generation to generation. Among them were many small holders also, not tenants in the present sense of the word, but people who had their land handed down from their fathers, either by hereditary lease, or by force of ancient custom, and had hitherto held it as securely as if it had actually been their own property. When the industrial workers withdrew from agriculture, a great number of small holdings fell idle, and upon these the new class of large tenants established themselves, tenants-at-will, holding fifty, one hundred, two hundred or more acres, liable to be turned out at the end of the year, but able by improved tillage and larger farming to increase the yield of the land. They could sell their produce more cheaply than the yeoman, for whom nothing remained when his farm no longer supported him but to sell it, procure a jenny or a loom, or take service as an agricultural labourer in the employ of a large farmer. His inherited slowness and the inefficient methods of cultivation bequeathed by his ancestors, and above which he could not rise, left him no alternative when forced to compete with men who managed their holdings on sounder principles and with all the advantages bestowed by farming on a large scale and the investment of capital for the improvement of the soil.

Meanwhile, the industrial movement did not stop here. Single capitalists began to set up spinning jennies in great buildings and to use water-power for driving them, so placing themselves in a position to diminish the number of workers, and sell their yarn more cheaply than single spinners could do who moved their own machines by hand. There were constant improvements in the jenny, so that machines continually became antiquated, and must be altered or even laid aside; and though the capitalists could hold out by the application of water-power even with the old machinery, for the single spinner this was impossible. And the factory system, the beginning of which was thus made, received a fresh extension in 1767, through the spinning throstle invented by Richard Arkwright, a barber, in Preston, in North Lancashire. After the steam-engine, this is the most important mechanical invention of the 18th century. It was calculated from the beginning for mechanical motive power, and was based upon wholly new principles. By the combination of the peculiarities of the jenny and throstle, Samuel Crompton, of Firwood, Lancashire, contrived the mule in 1785, and as Arkwright invented the carding engine, and preparatory ("slubbing and roving") frames about the same time, the factory system became the prevailing one for the spinning of cotton. By means of trifling modifications these machines were gradually adapted to the spinning of flax, and so to the superseding of handwork here, too. But even then, the end was not yet. In the closing years of the last century, Dr. Cartwright, a country parson, had invented the power-loom, and about 1804 had so far perfected it, that it could successfully compete with the hand-weaver; and all this machinery was made doubly important by James Watt's steam-engine, invented in 1764 and used for supplying motive power for spinning since 1785.

With these inventions, since improved from year to year, the victory of machine-work over hand-work in the chief branches of English industry was won; and the history of the latter from that time forward simply relates how the hand-workers have been driven by machinery from one position after another. The consequences of this were, on the one hand, a rapid fall in price of all manufactured commodities, prosperity of commerce and manufacture, the conquest of nearly all the unprotected foreign markets, the sudden multiplication of capital and national wealth; on the other hand, a still more rapid multiplication of the proletariat, the destruction of all property-holding and of all security of employment for the working-class, demoralisation, political excitement, and all those facts so highly repugnant to Englishmen in comfortable circumstances, which we shall have to consider in the following pages. Having already seen what a transformation in the social condition of the lower classes a single such clumsy machine as the jenny had wrought, there is no cause for surprise as to that which a complete and interdependent system of finely adjusted machinery has brought about, machinery which receives raw material and turns out woven goods.

● Building the Frame Through Writing

1. Engels dedicated *The Condition of the Working Class in England* to those who comprised that class, the workers themselves.

   • What does his language, style, or choice of examples tell you about his attitudes toward that audience? Can you identify ways that Engels appears to be clearly trying to appeal to working men?

   • Find some specific sentences that you think best show Engels's argument from pathos. Why do you think he characterizes the lives of working people as being petty and uninspiring, even while he says he's writing for and to them?

   • Notice Engels's use of "vegetating" in describing the lives of agricultural workers. Is this just his attempt at humor?

2. Most of the excerpt from *The Condition* focuses on how the invention of seemingly basic machinery changed the social structure in England. Following Engels's descriptions of technological "progress" and what it meant to the majority of the population, consider the kinds of technological innovations that have occurred in your own lifetime.

   • How do you see those advancements affecting social relations? Are you able to identify members of different economic classes by their use of, their ownership of, their familiarity with the newest technology?

- If you were to approach writing an essay that analyzed the relationships between technological innovations and changing social values, how would you begin? Can you imagine, for instance, students who might have access to computers at school, but not at home? If this is a plausible case, then how would you establish your thesis that access to technology varies according to economic conditions?

3. In the following short excerpt, Engels describes the physical layout of the British industrial city of Manchester. How do you see his attitudes above also being evident in this piece? In other words, see if you can find specific statements here that reenforce, substantiate, or otherwise bolster the arguments made above; then answer the questions that follow.

> Manchester itself is peculiarly built, so that a person may live in it for years, and go in and out daily without coming into contact with a working-people's quarter or even with workers, that is, so long as he confines himself to his business or to pleasure walks. This arises chiefly from the fact, that by unconscious tacit agreement, as well as with out-spoken conscious determination, the working-people's quarters are sharply separated from the sections of the city reserved for the middle-class; or, if this does not succeed, they are concealed with the cloak of charity.
>
> The finest part of the arrangement is this, that the members of this money aristocracy can take the shortest road through the middle of all the labouring districts to their places of business, without ever seeing that they are in the midst of the grimy misery that lurks to the right and the left. For the thoroughfares leading from the Exchange in all directions out of the city are lined, on both sides, with an almost unbroken series of shops, and are so kept in the hands of the middle and lower bourgeoisie, which, out of self-interest, cares for a decent and cleanly external appearance and can care for it. True, these shops bear some relation to the districts which lie behind them, and are more elegant in the commercial and residential quarters than when they hide grimy working-men's dwellings; but they suffice to conceal from the eyes of the wealthy men and women of strong stomachs and weak nerves the misery and grime which form the complement of their wealth.
>
> In this way any one who knows Manchester can infer the adjoining districts, from the appearance of the thoroughfare, but one is seldom in a position to catch from the street a glimpse of the real labouring districts. I know very well that this hypocritical plan is more or less common to all great cities; I know, too, that the retail dealers are forced by the nature of their business to take possession of the great highways: I know that there are more good buildings than bad ones upon such streets everywhere, and that the value of land is greater near them than in remoter districts; but at the same time I have never seen so systematic a shutting out of the working-class from the thoroughfares, so tender a concealment of everything which might affront the eye and the nerves of the bourgeoisie, as in Manchester. And yet, in other respects, Manchester is less built according to a plan, after official

regulations, is more an outgrowth of accident than any other city; and when I consider in this connection the eager assurances of the middle-class, that the working-class is doing famously, I cannot help feeling that the liberal manufacturers, the "Big Wigs" of Manchester, are not so innocent after all, in the matter of this sensitive method of construction.

- What is Engels saying about the demography of Manchester? Who lives where, and how does he explain why the "working class" is segregated? Can you identify the same processes from your own experience?

- In your hometown, were there wealthy sections? Poor sections? Can you describe the differences to others? Can you learn from others in your class about their own hometown demographics? What constants can you observe and how would you explain them?

4. If the demographics of a city, with its enclaves of specific and different ethnicities, or races, or income levels, is a "material phenomenon"—it's physically "there" and wasn't caused by nature—then we should be able to draw conclusions about how class competition in some form helps shape that city.

- How would you describe those conclusions to others in writing? What makes your writing easier to construct by knowing that the "others" you're writing to have just read the same article in question 2 about Manchester? Perhaps you can make some connections between what Engels describes and what you saw happening in the wake of Hurricane Katrina in the gulf states or in New Orleans?

- Can you use information about Katrina to argue Engels's position about demography being a result of class differences? Think of questions like: Who got aid first? Who still hasn't received aid? Who left their homes and haven't returned? What's being done today, and for whom? Who's making money in reconstruction?

The German Ideology

KARL MARX and FRIEDRICH ENGELS

In this selection from their book, a critique written in 1845–1846, Marx and Engels try to make clear what they call the "social nature" of consciousness. Consider the discussions earlier in this chapter about the relationships between language and social organization. This is where Marx and Engels explain that "consciousness" is determined by the life one lives, by material "events" in one's life, by the material conditions of existence.

Men are the producers of their conceptions, ideas, etc.—real, active men, as they are conditioned by a definite development of their productive forces and of the intercourse corresponding to these, up to its furthest forms. Consciousness can never be anything else than conscious existence, and the existence of men is their actual life process. If in all ideology men and their circumstances appear upside down as in a *camera obscura*, this phenomenon arises just as much from their historical life process as the inversion of objects on the retina does from their physical life process.

In direct contrast to German philosophy which descends from heaven to earth, here we ascend from earth to heaven. That is to say, we do not set out from what men say, imagine, conceive, nor from men as narrated, thought of, imagined, conceived, in order to arrive at men in the flesh. We set out from real, active men, and on the basis of their real life process we demonstrate the development of the ideological reflexes and echoes of this life process. The phantoms formed in the human brain are also, necessarily, sublimates of their material life process, which is empirically verifiable and bound to material premises. Morality, religion, metaphysics, all the rest of ideology and their corresponding forms of consciousness, thus no longer retain the semblance of independence. They have no history, no development; but men, developing their material production and their material intercourse, alter, along with this their real existence, their thinking, and the products of their thinking. Life is not determined by consciousness, but consciousness by life. In the first method of approach the starting point is consciousness taken as the living individual; in the second it is the real living individuals themselves, as they are in actual life, and consciousness is considered solely as *their* consciousness.

This method of approach is not devoid of premises. It starts out from the real premises and does not abandon them for a moment. Its premises are men, not in any fantastic isolation or abstract definition, but in their actual, empirically perceptible process of development under definite conditions. As soon as this active life process is described, history ceases to be a collection of dead facts as it is with the empiricists (themselves still abstract), or an imagined activity of imagined subjects, as with the idealists.

Where speculation ends—in real life—there real, positive science begins; the representation of the practical activity, of the practical process of development of men. Empty talk about consciousness ceases, and real knowledge has to take its place. When reality is depicted, philosophy as an independent branch of activity loses its medium of existence. At the best its place can only be taken by a summing-up of the most general results, abstractions which arise from the observation of the historical development of men. Viewed apart from real history, these abstractions have in themselves no value whatsoever.

● Building the Frame Through Writing

1. At paragraph 4 we read: "When reality is depicted, philosophy as an independent branch of activity loses its medium of existence." Can you translate this for someone else in your class?

- What do Marx and Engels mean by saying, "When reality is depicted"? Depicted how? by whom? Think of these questions as you write out your "translation." What other sentences or ideas in this selection help to argue your interpretation? Why does philosophy lose its medium of existence?

- What *is* philosophy's medium of existence? The questions in this selection revolve around the differences between "idealism" and "materialism." See if you can elaborate these differences in your own terms, using examples from your own life.

2. Marx and Engels have written, "[T]he same men [*sic*] who establish their social relations in conformity with their material productivity, produce also principles, ideas and categories in conformity with their social relations."

- What does it mean to "establish social relations in conformity with . . . material productivity"? Are they talking about hierarchies? about chains of command? Is this their way of trying to talk about "class"?

- Can you identify some "principles, ideas" or "categories" that are "produced" by some section of your culture for its own ends? For example: *Nascar Dads* or *Soccer Moms* have become categories of classification in our present culture. Who do you think of when you hear these phrases? Why? What kinds of evidence do you have to support your conceptual category, your own stereotype?

3. The readings in this section have been concerned with explaining and identifying a "class struggle" that Marx and Engels (and many others) see as a basic dynamic of all social interaction.

How do you define *class*, as an economic term? Do you see different classes in your own social environments? How would you explain the differences that define the classes? What about the phrase, she or he "has class"? What does this mean in relation to your own experience and in relation to the ideas presented by this critical method? In other words, if Marx's theories rely on the existence of "class struggle," what problems do you see in applying his theories to your own "lived" experience?

Writings for a Liberation Psychology
IGNACIO MARTÍN-BARÓ

Ignacio Martín-Baró was a Jesuit priest and educator in El Salvador who taught at the University of Central America in San Salvador. In 1989 he was murdered by the Salvadoran military along with five other Jesuits, their housekeeper, and her daughter. These Jesuits were advocates of liberation theology, a doctrine that stresses the Church's obligation to address the needs of the poor. El Salvador, at the time, was in the midst of a particularly brutal 12-year civil war that officially ended in 1992 with peace accords signed in Mexico City. This excerpt is from Chapter 4 of Writings for a Liberation Psychology.

Introduction

From the perspectives of both sociology and psychology, socialization tends   1
to be conceived as a series of mediating processes to explain the connection
between individual and society (for a fuller discussion of this point see
Martín-Baró, 1983a, pp. 113–120). Some writers see it in terms of individuals
acquiring the norms and abilities for living in society and getting their needs
satisfied; others see it as a molding of the individual to a society's values,
demands, and requirements. But whether the emphasis falls on the individual or
on society, socialization is understood as a kind of intermediate bridge between
the two.

It becomes clearer all the time, though, that the standard conceptions of
socialization are too abstract and fall short as explanatory principles. Their flaw
lies in having adopted a particular unit for analysis, and then—as often happens—treating the analytic unit as a reality in itself. With individual and society
we are dealing with historical entities, not abstract realities, and while it is
perfectly all right to speak of individuals and societies, it will not do to think
of them as independent realities, as absolute totalities. It goes without saying
that individuals do not exist without society, nor society without individuals,
but this almost self-evident assertion has important consequences for the subject
of socialization.

If society and individual exist as mutually dependent realities, in a dependency running through the backbone of history, then we have to consider socialization dialectically, recognizing that neither society nor the individual is real in
itself, but rather, both exist to the extent that they mutually give each other existence. If the individual is a human individual, it is because he or she is shaped by
society; if a human society exists, it is because there are individuals who make it
up. From a psychosocial perspective, this means that there does not first exist a
person, who then goes on to become socialized, but rather that the individual
becomes an individual, a human person, by virtue of becoming socialized.

This assertion does not deny that society—for instance, Salvadoran society—exists apart from any particular individual. Nor does it deny that each individual has a genetic endowment which is extremely important for understanding
who that person is. Individual and society do not come from nowhere, and
clearly they have unique characteristics that cannot be explained solely by mutual
reference. But if we want to understand real individuals, Juan and María, we will
have to consider their genetic heritage in reference to a social context. What
Juan and María become is not simply a function of their genetic endowment, nor
a linear function of their genes plus social influence; they are, rather, the living
result of a complex process in which the two factors interact and mutually shape
each other.

We may consider socialization, then, as those processes through which an   5
individual becomes a person in history. This dialectical understanding has important consequences for the analysis of specific socialization processes, for it
means that the variables we study can never be considered as orthogonal, and

microprocesses must always be understood as connected in their essence to more fundamental macroprocesses. Berger and Luckman (1966) maintain that when we perform a micro-sociological or social-psychological analysis of the phenomena of internalization, we must always do so with a macro-sociological understanding of their structural aspects. To this we should add that externalization is no simple mechanical consequence of internalization, but rather has to be understood in terms of how a particular individual actively and dynamically works things out.

. . .

For the ancient Greeks, the political domain was characterized by liberty and equality, as distinguished from the household, the domain of necessity and inequality. As Hannah Arendt (1958) points out, the emergence of the social in the modern era has erased that distinction and brought necessity into the sphere of the political. For the Greeks, it was taken as a given that human needs would have to be satisfied before political participation could begin. In modern society, by contrast, the political has penetrated every part of human existence, including the family home, and is seen as essential to the satisfaction of all sorts of needs.

The satisfaction of human needs is no longer simply a private or individual matter; on the contrary, it is a point of reference and a basic objective of all political activity. Accordingly, political socialization cannot be reduced to the process by which we acquire norms and behaviors directly related to formal political objects, though this cannot be excluded. More fundamentally, it involves the social shaping of the human needs of a given population, and specifically, of each individual person within it.

Human needs are not formed and developed in the abstract. They arise initially from biological demands and the organism's adaptation, but they develop, are modified, and are organized according to social patterns. In other words, the particular historical needs psychologists discover in people are not simply biological ("natural") facts, but also social phenomena (see Sève, 1975).

Clearly, society does not determine primary needs: regardless of the type of society in which they live, all human beings have to eat and sleep. Still, what we find in actual human beings is not the simple need for eating and sleeping but the need for eating certain things and sleeping under particular conditions, and both needs are manifested in a very specific reference system. If instead of primary needs we look at what psychologists call secondary needs—needs that are less biological and more specifically human, like the "need to have one's own car"—the argument becomes yet more compelling.

To be sure, the social configuration and historical reality of needs is a psychosocial phenomenon with political meaning. How the needs of a particular population are shaped, what kinds of needs the members of a given group or social class develop, how needs are hierarchically organized in different strata—all these are processes that have to do directly and essentially with a society's political organization. To the extent that a set of needs corresponds to the demands of the established political order, it will benefit the interests of the dominant classes, whose social power will tend to be bolstered by this good match. Likewise, if needs fall outside the bounds of the ruling order's interests, or contradict them, those needs turn into a potential for rebellion and political subversion. Thus, people's political socialization is necessarily tied to the way their needs are formed and organized, both in terms of how their primary needs were historically shaped and in terms of the types of secondary needs they have gone on to elaborate (see Knutson, 1973).

According to Dawson and Prewitt (1969, p. 13 ffnt), "political socialization processes operate at both the individual and community levels," with the former involving the development of a self, or political subject, and the latter the transmission of culture. The argument is that the self, even when it has no explicit political orientation, is necessarily a political self, for its needs, orientations, and attitudes have direct implications for the political system. The difference between a political self and a nonpolitical self is in the degree to which one is conscious of how one's needs relate to political consequences; or stated differently, the extent to which one's values, principles, and actions are or are not consistent with one's needs.

"The political self," Dawson and Prewitt (1969, p. 19) point out, "is made—not born. . . . It is political socialization which molds and shapes the citizen's relationship to the political community. Part of this process can be seen as taking general predispositions of the child and directing them toward political objects." This is an acceptable point of view; however, one would have to add that the molding of a relationship between the citizen and the political community is already implicit in the shaping of needs, values, and lifestyle.

The organization of a frame of reference presupposes an implicit political attitude, whether or not the individual comes to recognize that organization in his or her life or consciously reflects on it. Some predispositions become political by coming into contact with explicitly political objects; but, even when this process does not take place, the standard of living and lifestyle of any given person will incorporate a number of the political order's demands. The need to have one's own car is a political demand, even when it is not made explicit. As Frey (1964) points out, political socialization goes beyond the transmission of information and evaluation of the formal government. It also includes more general attitudes about the use and distribution of power, so that even if a particular family never discusses politics, the children of that family are still undergoing political socialization. They are acquiring some basic attitudes toward authority and toward what kinds of influence and forms of conduct should be accepted as legitimate, and they are gaining a general impression about the distribution of power in a particular system or some of its subsystems. From this perspective we can accept the position of Langton (1969, p. 5), who defines political socialization as "the process by which an individual learns politically relevant attitudinal dispositions and behavior patterns." Thus, not only what is transmitted in socialization but also what is not transmitted has political significance. An intentionally depoliticized socialization is a type of socialization that is very politicized.

Many researchers have pointed out that most families in the United States are not very interested in politics. While this may be true, it does not mean that North American children are lacking in political socialization. The values they receive at home or at school, the lifestyle ("the American Way of Life") to which they are introduced very early, constitute a political posture, or at least directly imply one. It is not by sheer accident that political figures like Nixon tend to appeal to "the silent majority," or that mediocrities like Reagan can achieve a high level of popularity and political success with the North American population.

Frey's observation cited above turns us toward a very important aspect of 15
socialization: the acquisition of a social identity. We have asserted that the individual becomes a person through socialization, that is, by becoming a social being. This means that the personal identity each individual acquires through socialization is conditioned, though not completely determined, by the particular society in which he or she grows up. All personal identity is tied to a social status and a variety of social roles that presuppose a politically sanctioned social structure. Even something as apparently remote from the political as sex has a political meaning, as the contemporary women's liberation movements have shown. To be a woman and identify as such has immediate political significance: note what happens if someone tries to reject certain aspects of what this identity has stood for.

Paulo Freire (1971) has analyzed the way in which Latin Americans acquired as part of their personal identity a host of implicit attitudes that determine individuals' basic relationships with most institutionalized political objects. For example, the needs developed by the "oppressor" demand a political system with built-in structures to maintain inequality in the distribution of wealth. Most people are not conscious of the political implications of their needs; nevertheless, as soon as something comes along to call attention to those implications, their political dimension becomes perfectly clear. Salvadoran women of the bourgeoisie, who had always valued "not mixing in politics," took to the streets in 1979 when a growing popular uprising demanded social reforms that threatened their class interests.

Berger and Luckman (1966) hold that through socialization individuals introject the objective world of the society in which they were born. Identity, objectively defined as location within a particular world, is understood subjectively as something that is appropriated *together with* that world. The world the individual internalizes, the reality that he or she constructs as *the* reality, is not abstract; it is *this* concrete, historical reality, this concrete symbolic universe, congruent with the ruling political system or at odds with it. The reality internalized by the individual, inherent in his or her political identity, involves a distribution of power, a hierarchy of values, an organization of social needs—that serve to a greater or lesser degree the interests of the dominant classes.

What, then, is political socialization? In keeping with what has been said so far, we can define it as *the individual construction of a reality and a personal identity that are or are not consistent with a particular political system.* Let me explain this definition.

Political socialization is, above all, a process of personal formation. Each individual becomes a person through the socialization process, which is to say, through those processes which, in a dialectical interaction between one's genetic heritage and a particular society or social group, narrow down the possibilities of what one will become.

On becoming socialized, the individual internalizes a reality, an objective world, and shapes his or her own personal identity. Basically, to accept an internalized reality is to incorporate a scheme of values, a frame of reference, that will work as a system for decoding objective acts and subjective experiences. Csikszentmihalyi and Beattie (1979) maintain that the pattern of affective and cognitive "coding" one holds comes mainly from the family in which one grows up. Using the available codes, a person is able to perceive the surrounding environment in a consistent way, to interpret events in terms of an underlying causal order, to discriminate between relevant and irrelevant stimuli, and to decide what actions are appropriate in a given situation.

It should be stressed that this cognitive structure is not simply a style of knowing; it also includes contents and values. It has to do with what certain European social psychologists, following Durkheim, have termed *social representations* (see Farr, 1984; Jodelet, 1984). In the case analyzed by Freire (1971) the "oppressors" not only perceive the world from a perspective of domination and superiority, but feel that in the natural order of things everything—both objects and persons—belongs to them. Hence, reality is shaped not simply by the transmission of an objective structure of knowledge but by the acceptance of an evaluative scheme for analyzing that supposedly objective reality. Socialization involves both the formation of people's ways of knowing and the criteria they use for evaluating what is known.

Through socialization, the individual also acquires a personal identity. This identity or personal "I" locates individuals in the world with respect to others, placing them within the matrix of interpersonal relations that characterizes all societies of history. Identity constitutes, at least in part, the human condition Marx perceived so clearly when he defined the essence of humankind as "the ensemble of the social relations" (Marx, 1845, p. 122). This is not to say that the human being is not "more than" that confluence of social relations. What it argues is that the individual's personal identity grows out of the combined social influences of his or her particular historical situation. What an individual comes to be or not be that is "more than" that, I see as a different problem.

Our discussion up to now has not been specifically about political socialization, but applies rather to the whole socialization process. More specific to political socialization is the question of how an individual's personal identity and reality relate to a given political system. Political character comes from the way an individual's identity and world fit the political system of the society in which he or she lives. A successful political socialization from the point of view of the established system would be one in which the individual's thoughts, values, and abilities are congruent with those of the political system—with the interests of the dominant classes and the hierarchy of values the system implicitly or explicitly defends.

This conception of political socialization does not deny the part played by what are usually considered socialization processes; for example, the experience the individual has with authority figures, or people's relations with formal political objects and symbols such as the government, the president, the army, the national flag, or political parties. What it claims is that these types of experiences and relationships are concrete instances through which a more general cognitive structure is actualized or by which more fundamental values become concretized. But those are not the only instances shaped by the cognitive-evaluative schemes, or even the most important ones. The child is learning constantly how to behave according to certain values and to judge life from certain frames of reference. Moreover, day after day the child is learning the theoretical and practical ways of organizing needs and getting them met by means of these cognitive-evaluative structures. And these structures and needs either are or are not congruent with the interests of the dominant classes, with the ruling political system.

In his distinction between a "latent" and a "manifest" political socialization, 25 Almond (1960) sets forth something similar to this, though not identical. His idea of latent political socialization includes personality formation and the learning of basic values that are not necessarily political but have political consequences. Manifest political socialization consists in "the explicit transmission of information, values, or feelings vis-à-vis the roles, inputs, and outputs of other social systems such as the family which affect attitudes toward analogous roles, inputs and outputs of the political system" (Almond, 1960, p. 28).

Time and again, political revolutions have found upon taking power that one of their staunchest enemies is the cognitive-evaluative structure—the personal reference scheme internalized by large sectors of the population during their socialization under the "old regime" (see Le Vine, 1963). That was so in the Cuban revolution, for example, as Oscar Lewis had occasion to confirm personally (see Lewis, Lewis, and Rigdon, 1977a), and as was made manifest by the exodus of the [disaffected] Marielitos from Cuba [in 1980]. Wilhelm Reich (1933) captured the essence of the problem when he held that a political system could survive only if it succeeded in molding the basic character of its citizens to fit its political agenda.

The absence of an explicitly political posture in no way proves "apoliticism." This was shown in the case of Chile during the Popular Unity government [of Salvador Allende, 1970–1973] (Zúñiga, 1975) and in the case of the Salvadoran oligarchy when its government tried to bring about a very timid project of "agrarian transformation" (Martín-Baró, 1977c). In El Salvador, values such as "development," "productivity," "technology," and "Christian faith," apparently innocuous and apolitical, show their political essence and consequences the minute practical measures are introduced that challenge not the values per se but the political system. When the agrarian reform was enacted, the Salvadoran oligarchy in the name of those values demanded a retention of the established political system, and in the name of those values fought all political change, first peacefully, then violently (see also Martín-Baró, 1985j). What we can conclude from this is that the individual socialized in those values has, through the very same socialization process, also been politically socialized, for those internalized values and those cognitive structures were congruent with one particular political system but incongruent with alternative possibilities.

The study of political socialization has to focus on the processes by which individual needs, thoughts, and values are formed with respect to the needs, thoughts, and values demanded by a given sociopolitical system. A congruence or incongruence may be expressed in a child's relationship to explicitly political objects and symbols, but this expression is not the one with the greatest political importance, and surely not the only one that exists. An examination of the standard of living, of the way activities are organized and how much time is devoted to each one, of the kinds of experiences most frequently sought, could supply excellent information on the type of political system to which the individual is being socialized. In the long run, it is this type of congruence or incongruence that will determine most decisively the explicit political actions the individual adopts in his or her adult life.

Bibliography

Almond, G. 1960. "A Functional Approach to Comparative Politics." In G. A. Almond and J. S. Coleman, eds., *The Politics of Developing Areas*. Princeton: Princeton UP.

Arendt, H. 1958. *The Human Condition*. Chicago: U. of Chicago Press.

Berger, P. L., and T. Luckman. 1966. *The Social Construction of Reality*. New York: Doubleday.

Czikszentmihalyi, M., and O. Beattie. 1979. "Life Themes: A Theoretical and Empirical Exploration of Their Origins and Effects." *Journal of Humanistic Psychology* 19: 45–63.

Dawson, R. E., and K. Prewitt. 1969. *Political Socialization*. Boston: Little, Brown.

Farr, R. M. 1984. "Les representations Sociales." In Moscovici, 1984.

Freire, P. 1971. *Pedagogy of the Oppressed*. New York: Herder and Herder.

Frey, F. W. 1964. "Political Socialization in Developing Nations." Presented at a Political Research Development Conference at the Interuniversity Consortium for Political Research, Ann Arbor, July-Aug.

Jodelet, D. 1984. "Representation Sociale: Phenomenes, Concept et Theorie." In Moscovici, 1984.

Knutson, J. N. 1973. "Personality in the Study of Politics." In, J. N. Knutson, ed., *Handbook of Political Psychology*. San Francisco: Jossey-Bass.

Langton, K. 1969. *Political Socialization*. New York: Oxford UP.

Lasswell, H. D. 1949. "The Language of Power." In H. D. Lasswell and N. Leites, eds., *Language of Politics*. New York: G. W. Stewart.

Le Vine, R.A. 1963. "Political Socialization and Culture Change." In C. Geertz, ed., *Old Societies and New States.* New York: Free Press.

Lewis, O., R. M. Lewis, and S. Rigdon. 1977a. *Four Men—Living the Revolution: An Oral History of Contemporary Cuba.* Urbana: U. of Illinois Press.

Martín-Baró, Ignacio. 1985j. "Conflicto Social e Ideologia Cientifica: De Chile a El. Salvador." Presented at 20th Interamerican Congress of Psychology, Caracas.

_____1983a. *Accion e Ideologia: Psicologia Social desde Centroamerica.* San Salvador: UCA Editories.

_____1977c. "Social Attitudes and Group Conflict in El Salvador." Master's Thesis, U. of Chicago.

Marx, K. 1845. "Theses on Feuerbach." In K. Marx and F. Engels, *The German Ideology*, ed., C. J. Arthur. New York: International Publishers, 1969.

Moscovici, S. 1972. "Society and Theory in Social Psychology." In J. Isreal and H. Tajfel, eds., *The Context of Social Psychology: A Critical Assessment.* London: Academic Press.

_____ed. 1984. *Psychologie Sociale.* Paris: Presses Universitaires de France.

Reich, W. 1933. *The Mass Psychology of Fascism.* New York: Farrar, Straus and Giroux, 1970.

Sève, L. 1975. *Marxism and the Theory of Human Personality.* London: Lawrence and Wishart.

Sherif, M., and C. W. Sherif. 1964. *Reference Groups: Exploration into Conformity and Deviation of Adolescents.* Chicago: Henry Regnery.

Zúñiga, R. 1975. "The Experimenting Society and Radical Social Reform: The Role of the Social Scientist in Chile's Unidad Popular Experience." *American Psychologist* 30: 99–115.

● Building the Frame Through Writing

1. Martín-Baró maintains in paragraph 3 that "there does not first exist a person, who then goes on to become socialized, but rather that the individual becomes an individual, a human person, by virtue of becoming socialized."

   • How does this idea fit with Voloshinov's argument (see p. 171)? Are these two essentially saying the same things?

   • Does this quote mean that to be socialized essentially means to become an ideological being? Explain how these ideas might contradict or complicate your own beliefs about yourself as an individual, as a unique personality.

2. In discussing the relationship between individuals and societies, Martín-Baró says, "the personal identity each individual acquires through socialization is conditioned, though not completely determined, by the particular society in which he or she grows up" (para. 15). One of the recurrent complaints about materialist thinking is that it's formulaic or overly mechanistic—that systems

are given priority in terms of analysis at the expense of the possibilities for individual creativity or action.

- How does Martín-Baró address this complaint in the sentence above?
- How does *dialectical* thinking explain Martín-Baró's point?

3. Can you identify specific passages in this excerpt that you think could help explain why the Salvadoran military would consider Martín-Baró to be a subversive, and therefore someone to be silenced? What ideas might be threatening to an authoritarian government?

4. Here's a portion of the listing of murder victims from the El Mozote region of El Salvador, a systematic killing spree in December 1981. In his book *Massacre at El Mozote*, author Mark Danner supplies copious data to back up his contentions. The simple, short descriptions in this list are not without rhetorical "positioning." See if you can explain how even simple lists can help create narratives or stories. What stories can you construct just from using this list?

78. CHILD, 9 months old, daughter of Eugenia Claros and granddaughter of Moisés Claros
79. BENJAMÍN ANTONIO CLAROS, 45, son of Moisés Claros
80. ANASTACIA MÁRQUEZ, 40, pregnant at time of death, companion of Benjamín Antonio Claros
81. MATÍAS MÁRQUEZ, 75, carpenter, father of Anastacia Márquez
82. MARÍA ARGUETA, 30, companion of Matías Márquez
83. DOLORES MÁRQUEZ, 25, pregnant at time of death, daughter of Matías Márquez
84. LUCÍO MÁRQUEZ, 45, day laborer, companion of Dolores Márquez
85. CHILD, 7, son of Dolores Márquez and Lucío Márquez
86. CHILD, 5, son of Dolores Márquez and Lucío Márquez
87. DOMINGA MÁRQUEZ, 70, mother of Lucío Márquez
88. CHILD, 5, daughter of Benjamín Claros (victim #79) and Anastacia Márquez (victim #80)
89. CHILD, 6, son of Benjamín Claros (victim #79) and Anastacia Márquez (victim #80)
90. CHILD, 9, son of Benjamín Claros (victim #79) and Anastacia Márquez (victim #80)
91. CHILD, 11, son of Benjamín Claros (victim #79) and Anastacia Márquez (victim #80)
92. FRANCISCO CLAROS, 80, day laborer, cousin of Moisés Claros (victim #70)
93. ROGELIA DÍAZ, 76, wife of Francisco Claros
94. BOY, 16, paralyzed, grandson of Francisco Claros
95. PAULINA MÁRQUEZ CLAROS OR PAULINA CLAROS OR PAULINA DÍAZ, 60
96. TELÉSFORO MÁRQUEZ, 35, deaf and mute, son of Paulina Márquez
97. LORENZO CLAROS OR LORENZO DÍAZ, 25, son of Paulina Márquez and brother of Telésforo Márquez
98. EUGENIO VIGIL, 60, farmer

99. AGUSTINA VIGIL, 25, pregnant at time of death, daughter of Eugenio Vigil
100. CHILD, 7, daughter of Agustina Vigil
101. MARCELINA VIGIL, 22, daughter of Eugenio Vigil
102. DIONISIO MÁRQUEZ, 20, day laborer, husband of Marcelina Vigil
103. MIGUEL MÁRQUEZ, 70, day laborer, father of Dionisio Márquez
104. CHILD, 5, son of Dionisio Márquez
105. CHILD, 9 months old, daughter of Dionisio Márquez
106. MARÍA ANSELMA MÁRQUEZ, 25, pregnant at time of death, daughter of Miguel Márquez
107. ARTURO GIDIO CHICAS, 39, day laborer, companion of Anselma Márquez

. . .

759. CRESCENCIA PÉREZ, 18, sister of Máximo Pérez
760. CARLOS ORTÍZ, 48, day laborer
761. TERESO DE JESÚS LUNA, 14, day laborer, deaf and mute
762. NATIVIDAD LUNA, 18, cousin of Tereso de Jesús Luna
763. OCTAVIANA LUNA, 8 months old, daughter of Natividad Luna
764. JULIA N., 12
765. WOMAN, 50
766. GIRL, 15, daughter of victim #765
767. GIRL, 13, daughter of victim #765

Lying-In: A History of Childbirth in America
RICHARD WERTZ and DOROTHY WERTZ

The title of this 1997 book aptly describes its contents: a history of childbirth in America. The authors examine social and political factors that have helped define American medical practices for delivering babies, from colonial times to the present. These excerpts are from the chapter titled "The New Midwifery."

The **"Popular Health Movement,"** as historians have labeled it, peaked in the 1830s and 1840s but remained influential throughout the century. Both women and men attended public lectures, held separately for each sex, on physiology, and many doctored themselves rather than turn to regular physicians. The various local "Ladies' Physiological Societies" were the backbone of the popular health movement. The lecturers were men and women doctors— regular, irregular, and empiric—and women and men with an interest in women's health, such as Mary Gove Nichols, a water-cure advocate, and Samuel

Gregory, an opponent of man-midwifery. One of the most important influences of nineteenth-century feminism on birth was through the Popular Health Movement's admonition to women to know, and therefore implicitly to control, their own bodies. Such control eventually led to family limitation and to demands for less painful birth.

We have seen that nineteenth-century women could choose among a variety of therapies and practitioners. Their choice was usually dictated by social class. An upper-class woman in an Eastern city would see either an elite regular physician or a homeopath; if she were daring, she might visit a hydropathic establishment. A poor woman in the Midwest might turn to an empiric, a poorly-educated regular doctor, or a Thomsonian botanist. This variety of choice distressed regular doctors, who were fighting for professional and economic exclusivity. As long as doctors were organized only on a local basis, it was impossible to exclude irregulars from practice or even to set enforceable standards for regular practice. The American Medical Association was founded in 1848 for those purposes. Not until the end of the century, however, was organized medicine able to re-establish licensing laws. The effort succeeded only because the regulars finally accepted the homeopaths, who were of the same social class, in order to form a sufficient majority to convince state legislators that licensing was desirable.

Having finally won control of the market, doctors were able to turn to self-regulation, an ideal adopted by the American Medical Association in 1860 but not put into effective practice until after 1900. Although there had been progress in medical science and in the education of the elite and the specialists during the nineteenth century, the average doctor was still woefully undereducated. The Flexner Report in 1910 revealed that 90 percent of doctors were then without a college education and that most had attended substandard medical schools. Only after its publication did the profession impose educational requirements on the bulk of medical practitioners and take steps to accredit medical schools and close down diploma mills. Until then the average doctor had little sense of what his limits were or to whom he was responsible, for there was often no defined community of professionals and usually no community of patients.

Because of the ill-defined nature of the medical profession in the nineteenth century and the poor quality of medical education, doctors' insistence on the exclusion of women as economically dangerous competitors is quite understandable. As a group, nineteenth-century doctors were not affluent, and even their staunchest critics admitted that they could have made more money in business. Midwifery itself paid less than other types of practice, for many doctors spent long hours in attending laboring women and later had trouble collecting their fees. Yet midwifery was a guaranteed income, even if small, and it opened the way to family practice and sometimes to consultations involving many doctors and shared fees. The family and female friends who had seen a doctor "perform" successfully were likely to call him again. Doctors worried that, if midwives were allowed to deliver the upper classes, women would turn to them for treatment of other illnesses and male doctors would lose half their clientele.

As a prominent Boston doctor wrote in 1820, "If female midwifery is again introduced among the rich and influential, it will become fashionable and it will be considered indelicate to employ a physician." Doctors had to eliminate midwives in order to protect the gateway to their whole practice.

They had to mount an attack on midwives, because midwives had their   5
defenders, who argued that women were safer and more modest than the new man-midwives. For example, the *Virginia Gazette* in 1772 carried a "LETTER on the present State of MIDWIFERY," emphasizing the old idea that "Labour is Nature's Work" and needs no more art than women's experience teaches, and that it was safer when women alone attended births.

> It is a notorious fact that more Children have been lost since Women were so scandalously indecent as to employ Men than for Ages before that Practice became so general. . . . [Women midwives] never dream of having recourse to Force; the barbarous, bloody Crochet, never stained their Hands with Murder. . . . A long unimpassioned Practice, early commenced, and calmly pursued is absolutely requisite to give Men by Art, what Women attain by Nature.

The writer concluded with the statement that men-midwives also took liberties with pregnant and laboring women that were "sufficient to taint the Purity, and sully the Chastity, of any Woman breathing." The final flourish, "True Modesty is incompatible with the Idea of employing a MAN-MIDWIFE," would echo for decades, causing great distress for female patients with male attendants. Defenders of midwives made similar statements throughout the first half of the nineteenth century. Most were sectarian doctors or laymen with an interest in women's modesty. No midwives came forward to defend themselves in print.

The doctors' answer to midwives' defenders was expressed not in terms of pecuniary motives but in terms of safety and the proper place of women. After 1800 doctors' writings implied that women who presumed to supervise births had overreached their proper position in life. One of the earliest American birth manuals, the *Married Lady's Companion and Poor Man's Friend* (1808), denounced the ignorance of midwives and urged them to "submit to their station."

Two new convictions about women were at the heart of the doctors' opposition to midwives: that women were unsafe to attend deliveries and that no "true" woman would want to gain the knowledge and skills necessary to do so. An anonymous pamphlet, published in 1820 in Boston, set forth these convictions along with other reasons for excluding midwives from practice. The author, thought to have been either Dr. Walter Channing or Dr. Henry Ware, another leading obstetrician, granted that women had more "passive fortitude" than men in enduring and witnessing suffering but asserted that women lacked the power to act that was essential to being a birth attendant:

> They have not that power of action, or that active power of mind, which is essential to the practice of a surgeon. They have less power of restraining and

governing the natural tendencies to sympathy and are more disposed to yield to the expressions of acute sensibility . . . where they become the principal agents, the feelings of sympathy are too powerful for the cool exercise of judgment.

The author believed only men capable of the attitude of detached concern needed to concentrate on the techniques required in birth. It is not surprising to find the author stressing the importance of interventions, but his undervaluing of sympathy, which in most normal deliveries was the only symptomatic treatment necessary, is rather startling. Clearly, he hoped to exaggerate the need for coolness in order to discountenance the belief of many women and doctors that midwives could safely attend normal deliveries.

The author possibly had something more delicate in mind that he found hard to express. He perhaps meant to imply that women were unsuited because there were certain times when they were "disposed to yield to the expressions of acute sensibility." Doctors quite commonly believed that during menstruation women's limited bodily energy was diverted from the brain, rendering them, as doctors phrased it, idiotic. In later years another Boston doctor, Horatio Storer, explained why he thought women unfit to become surgeons. He granted that exceptional women had the necessary courage, tact, ability, money, education, and patience for the career but argued that, because the "periodical infirmity of their sex . . . in every case . . . unfits them for any responsible effort of mind," he had to oppose them. During their "condition," he said, "neither life nor limb submitted to them would be as safe as at other times," for the condition was a "temporary insanity," a time when women were "more prone than men to commit any unusual or outrageous act."

The author of the anonymous pamphlet declared that a female would find herself at times (i.e., during menstruation) totally unable to manage birth emergencies, such as hemorrhages, convulsions, manual extraction of the placenta, or inversion of the womb, when the newly delivered organ externally turned itself inside out and extruded from the body, sometimes hanging to the knees. In fact, an English midwife, Sarah Stone, had described in 1737 how she personally had handled each of these emergencies successfully. But the author's readers did not know that, and the author himself could have dismissed Stone's skill as fortuitous, exercised in times of mental clarity.

The anonymous author was also convinced that no woman could be trained [10] in the knowledge and skill of midwifery without losing her standing as a lady. In the dissecting room and in the hospital a woman would forfeit her "delicate feelings" and "refined sensibility"; she would see things that would taint her moral character. Such a woman would "unsex" herself, by which the doctors meant not only that she would lose her standing as a "lady" but also, literally, that she would be subject to physical exertions and nervous excitements that would damage her female organs irreparably and prevent her from fulfilling her social role as wife and mother.

Perhaps the epitome of this point of view about women was expressed by Dr. Charles Meigs of the Jefferson Medical College in Philadelphia in 1847 to his all-male gynecology class, in the form of a special introductory "Lecture on the Distinctive Characteristics of the Female." Meigs said, in part:

> The great administrative faculties are not hers. She plans no sublime campaign, leads no armies to battle, nor fleets to victory. The Forum is no threatre for her silver voice. . . . She discerns not the courses of the planets. . . . She composes no Iliad, no Aeneid. The strength of Milton's poetic vision was far beyond her fine and delicate perceptions. . . . Do you think that a Woman . . . could have developed, in the tender soil of her intellect, the strong idea of a Hamlet, or a Macbeth?
>
> Such is not woman's province, nature, power, or mission. She reigns in the heart; her seat and throne are by the hearthstone. The household altar is her place of worship and service. . . .
>
> She has a head almost too small for intellect and just big enough for love.

In recent years some social historians have been examining the character of Victorian separate-sex culture, the reasons for it, its extent, and its consequences. That culture expected women to be primarily wives and mothers, homebound, pious, and dependent upon husbands and other males, and it seems that some women were content in this arrangement. Doctors as a group helped both to define and to enforce the boundary between what men and women were expected to do. Thus, arguing that women could not and should not be midwives or doctoresses, male doctors were expressing a cultural judgment as well as protecting their own professional and economic interests. At the same time, they were also, of course, saying what men could and should sometimes do. Sex-linked attributes and prerogatives in birth became a central cultural event, a ritualistic definition of sexual place. In the most simple sense, it became unthinkable that a woman could both give birth and attend birth. Giving birth was the quintessential feminine act; attending birth was a fundamental expression of the controlling and performing actions suitable only for men.

Those women who sought to obtain medical training, despite the opposition of male doctors, were not merely attempting to serve the interests of female patients in modesty, morality, and more natural deliveries. They were also contesting the definition of social place determined by sex, as doctors and the dominant male culture defined and enforced it. When Harriot K. Hunt, a woman empiric who had been trained by apprenticeship to another woman, applied to Harvard Medical School in 1847, she was turned down. In 1850 she tried again and was admitted by the faculty, but the medical students' published objections forced her withdrawal. "We object," wrote the students, "to having the company of any female forced upon us, who is disposed to unsex herself and to sacrifice her modesty by appearing with men in the medical lecture room," where "no woman of any true delicacy" should be found.

Elizabeth Blackwell had greater success; after applying to twenty-nine medical schools, she was finally accepted by Geneva (New York) Medical College, a "regular" school, in 1847. Her acceptance was not intended by the school. The faculty, hesitating to reject the request of the Philadelphia Quaker physician who sponsored her, had allowed the students to cast the decisive vote, feeling confident that they would reject her. Some of the class believed the application was a hoax, others thought that a woman's presence would enliven their education, and others argued that "one of the radical principles of a Republican Government is the universal education of both sexes," which statement appeared in the formal resolution adopted by the class after a unanimous vote to admit her. Blackwell attended three four-month terms, the usual length of a medical course in rural schools, and graduated at the top of her class. She had to go to Paris and London to obtain clinical experience, as no American hospital would allow her to practice. On her return she established, with Quaker backing, the New York Infirmary for Women and Children in 1856, not only to serve the poor but to give women doctors an opportunity for clinical experience. Dr. Marie Zackrzewska, who had been the head midwife at the Royal Maternity Hospital in Berlin, became one of the leading clinicians; she was later joined by Dr. Mary Putnam Jacobi, an ardent suffragist and notable researcher on menstruation. In 1864 Elizabeth Blackwell and her sister Emily opened a medical college for women in conjunction with the infirmary. Their college was notable for having the first professorship of "hygiene," or preventive medicine, in America, a chair first occupied by Elizabeth Blackwell.

Blackwell was more interested in encouraging the entrance of women into the profession than in actually practicing medicine herself. She believed that her life work was "to open the profession to intelligent and cultivated women." The care of children, the sick, the wounded, and especially women in childbed, she argued, "has always been far more the special duty of women than of men," and "the medical practice of women is no new thing, but a necessity of society." She noted in 1855 that "the midwife has been entirely supplanted by the doctor," but she did not lament the passing of the "old midwife," who was "an imperfect institution" that "will disappear with the progress of society." "The midwife," she said, "must give place to the physician. Woman therefore must become physician." Women's practice of medicine would be a spiritual extension of maternity, which Blackwell considered women's "noblest thought," to all humanity, as the "great mothering spirit" was extended to patients.

The difficulties of admission to regular medical schools spurred the establishment of special colleges for women. The first was New England Female Medical College, originally founded in 1848 as a school for midwives by Samuel Gregory. It quickly became a regular medical school but merged in 1874 with Boston University's Homeopathic medical school. In Philadelphia, Quakers, who had always had an interest in the medical education of women, founded Woman's Medical College of Pennsylvania in 1850; it began as an Eclectic school, then became regular. Although no woman's name appeared on the opening announcement, the Quaker feminist Lucretia Mott was active in its establishment, and for many years Dr. Ann Preston, also a Quaker, was its moving spirit.

Women also founded irregular schools. New York Medical College for Women, a Homeopathic school, was founded in 1863 with the help of the suffragist Elizabeth Cady Stanton. During the nineteenth century, at least seventeen women's medical schools were founded, some of them irregular, most of them below the standards of the elite schools. Only one, Woman's Medical College of Philadelphia, survived after the Flexner Report raised medical-educational standards. Because the women's medical schools were mostly small, most women who sought medical degrees in the nineteenth century were forced to go to coeducational schools of irregular traditions such as Homeopathy, Botanism, Eclecticism, or Hydropathy, making their acceptance by the regular profession even more difficult. The first fully coeducational elite school was Johns Hopkins, opened in 1893, which had to accept women as a condition of its endowment by Mary Garrett.

Despite these problems, a number of women did acquire medical degrees of some sort during the nineteenth century. Blackwell estimated that there were two hundred women calling themselves doctors in 1855; by 1870 Federal Census records listed 527; by 1880, after some state university medical schools started admitting women, there were 2,432. In 1890 there were 4,557 and in 1900, 7,387. But these numbers seem less impressive when compared with the numbers of men in the profession. In 1905, for instance, out of 26,000 medical students, only about 1,000 were women.

Women doctors faced obstacles at every turn. They were often refused membership in local medical societies, and even the men who supported or taught them were sometimes ostracized by the profession. Hospitals usually refused to give women clinical training. Therefore women had to found their own institutions, as had Blackwell. These included the New England Hospital for Women and Children in Boston, the Woman's Hospital in Philadelphia, and the Mary Thompson Hospital in Chicago, all founded in the 1860s as institutions where women could be "physicians unto their own sex." Women's practice was small, professionally segregated from men's, and often restricted to serving the poor because many notable women doctors regarded medicine as a public service rather than a scientific or a pecuniary endeavor.

Women never entered medicine in sufficient numbers to take over as physicians to their own sex, as Blackwell had hoped. One reason for this was that the development of nursing as a profession for upper-class educated women attracted many who might otherwise have gone to medical schools. Although the nurse appeared as a necessary figure in all the "matron's manuals of midwifery" published throughout the nineteenth century, she was portrayed as an uneducated practical helper, a servant hired by the family to clean up before and after the birth and to run errands for the doctor. Her virtue lay in her obedience to the doctor, according to the manuals. Possibly some women who might have become midwives in an earlier century became practical nurses in the nineteenth century, an occupation accorded little autonomy or esteem. Toward the end of the century, under the influence of Florence Nightingale, nursing schools were established for the educated upper- or middle-class woman who desired to work at service for others rather than stay at home. Blackwell and other pioneer women physicians applauded and encouraged the upgrading of nursing, but the new nursing schools siphoned off some women who might otherwise have tried to become physicians. Instead, they were trained to obey physicians.

Women medical graduates specialized almost entirely in obstetrics and the diseases of women and children. They encountered difficulties in public acceptance, however, for they were sometimes confused with the "female physicians" who advertised in nineteenth-century newspapers and who were usually uneducated, illegal abortionists. Some male obstetricians lampooned women doctors as feminists, as unmarried, and, above all, as a threat to motherhood. The men implied that such women were promoting family limitation and abortion. In 1852 one doctor lecturing at King's College Medical School argued:

> We have lecturers and lecturesses, and female colleges, where the very large and highly intelligent classes are taught how to get children, and especially how not to get them. The Women's Rights Convention cannot see why women should bear children more than men, and while waiting some plan to equalize the matter, they refuse to bear them themselves.

As a final irony, men doctors charged that women physicians were vulgar and coarse and used street language. Real ladies should prefer gentlemen doctors, who would be courteous and treat them with delicacy.

Many early women doctors were indeed feminists, and many hoped that obstetrics would become the province of women. It is questionable, however, whether feminism had any direct effect upon the therapies used by women physicians. The number of women who practiced was so small and so far outside the mainstream of research and teaching that women could have no effect on the course of obstetric medicine. It is possible that women may have intervened less frequently in birth than did men, but even if their practices differed, and it is uncertain whether they did, women did not establish and teach a distinctly "female" form of obstetrics. Their own training had been dominated by traditions established by men.

The exclusion of women from obstetrical cooperation with men had important effects upon the "new practice" that was to become the dominant tradition in American medical schools. American obstetric education differed significantly from training given in France, where the principal maternity hospitals trained doctors clinically alongside student midwives. Often the hospital's midwives, who supervised all normal births, trained the doctors in normal deliveries. French doctors never lost touch with the conservative tradition that said "Dame Nature is the best midwife." In America, where midwives were not trained at all and medical education was sexually segregated, medicine turned away from the conservative tradition and became more interventionist.

Around 1810 the new midwifery in America appears to have entered a new phase, one that shaped its character and problems throughout the century. Doctors continued to regard birth as a fundamentally natural process, usually sufficient by itself to effect delivery without artful assistance, and understandable mechanistically. But this view conflicted with the exigencies of their medical practice, which called upon them to demonstrate skills. Gradually, more births seemed to require aid.

Young doctors rarely had any clinical training in what the theory of birth meant in practice. Many arrived at a birth with only lectures and book learning to guide them. If they (and the laboring patient) were fortunate, they had an older, experienced doctor or attending woman to explain what was natural and what was not. Many young men were less lucky and were embarrassed, confused, and frightened by the appearances of labor and birth. Lacking clinical training, each had to develop his own sense of what each birth required, if anything, in the way of artful assistance; each had to learn the consequence of misdirected aids.

If the doctor was in a hurry to reach another patient, he might be tempted to 25 hasten the process along by using instruments or other expedients. If the laboring woman or her female attendants urged him to assist labor, he might feel compelled to use his tools and skills even though he knew that nature was adequate but slow. He had to use his arts because he was expected to "perform." Walter Channing, Professor of Midwifery at Harvard Medical School in the early nineteenth century, remarked about the doctor, in the context of discussing a case in which forceps were used unnecessarily, that he "must do something. He cannot remain a spectator merely, where there are too many witnesses and where interest in what is going on is too deep to allow of his inaction." Channing was saying that, even though well-educated physicians recognized that natural processes were sufficient and that instruments could be dangerous, in their practice they also had to appear to *do* something for their patient's symptoms, whether that entailed giving a drug to alleviate pain or shortening labor by using the forceps. The doctor could not appear to be indifferent or inattentive or useless. He had to establish his identity by doing something, preferably something to make the patient feel better. And if witnesses were present there was perhaps even more reason to "perform." Channing concluded: "Let him be collected and calm, and he will probably do little he will afterwards look upon and regret."

If educated physicians found it difficult in practice to appeal before their patients to the reliability of nature and the dangers of instruments, one can imagine what less confident and less competent doctors did with instruments in order to appear useful. A number of horror stories from the early decades of the century have been detailed by men and women who believed that doctors used their instruments unfairly and incompetently to drive midwives from practice.

Whatever the truth may be about the harm done, it is easy to believe that instruments were used regularly by doctors to establish their superior status.

If doctors believed that they had to perform in order to appear useful and to win approval, it is very likely that women, on the other hand, began to expect that more might go wrong with birth processes than they had previously believed. In the context of social childbirth, which, we have noted, meant that women friends and kin were present at delivery, the appearance of forceps in one birth established the possibility of their being used in subsequent births. In short, women may have come to anticipate difficult births whether or not doctors urged that possibility as a means of selling themselves. Having seen the "best," perhaps each woman wanted the "best" for her delivery, whether she needed it or not.

Strange as it may sound, women may in fact have been choosing male attendants because they wanted a guaranteed performance, in the sense of both guaranteed safety and guaranteed fashionableness. Choosing the best medical care is itself a kind of fashion. But in addition women may have wanted a guaranteed audience, the male attendant, for quite specific purposes; namely, they may have wanted a representative male to see their pain and suffering in order that their femininity might be established and their pain verified before men. Women, then, could have had a range of important reasons for choosing male doctors to perform: for themselves, safety; for the company of women, fashion; for the world of men, femininity.

So a curious inconsistency arose between the principle of noninterference in nature and the exigencies of professional practice. Teachers of midwifery continued to stress the adequacy of nature and the danger of instruments. Samuel Bard, Dean of King's College Medical School, wrote a text on midwifery in 1807 in which he refused even to discuss forceps because he believed that interventions by unskilled men, usually inspired by Smellie's writings, were more dangerous than the most desperate case left to nature. Bard's successors made the same points in the 1830s and 1840s. Dr. Chandler Gilman, Professor of Obstetrics at the College of Physicians and Surgeons in New York from 1841 to 1865, taught his students that "Dame Nature is the best midwife in the world. . . . Meddlesome midwifery is fraught with evil. . . . The less done generally the better. Non-interference is the cornerstone of midwifery." This instruction often went unheeded, however, because young doctors often resorted to instruments in haste or in confusion, or because they were poorly trained and unsupervised in practice, but also, as we have indicated, because physicians, whatever their state of knowledge, were expected to do something.

What they could do—the number of techniques to aid and control natural 30 processes—gradually increased. In 1808, for example, Dr. John Stearns of upper New York State learned from an immigrant German midwife of a new means to effect the mechanics of birth. This was ergot, a powerful natural drug that stimulates uterine muscles when given orally. Ergot is a fungus that grows on rye and other stored grains. It causes powerful and unremitting contractions.

Stearns stressed its value in saving the doctor's time and in relieving the distress and agony of long labor. Ergot also quickens the expulsion of the placenta and stems hemorrhage by compelling the uterus to contract. Stearns claimed that ergot had no ill effects but warned that it should be given only after the fetus was positioned for easy delivery, for it induced an incessant action that left no time to turn a child in the birth canal or uterus.

There was in fact no antidote to ergot's rapid and uncontrollable effects until anesthesia became available in later decades. So if the fetus did not move as expected, the drug could cause the uterus to mold itself around the child, rupturing the uterus and killing the child. Ergot, like most new medical arts for birth, was a mix of danger and benefit. Critics of meddlesome doctors said that they often used it simply to save time. However true that was, ergot certainly fitted the mechanistic view of birth, posed a dilemma to doctors about wise use, and enlarged the doctors' range of arts for controlling birth. Doctors eventually determined that using ergot to induce labor without an antidote was too dangerous and limited its use to expelling the placenta or stopping hemorrhage.

Despite the theory of the naturalness of birth and the danger of intervention, the movement in midwifery was in the opposite direction, to less reliance on nature and more reliance on artful intervention. The shift appeared during the 1820s in discussions as to what doctors should call themselves when they practiced the new midwifery. "Male-midwife," "midman," "man-midwife," "physician man-midwife," and even "androboethogynist" were terms too clumsy, too reminiscent of the female title, or too unreflective of the new science and skill. "Accoucheur" sounded better but was French. The doctors of course ignored Elizabeth Nihell's earlier, acid suggestion that they call themselves "pudendists" after the area of the body that so interested them. Then an English doctor suggested in 1828 that "obstetrician" was as appropriate a term as any. Coming from the Latin meaning "to stand before," it had the advantage of sounding like other honorable professions, such as "electrician" or "geometrician," in which men variously understood and dominated nature.

The renaming of the practice of midwifery symbolized doctors' new sense of themselves as professional actors. In fact, the movement toward greater dominance over birth's natural processes cannot be understood unless midwifery is seen in the context of general medical practice. In that perspective, several relations between midwifery and general practice become clearly important. In the first place, midwifery continued during the first half of the nineteenth century to be one of the few areas of general practice where doctors had a scientific understanding and useful medical arts. That meant that practicing midwifery was central to doctors' attempts to build a practice, earn fees, and achieve some status, for birth was one physical condition they were confident they knew how to treat. And they were successful in the great majority of cases because birth itself was usually successful. Treating birth was without the risk of treating many other conditions, but doctors got the credit nonetheless.

In the second place, however, birth was simply one condition among many that doctors treated, and the therapeutic approach they took to other conditions tended to spill over into their treatment of birth. For most physical conditions of illness doctors did not know what processes of nature were at work. They tended therefore to treat the patient and the patient's symptoms rather than the processes of disease, which they did not see and were usually not looking for. By treating his or her symptoms the doctors did something for the patient and thereby gained approbation. The doctors' status came from pleasing the patients rather than from curing diseases. That was a risky endeavor, for sometimes patients judged the treatment offered to relieve symptoms to be worthless or even more disabling than the symptoms themselves. But patients expected doctors to do something for them, an expectation that carried into birth also. So neither doctors nor patients were inclined to allow the natural processes of birth to suffice.

There is no need to try to explain this contradiction by saying that doctors were ignorant, greedy, clumsy, hasty, or salacious in using medical arts unnecessarily (although some may have been), for the contradiction reflects primarily the kind of therapy that was dominant in prescientific medicine.

The relations between midwifery and general medical practice become clearer if one considers what doctors did when they confronted a birth that did not conform to their understanding of birth's natural processes. Their mechanistic view could not explain such symptoms as convulsions or high fevers, occasionally associated with birth. Yet doctors did not walk away from such conditions as being mysterious or untreatable, for they were committed to the mastery of birth. Rather, they treated the strange symptoms with general therapies just as they might treat regular symptoms of birth with medical arts such as forceps and ergot.

Bloodletting was a popular therapy for many symptoms, and doctors often applied it to births that seemed unusual to them. If a pregnant woman seemed to be florid or perspiring, the doctor might place her in a chair, open a vein in her arm, and allow her to bleed until she fainted. Some doctors bled women to unconsciousness to counter delivery pains. A doctor in 1851 opened the temporal arteries of a woman who was having convulsions during birth, "determined to bleed her until the convulsion ceased or as long as the blood would flow." He found it impossible to catch the blood thrown about during her convulsions, but the woman eventually completed her delivery successfully and survived. Bloodletting was also initiated when a woman developed high fever after delivery. Salmon P. Chase, Lincoln's Secretary of the Treasury and later Chief Justice, told in his diary how a group of doctors took 50 ounces of blood from his wife to relieve her fever. The doctors gave careful attention to the strength and frequency of her pulse, debating and deliberating upon the meaning of the symptom, until finally Mrs. Chase died.

For localized pain, doctors applied leeches to draw out blood from the affected region. A distended abdomen after delivery might merit the application of twelve leeches; a headache, six on the temple; vaginal pain also merited several.

35

Another popular therapy was calomel, a chloride of mercury that irritated the intestine and purged it. A woman suffering puerperal fever might be given extended doses to reduce swelling by purging her bodily contents. If the calomel acted too violently, the doctors could retard it by administering opium. Doctors often gave emetics to induce vomiting when expectant women had convulsions, for they speculated that emetics might be specifics for hysteria or other nervous diseases causing convulsions.

An expectant or laboring woman showing unusual symptoms might be subjected to a battery of such agents as doctors sought to restore her symptoms to a normal balance. In a famous case in Boston in 1833 a woman had convulsions a month before her expected delivery. The doctors bled her of 8 ounces and gave her a purgative. The next day she again had convulsions, and they took 22 ounces of blood. After 90 minutes she had a headache, and the doctors took 18 more ounces of blood, gave emetics to cause vomiting, and put ice on her head and mustard plasters on her feet. Nearly four hours later she had another convulsion, and they took 12 ounces, and soon after, 6 more. By then she had lapsed into a deep coma, so the doctors doused her with cold water but could not revive her. Soon her cervix began to dilate, so the doctors gave ergot to induce labor. Shortly before delivery she convulsed again, and they applied ice and mustard plasters again and also gave a vomiting agent and calomel to purge her bowels. In six hours she delivered a stillborn child. After two days she regained consciousness and recovered. The doctors considered this a conservative treatment, even though they had removed two-fifths of her blood in a two-day period, for they had not artificially dilated her womb or used instruments to expedite delivery.

Symptomatic treatment was intended not simply to make the patient feel better—often the treatment was quite violent, or "heroic"—but to restore some balance of healthy appearances. Nor were the therapies given to ailing women more intrusive or different from therapies given to suffering men. The therapies were not, in most instances, forced upon the patients without their foreknowledge or consent. People were often eager to be made healthy and willing to endure strenuous therapies to this end. Doctors did believe, however, that some groups of people were more susceptible to illness than others and that different groups also required, or deserved, different treatments.

These views reflected in large part the doctors' awareness of cultural classifications of people; in other words, the culture's position on the relative social worth of different social classes influenced doctors' views about whose health was likely to be endangered, how their endangered health affected the whole society, and what treatments, if any, were suitable. For birth this meant, for example, that doctors believed it more important for them to attend the delivery of children by middle- and upper-class women than the delivery of children by the poor. It meant that doctors expected "fashionable" women to suffer more difficult deliveries because their tight clothing, rich diet and lack of exercise were unhealthy and because they were believed to be more susceptible to nervous strain. It also meant that doctors thought it fitting for unmarried and otherwise disreputable mothers not to receive charitable care along with other poor but respectable women.

There is abundant evidence that doctors came to believe in time that middle- and upper-class women typically had more difficult deliveries than, for example, farm women. One cannot find an objective measure of the accuracy of their perception, nor, unfortunately and more to the point, can one find whether their perception that some women were having more difficult deliveries led doctors consistently to use more intervention in attending them than in attending poorer women with normal deliveries. Doctors' perception of the relative difficulty of deliveries was part of their tendency to associate different kinds of sickness with different social classes. They expected to find the symptoms of certain illnesses in certain groups of people, and therefore looked for those particular symptoms or conditions. In the nineteenth century upper-class urban women were generally expected to be sensitive and delicate, while farm women were expected to be robust. Some doctors even believed that the evolutionary result of education was to produce smaller pelves in women and larger heads in babies, leading to more difficult births among civilized women. There is no evidence that these beliefs were medically accurate. Whether a doctor considered a patient "sick" or "healthy" depended in part upon class-related standards of health and illness rather than on objective scientific standards of sickness.

Treatment probably varied according to the doctor's perception of a woman's class and individual character. At some times and places the treatment given probably reflected the patient's class as much as her symptoms. Thus some doctors may have withheld the use of instruments from their upper-class patients in the belief that they were too fragile to undergo instrumental delivery. The same doctors may have used instruments needlessly on poor patients, who were considered healthy enough to stand anything, in order to save the doctor's time and permit him to rush off to the bedside of a wealthier patient. On the other hand, some doctors may have used instruments on the upper-class women in order to shorten labor, believing that they could not endure prolonged pain or were too weak to bring forth children unassisted, and also in order to justify higher fees. The same doctors may have withheld forceps from poor women whom they considered healthy enough to stand several days of labor. Unfortunately, there is no way of knowing exactly how treatments differed according to class, for very few doctors kept records of their private patients. The records now extant are for the small number of people, perhaps 5 percent of the population, who were treated in hospitals in the nineteenth century. Only poor women, most unmarried, delivered in hospitals, so the records do not cover a cross-section of classes. These hospital records do indicate a large number of instrumental deliveries and sometimes give the reasons as the patient's own "laziness" or "stupidity" in being unable to finish a birth. It is likely that doctors' expectations of lower-class performance are reflected here. Hospital records also reflect the use of poor patients for training or experimentation, another reason for a high incidence of instrumental deliveries.

The fact that doctors' tendency to classify patients according to suscept-   45
ibility did not lead to consistent differences in treatment is an important indication that they were not merely slavish adherents to a mechanistic view of
nature or to cultural and class interests. Doctors were still treating individual
women, not machines and not social types. The possibility of stereotypical
classification and treatment, however, remained a lively threat to more subtle
discernments of individual symptoms and to truly artful applications of
treatment in birth.

At the same time, it was possible that patients would find even unbiased
treatments offensively painful, ineffective, and expensive, or would doubt that
the doctor had a scientific reason for giving them. Such persons could seek
other treatments, often administered by laypeople or by themselves. Yet those
treatments, including treatments for birth, were also directed toward symptoms.
At a time when diseases were unrecognized and their causes unknown, the test
of therapy was the patient's whole response, not the curing of disease. So
patients who resented treatments as painful, ineffective, or officious rejected the
doctor and the treatments. A woman who gave birth in Ohio in 1846 recalled
that the doctor bled her and then gave her ergot even though the birth was
proceeding, in her view, quite normally. She thought he was simply drunk and
in a hurry and angrily judged him a "bad man."

The takeover of birth by male doctors in America was an unusual phenomenon in comparison to France and England, where traditional midwifery
continued as a much more significant part of birth. Practice developed differently
in America because the society itself expanded more rapidly and the medical profession grew more quickly to doctor in ever new communities. American mobility
left fewer stable communities than in France or England, and thus networks
of women to support midwives were more often broken. The standards of the
American medical profession were not so high or so strictly enforced as standards
in other countries, and thus there were both more "educated" doctors and more
self-proclaimed doctors in America to compete with midwives. So American midwives disappeared from view because they had less support from stable communities of women and more competition from male doctors.

The exclusion of women from midwifery and obstetrics had profound
effects upon practice. Most obviously, it gave obstetrics a sexist bias; maleness
became a necessary attribute of safety, and femaleness became a condition in
need of male medical control. Within this skewed view of ability and need, doctors found it nearly impossible to gain an objective view of what nature could do
and what art should do, for one was identified with being a woman and the
other with being a man.

The bias identified functions, attributes, and prerogatives, which unfortunately could become compulsions, so that doctors as men may have often felt
that they had to impose their form upon the processes of nature in birth.
Obstetrics acquired a basic distortion in its orientation toward nature, a confusion of the need to be masterful and even male with the need for intervention.

Samuel Bard, one of the few doctors to oppose the trend, remarked that the   50
young doctor, too often lacking the ability to discriminate about natural processes,
often became alarmed for his patient's safety and his own reputation, leading him
to seek a speedy instrumental delivery for both. A tragedy could follow, com-
pounded because the doctor might not even recognize that he had erred and might
not, therefore, learn to correct his practice. But doctors may also have found the
"indications" for intervention in their professional work—to hurry, to impress, to
win approval, and to show why men rather than women should attend births.

The thrust for male control of birth probably expressed psychosexual needs
of men, although there is no basis for discussing this historically. The doctor
appears to history more as a ritualistic figure, a representative man, identifying
and enforcing sexual roles in critical life experiences. He also provided, as
a representative scientist, important rationalizations for these roles, particularly
why women should be content to be wives and mothers, and, as a representative
of dominant cultural morality, determined the classifications of women who
deserved various kinds of treatment. Thus the doctor could bring to the event of
birth many prerogatives that had little to do with aiding natural processes, but
which he believed were essential to a healthy and safe birth.

Expectant and laboring women lost a great deal from the exclusion of
educated female birth attendants, although, of course, they would not have chosen
men if they had not believed men had more to offer, at least in the beginning
decades of the century. Eventually there were only men to choose from. Although
no doubt doctors were often sympathetic, they could never have the same point of
view as a woman who had herself borne a child and who might be more patient and
discerning about birth processes. And female attendants would not, of course, have
laid on the male prerogatives of physical and moral control of birth.

Instead, women gave birth before a male attendant in a culture that separated the sexes into widely divergent spheres of life. Birth thereby took on the
additional problem of modesty; it became a social event that challenged codes of
purity and privacy. Further, as an initiation rite for women, birth became
a moral test and a physical trial in which the male doctor, not merely the
company of women, judged a woman's passage into adult society.

● Building the Frame Through Writing

1. Paragraph 4 makes explicit claims about the interrelatedness of economic status
   and gender. Explain in your own words why women were considered unfit for
   the medical profession. What arguments do you see being proposed by male
   doctors? What kinds of ideological positions do these doctors rely on to be persuasive?

2. The authors write, "Doctors as a group helped both to define and enforce the
   boundary between what men and women were expected to do."

- Can you explain this ability to "define and enforce" by referring to specific passages from *A Contribution to the Critique of Political Economy* (p. 185)?
- In what ways can you explain the point that "male doctors were expressing a cultural judgment as well as protecting their own professional and economic interests"?
- What do you see as the connection between "cultural judgment" and "economic interests"?

3. Explain the political and social repercussions of male doctors creating a separate, "nursing" profession. What do the authors suggest lies at the heart of such a medical decision? How would you explain this "professional" classification using what you've learned about materialist theory?

Writing from a Materialist Frame

a s a m p l e d r a f t i n g p r o c e s s

Using our now familiar example of the film *Jurassic Park*, we can use a materialist perspective to generate critical questions. Although virtually every element of the film, from scene composition, to musical score, to the characters' clothing and language, can be analyzed with this critical method, we'll restrict this discussion to the strictly "monied" interests, to the influence of economic concerns on the way we interpret the story.

When we first meet the park's creator, John Hammond, he has dropped in on the two paleontologists at their work site, which houses a laboratory in a cluttered trailer. What immediately becomes clear is that this cheery old fellow is pulling all the purse strings; he's funded the couple's research, and he's willing to offer them continued, greater funding if they assent to accompany him to an island he's developing. Money supersedes, funds, and controls science from the very beginning of the story. Paradoxically, money is hardly ever mentioned when the scientists are talking. Science is, after all, above money—supposedly "uncontaminated" by mundane matters of exchange value, salaries, or profit. And yet, while the two paleontologists are pictured as hard at work, before the film has hardly begun they're *persuaded* to abandon their trailer, their research, the "regular" people they were teaching, for a trip to an as-yet unknown location on the whim of their benefactor. What kinds of messages are being sent here? In what respects are they "free" to choose to go with him, or not?

And what about the park itself? What purpose was it supposed to serve in the social or cultural life of the world? What sense do you have of what this place is eventually supposed to look like? A museum, an educational venue for the world's inquisitive minds, or an amusement park, complete with rides, ice cream, and convention center? Given what we see, who are its paying customers likely to be? It's quite unlikely any normal person in the world would be able to afford the trip. So, in this light, the whole experiment can be seen as a diversion for the rich. Hammond says he wants all people to have access, but his investors' lawyer deflects that sentiment with a joke about offering "coupon days."

Even more interesting is the characterization of the security/computer wizard. In addition to being presented as rather disgustingly preoccupied with himself, he is the only character in the film who actually discusses money. In fact, his undoing is his attempt to steal embryos to sell for personal gain. This is the unspoken "problematic" of the film. Vast sums of money underwrite the entire project, but questions of who's paying and who's making a profit are never discussed. We all know, from numerous cultural messages we receive, that only crass or greedy people would bring up cash when the discussions are about "knowledge" or "science." Like religion or philosophy or art, science and scientists are not only *not* interested in economic matters, they're disinterested. And the distinction here means everything. Not to be interested suggests that they could be, but just choose to ignore such topics. To say they're disinterested, however, is to say that subjects of money are somehow ruled out as viable, meaningful, or acceptable in these contexts. Or, like aristocracy, they prove how rich they are by not having to talk about money at all. While people caught in the grist and grime of daily existence must think about bank accounts, the truly wealthy are beyond such contamination precisely because they're already well off.

From this perspective, the whole enterprise of *Jurassic Park* is emblematic of how topics of discussion, areas of investigation, systems of thought are influenced by issues of class and property. John Hammond already "owns" history in this story, and underneath all the puzzling questions about how to best show off the dinosaurs, or what people could learn from looking at them—beneath and foundational to all this, Hammond's ownership is dependent on convincing his financial "backers" that the place will make money. The backers' agent, conveniently identified as a lawyer, appears as a shallow-minded, sleazy moneygrubber. Appropriately, he's the first to be chomped while trying to hide in an outhouse; it's almost comic relief, and some of the audience actually cheer at his demise, he's such an unsympathetic character. Notice that, despite the very real necessity for large sums of capital in order to develop the park, despite the fact that the scientists are only visiting *because* Hammond needs someone to help convince his financers, these issues are brushed off from the beginning as almost "beside the point"—the "point" being scientific discovery. Class issues on the island are concealed behind that shade of "scientific inquiry" and property issues are never seriously considered.

When we get to the end of the film, the island is a site of supreme disaster. The lawyer and sloppy computer nerd are dead, along with some dispensable others. But who escapes? The creator/owner is shaken but still alive (as are his heirs) to come up with new options. From a more distanced perspective—looking at the film as a product itself being sold to millions of eager consumers—what does the ending tell us? As a helicopter skims across the water, leaving the chaos behind, did anyone wonder whether a sequel was in the works? The story isn't finished, by any means. All the dangers of rampant dinosaurial mayhem are still there. The narrative absolutely cries out for resolution, but at the cost of another admission ticket.

Drafting an Essay

A tag line from another popular film could provide a focused title for a materialist critique of *Jurassic Park*: "Show me the money!" If you've seen *All the President's Men*, you could borrow Deep Throat's advice to "follow the money" and see what story emerges. Your task as author is to show readers how revealing the economic interests in the story line also reveals a story of class and power. We'll work dialectically to get at the social conditions of the *Jurassic Park* enterprise. Remember that we're not asking you to just accept our interpretations as truth—we couldn't possibly make that claim. Use our analysis to spark your own ideas as to how you might write from a materialist frame.

Argument: Although *Jurassic Park* pretends to be a film about what happens when legitimate science runs amok, what the story tells us *between the lines* is that corporate greed is good while private, personal attempts to get money are seen as low class, deviant, and destructive of the "natural" order. In what ways can we see corporate greed as good and "natural"?

- Hammond's character is put forth as a jovial grandfather who's investing others' money in park. But *between the lines*, he's a snake oil salesman who used to run a flea circus; he's essentially just a con man. His character, however, is never shown to be less than a well-intentioned humanitarian.

- Paleontologists lend their support to validate the scientific mission of park. But *between the lines*, the pair has no choice—Hammond controls the purse strings. Their real job is to convince investors for Hammond so they can keep their research funding, but they're shown as truth-seeking scientists who have no personal interest.

- The park itself is supposed to be seen as a "gift" to humanity, a place of great scientific discovery. But *between the lines*, it's a corporate money-making scheme, a destination resort like Disneyland, Marine World, or Las Vegas. Capitalism appears as the "natural" order of reality.

- The private, personal desire for money is shown as a negative trait, destructive of the "natural" order. The computer expert is sloppy, stupid, and obviously low class. His attempt to sell the embryos brings about the entire catastrophe. A good-looking, suave, and brilliant character—like Dr. Ian Malcolm—would be above such crass self-interest.

- None of the positive characters ever hint that they're motivated by desire for personal gain. The story is developed so that the overall conceptual umbrella is one of well-intentioned and "naturally" good people caught in crises caused by the deviant, self-serving computer specialist.

A materialist critique would show that social attitudes are constructed and manipulated by those who stand to benefit most from those values. A materialist analysis of *Jurassic Park* would move inductively to describe a narrative that's *between the lines* of the surface story line. Using elements of materialist theory, focusing on the rhetorical issues in the critique, a writer can make a coherent and persuasive argument that this film mirrors those social realities that define desires for personal gain among the masses as ugly and deviant while simultaneously disguising that desire in the ruling classes as "right," "natural," or "good."

topics for writing

1. Since by now you've worked with different aspects of materialist theory, perhaps different students could provide the class with "working" definitions of some of the terms used most frequently in such discussions. Using the chapter readings and further research, develop a working knowledge of the following critical vocabulary:

base/superstructure	ideology	hegemony	use value
exchange value	praxis	surplus value	mode of production
alienation	proletariat	bourgeoisie	capital
determinism	Fordism		

2. Which came first in the United States: compulsory education laws or child labor laws? And in which states first? One textbook "truth" about children in factories, running geared machines that often maimed them, is that these conditions changed because they were considered to be inhuman and inhumane, the result of concentrated pressure of reform movements, often headed by women who denounced the cruelty of factory life—a layered social "story" that the culture tells itself *about* itself at that time.

   • Find out for yourself through research who lobbied for child labor laws. What were the arguments? When were the first laws passed and where? When were the last child labor laws passed, and in which states? How do you explain these events? What was the "story" you learned? How does your research match up with the textbook account or with your own prior learning?

   • Having done this work, how do you think the way this "history" was taught to you could be explained by a materialist critique?

3. Much of what you've been reading relies heavily on knowledge of European history.

   • Find a reference to some historical event or date mentioned that you don't thoroughly understand and see what you can learn about it.

   • Contextualize your discussion by referring to the excerpt from which you're working; frame a question for yourself that you hope your research will help you answer.

4. In El Salvador in the 1980s, peasants were often required to show evidence of voting in order to keep their jobs in the fields. Many believed that the *padrone* or the government would know how they'd voted, and so they supported the dominant group's candidate to protect themselves and their families from economic or military retribution—an example of how material interests help *determine* how people behave or think.

Identify mechanisms, customs, behaviors in your own communities that you think would be *determining* electoral decisions. To what extent do you see voting as an expression of ideological worldviews, or support for such?

chapter **8**

Reading Critically
About Social Values

- Reading from a materialist perspective
- Seeing how knowledge is constructed and reproduced
- Understanding social values as shared knowledge

The Individual, Society, and Education
CLARENCE J. KARIER

This is the introduction to The Individual, Society, and Education, *an historical analysis of the nature of American institutionalized education. The first edition was titled* Man, Society, and Education, *but the 1986 second edition exchanged "man" for the more politically correct "individual." This name-changing is itself an example of how social pressures affect many material decisions.*

> It is open to every man to choose the direction of his strivings; and also, every man may draw comfort from Lessing's fine saying, that the search for truth is more precious than its possession.
>
> —Albert Einstein

History is not the story of man's past but rather that which certain men have come to think of as their past. One may read a particular *interpretation* of a historic period but never *the* history of that period. Historians, as human beings, can neither live in the past, which is dead, nor divorce themselves from their own subjective values acquired in the present. While Leopold von Ranke's idea of objective history served a useful function in removing history from the realm of literary fiction, his work nonetheless suffered from the same problem of subjective value judgment that marks all historical study. One can agree with Carl L. Becker that "All historical writing, even the most honest, is unconsciously subjective, since every age is bound, in spite of itself, to make the dead perform whatever tricks it finds necessary for its own peace of mind," and with Frederick Jackson Turner that "Each age writes the history of the past anew with reference to the conditions uppermost in its own time." Such frank recognition of the subjective and tentative nature of historical study need not destroy the value of historical inquiry. It should, however, sharpen our awareness of those subjective factors which give meaning to a sequence of events and ideas, as well as redirect our attention to the uses of history.

If it is true that the past is dead, that history does not repeat itself, and that history cannot prove anything, it is equally true that men persist in trying to prove things with history. There are few current debates which do not begin with a historical interpretation. Nikita Khrushchev appreciated the function of the historian when he said, "Historians are dangerous people. They are capable of upsetting everything. They must be directed." History can be and is used to support or discredit every social institution created by men. The student of the past is inevitably involved with the issues of the present.

History can also have a more personal, individualized utility. For some, historical inquiry provides a sense of continuity, a sense of space and time which seems to lighten the burden of an existential loneliness; for others, it offers new insight into current phenomena; and for still others, it affords an escape from reality.[1] But while it might be pleasing to conclude that every man is his own historian and every function of history a legitimate function, there does exist an objective world to which men must reconcile their subjective values. In one sense, the clinical psychologist is faced with a historical problem when he attempts to reconstruct the history of his patient. He must rely on empirical data while interpreting the subjective perception of the patient as well as keeping check on his own selective perception. From such complex patterns, he draws meaning for the current situation. The historian must also rely on empirical data, already subjectively screened by another age he cannot experience, to which he adds his own structure to develop meaning. Subjective judgments are made in this process, but they cannot remain private judgments. In the final analysis, historical knowledge must be public knowledge,[2] open to critical review and subject to acceptance or rejection on the basis of various criteria. Beyond the individual inquiry, historical truth is that upon which the best-informed observers can reach substantial agreement.

A student of history of education invariably finds that his inquiry takes him through at least a three-dimensional view of education. First, he is concerned with the major ideas and values which seem to predominate in any given period; second, he is concerned with the material conditions of life which seem to influence educational practice as well as ideology;[3] and third, he is concerned with actual practices in both formal and informal education of the young.

---

[1]For differing views of the uses of history, see Herbert J. Muller, *The Uses of the Past* (New York: Oxford University Press, 1952). Also see Erich Kahler, *The Meaning of History* (New York: George Braziller, Inc., 1964).

[2]*Public knowledge* is defined as that knowledge which all men can obtain if they follow the same stated canons of inquiry.

[3]*Ideology* is used in this text to mean that system of ideas and values by which men profess to live.

Focus on Ideology

This book is not a definitive history of education; it is rather an interpretive study of certain American educational ideas. The focus of the book, therefore, is limited to those systems of ideas which have given form and purpose to educational practice in the United States. This does not mean, however, that major social forces and actual practice can be ignored. On the contrary, the expressed ideology may at any one time be as much a rationalization for economic and social forces as a controlling agent. The major emphasis of this book, then, is on ideology, which is used here as only one factor in a possible constellation of factors at work in any process of educational change.

Continuity and change occur simultaneously, and ideology is a part of both processes. In this respect one can agree with Butts and Cremin, who said, "The history of education must record the history of ideas as instruments of educational change as well as social conditions that serve to accelerate or thwart educational change."[4] Modern man, living in what has been described as a post-Christian era and an age of technological determinism, tends to underestimate the importance that religion, philosophy, literature, and general ideology have had in determining educational practice. While a strong case can be made for economic determinism in American formal educational institutions, the thesis breaks down when applied to individuals. The ideology one holds seems related to personality, and personality undoubtedly is markedly affected by child-rearing practices, which, in turn, seem as much related to ideological factors as to economic forces. Any single determinant can render only partial truth and partial insight.

Focus on the Last Century

Because of the rapid changes wrought in ideology and institutional education in the century from 1865 to 1965, those hundred years are overwhelmingly important in the history of American educational thought. As both the philosopher and the theologian were asked to take a lower seat at the table of culture, it became apparent that man's concept of man and society had shifted from a sectarian, supernatural view to a more secular, naturalistic position. Increasingly, men placed their faith in a science controlled by men rather than in a theology controlled by God.

This was the era when America passed from a rural to an urban to a "rurbanized" society; from a basically agrarian society to a laissez-faire industrial economy to an affluent industrial economy; and from a rather insignificant nation to an unsure-of-itself isolationist world power to an international leader. Such a massive cultural transformation had an inevitable impact on educational

[4]Freeman Butts and Lawrence Cremin, *A History of Education in American Culture* (New York: Henry Holt and Company, 1953), p. 66.

institutions as well as on educational ideology. With the closing of the Western frontier came the opening of the educational frontier. In advising a young man about his future, it might have been customary in 1865 to suggest that he "Go West," but by 1965 he was more often advised, "Go to college!"

Most of the present American educational system, from the standpoint of institutional structure, was completed during this period. The education of the American young passed from an informal, face-to-face, community kind of instruction to a formal, bureaucratic educational establishment. Such an establishment tended to reflect the virtues and vices of the culture at large as well as the most critical intellectual, moral, and social issues of that culture. As the informal educational agencies, such as the neighborhood and family, decreased in importance, the school increased in significance. Viewed as the single most important vehicle of social mobility and as the single most important educational agency, the American school inevitably became the center of social and ideological conflict. If the geographical frontier was fraught with physical conflict, the educational frontier was scarred by ideological conflict.

Fundamental Ideological Questions

In spite of vast economic, social, and ideological change, men have persisted in asking certain significant questions that lend themselves to a broader, more meaningful interpretation of the process of education in a cultural setting. While these questions are not assumed to have any metaphysical or transcendental reality, the persistence with which men have been concerned with them may be accounted for by the fact that man is a social animal with a need to define himself, his society, and what he accepts as truth. Since education begins and ends with man, one of the most basic questions is "What is the nature of man?" Going from the microcosm to the macrocosm, an equally revelant question is "What is the nature of the good society?" In defining himself and his society, man usually asks what criterion provides a basis for truth? The criterion he comes to accept often influences his answers to the prior questions. Men, movements, and periods may be generally classified with reference to these questions, and within this context continuity and change may be detected. These are the questions through which American educational thought will be considered in this book.

Concepts of Human Nature

How men conceive human nature usually influences educational practice. If one assumes that men are inherently good, as Rousseau proclaimed, as Walt Whitman, Thoreau, and Emerson envisioned, and as Earl Kelley, Carl Rogers, and Ashley Montagu have assumed, then one advocates a child-centered curriculum. Since nature is good and the child of nature is good, educators must look to the child for clues to his natural development. What the child needs is

10

freedom to develop his natural self to become that which he is naturally capable of becoming. Emerson advised teachers:

> It is not for you to choose what he shall know, what he shall do. It is chosen and foreordained, and he only holds the key to his own secret. Wait and see the new product of nature. Respect the child. Be not too much his parent. Trespass not on his solitude.[5]

His counsel has been reaffirmed throughout the history of American educational thought by men who have premised their own thinking on the assumption that human nature is essentially good.

On the other hand, there have been those who viewed nature as evil and natural man as depraved. Just as John Cotton referred to men as "vipers" and the Reverend John White referred to the first settlers as "the very scum of the land," so, too, Cotton Mather in *A Family Well-Ordered* advised parents that "your Children are the Children of Death and the Children of Hell, and the Children of Wrath, by Nature; and that from you, this Nature is derived and conveyed unto them!" The Puritan, in attempting to amplify the importance of God, weakened the significance of man. In so doing, he automatically increased man's dependency on revealed supernatural religion. The problem of supernaturalism, with God the measure, versus naturalism, with man the measure, has continued throughout the history of Western education. How this issue is temporarily resolved for any given historical period is usually reflected in the educational system of that period.

Concepts of the Ideal Society

While education begins and ends with man, it always functions through a social system. Thinkers from Aristotle to George H. Mead have proclaimed the obvious; i.e., that man is a social animal who achieves his humanity through a social system. Formal education becomes the vehicle through which the young are inducted into the social system. Conflict arises not only around the most efficient techniques for achieving the purpose but, more significantly, around the nature of the purpose itself. At first glance, it might seem relatively easy to define what "is" and proceed to "consensus" from there. But this approach proves illusory because of at least two factors. First, the social system existing at any one time is seldom viewed as altogether desirable, except in a very static society; and, second, the judgment about what does exist within the social system is distorted by the selective perceptions of the individual or group making the analysis. These selective perceptions are usually conditioned by what the individual or group considers to be the ideal social order; and what men consider a desirable social system or a "good" society is a highly effective tool in the analysis of American educational thought. It would be neater and easier to assume that informal and formal education of the young historically proceeded in a social vacuum. This would

---

[5]Ralph Waldo Emerson, *The Complete Writings of Ralph Waldo Emerson* (New York: Wm. H. Wise and Company, 1929), p. 993.

force us, however, to ignore not only considerable educational history but much of American social and intellectual thought. The history of the idea of progress, for example, and of its corollary, social meliorism, cannot be adequately treated without consideration of education as a vehicle of social reform.

The good society, to the Puritans, was the theocratic community, which unquestionably influenced the course of educational development for colonial New England. So, too, the good society for the Enlightenment, which was a society free from religious sanctions in the civil domain, had its effect on the institutionalizing of the principle of separation of Church and State. Horace Mann's conception of a good society as one being held together with a common set of values, welded in a common set of experiences in a common school, no doubt influenced his conception of the function of public education in America, just as John Dewey's conception of a pluralistic society conditioned what he advocated in American education.

The educational ideas of the social reconstructionist in the twentieth century, from Albion Small and George S. Counts to Theodore Brameld, cannot be appraised without careful consideration of what these men deem the desirable or "good" society. Nor does it seem possible to examine realistically the ideas of other major participants in the twentieth-century educational dialog—without concern for what they consider the desirable social order. Behind much of the educational conflict in the twentieth century has been disagreement not only on what human nature is and what is an acceptable criterion of truth but also on what is to be considered the good society toward which education must strive.

15

Bases of Truth

Throughout the history of the West, men not only have defined human nature differently and viewed society differently but have also devised different criteria or bases for truth. Of these, at least five can be clearly identified and are used as an analytic guide in this book. Within the realm of public knowledge, the criteria are those of the rationalist, the empiricist, and the esthetic. Within the realm of private knowledge, our concern will center on the criteria of the mystic and the romantic.

Public Knowledge   The rationalist relies on reason and assumed universal rules of logic as the basis for truth. He usually asserts that rules of logic are discovered rather than invented and that what can be proved logical can be accepted as true. The rationalist most often operates from *a priori* assumptions and arrives at truth deductively. Much of Western thought, from Plato to Hegel, has been within a rationalistic tradition.

Still within the field of public knowledge, but at a polar position from the rationalist, is the empiricist, who relies on sense observation and a sense-experience test for the basis of his truth. The empiricist views logic as a human invention, a tool which is useful in organizing his data. Much scientific inquiry from Francis Bacon to Albert Einstein is represented by this point of view. While the work of Bacon tended to be heavy in sense observation and that of Einstein in theoretical models, the chief characteristic of these men which permits us to place them in the same tradition is that both would profess that the ultimate test of truth is the empirical test. Rationalism and empiricism are intimately related through the history of mathematics. Both the rationalist and the empiricist tend to have similar views of social reality and are inclined toward building social systems.

While some men arrive at truth through logic and others through empirical test, another group finds truth through a disciplined esthetic taste, disciplined by the ideas of the great thinkers of antiquity, or what Paul Elmer More referred to as the "noble dead." This group of men knows the truth not through a cold logic or an emotionalized intuition but through an "educated" intuition which appreciates the balance and subtle nuances of classical thought. This is the tradition of the belles-lettres, more accurately labeled classical humanism. The classical humanists, from Isocrates to Cicero, from Quintilian to Petrarch, and from Vittorino da Feltre to Erasmus, deserve the title of Schoolmasters of Western Culture. It was this tradition which defined for centuries the meaning of an educated man and of a liberal education. It was also this tradition which fought the battle against the rationalistic mind of the scholastics during the Renaissance and proved to be the most serious obstacle to the advancement of empirical science in institutions of higher learning in the seventeenth and eighteenth centuries. With some modifications, it was this tradition, embodying an esthetic approach to truth, which came to life again in the twentieth century in the form of neo-humanism as expressed by Irving Babbitt, Paul Elmer More, and Norman Foerster.

Private Knowledge   In direct conflict with the rationalist, the empiricist, and   20
the esthetic are the mystic and the romantic. To these men, ultimate truth is always a private experience. Truth is discovered by using one's intuition to commune with the source of truth, which may be either God or nature. The mystic, who is a supernaturalist, has direct experience with God, whereas the romantic communes with a transcendental nature or a pantheistic God in nature. In this tradition, ultimate truth is always subjective and private and needs no confirmation by way of a logical or empirical test. Emerson said, "A foolish consistency is the hobgoblin of little minds"; and Pascal asserted that "The heart has its reasons which the reason does not know." It is the mystic and the romantic who emphasize the individual's importance over the needs of the social organization. In a very real sense, the mystic and the romantic have been the rebels of Western social systems, whether the system was an institutionalized church or a nationalized state. Having direct relations with the source of truth, these thinkers are usually impatient with organized bureaucracy. The history of the Roman Church is replete with cases reflecting the difficulty of keeping the mystic within the organized church. In the American tradition, it was a romantic who developed the doctrine of civil disobedience that Mahatma Gandhi found so significant. It was that same romantic, Henry David Thoreau, who

cautioned his countrymen that "They are to be men first, and Americans only at a late and convenient hour."

The Importance of Ideology

By identifying the rational, the empirical, the classical esthetic, the mystic, and the romantic bases of truth, we have by no means exhausted the field. Nevertheless, these selected concepts are useful in analyzing American educational thought. There is the danger, however, of adhering too strictly to these classifications. In practice, it is difficult to find a pure mystic, a pure rationalist, or a pure empiricist. Most men tend to be some of each, depending on the kinds of questions they are facing; but significant thinkers who tend to dominate an intellectual climate of opinion for any given period are usually not eclectic in these matters but rather tend to rely predominantly on one of these criteria as a basis of their thought. Why some men have been more attracted to one tradition than to another seems to be a condition less of the forcefulness of the argument than the personal temperament of a particular individual in a particular environment. William James may very well have been correct when he assumed that the psychology of the individual and the philosophy of the individual are really two sides of the same coin. When, however, men accept diametrically opposed criteria of truth within any formal institution, such as the school system, the educational dialog becomes laden with conflict. Behind much of the discord in twentieth-century American education lie not only conflicting concepts of human nature but also conflicting bases for truth.

Sometimes the major ideas of a particular period have reached such a consensus that the answers to the questions about human nature and society are merely assumed, or taken for granted. At other times, when a current ideology is threatened, conflicting answers to these questions can usually be found behind the dust and smoke of battle. Indeed, when education becomes a battleground, it often does so for reasons far deeper than the usual problem of determining the most efficient method of educating children. Almost in an orchestral fashion, different positions come to the fore, are heard, and then fade into the background, only to return again in a different context. What causes these changes will probably remain an unanswered question. From one perspective, the ideology of one period can be viewed as a reaction to another; but from another perspective, the same ideology may be viewed as a consequence of economic and social conditions.

Perhaps the dilemma lies fundamentally in man's unique existence, which allows him to be tomorrow that which he is not today. Man is the creator who makes over not only his physical and social environment but also himself. Man the creator is a restless being who always dies a little when he fails to create and nothing inhibits his creating more than *the* truth. In this context one can agree with Lessing that "the search for truth is more precious than its possession."

● Applying a Materialist Frame

1. Karier quotes Carl L. Becker in saying, "All historical writing, even the most honest, is unconsciously subjective, since every age is bound, in spite of itself, to make the dead perform whatever tricks it finds necessary for its own peace of mind" (para 1). This is quite a damning statement for anyone who wants to say he or she can learn any "truth" from historical records. Does this imply that there's never been or going to be anything like "historical accuracy"? If that's the case, how do you move forward in any meaningful matter to try to make sense of the past?

   • How do you explain this seeming impossibility of "knowing?" How do you think we convince ourselves we know what we're talking about when we discuss what life was like in the seventh-century Scottish highlands for a clan member, or any other such information that seems to be so clear-cut? If ideologies are the stories we tell ourselves *about* ourselves, and if materialism claims to be an economic explanation for ideology, then how does this work from a materialist frame?

   • Where do you think we're going to find arguments that carry weight if we're squinting through materialist lenses? The following statement might be helpful: "While a strong case can be made for economic determinism in American formal educational institutions, the thesis breaks down when applied to individuals."

2. What would be the specific differences you might expect to see in a school predicated on "God, the measure" versus "naturalism, with man the measure"? Try to follow up on your expectations by doing some Web research to find published curricula from different religiously affiliated, private institutions and different state schools. You might, for example, just use your own major or interest area as a focus and look for how these other programs differ or jibe with yours.

   Can you draw any conclusions about the underlying ideology of the institution from looking at how it markets its curricula?

3. Do you have any personal experiences with what Karier refers to as the "conflict" and "discord" in American educational systems? What form did the conflict take? How did you recognize that discord existed?

4. Do you remember any specific issues, or events, or textbooks that caused controversy in your schooling? How were the battle lines drawn? Who voiced the positions? What happened? Did student organizations, for instance, ever get censored? events banned? clothing standards enforced?

   Where were you led to believe these decisions came from? What was the rationale given? How well did you accept that rationale?

5. Compare your own experiences with controversy with others in your class or group. What commonalities, if any, can you find? What conclusions can you draw?

Cultural Literacy: What Every American Needs to Know

E. D. HIRSCH JR.

E. D. Hirsch's 1988 book Cultural Literacy *was a bestseller when it first appeared. It attracted commentary from a variety of political positions, but could safely be said to represent the "back to basics" point of view that was popular at the time. Hirsch's ideas of cultural literacy stimulated much debate both on and off campuses, appearing as it did on the heels of open enrollment policies that brought historically marginalized students to universities and colleges. The following excerpt is from Chapter 1, "Literacy and Cultural Literacy."*

The Decline of Literate Knowledge

This book explains why we need to make some very specific educational changes in order to achieve a higher level of national literacy. It does not anatomize the literacy crisis or devote many pages to Scholastic Aptitude Test scores. It does not document at length what has already been established, that Americans do not read as well as they should. It takes no position about methods of initial reading instruction beyond insisting that content must receive as much emphasis as "skill." It does not discuss teacher training or educational funding or school governance. In fact, one of its major purposes is to break away entirely from what Jeanne S. Chall has called "the great debate" about methods of reading instruction. It focuses on what I conceive to be the great hidden problem in American education, and I hope that it reveals this problem so compellingly that anyone who is concerned about American education will be persuaded by the book's argument and act upon it.

The standard of literacy required by modern society has been rising throughout the developed world, but American literacy rates have not risen to meet this standard. What seemed an acceptable level in the 1950s is no longer acceptable in the late 1980s, when only highly literate societies can prosper economically. Much of Japan's industrial efficiency has been credited to its almost universally high level of literacy. But in the United States, only two thirds of our citizens are literate, and even among those the average level is too low and should be raised. The remaining third of our citizens need to be brought as close to true literacy as possible. Ultimately our aim should be to attain universal literacy at a very high level, to achieve not only greater economic prosperity but also greater social justice and more effective democracy. We Americans have long accepted literacy as a paramount aim of schooling, but only recently have some of us who have done research in the field begun to realize that literacy is far more than a skill and that it requires large amounts of specific information. That new insight is central to this book.

Professor Chall is one of several reading specialists who have observed that "world knowledge" is essential to the development of reading and writing skills.

What she calls world knowledge I call cultural literacy, namely, the network of information that all competent readers possess. It is the background information, stored in their minds, that enables them to take up a newspaper and read it with an adequate level of comprehension, getting the point, grasping the implications, relating what they read to the unstated context which alone gives meaning to what they read. In describing the contents of this neglected domain of background information, I try to direct attention to a new opening that can help our schools make the significant improvement in education that has so far eluded us. The achievement of high universal literacy is the key to all other fundamental improvements in American education.

Why is literacy so important in the modern world? Some of the reasons, like the need to fill out forms or get a good job, are so obvious that they needn't be discussed. But the chief reason is broader. The complex undertakings of modern life depend on the cooperation of many people with different specialties in different places. Where communications fail, so do the undertakings. (That is the moral of the story of the Tower of Babel.) The function of national literacy is to foster effective nationwide communications. Our chief instrument of communication over time and space is the standard national language which is sustained by national literacy. Mature literacy alone enables the tower to be built, the business to be well managed, and the airplane to fly without crashing. All nationwide communications, whether by telephone, radio, TV, or writing are fundamentally dependent upon literacy, for the essence of literacy is not simply reading and writing but also the effective use of the standard literate language. In Spain and most of Latin America the literate language is standard written Spanish. In Japan it is standard written Japanese. In our country it is standard written English.

Linguists have used the term "standard written English" to describe both our written and spoken language, because they want to remind us that standard spoken English is based upon forms that have been fixed in dictionaries and grammars and are adhered to in books, magazines, and newspapers. Although standard written English has no intrinsic superiority to other languages and dialects, its stable written forms have now standardized the oral forms of the language spoken by educated Americans. The chief function of literacy is to make us masters of this standard instrument of knowledge and communication, thereby enabling us to give and receive complex information orally and in writing over time and space. Advancing technology, with its constant need for fast and complex communications, has made literacy ever more essential to commerce and domestic life. The literate language is more, not less, central in our society now than it was in the days before television and the silicon chip.

The recently rediscovered insight that literacy is more than a skill is based upon knowledge that all of us unconsciously have about language. We know instinctively that to understand what somebody is saying, we must understand more than the surface meanings of words; we have to understand the context as well. The need for background information applies all the more to reading and writing. To grasp the words on a page we have to know a lot of information that isn't set down on the page.

Consider the implications of the following experiment described in an article in *Scientific American*. A researcher goes to Harvard Square in Cambridge, Massachusetts, with a tape recorder hidden in his coat pocket. Putting a copy of the *Boston Globe* under his arm, he pretends to be a native. He says to passers-by, "How do you get to Central Square?" The passers-by, thinking they are addressing a fellow Bostonian, don't even break their stride when they give their replies, which consist of a few words like "First stop on the subway."

The next day the researcher goes to the same spot, but this time he presents himself as a tourist, obviously unfamiliar with the city. "I'm from out of town," he says. "Can you tell me how to get to Central Square?" This time the tapes show that people's answers are much longer and more rudimentary. A typical one goes, "Yes, well you go down on the subway. You can see the entrance over there, and when you get downstairs you buy a token, put it in the slot, and you go over to the side that says Quincy. You take the train headed for Quincy, but you get off very soon, just the first stop is Central Square, and be sure you get off there. You'll know it because there's a big sign on the wall. It says Central Square." And so on.

Passers-by were intuitively aware that communication between strangers requires an estimate of how much relevant information can be taken for granted in the other person. If they can take a lot for granted, their communications can be short and efficient, subtle and complex. But if strangers share very little knowledge, their communications must be long and relatively rudimentary.

In order to put in perspective the importance of background knowledge in language, I want to connect the lack of it with our recent lack of success in teaching mature literacy to all students. The most broadly based evidence about our teaching of literacy comes from the National Assessment of Educational Progress (NAEP). This nationwide measurement, mandated by Congress, shows that between 1970 and 1980 seventeen-year-olds declined in their ability to understand written materials, and the decline was especially striking in the top group, those able to read at an "advanced" level. Although these scores have now begun to rise, they remain alarmingly low. Still more precise quantitative data have come from the scores of the verbal Scholastic Aptitude Test (SAT). According to John B. Carroll, a distinguished psychometrician, the verbal SAT is essentially a test of "advanced vocabulary knowledge," which makes it a fairly sensitive instrument for measuring levels of literacy. It is well known that verbal SAT scores have declined dramatically in the past fifteen years, and though recent reports have shown them rising again, it is from a very low base. Moreover, performance on the verbal SAT has been slipping steadily *at the top*. Ever fewer numbers of our best and brightest students are making high scores on the test.

Before the College Board disclosed the full statistics in 1984, antialarmists could argue that the fall in average verbal scores could be explained by the rise in the number of disadvantaged students taking the SATs. That argument can no longer be made. It's now clear that not only our disadvantaged but also our best educated and most talented young people are showing diminished verbal skills. To be precise, out of a constant pool of about a million test takers each year, 56 percent more students scored above 600 in 1972 than did so in 1984. More startling yet, the percentage drop was even greater for those scoring above 650—73 percent.

In the mid 1980s American business leaders have become alarmed by the lack of communication skills in the young people they employ. Recently, top executives of some large U.S. companies, including CBS and Exxon, met to discuss the fact that their younger middle-level executives could no longer communicate their ideas effectively in speech or writing. This group of companies has made a grant to the American Academy of Arts and Sciences to analyze the causes of this growing problem. They want to know why, despite breathtaking advances in the technology of communication, the effectiveness of business communication has been slipping, to the detriment of our competitiveness in the world. The figures from NAEP surveys and the scores on the verbal SAT are solid evidence that literacy has been declining in this country just when our need for effective literacy has been sharply rising.

I now want to juxtapose some evidence for another kind of educational decline, one that is related to the drop in literacy. During the period 1970–1985, the amount of shared knowledge that we have been able to take for granted in communicating with our fellow citizens has also been declining. More and more of our young people don't know things we used to assume they knew.

A side effect of the diminution in shared information has been a noticeable increase in the number of articles in such publications as *Newsweek* and the *Wall Street Journal* about the surprising ignorance of the young. My son John, who recently taught Latin in high school and eighth grade, often told me of experiences which indicate that these articles are not exaggerated. In one of his classes he mentioned to his students that Latin, the language they were studying, is a dead language that is no longer spoken. After his pupils had struggled for several weeks with Latin grammar and vocabulary, this news was hard for some of them to accept. One girl raised her hand to challenge my son's claim. "What do they speak in Latin America?" she demanded.

At least she had heard of Latin America. Another day my son asked his Latin class if they knew the name of an epic poem by Homer. One pupil shot up his hand and eagerly said, "The Alamo!" Was it just a slip for *The Iliad*? No, he didn't know what the Alamo was, either. To judge from other stories about information gaps in the young, many American schoolchildren are less well informed than this pupil. The following, by Benjamin J. Stein, is an excerpt from one of the most evocative recent accounts of youthful ignorance.   15

> I spend a lot of time with teen agers. Besides employing three of them part-time, I frequently conduct focus groups at Los Angeles area high schools to learn about teen agers' attitudes towards movies or television shows or nuclear arms or politicians. . . .

I have not yet found one single student in Los Angeles, in either college or high school, who could tell me the years when World War II was fought. Nor have I found one who could tell me the years when World War I was fought. Nor have I found one who knew when the American Civil War was fought. . . .

A few have known how many U.S. senators California has, but none has known how many Nevada or Oregon has. ("Really? Even though they're so small?") . . . Only two could tell me where Chicago is, even in the vaguest terms. (My particular favorite geography lesson was the junior at the University of California at Los Angeles who thought that Toronto must be in Italy. My second-favorite geography lesson is the junior at USC, a pre-law student, who thought that Washington, D.C., was in Washington State.) . . .

Only two could even approximately identify Thomas Jefferson. Only one could place the date of the Declaration of Independence. None could name even one of the first ten amendments to the Constitution or connect them with the Bill of Rights. . . .

On and on it went. On and on it goes. I have mixed up episodes of ignorance of facts with ignorance of concepts because it seems to me that there is a connection. . . . The kids I saw (and there may be lots of others who are different) are not mentally prepared to continue the society because they basically do not understand the society well enough to value it.

My son assures me that his pupils are not ignorant. They know a great deal. Like every other human group they share a tremendous amount of knowledge among themselves, much of it learned in school. The trouble is that, from the standpoint of their literacy and their ability to communicate with others in our culture, what they know is ephemeral and narrowly confined to their own generation. Many young people strikingly lack the information that writers of American books and newspapers have traditionally taken for granted among their readers from all generations. For reasons explained in this book, our children's lack of intergenerational information is a serious problem for the nation. The decline of literacy and the decline of shared knowledge are closely related, interdependent facts.

The evidence for the decline of shared knowledge is not just anecdotal. In 1978 NAEP issued a report which analyzed a large quantity of data showing that our children's knowledge of American civics had dropped significantly between 1969 and 1976. The performance of thirteen-year-olds had dropped an alarming 11 percentage points. That the drop has continued since 1976 was confirmed by preliminary results from a NAEP study conducted in late 1985. It was undertaken both because of concern about declining knowledge and because of the growing evidence of a causal connection between the drop in shared information and in literacy. The Foundations of Literacy project is measuring some of the specific information about history and literature that American seventeen-year-olds possess.

Although the full report will not be published until 1987, the preliminary field tests are disturbing. If these samplings hold up, and there is no reason to think they will not, then the results we will be reading in 1987 will show that two thirds of our seventeen-year-olds do not know that the Civil War occurred between 1850 and 1900. Three quarters do not know what *reconstruction* means. Half do not know the meaning of *Brown decision* and cannot identify either Stalin or Churchill. Three quarters are unfamiliar with the names of standard American and British authors. Moreover, our seventeen- year-olds have little sense of geography or the relative chronology of major events. Reports of youthful ignorance can no longer be considered merely impressionistic.

My encounter in the seventies with this widening knowledge gap first caused me to recognize the connection between specific background knowledge and mature literacy. The research I was doing on the reading and writing abilities of college students made me realize two things. First, we cannot assume that young people today know things that were known in the past by almost every literate person in the culture. For instance, in one experiment conducted in Richmond, Virginia, our seventeen- and eighteen-year-old subjects did not know who Grant and Lee were. Second, our results caused me to realize that we cannot treat reading and writing as empty skills, independent of specific knowledge. The reading skill of a person may vary greatly from task to task. The level of literacy exhibited in each task depends on the relevant background information that the person possesses.

The lack of wide-ranging background information among young men and women now in their twenties and thirties is an important cause of the illiteracy that large corporations are finding in their middle-level executives. In former days, when business people wrote and spoke to one another, they could be confident that they and their colleagues had studied many similar things in school. They could talk to one another with an efficiency similar to that of native Bostonians who speak to each other in the streets of Cambridge. But today's high school graduates do not reliably share much common information, even when they graduate from the same school. If young people meet as strangers, their communications resemble the uncertain, rudimentary explanations recorded in the second part of the Cambridge experiment.

My father used to write business letters that alluded to Shakespeare. These allusions were effective for conveying complex messages to his associates, because, in his day, business people could make such allusions with every expectation of being understood. For instance, in my father's commodity business, the timing of sales and purchases was all-important, and he would sometimes write or say to his colleagues, "There is a tide," without further elaboration. Those four words carried not only a lot of complex information, but also the persuasive force of a proverb. In addition to the basic practical meaning, "Act now!" what came across was a lot of implicit reasons why immediate action was important.

For some of my younger readers who may not recognize the allusion, the passage from *Julius Caesar* is:

20

> There is a tide in the affairs of men
> Which taken at the flood leads on to fortune;
> Omitted, all the voyage of their life
> Is bound in shallows and in miseries.
> On such a full sea are we now afloat,
> And we must take the current when it serves,
> Or lose our ventures.

To say "There is a tide" is better than saying "Buy (or sell) now and you'll cover expenses for the whole year, but if you fail to act right away, you may regret it the rest of your life." That would be twenty-seven words instead of four, and while the bare message of the longer statement would be conveyed, the persuasive force wouldn't. Think of the demands of such a business communication. To persuade somebody that your recommendation is wise and well- founded, you have to give lots of reasons and cite known examples and authorities. My father accomplished that and more in four words, which made quoting Shakespeare as effective as any efficiency consultant could wish. The moral of this tale is not that reading Shakespeare will help one rise in the business world. My point is a broader one. The fact that middle-level executives no longer share literate background knowledge is a chief cause of their inability to communicate effectively.

The Nature and Use of Cultural Literacy

The documented decline in shared knowledge carries implications that go far beyond the shortcomings of executives and extend to larger questions of educational policy and social justice in our country. Mina Shaughnessy was a great English teacher who devoted her professional life to helping disadvantaged students become literate. At the 1980 conference dedicated to her memory, one of the speakers who followed me to the podium was the Harvard historian and sociologist Orlando Patterson. To my delight he departed from his prepared talk to mention mine. He seconded my argument that shared information is a necessary background to true literacy. Then he extended and deepened the ideas I had presented. Here is what Professor Patterson said, as recorded in the *Proceedings* of the conference.

> Industrialized civilization [imposes] a growing cultural and structural complexity which requires persons to have a broad grasp of what Professor Hirsch has called cultural literacy: a deep understanding of mainstream culture, which no longer has much to do with white Anglo-Saxon Protestants, but with the imperatives of industrial civilization. It is the need for cultural literacy, a profound conception of the whole civilization, which is often neglected in talk about literacy.

Patterson continued by drawing a connection between background information and the ability to hold positions of responsibility and power. He was particularly concerned with the importance for blacks and other minorities of possessing this information, which is essential for improving their social and economic status.

> The people who run society at the macro-level must be literate in this culture. For this reason, it is dangerous to overemphasize the problems of basic literacy or the relevancy of literacy to specific tasks, and more constructive to emphasize that blacks will be condemned in perpetuity to oversimplified, low-level tasks and will never gain their rightful place in controlling the levers of power unless they also acquire literacy in this wider cultural sense.

Although Patterson focused his remarks on the importance of cultural literacy   25
for minorities, his observations hold for every culturally illiterate person in our nation. Indeed, as he observed, cultural literacy is not the property of any group or class.

> To assume that this wider culture is static is an error; in fact it is not. It's not a WASP culture; it doesn't belong to any group. It is essentially and constantly changing, and it is open. What is needed is recognition that the accurate metaphor or model for this wider literacy is not domination, but dialectic; each group participates and contributes, transforms and is transformed, as much as any other group. . . . The English language no longer belongs to any single group or nation. The same goes for any other area of the wider culture.

As Professor Patterson suggested, being taught to decode elementary reading materials and specific, job-related texts cannot constitute true literacy. Such basic training does not make a person literate with respect to newspapers or other writings addressed to a general public. Moreover, a directly practical drawback of such narrow training is that it does not prepare anyone for technological change. Narrow vocational training in one state of a technology will not enable a person to read manuals that explain new developments in the same technology. In modern life we need general knowledge that enables us to deal with new ideas, events, and challenges. In today's world, general cultural literacy is more useful than what Professor Patterson terms "literacy to a specific task," because general literate information is the basis for many changing tasks.

Cultural literacy is even more important in the social sphere. The aim of universal literacy has never been a socially neutral mission in our country. Our traditional social goals were unforgettably renewed for us by Martin Luther King, Jr., in his "I Have a Dream" speech. King envisioned a country where the children of former slaves sit down at the table of equality with the children of former slave owners, where men and women deal with each other as equals and judge each other on their characters and achievements rather than their origins. Like Thomas Jefferson, he had a dream of a society founded not on race or class but on personal merit.

In the present day, that dream depends on mature literacy. No modern society can hope to become a just society without a high level of universal literacy. Putting aside for the moment the practical arguments about the economic uses of literacy, we can contemplate the even more basic principle that underlies our national system of education in the first place—that people in a democracy can be entrusted to decide all important matters for themselves because they can deliberate and communicate with one another. Universal literacy is inseparable from democracy and is the canvas for Martin Luther King's picture as well as for Thomas Jefferson's.

Both of these leaders understood that just having the right to vote is meaningless if a citizen is disenfranchised by illiteracy or semiliteracy. Illiterate and semiliterate Americans are condemned not only to poverty, but also to the powerlessness of incomprehension. Knowing that they do not understand the issues, and feeling prey to manipulative oversimplifications, they do not trust the system of which they are supposed to be the masters. They do not feel themselves to be active participants in our republic, and they often do not turn out to vote. The civic importance of cultural literacy lies in the fact that true enfranchisement depends upon knowledge, knowledge upon literacy, and literacy upon cultural literacy.

To be truly literate, citizens must be able to grasp the meaning of any piece   30
of writing addressed to the general reader. All citizens should be able, for instance, to read newspapers of substance, about which Jefferson made the following famous remark:

> Were it left to me to decide whether we should have a government without newspapers, or newspapers without a government, I should not hesitate a moment to prefer the latter. But I should mean that every man should receive those papers and be capable of reading them.

Jefferson's last comment is often omitted when the passage is quoted, but it's the crucial one.

Books and newspapers assume a "common reader," that is, a person who knows the things known by other literate persons in the culture. Obviously, such assumptions are never identical from writer to writer, but they show a remarkable consistency. Those who write for a mass public are always making judgments about what their readers can be assumed to know, and the judgments are closely similar. Any reader who doesn't possess the knowledge assumed in a piece he or she reads will in fact be illiterate with respect to that particular piece of writing.

Here, for instance, is a rather typical excerpt from the *Washington Post* of December 29, 1983.

> A federal appeals panel today upheld an order barring foreclosure on a Missouri farm, saying that U.S. Agriculture Secretary John R. Block has reneged on his responsibilities to some debt ridden farmers. The appeals panel

directed the USDA to create a system of processing loan deferments and of publicizing them as it said Congress had intended. The panel said that it is the responsibility of the agriculture secretary to carry out this intent "not as a private banker, but as a public broker."

Imagine that item being read by people who are well trained in phonics, word recognition, and other decoding skills but are culturally illiterate. They might know words like *foreclosure*, but they would not understand what the piece means. Who gave the order that the federal panel upheld? What is a federal appeals panel? Where is Missouri, and what about Missouri is relevant to the issue? Why are many farmers debt ridden? What is the USDA? What is a public broker? Even if culturally illiterate readers bothered to look up individual words, they would have little idea of the reality being referred to. The explicit words are just surface pointers to textual meaning in reading and writing. The comprehending reader must bring to the text appropriate background information that includes knowledge not only about the topic but also the shared attitudes and conventions that color a piece of writing.

Our children can learn this information only by being taught it. Shared literate information is deliberately sustained by national systems of education in many countries because they recognize the importance of giving their children a common basis for communication. Some decades ago a charming book called *1066 and All That* appeared in Britain. It dealt with facts of British history that all educated Britons had been taught as children but remembered only dimly as adults. The book caricatured those recollections, purposely getting the "facts" just wrong enough to make them ridiculous on their face. Readers instantly recognized that the book was mistaken in its theory about what Ethelred-the-Unready was unready for, but, on the other hand, they couldn't say precisely what he *was* unready for. The book was hilarious to literate Britons as a satire of their own vague and confused memories. But even if their schoolchild knowledge had become vague with the passage of time, it was still functional, because the information essential to literacy is rarely detailed or precise.

This haziness is a key characteristic of literacy and cultural literacy. To   35
understand the *Washington Post* extract literate readers have to know only vaguely, in the backs of their minds, that the American legal system permits a court decision to be reversed by a higher court. They would need to know only that a judge is empowered to tell the executive branch what it can or cannot do to farmers and other citizens. (The secretary of agriculture was barred from foreclosing a Missouri farm.) Readers would need to know only vaguely what and where Missouri is, and how the department and the secretary of agriculture fit into the scheme of things. None of this knowledge would have to be precise. Readers wouldn't have to know whether an appeals panel is the final judicial level before the U.S. Supreme Court. Any practiced writer who feels it is important for a reader to know such details always provides them.

Much in verbal communication is necessarily vague, whether we are conversing or reading. What counts is our ability to grasp the general shape of what we are reading and to tie it to what we already know. If we need details, we rely on the writer or speaker to develop them. Or if we intend to ponder matters in detail for ourselves, we do so later, at our leisure. For instance, it is probably true that many people do not know what a beanball is in baseball. So in an article on the subject the author conveniently sets forth as much as the culturally literate reader must know.

> Described variously as the knockdown pitch, the beanball, the duster and the purpose pitch—the Pentagon would call it the peacekeeper—this delightful stratagem has graced the scene for most of the 109 years the major leagues have existed. It starts fights. It creates lingering grudges. It sends people to the hospital. . . . "You put my guy in the dirt, I put your guy in the dirt."

To understand this text, we don't have to know much about the particular topic in advance, but we do require quite a lot of vague knowledge about baseball to give us a sense of the whole meaning, whether our knowledge happens to be vague or precise.

The superficiality of the knowledge we need for reading and writing may be unwelcome news to those who deplore superficial learning and praise critical thinking over mere information. But one of the sharpest critical thinkers of our day, Dr. Hilary Putnam, a Harvard philosopher, has provided us with a profound insight into the importance of vague knowledge in verbal communication.

> Suppose you are like me and cannot tell an elm from a beech tree. . . . [I can nonetheless use the word "elm" because] *there is a division of linguistic labor.* . . . It is not at all necessary or efficient that everyone who wears a gold ring (or a gold cufflink, etc.) be able to tell with any reliability whether or not something is really gold. . . . Everyone to whom the word "gold" is important for any reason has to *acquire* the word "gold"; but he does not have to acquire the *method of recognizing* if something is or is not gold.

Putnam does acknowledge a limit on the degrees of ignorance and vagueness that are acceptable in discourse. "Significant communication," he observes, "requires that people know something of what they are talking about." Nonetheless, what is required for communication is often so vague and superficial that we can properly understand and use the word *elm* without being able to distinguish an elm tree from a beech tree. What we need to know in order to use and understand a word is an initial stereotype that has a few vague traits.

> Speakers are *required* to know something about (stereotypic) tigers in order to count as having acquired the word "tiger"; something about elm trees (or

anyway about the stereotype thereof) to count as having acquired the word "elm," etc. . . . The nature of the required minimum level of competence depends heavily upon both the culture and the topic, however. In our culture speakers are not . . . required to know the fine details (such as leaf shape) of what an elm tree looks like. English speakers are *required by their linguistic community* to be able to tell tigers from leopards; they are not required to be able to tell beech trees from elm trees.

When Putnam says that Americans can be depended on to distinguish tigers and leopards but not elms and beeches, he assumes that his readers will agree with him because they are culturally literate. He takes for granted that one literate person knows approximately the same things as another and is aware of the probable limits of the other person's knowledge. That second level of awareness—knowing what others probably know—is crucial for effective communication. In order to speak effectively to people we must have a reliable sense of what they do and do not know. For instance, if Putnam is right in his example, we should not have to tell a stranger that a leopard has spots or a tiger stripes, but we would have to explain that an elm has rough bark and a beech smooth bark if we wanted that particular piece of information conveyed. To know what educated people know about tigers but don't know about elm trees is the sort of cultural knowledge, limited in extent but possessed by all literate people, that must be brought into the open and taught to our children.

Besides being limited in extent, cultural literacy has another trait that it is   40
important for educational policy—its national character. It's true that literate English is an international language, but only so long as the topics it deals with are international. The background knowledge of people from other English-speaking nations is often inadequate for complex and subtle communications within our nation. The knowledge required for national literacy differs from country to country, even when their national language is the same. It is no doubt true that one layer of cultural literacy is the same for all English-speaking nations. Australians, South Africans, Britons, and Americans share a lot of knowledge by virtue of their common language. But much of the knowledge required for literacy in, say, Australia is specific to that country, just as much of ours is specific to the United States.

For instance, a literate Australian can typically understand American newspaper articles on international events or the weather but not one on a federal appeals panel. The same holds true for Americans who read Australian newspapers. Many of us have heard "Waltzing Matilda," a song known to every Australian, but few Americans understand or need to understand what the words mean.

Once a jolly swagman camped beside a billabong,
Under the shade of a coolibah tree,

And he sang as he sat and waited while his billy boiled,
"You'll come a'waltzing Matilda, with me."

Waltzing Matilda doesn't mean dancing with a girl; it means walking with a kind of knapsack. A *swagman* is a hobo, a *billabong* is a pond, a *coolibah* is a eucalyptus, and a *billy* is a can for making tea.

The national character of the knowledge needed in reading and writing was strikingly revealed in an experiment conducted by Richard C. Anderson and others at the Center for the Study of Reading at the University of Illinois. They assembled two paired groups of readers, all highly similar in sexual balance, educational background, age, and social class. The only difference between the groups was that one was in India, the other in the United States. Both were given the same two letters to read. The texts were similar in overall length, word-frequency distribution, sentence length and complexity, and number of explicit propositions. Both letters were on the same topic, a wedding, but one described an Indian wedding, the other an American wedding. The reading performances of the two groups—their speed and accuracy of comprehension—split along national lines. The Indians performed well in reading about the Indian wedding but poorly in reading about the American one, and the Americans did the opposite. This experiment not only reconfirmed the dependence of reading skill on cultural literacy, it also demonstrated its national character.

Although nationalism may be regrettable in some of its world-wide political effects, a mastery of national culture is essential to mastery of the standard language in every modern nation. This point is important for educational policy, because educators often stress the virtues of multicultural education. Such study is indeed valuable in itself; it inculcates tolerance and provides a perspective on our own traditions and values. But however laudable it is, it should not be the primary focus of national education. It should not be allowed to supplant or interfere with our schools' responsibility to ensure our children's mastery of American literate culture. The acculturative responsibility of the schools is primary and fundamental. To teach the ways of one's own community has always been and still remains the essence of the education of our children, who enter neither a narrow tribal culture nor a transcendent world culture but a national literate culture. For profound historical reasons, this is the way of the modern world. It will not change soon, and it will certainly not be changed by educational policy alone.

● Applying a Materialist Frame

1. Hirsch goes to great lengths to assure his readers that his ideas of cultural literacy don't necessarily cut out marginalized or minority groups, but he also says that "multicultural education" should not "be the primary focus of national education. It should not be allowed to supplant or interfere with our schools' responsibility to ensure our children's mastery of American literate culture" (para. 43). Doesn't this really say that "multicultural education" and "American literate culture" don't share much?

- If you consider his choices of information everyone should know to be considered culturally literate, which is it—"everyone's included in deciding what matters" or "these are the important things because I said so"?
- What do you think of the examples he cites?
- Do you see any class-based implications for the kinds of data he says every "literate" American should know?

2. As a student yourself, how do you react to his use of so many examples that show students as almost comically ignorant?

- Are the topics those students didn't know anything about the same ones you'd see as fundamentally important to know? Why?
- What impressions about his *ethos*, his appeal to credibility do you form? How does he justify his own authorial position? What makes him an expert in this discussion?
- What about those references to the SAT as a "fairly sensitive instrument for measuring levels of literacy"? Were the vocabulary sections representative of the way you communicate with others in your daily life? What is your response to Hirsch's argument?

3. At the very beginning of this excerpt, Hirsch says his book focuses on "a hidden problem in American education," and that he hopes those concerned about the topic "will be persuaded by the book's argument and act upon it."

Can you imagine what he might mean by "act on it"? Let's assume that we can all agree that the hidden problem in education he refers to is that we all aren't equally culturally literate. What, then, would we do? If we are by chance someone who is culturally deficient, how should we act?

4. Hirsch says that "everyone needs to know certain basic things—and the people who already know those things will be the ones to make up the list of what needs to be known."

What conclusions would you draw from that line of thinking about who's going to set the standards, who's going to decide what needs to be known? How comfortable do you feel about Hirsch's "focus"?

5. Some educators who disagree with Hirsch's specific contentions nonetheless credit him with opening up important lines of discussion. What do you think these contributions might be? Why would those who disagree with his solution to "a hidden problem" or even his definition of the problem might also think he'd provided a service to the educational community?

Social Class and the Hidden Curriculum of Work

JEAN ANYON

In this selection, Jean Anyon uses empirical research to gather information about the class-based nature of some elementary schools. Her piece, written in 1980, was reprinted in a collection of essays called The Hidden Curriculum and Moral Education *in 1983. Anyon is a professor of educational policy who works on issues of race and class in urban education.*

Scholars in political economy and the sociology of knowledge have recently argued that public schools in complex industrial societies like our own make available different types of educational experience and curriculum knowledge to students in different social classes. Bowles and Gintis, for example, have argued that students in different social-class backgrounds are rewarded for classroom behaviors that correspond to personality traits allegedly rewarded in the different occupational strata—the working classes for docility and obedience, the managerial classes for initiative and personal assertiveness. Basil Bernstein, Pierre Bourdieu, and Michael W. Apple, focusing on school knowledge, have argued that knowledge and skills leading to social power and regard (medical, legal, managerial) are made available to the advantaged social groups but are withheld from the working classes, to whom a more "practical" curriculum is offered (manual skills, clerical knowledge). While there has been considerable argumentation of these points regarding education in England, France, and North America, there has been little or no attempt to investigate these ideas empirically in elementary or secondary schools and classrooms in this country.

This article offers tentative empirical support (and qualification) of the above arguments by providing illustrative examples of differences in student *work* in classrooms in contrasting social class communities. The examples were gathered as part of an ethnographical study of curricular, pedagogical, and pupil evaluation practices in five elementary schools. The article attempts a theoretical contribution as well and assesses student work in the light of a theoretical approach to social-class analysis. The organization is as follows: the methodology of the ethnographical study is briefly described; a theoretical approach to the definition of social class is offered; income and other characteristics of the parents in each school are provided, and examples from the study that illustrate work tasks and interaction in each school are presented; then the concepts used to define social class are applied to the examples in order to assess the theoretical meaning of classroom events. It will be suggested that there is a "hidden curriculum" in schoolwork that has profound implications for the theory—and consequence—of everyday activity in education.

Methodology

The methods used to gather data were classroom observation; interviews of students, teachers, principals, and district administrative staff; and assessment of curriculum and other materials in each classroom and school. All classroom events to be discussed here involve the fifth grade in each school. Except for that school where only one fifth-grade teacher could be observed, all the fifth-grade teachers (that is, two or three) were observed as the children moved from subject to subject. In all schools the art, music, and gym teachers were also observed and interviewed. All teachers in the study were described as "good" or "excellent" by their principals. All except one new teacher had taught for more than four years. The fifth grade in each school was observed by the investigator for ten three-hour periods between September 15, 1978, and June 20, 1979.

Before providing the occupations, incomes, and other relevant social characteristics of the parents of the children in each school, I will offer a theoretical approach to defining social class.

Social Class

One's occupation and income level contribute significantly to one's social class,   5
but they do not define it. Rather, social class is a series of relationships. A person's social class is defined here by the way that person relates to the process in society by which goods, services, and culture are produced. One relates to several aspects of the production process primarily through one's work. One has a relationship to the system of ownership, to other people (at work and in society), and to the content and process of one's own productive activity. One's relationship to all three of these aspects of production determines one's social class; that is, all three relationships are necessary, and none is sufficient for determining a person's relation to the process of production in society.

Ownership Relations

In a capitalist society, a person has a relation to the system of private ownership of capital. Capital is usually thought of as being derived from physical property. In this sense capital is property that is used to produce profit, interest, or rent in sufficient quantity so that the result can be used to produce more profit, interest, or rent—that is, more capital. Physical capital may be derived from money, stocks, machines, land, or the labor of workers (whose labor, for instance, may produce products that are sold by others for profit). Capital, however, can also be symbolic. It can be the socially legitimated knowledge of how the production process works, its financial, managerial, technical, or other "secrets." Symbolic capital can also be socially legitimated skills—cognitive (for example, analytical), linguistic, or technical skills that provide the ability to, say, produce the dominant scientific, artistic, and other culture or to manage the systems of industrial and cultural production. Skillful application of symbolic capital may yield social and cultural power and perhaps physical capital as well.

The ownership relation that is definitive for social class is one's relation to physical capital. The first such relationship is that of capitalist. To be a member of the capitalist class in the present-day United States, one must participate in the ownership of the apparatus of production in society. The number of such persons is relatively small; while one person in ten owns some stock, for example, a mere 1.6 percent of the population owns 82.2 percent of *all* stock, and the wealthiest one-fifth owns almost all the rest.

At the opposite pole of this relationship is the worker. To be in the United States working class, a person will not ordinarily own physical capital; on the contrary, his or her work will be wage or salaried labor that is either a *source* of profit (that is, capital) to others or that makes it possible for others to *realize* profit. Examples of the latter are white-collar clerical workers in industry and distribution (office and sales) as well as the wage and salaried workers in the institutions of social and economic legitimation and service (in state education and welfare institutions). According to the criteria to be developed here, the number of persons who presently comprise the working class in the United States is between 50 percent and 60 percent of the population.

In between the defining relationship of capitalist and worker are the middle classes, whose relationship to the process of production is less clear and whose relationship may indeed exhibit contradictory characteristics. For example, social service employees have a somewhat contradictory relationship to the process of production because, although their income may be at middle-class levels, some characteristics of their work are working class (they may have very little control over their work). Analogously, there are persons at the upper income end of the middle class, such as upper-middle-class professionals, who may own quantities of stocks and will therefore share characteristics of the capitalist class. As the next criterion to be discussed makes clear, however, to be a member of the present-day capitalist class in the United States, one must also participate in the social *control* of this capital.

Relationships Between People

The second relationship that contributes to one's social class is the relation one has to authority and control at work and in society. One characteristic of most working-class jobs is that there is no built-in mechanism by which the worker can control the content, process, or speed of work. Legitimate decision making is vested in personnel supervisors, in middle or upper management, or—as in an increasing number of white-collar working-class (and most middle-class) jobs— by bureaucratic rule and regulation. For upper-middle-class professional groups there is an increased amount of autonomy regarding work. Moreover, in middle- and upper-middle-class positions there is an increasing chance that one's work will also involve supervising the work of others. A capitalist is defined within these relations of control in an enterprise by having a position that participates in the direct control of the entire enterprise. Capitalists do not directly control workers in physical production and do not directly control ideas in the sphere of cultural production. However, more crucial to control, capitalists make the decisions over how resources are used (that is, where money is invested) and how profit is allocated.

Relations Between People and Their Work

The third criterion that contributes to a person's social class is the relationship between that person and his or her own productive activity—the type of activity that constitutes his or her work. A working-class job is often characterized by work that is routine and mechanical and that is a small, fragmented part of a larger process with which workers are not usually acquainted. These working-class jobs are usually blue-collar, manual labor. A few skilled jobs such as plumbing and printing are not mechanical, however, and an increasing number of working-class jobs are *white*-collar. These white-collar jobs, such as clerical work, may involve work that necessitates a measure of planning and decision making, but one still has no built-in control over the content. The work of some middle- and most upper-middle-class managerial and professional groups is likely to involve the need for conceptualization and creativity, with many professional jobs demanding one's full creative capacities. Finally, the work that characterizes the capitalist position is that this work is almost entirely a matter of conceptualization (planning and laying out) that has as its object management and control of the enterprise.

One's social class, then, is a result of the relationships one has, largely through one's work, to physical capital and its power, to other people at work and in society, and to one's own productive activity. Social class is a lived, developing process. It is not an abstract category, and it is not a fixed, inherited position (although one's family background is, of course, important). Social class is perceived as a complex of social relations that one develops as one grows up—as one acquires and develops certain bodies of knowledge, skills, abilities, and traits, and as one has contact and opportunity in the world. In sum, social class describes relationships that we as adults have developed, may attempt to maintain, and in which we participate every working day. These relationships in a real sense define our material ties to the world. An important concern here is whether these relationships are developing in children in schools within particular social-class contexts.

The Sample of Schools

With the above discussion as a theoretical backdrop, the social-class designation of each of the five schools will be identified, and the income, occupation, and other relevant available social characteristics of the students and their parents will be described. The first three schools are in a medium-sized city district in northern New Jersey, and the other two are in a nearby New Jersey suburb.

The first two schools I will call *working-class schools*. Most of the parents have blue-collar jobs. Less than a third of the fathers are skilled, while the majority are in unskilled or semiskilled jobs. During the period of the study (1978–1979), approximately 15 percent of the fathers were unemployed. The large majority (85 percent) of the families are white. The following occupations are typical: platform, storeroom, and stockroom workers; foundrymen, pipe welders, and boilermakers; semiskilled and unskilled assembly-line operatives; gas station attendants, auto mechanics, maintenance workers, and security guards. Less than 30 percent of the women work, some part-time and some full-time, on assembly lines, in storerooms and stockrooms, as waitresses, barmaids, or sales clerks. Of the fifth-grade parents, none of the wives of the skilled workers had jobs. Approximately 15 percent of the families in each school are at or below the federal "poverty" level; most of the rest of the family incomes are at or below $12,000, except some of the skilled workers whose incomes are higher. The incomes of the majority of the families in these two schools (at or below $12,000) are typical of 38.6 percent of the families in the United States.

The third school is called the *middle-class school*, although because of neigh- 15 borhood residence patterns, the population is a mixture of several social classes. The parents' occupations can be divided into three groups: a small group of blue-collar "rich," who are skilled, well-paid workers such as printers, carpenters, plumbers, and construction workers. The second group is composed of parents in working-class and middle-class white-collar jobs: women in office jobs, technicians, supervisors in industry, and parents employed by the city (such as firemen, policemen, and several of the school's teachers). The third group is composed of occupations such as personnel directors in local firms, accountants, "middle management," and a few small capitalists (owners of shops in the area). The children of several local doctors attend this school. Most family incomes are between $13,000 and $25,000, with a few higher. This income range is typical of 38.9 percent of the families in the United States.

The fourth school has a parent population that is at the upper income level of the upper middle class and is predominantly professional. This school will be called the *affluent professional school*. Typical jobs are: cardiologist, interior designer, corporate lawyer or engineer, executive in advertising or television. There are some families who are not as affluent as the majority (the family of the superintendent of the district's schools, and the one or two families in which the fathers are skilled workers). In addition, a few of the families are more affluent than the majority and can be classified in the capitalist class (a partner in a prestigious Wall Street stock brokerage firm). Approximately 90 percent of the children in this school are white. Most family incomes are between $40,000 and $80,000. This income span represents approximately 7 percent of the families in the United States.

In the fifth school the majority of the families belong to the capitalist class. This school will be called the *executive elite school* because most of the fathers are top executives (for example, presidents and vice-presidents) in major United States-based multinational corporations—for example, ATT, RCA, City Bank, American Express, U.S. Steel. A sizable group of fathers are top executives in financial firms in Wall Street. There are also a number of fathers who list their occupations as "general counsel" to a particular corporation, and these corporations are also among the large multinationals. Many of the mothers do volunteer work in the Junior League, Junior Fortnightly, or other service groups; some are intricately involved in town politics; and some are themselves in well-paid occupations. There are no minority children in the school. Almost all the family incomes are over $100,000, with some in the $500,000 range. The incomes in this school represent less than 1 percent of the families in the United States.

Since each of the five schools is only one instance of elementary education in a particular social class context, I will not generalize beyond the sample. However, the examples of schoolwork which follow will suggest characteristics of education in each social setting that appear to have theoretical and social significance and to be worth investigation in a larger number of schools.

Social Class and Schoolwork

There are obvious similarities among United States schools and classrooms. There are school and classroom rules, teachers who ask questions and attempt to exercise control and who give work and homework. There are textbooks and tests. All of these were found in the five schools. Indeed, there were other curricular similarities as well: all schools and fifth grades used the same math book and series (*Mathematics Around Us*, Scott Foresman, 1978); all fifth grades had at least one boxed set of an individualized reading program available in the room (although the variety and amounts of teaching materials in the classrooms increased as the social class of the school population increased); and, all fifth-grade language arts curricula included aspects of grammar, punctuation, and capitalization.

This section provides examples of work and work-related activities in each school that bear on the categories used to define social class. Thus, examples will be provided concerning students' relation to capital (for example, as manifest in any symbolic capital that might be acquired through schoolwork); students' relation to persons and types of authority regarding schoolwork; and students' relation to their own productive activity. The section first offers the investigator's interpretation of what schoolwork *is* for children in each setting and then presents events and interactions that illustrate that assessment.

The Working-Class Schools

In the two working-class schools, work is following the steps of a procedure. The procedure is usually mechanical, involving rote behavior and very little decision making or choice. The teachers rarely explain why the work is being assigned, how it might connect to other assignments, or what the idea is that lies behind the procedure or gives it coherence and perhaps meaning or significance. Available textbooks are not always used, and the teachers often prepare their own dittos or put work examples on the board. Most of the rules regarding work are designations of what the children are to do; the rules are steps to follow. These steps are told to the children by the teachers and are often written on the board. The children are usually told to copy the steps as notes. These notes are to be studied. Work is often evaluated not according to whether it is right or wrong but according to whether the children followed the right steps.

The following examples illustrate these points. In math, when two-digit division was introduced, the teacher in one school gave a four-minute lecture on what the terms are called (which number is the divisor, dividend, quotient, and remainder). The children were told to copy these names in their notebooks. Then the teacher told them the steps to follow to do the problems, saying, "This is how you do them." The teacher listed the steps on the board, and they appeared several days later as a chart hung in the middle of the front wall: "Divide, Multiply, Subtract, Bring Down." The children often did examples of two-digit division. When the teacher went over the examples with them, he told them what the procedure was for each problem, rarely asking them to conceptualize or explain it themselves: "Three into twenty-two is seven; do your subtraction and one is left over." During the week that two-digit division was introduced (or at any other time), the investigator did not observe any discussion of the idea of grouping involved in division, any use of manipulables, or any attempt to relate two-digit division to any other mathematical process. Nor was there any attempt to relate the steps to an actual or possible thought process of the children. The observer did not hear the terms *dividend*, *quotient*, and so on, used again. The math teacher in the other working-class school followed similar procedures regarding two-digit division and at one point her class seemed confused. She said, "You're confusing yourselves. You're tensing up. Remember, when you do this, it's the same steps over and over again—and that's the way division always is." Several weeks later, after a test, a group of her children "still didn't get it," and she made no attempt to explain the concept of dividing things into groups or to give them manipulables for their own investigation. Rather, she went over the steps with them again and told them that they "needed more practice."

In other areas of math, work is also carrying out often unexplained fragmented procedures. For example, one of the teachers led the children through a series of steps to make a 1-inch grid on their paper *without* telling them that they were making a 1-inch grid or that it would be used to study scale. She said, "Take your ruler. Put it across the top. Make a mark at every number. Then move your ruler down to the bottom. No, put it across the bottom. Now make a mark on top of every number. Now draw a line from . . ." At this point a girl said that she had a faster way to do it and the teacher said, "No, you don't; you don't even know what I'm making yet. Do it this way, or it's wrong." After they had made the lines up and down and across, the teacher told them she wanted them to make a figure by connecting some dots and to measure that, using the scale of 1 inch equals 1 mile. Then they were to cut it out. She said, "Don't cut until I check it."

In both working-class schools, work in language arts is mechanics of punctuation (commas, periods, question marks, exclamation points), capitalization, and the four kinds of sentences. One teacher explained to me, "Simple punctuation is all they'll ever use." Regarding punctuation, either a teacher or a ditto stated the rules for where, for example, to put commas. The investigator heard no classroom discussion of the aural context of punctuation (which, of course, is what gives each mark its meaning). Nor did the investigator hear any statement or inference that placing a punctuation mark could be a decision-making process, depending, for example, on one's intended meaning. Rather, the children were told to follow the rules. Language arts did not involve creative writing. There were several writing assignments throughout the year, but in each instance the children were given a ditto, and they wrote answers to questions on the sheet. For example, they wrote their "autobiography" by answering such questions as "Where were you born?" "What is your favorite animal?" on a sheet entitled "All About Me."

In one of the working-class schools, the class had a science period several times a week. On the three occasions observed, the children were not called upon to set up experiments or to give explanations for facts or concepts. Rather, on each occasion the teacher told them in his own words what the book said. The children copied the teacher's sentences from the board. Each day that preceded the day they were to do a science experiment, the teacher told them to copy the directions from the book for the procedure they would carry out the next day and to study the list at home that night. The day after each experiment, the teacher went over what they had "found" (they did the experiments as a class, and each was actually a class demonstration led by the teacher). Then the teacher wrote what they "found" on the board, and the children copied that in their notebooks. Once or twice a year there are science projects. The project is chosen and assigned by the teacher from a box of 3-by-5-inch cards. On the card the teacher has written the question to be answered, the books to use, and how much to write. Explaining the cards to the observer, the teacher said, "It tells them exactly what to do, or they couldn't do it."

Social studies in the working-class schools is also largely mechanical, rote work that was given little explanation or connection to larger contexts. In one school, for example, although there was a book available, social studies work was to copy the teacher's notes from the board. Several times a week for a period of several months the children copied these notes. The fifth grades in the district were to study United States history. The teacher used a booklet she had purchased called "The Fabulous Fifty States." Each day she put information from the booklet in outline form on the board and the children copied it. The type of information did not vary: the name of the state, its abbreviation, state capital, nickname of the state, its main products, main business, and a "Fabulous Fact" ("Idaho grew twenty-seven billion potatoes in one year. That's enough potatoes for each man, woman, and . . ."). As the children finished copying

25

the sentences, the teacher erased them and wrote more. Children would occasionally go to the front to pull down the wall map in order to locate the states they were copying, and the teacher did not dissuade them. But the observer never saw her refer to the map; nor did the observer ever hear her make other than perfunctory remarks concerning the information the children were copying. Occasionally the children colored in a ditto and cut it out to make a stand-up figure (representing, for example, a man roping a cow in the Southwest). These were referred to by the teacher as their social studies "projects."

Rote behavior was often called for in classroom work. When going over math and language art skills sheets, for example, as the teacher asked for the answer to each problem, he fired the questions rapidly, staccato, and the scene reminded the observer of a sergeant drilling recruits: above all, the questions demanded that you stay at attention: "The next one? What do I put here? . . . Here? Give us the next." Or "How many commas in this sentence? Where do I put them . . . The next one?"

The four fifth-grade teachers observed in the working-class schools attempted to control classroom time and space by making decisions without consulting the children and without explaining the basis for their decisions. The teacher's control thus often seemed capricious. Teachers, for instance, very often ignored the bells to switch classes—deciding among themselves to keep the children after the period was officially over to continue with the work or for disciplinary reasons or so they (the teachers) could stand in the hall and talk. There were no clocks in the rooms in either school, and the children often asked, "What period is this?" "When do we go to gym?" The children had no access to materials. These were handed out by teachers and closely guarded. Things in the room "belonged" to the teacher: "Bob, bring me my garbage can." The teachers continually gave the children orders. Only three times did the investigator hear a teacher in either working-class school preface a directive with an unsarcastic "please," or "let's" or "would you." Instead, the teachers said, "Shut up," "Shut your mouth," "Open your books," "Throw your gum away—if you want to rot your teeth, do it on your own time." Teachers made every effort to control the movement of the children, and often shouted, "Why are you out of your seat??!!" If the children got permission to leave the room, they had to take a written pass with the date and time.

The control that the teachers have is less than they would like. It is a result of constant struggle with the children. The children continually resist the teachers' orders and the work itself. They do not directly challenge the teacher's authority or legitimacy, but they make indirect attempts to sabotage and resist the flow of assignments:

Teacher: I will put some problems on the board. You are to divide.

Child: We got to divide?

Teacher: Yes.

Several children: (Groan) Not again. Mr. B., we done this yesterday.

Child: Do we put the date?

Teacher: Yes. I hope we remember we work in silence. You're supposed to do it on white paper. I'll explain it later.

Child: Somebody broke my pencil. (Crash—a child falls out of his chair.)

Child: (repeats) Mr. B., somebody broke my *pencil*!

Child: Are we going to be here all morning?

(Teacher comes to the observer, shakes his head and grimaces, then smiles.)

The children are successful enough in their struggle against work that there are long periods where they are not asked to *do* any work but just to sit and be quiet. Very often the work that the teachers assign is "easy," that is, not demanding and thus receives less resistance. Sometimes a compromise is reached where, although the teachers insist that the children continue to work, there is a constant murmur of talk. The children will be doing arithmetic examples, copying social studies notes, or doing punctuation or other dittos, and all the while there is muted but spirited conversation—about somebody's broken arm, an after-school disturbance the day before, and so on. Sometimes the teachers themselves join in the conversation because, as one teacher explained to me, "It's a relief from the routine."

Middle-Class School

In the middle-class school, work is getting the right answer. If one accumulates enough right answers, one gets a good grade. One must follow the directions in order to get the right answers, but the directions often call for some figuring, some choice, some decision making. For example, the children must often figure out by themselves what the directions ask them to do and how to get the answer: what do you do first, second, and perhaps third? Answers are usually found in books or by listening to the teacher. Answers are usually words, sentences, numbers, or facts and dates; one writes them on paper, and one should be neat. Answers must be given in the right order, and one cannot make them up.

The following activities are illustrative. Math involves some choice: one may do two-digit division the long way or the short way, and there are some math problems that can be done "in your head." When the teacher explains how to do two-digit division, there is recognition that a cognitive process is involved; she gives several ways and says, "I want to make sure you understand what you're doing—so you get it right"; and, when they go over the homework, she asks the *children* to tell how they did the problem and what answer they got.

In social studies the daily work is to read the assigned pages in the textbook and to answer the teacher's questions. The questions are almost always designed to check on whether the students have read the assignment and understood it: who did so-and-so; what happened after that; when did it happen, where, and sometimes, why did it happen? The answers are in the book and in one's understanding of the book; the teacher's hints when one doesn't know the answers are to "read it again" or to look at the picture or at the rest of the paragraph. One is to search for the answer in the "context," in what is given.

Language arts is "simple grammar, what they need for everyday life." The language arts teacher says, "They should learn to speak properly, to write business letters and thank-you letters, and to understand what nouns and verbs and simple subjects are." Here, as well, actual work is to choose the right answers, to understand what is given. The teacher often says, "Please read the next sentence and then I'll question you about it." One teacher said in some exasperation to a boy who was fooling around in class, "If you don't know the answers to the questions I ask, then you can't stay in this *class*! [pause] You *never* know the answers to the questions I ask, and it's not fair to me—and certainly not to you!"

Most lessons are based on the textbook. This does not involve a critical perspective on what is given there. For example, a critical perspective in social studies is perceived as dangerous by these teachers because it may lead to controversial topics; the parents might complain. The children, however, are often curious, especially in social studies. Their questions are tolerated and usually answered perfunctorily. But after a few minutes the teacher will say, "All right, we're not going any farther. Please open your social studies workbook." While the teachers spend a lot of time explaining and expanding on what the textbooks say, there is little attempt to analyze how or why things happen, or to give thought to how pieces of a culture, or, say, a system of numbers or elements of a language fit together or can be analyzed. What has happened in the past and what exists now may not be equitable or fair, but (shrug) that is the way things are and one does not confront such matters in school. For example, in social studies after a child is called on to read a passage about the pilgrims, the teacher summarizes the paragraph and then says, "So you can see how strict they were about everything." A child asks, "Why?" "Well, because they felt that if you weren't busy you'd get into trouble." Another child asks, "Is it true that they burned women at the stake?" The teacher says, "Yes, if a woman did anything strange, they hanged them. [sic] What would a woman do, do you think, to make them burn them?" [sic] See if you can come up with better answers than my other [social studies] class." Several children offer suggestions, to which the teacher nods but does not comment. Then she says, "Okay, good," and calls on the next child to read.

Work tasks do not usually request creativity. Serious attention is rarely given in school work on *how* the children develop or express their own feelings and ideas, either linguistically or in graphic form. On the occasions when creativity or self-expression is requested, it is peripheral to the main activity or it is "enrichment" or "for fun." During a lesson on what similes are, for example, the teacher explains what they are, puts several on the board, gives some other examples herself, and then asks the children if they can "make some up." She calls on three children who give similes, two of which are actually in the book

35

they have open before them. The teacher does not comment on this and then asks several others to choose similes from the list of phrases in the book. Several do so correctly, and she says, "Oh good! You're picking them out! See how good we are?" Their homework is to pick out the rest of the similes from the list.

Creativity is not often requested in social studies and science projects, either. Social studies projects, for example, are given with directions to "find information on your topic" and write it up. The children are not supposed to copy but to "put it in your own words." Although a number of the projects subsequently went beyond the teacher's direction to find information and had quite expressive covers and inside illustrations, the teacher's evaluative comments had to do with the amount of information, whether they had "copied," and if their work was neat.

The style of control of the three fifth-grade teachers observed in this school varied from somewhat easygoing to strict, but in contrast to the working-class schools, the teachers' decisions were usually based on external rules and regulations—for example, on criteria that were known or available to the children. Thus, the teachers always honor the bells for changing classes, and they usually evaluate children's work by what is in the textbooks and answer booklets.

There is little excitement in schoolwork for the children, and the assignments are perceived as having little to do with their interests and feelings. As one child said, what you do is "store facts up in your head like cold storage—until you need it later for a test or your job." Thus, doing well is important because there are thought to be *other* likely rewards: a good job or college.

Affluent Professional School

In the affluent professional school, work is creative activity carried out independently. The students are continually asked to express and apply ideas and concepts. Work involves individual thought and expressiveness, expansion and illustration of ideas, and choice of appropriate method and material. (The class is not considered an open classroom, and the principal explained that because of the large number of discipline problems in the fifth grade this year they did not departmentalize. The teacher who agreed to take part in the study said she is "more structured" this year than she usually is.) The products of work in this class are often written stories, editorials and essays, or representations of ideas in mural, graph, or craft form. The products of work should not be like everybody else's and should show individuality. They should exhibit good design, and (this is important) they must also fit empirical reality. Moreover, one's work should attempt to interpret or "make sense" of reality. The relatively few rules to be followed regarding work are usually criteria for, or limits on, individual activity. One's product is usually evaluated for the quality of its expression and for the aproppriateness of its conception to the task. In many cases, one's own satisfaction with the product is an important criterion for its evaluation. When right answers are called for, as in commercial materials like

SRA (Science Research Associates) and math, it is important that the children decide on an answer as a result of thinking about the idea involved in what they're being asked to do. Teacher's hints are to "think about it some more."

The following activities are illustrative. The class takes home a sheet   40 requesting each child's parents to fill in the number of cars they have, the number of television sets, refrigerators, games, or rooms in the house, and so on. Each child is to figure the average number of a type of possession owned by the fifth grade. Each child must compile the "data" from all the sheets. A calculator is available in the classroom to do the mechanics of finding the average. Some children decide to send sheets to the fourth-grade families for comparison. Their work should be "verified" by a classmate before it is handed in.

Each child and his or her family has made a geoboard. The teacher asks the class to get their geoboards from the side cabinet, to take a handful of rubber bands, and then to listen to what she would like them to do. She says, "I would like you to design a figure and then find the perimeter and area. When you have it, check with your neighbor. After you've done that, please transfer it to graph paper and tomorrow I'll ask you to make up a question about it for someone. When you hand it in, please let me know whose it is and who verified it. Then I have something else for you to do that's really fun. [pause] Find the average number of chocolate chips in three cookies. I'll give you three cookies, and you'll have to *eat* your way through, I'm afraid!" Then she goes around the room and gives help, suggestions, praise, and admonitions that they are getting noisy. They work sitting, or standing up at their desks, at benches in the back, or on the floor. A child hands the teacher his paper and she comments, "I'm not accepting this paper. Do a better design." To another child she says, "That's fantastic! But you'll never find the area. Why don't you draw a figure inside [the big one] and subtract to get the area?"

The school district requires the fifth grade to study ancient civilization (in particular, Egypt, Athens, and Sumer). In this classroom, the emphasis is on illustrating and re-creating the culture of the people of ancient times. The following are typical activities: The children made an 8mm film on Egypt, which one of the parents edited. A girl in the class wrote the script, and the class acted it out. They put the sound on themselves. They read stories of those days. They wrote essays and stories depicting the lives of the people and the societal and occupational divisions. They chose from a list of projects, all of which involved graphic representations of ideas: for example, "Make a mural depicting the division of labor in Egyptian society."

Each child wrote and exchanged a letter in hieroglyphics with a fifth grader in another class, and they also exchanged stories they wrote in cuneiform. They made a scroll and singed the edges so it looked authentic. They each chose an occupation and made an Egyptian plaque representing that occupation, simulating the appropriate Egyptian design. They carved their design on a cylinder of wax, pressed the wax into clay, and then baked the clay. Although one girl did not choose an occupation but carved instead a series of gods and slaves, the teacher said, "That's all right, Amber, it's beautiful." As they were working the teacher said, "Don't cut into your clay until you're satisfied with your design."

Social studies also involves almost daily presentation by the children of some event from the news. The teacher's questions ask the children to expand what they say, to give more details, and to be more specific. Occasionally she adds some remarks to help them see connections between events.

The emphasis on expressing and illustrating ideas in social studies is accompanied in language arts by an emphasis on creative writing. Each child wrote a rhebus story for a first grader whom they had interviewed to see what kind of story the child liked best. They wrote editorials on pending decisions by the school board and radio plays, some of which were read over the school intercom from the office and one of which was performed in the auditorium. There is no language arts textbook because, the teacher said, "The principal wants us to be creative." There is not much grammar, but there is punctuation. One morning when the observer arrived, the class was doing a punctuation ditto. The teacher later apologized for using the ditto. "It's just for review," she said. "I don't teach punctuation that way. We use their language." The ditto had three unambiguous rules for where to put commas in a sentence. As the teacher was going around to help the children with the ditto, she repeated several times, "Where you put commas depends on how you say the sentence; it depends on the situation and what you want to say." Several weeks later the observer saw another punctuation activity. The teacher had printed a five-paragraph story on an oak tag and then cut it into phrases. She read the whole story to the class from the book, then passed out the phrases. The group had to decide how the phrases could best be put together again. (They arranged the phrases on the floor.) The point was not to replicate the story, although that was not irrelevant, but to "decide what you think the best way is." Punctuation marks on cardboard pieces were then handed out, and the children discussed and then decided what mark was best at each place they thought one was needed. At the end of each paragraph the teacher asked, "Are you satisfied with the way the paragraphs are now? Read it to yourself and see how it sounds." Then she read the original story again, and they compared the two.

Describing her goals in science to the investigator, the teacher said, "We use ESS (Elementary Science Study). It's very good because it gives a hands-on experience—so they can make *sense* out of it. It doesn't matter whether it [what they find] is right or wrong. I bring them together and there's value in discussing their ideas."

The products of work in this class are often highly valued by the children and the teacher. In fact, this was the only school in which the investigator was not allowed to take original pieces of the children's work for her files. If the work was small enough, however, and was on paper, the investigator could duplicate it on the copying machine in the office.

The teacher's attempt to control the class involves constant negotiation. She does not give direct orders unless she is angry because the children have been too noisy. Normally, she tries to get them to foresee the consequences of

45

their actions and to decide accordingly. For example, lining them up to go see a play written by the sixth graders, she says, "I presume you're lined up by someone with whom you want to sit. I hope you're lined up by someone you won't get in trouble with." The following two dialogues illustrate the process of negotiation between student and teacher.

> **Teacher:** Tom, you're behind in your SRA this marking period.
>
> **Tom:** So what!
>
> **Teacher:** Well, last time you had a hard time catching up.
>
> **Tom:** But I have my [music] lesson at 10:00.
>
> **Teacher:** Well, that doesn't mean you're going to sit here for twenty minutes.
>
> **Tom:** Twenty minutes! OK. (He goes to pick out an SRA booklet and chooses one, puts it back, then takes another, and brings it to her.)
>
> **Teacher:** OK, this is the one you want, right?
>
> **Tom:** Yes.
>
> **Teacher:** OK, I'll put tomorrow's date on it so you can take it home tonight or finish it tomorrow if you want.
>
> **Teacher:** (to a child who is wandering around during reading) Kevin, why don't you do *Reading for Concepts*?
>
> **Kevin:** No, I don't like *Reading for Concepts*.
>
> **Teacher:** Well, what are you going to do?
>
> **Kevin:** (pause) I'm going to work on my DAR. (The DAR has sponsored an essay competition on "Life in the American Colonies.")

One of the few rules governing the children's movement is that no more than three children may be out of the room at once. There is a school rule that anyone can go to the library at any time to get a book. In the fifth grade I observed, they sign their name on the chalkboard and leave. There are no passes. Finally, the children have a fair amount of officially sanctioned say over what happens in the class. For example, they often negotiate what work is to be done. If the teacher wants to move on to the next subject, but the children say they are not ready, they want to work on their present projects some more, she very often lets them do it.

Executive Elite School

In the executive elite school, work is developing one's analytical intellectual powers. Children are continually asked to reason through a problem, to produce intellectual products that are both logically sound and of top academic quality. A primary goal of thought is to conceptualize rules by which elements may fit together in systems and then to apply these rules in solving a problem. Schoolwork helps one to achieve, to excel, to prepare for life.

The following are illustrative. The math teacher teaches area and perimeter by having the children derive formulas for each. First she helps them, through discussion at the board, to arrive at A = W × L as a formula (not *the* formula) for area. After discussing several, she says, "Can anyone make up a formula for perimeter? Can you figure that out yourselves? [pause] Knowing what we know, can we think of a formula?" She works out three children's suggestions at the board, saying to two, "Yes, that's a good one," and then asks the class if they can think of any more. No one volunteers. To prod them, she says, "If you use rules and good reasoning, you get many ways. Chris, can you think up a formula?"

She discusses two-digit division with the children as a decision-making process. Presenting a new type of problem to them, she asks, "What's the *first* decision you'd make if presented with this kind of example? What is the first thing you'd *think*? Craig?" Craig says, "To find my first partial quotient." She responds, "Yes, that would be your first decision. How would you do that?" Craig explains, and then the teacher says, "OK, we'll see how that works for you." The class tries his way. Subsequently, she comments on the merits and shortcomings of several other children's decisions. Later, she tells the investigator that her goals in math are to develop their reasoning and mathematical thinking and that, unfortunately, "there's no *time* for manipulables."

While right answers are important in math, they are not "given" by the book or by the teacher but may be challenged by the children. Going over some problems in late September the teacher says, "Raise your hand if you do not agree." A child says, "I don't agree with sixty-four." The teacher responds, "OK, there's a question about sixty-four, [to class] Please check it. Owen, they're disagreeing with you. Kristen, they're checking yours." The teacher emphasized this repeatedly during September and October with statements like "Don't be afraid to say you disagree. In the last [math] class, somebody disagreed, and they were right. Before you disagree, check yours, and if you still think we're wrong, then we'll check it out." By Thanksgiving, the children did not often speak in terms of right and wrong math problems but of whether they agreed with the answer that had been given.

There are complicated math mimeos with many word problems. Whenever they go over the examples, they discuss how each child has set up the problem. The children must explain it precisely. On one occasion the teacher said. "I'm more—just as interested in *how* you set up the problem as in what answer you find. If you set up a problem in a good way, the answer is *easy* to find."

Social studies work is most often reading and discussion of concepts and independent research. There are only occasional artistic, expressive, or illustrative projects. Ancient Athens and Sumer are, rather, societies to analyze. The following questions are typical of those that guide the children's independent research. "What mistakes did Pericles make after the war?" "What mistakes did the citizens of Athens make?" "What are the elements of a

55

civilization?" "How did Greece build an economic empire?" "Compare the way Athens chose its leaders with the way we choose ours." Occasionally the children are asked to make up sample questions for their social studies tests. On an occasion when the investigator was present, the social studies teacher rejected a child's question by saying, "That's just fact. If I asked you that question on a test, you'd complain it was just memory! Good questions ask for concepts."

In social studies—but also in reading, science, and health—the teachers initiate classroom discussions of current social issues and problems. These discussions occurred on every one of the investigator's visits, and a teacher told me, "These children's opinions are important—it's important that they learn to reason things through." The classroom discussions always struck the observer as quite realistic and analytical, dealing with concrete social issues like the following: "Why do workers strike?" "Is that right or wrong?" "Why do we have inflation, and what can be done to stop it?" "Why do companies put chemicals in food when the natural ingredients are available?" and so on. Usually the children did not have to be prodded to give their opinions. In fact, their statements and the interchanges between them struck the observer as quite sophisticated conceptually and verbally, and well-informed. Occasionally the teachers would prod with statements such as, "Even if you don't know [the answers], if you think logically about it, you can figure it out." And "I'm asking you [these] questions to help you think this through."

Language arts emphasizes language as a complex system, one that should be mastered. The children are asked to diagram sentences of complex grammatical construction, to memorize irregular verb conjugations (he lay, he has lain, and so on . . .), and to use the proper participles, conjunctions, and interjections in their speech. The teacher (the same one who teaches social studies) told them, "It is not enough to get these right on tests; you must use what you learn [in grammar classes] in your written and oral work. I will grade you on that."

Most writing assignments are either research reports and essays for social studies or experiment analyses and write-ups for science. There is only an occasional story or other "creative writing" assignment. On the occasion observed by the investigator (the writing of a Halloween story), the points the teacher stressed in preparing the children to write involved the structural aspects of a story rather than the expression of feelings or other ideas. The teacher showed them a filmstrip, "The Seven Parts of a Story," and lectured them on plot development, mood setting, character development, consistency, and the use of a logical or appropriate ending. The stories they subsequently wrote were, in fact, well-structured, but many were also personal and expressive. The teacher's evaluative comments, however, did not refer to the expressiveness or artistry but were all directed toward whether they had "developed" the story well.

Language arts work also involved a large amount of practice in presentation of the self and in managing situations where the child was expected to be in charge. For example, there was a series of assignments in which each child had to be a "student teacher." The child had to plan a lesson in grammar, outlining, punctuation, or other language arts topic and explain the concept to the class. Each child was to prepare a worksheet or game and a homework assignment as well. After each presentation, the teacher and other children gave a critical appraisal of the "student teacher's" performance. Their criteria were: whether the student spoke clearly, whether the lesson was interesting, whether the student made any mistakes, and whether he or she kept control of the class. On an occasion when a child did not maintain control, the teacher said, "When you're up there, you have authority and you have to use it. I'll back you up."

The teacher of math and science explained to the observer that she likes   60
the ESS program because "the children can manipulate variables. They generate hypotheses and devise experiments to solve the problem. Then they have to explain what they found."

The executive elite school is the only school where bells do not demarcate the periods of time. The two fifth-grade teachers were very strict about changing classes on schedule, however, as specific plans for each session had been made. The teachers attempted to keep tight control over the children during lessons, and the children were sometimes flippant, boisterous, and occasionally rude. However, the children may be brought into line by reminding them that "It is up to you." "You must control yourself," "you are responsible for your work," you must "set your priorities." One teacher told a child, "You are the only driver of your car—and only you can regulate your speed." A new teacher complained to the observer that she had thought "these children" would have more control.

While strict attention to the lesson at hand is required, the teachers make relatively little attempt to regulate the movement of the children at other times. For example, except for the kindergartners the children in this school do not have to wait for the bell to ring in the morning; they may go to their classroom when they arrive at school. Fifth graders often came early to read, to finish work, or to catch up. After the first two months of school, the fifth-grade teachers did not line the children up to change classes or to go to gym, and so on, but, when the children were ready and quiet, they were told they could go—sometimes without the teachers.

In the classroom, the children could get materials when they needed them and took what they needed from closets and from the teacher's desk. They were in charge of the office at lunchtime. During class they did not have to sign out or ask permission to leave the room; they just got up and left. Because of the pressure to get work done, however, they did not leave the room very often. The teachers were very polite to the children, and the investigator heard no sarcasm, no nasty remarks, and few direct orders. The teachers never called the children "honey" or "dear" but always called them by name. The teachers were expected to be available before school, after school, and for part of their lunchtime to provide extra help if needed.

Discussion and Conclusion

One could attempt to identify physical, educational, cultural, and interpersonal characteristics of the environment of each school that might contribute to an empirical explanation of the events and interactions. For example, the investigator could introduce evidence to show that the following *increased* as the social class of the community increased (with the most marked differences occurring between the two districts): increased variety and abundance of teaching materials in the classroom; increased time reported spent by the teachers on preparation; higher social-class background and more prestigious educational institutions attended by teachers and administrators; more stringent board of education requirements regarding teaching methods; more frequent and demanding administrative evaluation of teachers; increased teacher support services such as in-service workshops; increased parent expenditure for school equipment over and above district or government funding; higher expectations of student ability on the part of parents, teachers, and administrators; higher expectations and demands regarding student achievement on the part of teachers, parents, and administrators; more positive attitudes on the part of the teachers as to the probable occupational futures of the children; an increase in the children's acceptance of classroom assignments; increased intersubjectivity between students and teachers; and increased cultural congruence between school and community.

All of these—and other—factors may contribute to the character and scope   65 of classroom events. However, what is of primary concern here is not the immediate causes of classroom activity (although these are in themselves quite important). Rather, the concern is to reflect on the deeper social meaning, the wider theoretical significance, of what happens in each social setting. In an attempt to assess the theoretical meaning of the differences among the schools, the work tasks and milieu in each will be discussed in light of the concepts used to define social class.

What potential relationships to the system of ownership of symbolic and physical capital, to authority and control, and to their own productive activity are being developed in children in each school? What economically relevant knowledge, skills, and predispositions are being transmitted in each classroom, and for what future relationship to the system of production are they appropriate? It is of course true that a student's future relationship to the process of production in society is determined by the combined effects of circumstances beyond elementary schooling. However, by examining elementary school activity in its social-class context in the light of our theoretical perspective on social class, we can see certain potential relationships already developing. Moreover, in this structure of developing relationships lies theoretical—and social—significance.

The working-class children are developing a potential *conflict* relationship with capital. Their present schoolwork is appropriate preparation for future wage labor that is mechanical and routine. Such work, insofar as it denies the human capacities for creativity and planning, is degrading; moreover, when performed in industry, such work is a source of profit to others. This situation produces industrial conflict over wages, working conditions, and control. However, the children in the working-class schools are not learning to be docile and obedient in the face of present or future degrading conditions or financial exploitation. They are developing abilities and skills of resistance. These methods are highly similar to the "slowdown," subtle sabotage, and other modes of indirect resistance carried out by adult workers in the shop, on the department store sales floor, and in some offices. As these types of resistance develop in school, they are highly constrained and limited in their ultimate effectiveness. Just as the children's resistance prevents them from learning socially legitimated knowledge and skills in school and is therefore ultimately debilitating, so is this type of resistance ultimately debilitating in industry. Such resistance in industry does not succeed in producing—nor is it intended to produce—fundamental changes in the relationships of exploitation or control. Thus, the methods of resistance that the working-class children are developing in school are only temporarily and *potentially* liberating.

In the middle-class school the children are developing somewhat different potential relationships to capital, authority, and work. In this school the work tasks and relationships are appropriate for a future relation to capital that is *bureaucratic.* Their schoolwork is appropriate for white-collar working-class and middle-class jobs in the supportive institutions of United States society. In these jobs one does the paperwork, the technical work, the sales and the social service in the private and state bureaucracies. Such work does not usually demand that one be creative, and one is not often rewarded for critical analysis of the system. One is rewarded, rather, for knowing the answers to the questions one is asked, for knowing where or how to find the answers, and for knowing which form, regulation, technique, or procedure is correct. While such work does not usually satisfy human needs for engagement and self-expression, one's salary can be exchanged for objects or activities that attempt to meet these needs.

In the affluent professional school the children are developing a potential relationship to capital that is instrumental and expressive and involves substantial negotiation. In their schooling these children are acquiring *symbolic capital*: they are being given the opportunity to develop skills of linguistic, artistic, and scientific expression and creative elaboration of ideas into concrete form. These skills are those needed to produce, for example, culture (for example, artistic, intellectual, and scientific ideas and other "products"). Their schooling is developing in these children skills necessary to become society's successful artists, intellectuals, legal, scientific, and technical experts and other professionals.

The developing relation of the children in this school to their work is creative and relatively autonomous. Although they do not have control over which ideas they develop or express, the creative act in itself affirms and utilizes the human potential for conceptualization and design that is in many cases valued as intrinsically satisfying.

Professional persons in the cultural institutions of society (in, say, academe, publishing, the nonprint media, the arts, and the legal and state bureaucracies) are in an expressive relationship to the system of ownership in society because the ideas and other products of their work are often an important means by which material relationships of society are given ideological (for example, artistic, intellectual, legal, and scientific) expression. Through the system of laws, for example, the ownership relations of private property are elaborated and legitimated in legal form; through individualistic and meritocratic theories in psychology and sociology, these individualistic economic relations are provided scientific "rationality" and "sense." The relationship to physical capital of those in society who create what counts as the dominant culture or ideology also involves substantial negotiation. The producers of symbolic capital often do not control the socially available physical capital nor the cultural uses to which it is put. They must therefore negotiate for money for their own projects. However, skillful application of one's cultural capital may ultimately lead to social (for example, state) power and to financial reward.

The executive elite school gives its children something that none of the other schools does: knowledge of and practice in manipulating the socially legitimated tools of analysis of systems. The children are given the opportunity to learn and to utilize the intellectually and socially prestigious grammatical, mathematical, and other vocabularies and rules by which elements are arranged. They are given the opportunity to use these skills in the analysis of society and in control situations. Such knowledge and skills are a most important kind of *symbolic capital*. They are necessary for control of a production system. The developing relationship of the children in this school to their work affirms and develops in them the human capacities for analysis and planning and helps to prepare them for work in society that would demand these skills. Their schooling is helping them to develop the abilities necessary for ownership and control of physical capital and the means of production in society.

The foregoing analysis of differences in schoolwork in contrasting social class contexts suggests the following conclusion: the "hidden curriculum" of schoolwork is tacit preparation for relating to the process of production in a particular way. Differing curricular, pedagogical, and pupil evaluation practices emphasize different cognitive and behavioral skills in each social setting and thus contribute to the development in the children of certain potential relationships to physical and symbolic capital, to authority, and to the process of work. School experience, in the sample of schools discussed here, differed qualitatively by social class. These differences may not only contribute to the development in the children in each social class of certain types of economically significant relationships and not others but would thereby help to *reproduce* this system of relations in society. In the contribution to the reproduction of unequal social relations lies a theoretical meaning and social consequence of classroom practice.

The identification of different emphases in classrooms in a sample of contrasting social class contexts implies that further research should be conducted in a large number of schools to investigate the types of work tasks and interactions in each to see if they differ in the ways discussed here and to see if similar potential relationships are uncovered. Such research could have as a product the further elucidation of complex but not readily apparent connections between everyday activity in schools and classrooms and the unequal structure of economic relationships in which we work and live.

● Applying a Materialist Frame

1. Elsewhere in the volume in which Anyon's essay appears, Henry Giroux writes: "Prior to the advent of the twentieth century and rise of scientific management movement that swept the curriculum field, there was no pretense on the part of educational leaders as to the purpose and function of public schooling. Schools, with few exceptions, were training grounds for character development and economic and social control."

   How might you make the same claim for the schools Anyon analyzes? In what ways do you see the educational practices she describes as being "training grounds" for "economic and social control"?

2. How do you relate to Anyon's writing? Do you find it persuasive? She blends firsthand observation of teachers with data about social and economic stratification. It's obvious she's not "unbiased" in that she has a motive for writing and a specific attitude about her subject. Does her account convince you of the conclusions she draws? Given the descriptions and data she provides, can you see how you might come to different conclusions? What would they be?

3. Do your own educational experiences match any of those she describes? Share your own history with others in your class or group. What can you learn about the kinds of schools they attended? Are you able to come to any "across the board" conclusions based on what students share with each other?

   How does your discussion help you see the materialist assumption that "the beliefs and attitudes of the social elite become the 'natural' or 'correct' beliefs and attitudes—those perpetuated in schools and in popular culture"?

topics for writing

1. In groups, identify public school teachers to interview who are all at the same grade level. Borrow a video camera and tripod from your school's media center and film the teachers as they answer your questions. (If you save the interviews as digital files, you can burn them onto a CD for viewing by the rest of your class.) You might consider beginning a research base of interviews that students in other courses or classes could use as sources.

   Write a group report based on what you learn from the interviews. Below is a list of questions you might ask, created by a liberal studies class.

   - To what extent are ideological attitudes acknowledged, ignored, dismissed, or discussed in depth by the teachers?
   - What do you learn about the structures in which they teach from the information you get?

   Teacher Survey Questions

   How old are you?

   How long have you been teaching?

   What is the socioeconomic background of your school?

   I teach because . . .

   What percentage of your personal household income do you contribute?

   What is the most important quality in a teacher?

   How would (or can) you describe your teaching style?

   What do you perceive as the major issues in education today?

   Do you develop or own curriculum, or is it given to you?

   What is it you do not like about teaching today, versus when you started out?

   Are you fairly compensated?

   What do you feel about the public's perception of your occupation, and the job you do?

   To what extent does job security influence what and how you teach?

   Do you try to keep religion or politics out of your teaching?

   Have you ever suffered for teaching from a religious or political foundation?

   What would you teach if you could teach *your own* curriculum?

   What would you expand upon—sex education, religion, politics—that you do not today?

   How fair do you think the grading systems *you* use are? Why?

2. What can you find out about the "back to basics" movement in United States educational theory? See if you can reconstruct the major arguments of those who proposed this doctrine. What was the impact of the movement on educational systems? Present your information either as an oral presentation or as a research project.

3. A publication called "College Bound Seniors, 1973–1974" printed the following chart that compares SAT scores on the verbal test with family income.

SAT Average	Parent's Mean Income
750–800	$24,124
700–749	21,980
650–699	21,292
600–649	20,330
550–599	19,481
500–549	18,824
450–499	18,122
400–449	17,387
350–399	16,182
300–349	14,355
250–299	11,428
200–249	8,639

Find a similar chart for a more recent year. Do the same relationships still hold true—that there's a direct correlation between SAT scores and family income?

Do further research on the relationship between income levels and collegiate attendance, acceptance to "elite" schools, SAT scores. Use your data to write a methodological analysis following Anyon's model.

4. Hirsch's book *Cultural Literacy* comes complete with an alphabetized list of what he thinks any American ought to know in order to consider himself or herself culturally literate. Following are some of the A's:

actions speak louder	Adams, John	Adirondack	Aeneas
than words	Quincy	Mountains	*Aeneid*, the
act of God	adaptation	adjective	aerobic
actuary	Addams, Jane	Adonis	Aeschylus
acupuncture	Addis Ababa	adrenal gland	Aesop's fables
A.D.	ad hoc	adrenaline	aesthetics
ad absurdum	ad hominem	adultery	affirmative
adagio	adieu	adverb	action
Adam and Eve	ad infinitum	AEC	affluent society
Adams, John	adios	Aegean, the	Afghanistan

Draw some conclusions from examining the list. What's being asked? Who would typically know these things?

- What would it mean to tell someone else they were culturally illiterate if they didn't score well? Hirsch maintains that creating such a knowledge base as he describes is "inherently democratic." What do you think?

- Is Hirsch's idea of teaching what he calls "contexts" a form of commodity exchange, memorization, assimilating a certain social groups' set of standards because that group controls curricula?

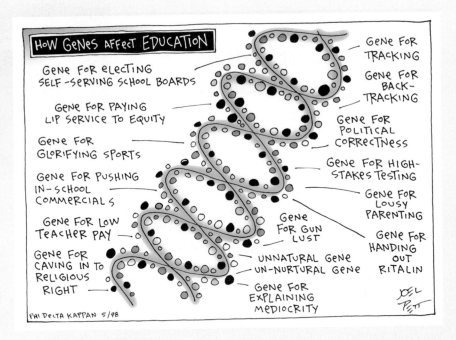

5. See the cartoon. It's meant to be a satire on those who claim that intelligence or success in school is genetically based. If you were to analyze this cartoon from the perspective of what you read in this chapter, how would you write it up?

   Discuss with others what form (essay, report, another cartoon) your response might take and then analyze accordingly.

6. Gary Peller, in an article titled "Reason and the Mob: Politics of Representation," argues the following:

   [W]hat has been presented in our social-political and our intellectual traditions as knowledge, truth, objectivity and reason are actually merely the effects of a particular form of social power, the victory of a particular way of representing the world that then presents itself as beyond mere interpretation, as truth itself.

   Using Peller's statement as a thesis, argue his point (or use it to make your own point) by drawing from the readings in this chapter.

7. Use Anyon's article to "prove" Marx's *A Contribution to the Critique of Political Economy* from Chapter 7. What ideological "fights" are taking place between the different classrooms Anyon describes for you?

   Show through your writing how Anyon's research reflects the relationships between culture and social class that Marx described.

chapter 9

Reading Critically About Legal Values

This Chapter's Rhetorical Concepts

- Understanding the ways in which social needs for stability create culture
- Thinking through structured frames
- Finding avenues for authorship

Reflections on the Civil War

BRUCE CATTON

Bruce Catton is a well-known United States Civil War historian. In 1954, he received the Pulitzer Prize for his book A Stillness at Appomattox. *His other many works on Civil War history include* Mr. Lincoln's Army *(1951),* Glory Road *(1952),* This Hallowed Ground *(1956),* Grant Moves South *(1960),* Grant Takes Command *(1969),* The Centennial History of the Civil War *(3 vol., 1961–65), and* Prefaces to History *(1970). This chapter, "A Rich Man's War—a Poor Man's Fight," is from his book,* Reflections on the Civil War, *which appeared in 1982.*

What we have been talking about so far are the early regiments—the volunteer regiments, which were made up largely of men who were in the army simply because they wanted to be in it.

After the first year or two the crop of volunteers dwindled almost to the vanishing point. The Federal Government, like the Confederate government, was obliged to resort to conscription. The only trouble was that the Congress in Washington adopted probably the worst conscription law anybody ever imagined. It had two very bad features; first, a man whose number was drawn for drafting could pay a $300 commutation fee and get excused from service. His number might be drawn again later, but, unless and until it was, his payment of a $300 fee excused him. Consequently the well-to-do man could not be forced into the army and the poor man could. Bear in mind that in 1862, $300 was a very fair year's income for an unskilled laborer. Even a skilled mechanic would not make twice that much money in a year, and in the ordinary course of things, never actually saw as much as $300 in cash.

An even worse feature of the draft act was the fact that it permitted a man who had been drafted to hire a substitute. If he could find some man who was willing to fight if paid, he would pay him whatever the market rate called for and the man would go and fill the draftee's place. If he got killed, that was too bad; but the draftee himself was off the hook. The Civil War had quickly become what the common soldiers on both sides called it—a Rich Man's War, and a Poor Man's Fight.

Technically, the draft did not put a great many men into uniform. That is, the number of drafted men who became soldiers was comparatively small. What the draft did do and what made it very important to the Government, was to stimulate recruiting drives by states, cities, and other government organizations. The draft, which was very unpopular, would not be applied in any locality that had met its quota of recruits. The country was divided up into Congressional Districts; its need for men was apportioned to those districts, and each district was supposed to provide a specific number of men. If that proper number of men had volunteered in a given district, the draft would not apply there. So, it was in the interest of government authorities in the counties and cities to recruit men as vigorously as they could, simply to keep the draft from affecting the people in that area. In that way, the draft was extremely effective. It stirred recruiting drives all over the country and resulted in a great many men going into the army who probably would not have enlisted if they were left to their own devices.

The draft also caused a great many substitutes to go to war; at least 75,000 men were hired by drafted civilians. In addition, about 42,000 men were paid to go into the army as substitutes by men who were enrolled in the draft and were simply trying to do their best to support the war effort. Oddly enough, one of the men who sent a substitute in his place was Abraham Lincoln himself. He, of course, was not subject to the draft, but he did hire a substitute and the man served a full term in the army and apparently acquitted himself very well.

So, between the added number of volunteers and the substitutes who were paid directly by draftees or other stay-at-homes, the Conscription Act did bring a large number of men into the army.

With all of the great defects in the Civil War Draft Law, it was inevitable that the enforcement of the law would be attended by grave difficulties. These were much more serious than anything we have seen in this country since then. In New York City, for instance, in the summer of 1863, very shortly after the time of the Battle of Gettysburg, one of the worst riots that ever afflicted any American city broke out because of the draft. The riot started at a Provost Marshal's office in mid-Manhattan, where draft numbers were being drawn. People gathered outside, objecting to the whole process, and soon started throwing bricks through the windows. Emotions exploded, and the mob destroyed the office, beat up the people who were in it, and went rampaging through town. Because of the violence, the Draft Act had to be suspended in New York City and the militia had to be called out. But the militia was unable to cope with the situation and the mob got completely out of control. It set fires and lynched as many black people as it could lay its hands on. It burned down a black orphanage and did its best to destroy the people who came out of the burning building. All in all, in the course of a week about a thousand were killed or wounded. In the end, regiments had to be brought in from the Army of the Potomac, fresh from the battlefield at Gettysburg, to restore order.

Whereas the draft riots in New York City were by far the worst of any during the Civil War, they were by no means the only ones. A very serious situation developed in the anthracite coal-mining regions of Pennsylvania, where the coal miners, who tended to be a downtrodden class of laborers at that period of the country's development, were trying to form a union and get some sort of decent pay and working conditions in the mines. While they were doing this, the draft came along, and it did seem to happen that very often the men who had been the most active in promoting unionization were the first ones to be picked up by the Provost Marshal and taken off to the army. The coal miners rioted up and down the countryside, tearing down draft offices and in general defying the authorities. Again, troops had to be sent in to tone things down and restore order.

As a matter of fact, order was restored finally by dint of some fast footwork on the part of President Lincoln who, I think, had a certain amount of sympathy for what the coal miners were up against. Lincoln worked out, or at least consented to, a very neat little arrangement that rested on the Congressional District allocation. There was an obscure provision in the Draft Act stating that a man should be credited to the Congressional District from which he came, rather than the one in which he actually enlisted. That is, if a man living in Meadeville, Pennsylvania, happened to be in Philadelphia and enlisted there, his enlistment should be credited to the district back home in Meadeville. It rarely happened, but that was the theory.

Some people got to work and examined the returns in Eastern Pennsyl-   10
vania and discovered, or claimed they discovered, that hundreds of men who had been enlisted in Philadelphia actually came from the anthracite regions and that these regions had, consequently, met their quotas. As a result, the draft was finally suspended in the anthracite areas, and things went on very smoothly.

There were other cases where troops had to be called in. There was actually a small military engagement in north-central Ohio where the farmers dug in around some isolated woodland and announced their defiance of the Government. Troops were sent up from Columbus, and a few shots were fired, without doing a great deal of harm to anybody, before this uprising was put down.

The draft was obviously extremely unpopular. No Congressman and no member of the State Legislature wanted to see his people drafted, so the state and local governments came to the rescue.

A city or town would offer a bounty to any man who enlisted voluntarily; the County Board of Commissioners would add its own fee to that; the State Legislature might add some more, and leading citizens might raise a fund. Toward the final year and a half of the war, the bounties got so high that a man could get anywhere from five hundred to a thousand dollars simply for enlisting. Substitute brokers began to appear in the cities; that is, men who would find volunteers for a man who didn't want to serve the time himself. They would get paid out of the bounty which the enlistee would get, and they rode herd on him to see that they got it.

It also led to the development, all across the North, of a class of men known as bounty jumpers. A man would come in and enlist, draw his bounty, desert again, enlist in still a third place, and keep this up as long as he could get away with it. There are reports of men who had enlisted as many as six or eight times. These men, of course, were of no earthly use as soldiers. It was hard enough to get them to the front at all; they had to be kept constantly under guard. There are a number of accounts of convoys accompanied by armed guards coming down from the North to the camps in Virginia. As deserters or bounty jumpers tried to jump off the train, they came under fire—and some were killed. Many, of course, got away.

If they actually had to join the army in camp, they would desert the first   15 time they got into battle. Often they would allow themselves to be captured, for the Confederacy let it be known that they needed workers in war plants in the South, that wages were high, that any prisoner of war who wanted to go to work in a factory in Richmond, Atlanta, or where ever, would be welcomed and well paid. They got quite a lot of men that way. The men, of course, were not worth any more as workers than they were as soldiers, and, in 1864 the Confederacy withdrew this offer.

General Grant remarked at the end of the war that not one soldier in eight who was brought in by the high-bounty system ever did any useful service at the front. The men in the ranks, themselves, abominated these high-bounty troops; they ostracized them. They did their best to shove them up into the front lines where they would at least get shot at before they could surrender. Whenever they could, they made life uncomfortable for them, and there are lots of ways you can do that in the army.

Amid all of this, the men who were actually drafted, the men who couldn't hire a substitute and couldn't pay the commutation fee, usually turned out to be fairly good soldiers. Even to the end, the Union army depended primarily on the volunteers. In the winter of 1863–64, especially along in January and February of 1864, the army had to do an enormous job of recruiting because the term of service for most of the soldiers in those days was three years. Those men who had enlisted at the start of the war, the enthusiastic, ardent men, the men who made by far the best soldiers, were running out of time; their enlistments were about to expire. There was no way on earth the government could compel them to stay in the army if they didn't want to. The government had already given these soldiers an object lesson about the folly of volunteering through its abominable conscription act. Then, it suddenly had to go to these men, hat in hand, and ask them to reenlist.

It's amazing, but many of them did stay on. These were men who had been through the mill. They had been through the terrible battles—Shiloh, Chancellorsville, Gettysburg, and Chickamauga. They had survived them, knew what it was like, and knew that even worse fights were coming. They had done their duty and were entitled to go home. In spite of all this, many of them voluntarily reenlisted. The percentage was a good deal higher in the Western armies than it was in the Army of the Potomac, but even in the Army of the Potomac, close to 30,000 volunteers reenlisted that winter of 1863–64; a larger number did so in the West.

If a regiment could show a certain percentage of its number reenlisting, it was entitled thereafter to call itself a Veteran Volunteer Regiment, and that was a title the men prized very, very highly, particularly after the war. If they had belonged to a Veteran Volunteer Regiment, they were sure to mention the fact.

In one way or another, the Union army managed to keep itself at adequate   20
strength and carry on with the war. It should be noted that the Confederate government was a great deal wiser. It came to a draft act earlier and, after a very brief experience with such loopholes as substitutes, it tightened its rules and made the draft a fair, workable act. It did not have nearly the trouble the Northern government had; its major problem was that it didn't have as many men from which to draw. What helped to cripple the Confederacy as much as anything, probably, was the fact that so many of its factories and its railroad system—actually all of its transportation systems—were fatally handicapped because the army had drained off the manpower. It didn't have enough men to both run the war plants and keep the army at proper strength. It could do one or the other, but it couldn't do both. Because the war plants couldn't operate at full strength, because the railroads were so run down that the supply services kept collapsing, the strain on the soldiers was great. They had to get along with inadequate food and clothing; they were poorly shod, as often as not, and they had no tents. Toward the final year of the war, when the picture was getting even darker and the Northern armies were advancing deeper and deeper into the South, the Confederate armies were profoundly affected by a very high rate of desertion.

By the end of 1864, of the men on the Southern army rolls, there were probably as many at home as with the colors. The mainspring had broken; the men who elected to go home and look after their families can't be blamed. Their government was unable to take care of their families for them, and they had stood all that any soldiers could properly be asked to stand.

So, in the final months of the war, the Confederate armies ran down and, as they did so, the Union armies began to get a new source of recruits. A great many of the veterans whose time had expired in the spring of 1864 and who went back home to enjoy life as civilians, began, by the end of the year, to drift back into the army. Some of the regiments that were formed at the end of 1864 and the beginning of 1865 were first-rate regiments because they were full of veteran soldiers—not bounty jumpers, not hired substitutes, but men who knew their way around in the army and who had come back because they apparently wanted to be in at the finish. They could see the war being won, and they wanted to be there when it was won.

● Applying a Materialist Frame

1. Catton cites two serious drawbacks to the Union's draft law: an "excuse" fee of $300 and the hiring of substitutes.

   - How would a materialist perspective explain these draft law features?
   - What passages or quotations from anything in the materialist critiques at the start of this section can help argue your point?

2. Catton suggests here that "the draft was extremely effective." He also suggests that it was not primarily by drafting men that the draft law was effective. How does he describe this effectiveness?

   Though Catton doesn't examine his own statements to any degree, what kinds of issues is he raising here, between what men "intend" and what they "experience"? Did you notice this same distinction being made in the materialist readings? Where? How do you see the connections?

3. If men could pay to have someone take their place in the Civil War, who do you think these men were who would agree to such a proposal?

   From the other perspective, Catton says that the men who paid others to serve for them were "simply trying to do their best to support the war effort." Do you believe his conclusions here? In your opinion, what *other* motivations might explain why they paid for substitutes? What "class" attitudes are being defended or deflected in Catton's statement?

4. You may never have read about the 1863 New York City draft riots, when armies had to be brought in "fresh from the battle at Gettysburg" to suppress the disturbances, and blacks were targeted. Why do you think this was happening in a Northern city? How did the press at the time explain it?

   - Try to locate firsthand accounts or reports of the 1863 riots and see if you can identify how language was used to *create* social attitudes through popular media.
   - What do you make of Catton's rather tongue-in-cheek reference (para. 8) that "it did seem to happen that very often the men who had been the most active in promoting unionization were the first ones to he picked up by the Provost Marshal and taken off to the army"?
   - What do you think about the way President Lincoln "solved" the crises? What does this incident tell you about how political decisions are often dependent upon unspoken, hidden motives? Why do you think the motives have to be unspoken? What would be the dangers to those in power of open discussion?

5. What is Catton's attitude toward the "bounty" soldiers? In what ways would you say this attitude reflects the state's attitude?

   - What ideological stories does Catton's attitude bring to mind? Why do you think he says, "[T]he men, of course, were not worth any more as workers than they were as soldiers" (para. 15)?
   - How were these men different from those who would have been "hired" to fight by those who had the means to pay?

The Labor Wars

SIDNEY LENS

Sidney Lens has written about American labor for over three decades. His works include The Crisis of American Labor *(1959);* Working Men: The Story of Labor *(1960);* The Forging of the American Empire *[1971] (2003);* The Labor Wars: From the Molly Maguires to the Sitdowns *(1973).*

For ten weeks in 1970 the largest industrial corporation in the United States, General Motors, confronted the largest industrial union in the United States, the United Auto Workers. The firm, with resources larger than the gross national product of many countries, was shut tight as 400,000 card-carrying members of the UAW "hit the bricks."

In an earlier day, four or five decades ago, a strike of this sort would have provoked a burst of corporate energy. The company would have prepared itself with a small army of "guards" and Pinkerton spies; would have stockpiled guns and tear gas; and organized a "citizens' committee" to prepare a "back-to-work" movement. Its personnel department would have combed the hinterlands for strikebreakers, professional and amateur; its lawyers would have drafted injunctions to be presented by pliable district attorneys to equally pliable judges. The tenor at the GM offices would have been one of war and accelerated activity. In the union offices throughout the country the pulse would have been equally rapid. Flying squadrons would have been formed to guard against an influx of strikebreakers at railroad stations or highways. Visiting committees would have been delegated to talk with scabs. Plans would have been formulated for mass picketing. Calls would have been made to other unions in other shops to alert them to the possible need for help on the picket lines. And as the lines formed on the first day of the walkout—September 14—there would be an air of tension. Would Johnny So-and-So of the tool and die shop go through? Were the men on the assembly line solid? Would the police attack this morning? A judge issue an injunction?

Among those outside the plant gates in September 1970 were some who had participated in the sitdown strikes against GM back in 1936–37. Many still remembered the Battle of Bulls Run outside Fisher Body No. 2 in Flint on January 11, 1937. While the strikers sat inside the plant that cold, wintry afternoon, hoping for Governor Frank Murphy to get talks started with the great corporation, the company shut off the heat, and police prevented food from being sent in. Soon the battle lines formed. Strikers on the outside crashed through the small wall of police to carry bread and coffee to their beleaguered comrades within, and when the cops reformed their ranks two hours later a three-hour battle ensued in which the men in blue used tear gas, clubs, and guns; the unionists metal pipes, nuts, bolts, sticks, bottles, coffee mugs, and two-pound auto-door hinges. "We wanted peace," said strike leaders over the microphone in their sound truck, "General Motors chose war. Give it to them." Within minutes the sedan of Sheriff Thomas Wolcott was toppled over, and before hostilities ended, three other police vehicles were similarly treated. At midnight, as the sitdown strikers turned a powerful water hose on the officers, the fighting came to a halt. Fourteen strikers had been taken to the hospital with bullet wounds that day. Across the country thousands of unionists faced the police and National Guardsmen in front of GM plants, and not a few were injured in the ensuing melees.

Now in 1970 the strike situation evoked very different responses. The company did not try to keep its plants open, except for those that the union agreed were needed to feed parts to other manufacturers. There were no strikebreakers, scabs, back-to-work movements, or citizens' committees. There were no shootings, tear-gassings, clubbings, nothing even remotely resembling the Battle of Bulls Run—and, no arrests. The union organized no flying squadrons, sent no urgent alerts to anyone, and its members picketed perfunctorily in order to qualify for strike benefits. There was no fear of attack by the police or National Guard and small likelihood that management would seek injunctions in the courts. The most lethal weapon used by the UAW this time was a strike fund, upward of a hundred million dollars, collected from dues and assessments, out of which weekly benefits were paid to those on the picket line.

By and large this kind of non-violent confrontation was now the pattern in all the strikes between so-called big labor and big business—in auto, steel, trucking, aircraft, railroads—and in most of the 3,000 to 6,000 work stoppages each year of lesser import. During the 1956 national steel strike, U.S. Steel at its South Works mill in Chicago furnished the picket captain with a desk just inside the gate and ran a power line and water to the union's six trailers. One night it supplied the pickets with beer. In another mill, management provided portable toilets for the men who had walked off the job. Republic Steel, which a generation before had relentlessly opposed the right of its men to be represented by a union of their choice, told its workers to take their vacations during the strike so that they would lose little or no pay, and would be ready and fit when the mills stoked up again. Not everyone, of course, conformed to the new "rules." The Kohler Company near Sheboygan, Wisconsin, precipitated a strike in 1954 that lasted eight long years. General Electric usually gave the two electrical unions it dealt with much more trouble than GM gave UAW. Yet picket line fights and arrests were comparatively rare, and bloodshed even more so.

The labor wars seemed to be over. If the adversaries had not exactly found a *modus vivendi* whereby all disputes could be adjusted automatically, nevertheless their quarrels usually were as bland as those of two corporate lawyers negotiating a contract for real estate. And the strikes were simply waiting games to see which side would feel the economic pinch first, rather than wars of extermination. A truce of sorts existed between labor and capital in which neither side exactly learned to love the other but did not go to former extremes either.

A generation of young zealots today has deduced from such circumstances either that labor has always been a quiescent adjunct to the American establishment, or that its struggles in the long past have been somehow irrelevant. Oriented as the younger generation is to the quest for peace, and racial and sexual equality, it has downgraded the battles of another epoch, though they were far bloodier, far more militant and most certainly "relevant" to today's struggles. It has closed its eyes so tightly to the earlier efforts, that it seldom bothers to study strikers' tactics or strategies, though they bear great resemblance to those of the present. For all practical purposes the labor wars—that was the term applied by the New York *Tribune* to the 1877 railroad strikes and used frequently thereafter—are now all but forgotten. It is as if they have been drawn into and covered by historical quicksand, with no one to mourn their martyrs and no one to remember their import and legacy.

II

The labor wars were a specific response to a specific set of injustices at a time when industrial and financial capitalism was establishing its predominance over American society. In a sense the battles were no different from the hundreds of other violent clashes against social injustice, as normal as the proverbial apple pie in the nation's annals.

Colonial America witnessed armed uprisings of small farmers and backwoodsmen against authoritarian governments, or tenants against landlords, and at least forty conspiracies and revolts by black slaves and white "indentured" servants. The colonial equivalents of Eugene V. Debs, Big Bill Haywood, and Harry Bridges were Nathaniel Bacon, Jacob Leisler, the North Carolina Regulators, and a dozen blacks whose names have slipped into the recesses of history. In post-revolutionary America, from 1783 to the Civil War, social opposition took a dozen forms, varying from Shays' Rebellion and the bloody collisions between Jeffersonians and Hamiltonians in the 1790s, to the hesitant efforts of unions to establish themselves in the face of "conspiracy" prosecutions, to the workingmen's parties of the 1820s, to the utopian communities of Robert Owen and the Fourierists, and to George Henry Evans' "new agrarianism" which in much-diluted form became the Homestead Act.

In this tempestuous period, when the nation threatened to burst asunder on more than one occasion, the United States was still an agricultural and rural nation. In 1840 only one out of twelve people lived in cities of more than 8,000, and in 1860 the ratio was still a mere one out of six. But industry was flexing its muscles and would soon burst the shackles of technological backwardness and

10

political restraint. From 1840 to 1860 the value of industrial products quadrupled, from a half-billion dollars a year to 2 billion, and from 1860 to 1889 quadrupled again to 9 billion. As of 1909 factory production had jumped to $21 billion and as of 1919 to $62 billion. The railroads, a barometer of industrial advance, boasted 2,800 miles of track in 1840; 30,600 miles in 1860; and approximately 200,000 miles at the end of the century. In this development heavy industry, such as steel, relentlessly and inexorably replaced light industry, such as shoemaking, as the core of the economy. And as industries mushroomed and the railroads crisscrossed the land, some men made fabulous fortunes, grew fat and arrogant. The merchant-capitalist of the first half of the century was considered rich if his wealth spiraled to a few hundred thousand dollars. The industrial-capitalist of the last half of the century measured his wealth in millions, sometimes tens of millions. "Commodore" Cornelius Vanderbilt, the railroad magnate who died in 1877, left an estate of $105 million and a heritage of contempt for the populace that was epitomized in his famous statement: "Law? What do I care about law? Hain't I got the power?"

Growth was accompanied by an orgy of corruption and thievery such as the nation had never seen before. Men like Vanderbilt, J. P. Morgan, E. H. Harriman, and Jay Cooke flouted all the rules in an unmatched display of materialism. Typical was the transaction of J. P. Morgan during the Civil War, by which he bought defective rifles, already condemned, *from* the government, for $17,500 one day, and resold them *to* the government the next day for $110,000. Philip Armour, just twenty-six years old, bought pork at $18 a barrel and sold it in quick turnover for $40.

A symbol of the time was the rail tycoon Jay Gould, about whom it may be said that nothing illegal or immoral was alien to his character. He got his start by cheating two partners in a leather business. He printed and sold counterfeit share certificates in the Erie Railroad, and, when the fraud was discovered, slipped away to New Jersey with his partner, Jim Fisk, and a tidy $6 million in cash, plus the Erie's financial records. Later he bribed New York legislators to pass a law making his act legal. Ironically, with the haul from the Erie brigandage Gould set out to corner the $15 million in gold then in circulation.

It would be false to say that all entrepreneurs were as bereft of conscience as Gould or Vanderbilt. But for the acquisitive classes money became a religion and "Social Darwinism" a salient dogma. "Under the natural order of things," wrote the oracle of Social Darwinism, Herbert Spencer, "society is constantly excreting its unhealthy, imbecile, slow, vacillating, faithless members" in order to leave room for the competent ones entitled to reward. As in the animal world the fit survived; the unfit were rightly ground under. Gould and Vanderbilt became buccaneers before Spencer arrived on the scene, but they and their contemporaries operated on the simple thesis that the capitalists, by their proven superiority, were entitled to rule; the workers, by their proven ineptness, obligated to accept their judgments. And when workers strayed from the prescribed path—to form unions and go on strike, for instance—it was only just and proper that they be spanked with strikebreakers, Pinkerton spies, and blacklisting. They had trespassed the area of decision-making allotted to their "betters," and their due was the stick—not the carrot. Thus it was that for six decades, from the panic of 1873 to the end of the New Deal, an autocratic capitalist class fought one war after another against a working class made desperate by the hard-nosed abuse it had absorbed.

III

Properly speaking, the labor wars were wars of capital—and its unswerving ally, government—*against* labor. The owners of capital justified their attacks on the lofty theory that they were defending society from rabble, scum, and outsiders, intent on desecrating law and order and uprooting the great free enterprise system which allegedly was responsible for America's high living standards. They were upholding, they said, the inalienable democratic right of a man to work wherever he pleased, even as a strikebreaker. The record shows, however, that the corporations' true objective was to limit wages or reduce them, to retain or lengthen the work week, and to wring as much work for each dollar of pay as human energy could deliver. The rest of what was said was persiflage to allay possible public criticism. The government too justified its dispatch of troops and its requests for injunctions on the theory that it was defending society against lawlessness. In reality, however, the lawlessness was usually created by the troops and by the government's own denial of civil liberties. The real purpose, thinly disguised in phrases of "impartiality," was to aid management in emasculating the unions.

The labor wars, then, played a pivotal role in American history. They were   15
the antidote to an insolent philosophy, expressed best in robber baron Jay Gould's classic remark: "I can hire one-half of the working class to kill the other half." The labor wars were indispensable to achieving the present levels of consumption. They helped win a measure of industrial and political freedom for the underclasses. They placed limits on the power of the robber barons and financial goliaths. And toward the end, in the 1930s, they were part of a social upheaval that transformed *laissez-faire* capitalism to controlled capitalism.

Along with the Revolution and certain farm and slave uprisings during colonial days, the labor wars were among the most heroic events in the American epic. They typified the ageless conflict between the privileged and underprivileged, the oppressor and oppressed. In an era of unbridled *laissez-faire*, the prevailing thesis was every man for himself, devil take the hindmost. A worker was deemed to have no other right—if he were dissatisfied, as he was all too often—but to leave his job and seek another. If there were no jobs to be had, he could move in with relatives, join the soup line, or starve. Even some "socialists" questioned whether the proletariat was justified in taking concerted action. Thus, *The American Socialist*, published by John Humphrey Noyes' communitarian group at

Oneida, New York, wrote during the 1877 railroad riots: "The laborers . . . have no legal or moral right to insist that certain men who have been employing them shall pay them whatever wages they demand. They have a right to quit work and seek better pay elsewhere, but have no right to make war or destroy property, or prevent others from taking their places at the reduced wages."

The labor wars, after torturous decades and innumerable picket line murders, secured for the workingman a right which he had been previously denied, totally or partially: the right to collective action. Without that right much of what we consider progressive today in the American way of life would have been impossible—the abolition of child labor, workmen's compensation for accidents, safety standards, protection of women and immigrants, unemployment compensation, social security, low-cost housing (inadequate as it is), Medicare, and many other reforms. Tens of millions of proletarians would be chained to their machines without benefit of shorter hours, seniority rights, grievance machinery, paid vacations and holidays, sick pay, supplemental unemployment compensation, and health insurance.

All of these benefits had to be won through bitter contention. The battles were related to that ceaseless struggle for power between the radical and reactionary strains of American life, between Jeffersonians and Hamiltonians in early America, between something vaguely called the New Left and the military-industrial complex today. The struggle always has been unequal, but in the last third of the nineteenth century the gap widened to a chasm. Tenuous labor unions fell more and more on the defensive against the escalating might of the new transport and mass-production industries that were fast replacing the old small-producer economy. In the beginning, labor made no headway at all, suffering one defeat and bloodbath after another. Then, in the last decade and a half of the century, it was able to sink stable roots in one corner of the economy, the decentralized industries—such as construction. The bastions where the giant corporations prevailed, however, still eluded working-class penetration. Indeed it took six stinging decades before the underclasses achieved sufficient countervailing power against the impersonal industrial and financial duchies that even today still tower over society. Along the way the road was strewn with the martyrs of the Pennsylvania coal fields of the 1870s, the so-called Molly Maguires; of the railroad workers of 1877 and 1894; the Homestead strikers; the metal miners in the West and the coal miners in the East; the garment workers; the steel workers of 1919 and 1937; and of the auto, rubber, and other mass production laborers of 1933–38. During those three or four generations the American proletariat was preyed upon by industrial spies, company police, sheriffs' deputies, National Guardsmen, federal troops, unsympathetic judges, and a hostile press. The end result was not a final victory by any means, but a victory nonetheless. The labor movement made a quantum jump in numbers and influence; its struggles in the 1940s and 1950s were no longer primarily for union recognition or against wage cuts, but for positive benefits such as wages, seniority rights, supplementary unemployment compensation. And, above all, they no longer met the persistent violent reaction of employers and government so characteristic of an earlier day.

In this grand scenario three distinct features are evident:

1. The labor wars were conducted outside the pall of narrow legality. Had the workers abided by court injunctions against picketing and had they shown the expected respect for the organs of law and order—police, militia, federal troops—unions today would have been dwarfs in size and impotent in influence.

2. The ultimate enemy was almost always the city, state, and federal governments. Had government been truly impartial, let alone oriented toward the exploited classes, unions would have attained decisive power before the end of the nineteenth century.

3. The labor wars, at first two-sided encounters between labor and capital, became triangular as a progressively entrenched AFL hierarchy gave both witting and unwitting aid to the scions of business. Certainly the mass production industries would have yielded to unionism decades before it did if it had not been for the Tory attitudes of AFL leadership; and the unions would unquestionably have been more dynamic if their own reactionary officials had not signed backdoor contracts in the 1930s to prevent militant unions from organizing.

When great events pass into history they are given the cosmetic treatment. 20 Violence, bitterness, deception, illegality, immorality, conflict, are scraped away to give the appearance of friendly, orderly progress. But it didn't happen that way between labor and capital in America, and it is well to remember that what was won was won by flouting both institutionalized conformity and one-sided legality.

● Applying a Materialist Frame

1. How does Sidney Lens go about trying to capture your interest in his writing? When he talks about the "Labor Wars" of 1877, how does he try to convince you of their importance? Is he successful? Why or why not? What does your answer tell you about a "persuasive" way to get your attention?

2. What do you think Lens means when he says, "for the acquisitive classes money became a religion and 'Social Darwinism' a salient dogma"? What is Social Darwinism, and how can you relate it to materialist thought?

3. Lens writes of a time in American history when "labor wars were wars of capital—and its unswerving ally, government—*against* labor." What do you know about such "wars"? Find examples from as many sources as you can: history, movies, family stories, old newspaper items, and so on.

4. In what ways do you think Lens uses language to "load" his arguments? In other words, find examples of what you'd consider to be "loaded" terms, terms that carry with them value judgments you recognize clearly.

   • Could you rewrite passages, substituting what you'd call more "neutral" terms for those of his you consider too biased?

   • Has your substitution of terms changed Lens's meaning in any way? Would his conclusions be different, do you think, if he were to use your language?

5. Lens cites three distinct features of the labor wars. All three of these features argue that labor has always operated from a position outside the interests of the dominant class. What arguments does he offer here, and how persuasive do you find them?

6. "When great events pass into history," Lens writes in his conclusion, "they are given the cosmetic treatment. Violence, bitterness, deception, illegality, immorality, conflict, are scraped away to give the appearance of friendly, orderly progress."

   • What other "great events" that have "passed into history" do you know about that have essentially been sanitized or rewritten after the fact?

   • Is Lens really saying that "winners write the histories"? Where can you find evidence of such "historical" accounts? Why do you think people generally accept such accounts?

Three Days of Hell in L.A.

CLARK STATEN

These Web accounts all come from the same source and profess to have been written in "real-time" as the South-Central Los Angeles riots occurred in 1992. These accounts are reprinted in substantially unedited form.

L.A. Police Acquitted, Rioting Strikes S.E. Los Angeles

Los Angeles, CA—In an unexpected climax to a year of racial strife surrounding the alleged L.A.P.D. beating of Rodney King, a jury of six men and six women found the officers not guilty. The jurors were unable to reach a conclusion regarding one charge against Officer Laurence Powell, age 29, for using excessive force under the color of authority. A mistrial was declared by Judge Stanley Weisberg on that one count, with eight jurors voting for acquittal and four for a guilty verdict.

Sgt. Stacey Koon, Officer Theodore Briseno, and Officer Timothy Wind were found completely not guilty on all counts of official misconduct, excessive force, filing false police reports, and assault with a deadly weapon. District Attorney Ira Reiner said that no decision had been reached in regard to whether or not to retry Officer Powell on the one count that was declared indecisive.

An eighty-one second video tape, captured by a concerned citizen, sparked the controversy regarding police brutality and led to eventual indictments of the officers. Many months of investigation, charges, and counter-charges followed the release of the video tape. Various segments of the community in Los Angeles were polarized as the details of the event played out daily on local television stations.

A trial ensued. It was moved to suburban Simi Valley, CA, due to pre-trial publicity and the seemingly premature release of the now "infamous" tape of the police wielding batons and striking King repeatedly. A jury was chosen that contained eleven white jurors and one of Filipino descent. Black civil rights activists complained that no blacks were chosen for the jury and that the choice of jurors was another example of racism.

The trial and surrounding investigations also sparked unprecedented   5
criticism of Police Chief Daryl Gates and the entire Los Angeles Police Department. The Christopher Commission was formed and did find occasions of racism and institutional brutality. Police officers in Los Angeles were also found to have used official computer systems for insensitive and racist remarks. Calls were received for the resignation of the Chief Gates.

Lawyers for the officers charged in the allegations argued that the policemen believed that King was acting under the influence of the animal tranquilizer PCP, which often causes violent and unpredictable behavior that has resulted in the injury of numerous emergency responders and law enforcement officers. They also testified as to King's combativeness that didn't appear on the tape. King was not found to have been using PCP, but was found to have a blood alcohol level of .19, which is more than double that allowed in most states as indicative of "drunken driving." The evidence was weighed and the jury found the four officers not guilty after seven days of deliberations.

A reaction to the acquittal of the four officers was immediately received from blacks and civilrights activists. The Mayor of Los Angeles, Tom Bradley, said: "We must express our profound anger and outrage (at the acquittal), but we also must not endanger the reforms that we have made by striking out blindly." He continued, "We must demand that the L.A.P.D. fire the officers who beat Rodney King and take them off the streets once and for all."

California State Senator Ed Smith said that he was also shocked. Smith was quoted by the United Press as saying, "It's hard to beleive that there was no sustaining of the charges at all . . . the world saw the videotape and if that conduct is sanctioned by law in California, then we have to re-write the law." Exec. Director Ramona Ripston of the American Civil Liberties Union called the verdicts "a travesty of justice."

Response to the Jury Verdict

According to late afternoon and early evening news reports, citizens of the Southeast and Southcentral area of Los Angeles have decided that they can't wait for laws to be changed. Reportedly, numerous occasions of rioting, arson, and looting are taking place at the time of this report. Live helicopter news reports showed the air over several neighborhoods appeared to be filled with smoke. Los Angeles Fire Department officials report that as many as nine (9) large stores are burning, and that numerous cars have been "torched" in an attempt to block intersections.

The Los Angeles Police 77th Station is said to have requested reinforcements due to the violence that is believed sparked by the police acquittal. The Cable News Network (CNN) reported that they had received a report of "white motorists" being pulled from their cars and "beaten" by a crowd of black youths. No official source would confirm the type of injuries in the area of the disturbance, but an Emergency Medical Services (EMS) source said that the situation was "extremely fluid" and that fire department medic units had been called to several locations.

An L.A.P.D. police sergeant, who asked not to be identified, said that the police department was activating a "tactical recall," which would cancel days off for all police officers and cause them to immediately report for work. Officers were seen at several locations to be wearing the standard "riot gear" that is used during periods of unrest and to protect officers from assaults. A Los Angeles Television station (KTLA) is reporting that few officers were in evidence in the area of the reported violence and looting, but that they appeared to be assembling at area police stations.

As the story continues to unfold, senseless violence seems to beget senseless violence. Parker Center in downtown Los Angeles reportedly has been under "seige" by a large crowd of protestors since shortly after the jury's announcement. Several reports of arrests have been received, but most observers agree that the police officers there appear subdued and restrained in their actions. Sporadic events of violence and arson, in predomantly black neighborhoods, continue to be reported.

One witness said that the atmosphere and conditions were reminiscent of those at the onset of the "Watts Riots" that shook Los Angeles following the death of Martin Luther King. City residents are said to be "holding their breath" and praying that the seemingly isolated "lawlessness" doesn't spread to engulf the entire city in vengence for the actions of a jury that made a decision.

10

Major Riot in Los Angeles, Thirteen Dead, 192 Injuried

Los Angeles, CA—Following a jury verdict which acquitted four L.A.P.D. officers of charges resulting from the videotaped beating of motorist Rodney King, Southcentral Los Angeles erupted in a violent and deadly outburst of arson and shooting. Local police and emergency medical services officials report the deaths of as many as nine (9) people and injuries to another 138.

As the sun rose over Los Angeles, more than forty (40) major fires still   15
burned out of control. They were part of an estimated 140 fires that were set in
the Southeast and Southcentral parts of the city. During the night, firefighters
and paramedics were hardpressed to keep up with the requests for emergency
response to more than 140 fires. Reportedly, they came under sniper fire on
several occasions, from rooftops surrounding the fire scenes. One Los Angeles
firefighter is reported in stable, but serious, condition at an area hospital
following his being shot in the face while fighting a blaze.

According to a police spokesman at least five (5) people have been shot
by police and one was killed in a gun-battle in the city's Inglewood area.
A spokesperson for the Daniel Freeman Hospital says that they have treated at
least fifty (50) citizens with "riot-related" injuries. Emergency Medical Services
(EMS) officers say that all available city ambulances are "on calls" and that
mutual aid from Los Angeles County and Orange County has been requested.
At least 192 people are reported to have been taken to various hospitals in the
L.A. metropolitan area.

Los Angeles Mayor Thomas Bradley has been following the rise of
violence and has repeatedly called for calm among the city's black citizens.
Observers report, however, that many of those participating in looting and
arson are not black, but rather, youths of hispanic and caucasian origin. Reports
were also received that numerous reputed "street gang" members were seen to
be participating in the violence and shooting.

Mayor Bradley is said to have declared a local "State of Emergency" and
requested a California disaster declaration. Mayor Bradley is also reported to
have issued a "dusk to dawn" curfew which prohibits people from being on the
street during nighttime hours. He also issued orders prohibiting the sale of
firearms and gasoline (other than into vehicle tanks) to Los Angeles citizens.
The Mayor also announced that all Catholic and public schools in the southern
part of Los Angeles have been closed and will not reopen until further notice.

According to California Governor Pete Wilson, he has activated more than
2,000 National Guardsmen to help quell the rampage in Los Angeles. The Guards-
man are reportedly members of Military Police Units and are said to be armed with
sidearms and M-16 rifles. Police spokespersons indicate that the Gueardsmen have
not been used for law enforcement duties, but to secure areas that have been previously cleared by police. An unidentified army sergeant was reported to have said
that the guard is "on standby" awaiting the orders of police officials.

As the morning progressed, numerous eyewitness reports of additional   20
looting were seen on KPLA T.V. and the Cable News Network. Hundreds of
citizens of all colors were seen to be breaking into stores, almost at will, and
leaving with armloads of merchandise. Several new fires were reported by the
L.A. Fire Dept., these in addition to those that still burned out of control in
several locations. Fire Chief Donald Manning appealed to L.A. citizens to
discontinue the practice of assaulting and shooting at firefighters who were
attempting to fight the conflagrations.

In afternoon developments, the Bank of America is reported to have been closing all of its Los Angeles branch banks and moving money to safer locations, away from the chaos that is spreading through various neighborhoods. Other businesses are said to be closing and boarding up their windows in an attempt to prevent future looting. Reports were received that the crowds of looters were said to be moving into an area on Hollywood Blvd. and that the thievery seems to be spreading as the day progresses.

As lawlessness continued, President George Bush called for calm and a stop to "anarchy" on the streets of Los Angeles. He said that he had conferred with U.S. Attorney William Barr, Mayor Tom Bradley, and Governor Pete Wilson in an effort to provide whatever assistance might be needed to stop the senseless arson, violence, and looting. President Bush is said to have several key staff members monitoring the situation closely and available to provide federal assistance should it be needed.

An unidentified Los Angeles Police officer provided a concise commentary on the state of affairs in Los Angeles: "Things are totally out of control here . . . and we expect it to get worse when it gets dark . . . I hope we all live to see tommorow."

L.A. Insurrection Surpasses 1965 Watts Riots, 38 Dead, More Than 1,200 Injured

Los Angeles, CA—The latest reported deaths in Los Angeles bring to thirty-eight the total that have been killed as the result of the fires, riots, and shooting that has plagued this second largest American city. The death toll has risen following another night of violence and mayhem that is said, by some, to be the consequences for the acquittal of four L.A.P.D. officers in Simi Valley, CA, on Wednesday.

The current totals of dead, injured, and damage done now exceed those that occured in 1965, when residents of the Watts section of Los Angeles erupted after the arrest of a black man by a white highway patrol officer. Thirty-four (34) people died in the following six days of chaos, 1,000 were injuried, and $200 million dollars in damage was done. Older eyewitnesses say that the most current riots far exceed the days of the Watts riots, both in intensity and level of violence.

As 4,000 regular Army troops and 1,000 federal law enforcement officers move into Los Angeles, people have begun to actually assess the severity of this latest day of "revolution." They find thirty-eight (38) people dead, 1,250 people injuried, 3,600 structural fires, hundreds of businesses looted and closed, and more than 3,000 people arrested. At least four (4) police officers and three (3) firefighters have been shot and hundreds of other injuried as they attempted to control the fires and lawlessness of the past three days.

A "Dusk to Dawn" curfew has been imposed by Mayor Tom Bradley, in an effort to prevent citizens from congregating into the groups that have controlled the streets in recent days. The curfew also finally has "teeth" as 4,000 California

National Guardsmen assist the police in securing areas of previous violence. This evening, the National Guard Units were also "federalized" by President Bush and supplemented by another 4,000 Army and Marine troops with orders to act as "Light-Infantry" and to "return fire if fired upon."

Reports are received at the time of this report that authorities may be gaining a tactical advantage and that, with the help of an added 9,000 law enforcement and military personnel, the situation may be under control by the weekend. According to current reports, there have been fewer fires and shooting incidents since the curfew was instituted on Friday evening.

The wave of destruction, which had spread from Southcentral Los Angeles to Downtown, to Pasadena, to Hollywood, and to Koreatown, has not always seemed just a response to the Rodney King verdict. Often in its intensity, the "rioting beast" did not pay attention to the race, color, or creed of its victims; it struck indiscriminately. Early video tapes of the "rioters" sometimes showed middle-class white youths, street gang members, and those that have been associated with radical organizations such as the American Communist Party.

Differing agendas seemed to be "at play" in differing circumstances. Much   30
looting appeared to "opportunistic" in scope and origin. Entire families were seen working together to steal from stores in their own neighborhoods. Often, what was being stolen was not of any necessity, but rather luxury items such as designer gym shoes, radios, and starter jackets. Frequently, it just appeared that it was those "without" were taking from those "with," because they could.

In other situations, the anger and frustration was expressed by pulling white motorists from cars and trucks and brutally beating and kicking them. In one such case, Reginald Oliver Denny was pulled from his truck as he stopped to prevent hitting looters who filled the street. The incident was captured by a helicopter television news crew as it occured and was broadcast live. Some viewers said that the violence that was portrayed was as "violent and sickening" as any that occured to Rodney King. Denny was taken to Daniel Freeman Hospital after the furious beating, and has been upgraded from critical to serious, following brain sugery to remove a blood clot.

Arson was another way that some people vented their rage of various kinds. Fire Chief Donald Manning was quoted as saying that the Los Angeles Fire Dept. has responded to more than 3,600 fires in the past three days. Further, he commented that at given times during the past two days, the L.A.F.D. was receiving calls for three (3) fires every minute. He said that this level of need for service far exceeded the department's ability to respond and that this call volume was five (5) times that of normal.

Manning said that additional fire units were called from all over California to help fight the conflagrations that spread through neighborhood after neighborhood. Efforts were also reportedly hampered on numerous occasions by sniper fire and direct confrontations against firefighters. One firefighter was quoted as saying yesterday: "I'd feel a lot more secure if they gave me a rifle." He was responding to the fact that at least three firefighters have been reportedly shot while in the performance of their duties, and that often police officers were not available to accompany and protect fire units while they performed their already dangerous duties.

Los Angeles Police say that the circumstances also "unleashed" criminals, street gangs, and others whose only motive in involvement in the riots was that of profit. They point out the fact that this was also felt to be the perfect opportunity to justify acts of violence by street gang members against members of the police department. Police Chief Daryl Gates admitted that on several occasions his forces had also been "overwhelmed" and unable to respond to even calls for assistance from fellow officers and firefighters. This reportedly enabled those that would engage in revenge against any official agency to feel that they could do so with impunity.

As the senseless violence reached it's peak in Los Angeles on Thursday   35
night, reports began to be received that it had spread to other cities and states across the country.

- In Northern California, 1,400 people were arrested in San Francisco as rioting engulfed the city's downtown area. A State of Emergency was declared there and a curfew established.

- In Los Vegas, a mob of two-hundred (200) people went on a rampage, setting fires, and engaged in sniper fire and drive-by shootings. Local law enforcement officials admitted that they were overwhelmed and requested the activation of the Nevada National Guard. The Governor complied and control has reportedly been somewhat reestablished. Reports were received of several arson fires.

- Seattle was struck by mobs of 50–100 people, who randomly broke windows and and looted numerous cars in downtown Seattle during the night Thursday and early Friday. Police say that forty-five (45) people were arrested and five (5) injured during the violent spree. Firefighters responded to twenty-eight (28) fire calls during the unrest, including five (5) buildings that were termed "suspicious in nature."

- Further east, Black protestors in New York City reportedly pulled two white men from a truck, stabbed one and beat the other. An estimated two hundred (200) protestors attacked the doors at Madison Square Garden causing injuries and property damage. Another crowd of four hundred (400) black youths reportedly stormed a popular shopping mall and smashed windows and stole merchandise. Shops and businesses were damaged as the "melee" traveled over several blocks. As many as eighty (80) arrests were made and several police officers injuried. Many NYC employers were said to have released workers from work early to avoid further occurances.

- Police in Atlanta, GA, were confronted on Friday by hundreds of black protestors. This followed a night of three hundred (300) arrests and fifty-seven (57) injuries. It also prompted the use of teargas and a call for the Georgia National Guard to help combat large crowds of people looting and throwing rocks and bricks. Mayor Maynard Jackson called for calm and understanding, as he counseled college students that had originally begun peaceful protests which escalated into widespread violence.

Sporadic acts of violence, arson, and property damage were also associated with the Los Angeles Riots in such cities as Tampa, FL, Pittsburg, PA, Birmingham, MS, Omaha, NE, and several other locations.

As night settled over several cities, residents took to their homes, prayed for an end to senseless violence, and waited for the morning light to see if the fragile peace was to endure. Fire, Police, and EMS Officials hoped for even a brief respite from the constant stress and danger of angry citizens and harrowing rescues. Everyone wished that the madness would be over.

● Applying a Materialist Frame

1. What do you notice about the accounts of the Los Angeles or "Rodney King" riots, as they're called, that's markedly different from either Catton's or Lens's account of civil unrest? What do you think explains this difference?

   - How does the appeal to *ethos* figure into the way you react to these Net press releases?

   - In what ways do you see government's (federal, state, or local) reactions and actions as being similar when you compare cases of civil unrest in different eras? How would the materialists you've studied explain this similarity, if you were to refer to their writing?

2. See what you can find out about Emergencynet News Service (ENN). Who is compiling this information? How are they funded?

   - What kinds of attitudes *toward* the Los Angeles riots do you perceive from this writing? How do you explain those attitudes?

   - What effect does the authorial tone or voice have on your willingness to be persuaded? Are these articles more believable, for instance, than the excerpt from Professor Fowler's 1898 history book (pp. 169 and 170) at the beginning of this section? Why or why not?

3. This report notes that "Los Angeles Police say that the circumstances also 'unleashed' criminals, street gangs, and others whose only motive in involvement in the riots was that of profit" (para. 34). Does this mean that if one's motive for rioting weren't primarily to get profit, then such a rioter wouldn't be a criminal?

4. What do you think about the connection between the Rodney King trial verdict and the subsequent rioting? Do you think people used the verdict as an excuse for rioting? What's your evidence for thinking the way you do?

5. See what you can learn about another civil disturbance in our nation's past. What were the causes? What were the government's reactions? How were the crises resolved?

   From a materialist frame, how would you explain the events and circumstances you learn about?

6. How reliable do you consider these Web reports to be? What's the credibility of the author? How *do* you go about making decisions about which sources are "legitimate" and which aren't? Why?

topics for writing

1. Compare the introductory headnotes to each selection of this chapter.
   - What rhetorical appeal do you see us using for Catton and Lens that we don't use for the Web page section? Why?
   - How does our rhetorical treatment of Lens and Catton differ from the Los Angeles riot pieces?
   - Does our introductory commentary affect your way of reading these different selections?

2. Urban riots have always been part of U.S. history. From the Boston Massacre before the War of Independence, through the tumultuous "Days of Rage" in the late 1960s, to South Central Los Angeles in 1992, cities have been the sites of civil disturbance that have resulted in loss of life. Most of these events disappear from public conversation almost immediately after their occurrence.

   Examine the causes and repercussions of some of these riots in a research paper that singles out specific occasions, provides some historical background for them, and draws conclusions from how U.S. society reacted to them.
   - Did anything change after these occasions to resolve the dissatisfaction that caused them?
   - To what extent were you taught about these riots? If you were made aware of the number of instances of civil unrest, how were they described to you?
   - If not, why do you think this information was missing from your education?

3. How do you see the rapid emergence of the World Wide Web as changing the nature of how news is made available to you? What questions of credibility do this new media bring to mind?

- In what ways are these questions *not* part of the way you react to network television, for example, or other mainstream corporate news agencies? Do some research on how scholars or media experts suggest the Internet or Web will alter how public opinion is formed or will be utilized to influence political decisions in the future.

- National office-seekers are now using the Web as a fundraising and marketing tool. Can you find any evidence to suggest what such an innovation might mean for electoral politics in the United States?

4. Select a major U.S. weekly news magazine and find some articles published the week of or the week after the South-Central Los Angeles riot. Write a rhetorical analysis of one such article in which you evaluate the authorial position.

- What means of persuasion do you see in play? Are photos used to intensify certain "slants," or perhaps to complicate issues?

- How does the story "sell" itself through highlighted boxes and headings? What kinds of statements are used to attract the reader? Find out what you can about the readership of the magazine you're using and try to explain how that particular major audience may have shaped the news article itself.

5. A materialist would most likely describe warfare as being precipitated by "real, physical, material" interests. Examine recent news articles or magazine articles that give you information on who made the most money from Operation Iraqi Freedom. Some have said that this military expedition was the first in history to be mostly "subcontracted." See what you can learn about this topic and write your conclusions in either a report or an argumentative essay.

- What does "subcontracted" mean in this context?

- Is there a profit motive visible for any one of the players?

- To what extent, if any, would the fact that someone is making money from the war affect your attitude about how the war is being conducted?

- What other questions can you come up with that will help you shape your writing? Ask your classmates.

chapter **10**

Reading Critically About Corporate Values

This Chapter's Rhetorical Concepts

- Reading critically from a materialist frame
- Synthesizing sources
- Moving an audience

The Greening of America

CHARLES A. REICH

In his preface to the twenty-fifth anniversary edition of his 1970 bestseller, the author recontextualizes his book for a different, younger audience: "If there was any doubt about the need for social transformation in 1970, that need is clear and urgent today. . . . I am now more convinced than ever that the conflict and suffering now threatening to engulf us are entirely unnecessary, and a tragic waste of our energy and resources. We can create an economic system that is not at war with human beings or nature, and we can get from here to there by democratic means." The following excerpt is from Chapter 5, "Anatomy of the Corporate State."

What is the nature of the social order within which we all live? Why are we so powerless? Why does our state seem impervious to democratic or popular control? Why does it seem to be insane, destroying both self and environment for the sake of principles that remain obscure? Our present social order is so contrary to anything we have learned to expect about a government or a society that its structure is almost beyond comprehension. Most of us, including our political leaders and those who write about politics and economics, hold to a picture that is entirely false. Yet children are not entirely deceived, teen-agers understand some aspects of the society very well, and artists, writers and especially moviemakers sometimes come quite close to the truth. The corporate state is an immensely powerful machine, ordered, legalistic, rational, yet utterly out of human control, wholly and perfectly indifferent to any human values.

It is hard to say exactly when our society assumed this shape; it came on slowly, imperceptibly to those living with it day by day. The major symptoms started appearing after the conclusion of World War II, and especially in the 1950's. Those symptoms, such as the Cold War, a trillion dollars spent for defense, destruction of environment, production of unneeded goods, were not merely extensions of the familiar blunders and corruption of America's past.

They were of a different order of magnitude, they were surrounded by a growing atmosphere of unreality, and they were all an integral part of a seemingly
rational and legal system. The stupidities and thefts of the Grant era were not
insane; they were human departures from a reasonably human standard. In the
1950's the norm itself—the system itself—became deranged.

Our present system has gone beyond anything that could properly be
called the creation of capitalism or imperialism or a power elite. That, at least,
would be a human shape. Of course a power elite does exist and is made rich by
the system, but the elite are no longer in control, they are now merely taking
advantage of forces that have a life of their own. Nor is our system a purely
technological society, although technology has increasingly supplied the basis
for our choices and superseded other values. What we have is technology, organization, and administration out of control, running for their own sake, but at
the same time subject to manipulation and profiteering by the power interests of
our society for their own non-human ends. And we have turned over to this system the control and direction of everything—the natural environment, our
minds, our lives. Other societies have had bad systems, but have endured
because a part of life went on outside the system. We have turned over everything, rendered ourselves powerless, and thus allowed mindless machinery to
become our master.

The American Corporate State today can be thought of as a single vast
corporation, with every person as an involuntary member and employee. It consists primarily of large industrial organizations, plus nonprofit institutions such
as foundations and the educational system, all related to the whole as divisions to
a business corporation. Government is only a part of the state, but government
coordinates it and provides a variety of needed services. The Corporate State is a
complete reversal of the original American ideal and plan. The State, and not the
market or the people or any abstract economic laws, determines what shall be
produced, what shall be consumed, and how it shall be allocated. It determines,
for example, that railroads shall decay while highways flourish; that coal miners
shall be poor and advertising executives rich. Jobs and occupations in the society
are rigidly defined and controlled, and arranged in a hierarchy of rewards, status,
and authority. An individual can move from one position to another, but he gains
little freedom thereby, for in each position he is subject to conditions imposed
upon it; individuals have no protected area of liberty, privacy, or individual sovereignty beyond the reach of the State. The State is subject neither to democratic
controls, constitutional limits, or legal regulation. Instead, the organizations in
the Corporate State are motivated primarily by the demands of technology and
of their own internal structure. Technology has imperatives such as these: if computers have been developed, they must be put to use; if faster planes can be produced, they must be put into service; if there is a more efficient way of organizing
an office staff, it must be done; if psychological tests provide added information
for personnel directors, they must be used on prospective employees. A general
in charge of troops at Berkeley described the use of a helicopter to attack

students with chemicals as "logical." As for organizations, their imperative is to grow. They need stability, freedom from outside interference, constantly increasing profits. Everyone in the organization wants more and better personnel, more functions, increased status and prestige—in a word, growth. The medium through which these forces operate is law. The legal system is not primarily concerned with justice, equality, or individual rights; it functions as an instrument of State domination, and it acts to prevent the intervention of human values or individual choice. Although the forces driving the State are impersonal rather than evil, they are wholly indifferent to man's needs, and tend to have the same consequences as would a system expressly designed for the purpose of destroying human beings and their society.

The essence of the Corporate State is that it is relentlessly single-minded;   5
it has only one value, the value of technology-organization-efficiency-growth-progress. The State is perfectly rational and logical. It is based upon principle. But life cannot be supported on the basis of any single principle. Yet no other value is allowed to interfere with this one, not amenity, not beauty, not community, not even the supreme value of life itself. Thus the State is essentially mindless; it has only one idea and it rolls along, never stopping to think, consider, balance, or judge. Only such single-valued mindlessness would cut the last redwoods, pollute the most beautiful beaches, invent machines to injure and destroy plant and human life. To have only one value is, in human terms, to be mad. It is to be a machine.

In the remainder of this chapter, we shall attempt to outline the main features of the Corporate State. We shall build our picture out of several elements, but the description is cumulative, for it is the *interrelationship* of the elements that gives the State its extraordinary form. In the case of the Corporate State, the whole is more than the sum of the parts, and the truth is in the whole, not the parts.

1. *Amalgamation and Integration.* We normally consider the units of the Corporate State, such as the federal government, an automobile company, a private foundation, as if they were separate from each other. This is, however, not the case. In the first place, there is a marked tendency for "separate" units to follow parallel policies, so that an entire industry makes identical decisions as to pricing, kind of product, and method of distribution; the automobile and the air travel industries show this. Second, very different companies are coming under combined management through the device of conglomerates, which place vast and diverse empires under a single unified control. But even more significant is the disappearance of the line between "public" and "private." In the Corporate State, most of the "public" functions of government are actually performed by the "private" sector of the economy. And most "government" functions are services performed for the private sector.

Let us consider first how government operations are "privately" performed. To a substantial degree, this relationship is formalized. The government hires "private" firms to build national defense systems, to supply the space program, to construct the interstate highway system, and sometimes, in the case of the think institutes, to do its "thinking" for it. An enormous portion of the federal budget is spent in simply hiring out government functions. This much is obvious, although many people do not seem to be aware of it. What is less obvious is the "deputizing" system by which a far larger sector of the "private" economy is enlisted in government service.

An illustration will indicate what is meant by "deputizing." A college teacher receives a form from the Civil Service Commission, asking him for certain information with respect to an individual who is applying for a government job. When he fills in the form, the teacher has acted as if he had been "deputized" by the government; i.e., he is performing a service for the government, one for which he might even feel himself entitled to compensation. Now consider a foundation which receives a special tax-exempt status. The foundation is in this favored position because it is engaged in activities which are of "public benefit." That is, it is the judgment of the government that some types of activities are public services although performed under private auspices. The government itself could do what private foundations now do: aid education, sponsor research, and other things which do not command a profit in the commercial sense. It is the government's decision that these same functions are better performed by foundations. It is the same judgment that government makes when it hires Boeing to build bombers, or a private construction firm to build an interstate highway. Public utilities—airlines, railroads, truck carriers, taxicabs, oil pipe lines, the telephone company—all are "deputized" in this fashion. They carry on *public* functions—functions that in other societies might be performed by the government itself.

Let us now look at the opposite side of the coin: government as the servant   10
of the "private" sector. Once again, sometimes the relationship is formal and obvious. The government spends huge amounts for research and development, and private companies are often able to get the benefits of this. Airports are built at public expense for private airlines to use. Highways are built for private trucking firms to use. The government pays all sorts of subsidies, direct and indirect, to various industries. It supplies credit services and financial aid to homeowners. It grows trees on public forest lands and sells them at cut-rate prices to private lumber companies. It builds roads to aid ski developments.

It is true that government has always existed to serve the society; that police and fire departments help business too; that paving streets helps business, and so do wars that open up new markets—and that is what government is and always has been all about. But today, governmental activity in aid of the private sector is enormously greater, more pervasive, more immediately felt than ever before. The difference between the local public services in 1776 and millions of dollars in subsidies to the shipping industry may be a difference of degree but it is still quite a difference. But the difference is not only one of degree. In the difference between a highly autonomous, localized economy and a highly interdependent one, there is a difference of principle as well as one of degree. Government help today is *essential*, not a luxury. The airlines could not operate without allocation of routes and regulation of landing and take-offs, nor could the television industry. The educational system, elementary school through high school, is essential for the production of people able to work in today's industry. Thus it may be said that everyone who operates "privately" really is aided and subsidized, to one degree or another, by the public; the sturdy, independent rancher rides off into the sunset on land irrigated by government subsidy, past sheep whose grazing is subsidized and crops whose prices are artificially maintained by governmental action; he does not look like a welfare client, but he is on the dole nevertheless.

Regulation itself is a service to industry. The film industry and the professional sports industry have elaborate systems of private regulation, including "commissioners," a system of laws and government, fines and penalties, all designed to place the industry on the best and most united basis to sell its product. Such "regulation" as is performed by such federal agencies as FCC, SEC, FTC, and CAB, is remarkably similar in general effect, but it is a service rendered at taxpayers' expense. Indeed, there is a constant interchange of personnel between the regulatory agencies and industry; government men leave to take high-paying positions with the corporations they formerly regulated; agency officials are frequently appointed from industry ranks.

This public-private and private-public integration, when added to the inescapable legislative power we have already described, gives us the picture of the State as a single corporation. Once the line between "public" and "private" becomes meaningless and is erased, the various units of the Corporate State no longer appear to be parts of a diverse and pluralistic system in which one kind of power limits another kind of power; the various centers of power do not limit each other, they all weigh in on the same side of the scale, with only the individual on the other side. With public and private merged, we can discern the real monolith of power and realize there is nothing at all within the system to impose checks and balances, to offer competition, to raise even a voice of caution or doubt. We are all involuntary members, and there is no zone of the private to offer a retreat.

One way to appreciate the true nature of the public-private amalgamated State, is to list some examples of power that can be found in the United States:

Power to determine the hour at which employees come to work, the hour at which they have lunch, the hour when they go home;   15

Power to make *Business Week* available to airline passengers but not *The Nation*;

Power to raise bank interest rates;

Power to wake all patients in a hospital at 6 A.M.;

Power to forbid apartment dwellers to have pets or children;

Power to require peanut butter eaters to choose between homogenized or   20 chunky peanut butter and to prevent them from buying "real" peanut butter;

Power to force all young people who want to go to college to do a certain kind of mechanical problem-solving devised by the College Entrance Examination Board;

Power to require that all public school teachers be fingerprinted;

Power to popularize snowmobiles instead of snowshoes, so that the winter forests screech with mechanical noise;

Power to force all riders in automobiles to sit in seats designed to torture the lower lumbar regions of the human anatomy;

Power to use forest products in constructing homes, making furniture, and publishing newspapers, thereby creating a demand for cutting timber;

Power to dominate public consciousness through the mass media;

Power to induce lung cancer in thousands of persons by promoting the sale of cigarettes;

Power to turn off a man's telephone service;

Power to provide railroad passengers with washrooms that are filthy;

Power to encourage or discourage various forms of scholarship, educational 30 activity, philanthropy, and research;

Power to construct office buildings with windows that will not open, or without any windows at all;

Power to determine what life-styles will not be acceptable for employees;

Power to make relatively large or small investments in the safety of consumer products;

Power to change the culture of a foreign country.

Were we confronted by this list and told that all of this power was held by a 35 single tyrannical ruler, we would find the prospect frightening indeed. We are likely to think, however, that, although the power may exist, it is divided in many ways, held by many different entities, and subject to all sorts of procedures, checks, balances, and controls; mostly it applies only to persons who subject themselves to it voluntarily, as by taking a job with a corporation. But power in the corporate state is not so easily escaped. The refugee from a job with one corporation will find a choice of other corporations—all prepared to subject him to similar control over employees. The television viewer who tires of one network finds the others even more tiresome. Can railroad or automobile passengers do anything about conditions they object to? Do they find alternative means of transportation readily available?

Editorials which denounce students usually say that a student who does not like the way a university is run should leave. But society makes it practically mandatory for a young person to complete his education, and, so far as rules and practices go, most universities are extraordinarily alike. Under these circumstances, it is hardly accurate to say that a student "voluntarily" submitted to university rule. The student's case is the case of the railroad traveler, the peanut butter eater, the man who wants a bank loan, the corporate employee, the apartment house dweller who wants to keep a pet. The integration of the Corporate State makes what was formerly voluntary inescapable. Like the birds in Alfred Hitchcock's apocalyptic film, powers that once were small and gentle become monstrous and terrifying. The better organized, the more tightly administered, the more rational and inclusive the Corporate State becomes, the more every organization turns into a government, and all forms of power take on the aspect of government decrees.

2. *The Principle of Administration and Hierarchy.* The activities, policies, and decisions of a society might theoretically be carried out by a variety of methods—voluntary co-operation by individuals, the physical coercion of a military tyranny, or the psychological conditioning of B. F. Skinner's *Walden Two.* The Corporate State has chosen to rely on the method of administration and hierarchy. So pervasive, indeed, is the principle of administration that in many ways the Corporate State is in its essence an administrative state. The theory of administration is that the best way to conduct any activity is to subject it to rational control. A framework of organization is provided. Lines of authority, responsibility, and supervision are established as clearly as possible; everyone is arranged in a hierarchy. Rules are drawn for every imaginable contingency, so that individual choice is minimized. Arrangements are made to check on what everyone does, to have reports and permanent records. The random, the irrational, and the alternative ways of doing things are banished.

It is worth recalling how this State derived from classic liberalism, and, more proximately, from the New Deal and the welfare state. Liberalism adopted the basic principle that there is no need for management of society itself; the "unseen hand" is all that is needed. The New Deal modified this by requiring activities to be subject to "the public interest." Gradually this came to mean ever-tightening regulation in directions fixed by the demands of a commercial, technological, mass society. Gradually it came to mean the replacement of a "political" state with an "administrative" state. A "political" state, in our present meaning, is one in which differences, conflicts, and cultural diversity are regarded as aspects of pluralism to be represented in the political process and allowed a life of their own within the body politic. Thus political radicals, marijuana users, or culturally distinct groups would all coexist, have political voices, and contribute to the diversity and balance of the nation. This "political" model has also been called the "conflict" model, not because there are actual conflicts, but because conflicting opinions and ways of life are allowed to exist side by side. Administration means a rejection of the idea of conflict as a desirable element in society. Administration wants extremes "adjusted"; it wants differences "settled"; it wants to find out which way is "best" and use it exclusively. That which refuses to be adjusted is considered by administration as "deviance," a departure from the norm needing to be treated and cured. It is a therapeutic model of society, in which variety is compromised and smoothed over in an effort to make everything conform to "the public interest." This society defines that which does not fit "the public interest" as "deviance." Marijuana use is made a crime, and people using it are punished, cured, or "helped." Political radicals are expected to be "responsible"; blacks are expected to be "integrated." The society "knows what is best" for everyone; its massive energies, power, and apparatus are focused on making sure that everyone accepts "what is best."

The structure of the administrative state is that of a hierarchy in which every person has a place in a table of organization, a vertical position in which he is subordinate to someone and superior to someone else. This is the structure of any bureaucracy; it represents a "rationalization" of organization ideals. When an entire society is subjected to this principle, it creates a small ruling elite and a large group of workers who play no significant part in the making of decisions. While they continue to vote in political elections, they are offered little choice among the candidates; all the major decisions about what is produced, what is consumed, how resources are allocated, the conditions of work, and so forth, are made administratively.

Administration seeks to remove decision-making from the area of politics to the area of "science." It does not accept democratic or popular choice; this is rejected in favor of professionals and experts and a rational weighing of all of the factors. Procedures are set up by which decision-making is channeled, and care is taken to define exactly which institution shall make which decisions. For each type of decision, there is someone "best" qualified to decide it; administration avoids participation in decisions by the less qualified. Its greatest outrage is directed toward a refusal to enter into its procedures—this seems almost a denial of the very principle of administration. If followed, these procedures usually produce a decision that is a compromise or balance which rejects any particular choice in its pure, uncompromised form. Choice takes place within narrow limits. A weighing of all the factors produces a decision somewhere in between, rather than one or another "extreme." 40

Administration has no values of its own, except for the institutional ones just described. It has no ideas; it is just professional management. Theoretically, it could accept any values. In practice, however, it is strongly conservative. Things go most smoothly when the status quo is maintained, when change is slow, cautious, and evolutionary. The more elaborate the machinery of administration, the less ready it is for new, disquieting values. And "rationality" finds some values easier to understand, to justify, to put into verbal terms than other values. It can understand quantity better than quality. Rationality does not like to blow its mind. Administration is neutral in favor of the Establishment.

Public welfare offers an example of the administrative model of society. The object of public welfare, apart from administration, is to protect people against the hazards of forces in an industrial society beyond their control, and the other hazards of life against which neither family nor local community any longer offer help; to provide every person with a minimum standard of security, well-being, and dignity. With the introduction of administration and hierarchy as the means for carrying out public welfare, the emphasis shifts to regulation of exactly who is qualified for welfare, how much is allotted, how it is spent, whether regulations are being followed. A large apparatus is developed for checking up, for keeping records, for making and enforcing rules, for punishing infractions. Some of this may save money, but the money saved is minimized by the costs of administration. Some of this may also serve the purpose of punishing the poor for not working, even though many are unable to work. But the "accomplishments" of administration are almost secondary; after a while what it does ceases to have an outside reference; it acquires an autonomous life of its own.

The tendency of administration, while it may appear to be benign and peaceful, as opposed to the turbulence of conflict, is actually violent. For the very idea of imposed order is violent. It demands compliance; nothing less than compliance will do; and it must obtain compliance, by persuasion or management if possible, by repression if necessary. It is convinced that it has "the best way" and that all others are wrong; it cannot understand those who do not accept the rightness of its view. A growing tension and anger develops against those who would question what is so carefully designed to be "best"—for them as well as for everybody else. Administration wants the best for everybody, and all that it asks is that individuals conform their lives to the framework established by the State.

3. *The Corporate State Is Autonomous.* What controls the amalgamated power of the Corporate State? We usually make at least three reassuring assumptions. One: power is controlled by the people through the democratic process and pluralism in the case of government, and through the market in the case of the "private" sector. Two: power is controlled by the persons who are placed in a position of authority to exercise it. Three: power is subject to the Constitution and the laws. These assumptions stand as a presumed barrier to the state power we have described. We will deal with the first two in this section, and the third in a later section on law.

As machinery for translating popular will into political effect, the American 45 system functions impossibly badly. We can hardly say that our political process makes it possible for voters to enforce their will on such subjects as pollution, the supersonic plane, mass transportation, the arms race, or the Vietnam War. On the contrary, if there are any popularly held views, it is impossible for them to be expressed politically; this was demonstrated for all to see in the 1968 presidential campaign, where both candidates supported the Vietnam War. Even if the political machinery did allow the electorate to express its views, it is difficult for citizens to get the information necessary to form an opinion.

What we have said with respect to the failure of the political process is also true with respect to the "private" economic process which supposedly is governed by a market. There is nothing at all to "stockholder democracy" in the control of corporations; it has long been true that stockholders have no realistic power in the government of corporate affairs. But the more important fact is that producers largely create their own demand for products. This is the central thesis of Galbraith's *The New Industrial State*, and it is hard to see how it can be disputed. Corporations decide what they want to produce, and they convince people that they want it, thus fashioning their own market. What we now produce and consume, the way we use our resources, the plans we make for future use of resources, are therefore not directed by what the people want. We do not know if they would prefer to have snowmobiles rather than new hospital equipment; no one asks them, and they cannot make their voices heard.

If pure democratic theory fails us in both the public and private spheres, we must nevertheless consider whether a modified version of democracy can permit large competing interests to achieve a balance which represents a rough approximation of what people want; this is the theory of pluralism. Here again, the theory simply does not work out. Robert Paul Wolff has effectively discussed this type of pluralism in his book *The Poverty of Liberalism* (the same essay also appears in a volume called *A Critique of Pure Tolerance*). The interests that make up the spectrum of political "pluralism" are highly select; many important interests are entirely omitted. Thus, as Wolff points out, we have recognized the three major religions but no agnostics; we have virtually no representation of the poor, the blacks, or other outsiders; no representation of youth, no radicals. "Pluralism" represents not interests, but *organized* interests. Thus, "labor" means large labor organizations, but these do not necessarily represent the real interests of individual employees. "Labor" may support heavy defense expenditures, repressive police measures, and emphasis on economic growth, but this may not be at all an expression of the true interests of the industrial worker. Likewise the three major religions may fail to represent the more individual spiritual strivings of persons which might take such forms as resistance to the draft. Indeed, at the organizational level there is far more agreement than difference among the "competing interests," so that they come to represent the same type of cooperation as conglomerate mergers produce among interests in the private sphere.

Even if the people had power to give orders, the orders might have little or no effect. Increasingly, the important part of government is found in the executive departments, which are staffed by career men, experts, professionals, and civil servants who have specialized knowledge of technical fields. These persons are not elected, nor are they subject to removal on political grounds. They are thus immunized from direct democratic control. Congress and the state legislatures, however, have neither the time nor the specialized knowledge to oversee all of these governmental activities. Instead, the legislatures have increasingly resorted to broad delegations of authority. Even if a statute tries to set more definite standards, such as the Federal Power Act, which lists some factors to be considered in building hydroelectric projects, the factors are simply left to be considered and weighed in the agency's discretion. What really happens is that government becomes institutionalized in the hands of professionals, experts, and managers, whose decisions are governed by the laws of bureaucratic behavior and the laws of professional behavior. These laws mean that decisions will be within narrow compass, tend to the status quo, tend to continue any policy once set, tend to reflect the interests of the organization.

These organizations, then, are unprepared to respond to any outside direction even if the people were in a position to give it. The same is true of the private corporate bureaucracies.

If the people do not control the Corporate State, is it at least controlled by those who give the orders—the executives and the power elite behind them? Such control might not satisfy those who favor democracy or the rule of law, but it would still be control that had to consider the broad trends of public opinion—still a major difference from no control at all.

Let us focus on an imaginary organization—government or private (an agency or corporation)—and its executive head—the personification of the "power elite." We enter into the paneled executive suite or, in the case of a more sophisticated organization, a suite in the most advanced taste, and there we expect to find an individual or "team" who really do exercise power. But the trappings, from the modern sculpture to the console telephone, do not tell the whole story. Any organization is subject to the demands of technology, of its own organization, and to its own middle-management. The corporation *must* respond to advances in technology. It *must* act in such a way as to preserve and foster its own organization. It is subject to the decision-making power of those in middle-management whose interests lie with the advance of organization and technology.

If the organization is a private corporation, the power elite must take much else into consideration; the fact that there are financial interests: bondholders, stockholders, banks and bankers, institutional owners (such as pension funds and mutual funds), potential raiders seeking financial control, possible financial control by a system of conglomerate ownership. This is not to suggest that stockholders or bondholders have any significant part in management, that there is any investor democracy, or that conglomerate structure necessarily means guidance of management. But the very existence of these interests creates certain impersonal demands upon the corporation; for example, the demand for profit, for growth, for stability of income. The manager cannot act without an awareness of the constant demand for profits. Thus a television executive's decision about whether to put on a special news broadcast and "sacrifice" a paying program is made in the oppressive awareness of the demand for profit—a demand which, because it is so institutional and impersonal, literally "cares" about nothing else than profits. The business executive is also required to be aware of many different kinds of state and federal law. The corporation is quite likely to be influenced by another set of relationships to government. It may possess valuable government contracts, subsidies, franchises or licenses, any of which can be modified or revoked. It may be the beneficiary of favored tax treatment that can be changed. It must therefore act in such a manner as to preserve whatever special privileges and advantages it has.

Inside a corporation, there is the important influence of the system of decision-making. Most managements consist of a committee rather than a single head; all students of group behavior know how a committee is limited in

50

ways that a single executive is not. Beyond this, management is limited by the many kinds of specialists and experts whose views must be consulted: the experts in marketing, in business management methods, the technicians, the whole class of people who occupy what Galbraith calls the "techno-structure." The structure of any large organization is bureaucratic, and all bureaucracies have certain imperatives and rules of their own. The bureaucracy acts to preserve itself and its system, to avoid any personal responsibility, to maintain any policy once set in motion. Decisions become "institutional decisions" that can be identified with no one person, and have the qualities of the group mind. The bureaucracy is so powerful that no executive, not even the President of the United States, can do much to budge it from its course. Top executives are profoundly limited by lack of knowledge. They know only what they are told. In effect, they are "briefed" by others, and the briefing is both limiting and highly selective. The executive is far too busy to find anything out for himself; he *must* accept the information he gets, and this sets absolute limits to his horizons. The briefing may be three steps removed from the facts, and thus be interpretation built upon interpretation—nearer fiction than fact by the time it reaches the top.

Thus the man in the chic office turns out to be a broker, a decider between limited alternatives, a mediator and arbitrator, a chairman, but not an originator. And such a position tends to be utterly inconsistent with thought, reflection, or originality. The executive cannot come up with reflections on policy, he cannot be the contemplative generalist, because he is too pressed and harried by the demands upon him. Increasingly, it is also inconsistent with the realities of the outside world, as the executive is insulated from them.

From all of this, there emerges the great revelation about the executive suite—the place from which power-hungry men seem to rule our society. The truth is far worse. In the executive suite, there may be a Léger or Braque on the wall, or a collection of African masks, there may be a vast glass-and-metal desk, but there is no one there. No one at all is in the executive suite. What looks like a man is only a representation of a man who does what the organization requires. He (or it) does not run the machine; he *tends* it.

● Applying a Materialist Frame

1. Reich says, "In the Corporate State, most of the 'public' functions of government are actually performed by the 'private' sector of the economy. And most of the 'government' functions are services performed for the private sector." How do the photograph and headlines on the next page that appeared on the first day of the first Gulf War affirm Reich's point?

2. In reading this chapter you no doubt noticed references to the Vietnam War. What else was going on in 1970—what did U.S. "culture" look like?

Markets React to War's First Day

Dow Soars 115 Points For Gain Of 4.6%

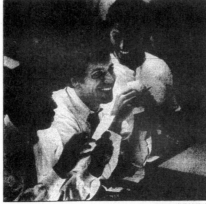

BY BRANT WARD/THE CHRONICLE

The soaring stock market made Pacific Stock Exchange traders in S.F. smile

Oil Dives $10.56 for Single-Day Record

- Create a "time capsule" out of researched information about U.S. popular culture, political controversies, music, film, advertisements—whatever you find that was in the news at the time. Your intention here would be to give yourselves and any others who might see your "time capsule" a look at the way our culture "represented" itself.

- What were the stories Americans were telling themselves *about* themselves? What conclusions do you draw as to whether substantive material issues were open topics of public discussion or were "hidden" beneath other issues?

3. One of the primary arguments of materialism is that human societies operate according to structural principles that always favor a small, elite ruling class's interests, and that the dominant ideologies that favor such a small segment of the population are not just accepted by the majority but are *adopted* by mass culture. The cultural value systems of the economically dominant are *pursued* by those who are not economically dominant.

   Can you examine Reich's "Anatomy of the Corporate State" to see evidence of this dynamic? If Reich was writing about 1970s corporate culture, what about the structures you see in your own lives today? How closely do 1970s descriptions still apply? What has changed, and why?

4. Reich describes different "consciousnesses" that he saw differentiating Americans. He identifies and classifies each "consciousness" as being rooted in and grounded on certain basic attitudes (or ideologies). Go to the text itself and pull out those descriptions. Share them with others in your class or group and see

   - whether you accept those classifications as described.

   - whether you see the same classifications still applying to your own national culture.

Amusing Ourselves to Death

NEIL POSTMAN

In critic Neil Postman's words, Amusing Ourselves to Death *(1986) is "an inquiry into and a lamentation about the most significant American cultural fact of the second half of the twentieth century: the decline of the Age of Typography and the ascendancy of the Age of Television." The following excerpt is Chapter 6, "The Age of Show Business."*

A dedicated graduate student I know returned to his small apartment   1
the night before a major examination only to discover that his solitary lamp was broken beyond repair. After a whiff of panic, he was able to restore both his equanimity and his chances for a satisfactory grade by turning on the television set, turning off the sound, and with his back to the set, using its light to read important passages on which he was to be tested. This is one use of television—as a source of illuminating the printed page.

But the television screen is more than a light source. It is also a smooth, nearly flat surface on which the printed word may be displayed. We have all stayed at hotels in which the TV set has had a special channel for describing the day's events in letters rolled endlessly across the screen. This is another use of television—as an electronic bulletin board.

Many television sets are also large and sturdy enough to bear the weight of a small library. The top of an old-fashioned RCA console can handle as many as thirty books, and I know one woman who has securely placed her entire collection of Dickens, Flaubert, and Turgenev on the top of a 21-inch Westinghouse. Here is still another use of television—as a bookcase.

I bring forward these quixotic uses of television to ridicule the hope harbored by some that television can be used to support the literate tradition. Such a hope represents exactly what Marshall McLuhan used to call "rear-view mirror" thinking: the assumption that a new medium is merely an extension or amplification of an older one; that an automobile, for example, is only a fast horse, or an electric light a powerful candle. To make such a mistake in the matter at hand is to misconstrue entirely how television redefines the meaning of public discourse. Television does not extend or amplify literate culture. It attacks it. If television is a continuation of anything, it is of a tradition begun by the telegraph and photograph in the mid-nineteenth century, not by the printing press in the fifteenth.

What is television? What kinds of conversations does it permit? What are   5
the intellectual tendencies it encourages? What sort of culture does it produce?

These are the questions to be addressed in the rest of this book, and to approach them with a minimum of confusion, I must begin by making a distinction between a technology and a medium. We might say that a technology is to a medium as the brain is to the mind. Like the brain, a technology is a physical apparatus. Like the mind, a medium is a use to which a physical apparatus is put. A technology becomes a medium as it employs a particular symbolic code, as it finds its place in a particular social setting, as it insinuates itself into economic and political contexts. A technology, in other words, is merely a machine. A medium is the social and intellectual environment a machine creates.

Of course, like the brain itself, every technology has an inherent bias. It has within its physical form a predisposition toward being used in certain ways and not others. Only those who know nothing of the history of technology believe that a technology is entirely neutral. There is an old joke that mocks that naive belief. Thomas Edison, it goes, would have revealed his discovery of the electric light much sooner than he did except for the fact that every time he turned it on, he held it to his mouth and said, "Hello? Hello?"

Not very likely. Each technology has an agenda of its own. It is, as I have suggested, a metaphor waiting to unfold. The printing press, for example, had a clear bias toward being used as a linguistic medium. It is *conceivable* to use it exclusively for the reproduction of pictures. And, one imagines, the Roman Catholic Church would not have objected to its being so used in the sixteenth century. Had that been the case, the Protestant Reformation might not have occurred, for as Luther contended, with the word of God on every family's kitchen table, Christians do not require the Papacy to interpret it for them. But in fact there never was much chance that the press would be used solely, or even very much, for the duplication of icons. From its beginning in the fifteenth century, the press was perceived as an extraordinary opportunity for the display and mass distribution of written language. Everything about its technical possibilities led in that direction. One might even say it was invented for that purpose.

The technology of television has a bias, as well. It is conceivable to use television as a lamp, a surface for texts, a bookcase, even as radio. But it has not been so used and will not be so used, at least in America. Thus, in answering the question, What is television? we must understand as a first point that we are not talking about television as a technology but television as a medium. There are many places in the world where television, though the same technology as it is in America, is an entirely different medium from that which we know. I refer to places where the majority of people do not have television sets, and those who do have only one; where only one station is available; where television does not operate around the clock; where most programs have as their purpose the direct furtherance of government ideology and policy; where commercials are unknown, and "talking heads" are the principal image; where television is mostly used as if it were radio. For these reasons and more television will not have the same meaning or power as it does in America, which is to say, it is possible for a technology to be so used that its potentialities are prevented from developing and its social consequences kept to a minimum.

But in America, this has not been the case. Television has found in liberal 10
democracy and a relatively free market economy a nurturing climate in which its full potentialities as a technology of images could be exploited. One result

of this has been that American television programs are in demand all over the world. The total estimate of U.S. television program exports is approximately 100,000 to 200,000 hours, equally divided among Latin America, Asia and Europe. Over the years, programs like "Gunsmoke," "Bonanza," "Mission: Impossible," "Star Trek," "Kojak," and more recently, "Dallas" and "Dynasty" have been as popular in England, Japan, Israel and Norway as in Omaha, Nebraska. I have heard (but not verified) that some years ago the Lapps postponed for several days their annual and, one supposes, essential migratory journey so that they could find out who shot J.R. All of this has occurred simultaneously with the decline of America's moral and political prestige, worldwide. American television programs are in demand not because America is loved but because American television is loved.

We need not be detained too long in figuring out why. In watching American television, one is reminded of George Bernard Shaw's remark on his first seeing the glittering neon signs of Broadway and 42nd Street at night. It must be beautiful, he said, if you cannot read. American television is, indeed, a beautiful spectacle, a visual delight, pouring forth thousands of images on any given day. The average length of a shot on network television is only 3.5 seconds, so that the eye never rests, always has something new to see. Moreover, television offers viewers a variety of subject matter, requires minimal skills to comprehend it, and is largely aimed at emotional gratification. Even commercials, which some regard as an annoyance, are exquisitely crafted, always pleasing to the eye and accompanied by exciting music. There is no question but that the best photography in the world is presently seen on television commercials. American television, in other words, is devoted entirely to supplying its audience with entertainment.

Of course, to say that television is entertaining is merely banal. Such a fact is hardly threatening to a culture, not even worth writing a book about. It may even be a reason for rejoicing. Life, as we like to say, is not a highway strewn with flowers. The sight of a few blossoms here and there may make our journey a trifle more endurable. The Lapps undoubtedly thought so. We may surmise that the ninety million Americans who watch television every night also think so. But what I am claiming here is not that television is entertaining but that it has made entertainment itself the natural format for the representation of all experience. Our television set keeps us in constant communion with the world, but it does so with a face whose smiling countenance is unalterable. The problem is not that television presents us with entertaining subject matter but that all subject matter is presented as entertaining, which is another issue altogether.

To say it still another way: Entertainment is the supra-ideology of all discourse on television. No matter what is depicted or from what point of view, the overarching presumption is that it is there for our amusement and pleasure. That is why even on news shows which provide us daily with fragments of tragedy and barbarism, we are urged by the newscasters to "join them tomorrow." What for? One would think that several minutes of murder and mayhem would suffice as material for a month of sleepless nights. We accept the newscasters' invitation because we know that the "news" is not to be taken seriously, that it is all in fun, so to say. Everything about a news show tells us this—the good looks and amiability of the cast, their pleasant banter, the exciting music that opens and closes the show, the vivid film footage, the attractive commercials—all these and more suggest that what we have just seen is no cause for weeping. A news show, to put it plainly, is a format for entertainment, not for education, reflection or catharsis. And we must not judge too harshly those who have framed it in this way. They are not assembling the news to be read, or broadcasting it to be heard. They are televising the news to be seen. They must follow where their medium leads. There is no conspiracy here, no lack of intelligence, only a straightforward recognition that "good television" has little to do with what is "good" about exposition or other forms of verbal communication but everything to do with what the pictorial images look like.

I should like to illustrate this point by offering the case of the eighty-minute discussion provided by the ABC network on November 20, 1983, following its controversial movie *The Day After*. Though the memory of this telecast has receded for most, I choose this case because, clearly, here was television taking its most "serious" and "responsible" stance. Everything that made up this broadcast recommended it as a critical test of television's capacity to depart from an entertainment mode and rise to the level of public instruction. In the first place, the subject was the possibility of a nuclear holocaust. Second, the film itself had been attacked by several influential bodies politic, including the Reverend Jerry Falwell's Moral Majority. Thus, it was important that the network display television's value and serious intentions as a medium of information and coherent discourse. Third, on the program itself no musical theme was used as background—a significant point since almost all television programs are embedded in music, which helps to tell the audience what emotions are to be called forth. This is a standard theatrical device, and its absence on television is always ominous. Fourth, there were no commercials during the discussion, thus elevating the tone of the event to the state of reverence usually reserved for the funerals of assassinated Presidents. And finally, the participants included Henry Kissinger, Robert McNamara, and Elie Wiesel, each of whom is a symbol of sorts of serious discourse. Although Kissinger, somewhat later, made an appearance on the hit show "Dynasty," he was then and still is a paradigm of intellectual sobriety; and Wiesel, practically a walking metaphor of social conscience. Indeed, the other members of the cast—Carl Sagan, William Buckley and General Brent Scowcroft—are, each in his way, men of intellectual bearing who are not expected to participate in trivial public matters.

The program began with Ted Koppel, master of ceremonies, so to speak, indicating that what followed was not intended to be a debate but a *discussion*. And so those who are interested in philosophies of discourse had an excellent opportunity to observe what serious television means by the word "discussion." Here is what it means: Each of six men was given approximately five minutes to say something about the subject. There was, however, no agreement on exactly   15 what the subject was, and no one felt obliged to respond to anything anyone else said. In fact, it would have been difficult to do so, since the participants were called upon seriatim, as if they were finalists in a beauty contest, each being given his share of minutes in front of the camera. Thus, if Mr. Wiesel, who was called upon last, had a response to Mr. Buckley, who was called upon first, there would have been four commentaries in between, occupying about twenty minutes, so that the audience (if not Mr. Wiesel himself) would have had difficulty remembering the argument which prompted his response. In fact, the participants—most of whom were no strangers to television—largely avoided addressing each other's points. They used their initial minutes and then their subsequent ones to intimate their position or give an impression. Dr. Kissinger, for example, seemed intent on making viewers feel sorry that he was no longer their Secretary of State by reminding everyone of books he had once written, proposals he had once made, and negotiations he had once conducted. Mr. McNamara informed the audience that he had eaten lunch in Germany that very afternoon, and went on to say that he had at least fifteen proposals to reduce nuclear arms. One would have thought that the discussion would turn on this issue, but the others seemed about as interested in it as they were in what he had for lunch in Germany. (Later, he took the initiative to mention three of his proposals but they were not discussed.) Elie Wiesel, in a series of quasi-parables and paradoxes, stressed the tragic nature of the human condition, but because he did not have the time to provide a context for his remarks, he seemed quixotic and confused, conveying an impression of an itinerant rabbi who has wandered into a coven of Gentiles.

In other words, this was no discussion as we normally use the word. Even when the "discussion" period began, there were no arguments or counterarguments, no scrutiny of assumptions, no explanations, no elaborations, no definitions. Carl Sagan made, in my opinion, the most coherent statement—a four-minute rationale for a nuclear freeze—but it contained at least two questionable assumptions and was not carefully examined. Apparently, no one wanted to take time from his own few minutes to call attention to someone else's. Mr. Koppel, for his part, felt obliged to keep the "show" moving, and though he occasionally pursued what he discerned as a line of thought, he was more concerned to give each man his fair allotment of time.

But it is not time constraints alone that produce such fragmented and discontinuous language. When a television show is in process, it is very nearly impermissible to say, "Let me think about that" or "I don't know" or "What do you mean when you say . . . ?" or "From what sources does your information come?" This type of discourse not only slows down the tempo of the show but creates the impression of uncertainty or lack of finish. It tends to reveal people in the *act of thinking*, which is as disconcerting and boring on television as it is on a Las Vegas stage. Thinking does not play well on television, a fact that television directors discovered long ago. There is not much to *see* in it. It is, in a phrase, not a performing art. But television demands a performing art, and so what the ABC network gave us was a picture of men of sophisticated verbal skills and political understanding being brought to heel by a medium that requires them to fashion performances rather than ideas. Which accounts for why the eighty minutes were very entertaining, in the way of a Samuel Beckett play: The intimations of gravity hung heavy, the meaning passeth all understanding. The performances, of course, were highly professional. Sagan abjured the turtle-neck sweater in which he starred when he did "Cosmos." He even had his hair cut for the event. His part was that of the logical scientist speaking in behalf of the planet. It is to be doubted that Paul Newman could have done better in the role, although Leonard Nimoy might have. Scowcroft was suitably military in his bearing—terse and distant, the unbreakable defender of national security. Kissinger, as always, was superb in the part of the knowing world statesman, weary of the sheer responsibility of keeping disaster at bay. Koppel played to perfection the part of a moderator, pretending, as it were, that he was sorting out ideas while, in fact, he was merely directing the performances. At the end, one could only applaud those performances, which is what a good television program always aims to achieve; that is to say, applause, not reflection.

I do not say categorically that it is impossible to use television as a carrier of coherent language or thought in process. William Buckley's own program, "Firing Line," occasionally shows people in the act of thinking but who also happen to have television cameras pointed at them. There are other programs, such as "Meet the Press" or "The Open Mind," which clearly strive to maintain a sense of intellectual decorum and typographic tradition, but they are scheduled so that they do not compete with programs of great visual interest, since otherwise, they will not be watched. After all, it is not unheard of that a format will occasionally go against the bias of its medium. For example, the most popular radio program of the early 1940's featured a ventriloquist, and in those days, I heard more than once the feet of a tap dancer on the "Major Bowes' Amateur Hour." (Indeed, if I am not mistaken, he even once featured a pantomimist.) But ventriloquism, dancing and mime do not play well on radio, just as sustained, complex talk does not play well on television. It can be made to play tolerably well if only one camera is used and the visual image is kept constant—as when the President gives a speech. But this is not television at its best, and it is not television that most people will choose to watch. The single most important fact about television is that people *watch* it, which is why it is called "tele*vision*." And what they watch, and like to watch, are moving pictures—millions of them, of short duration and dynamic variety. It is in the nature of the medium that it must suppress the content of ideas in order to accommodate the requirements of visual interest; that is to say, to accommodate the values of show business.

Film, records and radio (now that it is an adjunct of the music industry) are, of course, equally devoted to entertaining the culture, and their effects in altering the style of American discourse are not insignificant. But television is different because it encompasses all forms of discourse. No one goes to a movie to find out about government policy or the latest scientific advances. No one buys a record to find out the baseball scores or the weather or the latest murder. No one turns on radio anymore for soap operas or a presidential address (if a television set is at hand). But everyone goes to television for all these things and more, which is why television resonates so powerfully throughout the culture. Television is our culture's principal mode of knowing about itself. Therefore—and this is the critical point—how television stages the world becomes the model for how the world is properly to be staged. It is not merely that on the television screen entertainment is the metaphor for all discourse. It is that off the screen the same metaphor prevails. As typography once dictated the style of conducting politics, religion, business, education, law and other important social matters, television now takes command. In courtrooms, classrooms, operating rooms, board rooms, churches and even airplanes, Americans no longer talk to each other, they entertain each other. They do not exchange ideas; they exchange images. They do not argue with propositions; they argue with good looks, celebrities and commercials. For the message of television as metaphor is not only that all the world is a stage but that the stage is located in Las Vegas, Nevada.

In Chicago, for example, the Reverend Greg Sakowicz, a Roman Catholic   20 priest, mixes his religious teaching with rock 'n' roll music. According to the Associated Press, the Reverend Sakowicz is both an associate pastor at the Church of the Holy Spirit in Schaumberg (a suburb of Chicago) and a disc jockey at WKQX. On his show, "The Journey Inward," Father Sakowicz chats in soft tones about such topics as family relationships or commitment, and interposes his sermons with "the sound of *Billboard*'s Top 10." He says that his preaching is not done "in a churchy way," and adds, "You don't have to be boring in order to be holy."

Meanwhile in New York City at St. Patrick's Cathedral, Father John J. O'Connor put on a New York Yankee baseball cap as he mugged his way through his installation as Archbishop of the New York Archdiocese. He got off some excellent gags, at least one of which was specifically directed at Mayor Edward Koch, who was a member of his audience; that is to say, he was a congregant. At his next public performance, the new archbishop donned a New York Mets baseball cap. These events were, of course, televised, and were vastly entertaining, largely because Archbishop (now Cardinal) O'Connor has done Father Sakowicz one better: Whereas the latter believes that you don't have to be boring to be holy, the former apparently believes you don't have to be holy at all.

In Phoenix, Arizona, Dr. Edward Dietrich performed triple bypass surgery on Bernard Schuler. The operation was successful, which was nice for Mr. Schuler. It was also on television, which was nice for America. The operation was carried by at least fifty television stations in the United States, and also by the British Broadcasting Corporation. A two-man panel of narrators (a play-by-play and color man, so to speak) kept viewers informed about what they were seeing. It was not clear as to why this event was televised, but it resulted in transforming both Dr. Dietrich and Mr. Schuler's chest into celebrities. Perhaps because he has seen too many doctor shows on television, Mr. Schuler was uncommonly confident about the outcome of his surgery. "There is no way in hell they are going to lose me on live TV," he said.

As reported with great enthusiasm by both WCBS-TV and WNBC-TV in 1984, the Philadelphia public schools have embarked on an experiment in which children will have their curriculum sung to them. Wearing Walkman equipment, students were shown listening to rock music whose lyrics were about the eight parts of speech. Mr. Jocko Henderson, who thought of this idea, is planning to delight students further by subjecting mathematics and history, as well as English, to the rigors of a rock music format. In fact, this is not Mr. Henderson's idea at all. It was pioneered by the Children's Television Workshop, whose television show "Sesame Street" is an expensive illustration of the idea that education is indistinguishable from entertainment. Nonetheless, Mr. Henderson has a point in his favor. Whereas "Sesame Street" merely attempts to make learning to read a form of light entertainment, the Philadelphia experiment aims to make the classroom itself into a rock concert.

In New Bedford, Massachusetts, a rape trial was televised, to the delight of audiences who could barely tell the difference between the trial and their favorite mid-day soap opera. In Florida, trials of varying degrees of seriousness, including murder, are regularly televised and are considered to be more entertaining than most fictional courtroom dramas. All of this is done in the interests of "public education." For the same high purpose, plans are afoot, it is rumored, to televise confessionals. To be called "Secrets of the Confessional Box," the program will, of course, carry the warning that some of its material may be offensive to children and therefore parental guidance is suggested.

On a United Airlines flight from Chicago to Vancouver, a stewardess   25 announces that its passengers will play a game. The passenger with the most credit cards will win a bottle of champagne. A man from Boston with twelve credit cards wins. A second game requires the passengers to guess the collective age of the cabin crew. A man from Chicago guesses 128, and wins another bottle of wine. During the second game, the air turns choppy and the Fasten Seat Belt sign goes on. Very few people notice, least of all the cabin crew, who keep up a steady flow of gags on the intercom. When the plane reaches its destination, everyone seems to agree that it's fun to fly from Chicago to Vancouver.

On February 7, 1985, *The New York Times* reported that Professor Charles Pine of Rutgers University (Newark campus) was named Professor of the Year by the Council for the Support and Advancement of Education. In explaining why he has such a great impact on his students, Professor Pine said: "I have some gimmicks I use all the time. If you reach the end of the blackboard, I keep writing on the wall. It always gets a laugh. The way I show what a glass molecule does is to run over to one wall and bounce off it, and run over to the other wall." His students are, perhaps, too young to recall that James Cagney used this "molecule move" to great effect in *Yankee Doodle Dandy*. If I am not mistaken,

Donald O'Connor duplicated it in *Singin' in the Rain*. So far as I know, it has been used only once before in a classroom: Hegel tried it several times in demonstrating how the dialectical method works.

The Pennsylvania Amish try to live in isolation from mainstream American culture. Among other things, their religion opposes the veneration of graven images, which means that the Amish are forbidden to see movies or to be photographed. But apparently their religion has not got around to disallowing seeing movies *when* they are being photographed. In the summer of 1984, for example, a Paramount Pictures crew descended upon Lancaster County to film the movie *Witness*, which is about a detective, played by Harrison Ford, who falls in love with an Amish woman. Although the Amish were warned by their church not to interfere with the film makers, it turned out that some Amish welders ran to see the action as soon as their work was done. Other devouts lay in the grass some distance away, and looked down on the set with binoculars. "We read about the movie in the paper," said an Amish woman. "The kids even cut out Harrison Ford's picture." She added: "But it doesn't really matter that much to them. Somebody told us he was in *Star Wars* but that doesn't mean anything to us." The last time a similar conclusion was drawn was when the executive director of the American Association of Blacksmiths remarked that he had read about the automobile but that he was convinced it would have no consequences for the future of his organization.

In the Winter, 1984, issue of the *Official Video Journal* there appears a full-page advertisement for "The Genesis Project." The project aims to convert the Bible into a series of movies. The end-product, to be called "The New Media Bible," will consist of 225 hours of film and will cost a quarter of a billion dollars. Producer John Heyman, whose credits include *Saturday Night Fever* and *Grease*, is one of the film makers most committed to the project. "Simply stated," he is quoted as saying, "I got hooked on the Bible." The famous Israeli actor Topol, best known for his role as Tevye in *Fiddler on the Roof*, will play the role of Abraham. The advertisement does not say who will star as God but, given the producer's background, there is some concern that it might be John Travolta.

At the commencement exercises at Yale University in 1983, several honorary degrees were awarded, including one to Mother Teresa. As she and other humanitarians and scholars, each in turn, received their awards, the audience applauded appropriately but with a slight hint of reserve and impatience, for it wished to give its heart to the final recipient who waited shyly in the wings. As the details of her achievements were being recounted, many people left their seats and surged toward the stage to be closer to the great woman. And when the name Meryl Streep was announced, the audience unleashed a sonic boom of affection to wake the New Haven dead. One man who was present when Bob Hope received his honorary doctorate at another institution said that Dr. Streep's applause surpassed Dr. Hope's. Knowing how to please a crowd as well as anyone, the intellectual leaders at Yale invited Dick Cavett, the talk-show host, to deliver the commencement address the following year. It is rumored that this year, Don Rickles will receive a Doctorate of Humane Letters and Lola Falana will give the commencement address.

Prior to the 1984 presidential elections, the two candidates confronted each other on television in what were called "debates." These events were not the least like the Lincoln/Douglas debates or anything else that goes by the name. Each candidate was given five minutes to address such questions as, What is (or would be) your policy in Central America? His opposite number was then given one minute for a rebuttal. In such circumstances, complexity, documentation and logic can play no role, and, indeed, on several occasions syntax itself was abandoned entirely. It is no matter. The men were less concerned with giving arguments than with "giving off" impressions, which is what television does best. Post-debate commentary largely avoided any evaluation of the candidates' ideas, since there were none to evaluate. Instead, the debates were conceived as boxing matches, the relevant question being, Who KO'd whom? The answer was determined by the "style" of the men—how they looked, fixed their gaze, smiled, and delivered one-liners. In the second debate, President Reagan got off a swell one-liner when asked a question about this age. The following day, several newspapers indicated that Ron had KO'd Fritz with his joke. Thus, the leader of the free world is chosen by the people in the Age of Television.

What all this means is that our culture has moved toward a new way of conducting its business, especially its important business. The nature of its discourse is changing as the demarcation line between what is show business and what is not becomes harder to see with each passing day. Our priests and presidents, our surgeons and lawyers, our educators and newscasters need worry less about satisfying the demands of their discipline than the demands of good showmanship. Had Irving Berlin changed one word in the title of his celebrated song, he would have been as prophetic, albeit more terse, as Aldous Huxley. He need only have written, There's No Business But Show Business.

● Applying a Materialist Frame

1. *Amusing Ourselves to Death* appeared before the World Wide Web and became a household fact of life. When he talks about "technology" in this piece, he's referring almost exclusively to the technologies associated with television. As he says, "A technology becomes a medium as it employs a particular symbolic code, as it finds its place in a particular social setting, as it insinuates itself into economic and political contexts." Clearly, Postman believes that television has "insinuated" itself into "economic and political contexts." What does he mean by this?

   • Trace his argument in your own words. Did everyone in the class see the same points?

   • What kind of variety do you see in how others "read" Postman? How do you explain that variety?

2. Postman says, "Entertainment is the supra-ideology of all discourse on television." Explain what he means by this, using what you've read about ideology. What would it mean to have an "ideology of discourse on television"? Refer to specific television programs you're familiar with in your explanation.

3. If "thinking does not play well on television," how would you explain the way media transmit and help create ideologies *of* "spectacle"—*for* spectators? Are there clear lines, in your own mind, between "participants" and "spectators"?

   • In what ways are you participating in an event that is being broadcast on television?

   • If "thinking does not play well on television," then how have you been persuaded to participate/spectate?

   • How can something called "reality programming" make any sense? Aren't cameras on all the time and wouldn't you think that might alter "reality"?

4. Examine the lyrics of the following Christmas song. In what ways does Reich's chapter help you see corporate values in play?

   > Oh! You better watch out, You better not cry,
   > You better not pout, I'm telling you why:
   > Santa Claus is coming to town!
   > He's making a list, He's checking it twice,
   > He's gonna find out who's naughty or nice.
   > Santa Claus is coming to town!
   > He sees you when you're sleeping, He knows when you're awake.
   > He knows when you've been bad or good,
   > So be good for goodness sake!
   > So . . . You better watch out, You better not cry,
   > You better not pout, I'm telling you why:
   > Santa Claus is coming to town!

   What do you know about the *Panopticon*? Research this term and write about how it reflects the same concepts as the song above.

The Numbing of the American Mind: Culture as Anesthetic

THOMAS DE ZENGOTITA

Thomas de Zengotita teaches at the Dalton School and New York University's Draper Graduate Program. As a contributing editor for Harper's Magazine, *his frequent essays usually focus on the relationships between "culture" and "epistemology," or knowing—what we know, how we know it, why we know what we know. This essay appeared in 2002.*

. . . the massive influx of impressions is so great; surprising, barbaric, and violent things press so overpoweringly—"balled up into hideous clumps"— in the youthful soul; that it can save itself only by taking recourse in premeditated stupidity.

—Friedrich Nietzsche

It was to have been the end of irony, remember? Superficial celebrity culture was over; a new age of seriousness was upon us. Of course, the way media celebrities focused on their own mood as the consequence of September 11 was in itself an irony so marvelous you knew immediately how wrong they were. And sure enough, the spotlight never wavered. It went on shining as it always had, on those it was meant for—on them. A guarantee of continuing superficiality right there, quite apart from unintended irony.

So we shared Dan Rather's pain, marveled at intrepid Ashleigh Banfield, scrutinizing those ferocious tribal fighters through her designer specs, and Tom Brokaw, arbiter of greatness among generations, took us on a tour of the real West Wing. But these iconic moments swam into focus only momentarily, soon to be swept away in a deluge of references, references so numerous, so relentlessly repeated, that they came at last to constitute a solid field, a new backdrop for all our public performances. How often did you hear, how often did you say, "Since the events of 9/11"? A new idiom had been deposited in the language, approaching the same plane of habituality as "by the way" or "on the other hand." And in the process we got past it after all. Six months or so was all it took. The holidays came and went, and—if you were not personally stricken by the terror of September—chances are you got over it. You moved on.

How is that possible?

Nietzsche was not thinking I.Q. or ignorance when he used the word "stupidity." He meant stupidity as in clogged, anesthetized. Numb. He thought people at the end of the *nineteenth* century were suffocating in a vast goo of meaningless stimulation. Ever notice how, when your hand is numb, everything feels thin? Even a solid block of wood lacks depth and texture. You can't feel the wood; your limb just encounters the interrupting surface. Well, numb is to the soul as thin is to a mediated world. Our guiding metaphor. And it isn't just youthful souls either.

Here's the basic situation. On the one hand: the Web, satellite cable TV, Palm Pilot, DVD, Ethernet—Virtual Environments everywhere. On the other hand: cloning, genetic engineering, artificial intelligence, robotics—Virtual Beings everywhere. Someday, when people (or whatever they are) look back on our time, all this will appear as a single development, called something like "The Information Revolution," and the lesson of that revolution will have been this: what counts is the code. Silicon- or carbon-based. Artifact or animate. The difference between them is disappearing. This is not science fiction. This is really happening. Right now, in an Atlanta hospital, there is a quadriplegic with his brain directly wired to a computer. He can move the cursor with his thoughts.

The moving cursor doesn't really need explaining—it comes down to digital bytes and neurochemical spikes. What needs explaining is our equanimity in the face of staggering developments. How can we go about our business when things like this are happening? How can we just read the article, shake our heads, turn the page? If creatures from outer space sent a diplomatic mission to the U.N., how long would it be before we were taking that in stride? Before Comedy Central send-ups were more entertaining than the actual creatures? About six months?

Soap-opera politics. The therapy industry. Online communities. Digital effects. Workshops for every workplace. Viagra, Prozac, Ritalin, Reality TV. Complete makeovers. Someday, it will be obvious that all the content on our information platforms converges on this theme: there is no important difference between fabrication and reality, between a chemical a pill introduces and one your body produces, between role-playing in marital therapy and playing your role as a spouse, between selling and making, campaigning and governing, expressing and existing. And that is why we moved on after September 11, after an event that seemed so enormous, so horrific, so stark, that even the great blob of virtuality that is our public culture would be unable to absorb it. But it could. It has. Here's how.

Fabrication

Some people refuse to believe that reality has become indistinguishable from fabrication. But beliefs are crude reflections of the psychological processes that actually determine how we function. Fat people believe they are on the stocky side. Abject drunks believe they are poetical free spirits. Malicious prudes believe they are selfless do-gooders. And a lot of people still believe that, with some obvious exceptions involving hoaxes and errors, we know what's real and what's not. We can tell the difference between the *Kursk* and the *Titanic* (meaning the movie, of course), for example.

And maybe we can—when specifically focused on the issue. It might take a while, of course, because there *are* so many gradations when you stop to think about it. For example:

- Real real: You fall down the stairs. Stuff in your life that's so familiar you've forgotten the statement it makes.
- Observed real: You drive by a car wreck. Stuff in your life in which the image-statement is as salient as the function.
- Between real real and observed real: Stuff that oscillates between the first two categories. Like you're wearing something you usually take for granted but then you meet someone attractive.
- Edited real real: Shtick you have down so pat you don't know it's shtick anymore, but you definitely only use it in certain situations. Documentaries

and videos in which people are unaware of the camera, though that's not easy to detect, actually. Candid photographs.

- Edited observed real: Other people's down-pat shtick. Shtick you are still working on. Documentaries in which people are accommodating the camera, which is actually a lot of the time, probably.
- Staged real: Formal events like weddings. Retail-clerk patter.
- Edited staged real: Pictures of the above. Homemade porn.
- Staged observed real unique: Al kisses Tipper. *Survivor.*
- Staged observed real repeated: Al kisses Tipper again and again. Anchor-desk and talk-show intros and segues. Weather Channel behavior.

(In the interests of time, we can skip the subtler middle range of distinc- 10 tions and go to the other end of the spectrum:)

- Staged realistic: *The English Patient* and *NYPD Blue.*
- Staged hyperreal: Oliver Stone movies and *Malcolm in the Middle.*
- Overtly unreal realistic: S.U.V.'s climbing buildings. Digitized special effects in general, except when they are more or less undetectable.
- Covertly unreal realistic: Hair in shampoo ads. More or less undetectable digital effects, of which there are more every day.
- Between overtly and covertly unreal realistic: John Wayne in a beer ad (you have to know he's dead to know he isn't "really" in the ad).
- Real unreal: Robo-pets.
- Unreal real: Strawberries that won't freeze because they have fish genes in them.

See? No problem. The differences are perfectly clear.

But the issue isn't *can* we do it; it's *do* we do it—and the answer is, of course not. Our minds are the product of total immersion in a daily experience saturated with fabrications to a degree unprecedented in human history. People have never had to cope with so much stuff, so many choices. In kind and number.

Flood

And sheer quantity really matters, because here we collide with a real limit, one of the few that remain—namely, how much a person can register at a given instant. No innovation in techno-access or sensationalism can overcome this bottleneck. It determines the fundamental dynamic, the battle to secure attention, in every domain of our lives.

Compare, say, the cereal and juice sections of a supermarket today with those of years ago. For you youngsters out there, take it from Dad: it used to be

Wheaties, Corn Flakes, Cheerios (oats), Rice Krispies—and that was about it. One for each grain, see? Same for fruit juice. But now? Pineapple/Banana/Grape or Strawberry/Orange/Kiwi anyone? And that's just a sample from Tropicana— check out Nantucket Nectars. Makes of cars? Types of sunglasses? Sneaker species? Pasta possibilities? On and on. It's all about options, as they say.

Umbrella brands toss off diverse and evolving lines of market-researched products for niches of self-inventing customers with continual access to every representational fabrication ever produced in the whole of human history. That's "the environment." You like Vedic ankle tattoos? 1930s cockney caps? Safari jackets? Inca ponchos? Victorian lace-up high-heel booties? Whatever.   15

No wonder that word caught on.

The moreness of everything ascends inevitably to a threshold in psychic life. A change of state takes place. The discrete display melts into a pudding, and the mind is forced to certain adaptations if it is to cohere at all.

When you find out about the moving cursor, or hear statistics about AIDS in Africa, or see your 947th picture of a weeping fireman, you can't help but become fundamentally indifferent because you are exposed to things like this all the time, just as you are to the rest of your options. Over breakfast. In the waiting room. Driving to work. At the checkout counter. *All the time*. I know you know this already. I'm just reminding you.

Which is not to say you aren't moved. On the contrary, you are moved, often deeply, very frequently—never more so, perhaps, than when you saw the footage of the towers coming down on 9/11. But you are so used to being moved by footage, by stories, by representations of all kinds—that's the point. It's not your fault that you are so used to being moved, you just are.

So it's not surprising that you have learned to move on so readily to the next,   20 sometimes moving, moment. It's sink or surf. Spiritual numbness guarantees that your relations with the moving will pass. And the stuffed screen accommodates you with moving surfaces that assume you are numb enough to accommodate them. And so on, back and forth. The dialectic of postmodern life.

One might say, "Well, people didn't respond deeply to every development in the world 200 years ago either." And that's true, but it isn't an objection, it's a confirmation. Until the new media came along, people didn't even *know* about such developments, or not as quickly, and above all not as dramatically or frequently. Also, there weren't as many developments, period. This is crucial, another aspect of sheer moreness that gets overlooked. *Less was happening*.

The contrast is stark with, say, the Middle Ages. By the industrial era, a lot more was happening, and numbness became an issue then. Think of Baudelaire, adrift in the crowd, celebrating the artist for resisting numbness, for maintaining vulnerability—thus setting the standard for the genius of modernism. But a qualitative threshold has since been breached. Cities no longer belong to the soulful *flâneur* but to the wired-up voyeur in his soundproofed Lexus. Behind his tinted windows, with his cell phone and CD player, he gets more input, with less static, from more and different channels, than Baudelaire ever dreamed of. But it's all insulational—as if the deities at Dreamworks were invisibly at work around us, touching up the canvas of reality with existential airbrushes. Everything has that edgeless quality, like the lobby of a high-end Marriott/Ramada/Sheraton. Whole neighborhoods feel like that now. And you can be sure that whatever they do at "the site" will feel like that, too: Even if they specifically set out to avoid having it feel like that—it will still feel like that. They can't control themselves. They can't stop.

Take the new Times Square, everybody's icon for this process. All the usual observations apply—and each contributes its iota to muffling what it meant to expose. But the point here is the way everything in that place is *aimed*. Everything is firing message modules, straight for your gonads, your taste buds, your vanities, your fears. These modules seek to penetrate, but in a passing way. A second of your attention is all they ask. Nothing is firing that rends or cuts. It's a massage, really, if you just go with it. And why not? Some of the most talented people on the planet have devoted their lives to creating this psychic sauna, just for you.

And it's not just the screens and billboards, the literal signs; it's absolutely everything you encounter. Except for the eyes of the people, shuffling along, and the poignant imperfections of their bodies; they are so manifestly unequal to the solicitations lavished upon them. No wonder they stuff themselves with junk— or, trying to live up to it all, enslave themselves to regimes of improvement.

Yes, there were ersatz environments and glitzy ads back in the fifties, but this is a new order of quality and saturation. Saying that it's just more of what we had before is like saying a hurricane is just more breeze. For here, too, there is a psychological threshold. Today, your brain is, as a matter of brute fact, full of stuff that was *designed* to affect you. As opposed to the scattered furniture of nature and history that people once registered just because it happened to be there. September 11 had to accommodate the fact that our inner lives are now largely constituted by effects.

To get relief, you have to stumble into the Greyhound bus station in Albany, or some old side-street barbershop that time forgot, into someplace not yet subjected to the renovating ministrations of the International Red Brick and Iron Filigree Restoration Corporation. And "stumble" is the key concept here. Accidental places are the only real places left.

That's why a couple of weeks out in Nature doesn't make it anymore. Even if you eschew the resonant clutter of The Tour and The Gear, you will virtualize everything you encounter anyway, all by yourself. You won't see wolves, you'll see "wolves." You'll be murmuring to yourself, at some level, "Wow, look, a real wolf, not in a cage, not on TV, I can't believe it."

That's right, you can't. Natural things have become their own icons.

And you will get restless really fast if that "wolf" doesn't do anything. The kids will start squirming in, like, five minutes; you'll probably need to pretend you're not getting bored for a while longer. But if that little smudge of canine out there in the distance continues to just loll around in the tall grass, and you don't have a really powerful tripod-supported telelens gizmo to play with, you

25

will get bored. You will begin to appreciate how much technology and editing goes into making those nature shows. The truth is that if some no-account chipmunk just happens to come around your campsite every morning for crumbs from your picnic table, it will have meant more to you than any "wolf."

Precious accidents.

Back to the new Times Square—do you parse out the real from the fabricated in that mélange? Not *can* you, but *do* you. The Fox screen is showing Elián in his Cuban school uniform on the side of a building—real or not? Some glorious babe in her underwear is sprawled across 35 percent of your visual field. She's looking you right in the eye. You feel that old feeling—real or not? A fabulous man, sculpted to perfection by more time in the health club than most parents have for their kids, is gliding by on Day-Glo Rollerblades eight inches high. He's wearing Tex-tex gear so tight it looks like it's under his skin, and the logos festooning his figure emit meaning-beeps from every angle—real or not? What about the pumped-up biceps? If he uses steroids? But, once again, the issue isn't what you *can* do when I call your attention to it. The real issue is *do* you do it as a matter of routine processing? Or do you rely instead on a general immunity that only numbness can provide, an immunity that puts the whole flood in brackets and transforms it all into a play of surfaces—over which you hover and glide like a little god, dipping in here and there for the moving experience of your choice, with the ultimate reaches of your soul on permanent remote?

30

Finitude

What about that feeling that it's all been done? Not in the techie department, of course; there, the possibility of novelty seems to be unlimited. But in those areas occupied by what platform proprietors call "content providers." What a phrase! Could anything register devastation of the spirit more completely than that little generic? Could meaning suffer more complete evacuation? Not since we landed on the moon and found nothing has our cultural unconscious encountered so traumatic a void.

Maybe the postmodern taste for recycling and pastiche is more than a phase? Maybe it's necessity. Maybe more or less everything that can be done in the plastic arts, say, has been done? How many different ways can a finite set of shapes and colors be arranged in a finite space? We aren't talking infinitely divisible Platonic geometry here. Maybe there just isn't any really new way to put x shapes and y colors into z permutations. Maybe some day it will be obvious that the characteristic gestures of twentieth-century art were flailing against this fact. Cézanne's planes, Magritte's pipe, Pollock's swirls, Warhol's soup can, Christo's draperies, Serrano's piss, the "installations"—so many desperate efforts to elude the end of originality?

Likewise with music? How many distinguishable sounds can be put in how many patterns? There has to be some limit. After you've integrated techno and Brazilian-Afro and Tibetan monko and Hump-backed Whalo, at some point, surely, there's going to be nothing left but play it again, Sam. Maybe that's why it's the age of the mix. And characters and plots, in stories and shows? What's the raw material? Sex, outlaws, illness, death, master villains, guilt, the fall of giants, fate, just deserts, the dark side, redemption by the little things, a few other themes—we all know the repertoire. Maybe it's just impossible to think of anything that couldn't be described, after the fashion of all contemporary pitches, as "It's *To the Lighthouse* meets *Married with Children*" or "It's Hannibal Lecter meets Peter Pan."

The prospect of finitude helps to account for the turn to sensation, as if   35 intensity of presentation could make up for repetition. Of course, sensation is also a response to sheer clutter on the screen, a way to grab the most possible attention in the least amount of time. But that clutter also accounts for why everything's already been done, and so it cycles on relentlessly—fill the pages, fill the time slots, fill the channels, the websites, the roadsides, the building facades, the fronts and backs of shirts and caps, everything, everything must be saying something, every minute. But what? What's left to say? It doesn't matter. Cut to the response.

Zap. Whimper. Flinch. Cringe, Melt. Assert! Exult! Weep. Subside. Ahhh . . .

Eventually we can just wire our glands directly to a console of sensation buttons, platform to platform, and be done with this tiresome content altogether. Call it P2P communication. Talk about interactive. Thus will the human soul be compensated for the despair of finitude.

Fast

Remember that T-shirt from the eighties that said "High on Stress"? It was sort of true and sort of a way to bluff it out and sort of a protest—it had that "any number of meanings" quality we now prefer to depth. That's because the any-number-of-meanings quality keeps you in motion, but depth asks you to stop. Depth is to your life what dead air is to a talk show.

Being numb isn't antithetical to being totally stressed, 24–7—and asking for more. Over-scheduled busyness might seem like the opposite of numbness, but it is just the active aspect of living in a flood of fabricated surfaces. Consider the guiding metaphor again. The (absence of) sensation that is physical numbness is constituted by a multitude of thrills and tingles at a frequency beyond which you feel nothing. The numbness of busyness works on the same principle, but it relies upon its agents to abide by an agreement they must keep secret, even from themselves. The agreement is this: we will so conduct ourselves that everything becomes an emergency.

Under that agreement, stress is how reality feels. People addicted to busy-   40 ness, people who don't just use their cell phones in public but display in every nuance of cell-phone deportment their sense of throbbing connectedness to Something Important—these people would suffocate like fish on a dock if they were cut off from the Flow of Events they have conspired with their fellows to create. To these plugged-in players, the rest of us look like zombies, coasting on fumes. For them, the feeling of being busy *is* the feeling of being alive.

Partly, it's a function of speed, like in those stress dramas that television provides to keep us virtually busy, even in our downtime. The bloody body wheeled into the ER, every personjack on the team yelling numbers from monitors, screaming for meds and equipment, especially for those heart-shocker pads—that's the paradigm scene. All the others derive from it: hostage-negotiator scenes, staffers pulling all-nighters in the West Wing, detectives sweeping out of the precinct, donning jackets, adjusting holsters, snapping wisecracks. Sheer speed and Lives on the Line. That's the recipe for feeling real.

The irony is that *after* we have worked really hard on something urgent for a long time, we do escape numbness for a while—stepping out of the building, noticing the breeze, the cracks in the sidewalk, the stillness of things in the shop window. During those accidental and transitional moments, we actually get the feeling of the real we were so frantically pursuing when we were busy. But we soon get restless. We can't take the input reduction. Our psychic metabolism craves more.

Actually, stress dramas are about the lives of the media people who make them. They purport to be about hospitals or law firms, but they are actually about what it is like to make TV shows, about high-stakes teamwork in the land of celebrity, where, by definition, everything matters more than it does anywhere else, a land that welcomes diversity and foibles as long as The Job Gets Done, a land where everything personal, unconditional, intimate—everything unbounded by the task—takes place on the side. That's why, in these shows through which the celebrated teach the rest of us how to be like them, the moments of heartfelt encounter that make it all worthwhile are stolen in the corridors of power, while the verdict is awaited. If we get that real-folks-rushing-to-get-out-of-the-house-in-the-morning scene, it's just to underscore the priority of the Flow of Events that protects the busy from being left alone in the stillness with what makes it all worthwhile. Lest direction be lost, motion must be maintained.

Moving On

So life in a flood of surfaces means a life of perpetual motion, and TV provides the model in other modes as well. Take the transitions from story to story in news-casts, that finishing-with-a-topic moment. "Whether these supplies, still piling up after weeks of intense effort by these humanitarian workers, will actually reach the victims (pause) remains to be seen." A hint of a sigh, a slight shake of the head, eyes down-turning; the note of seasoned resignation. Profound respect is con-veyed for the abandoned topic even as a note of anticipation rises to greet the (also interesting, but less burdensome) next topic—and the new camera angle at the anchor desk makes it clear that stem and external necessity, rather than any human agency, governs the shift from two minutes on mass starvation to the next episode of The Fall of the House of Enron.

Judy Woodruff is especially good at this, her particular little head nod, or   45
shake, as the case may be, and the way her lips tighten up a tad. "If it were up to
me as a human being I would *never* leave this coverage of thousands of dying
innocents, but, as a newscaster, of course, I have to." And her speaking voice
says, "All right, Jim, we have to go to a break now, but we will be following this
story as it develops—and thanks again." "Thank you, Judy," says Jim, echoing
her gesture, and we understand that he, too, as a human being, would never
allow us to move on from so ghastly and demanding a reality, but it isn't up to
him as a human being either. It isn't up to anybody, actually. That's the one real
reality. Moving on.

It would be irrelevant to object by asking, "Well, how else are we supposed
to do it?" There isn't any other way to do it. That's the point. This isn't a consultant's memo. This is a serious diagnosis of a serious condition. Would we
rather not know about it because it happens to be incurable? This goes much
deeper than subject matter, or political bias, the usual fodder. It determines the
way we frame everything. Like all that is most profound in human custom, this
agreement is almost physical, an attunement, more music than semantics. It
instills and expresses, moment by moment, the *attitude* we bring to living in this
world of surfaces.

So, for example, you don't have to wait for the anchorperson to change the
topic. You can change it yourself, and you don't have to sigh or tighten your lips
as you make the transition. But you do. Monitor yourself next time you zap
away from some disturbing something on *Lehrer* to catch the action on the *Law
& Order* reruns. You mime those little gestures as you punch the buttons. These
are the constituting habit structures of our culture.

And we've touched already on what awaits you when you join the gang
on *Law & Order*. The stress drama re-creating, more elaborately, the basic
gesture of the news show, the one you just performed when you slid away from
those refugee visuals. Everything's in motion, elliptical, glancing, fungible. You
see the sides of faces, the slope of shoulders, the beginnings of expressions but
not the ends, the ends of expressions but not the beginnings. No matter the
horror, no matter the injustice, no matter how passionate McCoy may feel, no
matter how angry Bratt gets at Briscoe (actors or characters?), no matter how
obnoxious the defense attorney or impatient the judge (especially in chambers),
they all keep moving. And the camera keeps moving, too, gliding, peeking,
glimpsing. Frightened witnesses, incoming lawyers, outgoing suspects, they're
all moving—as is the traffic, the doors, hands, phones, everything. Meaningful
personal encounters are bound to be interrupted, and the performers,
like would-be fighters in a bar relying on friends to keep them apart, anticipate
the interruption. Ferociously or tenderly, they emote in transitional interlude,
awaiting inevitable rescue by events, and, gratefully regretting the passing of
the moment of communion, they watch the D.A. step into the elevator and
deliver the homily as the door slides shut across his grizzled visage, a homily
that is never merely upbeat or despairing, never final or conclusive in any way.

Because the one thing people in a TV series know is that tomorrow is another show, and they will be ready to roll. For they are pros, and pros know how to deal. It's not that they're indifferent or cynical. They care. Sometimes they win, sometimes they lose—but, either way, they move on. That's the lesson, the ultimate homily of all shows. The way we live now.

So, if we were spared a gaping wound in the flesh and blood of personal life, we inevitably moved on after September 11. We were carried off by endlessly proliferating representations of the event, and by an ever expanding horizon of associated stories and characters, and all of them, in their turn, represented endlessly, and the whole sweep of it driven by the rhythms of The Show—anthrax, postal workers, the Bronx lady, the Saddam connection, Osama tapes, Al Jazeera's commentary on Osama tapes, Christiane Amanpour's commentary on Al Jazeera's commentary on Osama tapes, a magazine story about Christiane Amanpour . . .

And that's just one thread in this tapestry of virtuality. The whole is so 50
densely woven and finely stranded that no mind could possibly comprehend it, escape it, govern it. It's the dreamwork of culture. It just proceeds and we with it, each of us exposed to thousands, probably millions of 9/11-related representations—everything from the layout of the daily paper to rippling-flag logos to NYPD caps on tourists to ads for *Collateral Damage*. Conditioned thus relentlessly to move from representation to representation, we got past the thing itself as well; or rather, the thing itself was transformed into a sea of signs and upon it we were borne away from every shore, moving on, moving on.

What else could we do?

● Applying a Materialist Frame

1. De Zengotita sums up his basic premise like this: "Someday, it will be obvious that all the content on our information platforms converges on this theme: there is no important difference between fabrication and reality, between a chemical a pill introduces and one your body produces, between role-playing in marital therapy and playing your role as a spouse, between selling and making, campaigning and governing, expressing and existing," (para. 7). He uses this premise to explain why "we moved on after September 11th."

   How does this work? How does he say our culture "moved on"? What's his point in making these connections, do you think?

2. "Our minds are the product of total immersion in a daily experience saturated with fabrications to a degree unprecedented in human history." How can you see the roots of this experience of fabrication in *The Condition of the Working Class in England* (p. 188)? In other words, from a materialist perspective, how can you explain why the patterns de Zengotita describes could be called "inevitable"?

3. The July 2003 issue of *Harper's Magazine* has an essay by de Zengotita titled "The Romance of Empire." Read this article and compare its basic assumptions with those from "The Numbing of the American Mind." What differences do you notice, either in content or in style? Is one article more persuasive to you than the other? Why?

4. What is de Zengotita's rhetorical position as author in relation to his intended audience?

   • Who is his intended audience? How does he situate himself as an author of ideas that he obviously thinks others ought to think about?

   • What is his rhetorical appeal in this essay based on?

topics for writing

1. One could conceivably write a logically based argument that begins with "Anatomy of the Corporate State" (from *The Greening of America*), includes references to "The Age of Show Business" (from *Amusing Ourselves to Death*), and concludes with "The Numbing of the American Mind." What kinds of logically connected ideas do you find running like a thread through these different pieces? Write an analysis that ties them together by using the materialist critique as your framing lens.

2. As a way of summing up his article, de Zengotita concludes: "Conditioned thus relentlessly to move from representation to representation, we got past the thing itself as well; or rather, the thing itself was transformed into a sea of signs and upon it we were borne away from every shore, moving on, moving on. What else could we do?"

   What else *could* you imagine "us" doing? If we are "borne away" on a "sea of signs," then where is any individual's opportunity for personal agency, for making decisions about the nature or quality of one's life?

   • If one of the materialist premises is

     In order to successfully change the world from a place of constant misery and struggle for most of its inhabitants, we must understand that the underlying organizing principle for *all of social existence* is both material (physical) and economic.

     then how do you respond to de Zengotita?

   • How would you visualize moving from "numbing" yourself in response to modern (or postmodern) pressures to "changing" the pressures themselves?

3. Materialism tells us we can gain knowledge of "who" we are by examining what we "do" to live. How we worship. How we play. What we consider entertainment. What attitudes we have about others.

- Analyze some aspect of your own technological culture with an eye to explaining it to someone from an older generation, someone who doesn't participate in your culture.

- Describe your own popular interests as a way of telling someone "who" you are. Let your older audience in on what makes you tick by explaining to them how and why you behave as you do, play as you do, entertain yourself the way you do. Obviously, you won't be able to just drop the name of your favorite band and expect your audience to "get" it. You'll have to try to use examples or images or ideas that you think this audience can understand—something we all see, something common to everyone. Perhaps you can use references to national or international news events.

Framing and Composing from a Materialist Perspective

1. How many recent news stories have focused on people who exhibit different "rage" behaviors? "Road rage" is a frequent subject of nightly news exposes; we hear stories of drivers, even celebrities, who lose their tempers because of real or perceived driving insults from others and inflict bodily harm or property damage. Some passengers have exploded with "air rage" while on flights or waiting in airport lines; these people demand a certain seat, a piece of luggage to be stowed, or some other kind of "special" attention. Shoppers bent on beating others to the best bargain often are categorized as having "shopping mall rage" as they push and shove to be the first to buy.

   - What kind of thinking would explain how someone just decides that she or he is "better" than others, more deserving—that they have more "status"? You're probably aware of instances in our country's recent past that illustrate "workplace rage"—aberrant and violent behavior from those passed over for promotion, "downsized," laid off.

   - What do all these "rages" have in common? Of course, often the perpetrators are classified as "deranged," "psychotic," or "disturbed." But can we explain their behavior, instead of just condemning it?

   - Can we explain such behavior from the point of view that these people might be trying to assert themselves, if in an antisocial way, trying to make themselves seen or heard? Is this a case of "status-seeking" gone awry?

   Decide with others in your class how you might write about different "rage" disorders and how you might collectively write a synthesis of what you've all learned individually.

2. We've written in the Part Three introduction:

   > Consider what happens every time you enter a writing class. Questions of what specific readings are assigned, where the instructor places grading emphasis, even the style or *mode* of writing encouraged in any individual course—these basic assumptions about what you ought to do or be as a writer in a college classroom—are *ideologically informed*.

   Take a look at the guidelines for "Professionalism in the Written Paper." It was handed to each student enrolling in a graduate level sociology class.

   - Write a cohesive analysis that explains how this approach to teaching/grading writing might be "ideologically informed" to foster certain attitudes and ideas about learning, about student authority, about what "professionalism" means.

Professionalism in the Written Paper

The following is a description of what I mean by a professionally presented paper. This won't guarantee you an "A" grade, as it doesn't address the content area. However, following these guidelines will influence the overall grade of the paper.

Cover (title) page.

Table of Contents (for papers over 10 pages).

Research papers draw from multiple sources that include sources outside of assigned course texts (minimum of 3 additional sources). Original sources are best. Secondary sources are OK; however they must be reflected as secondary on the reference page.

Proper use of citations, following APA (American Psychological Association) guidelines. Citations within text match reference list.

Objective writing style.[1] However, a certain level of *passion* is appropriate.

Clearly presents well-developed argument(s) backed up with evidence—presents concept/theory, develops it with clarity and thoroughness, using *supportive* quotes/citations. When presenting your opinion that is not supported by any author, this is clearly stated as your opinion.

Addresses all points/questions posed in the assignment in depth and detail. *In addition* includes points/questions of your own.[2] Your voice is clearly heard—the paper is not a running sequence of quotes to form the ideas presented.

Begins with an introduction, and ends with a summary.[3] Follows a logical path. Paper is written with clarity.

Appropriate use of headings and subheadings. Topics are linked with appropriate transition statements.

Grammatically correct.

Free of spelling errors.

The paper is bound in an appropriate manner.

---

[1] You are a scholar, therefore responsible for presenting your arguments in a manner that addresses multiple perspectives of a given topic, i.e., pros and cons. Even when writing a paper that is about "you," assume a researcher perspective in order to gain objectivity.

[2] It is expected that you will not simply repeat what the text or instructor has said, but that you will demonstrate your knowledge and understanding through your own voice. When I present "things to think about," they are usually stated, "At a minimum. . . ." Discussing only these items does not represent excellent/exceptional work.

[3] "Tell them what you're going to tell them; tell them; tell them what you told them."

- What do you think when you're told that guidelines don't cover "the content" areas?
- How exactly do you interpret commands such as to write with "clarity" or "thoroughness"? What would you *do* as a writer to ensure success here?
- What about this reliance on "objectivity"? How can you "assume" such a stance and still use your "own voice"?
- Look at footnote 1. Notice how "multiple perspective" turns into "i.e., pros and cons." What does this quick redefinition tell you about the mindset that produced it?

3. A Hollywood star opens an "air bar" in Los Angeles. For $30 or so, the client can lie on pillows with hoses in the nose, like patients in the trauma clinic, and breathe "clean" air. At the current time, these "salons" seem to be mostly populated by the well-to-do and are fadish. But what if, due to some catastrophe of nature or humanity, bottled air was needed to keep you healthy? Would you want to find some more democratic way to use the supply? Do you think this would be necessary? What tells you (in your experience, research, or intellect) what to expect?

   In writing, see if you can explain how your own ideas make sense through a materialist frame. If everyone in your class, for instance, has read the same excerpts, then quoting from them is a valid way to establish credibility, using *others'* voices to make *your* points.

4. Status—people seem to have been caught up in this for centuries. According to the book *News and Rumor in Renaissance Europe* (the Fugger Newsletters), in an account of Seville's *auto de fe* (a public ritual of penance during the Spanish Inquisition), status was strongly at play. This was a report of the "persons who were brought as penitents to the public [court] held by the Holy Court of the Inquisition upon Sunday the 3rd day of May in the year 1579:

   > Thirty-eight: Juan Astruez, a locksmith, Juan Lipiotol and Fernando Gil have said that they were relations of the Inquisitors. Since this is not true, they have had a rope placed round their Necks and have been exposed to public shame."

- What do you know about the Spanish Inquisition? Church officials were judges or "inquisitors," so their status was of the most divine kind. What kinds of social power relationships can you uncover?
- How was social power distributed in the medieval church? By what standards could one gain in status, or social power, in these contexts?
- See if you can explain your perspectives by referring to contemporary events or attitudes your audience would recognize.

5. Research the savings and loan scandals of the late 1980s.
   - Who lost money? How much? Who paid it back?
   - What happened to the people responsible?
   - How did such a fiasco happen?

Perhaps you can relate these events with some more recent corporate scandals, such as Enron. As you write the results of your research, you might experiment with genres other than the "essay". You could write an expose, an editorial, a personal response. Use a materialist frame to contextualize your own "position" as author.

6. Look at holidays as "ritualized" consuming events. Notice the calendar we've created below. What strikes you about the events listed? Try concentrating on each of these holidays as "ritualized spending occasions." Think of the traditions and practices that accompany these holidays and try to apply materialist theory to them.

Looking at Holidays as "Ritualized" Consuming Events

January	**February**	**March**	**April**
New Year's Day	Valentine's Day	St. Patrick's Day	Passover
Martin Luther		Purim/Easter	
King Jr.'s B.D.			

May	**June**	**July**	**August**
Mother's Day	Father's Day	Independence	(summer
Memorial Day		Day	vacations)

September	**October**	**November**	**December**
Labor Day	Rosh Hashanah	Thanksgiving	Christmas
	Yom Kippur		Hanukkah
	Halloween		Boxing Day

- What other events can you think of that you'd describe as "ritualized" spending? Birthdays? Weddings? Graduations?
- How do you think about the giving and receiving of gifts as a way of demonstrating your love, care, or concern?
- What do you see as disadvantages of thinking in these ritualistic ways?

7. Have you ever been "put out" with your parents because they bought you an article of clothing or other commodity that you thought made you seem "cheap" or "out of style"? How did you express that dissatisfaction?

- Are there any telling stories here about your own relationship to how others might think of you?
- What place does social status have, do you think, in your own life? How much are you influenced by popular trends, fads, styles, and how do you feel about being so influenced?

Your instructor will determine a specific writing genre that's appropriate, or perhaps such choices will be topics of discussion before writing.

8. Go to a popular café, a student union, or pay particular attention in your classes to see how much the Name Brand phenomenon is prevalent in your culture.

Keep some kind of record. Draw conclusions from your record as to what brand names seem to be most popular and why you think this is so. Perhaps you could ask someone who's displaying the name why they do so. Note the person's reaction to your question; what do you think you've learned by asking? What's the best way of writing your conclusions if the audience is your instructor?

9. The creator of *The Simpsons* produced the "Life in Hell" cartoon below. What makes it humorous? Why is school being labeled as "Life in Hell"? What's the message coming from the "mother," and why is it the punch line? Notice the child's eyes in each panel. Where are they looking in the last one? What kind of attitude does this change reflect? How is this minor change in the drawing representative of someone who understands the rhetorical appeal to audience?

- On a similar tact, how do you react to those perpetual college-isms such as saying that all a university education teaches you is to "masticate and regurgitate"? How does this complaint fit in with a materialist concept of institutionalized education being the process by which dominant social values are replicated? You're the author, but you'll need to establish your audience and purpose.

10. One of the authors has come up with the following *truism*: "People can be socialized into and out of almost any kind of mass behavior, as long as the infrastructural conditions are present." Read the personal accounts that follow of some who took part in the Rwandan genocide in the spring of 1994. These passages are from *Machete Season* by Jean Hatzfeld; see if you can identify what "infrastructural conditions" made socialization into slaughter possible.

> **Leopord**: Since that morning people had begun getting up the courage to kill in the streets. You could hear gunshots on the summit of Kayumba hill: it was soldiers, driving a group of fugitives back toward the parish* and church of Nyamata. This told us that the day would heat up. I took my machete, left the house, and went to the center of town. On this side and that, people were already giving chase.
>
> At the marketplace I saw a man running toward me. He was coming down from Kayumba, all breathless and scared, looking only for escape, and he didn't see me. I was heading up, and in passing, I gave him a machete blow at neck level, on the vulnerable vein. It came to me naturally, without thinking. Aiming was simple, since the gentleman did not fight back. He made no defensive move—he fell without shouting, without moaning. I felt nothing, just let him lie. I looked around; killing was going on every which way. I kept chasing after runaways all day long.
>
> It was sweaty-hard and stimulating, like an unforeseen diversion. I did not even keep count. Not during the action, not afterward, since I knew it would be starting up again. I cannot tell you, sincerely, how many I killed, because I forgot some along the way.
>
> This gentleman I killed at the marketplace, I can tell you the exact memory of it because he was the first. For others, it's murky—I cannot keep track anymore in my memory. I considered them unimportant; at the time of those murders I didn't even notice the tiny thing that would change me into a killer.
>
> . . .
>
> **Alphonse**: The first evening, coming home from the massacre in the church, our welcome was very well put together by the organizers. We all met up again back on the soccer field. Guns were shooting into the air, whistles and suchlike musical instruments were sounding.

---

*The cluster of buildings—schools, clinics, hospitals, residences—around a church. —Translator's note

The children pushed into the center all the cows rounded up during the day. Burgomaster Bernard offered the forty fattest ones to the *interahamwe*, to thank them, and the other cows to the people, to encourage them. We spent the evening slaughtering the cattle, singing, and chatting about the new days on the way. It was the most terrific celebration.

Jean-Baptiste: Evenings the gang would get together in a *cabaret*, in Nyarunazi or Kibungo, it depended. We might also go from one to the other. We ordered cases of Primus, we drank, and we fooled around to rest up from our day.

Some spent sleepless nights emptying bottles and became even wilder. Others went on home to rest after having an ordinary relaxing evening. Rowdies kept on slaughtering cows after the killings because they couldn't put down their machetes. So it wasn't possible to herd the cows for the future, and they had to be eaten on the spot.

Me, I went through those festivities with a pretend smile and a worried ear. I had posted a young watcher to make rounds about my house, but I stayed on the alert. The safety of my Tutsi wife tormented me, especially during the drinking sessions.

Fulgence: In the *cabaret*, we made comparisons and had contests. Many upped their numbers to increase their shares. Others lowered their numbers because it bothered them to recount the blood spilled and to boast about it. People cheated both ways and made fun of those who exaggerated too obviously. There is one, however, well known today in prison, who bragged of more than thirty victims in one big day, without anyone accusing him of lying.

Pancrace: The evening atmosphere was festive, but some came spoiling for a fight, their fists clenched or machetes still dirty in their hands, because of badly distributed land. For fields, negotiations got very serious. Since many drank Primus without counting, it could get chancy.

At night the bosses were gone and their authority with them: conditions in town were no longer controlled, as they were in the marshes during the day. It was heated and disreputable. So the women would come looking for their husbands and take them home if they heard they were in bad company.

Adalbert: Vagabond children, children from the streets of Nyamata, more or less abandoned by misfortune, took part in the marshes. Little good-for-nothings, so to speak. But the educated children of the farmers—they could not go. They contented themselves with the looting activities and the merrymaking on the hills.

Alphonse: During the killings, we had not one wedding, not one baptism, not one soccer match, not one religious service like Easter. We did not find that kind of celebration interesting anymore. We did not care spit for that Sunday silliness. We were dead tired from work, we were getting greedy, we celebrated whenever we felt like it, we drank as much as we wanted. Some turned into drunks.

Anyone who felt sad about someone he had killed really had to hide his words and his regrets, for fear of being seen as an accomplice and being treated roughly. Sometimes drinkers went mean when they had found no one to kill that day; others went mean because they had killed too much. You had to show them a smiling face, or watch out.

Clémentine: In the evening, families listened to music, folk dances, Rwandan or Burundian music. Thanks to the many stolen audiocassettes, families in every house could enjoy music. They all felt equally richer, without jealousy or backbiting, and they congratulated themselves. The men sang, everyone drank, the women changed dresses three times in an evening. It was noisier than weddings, it was drunken reveling every day.

From a materialist perspective, see if you can find specific examples from these Rwandans that would help prove the author's *truism*. Write your findings in an appropriate genre and under conditions defined by your instructor, or by your class itself.

- Is your purpose to explain? to persuade? to inform? to shock? all of these?
- In what ways will your choice of audience in this exercise help you shape your genre choices?

The Postcolonial Frame

Introduction and Historical Origins

In order to understand "postcolonialism"—the situation and study of peoples and nations after a period of physical and/or cultural occupation by a foreign power—we need to begin with a discussion of what preceded it, and that is colonialism, which can be seen as both an attitude and a set of historical practices. In practical terms, colonialism can be simply defined: one nation takes control of another nation or geographic area, making it a colony, a dependent entity under the conquering nation's control. A colonizer may use military force to gain power over a "foreign" land, but other means of colonization exist as well, such as cultural influence or coercive economic relations. Global history is to a large extent the story of colonization of the weak by the strong, a history often justified in just those terms—through colonization, the "strong" nation or culture "guides" or "administers" the "weak."

If you look at a globe or world map, it's difficult to find a geographic area that has not been or isn't currently a colonized spot and/or the home of colonialist practices. Great Britain, for example, was colonized by multiple groups, including imperial Rome, and went on, after solidifying its nationhood, to form one of the most powerful and far-reaching colonialist empires of the modern era. (The once-familiar saying, "The sun never sets on the British Empire," was literally true: it was so vast that it was always daylight somewhere in its colonial holdings.) The United States is a colonial and colonialist nation, since its nationhood began with colonists from Europe taking over Native American land, and much of its economic strength and cultural influence has resulted from its subsequent physical, economic, and cultural colonizing of others. Every continent, including Antarctica, has been or is the site of colonial domination or conquest.

Colonization is pervasive in time and place because it greatly benefits the colonizing nation. The specific motives are varied, and are influenced by the prevailing political system of a place and time: a country concerned about secure borders (a continuing source of intense conflict in the Middle East, for example) might seek to colonize/dominate its neighbors or to gain military tactical advantage (seen in U.S. colonial activity in places such as Puerto Rico, Hawaii, or the Philippines). Or it might have explicitly capitalist purposes. Colonizers gain access to the colonized nation's markets, and they can force the nation into trade with the colonizer, to its economic enrichment. Colonizers also gain access to a colony's valuable raw materials. In the West, for example, we have come to associate certain nations and regions with these materials—diamonds and South Africa; cocoa and West Africa; tin and South America. The phrase "not for all the tea in China" reveals a commodity-driven notion of that nation from past Western attempts to force open trade routes (as well as a way of totalizing its cultures according to stereotypes about their cultural practices). Cheap labor is another colonial interest, as is the opportunity to export surplus labor from the colonizing nation. Today, as the cost of American labor rises, U.S. manufacturers often shift production to cheap labor areas such as Mexico or Southeast Asia. In the past, Great Britain sent its "civil servants" to India to "administer" that country, providing professional careers to a privileged class of British workers.

In capitalist systems, colonialism also makes native cultures a kind of commodity. A native, or indigenous, culture can be made into a line of products and then "sold." Its artifacts can be marketed: Indian blankets, Mexican tiles, African sculptures—these are objects that can be bought or produced cheaply in the colonized country/region and sold at high prices as "exotic art" in the colonizer's home culture. But it's not only objects that can be imported. Colonizers also produce and bring into their home cultural ideas about indigenous peoples. Consider the American appetite for information on Asian religions, philosophies, and business practices (or the *ideas* that colonialist practices create of these cultural systems), which are reified—made into objects—in sellable forms such as books, classes, clothes, and so on. These are then presented for consumption as "authentic" cultural experience and knowledge.

Along with creating and marketing these cultural commodities, capitalist colonial practices spread and authorize attitudes toward them—attitudes that then affect how the culture/nation is acted on by the colonizing culture. If as a result of our culture's colonizing activity in Nation X, for example, we are presented with a picture of that nation as uneducated, unable to develop its resources, and unable to govern itself, then as a culture and government we are able and likely to impose our power, control, and values on that "underdeveloped" or "developing" nation. In other words, we take the picture we ourselves have produced and act in our relations with this culture as if the picture is real, accurate, and historical. We don't compare impressions with the culture's own self-presentation (we have already established that this nation is incapable of competently representing itself, after all). We act instead from the representation of it that we have developed, a representation that is more likely to reflect our own culture's values and needs—and to reinforce its sense of power and superiority—than to present a complex picture of the "other" culture. Thus, stereotypes become the basis for action. From Operation Desert Storm, during the Persian Gulf war, in which the United States used what was then highly unusual direct military intervention, to the recent and ongoing Iraq war, the administration capitalized on U.S. stereotypes of Arabs as being warlike and terrorists. Whole states are also represented in a totalizing way, a picture which is then used as the basis for interaction: Japan has traditionally been pictured as well organized, and this image bolsters capitalist production and technological development; but Tahiti is pictured as "natural" and sensual, a picture that helps maintain an essentialized view of the "Orient" as an exotic, different, and exploitable resource outside of the American cultural identity. These representations, which become the frame for any experience of and relation to the culture, create a closed system that the indigenous voice cannot alter—at least not within the terms of colonial discourse. The frame itself controls how we see and act toward the "other" culture—the marginal one that is not like "us," who are (we imagine) the ones at the center of the world.

This notion of cultural colonization and marginalization can occur within a given nation's borders as well. Such a condition is called "internal colonization." This situation can be clearly seen in the history of African Americans—and in the term *African American* itself. Most nonwhite minority populations in the United States have struggled and continue to struggle with the representations made of them by the dominant, or hegemonic, group, and with the economic problems that accompany these cultural frames. While most first-generation immigrants have faced prejudice, native-born Americans from certain minority groups are also the object of discrimination (as Victor Villanueva, p. 446, argues in the excerpt from his book *Bootstraps*), and as a result suffer continued curtailed opportunity over the course of generations, contrary to the progressively improved conditions that children and grandchildren of caucasian/European immigrants can expect. Those who face internal colonization struggle to find a place in their own larger culture, a sense of home within their own home, and the sense of social entitlement that their neighbors typically enjoy. Internal colonization can result from racial, ethnic, social class, gender, or sexual "difference" (or a combination of these) in a culture or nation where whiteness, European ancestry, middle-class standing, maleness, and heterosexuality are "normative," meaning taken as what is normal, central, and so "good." Those who are different from these norms are therefore not central but marginal—the "other," the internally colonized. Their worth is put into question by their difference.

Colonization, because it alters a nation's or group's cultural identity, has extreme effects on the colonized individual and his or her sense of self. As Frantz Fanon (p. 439) explains in the excerpt from his book *Black Skin, White Masks*, colonization brings about psychological changes in the colonized individual. One's sense of identity, of a self that is unified, acceptable, and normal, is radically altered; one is *re*-figured and *dis*-figured. One's actual home place may be destroyed; much colonization in the past involved relocation of cultural groups, redrawing of national boundaries, and imposition of the dominator's language and systems of education and government. One's own body and language thus become the sources of social alienation. To "count," one must become like the dominant group. But such things as skin color, gender, sexual orientation, and birth language make true membership impossible, and membership in any case comes at the cost of rejection of fundamental parts of the self.

The rhetorical and critical questions implicit in postcolonial critique have gained new importance since the 9/11 attacks and the war in Iraq, all of which has reactivated world suspicions of U.S. colonialist intentions. How we as a nation (a concept that much postcolonial and globalization theory questions—is the nation giving way to much broader units of social and economic organization, like multinational corporations?) see ourselves in relation to other nations, regions, and affiliated groups has become a troubled issue. Having a grasp of the issues raised by postcolonial critique can give you new ways to frame this urgent conversation.

● Adding to the Conversation

In a notebook or journal, reflect on the above ideas, perhaps considering the following questions:

1. What do you already know about colonialism, colonial practices, national liberations?

2. The United States began as thirteen colonies; what were the later reasons for the revolution against Great Britain, as Americans are taught in elementary school? How do you think most Americans are taught to view their historical resistance to English rule?

3. What reasons can you think of for Columbus Day having become in recent times a contested celebration?

4. How do you think the loss of the native language or its secondary status to a colonizer's language affects cultural identity and practices? Can you draw examples from your own cultural heritage?

5. Which cultural groups in the United States do you think might consider themselves internally colonized?

6. Think about what you know of globalization. Is globalization necessarily a form of colonization?

7. Think of an example of a marginalized group's discursive resistance in popular culture—in music, for example.

8. What have been some reasons for and responses to the charge that U.S. intervention in Iraq is a colonialist move? How do you see this intervention?

Rhetorical Issues in Postcolonial Critique

Postcolonialism is the situation and study of a culture/nation after colonization, though not necessarily after liberation from the colonizing force. It's also a *reading* and *writing* strategy, and it's this form of the concept that is of critical and rhetorical interest for us. To read and write from a postcolonial perspective is to deconstruct a text (to read it for its contradictory claims) and to offer a revision of it—a "counter discourse" that seeks out the biases within a text and shows how a text (mis)represents the "other," "foreign" entities that are outside of the powerful group, the group that has the power to represent them. A major rhetorical goal is then to give voice to the "subaltern," the person or location being (mis)represented. If as authors we speak of "students," for example, we are, first, totalizing this immensely complex and diverse group, treating it as a single entity. We can then "essentialize" students, assigning particular traits as we wish to represent this vast group, thus making a claim about its members' absolute, defining characteristics. If we write, "Students are likely to resist difficult, abstract readings," we represent you—we speak of you and for you, and then we can act on this "truth" about you (perhaps, for example, by producing a textbook that assumes students do best with "easy," "familiar" readings). Since we are college instructors, the culture tends to view us as authorities on students. We have access to mass media—to textbook publication, for instance. We can claim in-depth knowledge of "students" because we can claim to have taught many (though "many" is a term that needs investigation in relation to the total number of American students). We can speak of and for you; you in all likelihood don't have access to equivalent cultural power to refute us, or even to be heard as serious voices. In postcolonial terms, the subaltern—in this case, the student—is silenced.

As college instructors, what we say about students can have real, material consequences—we influence the texts you'll read, the nature of the work you'll do, the ideas you will and won't be asked to learn and work with (as in the claim about student resistance to complex material, which could be used to "dumb down" curricula, or to create different curricular tracks, as in postsecondary programs that are college prep or vocational, or to make social class distinctions between university and community college degrees). We occupy positions made different by the differing degree of power that instructors and students have. And yet our power, our jobs, depend on you: we need you to be in your dependent position for us to be in our powerful one. The same is true of those in political and economic power, the hegemonic group: they are dependent on the "other" for this system of privilege/oppression to continue. But postcolonial critique lets us examine this system of inequality whose interdependence is often unrecognized or suppressed, and to explore ways in which the "other" might claim a voice and presence. It teaches us how to "read" situations of differing power and to question how such imbalance historically came to be, how it is perpetuated, what effects it has on the participants, and how one might counter the discourse that imposes and attempts to preserve this inequitable power relation.

A postcolonial critique of a given text, then, attempts to reveal and undo the value system that the text employs. A critical reader already reads with questions about a writer's assumptions in mind—how the writer defines good and bad, what kinds of evidence are treated as convincing, what authority the author claims, how he or she uses language to "color" perceptions, and so on. A reader who invokes postcolonial reading strategies does all this plus considers how the text is rhetorically constructed to make the author (and the group he or she represents) seem "right" and more powerful and justified in that power over his or her subject, and how the "other" is silenced. How, for instance, is the U.S. colonial period presented in grade school texts? What role do Native Americans play in the history as it's commonly written? Which Native American writers who specialize in that time period have you read? Now consider the textual sources of your knowledge about any particular nonmainstream group. How many works by African and Asian writers have you read? How many countries in each of these continents can you name? How many native inhabitants have you spoken to? Who and what are the sources of your knowledge? And just what does "knowledge" mean if it derives from non-native sources of information? What are the nation's/group's primary social, cultural, and political concerns as members of this nation or group define them?

Reading from a postcolonial perspective, the reader analyzes the ways in which the text "silences" the subject and considers what sort of topics *don't* get covered. Postcolonial critique tries to reveal these systems of representation and silencing and then to provide a space for the voice of the other, enabling him/her/them to represent themselves and resist the writing—and therefore power—of the dominating group. A new voice emerges, one that is inevitably marked by the colonial experience (sometimes called a "hybrid" voice), but which is able to assert an identity of its own, separate from the representation made of the group and able to speak back to the colonizing power.

In U.S. civil rights' history, we can point to the powerful voices of Martin Luther King Jr. and Malcolm X, both of whom used African American rhetorical traditions—formerly restricted to the marginalized African American community—to create (very different) black identities, resisting the negative, essentialized identity imposed on blacks by white-dominated society. King drew on religious protest language and "pulpit" oratory, Malcolm on vernacular, or "street" language. They spoke and wrote from new positions, as new voices—as powerful, audible black men.

Mohandas Gandhi did the same for Indian resistance to British rule. Later, in 1963, Betty Friedan wrote about "The Problem That Has No

Name," in fact naming U.S. women's discontent with their restricted family and social roles, setting off the modern feminist movement and opening up public opportunities for women's voices to be heard (though more recent critiques of her work have pointed out how it privileged the views and interests of middle-class white women, silencing minority and other non-normative voices within women's groups).

To speak and write powerfully from a position of powerlessness: this might be the defining agenda of a postcolonial leader. The leader's voice helps begin a process of redefinition, and a new, postcolonial identity emerges from the colonial situation.

This voice by historical necessity is not unified. King was not the sole voice of black Americans, even at the time of his earliest public speeches; he helped to provide a means for other blacks to speak—figures such as Malcolm and Stokely Carmichael (Kwame Toure), and radical groups like the Black Panthers and others. He helped them seek immediate social and political change through his program of gradual, nonviolent progress toward equality. All these voices challenge racist American practices, however, and this resistance to internal colonization is one means to cultural identity. In Chapter 14, Gloria Anzaldúa defines her "mestiza"—mixed—rhetoric, which accommodates multiple voices, identities, and languages. Postcolonial voices thus carry the trace of the colonial past but assert themselves in new positions of power, upsetting the past relation of colonizer and subaltern, center and margin, and insisting on *multiple* voices to accommodate complexity and deny the monolithic representation of diverse cultural groups. They create new voices and texts, claiming the power of self-representation and reframing historical and social narratives.

Approaching a text from a postcolonial perspective engages us in a rhetorical questioning process. We become "resistant" readers who talk back to the text instead of receiving it as automatically authoritative. We consider specific issues related to the power of language. Applied to a given text, the rhetorical reading process that postcolonial critique offers includes asking questions such as the following:

- Who is speaking in this text, and who does this speaker claim/presume to speak *for*?
- Who is made the object of the speaker's and reader's gaze, the subject who is being represented?
- Whose voice is central, and whose is marginalized or silenced altogether?
- Who and what is "right" and "normal"? Who is represented as different, the "other," and how is this "other" described, totalized, and essentialized?
- What forms of writing are seen as correct, refined, standard? What forms are devalued as uneducated, simplistic, offbeat?

- Does the speaker make claims for the universal truth and value of his/her statements and views?
- Does the text serve hegemonic interests—the preservation and furthering of the good of the dominant group? Does it have any resistant rhetorical features?

Writing from this critical perspective entails *re*-writing—a questioning and reformulating of the text's claims, amounting to the assertion of a new voice and vision. Such a voice is likely to include but also transgress the "rules" of the dominant, or "master," discourse—to sound less standard, since its goal is to challenge and open up what "standard" means and does. bell hooks, Aimé Césaire, Frantz Fanon, Victor Villanueva, and Gloria Anzaldúa, in the readings in the following chapters, all write in a multiplicity of transgressive voices and forms. Their writing strategies include the following techniques:

- The creation of a "counter" or alternative discourse, a critique of a dominant text's rhetorical practices, and a retelling, a re-presentation, of the text's events and ideas.
- Resistance to adopting a single, uniform voice, identity, and position, seen in the use of a variety of discourses (formal academic writing, "street" or "vulgar" language, a "personal" voice) and languages (use of non-English phrases, rhetorical patterns, and values) and mixing of forms (argument, reflection, journal entry, direct address, fiction/ nonfiction, etc.).
- A willingness to be self-critical, to acknowledge the provisional, relative nature of truth and cultural values.

Consider reading and writing about Shakespeare's *The Tempest*[1]—a "masterpiece," a traditional, canonical text—from a postcolonial perspective. We can begin analyzing the text's representations of groups in different social relations to each other—political leaders in a struggle for power; parents and children; males and females; masters and slaves; Europeans and non-Europeans. We ask who the controlling figure in the play is and who and what he speaks for. We consider how the non-Europeans—the spirit Ariel and the slave Caliban—are represented, and by whom. How are they depicted as being different? Are they seen as positive or negative figures, and what value system is used to establish their worth? Who "wins"—whose values (and lives) are

---

[1]In this play, a former Italian duke, Prospero, unlawfully deposed by his brother, is shipwrecked with his daughter on a magical island. He enslaves the island's owner, who is described as a monster that is half-fish. Later, Prospero causes the ship of his betrayers and their crew to be wrecked on the island's shore. Prospero tricks his betrayers into confessing and repenting their deeds. All are reconciled in the end: Prospero regains his dukedom, his former enemy's son marries his daughter, and his servant, a spirit, is freed. His slave remains a slave.

preserved in the end? A play that is traditionally interpreted as a defense of state and family order can be understood further as a defense of colonial domination (the former duke's takeover of Caliban's island and body, control of Ariel's labor and freedom, control of his daughter's body and social functions), a justification of the use of physical force, a division of beings into "more" and "less" human, with an accompanying claim of the justice of the "higher" being dominating the "lower." One can write from the usually unheard position of the slave, for example, refiguring Caliban as a colonized being whose human and state rights have been violated. We can interpret his lines from a new rhetorical frame: he becomes a resistant voice, rather than a rebellious, animal-like slave unworthy to be in human company. And we can see how he is degraded to the point of self-loathing, leading him ultimately to consider his enslaved position a just and "natural" condition, showing how colonial discourse seeks to silence those who challenge its dominance.

The strategies for discursive resistance—for being critically aware of how language is used to establish power relations—can be enacted with all kinds of texts: with visual texts, such as film, television, and advertising images; with nonfiction texts, including historical and journalistic works; with oral language—speeches, conversations, and lectures; with fiction, and with all other language forms. Postcolonial theory is itself a powerful means to broaden one's critical understanding and to change social and cultural practices that support inequality.

Exploring Postcolonial Critique

Introduction to Culture and Imperialism

EDWARD W. SAID

The Palestinian-American critic Edward W. Said (1935–2003; pronounced "Sah-eed") was one of the first theorists of postcolonial critique. His greatly influential work Orientalism *(1978) is a complex, highly detailed analysis of the discourse of colonialism—the uses and privileged cultural sites of Western writing about the "Orient," specifically, about the countries and cultures of the Middle East. Said helped establish the fundamental concepts and methods of postcolonial critique. In* Culture and Imperialism *(1993), he explores how the colonial contact brought about by the West's imperialist expansion during the nineteenth and twentieth centuries shaped Western culture, and how this contact was met with the resistance of those colonized. This cultural contact helped the West define itself against the "other" and strengthen the sense of powerful, individual Western nations. But through contact, the "other" became an increasingly important part of Western culture, a first step in the globalization, multiculturalism, and, to use a postcolonial term,* cultural hybridity *of today. In this introductory essay to his book, Said dissects the concepts of a colonial discourse, national culture, and the myth of cultural purity.*

About five years after *Orientalism* was published in 1978, I began to gather together some ideas about the general relationship between culture and empire that had become clear to me while writing that book. The first result was a series of lectures that I gave at universities in the United States, Canada, and England in 1985 and 1986. These lectures form the core argument of the present work, which has occupied me steadily since that time. A substantial amount of scholarship in anthropology, history, and area studies has developed arguments I put forward in *Orientalism*, which was limited to the Middle East. So I, too, have tried here to expand the arguments of the earlier book to describe a more general pattern of relationships between the modern metropolitan West and its overseas territories.

What are some of the non–Middle Eastern materials drawn on here? European writing on Africa, India, parts of the Far East, Australia, and the

Caribbean; these Africanist and Indianist discourses, as some of them have been called, I see as part of the general European effort to rule distant lands and peoples and, therefore, as related to Orientalist descriptions of the Islamic world, as well as to Europe's special ways of representing the Caribbean islands, Ireland, and the Far East. What are striking in these discourses are the rhetorical figures one keeps encountering in their descriptions of "the mysterious East," as well as the stereotypes about "the African [or Indian or Irish or Jamaican or Chinese] mind," the notions about bringing civilization to primitive or barbaric peoples, the disturbingly familiar ideas about flogging or death or extended punishment being required when "they" misbehaved or became rebellious, because "they" mainly understood force or violence best; "they" were not like "us," and for that reason deserved to be ruled.

Yet it was the case nearly everywhere in the non-European world that the coming of the white man brought forth some sort of resistance. What I left out of *Orientalism* was that response to Western dominance which culminated in the great movement of decolonization all across the Third World. Along with armed resistance in places as diverse as nineteenth-century Algeria, Ireland, and Indonesia, there also went considerable efforts in cultural resistance almost everywhere, the assertions of nationalist identities, and, in the political realm, the creation of associations and parties whose common goal was self-determination and national independence. Never was it the case that the imperial encounter pitted an active Western intruder against a supine or inert non-Western native; there was *always* some form of active resistance, and in the overwhelming majority of cases, the resistance finally won out.

These two factors—a general world-wide pattern of imperial culture, and a historical experience of resistance against empire—inform this book in ways that make it not just a sequel to *Orientalism* but an attempt to do something else. In both books I have emphasized what in a rather general way I have called "culture." As I use the word, "culture" means two things in particular. First of all it means all those practices, like the arts of description, communication, and representation, that have relative autonomy from the economic, social, and political realms and that often exist in aesthetic forms, one of whose principal aims is pleasure. Included, of course, are both the popular stock of lore about distant parts of the world and specialized knowledge available in such learned disciplines as ethnography, historiography, philology, sociology, and literary history. Since my exclusive focus here is on the modern Western empires of the nineteenth and twentieth centuries, I have looked especially at cultural forms like the novel, which I believe were immensely important in the formation of imperial attitudes, references, and experiences. I do not mean that only the novel was important, but that I consider it *the* aesthetic object whose connection to the expanding societies of Britain and France is particularly interesting to study. The prototypical modern realistic novel is *Robinson Crusoe,* and certainly not accidentally it is about a European who creates a fiefdom for himself on a distant, non-European island.

A great deal of recent criticism has concentrated on narrative fiction, yet   5
very little attention has been paid to its position in the history and world of empire. Readers of this book will quickly discover that narrative is crucial to my
argument here, my basic point being that stories are at the heart of what explorers and novelists say about strange regions of the world; they also become the
method colonized people use to assert their own identity and the existence of
their own history. The main battle in imperialism is over land, of course; but
when it came to who owned the land, who had the right to settle and work on it,
who kept it going, who won it back, and who now plans its future—these issues
were reflected, contested, and even for a time decided in narrative. As one critic
has suggested, nations themselves *are* narrations. The power to narrate, or to
block other narratives from forming and emerging, is very important to culture
and imperialism, and constitutes one of the main connections between them.
Most important, the grand narratives of emancipation and enlightenment mobi-
lized people in the colonial world to rise up and throw off imperial subjection;
in the process, many Europeans and Americans were also stirred by these stories
and their protagonists, and they too fought for new narratives of equality and
human community.

Second, and almost imperceptibly, culture is a concept that includes a
refining and elevating element, each society's reservoir of the best that has
been known and thought, as Matthew Arnold put it in the 1860s. Arnold
believed that culture palliates, if it does not altogether neutralize, the ravages
of a modern, aggressive, mercantile, and brutalizing urban existence. You read
Dante or Shakespeare in order to keep up with the best that was thought and
known, and also to see yourself, your people, society, and tradition in their
best lights. In time, culture comes to be associated, often aggressively, with
the nation or the state; this differentiates "us" from "them," almost always
with some degree of xenophobia. Culture in this sense is a source of identity,
and a rather combative one at that, as we see in recent "returns" to culture and
tradition. These "returns" accompany rigorous codes of intellectual and moral
behavior that are opposed to the permissiveness associated with such relatively liberal philosophies as multiculturalism and hybridity. In the formerly
colonized world, these "returns" have produced varieties of religious and
nationalist fundamentalism.

In this second sense culture is a sort of theater where various political and
ideological causes engage one another. Far from being a placid realm of Apol-
lonian gentility, culture can even be a battleground on which causes expose
themselves to the light of day and contend with one another, making it apparent
that, for instance, American, French, or Indian students who are taught to read
their national classics before they read others are expected to appreciate and belong loyally, often uncritically, to their nations and traditions while denigrating
or fighting against others.

Now the trouble with this idea of culture is that it entails not only venerating one's own culture but also thinking of it as somehow divorced from, because

transcending, the everyday world. Most professional humanists as a result are unable to make the connection between the prolonged and sordid cruelty of practices such as slavery, colonialist and racial oppression, and imperial subjection on the one hand, and the poetry, fiction, philosophy of the society that engages in these practices on the other. One of the difficult truths I discovered in working on this book is how very few of the British or French artists whom I admire took issue with the notion of "subject" or "inferior" races so prevalent among officials who practiced those ideas as a matter of course in ruling India or Algeria. They were widely accepted notions, and they helped fuel the imperial acquisition of territories in Africa throughout the nineteenth century. In thinking of Carlyle or Ruskin, or even of Dickens and Thackeray, critics have often, I believe, relegated these writers' ideas about colonial expansion, inferior races, or "niggers" to a very different department from that of culture, culture being the elevated area of activity in which they "truly" belong and in which they did their "really" important work.

Culture conceived in this way can become a protective enclosure: check your politics at the door before you enter it. As someone who has spent his entire professional life teaching literature, yet who also grew up in the pre–World War Two colonial world, I have found it a challenge *not* to see culture in this way—that is, antiseptically quarantined from its worldly affiliations—but as an extraordinarily varied field of endeavor. The novels and other books I consider here I analyze because first of all I find them estimable and admirable works of art and learning, in which I and many other readers take pleasure and from which we derive profit. Second, the challenge is to connect them not only with that pleasure and profit but also with the imperial process of which they were manifestly and unconcealedly a part; rather than condemning or ignoring their participation in what was an unquestioned reality in their societies, I suggest that what we learn about this hitherto ignored aspect actually and truly *enhances* our reading and understanding of them.

Let me say a little here about what I have in mind, using two well-known and very great novels. Dickens's *Great Expectations* (1861) is primarily a novel about self-delusion, about Pip's vain attempts to become a gentleman with neither the hard work nor the aristocratic source of income required for such a role. Early in life he helps a condemned convict, Abel Magwitch, who, after being transported to Australia, pays back his young benefactor with large sums of money; because the lawyer involved says nothing as he disburses the money, Pip persuades himself that an elderly gentlewoman, Miss Havisham, has been his patron. Magwitch then reappears illegally in London, unwelcomed by Pip because everything about the man reeks of delinquency and unpleasantness. In the end, though, Pip is reconciled to Magwitch and to his reality: he finally acknowledges Magwitch—hunted, apprehended, and fatally ill—as his surrogate father, not as someone to be denied or rejected, though Magwitch is in fact unacceptable, being from Australia, a penal colony designed for the rehabilitation but not the repatriation of transported English criminals.

Most, if not all, readings of this remarkable work situate it squarely within the metropolitan history of British fiction, whereas I believe that it belongs in a history both more inclusive and more dynamic than such interpretations allow. It has been left to two more recent books than Dickens's—Robert Hughes's magisterial *The Fatal Shore* and Paul Carter's brilliantly speculative *The Road to Botany Bay*—to reveal a vast history of speculation about and experience of Australia, a "white" colony like Ireland, in which we can locate Magwitch and Dickens not as mere coincidental references in that history, but as participants in it, through the novel and through a much older and wider experience between England and its overseas territories.

Australia was established as a penal colony in the late eighteenth century mainly so that England could transport an irredeemable, unwanted excess population of felons to a place, originally charted by Captain Cook, that would also function as a colony replacing those lost in America. The pursuit of profit, the building of empire, and what Hughes calls social *apartheid* together produced modern Australia, which by the time Dickens first took an interest in it during the 1840s (in *David Copperfield* Wilkins Micawber happily immigrates there) had progressed somewhat into profitability and a sort of "free system" where laborers could do well on their own if allowed to do so. Yet in Magwitch

Dickens knotted several strands in the English perception of convicts in Australia at the end of transportation. They could succeed, but they could hardly, in the real sense, return. They could expiate their crimes in a technical, legal sense, but what they suffered there warped them into permanent outsiders. And yet they were capable of redemption—as long as they stayed in Australia.

Carter's exploration of what he calls Australia's spatial history offers us another version of that same experience. Here explorers, convicts, ethnographers, profiteers, soldiers chart the vast and relatively empty continent each in a discourse that jostles, displaces, or incorporates the others. Botany Bay is therefore first of all an Enlightenment discourse of travel and discovery, then a set of travelling narrators (including Cook) whose words, charts, and intentions accumulate the strange territories and gradually turn them into "home." The adjacence between the Benthamite organization of space (which produced the city of Melbourne) and the apparent disorder of the Australian bush is shown by Carter to have become an optimistic transformation of social space, which produced an Elysium for gentlemen, an Eden for laborers in the 1840s. What Dickens envisions for Pip, being Magwitch's "London gentleman," is roughly equivalent to what was envisioned by English benevolence for Australia, one social space authorizing another.

But *Great Expectations* was not written with anything like the concern for native Australian accounts that Hughes or Carter has, nor did it presume or forecast a tradition of Australian writing, which in fact came later to include the literary works of David Malouf, Peter Carey, and Patrick White. The prohibition placed on Magwitch's return is not only penal but imperial: subjects can be taken to places like Australia, but they cannot be allowed a "return" to metropolitan space, which, as all Dickens's fiction testifies, is meticulously charted, spoken for, inhabited by a hierarchy of metropolitan personages. So on the one hand, interpreters like Hughes and Carter expand on the relatively attenuated presence of Australia in nineteenth-century British writing, expressing the fullness and earned integrity of an Australian history that became independent from Britain's in the twentieth century; yet, on the other, an accurate reading of *Great Expectations* must note that after Magwitch's delinquency is expiated, so to speak, after Pip redemptively acknowledges his debt to the old, bitterly energized, and vengeful convict, Pip himself collapses and is revived in two explicitly positive ways. A new Pip appears, less laden than the old Pip with the chains of the past—he is glimpsed in the form of a child, also called Pip; and the old Pip takes on a new career with his boyhood friend Herbert Pocket, this time not as an idle gentleman but as a hardworking trader in the East, where Britain's other colonies offer a sort of normality that Australia never could.

Thus even as Dickens settles the difficulty with Australia, another struc-   15
ture of attitude and reference emerges to suggest Britain's imperial intercourse through trade and travel with the Orient. In his new career as colonial businessman, Pip is hardly an exceptional figure, since nearly all of Dickens's businessmen, wayward relatives, and frightening outsiders have a fairly normal and secure connection with the empire. But it is only in recent years that these connections have taken on interpretative importance. A new generation of scholars and critics—the children of decolonization in some instances, the beneficiaries (like sexual, religious, and racial minorities) of advances in human freedom at home—have seen in such great texts of Western literature a standing interest in what was considered a lesser world, populated with lesser people of color, portrayed as open to the intervention of so many Robinson Crusoes.

By the end of the nineteenth century the empire is no longer merely a shadowy presence, or embodied merely in the unwelcome appearance of a fugitive convict but, in the works of writers like Conrad, Kipling, Gide, and Loti, a central area of concern. Conrad's *Nostromo* (1904)—my second example—is set in a Central American republic, independent (unlike the African and East Asian colonial settings of his earlier fictions), and dominated at the same time by outside interests because of its immense silver mine. For a contemporary American the most compelling aspect of the work is Conrad's prescience: he forecasts the unstoppable unrest and "misrule" of the Latin American republics (governing them, he says, quoting Bolívar, is like plowing the sea), and he singles out North America's particular way of influencing conditions in a decisive yet barely visible way. Holroyd, the San Francisco financier who backs Charles Gould, the British owner of the San Tomé mine, warns his protégé that "we won't be drawn into any large trouble" as investors. Nevertheless,

We can sit and watch. Of course, some day we shall step in. We are bound to. But there's no hurry. Time itself has got to wait on the greatest country in the whole of God's universe. We shall be giving the word for everything—industry, trade, law, journalism, art, politics, and religion, from Cape Horn clear over to Surith's Sound, and beyond it, too, if anything worth taking hold of turns up at the North Pole. And then we shall have the leisure to take in hand the outlying islands and continents of the earth. We shall run the world's business whether the world likes it or not. The world can't help it—and neither can we, I guess.

Much of the rhetoric of the "New World Order" promulgated by the American government since the end of the Cold War—with its redolent self-congratulation, its unconcealed triumphalism, its grave proclamations of responsibility—might have been scripted by Conrad's Holroyd: we are number one, we are bound to lead, we stand for freedom and order, and so on. No American has been immune from this structure of feeling, and yet the implicit warning contained in Conrad's portraits of Holroyd and Gould is rarely reflected on since the rhetoric of power all too easily produces an illusion of benevolence when deployed in an imperial setting. Yet it is a rhetoric whose most damning characteristic is that it has been used before, not just once (by Spain and Portugal) but with deafeningly repetitive frequency in the modern period, by the British, the French, the Belgians, the Japanese, the Russians, and now the Americans.

Yet it would be incomplete to read Conrad's great work simply as an early prediction of what we see happening in twentieth-century Latin America, with its string of United Fruit Companies, colonels, liberation forces, and American-financed mercenaries. Conrad is the precursor of the Western views of the Third World which one finds in the work of novelists as different as Graham Greene, V. S. Naipaul, and Robert Stone, of theoreticians of imperialism like Hannah Arendt, and of travel writers, filmmakers, and polemicists whose specialty is to deliver the non-European world either for analysis and judgement or for satisfying the exotic tastes of European and North American audiences. For if it is true that Conrad ironically sees the imperialism of the San Tomé silver mine's British and American owners as doomed by its own pretentious and impossible ambitions, it is also true that he writes as a man whose *Western* view of the non-Western world is so ingrained as to blind him to other histories, other cultures, other aspirations. All Conrad can see is a world totally dominated by the Atlantic West, in which every opposition to the West only confirms the West's wicked power. What Conrad cannot see is an alternative to this cruel tautology. He could neither understand that India, Africa, and South America also had lives and cultures with integrities not totally controlled by the gringo imperialists and reformers of this world, nor allow himself to believe that anti-imperialist independence movements were not all corrupt and in the pay of the puppet masters in London or Washington.

These crucial limitations in vision are as much a part of *Nostromo* as its characters and plot. Conrad's novel embodies the same paternalistic arrogance of imperialism that it mocks in characters like Gould and Holroyd. Conrad seems to be saying, "We Westerners will decide who is a good native or a bad, because all natives have sufficient existence by virtue of our recognition. We created them, we taught them to speak and think, and when they rebel they simply confirm our views of them as silly children, duped by some of their Western masters." This is in effect what Americans have felt about their southern neighbors: that independence is to be wished for them so long as it is the kind of independence *we* approve of. Anything else is unacceptable and, worse, unthinkable.

It is no paradox, therefore, that Conrad was both anti-imperialist and imperialist, progressive when it came to rendering fearlessly and pessimistically the self-confirming, self-deluding corruption of overseas domination, deeply re-actionary when it came to conceding that Africa or South America could ever have had an independent history or culture, which the imperialists violently disturbed but by which they were ultimately defeated. Yet lest we think patron-izingly of Conrad as the creature of his own time, we had better note that recent attitudes in Washington and among most Western policymakers and intellectu-als show little advance over his views. What Conrad discerned as the futility latent in imperialist philanthropy—whose intentions include such ideas as "making the world safe for democracy"—the United States government is still unable to perceive, as it tries to implement its wishes all over the globe, espe-cially in the Middle East. At least Conrad had the courage to see that no such schemes ever succeed—because they trap the planners in more illusions of omnipotence and misleading self-satisfaction (as in Vietnam), and because by their very nature they falsify the evidence.

All this is worth bearing in mind if *Nostromo* is to be read with some atten-tion to its massive strengths and inherent limitations. The newly independent state of Sulaco that emerges at the end of the novel is only a smaller, more tightly controlled and intolerant version of the larger state from which it has seceded and has now come to displace in wealth and importance. Conrad allows the reader to see that imperialism is a system. Life in one subordinate realm of experience is imprinted by the fictions and follies of the dominant realm. But the reverse is true, too, as experience in the dominant society comes to depend uncritically on natives and their territories perceived as in need of *la mission civilisatrice*.

However it is read, *Nostromo* offers a profoundly unforgiving view, and it has quite literally enabled the equally severe view of Western imperialist illusions in Graham Greene's *The Quiet American* or V. S. Naipaul's *A Bend in the River*, novels with very different agendas. Few readers today, after Vietnam, Iran, the Philippines, Algeria, Cuba, Nicaragua, Iraq, would disagree that it is precisely the fervent innocence of Greene's Pyle or Naipaul's Father Huismans, men for whom the native can be educated into "our" civilization, that turns out to

20

produce the murder, subversion, and endless instability of "primitive" societies. A similar anger pervades films like Oliver Stone's *Salvador*, Francis Ford Coppola's *Apocalypse Now*, and Constantin Costa-Gavras's *Missing*, in which unscrupulous CIA operatives and power-mad officers manipulate natives and well-intentioned Americans alike.

Yet all these works, which are so indebted to Conrad's anti-imperialist irony in *Nostromo*, argue that the source of the world's significant action and life is in the West, whose representatives seem at liberty to visit their fantasies and philanthropies upon a mind-deadened Third World. In this view, the outlying regions of the world have no life, history, or culture to speak of, no independence or integrity worth representing without the West. And when there is something to be described it is, following Conrad, unutterably corrupt, degenerate, irredeemable. But whereas Conrad wrote *Nostromo* during a period of Europe's largely uncontested imperialist enthusiasm, contemporary novelists and filmmakers who have learned his ironies so well have done their work *after* decolonization, *after* the massive intellectual, moral, and imaginative overhaul and deconstruction of Western representation of the non-Western world, *after* the work of Frantz Fanon, Amílcar Cabral, C. L. R. James, Walter Rodney, *after* the novels and plays of Chinua Achebe, Ngugi wa Thiongo, Wole Soyinka, Salman Rushdie, Gabriel García Márquez, and many others.

Thus Conrad has passed along his residual imperialist propensities, although his heirs scarcely have an excuse to justify the often subtle and unreflecting bias of their work. This is not just a matter of Westerners who do not have enough sympathy for or comprehension of foreign cultures—since there are, after all, some artists and intellectuals who have, in effect, crossed to the other side—Jean Genet, Basil Davidson, Albert Memmi, Juan Goytisolo, and others. What is perhaps more relevant is the political willingness to take seriously the alternatives to imperialism, among them the existence of other cultures and societies. Whether one believes that Conrad's extraordinary fiction confirms habitual Western suspicions about Latin America, Africa, and Asia, or whether one sees in novels like *Nostromo* and *Great Expectations* the lineaments of an astonishingly durable imperial worldview, capable of warping the perspectives of reader and author equally: *both* those ways of reading the real alternatives seem outdated. The world today does not exist as a spectacle about which we can be either pessimistic or optimistic, about which our "texts" can be either ingenious or boring. All such attitudes involve the deployment of power and interests. To the extent that we see Conrad both criticizing and reproducing the imperial ideology of his time, to that extent we can characterize our own present attitudes: the projection, or the refusal, of the wish to dominate, the capacity to damn, or the energy to comprehend and engage with other societies, traditions, histories.

The world has changed since Conrad and Dickens in ways that have surprised, and often alarmed, metropolitan Europeans and Americans, who now confront large non-white immigrant populations in their midst, and face an impressive roster of newly empowered voices asking for their narratives to be heard. The point of my book is that such populations and voices have been there for some time, thanks to the globalized process set in motion by modern imperialism; to ignore or otherwise discount the overlapping experience of Westerners and Orientals, the interdependence of cultural terrains in which colonizer and colonized co-existed and battled each other through projections as well as rival geographies, narratives, and histories, is to miss what is essential about the world in the past century.

For the first time, the history of imperialism and its culture can now be studied as neither monolithic nor reductively compartmentalized, separate, distinct. True, there has been a disturbing eruption of separatist and chauvinist discourse, whether in India, Lebanon, or Yugoslavia, or in Afrocentric, Islamocentric, or Eurocentric proclamations; far from invalidating the struggle to be free from empire, these reductions of cultural discourse actually prove the validity of a fundamental liberationist energy that animates the wish to be independent, to speak freely and without the burden of unfair domination. The only way to understand this energy, however, is historically: and hence the rather wide geographical and historical range attempted in this book. In our wish to make ourselves heard, we tend very often to forget that the world is a crowded place, and that if everyone were to insist on the radical purity or priority of one's own voice, all we would have would be the awful din of unending strife, and a bloody political mess, the true horror of which is beginning to be perceptible here and there in the re-emergence of racist politics in Europe, the cacophony of debates over political correctness and identity politics in the United States, and—to speak about my own part of the world—the intolerance of religious prejudice and illusionary promises of Bismarckian despotism, à la Saddam Hussein and his numerous Arab epigones and counterparts.

What a sobering and inspiring thing it is therefore not just to read one's own side, as it were, but also to grasp how a great artist like Kipling (few more imperialist and reactionary than he) rendered India with such skill, and how in doing so his novel *Kim* not only depended on a long history of Anglo-Indian perspective, but also, in spite of itself, forecast the untenability of that perspective in its insistence on the belief that the Indian reality required, indeed beseeched British tutelage more or less indefinitely. The great cultural archive, I argue, is where the intellectual and aesthetic investments in overseas dominion are made. If you were British or French in the 1860s you saw, and you felt, India and North Africa with a combination of familiarity and distance, but never with a sense of their separate sovereignty. In your narratives, histories, travel tales, and explorations your consciousness was represented as the principal authority, an active point of energy that made sense not just of colonizing activities but of exotic geographies and peoples. Above all, your sense of power scarcely imagined that those "natives" who appeared either subservient or sullenly uncooperative were ever going to be capable of finally making you give up India or Algeria. Or of saying anything that might perhaps contradict, challenge, or otherwise disrupt the prevailing discourse.

Imperialism's culture was not invisible, nor did it conceal its worldly affiliations and interests. There is a sufficient clarity in the culture's major lines for us to remark the often scrupulous notations recorded there, and also to remark how they have not been paid much attention. Why they are now of such interest as, for instance, to spur this and other books derives less from a kind of retrospective vindictiveness than from a fortified need for links and connections. One of imperialism's achievements was to bring the world closer together, and although in the process the separation between Europeans and natives was an insidious and fundamentally unjust one, most of us should now regard the historical experience of empire as a common one. The task then is to describe it as pertaining to Indians *and* Britishers, Algerians *and* French, Westerners *and* Africans, Asians, Latin Americans, and Australians despite the horrors, the bloodshed, and the vengeful bitterness. . . .

. . .

In fine, this is a book about the past and the present, about "us" and "them," as each of these things is seen by the various, and usually opposed and separated, parties. Its moment, so to speak, is that of the period after the Cold War, when the United States has emerged as the last superpower. To live there during such a time means, for an educator and intellectual with a background in the Arab world, a number of quite particular concerns, all of which have inflected this book, as indeed they have influenced everything I have written since *Orientalism*.

First is a depressing sense that one has seen and read about current American policy formulations before. Each great metropolitan center that aspired to global dominance has said, and alas done, many of the same things. There is always the appeal to power and national interest in running the affairs of lesser peoples; there is the same destructive zeal when the going gets a little rough, or when natives rise up and reject a compliant and unpopular ruler who was ensnared and kept in place by the imperial power; there is the horrifically predictable disclaimer that "we" are exceptional, not imperial, not about to repeat the mistake of earlier powers, a disclaimer that has been routinely followed by making the mistake, as witness the Vietnam and Gulf wars. Worse yet has been the amazing, if often passive, collaboration with these practices on the part of intellectuals, artists, journalists whose positions at home are progressive and full of admirable sentiments, but the opposite when it comes to what is done abroad in their name.

It is my (perhaps illusory) hope that a history of the imperial adventure rendered in cultural terms might therefore serve some illustrative and even deterrent purpose. Yet though imperialism implacably advanced during the nineteenth and twentieth centuries, resistance to it also advanced. Methodologically then I try to show the two forces together. This by no means exempts the aggrieved colonized peoples from criticism; as any survey of post-colonial states will reveal, the fortunes and misfortunes of nationalism, of what can be called separatism and nativism, do not always make up a flattering story. It too must be told, if only to show that there have always been alternatives to Idi Amin and Saddam Hussein. Western imperialism and Third World nationalism feed off each other, but even at their worst they are neither monolithic nor deterministic. Besides, culture is not monolithic either, and is not the exclusive property of East or West, nor of small groups of men or women.

Nonetheless the story is a gloomy and often discouraging one. What tempers it today is, here and there, the emergence of a new intellectual and political conscience. This is the second concern that went into the making of this book. However much there are laments that the old course of humanistic study has been subject to politicized pressures, to what has been called the culture of complaint, to all sorts of egregiously overstated claims on behalf of "Western" or "feminist" or "Afrocentric" and "Islamocentric" values, that is not all there is today. Take as an example the extraordinary change in studies of the Middle East, which when I wrote *Orientalism* were still dominated by an aggressively masculine and condescending ethos. To mention only works that have appeared in the last three or four years—Lila Abu-Lughod's *Veiled Sentiments*, Leila Ahmed's *Women and Gender in Islam*, Fedwa Malti-Douglas's *Woman's Body, Woman's World*—a very different sort of idea about Islam, the Arabs, and the Middle East has challenged, and to a considerable degree undermined, the old despotism. Such works are feminist, but not exclusivist; they demonstrate the diversity and complexity of experience that works beneath the totalizing discourses of Orientalism and of Middle East (overwhelmingly male) nationalism; they are both intellectually and politically sophisticated, attuned to the best theoretical and historical scholarship, engaged but not demagogic, sensitive to but not maudlin about women's experience; finally, while written by scholars of different backgrounds and education, they are works that are in dialogue with, and contribute to, the political situation of women in the Middle East.

Along with Sara Suleri's *The Rhetoric of English India* and Lisa Lowe's *Critical Terrains*, revisionist scholarship of this sort has varied, if it has not altogether broken up the geography of the Middle East and India as homogenous, reductively understood domains. Gone are the binary oppositions dear to the nationalist and imperialist enterprise. Instead we begin to sense that old authority cannot simply be replaced by new authority, but that new alignments made across borders, types, nations, and essences are rapidly coming into view, and it is those new alignments that now provoke and challenge the fundamentally static notion of *identity* that has been the core of cultural thought during the era of imperialism. Throughout the exchange between Europeans and their "others" that began systematically half a millennium ago, the one idea that has scarcely varied is that there is an "us" and a "them," each quite settled, clear, unassailably self-evident. As I discuss it in *Orientalism*, the division goes back to Greek thought about barbarians, but, whoever originated this kind of "identity" thought, by the nineteenth century it had become the hallmark of imperialist cultures as well as those cultures trying to resist the encroachments of Europe.

We are still the inheritors of that style by which one is defined by the nation, which in turn derives its authority from a supposedly unbroken tradition. In the United States this concern over cultural identity has of course yielded up the contest over what books and authorities constitute "our" tradition. In the main, trying to say that this or that book is (or is not) part of "our" tradition is one of the most debilitating exercises imaginable. Besides, its excesses are much more frequent than its contributions to historical accuracy. For the record then, I have no patience with the position that "we" should only or mainly be concerned with what is "ours," any more than I can condone reactions to such a view that require Arabs to read Arab books, use Arab methods, and the like. As C. L. R. James used to say, Beethoven belongs as much to West Indians as he does to Germans, since his music is now part of the human heritage.

Yet the ideological concern over identity is understandably entangled   35 with the interests and agendas of various groups—not all of them oppressed minorities—that wish to set priorities reflecting these interests. Since a great deal of this book is all about what to read of recent history and how to read it, I shall only quickly summarize my ideas here. Before we can agree on what the American identity is made of, we have to concede that as an immigrant settler society superimposed on the ruins of considerable native presence, American identity is too varied to be a unitary and homogenous thing; indeed the battle within it is between advocates of a unitary identity and those who see the whole as a complex but not reductively unified one. This opposition implies two different perspectives, two historiographies, one linear and subsuming, the other contrapuntal and often nomadic.

My argument is that only the second perspective is fully sensitive to the reality of historical experience. Partly because of empire, all cultures are involved in one another; none is single and pure, all are hybrid, heterogenous, extraordinarily differentiated, and unmonolithic. This, I believe, is as true of the contemporary United States as it is of the modern Arab world, where in each instance respectively so much has been made of the dangers of "un-Americanism" and the threats to "Arabism." Defensive, reactive, and even paranoid nationalism is, alas, frequently woven into the very fabric of education, where children as well as older students are taught to venerate and celebrate the uniqueness of *their* tradition (usually and invidiously at the expense of others). It is to such uncritical and unthinking forms of education and thought that this book is addressed—as a corrective, as a patient alternative, as a frankly exploratory possibility. In its writing I have availed myself of the utopian space still provided by the university, which I believe must remain a place where such vital issues are investigated, discussed, reflected on. For it to become a site where social and political issues are actually either imposed or resolved would be to remove the university's function and turn it into an adjunct to whatever political party is in power.

I do not wish to be misunderstood. Despite its extraordinary cultural diversity, the United States is, and will surely remain, a coherent nation. The same is true of other English-speaking countries (Britain, New Zealand, Australia, Canada) and even of France, which now contains large groups of immigrants. Much of the polemical divisiveness and polarized debate that Arthur Schlesinger speaks of as hurting the study of history in *The Disuniting of America* is there of course, but it does not, in my opinion, portend a dissolution of the republic. On the whole it is better to explore history rather than to repress or deny it; the fact that the United States contains so many histories, many of them now clamoring for attention, is by no means to be suddenly feared since many of them were always there, and out of them *an* American society and politics (and even a style of historical writing) were in fact created. In other words, the result of present debates over multiculturalism is hardly likely to be "Lebanonization," and if these debates point a way for political changes and changes in the way women, minorities, and recent immigrants see themselves, then that is not to be feared or defended against. What does need to be remembered is that narratives of emancipation and enlightenment in their strongest form were also narratives of *integration* not separation, the stories of people who had been excluded from the main group but who were now fighting for a place in it. And if the old and habitual ideas of the main group were not flexible or generous enough to admit new groups, then these ideas need changing, a far better thing to do than reject the emerging groups.

The last point I want to make is that this book is an exile's book. For objective reasons that I had no control over, I grew up as an Arab with a Western education. Ever since I can remember, I have felt that I belonged to both worlds, without being completely *of* either one or the other. During my lifetime, however, the parts of the Arab world that I was most attached to either have been changed utterly by civil upheavals and war, or have simply ceased to exist. And for long periods of time I have been an outsider in the United States, particularly when it went to war against, and was deeply opposed to, the (far from perfect) cultures and societies of the Arab world. Yet when I say "exile" I do not mean something sad or deprived. On the contrary belonging, as it were, to both sides of the imperial divide enables you to understand them more easily. Moreover New York, where the whole of this book was written, is in so many ways the exilic city *par excellence*; it also contains within itself the Manichean structure of the colonial city described by Fanon. Perhaps all this has stimulated the kinds of interests and interpretations ventured here, but these circumstances certainly made it possible for me to feel as if I belonged to more than one history and more than one group. As to whether such a state can be regarded as really a salutary alternative to the normal sense of belonging to only one culture and feeling a sense of loyalty to only one nation, the reader must now decide.

● Building the Frame Through Writing

1. Said argues that Western literature helped create and sustain an Orientalist discourse of domination. Think about the literary works you've read in your high school and college classes.

   • Do you see a curriculum that privileges Eurocentric texts?

   • Do you see texts that promote an Orientalist conception of non-Western cultures?

   • Do you see texts that promote a sense of pride in a national culture, what Said calls "venerating one's own culture . . . as somehow divorced from . . . the everyday world"?

   • Does this concept of culture as separate, "autonomous," and "higher" in value still inform our sense of what "art" is? Consider how we commonly see what are called "popular culture" media especially—pop music, many forms of graphic art, film, and television—in relation to literary works of art, such as novels.

2. Are you familiar with any Orientalist claims about the "mind" or "ways" of a culture in or beyond the United States, as Said discusses this concept in paragraph 2? Consider visual as well as print-based media. Do you think such generalizations are still employed in any academic contexts?

3. Do you agree with Said that narrative is an especially powerful form of writing? Think of some ways in which narratives have shaped your sense of culture: think of books, films, and television shows that have given you a sense of cultures beyond the United States, as well as the "grand narratives" we have constructed to tell our own history—the narrative of westward expansion, for example, or of the West as the "cradle of democracy."

   • Think back on the novels you're likely to have read in primary and secondary school: *The Adventures of Tom Sawyer; The Adventures of Huckleberry Finn; The Scarlet Letter; 1984; Lord of the Flies; The Catcher in the Rye, The Color Purple*, among others. Have you been asked to place narratives in relation to each other to study them as differing accounts of history?

   • What "grand narratives" have informed your educational decisions? What do you believe is the "story" of college education?

4. Work out in your own words Said's argument about Dickens's *Great Expectations*. How does the novel help establish "proper" relations between the colonizing nation and its colony/colonial subjects? Why can't Magwitch return to Britain, from a colonialist perspective?

5. The literary works of Joseph Conrad are often read as anticolonialist (*Heart of Darkness*, in particular). Said, however, offers a counter-reading. What do you understand to be Conrad's colonialist assumptions, his "residual imperialist propensities," as Said critiques them?

6. The last part of Said's argument relates to globalization, the contemporary interconnection of nations, cultures, and economies. Said's view of globalization is a very mixed one. Outline his points, and consider how you might reformulate the narrative of the contemporary world situation that he offers. Consider some of the following claims:

- The United States considers itself as "exceptional, not imperial" (para. 30).

- Despite increased contact, "the one idea that has scarcely varied is that there is an 'us' and a 'them' " (para. 33).

- "American identity is too varied to be a unitary and homogenous thing" (para. 35).

- "Defensive, reactive, and even paranoid nationalism is . . . woven into the very fabric of education" (para. 36).

- "If the old and habitual ideas of the main group were not flexible or generous enough to admit new groups, then these ideas need changing" (para. 37).

Postcolonial Studies

HANS BERTENS

The following selection, a chapter taken from an introductory literary theory text, focuses on three central postcolonial concepts. The first is Said's concept of "Orientalism," or the process through which another culture gets represented as an "other" culture—an alien, exotic, different, and inferior group. In the preceding selection, Said emphasizes discourse *as the means of creating "knowledge" about an "alien" group, which then becomes the basis for how the more powerful group relates to (and attempts to dominate) the "other." The second concept is the relationship of colonizer and colonized, especially the effect on the colonized individual's sense of identity. Postcolonial writers also call attention to the mutual effects of colonization; you'll read in Aimé Césaire, for example, about the dehumanizing effect of colonization on the colonizer. In his chapter, Bertens explains the postcolonial concept of mimicry, or how the colonized individual adopts but also changes the cultural identity of the colonizers, distorting the image of the supposedly powerful ones. The third concept is the subaltern, or the doubly disempowered colonized subject, whose voice is silenced by class and gender as well as by the position as a colonized subject. Note that these concepts are all rhetorical in that they deal with how language is used to construct a relationship between a speaker and audience, sometimes to silence the audience, but this same language can be used to reveal oppressive motives and to resist them. Note: We've highlighted key terms.*

Orientalism

[P]ostcolonial studies in its current theoretically oriented form starts with the publication, in 1978, of the Palestinian-American critic Edward Said's book *Orientalism*. Drawing on Foucault and, to a lesser extent, Gramsci, Said's study completely changed the agenda of the study of non-Western cultures and their literatures and pushed it in the direction of what we now call postcolonial theory.

Orientalism is a devastating critique of how through the ages, but particularly in the nineteenth century—the heyday of imperialist expansion—which is the book's focus, Western texts have represented the East, and more specifically the Islamic Middle East (for the sake of convenience I will simply refer to "the Orient" or "the East" here). Using British and French "scholarly works . . . works of literature, political tracts, journalistic texts, travel books, religious and philological studies," Said examines how these texts *construct* the Orient through imaginative representations (in novels, for instance), through seemingly factual descriptions (in journalistic reports and travel writing), and through claims to knowledge about Oriental history and culture (histories, anthropological writings, and so on). Together, all these forms of Western writing form a **Foucauldian** *discourse*—a loose system of statements and claims that constitutes a field of supposed knowledge and through which that "knowledge" is constructed. Such discourses, although seemingly interested in knowledge, always establish relationships of power. In Foucault's work, power is first of all a force that serves itself. We may think we use it for our own purposes in our capacity as free agents, but in reality it works first of all *through* us and not *for* us. From Foucault's anti-humanistic perspective we are functions within networks of power. For Said, however, the West's representations of the East ultimately work within the framework of a conscious and determined effort at subordination. For Said, Orientalism—this Western discourse about the Orient—has traditionally served *hegemonic* purposes. As we have seen, Antonio Gramsci thought of **"hegemony" as domination by consent**—the way the ruling class succeeds in oppressing other classes with their apparent approval. In Gramsci's analysis it does so through culture: the ruling class makes its own values and interests central in what it presents as a common, neutral, culture. Accepting that "common" culture, the other classes become complicit in their own oppression and the result is a kind of **velvet domination**. Orientalism, then, has traditionally served two purposes. It has legitimized Western expansionism and imperialism in the eyes of Western governments and their electorates and it has insidiously worked to convince the "natives" that Western culture represented universal civilization. Accepting that culture could only benefit them—it would, for instance, elevate them from the "backward" or "superstitious" conditions in which they still lived—and would make them participants in the most advanced civilization the world had ever seen.

For Said, Western representations of the Orient, no matter how well intentioned, have always been part of this damaging discourse. Wittingly or unwittingly, they have always been complicit with the workings of Western power. Even those Orientalists who are clearly in sympathy with Oriental peoples and their cultures—and Said finds a substantial number of them—cannot overcome their Eurocentric perspective and have unintentionally contributed to Western domination. So instead of the disinterested objectivity in the service of the higher goal of true knowledge that Western scholarship has traditionally claimed for itself, we find invariably false representations that have effectively paved the way for military domination, cultural displacement, and economic exploitation. . . . *Orientalism*, whatever its shortcomings may have been, revolutionized the way Western scholars and critics looked at representations of non-Western subjects and cultures (just like feminism had somewhat earlier revolutionized the way we look at representations of women and African-American studies had revolutionized the way in which in particular American criticism looks at representations of African-Americans). Said's book also drew attention to the way in which the discourse of Orientalism serves to create the West as well it creates the East. West and East form a **binary opposition** in which the two poles define each other. The inferiority that Orientalism attributes to the East simultaneously serves to construct the West's superiority. The sensuality, irrationality, primitiveness, and despotism of the East constructs the West as rational, democratic, progressive, and so on. The West always functions as the "**centre**" and the East is a marginal "**other**" that simply through its existence confirms the West's centrality and superiority. Not surprisingly perhaps, the opposition that the West's discourse about the East sets up makes use of another basic opposition, that between the masculine and the feminine. Naturally the West functions as the masculine pole—enlightened, rational, entrepreneurial, disciplined—while the East is its feminine opposition—irrational, passive, undisciplined, and sensual.

. . .

Colonized and Colonizer

One of the questions that Said does not address but that is central to the work of Homi Bhabha is what actually happens in the cultural interaction between colonizer and colonized. In earlier writings on colonialism, such an interaction had often been denied. Aimé Césaire, for instance, claimed in his 1955 *Discourse on Colonialism* that between colonizer and colonized there is "[n]o human contact, but relations of domination and submission which turn the colonizing man into a classroom monitor, an army sergeant, a prison guard, a slave driver, and the indigenous man into an instrument of production." British and French accounts of colonial life had standardly presented a wholly different, and benign, view of colonialism, but had seen as little interaction between colonizer and colonized as Césaire. The colonizers remained their civilized and disciplined European selves even in the most trying circumstances. The West has always been convinced that its presence overseas greatly affected the "natives" (to the point that it told itself that the smartest and most sensitive of them immediately started scrambling to adopt Western ways and values), but has never been comfortable with the idea that its sons and daughters might in their turn be affected by the cultures they encountered. It is mostly in literature that we find alternative perspectives. In Joseph Conrad's *Heart of Darkness* (1899) the colonial experience has the effect of turning the ivory collector Kurtz into a megalomaniacal barbarian and in E.M. Forster's *A Passage to India* (1924) two British women also pay a price for leaving familiar territory and suffer permanently unsettling experiences in India.

For Bhabha, the encounter of colonizer and colonized always affects both. 5 Colonialism, with the displacements and terrible uncertainties that it brings, is such a radically unsettling "affective experience of **marginality**." . . . But the colonial experience also affects the colonizer. More specifically, for Bhabha the colonizer cannot escape a complex and paradoxical relationship with the colonized. . . . Instead of being self-sufficient with regard to his identity ("his" because colonialism is an almost exclusively male enterprise), the colonizer at least partly constructs it through interaction with the colonized. The colonizer's identity has no "origin" in himself and is not a fixed entity, but is differential, a "meaning" generated by difference. Although that difference has in a sense been constructed beforehand—by Western discourses about the East—the "British" or "English" identity of the colonizer can only become a "reality" after the colonial contact which truly confirms it. . . .

Bhabha sees signs of the colonizer's partial dependency on none-too-friendly "others"—and the resulting inherent uncertainty—in a whole range of phenomena. Racial stereotyping, for instance, first of all repeats this process of identity-creation in that it construes not only those who are stereotyped, but also the stereotyper himself—in opposition to the stereotyped. It functions to construe or confirm the stereotyper's identity. However, the repetitiveness of acts of stereotyping points to a continuing uncertainty in the stereotyper: apparently the stereotyper has to convince himself over and over again of the truthfulness of the stereotype—and thus, by extension, of his own identity. The self-confidence of the colonizer is further undermined by what Bhabha calls *mimicry*—the always slightly alien and distorted way in which the colonized, either out of choice or under duress, will repeat the colonizer's ways and discourse. In mimicry the colonizer sees himself in a mirror that slightly but effectively distorts his image—that subtly and unsettlingly "others" his own identity. . . . But colonial power's lack of complete control is also the result of acts of conscious resistance on the part of the colonized. In the physical encounter between colonizer and colonized the latter may for instance refuse to meet his oppressor's gaze and in so doing reject "the narcissistic demand that [he] should be addressed directly, that the Other should authorize the self, recognize its priority, fulfill its outlines."

Perhaps the most influential of Bhabha's contributions to postcolonial theory is his notion of *hybridity*. While Said's *Orientalism* keeps the spheres of colonizer and colonized rather firmly apart, Bhabha, with his interest in their interaction, sees important movements going both ways. Shifting his focus from "the noisy command of colonial authority" and "the silent repression of native traditions," to "the colonial hybrid," Bhabha argues that the cultural interaction of colonizer and colonized leads to a fusion of cultural forms that from one perspective, because it signals its "productivity," confirms the power of the colonial presence, but that as a form of mimicry simultaneously "unsettles the mimetic or narcissistic demands of colonial power." . . .

The Subaltern

. . . Since colonized women almost by definition went unheard within their own patriarchal culture, they were doubly unheard under a colonial regime. [Gayatri] Spivak can be said to be the first postcolonial theorist with a fully feminist agenda. That agenda includes the complicity of female writers with imperialism. "It should not be possible to read nineteenth-century British fiction without remembering that imperialism, understood as England's social mission, was a crucial part of the cultural representation of England to the English," Spivak tells us in her 1985 essay "Three Women's Texts and a Critique of Imperialism." . . .

Of all postcolonial theorists, Spivak has most consistently focused on what in postcolonial studies has come to be called the *subaltern:* literally, the category of those who are lower in position or who, in the military terms that are always appropriate to the colonial situation, are lower in rank. Spivak employs the term (which derives from Gramsci) to describe the lower layers of colonial and postcolonial (or, as many would say, neo-colonial) society: the homeless, the unemployed, the subsistence farmers, the day labourers, and so on. . . . One result of this attentiveness to difference is Spivak's focus on the female subaltern, a very large—and of course differentiated—category among the colonized (and neo-colonized) that, she argues, has traditionally been doubly marginalized: "If, in the context of colonial production, the subaltern has no history and cannot speak, the subaltern as female is even more deeply in shadow."

This focus does not mean that she speaks for—or has the intention of speaking for—the female subaltern. Rather, she is motivated by the desire to save the female subaltern from misrepresentation. In a famous essay from 1988, "Can the Subaltern Speak?" Spivak . . . examines the nineteenth-century controversy between the colonized Indians and their British colonizers over what she calls "widow-sacrifice": the burning of widows on the funeral pyre of their deceased husbands. Spivak concludes that neither party allowed women—the potential victims of this practice—to speak. The British texts construct a position for the woman in which she is made to represent Western individualism and, by implication, a superior Western civilization that emphasizes modern freedom, while the Indian ones present her as choosing for duty and tradition. Although both parties claim that they have them on their side, the women themselves remain unheard. . . .

● **Building the Frame Through Writing**

1. Edward Said defined Orientalism as a "discourse," or, as Bertens writes, "a loose system of statements and claims that constitutes a field of supposed knowledge and through which that 'knowledge' is constructed"; this system also "establish[es] relationships of power" (para. 2). Where can you see "master" discourses defining a group and determining practices related to them in your daily lives? Consider the following:

   • In the introduction to this section, we noted that students can be the object of this kind of discursive construction and power imbalance. What are the common elements in the discourse about students?

   • How are you characterized when the speakers are educators and educational policy makers?

   • How and why does this discourse have power? How does it affect your experiences as a student?

   • Consider the same questions applied to the discourse of social class (working, middle, upper/elite); a racial or ethnic group; homosexuality; or another topic of your choosing.

2. What are some historical instances of "velvet domination"? What are some of the discourses that enabled this response that Gramsci called "domination by consent"? Think about

   • historical instances of pre- or antifeminist support for male dominance,

   • pro-assimilation views among ethnic and racial minorities, and

   • Anglophile (British-culture-loving) responses to Eurocentric cultural dominance.

3. In the U.S. conflicts in Vietnam, Afghanistan, Iraq, and other "exotic" places, what were some of the most direct assumptions about how U.S. influence on the native populations should and would change them? What have been some of the unexpected counterinfluences on U.S. culture?

4. Many African American and Asian American comedians use mimicry to create humorous but also socially critical effects. The film versions of Richard Pryor's comic routines (for example, *Live on the Sunset Strip*) are especially powerful examples. How does Homi Bhabha's theory help you see the purpose and effects of such mimicry?

5. In the United States, we can see many instances of cultural hybridity. Using Homi Bhabha's notion of the hybrid as evidence of both colonial power and mimcry as an "unsettling" of this power, consider where and how hybridity operates in this country—in, for example, such places as Hawaii, Puerto Rico, Florida, Native American lands, and border states (such as Texas and California).

6. Using Gayatri Spivak's concept of the subaltern, analyze the critical problems that you would face if you were asked to write an essay on the situation of the

following groups: African women; Latinas; "untouchables"/harijan caste; Maori or aborigines.

- Consider the rhetorical challenges: by writing about one of these groups, what relationship would you be establishing?
- What evidence would you likely depend on?

7. In the United States, we usually assume a positive view of international assistance groups such as the Peace Corps and educational ventures such as Study Abroad programs. Why might such a view come under challenge from social critics in other countries, including those whom we see as beneficiaries of Peace Corps work or passive hosts to U.S. students?

Discourse on Colonialism
AIMÉ CÉSAIRE

Born in the French Caribbean colony of Martinique in 1913, Aimé Césaire was a teacher, political leader, and poet. His critique of colonialism is foundational in its analysis of the role race plays in power relations, and he is known as a proponent of "negritude"—the power of black culture. The following excerpt from his long essay on colonialism, first published in France in 1955, is an early version of resistant discourse in the arguments it makes, in the ways in which it uses colonial writings against themselves, showing their hypocrisies, inconsistencies, and contradictions, and in constructing a voice of and for the colonized.

A civilization that proves incapable of solving the problems it creates   1
is a decadent civilization.

A civilization that chooses to close its eyes to its most crucial problems is a stricken civilization.

A civilization that uses its principles for trickery and deceit is a dying civilization.

The fact is that the so-called European civilization—"Western" civilization—as it has been shaped by two centuries of bourgeois rule, is incapable of solving the two major problems to which its existence has given rise: the problem of the proletariat and the colonial problem; that Europe is unable to justify itself either before the bar of "reason" or before the bar of "conscience"; and that, increasingly, it takes refuge in a hypocrisy which is all the more odious because it is less and less likely to deceive.

Europe is indefensible.   5

Apparently that is what the American strategists are whispering to each other.

That in itself is not serious.

What is serious is that "Europe" is morally, spiritually indefensible.

And today the indictment is brought against it not by the European masses alone, but on a world scale, by tens and tens of millions of men who, from the depths of slavery, set themselves up as judges.

The colonialists may kill in Indochina, torture in Madagascar, imprison in Black Africa, crack down in the West Indies. Henceforth the colonized know that they have an advantage over them. They know that their temporary "masters" are lying.

Therefore that their masters are weak.

And since I have been asked to speak about colonization and civilization, let us go straight to the principal lie which is the source of all the others.

Colonization and civilization?

In dealing with this subject, the commonest curse is to be the dupe in good faith of a collective hypocrisy that cleverly misrepresents problems, the better to legitimize the hateful solutions provided for them.

In other words, the essential thing here is to see clearly, to think clearly— that is, dangerously—and to answer clearly the innocent first question: what, fundamentally, is colonization? To agree on what it is not: neither evangelization, nor a philanthropic enterprise, nor a desire to push back the frontiers of ignorance, disease and tyranny, nor a project undertaken for the greater glory of God, nor an attempt to extend the rule of law. To admit once for all, without flinching at the consequences, that the decisive actors here are the adventurer and the pirate, the wholesale grocer and the ship owner, the gold digger and the merchant, appetite and force, and behind them, the baleful projected shadow of a form of civilization which, at a certain point in its history, finds itself obliged, for internal reasons, to extend to a world scale the competition of its antagonistic economies.

Pursuing my analysis, I find that hypocrisy is of recent date; that neither Cortez discovering Mexico from the top of the great teocalli, nor Pizzaro before Cuzco (much less Marco Polo before Cambaluc), claims that he is the harbinger of a superior order; that they kill; that they plunder; that they have helmets, lances, cupidities; that the slavering apologists came later; that the chief culprit in this domain is Christian pedantry, which laid down the dishonest equations *Christianity = civilization, paganism = savagery*, from which there could not but ensue abominable colonialist and racist consequences, whose victims were to be the Indians, the yellow peoples and the Negroes.

That being settled, I admit that it is a good thing to place different civilizations in contact with each other; that it is an excellent thing to blend different worlds; that whatever its own particular genius may be, a civilization that withdraws into itself atrophies; that for civilizations, exchange is oxygen; that the great good fortune of Europe is to have been a crossroads, and that because it was the locus of all ideas, the receptacle of all philosophies, the meeting place of all sentiments, it was the best center for the redistribution of energy.

But then I ask the following question: has colonization really *placed civilizations in contact*? Or, if you prefer, of all the ways of *establishing contact*, was it the best?

I answer *no*.

And I say that between *colonization* and *civilization* there is an infinite distance; that out of all the colonial expeditions that have been undertaken, out of all the colonial statutes that have been drawn up, out of all the memoranda that have been despatched by all the ministries, there could not come a single human value.

First we must study how colonization works to *decivilize* the colonizer, to *brutalize* him in the true sense of the word, to degrade him, to awaken him to buried instincts, to covetousness, violence, race hatred and moral relativism; and we must show that each time a head is cut off or an eye put out in Vietnam and in France they accept the fact, each time a little girl is raped and in France they accept the fact, each time a Madagascan is tortured and in France they accept the fact, civilization acquires another dead weight, a universal regression takes place, a gangrene sets in, a center of infection begins to spread; and that at the end of all these treaties that have been violated, all these lies that have been propagated, all these punitive expeditions that have been tolerated, all these prisoners who have been tied up and "interrogated," all these patriots who have been tortured, at the end of all the racial pride that has been encouraged, all the boastfulness that has been displayed, a poison has been instilled into the veins of Europe and, slowly but surely, the continent proceeds toward *savagery*.

And then one fine day the bourgeoisie is awakened by a terrific reverse shock: the gestapos are busy, the prisons fill up, the torturers around the racks invent, refine, discuss.

People are surprised, they become indignant. They say: "How strange! But never mind—it's Nazism, it will pass!" And they wait, and they hope; and they hide the truth from themselves, that it is barbarism, but the supreme barbarism, the crowning barbarism that sums up all the daily barbarisms; that it is Nazism, yes, but that before they were its victims, they were its accomplices; that they tolerated that Nazism before it was inflicted on them, that they absolved it, shut their eyes to it, legitimized it, because, until then, it had been applied only to non-European peoples; that they have cultivated that Nazism, that they are responsible for it and that before engulfing the whole of Western, Christian civilization in its reddened waters, it oozes, seeps and trickles from every crack.

Yes, it would be worthwhile to study clinically, in detail, the steps taken by Hitler and Hitlerism and to reveal to the very distinguished, very humanistic, very Christian bourgeois of the twentieth century that without his being aware of it, he has a Hitler inside him, that Hitler *inhabits* him, that Hitler is his *demon*, that if he rails against him, he is being inconsistent and that, at bottom, what he cannot forgive Hitler for is not *crime* in itself, *the crime against man*, it is not *the humiliation of man as such*, it is the crime against the white man, the humiliation of the white man, and the fact that he applied to Europe colonialist procedures which until then had been reserved exclusively for the Arabs of Algeria, the coolies of India, and the blacks of Africa.

And that is the great thing I hold against pseudo-humanism: that for too   25
long it has diminished the rights of man, that its concept of those rights has
been—and still is—narrow and fragmentary, incomplete and biased and, all
things considered, sordidly racist.

I have talked a good deal about Hitler. Because he deserves it: he makes
it possible to see things on a large scale and to grasp the fact that capitalist
society, at its present stage, is incapable of establishing a concept of the rights
of all men, just as it has proved incapable of establishing a system of individual ethics. Whether one likes it or not, at the end of the blind alley that is
Europe, I mean the Europe of Adenauer, Schuman, Bidault and a few
others, there is Hitler. At the end of capitalism, which is eager to outlive its
day, there is Hitler. At the end of formal humanism and philosophic renunciation, there is Hitler.

And this being so, I cannot help thinking of one of his statements: "We
aspire not to equality but to domination. The country of a foreign race must
become once again a country of serfs, of agricultural laborers, or industrial
workers. It is not a question of eliminating the inequalities among men but of
widening them and making them into a law."

That rings clear, haughty and brutal and plants us squarely in the middle of
howling savagery. But let us come down a step.

Who is speaking? I am ashamed to say it: it is the Western *humanist*, the
"idealist" philosopher. That his name is Renan is an accident. That the passage
is taken from a book entitled *La Réforme intellectuelle et morale*, that it was written in France just after a war which France had represented as a war of right
against might, tells us a great deal about bourgeois morals.

The regeneration of the inferior or degenerate races by the superior races is
part of the providential order of things for humanity. With us, the common
man is nearly always a déclassé nobleman, his heavy hand is better suited to
handling the sword than the menial tool. Rather than work, he chooses to fight,
that is, he returns to his first estate. *Regere imperio populos*, that is our vocation.
Pour forth this all-consuming activity onto countries which, like China, are
crying aloud for foreign conquest. Turn the adventurers who disturb European
society into a *ver sacrum*, a horde like those of the Franks, the Lombards, or the
Normans, and every man will be in his right role. Nature has made a race of
workers, the Chinese race, who have wonderful manual dexterity and almost no
sense of honor; govern them with justice, levying from them, in return for the
blessing of such a government, an ample allowance for the conquering race,
and they will be satisfied; a race of tillers of the soil, the Negro; treat him with
kindness and humanity, and all will be as it should; a race of masters and soldiers, the European race. Reduce this noble race to working in the *ergastulum*
like Negroes and Chinese, and they rebel. In Europe, every rebel is, more or
less, a soldier who has missed his calling, a creature made for the heroic life, before whom you are setting *a task that is contrary to his race*—a poor worker, too

good a soldier. But the life at which our workers rebel would make a Chinese or a fellah happy, as they are not military creatures in the least. *Let each one do what he is made for, and all will be well.*

Hitler? Rosenberg? No, Renan.   30
But let us come down one step further. And it is the long-winded politician. Who protests? No one, so far as I know, when M. Albert Sarraut, the former governor-general of Indochina, holding forth to the students at the Ecole Coloniale, teaches them that it would be puerile to object to the European colonial enterprises in the name of "an alleged right to possess the land one occupies, and some sort of right to remain in fierce isolation, which would leave unutilized resources to lie forever idle in the hands of incompetents."

And who is roused to indignation when a certain Rev. Barde assures us that if the goods of this world "remained divided up indefinitely, as they would be without colonization, they would answer neither the purposes of God nor the just demands of the human collectivity"?

Since, as his fellow Christian, the Rev. Muller, declares: "Humanity must not, cannot allow the incompetence, negligence, and laziness of the uncivilized peoples to leave idle indefinitely the wealth which God has confided to them, charging them to make it serve the good of all."

No one.

I mean not one established writer, not one academician, not one preacher,   35
not one crusader for the right and for religion, not one "defender of the human person."

And yet, through the mouths of the Sarrauts and the Bardes, the Mullers and the Renans, through the mouths of all those who considered—and consider—it lawful to apply to non-European peoples "a kind of expropriation for public purposes" for the benefit of nations that were stronger and better equipped, it was already Hitler speaking!

What am I driving at? At this idea: that no one colonizes innocently, that no one colonizes with impunity either; that a nation which colonizes, that a civilization which justifies colonization—and therefore force—is already a sick civilization, a civilization that is morally diseased, that irresistibly, progressing from one consequence to another, one repudiation to another, calls for its Hitler, I mean its punishment.

Colonization: bridgehead in a campaign to civilize barbarism, from which there may emerge at any moment the negation of civilization, pure and simple.

Elsewhere I have cited at length a few incidents culled from the history of colonial expeditions.

Unfortunately, this did not find favor with everyone. It seems that I was   40
pulling old skeletons out of the closet. Indeed!

Was there no point in quoting Colonel de Montagnac, one of the conquerors of Algeria: "In order to banish the thoughts that sometimes besiege me, I have some heads cut off, not the heads of artichokes but the heads of men."

Would it have been more advisable to refuse the floor to Count d'Hérisson: "It is true that we are bringing back a whole barrelful of ears collected, pair by pair, from prisoners, friendly or enemy."

Should I have refused Saint-Arnaud the right to profess his barbarous faith: "We lay waste, we burn, we plunder, we destroy the houses and the trees."

Should I have prevented Marshal Bugeaud from systematizing all that in a daring theory and invoking the precedent of famous ancestors: "We must have a great invasion of Africa, like the invasions of the Franks and the Goths."

Lastly, should I have cast back into the shadows of oblivion the memorable 45 feat of arms of General Gérard and kept silent about the capture of Ambike, a city which, to tell the truth, had never dreamed of defending itself: "The native riflemen had orders to kill only the men, but no one restrained them; intoxicated by the smell of blood, they spared not one woman, not one child. . . . At the end of the afternoon, the heat caused a light mist to arise: it was the blood of the five thousand victims, the ghost of the city, evaporating in the setting sun."

Yes or no, are these things true? And the sadistic pleasures, the nameless delights that send voluptuous shivers and quivers through Loti's carcass when he focuses his field glasses on a good massacre of the Annamese? True or not true? And if these things are true, as no one can deny, will it be said, in order to minimize them, that these corpses don't prove anything?

For my part, if I have recalled a few details of these hideous butcheries, it is by no means because I take a morbid delight in them, but because I think that these heads of men, these collections of ears, these burned houses, these Gothic invasions, this steaming blood, these cities that evaporate at the edge of the sword, are not to be so easily disposed of. They prove that colonization, I repeat, dehumanizes even the most civilized man; that colonial activity, colonial enterprise, colonial conquest, which is based on contempt for the native and justified by that contempt, inevitably tends to change him who undertakes it; that the colonizer, who in order to ease his conscience gets into the habit of seeing the other man as *an animal*, accustoms himself to treating him like an animal, and tends objectively to transform *himself* into an animal. It is this result, this boomerang effect of colonization, that I wanted to point out.

Unfair? No. There was a time when these same facts were a source of pride, and when, sure of the morrow, people did not mince words. One last quotation; it is from a certain Carl Siger, author of an *Essai sur la colonisation* (Paris 1907):

> The new countries offer a vast field for individual, violent activities which, in the metropolitan countries, would run up against certain prejudices, against a sober and orderly conception of life, and which, in the colonies, have greater freedom to develop and, consequently, to affirm their worth. Thus to a certain extent the colonies can serve as a safety value for modern society. Even if this were their only value, it would be immense.

Truly, there are stains that it is beyond the power of man to wipe out and that can never be fully expiated.

But let us speak about the colonized.   50

I see clearly what colonization has destroyed: the wonderful Indian civilizations—and neither Deterding nor Royal Dutch nor Standard Oil will ever console me for the Aztecs and the Incas.

I see clearly the civilizations, condemned to perish at a future date, into which it has introduced a principle of ruin: the South Sea islands, Nigeria, Nyasaland. I see less clearly the contributions it has made.

Security? Culture? The rule of law? In the meantime, I look around and wherever there are colonizers and colonized face to face, I see force, brutality, cruelty, sadism, conflict, and, in a parody of education, the hasty manufacture of a few thousand subordinate functionaries, "boys," artisans, office clerks and interpreters necessary for the smooth operation of business.

I spoke of contact.

Between colonizer and colonized there is room only for forced labor,   55
intimidation, pressure, the police, taxation, theft, rape, compulsory crops, contempt, mistrust, arrogance, self-complacency, swinishness, brainless élites, degraded masses.

No human contact, but relations of domination and submission which turn the colonizing man into a classroom monitor, an army sergeant, a prison guard, a slave driver, and the indigenous man into an instrument of production.

My turn to state an equation: colonization = "thingification."

I hear the storm. They talk to me about progress, about "achievements," diseases cured, improved standards of living.

I am talking about societies drained of their essence, cultures trampled underfoot, institutions undermined, lands confiscated, religions smashed, magnificent artistic creations destroyed, extraordinary *possibilities* wiped out.

They throw facts at my head, statistics, mileages of roads, canals and   60
railroad tracks.

I am talking about thousands of men sacrificed to the Congo-Océan. I am talking about those who, as I write this, are digging the harbor of Abidjan by hand. I am talking about millions of men torn from their gods, their land, their habits, their life—from life, from the dance, from wisdom.

I am talking about millions of men in whom fear has been cunningly instilled, who have been taught to have an inferiority complex, to tremble, kneel, despair and behave like flunkeys.

They dazzle me with the tonnage of cotton or cocoa that has been exported, the acreage that has been planted with olive trees or grapevines.

I am talking about natural *economies* that have been disrupted—harmonious and viable *economies* adapted to the indigenous population—about food crops destroyed, malnutrition permanently introduced, agricultural development oriented solely toward the benefit of the metropolitan countries, about the looting of products, the looting of raw materials.

They pride themselves on abuses eliminated.   65

I too talk about abuses, but what I say is that on the old ones—very real—they have superimposed others—very detestable. They talk to me about local tyrants brought to reason; but I note that in general the old tyrants get on very well with the new ones, and that there has been established between them, to the detriment of the people, a circuit of mutual services and complicity.

They talk to me about civilization, I talk about proletarianization and mystification.

For my part, I make a systematic defense of the non-European civilizations.

Every day that passes, every denial of justice, every beating by the police, every demand of the workers that is drowned in blood, every scandal that is hushed up, every punitive expedition, every police van, every gendarme and every militiaman, brings home to us the value of our old societies.

They were communal societies, never societies of the many for the few.   70

They were societies that were not only ante-capitalist, as has been said, but also *anti-capitalist*.

They were democratic societies, always.

They were cooperative societies, fraternal societies.

I make a systematic defense of the societies destroyed by imperialism.

They were the fact, they did not pretend to be the idea; despite their faults,   75 they were neither to be hated nor condemned. They were content to be. In them, neither the word *failure* nor the word *avatar* had any meaning. They kept hope intact.

Whereas those are the only words that can, in all honesty, be applied to the European enterprises outside Europe. My only consolation is that periods of colonization pass, that nations sleep only for a time, and that peoples remain.

This being said, it seems that in certain circles they pretend to have discovered in me an "enemy of Europe" and a prophet of the return to the ante-European past.

For my part, I search in vain for the place where I could have expressed such views; where I ever underestimated the importance of Europe in the history of human thought; where I ever preached a *return* of any kind; where I ever claimed that there could be a *return*.

The truth is that I have said something very different: to wit, that the great historical tragedy of Africa has been not so much that it was too late in making contact with the rest of the world, as the manner in which that contact was brought about; that Europe began to "propagate" at a time when it had fallen into the hands of the most unscrupulous financiers and captains of industry; that it was our misfortune to encounter that particular Europe on our path, and that Europe is responsible before the human community for the highest heap of corpses in history.

In another connection, in judging colonization, I have added that Europe   80 has gotten on very well indeed with the local feudal lords who agreed to serve, woven a villainous complicity with them, rendered their tyranny more effective and more efficient, and that it has actually tended to prolong artificially the survival of local pasts in their most pernicious aspects.

I have said—and this is something very different—that colonialist Europe has grafted modern abuse onto ancient injustice, hateful racism onto old inequality.

That if I am attacked on the grounds of intent, I maintain that colonialist Europe is dishonest in trying to justify its colonizing activity *a posteriori* by the obvious material progress that has been achieved in certain fields under the colonial regime—since *sudden change* is always possible, in history as elsewhere; since no one knows at what stage of material development these same countries would have been if Europe had not intervened; since the technical outfitting of Africa and Asia, their administrative reorganization, in a word, their "Europeanization," was (as is proved by the example of Japan) in no way tied to the European *occupation*; since the Europeanization of the non-European continents could have been accomplished otherwise than under the heel of Europe; since this movement of Europeanization *was in progress*; since it was even slowed down; since in any case it was distorted by the European takeover.

The proof is that at present it is the indigenous peoples of Africa and Asia who are demanding schools, and colonialist Europe which refuses them; that it is the African who is asking for ports and roads, and colonialist Europe which is niggardly on this score; that it is the colonized man who wants to move forward, and the colonizer who holds things back.

● Building the Frame Through Writing

1. Analyze Césaire's rhetorical choices in this powerful essay:
    - Where do you see him use logos, ethos, and pathos in his denunciation of colonialism?
    - How does he claim credibility as a fair speaker deserving to be heard?
    - What is his purpose in using Hitler as a symbol of the colonial enterprise? How do you think his use of Hitler is related to his claim that "colonization works to decivilize the colonizer"?
    - After quoting Hitler on domination, Césaire then quotes Renan and Muller, two religious humanists, and then five European military leaders. Why did he select this range of voices? How are we to read them against each other?

2. In his essay, Césaire is answering white Europeans who had criticized him as a radical, an "enemy of Europe." How does his essay go beyond addressing this critical audience? Who else does he speak to?

3. In Africa (and elsewhere) in the nineteenth century, European missionaries worked to convert natives to Christian beliefs and values, often establishing

village schools, teaching English, French, or other European languages along with religious doctrine, and cooperating with colonial leaders' efforts to impose European legal and governmental systems. Why and how does Césaire reject the European missionary?

4. Césaire argues that Europeans operate with the equation "*Christianity = civilization, paganism = savagery*" (para. 16). Explain this equation as a *discourse*, as Said uses the term.

5. Explain the colonialist process of "thingification," of reducing, or dehumanizing, native populations. What ideologies are evident in the justifications Césaire notes have been given for colonialism?

6. Césaire says he is not against contact among different cultures, but he passionately condemns the specific nature of European-African contact. What historical realities made this contact so destructive, as Césaire outlines them?

7. What are the psychological effects of colonization on both the colonized and colonizer, according to Césaire?

Afterword to M. Butterfly

DAVID HENRY HWANG

David Henry Hwang is a playwright, a creative writer, rather than an academic or political theorist, but his essay on his play M. Butterfly *(1988) enacts Said's critical concept of Orientalism. As Hwang explains, the play reworks the libretto (story line) of the opera* Madame Butterfly, *turning its colonialist stereotypes against itself, reversing roles and genders, and revealing the Orientalist lens that the West adopts in its relations with Asian cultures. The play is based on an actual historical event—the arrest, trial, and conviction of a French diplomat who passed information to his Chinese lover, a spy for the Chinese government, a man who posed as a woman and whose French lover assumed to be a woman throughout their 20-year affair.*

It all started in May of 1986, over casual dinner conversation. A friend asked, had I heard about the French diplomat who'd fallen in love with a Chinese actress, who subsequently turned out to be not only a spy, but a man? I later found a two-paragraph story in *The New York Times*. The diplomat, Bernard Bouriscot, attempting to account for the fact that he had never seen his "girlfriend" naked, was quoted as saying, "I thought she was very modest. I thought it was a Chinese custom."

Now, I am aware that this is *not* a Chinese custom, that Asian women are no more shy with their lovers than are women of the West. I am also aware, however, that Bouriscot's assumption was consistent with a certain stereotyped view of Asians as bowing, blushing flowers. I therefore concluded that the diplomat must have fallen in love, not with a person, but with a fantasy stereotype. I also inferred that, to the extent the Chinese spy encouraged these misperceptions, he must have played up to and exploited this image of the Oriental woman as demure and submissive. (In general, by the way, we prefer the term "Asian" to "Oriental," in the same way "Black" is superior to "Negro." I use the term "Oriental" specifically to denote an exotic or imperialistic view of the East.)

I suspected there was a play here. I purposely refrained from further research, for I was not interested in writing docudrama. Frankly, I didn't want the "truth" to interfere with my own speculations. I told Stuart Ostrow, a producer with whom I'd worked before, that I envisioned the story as a musical. I remember going so far as to speculate that it could be some "great *Madame Butterfly*–like tragedy." Stuart was very intrigued, and encouraged me with some early funding.

Before I can begin writing, I must "break the back of the story," and find some angle which compels me to set pen to paper. I was driving down Santa Monica Boulevard one afternoon, and asked myself, "What did Bouriscot think he was getting in this Chinese actress?" The answer came to me clearly: "He probably thought he had found Madame Butterfly."

The idea of doing a deconstructivist *Madame Butterfly* immediately appealed to me. This, despite the fact that I didn't even know the plot of the opera! I knew Butterfly only as a cultural stereotype; speaking of an Asian woman, we would sometimes say, "She's pulling a Butterfly," which meant playing the submissive Oriental number. Yet, I felt convinced that the libretto would include yet another lotus blossom pining away for a cruel Caucasian man, and dying for her love. Such a story has become too much of a cliche not to be included in the archtypal East–West romance that started it all. Sure enough, when I purchased the record, I discovered it contained a wealth of sexist and racist cliches, reaffirming my faith in Western culture.

Very soon after, I came up with the basic "arc" of my play: the Frenchman fantasizes that he is Pinkerton and his lover is Butterfly. By the end of the piece, he realizes it is he who has been Butterfly, in that the Frenchman has been duped by love; the Chinese spy, who exploited that love, is therefore the real Pinkerton. I wrote a proposal to Stuart Ostrow, who found it very exciting. (On the night of the Tony Awards, Stuart produced my original two-page treatment, and we were gratified to see that it was, indeed, the play I eventually wrote.)

I wrote a play, rather than a musical, because, having "broken the back" of the story, I wanted to start immediately and not be hampered by the lengthy process of collaboration. I would like to think, however, that the play has retained many of its musical roots. So *Monsieur Butterfly* was completed in six weeks between September and mid-October, 1986. My wife, Ophelia, thought *Monsieur Butterfly* too obvious a title, and suggested I abbreviate it in the French fashion. Hence, *M. Butterfly*, far more mysterious and ambiguous, was the result.

I sent the play to Stuart Ostrow as a courtesy, assuming he would not be interested in producing what had become a straight play. Instead, he flew out to Los Angeles immediately for script conferences. Coming from a background in the not-for-profit theater, I suggested that we develop the work at a regional institution. Stuart, nothing if not bold, argued for bringing it directly to Broadway.

It was also Stuart who suggested John Dexter to direct. I had known Dexter's work only by its formidable reputation. Stuart sent the script to John, who called back the next day, saying it was the best play he'd read in twenty years. Naturally, this predisposed me to like him a great deal. We met in December in New York. Not long after, we persuaded Eiko Ishioka to design our sets and costumes. I had admired her work from afar ever since, as a college student, I had seen her poster for *Apocalypse Now* in Japan. By January, 1987, Stuart had optioned *M. Butterfly*, Dexter was signed to direct, and the normally sloth-like pace of commercial theater had been given a considerable prod.

On January 4, 1988, we commenced rehearsals. I was very pleased that John   10 Lithgow had agreed to play the French diplomat, whom I named Rene Gallimard. Throughout his tenure with us, Lithgow was every inch the center of our company, intelligent and professional, passionate and generous. B. D. Wong was forced to endure a five-month audition period before we selected him to play Song Liling. Watching B. D.'s growth was one of the joys of the rehearsal process, as he constantly attained higher levels of performance. It became clear that we had been fortunate enough to put together a company with not only great talent, but also wonderful camaraderie.

As for Dexter, I have never worked with a director more respectful of text and bold in the uses of theatricality. On the first day of rehearsal, the actors were given movement and speech drills. Then Dexter asked that everyone not required at rehearsal leave the room. A week later, we returned for an amazingly thorough run-through. It was not until that day that I first heard my play read, a note I direct at many regional theaters who "develop" a script to death.

We opened in Washington, D.C., at the National Theatre, where *West Side Story* and *Amadeus* had premiered. On the morning after opening night, most of the reviews were glowing, except for *The Washington Post*. Throughout our run in Washington, Stuart never pressured us to make the play more "commercial" in reaction to that review. We all simply concluded that the gentleman was possibly insecure about his own sexual orientation and therefore found the play threatening. And we continued our work.

Once we opened in New York, the play found a life of its own. I suppose the most gratifying thing for me is that we had never compromised to be more "Broadway"; we simply did the work we thought best. That our endeavor should be rewarded to the degree it has is one of those all-too-rare instances when one's own perception and that of the world are in agreement.

Many people have subsequently asked me about the "ideas" behind the play. From our first preview in Washington, I have been pleased that people leaving the theater were talking not only about the sexual, but also the political, issues raised by the work.

From my point of view, the "impossible" story of a Frenchman duped by a   15
Chinese man masquerading as a woman always seemed perfectly explicable; given the degree of misunderstanding—between men and women and also between East and West—it seemed inevitable that a mistake of this magnitude would one day take place.

Gay friends have told me of a derogatory term used in their community: "Rice Queen"—a gay Caucasian man primarily attracted to Asians. In these relationships, the Asian virtually always plays the role of the "woman"; the Rice Queen, culturally and sexually, is the "man." This pattern of relationships had become so codified that, until recently, it was considered unnatural for gay Asians to date one another. Such men would be taunted with a phrase which implied they were lesbians.

Similarly, heterosexual Asians have long been aware of "Yellow Fever"— Caucasian men with a fetish for exotic Oriental women. I have often heard it said that "Oriental women make the best wives." (Rarely is this heard from the mouths of Asian men, incidentally.) This mythology is exploited by the Oriental mail-order bride trade which has flourished over the past decade. American men can now send away for catalogues of "obedient, domesticated" Asian women looking for husbands. Anyone who believes such stereotypes are a thing of the past need look no further than Manhattan cable television, which advertises call girls from "the exotic east, where men are king; obedient girls, trained in the art of pleasure."

In these appeals, we see issues of racism and sexism intersect. The catalogues and TV spots appeal to a strain in men which desires to reject Western women for what they have become—independent, assertive, self-possessed—in favor of a more reactionary model—the pre-feminist, domesticated geisha girl.

That the Oriental woman is penultimately feminine does not of course imply that she is always "good." For every Madonna there is a whore; for every lotus blossom there is also a dragon lady. In popular culture, "good" Asian women are those who serve the White protagonist in his battle against her own people, often sleeping with him in the process. Stallone's *Rambo II*, Cimino's *Year of the Dragon*, Clavell's *Shogun*, Van Lustbader's *The Ninja* are all familiar examples.

Now our considerations of race and sex intersect the issue of imperialism.   20
For this formula—good natives serve Whites, bad natives rebel—is consistent with the mentality of colonialism. Because they are submissive and obedient, good natives of both sexes necessarily take on "feminine" characteristics in a colonialist world. Gunga Din's unfailing devotion to his British master, for instance, is not so far removed from Butterfly's slavish faith in Pinkerton.

It is reasonable to assume that influences and attitudes so pervasively displayed in popular culture might also influence our policymakers as they consider the world. The neo-Colonialist notion that good elements of a native society, like a good woman, desire submission to the masculine West speaks precisely to the heart of our foreign policy blunders in Asia and elsewhere.

For instance, Frances Fitzgerald wrote in *Fire in the Lake*, "The idea that the United States could not master the problems of a country as small and underdeveloped as Vietnam did not occur to Johnson as a possibility." Here, as in so many other cases, by dehumanizing the enemy, we dehumanize ourselves. We become the Rice Queens of *realpolitik*.

M. Butterfly has sometimes been regarded as an anti-American play, a diatribe against the stereotyping of the East by the West, of women by men. Quite to the contrary, I consider it a plea to all sides to cut through our respective layers of cultural and sexual misperception, to deal with one another truthfully for our mutual good, from the common and equal ground we share as human beings. For the myths of the East, the myths of the West, the myths of men, and the myths of women—these have so saturated our consciousness that truthful contact between nations and lovers can only be the result of heroic effort. Those who prefer to bypass the work involved will remain in a world of surfaces, misperceptions running rampant. This is, to me, the convenient world in which the French diplomat and the Chinese spy lived. This is why, after twenty years, he had learned nothing at all about his lover, not even the truth of his sex.

● Building the Frame Through Writing

1. Giacomo Puccini's opera *Madame Butterfly* tells the story of the British naval officer Pinkerton's cruel exploitation of a young Japanese woman. He makes empty promises, then leaves her pregnant and alone and marries a U.S. woman. Butterfly loves and believes in him completely, but, once she realizes his betrayal, kills herself. In the historical account of French diplomat Bernard Bouriscot, Hwang argues that "the diplomat must have fallen in love, not with a person, but with a fantasy stereotype." How can you explain both the fictional and historical scenarios as Orientalist discourse, as Edward W. Said (p. 353) might read it?

2. In Hwang's play, one of the central characters (Song Liling, the Chinese "woman"), states that the "West has sort of an international rape mentality towards the East. . . . Her mouth says no, but her eyes say yes. The West believes the East, deep down, *wants* to be dominated—because a woman can't think for herself." Use these lines to develop your own articulation of Hwang's postcolonial critique, as you see it. Do you find that they reflect Aimé Césaire's (p. 374) view of colonial discourse as well?

3. Hwang describes his play as disrupting conventional notions of gender and sexuality. What do you see the "grand narrative" of each is in dominant culture? Do you agree that "racism and sexism intersect," as Hwang claims?

4. In popular entertainment forms (films, television shows, plays, comics, etc.), do you believe that we continue to see the definition of the "good" native as one who serves caucasian/Western interests? Hwang cites several films that feature this cultural script; consider recent examples of this "mentality of colonialism," as Hwang calls it.

Writing from a Postcolonial Frame

a sample drafting process

Even though we've visited and revisited the film *Jurassic Park* in previous parts of this textbook, framing it in a postcolonial perspective opens up whole new ways of seeing the film, because it allows us to watch it not from the center but from the margins, from the perspective of those who are tangential and silenced—and, not surprisingly, among the first eaten.

Think of the central theoretical and rhetorical issues that postcolonial critique offers us. These include the representation of the "other" by the dominant group, and the discourse used to construct the other and maintain unequal power relations. (Who is speaking in this text, and who does this speaker claim/presume to speak *for*? How does the speaker make claims for the universal truth and rightness of his or her statements and views? How does the text serve hegemonic interests—the preservation and furthering of the good of the dominant group?) Silencing and erasure are means of this discursive and material oppression, so we should look at the extent to which the "other" speaks or is spoken for/of. (Whose voice is central, and whose is marginalized or silenced altogether?) The effects on the identity of the colonized and the means of resistance available to them are also central issues. (Who is represented as different, the "other," and how is this other described, totalized, and essentialized?)

Writing about the film from a postcolonial perspective opens up possibilities for the writer to explore ways of creating hybrid, multivoiced responses, using mimicry and developing counter discourses (the creation of an alternative discourse, a critique of a dominant text's rhetorical practices and a retelling, a re-presentation, of the text's events and ideas). "Talking back" to the film is another possible frame for invention and composing; how might the "others" of the film retell the story of Jurassic Park? Such resistance might come in the form, as we suggested earlier, of a use of a variety of discourses (formal academic writing, "street" or "vulgar" language, a "personal" voice) and languages (use of non-English phrases, rhetorical patterns, and values) and mixing of forms (argument, reflection, journal entry, direct address, fiction/nonfiction, etc.). Or an author can speak from "within," from the center, in a self-critically analytic way; as we saw in a psychoanalytic approach, the film does play out major wish fulfillment fantasies, and these can be read in political terms using a postcolonial lens. Let's take on *Jurassic Park* with these issues as possible guides to invention and response. We'll focus here on the opening scenes as material for our critical lens.

Like most films, *Jurassic Park* has an "attention-catching" dramatic opening: we see a scene of some unexplained commotion set amid vegetation and darkness. (Actually, if you watch the tape/DVD from the very beginning, what you see first is the name and logo of the company that sponsored its production: "Universal Pictures," represented by a turning globe. That's an interesting preface, one that could bear some postcolonial analysis itself.) Amid the vegetation we see the face of a man, dark-skinned and wearing a uniform; he is silent, looking at a scene we cannot see. Then a face appears, possibly Latino; this man, too, is uniformed, silent, watching. Then we see a white man: he is holding a gun and giving verbal orders to the others. He is dressed differently—he is wearing what's known as "safari" clothing, the khaki outfit of big game hunters, the "bwana," the boss, in colonial Africa. His orders, uttered in English, are repeated by the workers under him, and we hear Spanish phrases as the action intensifies. The gun-toting white man is overseeing the other men; at this point, we don't yet know the gun is not for control of the workers. As the workers struggle to move some high-tech equipment, we hear what we will soon realize is a wild animal within a high-tech cage. Another apparently Latino worker is knocked off the cage, falls to the ground, and is then seized by the still-unseen animal, who begins dragging him into the enclosure. The white overseer acts immediately and attempts to pull the man free. We see a large reptilian eye and the white overseer's eye; the man yells, "Shoot her! Shoot her!" Shots ring out, and the scene fades.

At the start of this scene, lines appear that identify the setting: "Isla Nublar, 120 miles west of Costa Rica." From the start, we're placed into the third-world context of Central America. The first people we see are men of color in the relation of subordinate to a superior white "boss." The film invites us to participate in a familiar script of Western male power directing a group of non-caucasian/Europeans in a location outside Europe or the United States, with the white/Western enterprise the center of attention, importance, and power. The workers are incidental to this main line of interest. They are units of labor, not individuals; they don't speak except to repeat orders; they move under the gaze and direction of the white overseer. He is not only their boss but their benevolent protector. Their labor is necessary to what we will later learn is the European John Hammond's commercial project; they are not stakeholders in the project nor landholders on the island, despite its location in their apparently native land.

The entrepreneurial plan for Jurassic Park entails the colonizing of an island that John Hammond has bought, and his capital gives him the power to define it as he wishes. It is represented to us as remote, uninhabited, and available for use. It appears to be inaccessible except through advanced means of transportation—helicopters and power boats. Again we see the colonialist script: nature exists for (certain) men to exploit; development is progress; the social order that allows such progress should be reproduced. And so we get the unequal power relations of caucasian bosses and darker-skinned laborers serving the bosses' interests, even at the cost of their lives and land. The scene introduces some key binary oppositions that help organize the story: nature versus technology; savagery versus civilization; animal versus human. Technology, civilization, and humanity are all coded as Western and white.

We see the colonialist features of this scene repeated in the next two, where a caucasian authority figure—the lawyer—is placed in relation to a non-Western, non-caucasian location and group of people. The lawyer stands on a raft being pulled across a river by some "natives"; a subtitle appears announcing the setting as the Dominican Republic. A Latino man speaks to the workers in Spanish, then switches to English to greet the lawyer. He addresses the lawyer's many questions and demands, but he speaks and moves easily, while the lawyer is clearly awkward and out of place. The Latino man seems to be in charge; the workers do not speak except to report to him. Where does his power come from? We soon learn that he is overseeing a dig, and later we'll understand that his job is to find dinosaur DNA in fossilized mosquitoes. He works for John Hammond, and his authority derives from this connection. He is the lawyer's equal, perhaps superior (since the lawyer is frequently made to look ridiculous, in one way by wearing a business suit that consists of shirt, tie, jacket—and shorts), but his power is that of the colonial chief he serves. He willingly exploits resources and workers from his own culture to further the colonial effort. In this scene, too, the land appears to be unoccupied and unused except as the site of excavation for Hammond's needs, which reflects a common colonialist representation of desired land as empty waste. (And the next scene is set, we're told, in the "Badlands" of "Snakewater, Montana"—empty, high desert bearing no material trace of Native American culture.)

Two other scenes form the exposition portion of the film's opening part. One takes place, we're told by subtitle, in "San Jose, Costa Rica," and involves a meeting between a representative of a corporate rival of John Hammond's and Hammond's own computer expert, who, we learn, is disgruntled over his contract. Both are Western, caucasian men. The scene is filled with folk music, Spanish songs, shots of a fruit stall, some chickens clucking, a woman in "native costume"—all Orientalizing images of the exotic, the sensual, the primitive. When Dennis, the computer expert, calls out "Dodson!" to his coconspirator, Dodson objects; Dennis yells out his name and points to the man, then says, "See? No one cares." The natives are, for all intents and purposes, powerless, passive beings, easily dismissed. The men's business is central, and native life is simply a tropical backdrop to it.

We've gone through just a few of the opening scenes and already the colonialist script is fairly clear. We can now think about some means of critiquing and/or "speaking back" to the film's representation of first world–third world relations. Rhetorically, we want to avoid reinscribing colonialist values by speaking for/about the third-world people and places the film depicts. Using these points as means of invention, consider some possible topics.

- analysis of the colonial script/discourse
- the inherent paternalism of colonialism
- "flipping" the script to show the entrepreneurial team as the carnivores, the ones guilty of indiscriminate consumption

The first topic can be refined to focus on issues of silencing; construction and marginalization of the "other"; feminizing of the "other"; or other specific colonialist practices that you've read about in this chapter in Said, Bertens, Césaire, and Hwang. The second topic is a straightforward analysis of how the colonial figures create a sense of their own justified, "natural" authority as father figures taking up what's been called the "white man's burden."

Writing on this last topic, an author can draw on shared cultural notions of the traditional role of the father/husband, picking out its familiar elements of authority figure, protector, teacher/moral guide, provider, creating a subaltern role for the female (or feminized body). In outline form, the essay's argument and logical progression might look like the following:

The Feminized Role of Third-World Workers in *Jurassic Park*

Argument: The film reproduces a familiar, gendered relationship between Western male authority and third-world people. The first world serves as the masculine, dominant leader—the role of the traditional father/husband. The role of feminine dependent is played by third-world people, who serve the father/husband's interests, follow his directions, and use their bodies for reproducing his interests and power. The film's representation of first- and third-world relations reinforces the colonialist script of Western masters and non-Western subordinates, a system portrayed as natural and mutually beneficial.

- summary of opening scenes showing third-world workers
- analysis of their roles in contrast to "master" role
  - support from example plus theoretical readings
  - Hwang on feminized non-Western male
  - Said/Bertens on Orientalism
- workers as wives in the film
  - doing the labor for Hammond's enterprise
  - serving the gamekeeper, lawyer, and technician
  - feeding the dinosaurs, Hammond's "babies" (we see Hammond in a later scene assisting at a dinosaur's birth and playing a fatherly role to them)

- disappearance of workers in the main action, outside the "domestic" sphere
- conclusion: the film reproduces the colonizer/colonized positions of dominant-subaltern and makes of third-world workers a passive group in need of direction and useful in supporting positions only; their subordinate positions create the need for and justify the role of the strong father/husband.

The third topic, "flipping" the script to show the entrepreneurial team as colonialist carnivores, would let you explore the film from a subaltern perspective. How might John Hammond's theme park venture appear? You could explain how it might appear uninhabited to him, because his Western notion of civilization might demand cities, modern industry, and other Western markers of settlement. These can be contrasted with less industrialized uses of land and different attitudes toward it, including ecological balance and communal property ownership. What about the purpose to which he intends to put the land? How might a dinosaur park be seen? It renders the island mainly uninhabitable for a native population, allies the island with prehistoric beings, and creates a service industry only—no natives will be owners or bosses on it. It will be a tourist site, further marginalizing any native culture, using it only as exotic decoration. Ultimately, Hammond's plan runs amuck, and dinosaurs take over the island, effectively destroying it as a human habitat. Hammond has thus devoured the land and, once consumed, it cannot be replenished.

Reading "Jurassic Park" or any text from a postcolonial frame requires that you reread from this perspective of all parties, not just the dominant voice of the text. Writing from this frame requires that you question assumptions about "normal," "right," "authoritative" voices—including your own.

topics for writing

1. The entry under "Aimé Césaire" in an early version of Encarta, Microsoft's compact-disk encyclopedia, reads in part this way:

   Césaire, Aimé (1913–), French West Indian poet and political leader, born in Basse-Pointe, Martinique, and educated at the Sorbonne and the École Normale Supérieur, Paris. Césaire was discovered by the surrealist poet and critic André Breton, who wrote the preface to the 1942 edition of *Return to My Native Land* (1939; trans. 1968), in which Césaire explores what he calls *negritude*, black culture as a valid and independent entity. His verse, although influenced by surrealism, remains impassioned and clear.

   Read the biography through a postcolonial lens and analyze the colonialist discourse evident in it.

   - How do you see Césaire being constructed in relation to European culture?
   - Do you find the use of the term *discovered* problematic?

- How is Breton introduced compared to Césaire? Are they presented as cultural equals, as you read the line?
- What do you notice about dates of composition and translation?
- Césaire's "verse" is called "impassioned and clear"; what qualities do you think are being assigned to it?
- What binary oppositions are created—what, for example, is black culture "independent" of, as this discourse composes the concept?

Depending on your own background, you might consider presenting the analysis/critique from Césaire's likely perspective (and here the critical challenge becomes one of not presuming to speak *of* and *for* him in ways that reproduce the colonialist mentality). Or you can speak from the perspective of a postcolonial Western critic who seeks to explain the problematic elements of the biography to other Westerners. Or you might experiment with alternative discourse and speak back to the entry, using mimicry, multiple voices, and/or a variety of discourses to critique, rework, and complexify the entry. Quoting Césaire himself would be one way to represent and include one potentially very powerful voice.

2. Map out the Orientalist discourse that typically is employed for some "exotic" locale familiar to many of us in the United States—and including parts such as Hawaii, Alaska, Hopi or Navajo areas, or various Chinatowns. Because such discourses construct *ideas* about a culture, you can also consider topics such as the frontier, the old West, the antebellum South/plantation life.

   - How do you see the discourse working to create a totalizing picture of a place and/or culture that is "other," available for "our" use, subordinate, perhaps desirous of "conquering," and the other discursive moves that colonialism encourages?
   - Do you see any means of silencing or erasing the "natives"?
   - Are we led to see the land made as open, empty, ripe for development?
   - Do you see the colonizing figures represented as powerful or heroic?

   First, consider organizing the essay to lay out a shared image for readers (one could use quotations from the opening of *Shane*, for example, in Chapter 5, to establish the discourse of the frontier), then organize the analysis by the main points Bertens covers in his essay. Hwang's critique might also be useful in establishing how the creation of an exotic "other" helps also create the illusion of a powerful master of it.

3. Gayatri Spivak's analysis (in Bertens's "Postcolonial Studies") of the subaltern suggests that academic writers have a role to play in helping to give voice to the traditionally silenced groups of women, especially third-world women. She identifies a serious rhetorical problem: how do we help give voice to them if we are speaking for them? One way might be to look at the ways in which our own discourses help create subaltern status.

- How do common cultural images and stereotypes help create and maintain subaltern status for women in the United States? Consider the mainstream images associated with females in various ethnic, racial, and/or cultural groups or in traditional roles. The cultural image of the schoolteacher, for example, is one potentially useful way to explore how the subaltern can and cannot speak with cultural power.

- You might look at the cultural stereotypes about schoolteachers; their relation to dominant discourse(s); their dominant numbers in elementary and secondary schools; their concentration in language arts and, at the college level, in the humanities, and especially in writing classes. What cultural functions are they associated with? How are they used for cultural reproduction?

Reading Critically About the "Other"

● Analyzing authorial
  perspectives from a
  postcolonial frame

● Analyzing "master" and
  "resistant" discourses

● Writing from rhetorically
  resistant perspectives

Walkabout in Woop Woop

PAUL THEROUX

*Paul Theroux is both a prolific novelist and a writer of popular nonfiction works on travel,
especially rail travel (*Riding the Iron Rooster *details his travel by train through China;*
The Great Railway Bazaar *his trip through India; and* The Old Patagonian Express *his
trip from his home in Boston to the southernmost tip of South America). He is also known for
a generally misanthropic stance. In* The Happy Isles of Oceania, *from which this chapter is
taken, he records his tour of Pacific island cultures, beginning with Australia. A native of
Massachusetts, Theroux was a Peace Corps volunteer in the African nation of Malawi. Clearly,
he is very familiar with many non-U.S., non-Western cultures. His chapter might be read as a
kind of test of the theory that cultural contact breeds tolerance.*

Ask white Australians what "walkabout" means and they will tell you it
is an Aboriginal's furious fugue, shambling off the job or out of the shelter of the
humpy, and heading into the outback. It is a sudden departure, a bout of madness almost—after which the Aboriginal chases his tail. But is that so?

Back in Sydney, I looked for an Aboriginal to ask. "Don't call them Abos,"
people cautioned me—not that I ever called them that—but privately they
muttered a dozen or more different names for them, of which "boong," "bing,"
and "murky" were just a few. Yet those Australians who were bigoted were
completely impartial: "A boong with boots on" was a Japanese and "a Yank
boong" was a black American.

Searching for Aborigines in Australia was a bit like bird-watching. Birds
are everywhere, but only real birders see them clearly. Without warning, bird
experts lean slightly forward, then stiffen and whisper, "Yellow vented
bulbul," and you see nothing but fluttering leaves. In a similar spirit, making
a point of it, developing a knack, I began to spot Aborigines. They were
so often camouflaged by gum trees or splotches of shadow. They were

frequently motionless, usually in the shade, often in city parks, nearly always under trees. There were many.

"So poor," as the saying went, "they were licking paint off the fence."

Perhaps they were visible to everyone, but if so, Australians never pointed   5
them out. I began to think that Aborigines were only visible to those people who were looking for them. I kept track of my sightings, like a birder.

Mark Twain was in Australia for more than a month in 1895 and regretted the fact that he never saw either a kangaroo or an Aboriginal.

"We saw birds, but not a kangaroo," Twain wrote, in one of the Australian chapters of his round-the-world tour, *Following the Equator*, "not an emu, not an ornithorhyncus [sic], not a lecturer, not a native. Indeed, the land seemed quite destitute of game. But I have misused the word native. In Australia it is applied to Australian-born whites only. I should have said that we saw no Aboriginals—no 'blackfellows.' And to this day I have never seen one."

"I would walk thirty miles to see a stuffed one," he sighs towards the end of his Australian tour.

It seemed to me that the people and the problem were unavoidable. There was a tidy Aboriginal settlement in La Perouse, at Botany Bay, near Sydney's airport. I walked through it one wet afternoon with a man from Sydney who had told me about it, and we looked at the hundred or so prefab houses—down Elaroo Avenue, up Adina, across to Goolagong Place. There were very few people outside and, seeing us, some Aborigines who were gathered around their motorcycles mounted the machines and roared away, scowling into the wind.

"They're strange people," Tony said. He was Italian—first-generation   10
Australian. He was small, the sort of man Australians describe as being so short he had to stand on his head to get his foot into a stirrup. He didn't hate Aborigines, he said, but he pitied them—and he didn't understand them. "They never fix anything. If they break something it stays broken. If they knock a tooth out they don't bother to replace it."

Certainly there was a dark fatalism about many of the Aborigines I met; sometimes it made them seem sad, at other times it made them seem indestructible.

"There's no trouble here," Tony said. "It's not like Redfern, where there are pitched battles with the police."

Many of the Aborigines in the Sydney district of Redfern were notoriously scruffy. "Rough as guts," said the white Australians—these could be last month's immigrant Turks, or last year's Sicilians, or the pompous people who snobbishly boasted about their convict ancestry—and they went on to generalize about Aborigines on the basis of these rather derelict urban specimens. The Aborigines aroused pity or disgust, they provoked feelings of violence or mockery. They were joked about, especially by schoolchildren.

Q: Why are the garbage bins in Redfern made of glass?

A: So that the Abos can window-shop.

Everyone had an opinion and no one had a solution.

I tried to reach Patrick White, Australia's greatest living writer, who was a   15
vocal advocate of Aboriginal rights. He had created a memorable portrait of an
Aboriginal, Alf Dubbo, in his novel *Riders in the Chariot*—Alf's walkabout, his
vast vivid paintings, his confusion, his culture shock, his drinking, his martyr-
dom. What about the word "walkabout" as a sudden departure, I wanted to ask
him; indeed, what about *Walkabout*, the classic film by Nicolas Roeg, which—
with Mr. White's novels—had been my only previous experience of Australia?
I was having trouble with the meaning of the word and wished to leave white
Australia for the distant outback that is summed up in the name Woop Woop.
I felt that Patrick White could help me. In his advancing and opinionated old
age he had been pronouncing on most subjects.

"I can't meet Paul Theroux. I am too ill to meet celebrities," the Nobel
prize winner said, from his home in a Sydney suburb.

He died two days later—speaking of sudden departures—and the Australian
obituarists went to work on him. Nothing made national traits more emphatic
than a victory in an international sport or the death of a prominent citizen. In
this case, the obituarists kicked Patrick White's corpse from Maggoty Gully to
Cootamundra. There was almost no evidence that any of these people had
actually read the man's novels. The vindictive philistines on Rupert Murdoch's
national paper *The Australian* put a portrait of Patrick White's old enemy,
A. D. Hope, on the front page instead of a picture of the man himself, and in any
number of other papers White was depicted as a meddlesome old poofter.*
Never mind his novels, what about the dreadful things he had said about
Australia? True, he had been characteristically crisp.

"After I returned to this country," Mr. White had written, "one of the most
familiar sounds was the heavy plop-plop of Australian bullshit."

In a public lecture he had called Bob Hawke, the prime minister, "one of
the greatest bull artists ever," and said he had a hairstyle like a cockatoo. He had
been cruel about the British Royal Family—"Queen Betty" and "The Royal
Goons." He had ridiculed Dame Joan Sutherland.

But on the day the Nobel laureate was cooling quietly in his coffin in   20
Centennial Park, La Stupenda was being draped with paper streamers, the sort
you fling at ships. They were strung out from all tiers of the Sydney Opera
House, and her vast preponderant bulk could have been mistaken for an ocean
liner as, after her final bow in Meyerbeer's religious farrago "The Huge Nuts"
(as I heard it jocosely called), she said she was proud to be an Australian, sang

---

*From the Sydney *Daily Telegraph Mirror*, 21 Feb., 1991: "A magistrate has outraged police by ruling that it
is acceptable to describe them as 'f——— poofters.' . . . On Tuesday, magistrate Pat O'Shane dismissed
a charge of offensive language against Geoffrey Allan Langham, 43. Sitting at Lismore on the State's north
coast, Ms. O'Shane said the words 'f——— poofters' were not as upsetting as the term 'collateral damage,'
used by military officials to describe human casualties. In the past three months, the NSW magistrates
have ruled it acceptable to call police 'pigs' and to use the word 'shit' in public."

"There's No Place Like Home," announced that she would never sing again, and flew back to her mansion in Switzerland. It was all walkabouts that week.

Reminding myself of the details in the movie, I used Nicolas Roeg's *Walkabout* to guide me around the city, and beyond it to the outback, because that is precisely the direction of the movie's plot.

No one I met in Australia or elsewhere who had seen *Walkabout* had forgotten the film's power or denied that they had been enchanted by it. After being released in 1969, it soon vanished, and had never been rereleased. It was not available on video anywhere in the world. It was never shown on television. It languished, the victim of Hollywood infighting, in some obscure and spiteful limbo of litigation.

Yet it still existed as a notable conversation piece in the "Did-you-ever-see?" oral tradition among movie buffs, and it endures that way, because it has a simple tellable story. Those who have seen *Walkabout* always speak of their favorite scenes—the opening, a salt-white tower block in Sydney with its swimming pool smack against the harbor; the frenzied picnic in the outback where the father tries and fails to kill his two children; the father's sudden suicide against a burning VW; the desperate kids faced with an immensity of desert; the girl (Jenny Agutter, age sixteen) peeling off her school uniform; the shot of an ant made gigantic in front of tiny distant kids—and every other creature in the outback crossing their path—snakes, lizards, birds, beetles, kangaroos, koalas, camels; the discovery of water under the quondong tree, after which the ordeal turns into a procession into paradise, as they all swim naked together in the pools of sunlit oases; the close call with the rural ockers; the wrecked house and its curios; the lovestruck Aboriginal's dance, ending in his suicide; the madman in the dainty apron in the ghost town howling at the children, "Don't touch that!"—and no rescue, no concrete ending, only a return to the tower block (it seems to be years later) on a note of regret.

And that is the film, really, almost all except the spell it cast on me. In a seemingly modest way it encompassed the whole of Australia, nearly all its variations of landscape, its incomparable light, its drunks and desperadoes, all its bugs—from its most beautiful city to its hot red center. A work of art, and especially a film or a novel, with a strong sense of place is a summing up, fixing a landscape once and for all in the imagination.

The director was an adventurer who relished the difficulties and improvisa-   25
tions of filmmaking on location. His was a triumph over mud, dust, rain, heat, impassable roads, and deserters from the crew.

"A few went apeshit in the night and started smashing things," he had told me. "They couldn't take the isolation. One of the toughest sparks [electricians] deserted. The grip freaked out. The cook went crazy one night, and crept off and sat on a chair near the airstrip. This was in the outback. He flew off without speaking. It was his fear of all that empty space."

The movie seemed to me to contain the essential Australia, even its bizarre and rowdy humor—most notably in the scene in an abandoned mining town, miles from anywhere, where a loony man, hanging on, stands in a ruined build-ing wearing an apron and ironing a pair of pants.

"It doesn't have Ayers Rock in it," Roeg said. "Everyone expected that it would. I was determined to make a film in the Australian outback that didn't show Ayers Rock. But it has everything else."

And it was the first feature film in which an Aboriginal played a starring role. David Gulpilil had had no training as an actor—had probably never seen a film in his life. He had been about fifteen years old, a dancer on his Aboriginal reserve somewhere in the north, in Arnhem Land.

I wanted to look at Aboriginal Australia. Going on the trail of *Walkabout*, in   30 Woop Woop—the remote outback—meant going walkabout in the Aboriginal sense of the word—setting off in search of old visions and sacred sites.

The Botanic Gardens in Sydney were easy enough to find, and it is possible to sit under the spreading tree where the little boy hurries towards Wool-loomooloo Bay after school in one of the early sequences. But his home on the harbor, the tower block with the swimming pool, was harder for me to locate. I knew it lay next to the water, and there is a glimpse of Sydney Harbour Bridge in the distance, but there are no other landmarks.

Thinking the tower block might be at the far edge of the harbor, I took the Manly Ferry and on the way scrutinized the shoreline: south side going out, north side on the return. Any visitor to Sydney would be well advised to take the Manly Ferry soon after arriving in the city, just to get the lie of the land. It is a long inexpensive ferry ride that takes in the entire length of the harbor, from Sydney's Circular Quay to distant Manly—an Edwardian township by the sea, with tea shops and palm trees, its back turned to the harbor, and facing the breakers of a beautiful bay.

Manly's smug and tidy little houses have names like "Camelot" and "Woodside." The town was named by an early settler who regarded the local Aborigines as fine specimens of manhood. But no Aborigines are found there today. Manlyness in the municipal sense is the epitome of the Australian good life: a snug bungalow of warm bricks by the sea, with a privet hedge and a palm.

Here and there on Manly beach were delicate dying jellyfish, small and blue, and so thin, so bright, so finely shaped, fluttering on the sand, they reminded me of little hanks of Chinese silk. Beyond them, some boys were surfing the waves, which was appropriate, because the first surfing—body surf-ing—was first done here at Manly around 1890 by an islander from the New Hebrides. (It was not until 1915 that surfboards were introduced to Australia, when the technique was demonstrated by the great Hawaiian surfer and Olympic swimmer Duke Kahanamoku.)

Manlyites who commuted from here to their jobs in the city had the best of   35 both worlds, but the despairing father in *Walkabout* was obviously not one of them. I walked from one end of Manly to the other and could not locate the white tower block. Nor was it apparent on any of the bays on the harbor.

"You're looking for a needle in a haystack," a woman on a bench said to me one day as I searched nearer the city, among the bobbing sailboats.

And she explained. In the twenty years since the film was made, Sydney had become extremely prosperous—there were plenty of stylish tower blocks now, there were lots of swimming pools by the sea. It might have been torn down, she said. That is another aspect of a movie with a strong sense of place: It is an era in history, it is the past.

I was told by Grahame Jennings, a Sydney movie producer who had helped *Walkabout* get made, that the tower block was out by Yarmouth Point, past Rushcutter's Bay.

My taxi driver was Cambodian, six years in Australia, where he had arrived as a political refugee ("I would have gone anywhere except China"), but less than a year behind the wheel. He had struggled to pass his driving test. And his knowledge of Sydney's streets was shaky. He agreed that he was somewhat handicapped as a cabbie. Australian passengers often berated him.

"They say, 'You fucking stupid.' But I smile at them. I don't care. This is a   40
nice country."

I roamed the harborside back streets, I detoured up Yarranabee Road and saw a familiar tower block—the one from the movie, with improvements; and beneath it, at the water's edge, the greeny-blue swimming pool. I congratulated myself on this little piece of detection, but I was also thinking how lucky all these people were who lived around Sydney Harbour. Because of the jigs and jags of its contours it is one of the most extensive pieces of real estate in the world.

The taxi driver who plucked me from Rushcutter's Bay was an economic refugee from Pakistan. We talked about Islam, about the similar stories in the Old Testament and the Koran—Joseph (Yusof), Jonah (Yunis).

"This is the first time I have ever spoken of religion with one of my passengers," he said—he was pleased.

But this was merely ice-breaking on my part. I came to the point. Had he heard of Salman Rushdie?

In his monotonously singsong Pakistani accent, he said, "Salman Rushdie   45
must be punished with death."

"I don't agree with you," I said. I leaned forward, nearer his hairy ears. "And no one in this nice law-abiding country agrees with you."

"Rushdie is a bad man—devil, I should say."

"—And you know why people in Australia don't agree with you?" He was still muttering, but what I said next shut him up. "Because they're not fanatics."

The man's bony hands tightened on the steering wheel, and when I got out of his taxi he gave me the evil eye.

"*Walkabout* was quietly released," Grahame Jennings told me. "I collected the   50
reviews. Of the thirty-odd I saw from around the world, four were negative. Three of those negative reviews were written by Australian critics."

"Why Australians?" I asked.

"Tall poppy syndrome."

Anyone who spends even a little time in the country hears this odd phrase, which means simply that people who succeed in Australia—or who distinguish themselves in any way—can expect to be savagely attacked by envious fellow Australians. It is also used as a verb: To be "tall-poppied" means to be cut down to size. That was the reason that Patrick White, in spite of his Nobel prize—or perhaps because of it—was spoken of as an insignificant and nagging old gussie. This merciless national trait is regarded as the chief reason for gifted Australians emigrating to countries where they are—or so they say—properly appreciated.

"'What right does this foreigner have to come and make a film about Australia?' was one criticism."

"That's ridiculous."

" 'Too many contradictions about the geography in the film,' was another. 'You can't get to the outback by driving from Sydney—' "

But you can. You might be the desperate alcoholic father leaving Yarran-abee Road with his kids, intending to shoot them, or you might be a visitor to Syndey with a rental car, yearning for the open spaces. In either case, you head up George Street and keep driving, first following signs for Parramatta. In this sprawl of sunburned bungalows, each one with its own lizards and its own dead hedges and its own peculiar-smelling lantana (but this bush usually smelled of cats); the discount stores and bad hotels and bottle shops and used car lots with tacky flapping banners, through Emu Plains and Blacktown—almost until the road rises into the first wooded slopes of the Blue Mountains, you begin to understand the disgusted snarl with which people in Sydney always utter the phrase *the Western Suburbs*.

Ascending the escarpment that winds towards Kattoomba, I was in a different landscape—mountainous, cool, green, with ravines and canyons, the gum trees having given over to pines. After these heights, it is a long slow descent to Lithgow, and not many miles farther on I felt I was truly in sunset country. Here, near Wallerawang on the Great Western Highway, less than two hours from Sydney, the proof of it: a big brown kangaroo, lying dead by the side of the road.

Dubbo, where Alf the Aboriginal in *Riders in the Chariot* could have come from, is two or three hours more, and Bourke four or five. But out there in the west of New South Wales—Bourke in one direction, Wilcannia in the other—you will have achieved your simple goal of driving from Sydney to the outback in a long day.

"Back o' Bourke" is an Australian expression for any out-the-way place, and there are dozens more—perhaps more euphemisms in Australia for remoteness (outback, wayback, back o' sunset, behind death o'day, Woop Woop, and so forth) than in any other language; but this is obviously because there is more remoteness in Australia than in most other countries—more empty space. These words are like little lonely cries of being lost, speaking of a solitude that is like exile on this huge island.

Somewhere before Dubbo I was distracted by bewitching names on the map and found myself detouring to places like Wattle Flat or Oberon or Budgee

Budgee (turn right at Mudgee), just to look at the small round hills, the frisky sheep, and the gum trees. It is hard to imagine anywhere on earth so pretty and peaceful as these hamlets in Australia's hinterland, green and cool in springtime September.

I was halfway to Woop Woop. I continued the rest of the way, to Alice Springs in the dead red center of the island of Australia, leaving my collapsible kayak behind in Sydney with my butler, who still believed the two big bags contained clothes.

I have usually yawned at travelers who describe landscapes from the window of the plane passing overhead, but the Australian landscape is well suited to such treatment, the bird's-eye view.

After the hills and square patches and pockets of farmland just west of Sydney, the greeny-yellow crops vanish, the rivers and lakes turn white and great gray ribbons appear and fade like enormous drips and spills of a red that they seem like bloodstains a hundred miles long. This is the beginning of the Simpson Desert, and there is so much of it that it takes hours to cross it flying in a jet at 500 miles an hour, and even at that you are only halfway over the country. With every passing minute the colors change from gray to mauve to pink and to a bleached bone-white that is chalky enough to pass for the Chinese color of death. No road, no water, no life, not even names on the map. I remembered Bruce Chatwin in 1983 stabbing his finger excitedly onto a map of the outback, thrilled by its emptiness, and saying to me, "Nothing there! Nothing there! Nothing there! I want to go there!"

(Later that year, Chatwin sent me a postcard from the outback: *All going well down under. . . . Have become interested in a very extreme situation—of Spanish monks in an Aboriginal mission, and am about to start sketching an outline. Anyway the crisis of "shall-never-write-another-line" sort is now over. As always, Bruce.*) 65

The Australian surface is stubbly, the gravelly texture a wilderness of boulders and wind. Then there is the so-called Dingo Fence, or Vermin Proof Fence, put up by the Wild Dog Destruction Board to keep the dingos out. This structure is such a serious effort it is longer (they say) than the Great Wall of China, and much more secure, and more clearly visible from the moon.

Farther on, below the flight path the land is scooped out and whitened. It is drizzling with sand—vast streaks of it. It becomes a rucked-up and striped horse blanket, a thousand square miles of wool. And soon after there are ridges of red hills and black patches of trees and the gouges of dry creeks, literally billabongs (dead creeks).

And it occurs to me that this is not like another planet but like the bottom of the sea after an ocean has drained away. It is Oceania after someone has pulled the plug. And sure enough a few days later I was hiking in the cliffs of those same mountains, in the Macdonnell Ranges, and found small broken fossils in the red rock—"nautiloids," the distant cousins of squid deposited here when this was an inland sea.

Alice Springs is here in the middle of these red ranges, a jumbled little one-story town, which is a railhead and a road junction and the confluence of three rivers—billabongs once again, because there is not a drop of water in them, only hot sand and tilted gum trees and Aborigines squatting in family groups in the splotches of shade. The Todd River is the widest, and the driest. Like many Australian rivers—few of them contained water—it looked like a bad road, but wider than others I had seen. It is said that if you've seen the Todd River flow three times you can consider yourself a local.

I walked around town, noting the meeting places of Aborigines and gener-   70
ally chatting.

"I'm not a racist—I just hate Abos."

This neat and commonly uttered absurdity was put to me by a woman on my first day in Alice Springs. When I said that I had come to the town to meet some Aborigines she began seething. It is probably worth putting down what she said, because so many people I met said the same things and only the tone of voice varied—ranging from sorrowful to apoplectic. Hers was outraged.

"They drink—they're always drunk and hanging around town. They're slobs, they're stupid. Their clothes are in rags—and they have money too! They're always fighting, and sometimes they're really dangerous."

I always smiled ruefully at this rant, because it was a true description of so many white Australians I had seen. I could never keep a straight face when I heard one of these leathery diggers turn sententious over the drinking habits of Aborigines, for whom they themselves were the alcoholic role models.

"There was a blackfella, worked for Kerry's father as a stockman outside   75
Adelaide. He went walkabout. He comes back after aideen months and says, 'Where's my job?'"

The speaker, Trevor Something, was barefoot, twisting his greasy hat, a tattooed and ranting ringer, snatching at his three boisterous kids, and snarling at Kerry. He had stubbie of Castlemaine Four X in his fist.

I wanted to laugh, because he was another one, a white Australian imputing slovenly habits to Aborigines and then behaving in precisely the same way, except the white Australian always did it wearing a hat—a Sewell's Sweat-Free Felt for preference, and in certain seasons in a brown, ankle-length Driazabone raincoat.

"We're not racists anymore," Trevor said. "They're the racists!"

It was true that Trevor was a ringer, an ocker—a redneck—but I had heard the same twanging sentiments more prettily phrased from the mouths of accomplished and well-educated people in Sydney and Melbourne, and a well-bred woman from Perth had said to me, "All Abos are liars."

When I encouraged Trevor to reminisce, he said, "We used to come up here   80
to Alice Springs and get into fights with the blackfellas. Mind you, there are some first-class blackfellas. Some of the nicest blokes you'd ever want to meet."

"They've got some funny ideas, though," his wife Kerry said. "We just come up from Ayers Rock. Blackfella we met said he wouldn't set foot on it. It would be like climbing over a pregnant woman's belly. He says to me, 'That rock is the pregnancy of the earth—swelling up, see.' Yairs, but there were plenty of drunken blackfellas all around Ayers Rock, and they didn't look too bothered."

"Maybe they had gone walkabout?" I asked.

"Yeh. They disappear," Trevor said. "They go mental."

The notion was that the Aboriginal lost his grip and in a severely manic mood whirled out of sight, endlessly perambulating the outback.

The Aborigines I met denied this, and they were unanimous in agreeing on the meaning of "walkabout."

"It means walking," Roy Curtis said. Roy was an Aboriginal of the Walbiri people in Yuendumu, 400 dusty kilometers to the northwest.

It is in that simple sense of walking that the word is used in, for example, Psalm 23 in Aboriginal Pidgin: "*Big Name makum camp alonga grass takum blackfella walkabout longa, no frightem no more hurry watta.*" ("He maketh me to lie down in green pastures: he leadeth me beside the still waters.")

Big soft potbelly, skinny legs, long eyelashes, whispering Roy Curtis was a part-time painter of dot pictures, waiting under gum trees in Alice Springs for compensation from the idiot who cracked up his car.

"It means going home," he said, and sounded as though he yearned to do that very thing.

"The word has a specific meaning," Darryl Pearce, director of the Institute of Aboriginal Development, told me. "It is when a person leaves to go to the outback on ceremonial business or family business, to visit sacred sites, to be with people of his own nation."

I had left my car and walked across a wide dry riverbed in Alice Springs to reach Darryl's office. This river, a tributary of the Todd, was crammed with cast-off beer cans and wine jugs from Aboriginal drinkers, and here and there against its banks, under the gum trees, were little abandoned camps, tattered blankets, and a litter of torn paper.

Two Aborigines were sitting impassively under a gum tree like people cast in bronze, a man and woman holding hands. I talked to the man, who was named Eric, about a scheme to dam one of the rivers. It was one of the explosive Aboriginal issues in Alice Springs at the moment; if the scheme went ahead it would mean an Aboriginal sacred site would be underwater.

"How would you like it if Westminster Abbey were destroyed?" some people argued, fumbling about for an analogy.

They were often greeted with a reply something like, "That site's about as sacred as a fly's arse."

There were sacred sites all over town. One was a fenced-off rock protruding, like a small fallen asteroid, from a parking lot of a pub that had borrowed its name: The Dog Rock Inn.

What was more important—I asked these two people sitting on the bank of the dry river—saving the town from flooding, or preserving the sacred site?

Eric said, "Preserving the site, I reckon."

Then I walked on to the Institute and heard a fierce version of this view from Darryl.

As for the word "walkabout," Darryl said he understood the concept well, because he himself was an Aboriginal. He could have fooled me. He was pasty-faced, freckled, somewhat stocky, with brownish hair cut short. I would have guessed Irish. He looked like any number of the drinkers and shopkeepers and taxi drivers who denounced Aborigines as boongs and layabouts.

"The expression 'part-Aboriginal' is bullshit," Darryl said. "Either you are   100
an Aboriginal or you aren't. It's not a question of color but of identity. We are all colors."

His mother had been a full-blooded Aboriginal, one parent a Mudbara from the Barkly Tablelands, the other an Aranda from near Alice Springs.

"People ask us why we're angry," he said.

I had not asked him that. Angry was not a word I associated with any Aborigines I had met, who had seemed to me more waif-like and bewildered.

"We've been in Australia for forty thousand years, and what good has that done us? Before 1960 it was illegal for a white Australian to marry an Aboriginal. We had no status. Until 1964 it was illegal for an Aboriginal to buy or drink alcohol—and anyone supplying an Aboriginal with alcohol could be jailed. We weren't even citizens of Australia until 1967."

"If Aborigines weren't citizens, what were they?"   105

"We were wards of the state. The state had total power over us," Darryl said. "The 1967 Referendum gave us citizenship. Wouldn't it have made more sense to ask us whether we wanted to be citizens? Yet no one asked us."

"Isn't it better to be a full citizen than a ward of the state?"

"We don't want to be either one. Something was taken away from us in sixty-seven. It was the blackest day in our history."

Before I could ask him another question—and I wanted to, because I did not understand his reasons for seeing the citizenship issue as sinister—he went on, "We pay for things we don't use. Lots of things are offered to us, but what good are they? We're entitled to so many services that mean nothing to us. We don't access the mainstream. It doesn't matter whether roads and schools and hospitals are built for us if we don't want them."

I said, "Then what do you want?"   110

"Our aim is to control our own future," he said, "We want to make our own decisions."

In a word, Aborigines had no power. Keeping the Aborigines powerless, he said, was the hidden reason behind many government policies.

"Look at the Aboriginal languages—what do you know about them?"

I said I had been to the Central Land Council in Alice Springs, because so many of the Aboriginal issues related to land questions. I had asked an official there about Aboriginal languages. How many were there in the Northern Territory—his own area?

"Umpteen," he said. Then, "Maybe two hundred and fifty?"   115

In fact he had no idea. I subsequently learned that when the first colonists arrived in Australia 200 years ago, there were 500 different Aboriginal languages in use. Only a fraction of these are still spoken.

"Aboriginal languages are not taught in Australian schools," Darryl said. "Why not? Because it would empower us. We would have to be taken seriously. It's ridiculous. An Australian student can choose between French, German, Italian, Greek—even Japanese, for God's sake!—but not any Aboriginal language."

This powerlessness he saw as the condition of many other native peoples—Maoris, Fijians, Inuits, black South Africans. But Maori was taught in New Zealand schools (and, ironically, the highest marks in it had been attained by white Kiwis); ethnic Fijians had recently taken control of their islands—with illegal force and the imposition of martial law—and as for black South Africans, Nelson Mandela was very shortly to be visiting Australia on his round-the-world tour after his release from a South African prison, and Darryl was going to meet him with an Aboriginal delegation.

"Indigenous people all over the world get shit land that can't be farmed," Darryl was saying. "And then someone discovers minerals on it and the government wants it back."

"I've heard Australians say that in the course of time assimilation will occur   120 and—"

"Assimilation is a hated word. We don't want to assimilate. Why should we?"

It seemed to me that Darryl himself—Irish-looking Darryl—was already assimilated. But I said, "I don't know the arguments. But do you really want apartheid—separate development?"

"This whole country is our land," Darryl said. "White people need permits to go on our land. Now they're saying that we'll need special permits to come into town. And it's all our land!"

The lack of water in Alice Springs was no deterrent to the annual Henley-on-Todd Regatta, which is held in the dry riverbed. When I heard that it was happening I headed for it, in a walkabout way—you couldn't miss it: I followed the roar of the crowd and the plumes of dust rising like smoke from the gum trees.

The events were in full swing, "Eights," "Yachts"—bottomless boats   125 carried by running men, "Oxford Tubs"—six people carrying a bathtub with someone sitting in it, "Sand Shovelling"—a relay race to fill a forty-four-gallon drum with sand, and men racing each other lugging sacks of wet sand.

The announcer was yelling himself hoarse, but there was no cheering. The large audience—thousands, it seemed, looking like jackeroos and jillaroos and the sort of cattle rustlers known locally as poddy-dodgers and cattle duffers—stood in the blinding sunlight and dust, wearing sweaty T-shirts and wide-brimmed hats and rubber flip-flops, drinking beer. Like many another outback event—the

Birdsville Races, the rodeo in distant Laura—the Henley-on-Todd was merely another excuse to get plastered in the most good-humored way.

"This place is a dump," a photographer friend confided to me in Alice Springs. He was doing a photographic essay about Australia, and the stress was beginning to become apparent. "Birdsville is a madhouse. I hate the cities. I get depressed in the suburbs. I can't win. To me, Australia is one big beer can."

By midafternoon the spectators at the Henley-on-Todd were so drunk they hardly seemed to notice who was competing, and they paid no attention to the skinny biting flies that are a plague in the outback. These flies are pestilential but much too small to show up on photographs of Australia. If they did, prospective tourists might think twice about going.

From where I stood, in the sand in the middle of the Todd River bed, I could see dark clusters of Aborigines under the distant trees. They were no more than insubstantial shadows. Two of those shadows were Michael and Mary, an Aboriginal husband and wife. I introduced myself to them that day and met them again a few days later in town. They told me that when they were in town they slept under the gum trees. Today they were standing mute and barefoot not far from the Dreamtime Art Gallery. They were covered in buzzing flies and looked quite lost. Michael had a rolled-up painting under his arm. They were both drunk but reasonably coherent. I looked at the painting.

"It's a kangaroo," Michael said. "I painted it."   130

"Do you paint, Mary?"

"I help with the dots," she said.

It was almost all dots, an amorphous pattern—perhaps a kangaroo but one that had been squashed by a truckie with a 'roo bar on the road to Tennants Creek. Michael said he would sell me the painting for $200.

He turned towards the art gallery and said, "They know me in there."

He took me inside. The gallery owner was a white Australian woman in a   135
bright dress, sorting Aboriginal drawings in a folder.

Michael approached her. He said shyly, "You have my painting?"

"I think we sold it," she said.

"It was there," Michael said, pointing to a space on the gallery wall.

His wife in her torn dress stood on the sidewalk, staring through the plate glass and somewhat unsteady on her feet, sort of teetering.

The gallery was full of paintings in a similar pointillist style, dots on canvas,   140
some showing identifiable creatures—kangaroos, lizards, crocs, and other paintings depicted the collapsing geometry of Aboriginal designs, which occasionally had the look of those dotty eye charts that are used in tests for color blindness.

I said, "You understand these pictures?"

Michael nodded. He blinked. The flies had followed him into the gallery. Some flies hurried around his head and others rested on his shoulders.

I pointed to a painting showing two crescents and a blob. "What's that?"

"People sitting in a circle."

I pointed to one showing just a blob, dots of two colors.   145
"An egg."
"That's a goog?" I said, trying out an Australian word. Chooks laid googs.
"Yah."
"What's this?" I said, in front of a large canvas covered in squiggles.
"Water. Rain."   150
"And that?" It looked like an irregular horizon of dots.
"A snake."
Michael said he bought canvas and paint here in Alice Springs and took them back to his house in the reserve near Hermannsburg where he did the paintings. Many of the canvases in the gallery were priced in the thousands.
"How much do you get for your paintings?"
"Not much," he said. "But enough."   155

I wanted to go to a reserve. I had been told that I would need an official permit to enter an Aboriginal reserve, but in the event I simply drove into Amungoona, a reserve outside Alice Springs, and asked the man in charge—Ray Satour, formerly a bulldozer driver, now a headman—if I could look around.

"Sure thing, mate," he said. He said I should pay special attention to the tennis courts, the swimming pool, the gymnasium, and all the new houses.

Why had he said that so proudly? Amungoona Aboriginal Reserve was fenced and ramshackle and looked like a cross between a free-range chicken farm and a minimum security prison. It was very dirty. The tennis courts were derelict, there was no water in the swimming pool, the gym was a wreck and so were the houses. This was all something of a conundrum to me.

I thought: *Perhaps rather than build swimming pools, the authorities should plant more gum trees for Aborigines to sit under?* There was surely something amiss when almost no white person spoke an Aboriginal language, and this in a country where a good two-thirds of the place names had Aboriginal roots. It made for alienation and hard feelings.

My intention was to go to Palm Valley, which was part of Michael and   160
Mary's Aboriginal reserve, beyond Hermannsburg, about a four-hour drive west from Alice Springs.

"I wouldn't go if I were you," the clerk at the car rental agency told me.

A half a dozen times I was told this same thing, about other places. Some of my informants were Americans. There seemed to me many Americans in Alice Springs—they said they loved it there and wanted to stay as long as possible. They were the dependents, wives mostly, of the American soldiers who worked at the Joint Defense Facility at Pine Gap—a satellite tracking station or perhaps a nuclear missile base: It was secret, so no one knew.

"Whites aren't welcome in Palm Valley."

I could not determine whether these warnings were sound. I felt that much of it was just talk. After all, I had simply waltzed into the reserve at Amungoona—my being polite and respectful had worked. And I had made a point of saying that I was not an Australian. But that warning worked—in the end, I decided not to go to Palm Valley.

Being a foreigner helped me in so many ways. It sometimes provoked Australians to give advice. I kept noticing how Australians—the most urbanized people in the world—were full of warnings, full of anxieties about the sun and the sea and the creep-crawlies and what they call "bities," snakes, spiders, box jellyfish, crocodiles, kangaroos bursting through your windshield, wild pigs eating your lunch. It is apparently a fact that the Australian desert contains more species of reptile (250—many of them venomous) than any other desert in the world, and it has been proven scientifically that the Australian inland taipan is the most poisonous snake on earth—its bite will kill you in seconds. But none of this ought seriously to deter anyone from confronting the outback on foot, or even on all fours.

I was doing this very thing, perambulating on my hands and knees, at Glen Helen Gorge, 130 kilometers from Alice Springs, climbing the red cliffs, looking for the shy black-footed rock wallaby. Beneath this magnificent ridge of crumbly russet sandstone was the Finke River—one of the few rivers in the outback that actually had some water in it—and there was a large cold pool of black water at the gorge itself. I climbed to the top of the hill, a hot two-hour trek up a fissure in the cliffs, and wandered around and then lost my way—couldn't find the return fissure, only a sheer drop to the valley floor. But just when it seemed to me that *Walkabout* was turning into *Picnic at Hanging Rock* I saw a way down and followed it.

There were Australians swimming at the pool at Glen Helen. They were shrieking at their kids, they were munching sandwiches, they were drinking beer, they were sitting under trees with their white legs thrust out, and they had hiked up their T-shirts to cool their bellies. The T-shirts said *Freddy Krueger* and *These Here Are Strange Times* and *I Climbed Ayers Rock*. It was all families. They were having a wonderful time.

These white Australians were doing—perhaps a bit more boisterously—what Aborigines had always done there. Because there was always water at Glen Helen it had been a meeting place for the Aranda people, who wandered throughout the central and western Macdonnell Ranges. This water hole was known as Yapalpe, the home of the Giant Watersnake of Aboriginal myth, and over there where Estelle Digby was putting sun block on her nose (and there was something about the gummy white sun block that looked like Aboriginal body paint) the first shapeless Dreamtime beings emerged.

The pool at Ormiston Gorge was even prettier—shadier, more secluded, with pure white tree trunks looking stark against the cracked and branched red rock. It looked as serene as Eden, even under the bluest sky. And here too kids were yelling and adults snoozing and a few old women with scowling emu-like faces, totally unfazed, were kicking through the loose gravel. They happened to be white, but they could easily have been Aborigines. It just so happened that Aborigines chose to gather at other water holes—the large dark pool at Emily

Gap, east of Alice Springs, was one. There I saw Aborigines swimming or snoozing or dandling their babies, doing what they had done for tens of thousands of years, but now wearing shorts and T-shirts.

It is perhaps oversimple to suggest that white Australians are Aborigines in different T-shirts, but they are nearer to that than they would ever admit, even though they are rather trapped and blinded by the lower-middle-class English suburban culture they still cling to. After all, a bungalow is just another kind of humpy.

About twenty or thirty miles northwest of Alice Springs on the road to   170
Tanami, I stopped the car to look at a lizard squatting by the roadside, and heard the wind plucking at the thorn bushes and moaning in the telephone lines. And then I realized that some cattle behind a fence were looking up, with rapt expressions. It was the music I had on the cassette player, Kiri Te Kanawa, singing *"I know that my Redeemer Liveth."* I played it louder, and the cattle crowded closer, listening to that glorious voice.

I got out of the car and walked up the road. It was a typical outback road, with dust and corrugations, hardly distinguishable from a riverbed except that it was straighter.

A tin sign was nailed to a tree:

> This plaque in memory of Jonathan Smith
> who if he hadn't jumped the fence in Darwin
> would have been able to do kaig. 13-8-88.

I had no idea what it meant, but I was sure that Jonathan Smith had been an Aboriginal, and this was one of those gnomic expressions of Aboriginal grief.

Going walkabout myself had led me here, looking hard at some of Australia's empty places, and I realized it was not just a dramatically beautiful land but a unique one, full of wild creatures which were just as strange as its people—its skinks and snakes and adders and wasps. Some I saw a few feet off on a track of red dust, others squashed in the middle of the road to Tennant Creek, and many were the subject of horror stories.

Some of the ugliest creatures were harmless, such as the thorny lizard, a   175
horrible-looking but innocent spiny and scaly harlequin. Yet the Eastern brown snake—second most toxic in the world—was an unprepossessing reptile. There was Spencer's goanna, with its baggy yellow belly and black tongue, the gidgee skink, a spiny lizard with a fat prickly tail, and the shingle-back lizard that was so flat it looked as though it had been mashed by a car even when it was fully alive. The frilled-neck lizard looked like a lizard's version of Bozo the Clown, and the desert death adder tricked its prey with its grub-like tail. And if you went down the road slowly you might see, watching by the roadside, the military dragon, a patient creature that squatted on the shoulder of the road, scoffing up insects that had been smashed by oncoming cars. As for the carpet python, which hunted at night, it had heat receptors in its head and a whip-like response that allowed it to catch a bat blindfolded.

Aborigines had learned to live with these creatures. Some they caught and skinned and ate raw, others they chucked into a fire and left them until they were black and bursting like sausages, and then they stuffed them into their mouths. They were not frightened of snakes. They believed they were related to snakes—to kangaroos, to the whole earth; and they did not see the place where the earth began and their lives ended. It was all part of a continuum, a natural process, in which with the blessings of the gods they whirled around with the rocks and stones and trees.

They coped well with the inland taipan and the death adder. It was the white Australian who presented problems.

"Very little has been done to give [Aborigines] a sense of security in the country we invaded," Patrick White wrote on Australia Day in 1988, the year of the Australian Bicentenary. "In spite of a lot of last-minute face-saving claptrap from the Prime Minister—one of the greatest bull artists ever—Aborigines may not be shot and poisoned as they were in the early days of colonization, but there are subtler ways of disposing of them. They can be induced to take their own lives by the psychic torments they undergo in police cells. It's usually put down to drugs or drink—and some of them are on with these—they learned it from the whites. In a town like Walgett, prestigious white characters can be seen reeling about the streets on important occasions. In my boyhood when I used to go there to my uncle's sheep station on the Barwon, and he drove me in his buggy past the shanties on the outskirts of town, he said, 'There's nothing you can do for these people.'"

The statistics for Aboriginal suicides in jail are terrifying, because a jail cell is an Aboriginal's idea of hell on earth, and waking up sober after being hauled in for drunkenness—or for possession (being found with alcohol within 100 yards of a bottle shop)—the realization of being penned in is such a nightmare to a nomadic soul that many hang themselves in these hot little holding cells before guilt or innocence can ever be determined. But drinking was not the main reason for younger Aborigines entering the criminal justice system. They were usually arrested for petty nuisances—for breaches of "good order," or for property offenses, burglary, and vehicle theft. But seldom for traffic violations or shoplifting, offenses in Australia which were monopolized by whites. In the normal way, Aborigines did not kill themselves, though you would have expected them to be hanging themselves left and right from gum trees on the basis of the jail suicides—somehow deducing that they had a propensity for it. But no, it was the result of their having been taken captive.

There was no question that Aboriginal drunks had become a problem. But 180 were they more of a problem than white drunks? With the possible exception of Finns in winter, I had never in my life seen so many people, black and white, dedicated to intoxication than I did in Australia. And it was not socially disapproved of, not any more than football rambunctiousness, or obscene rugby songs, or the peculiarly insulting manner that in Australia was taken to be a form of matey-ness—"mate-ship" being the concept that helped Australia operate. In Australia generally a non-drinker was regarded as a much greater irritation, not to say a threat, than a shouting, puking drunk.

So why in a drinking and drunken land were Aborigines blamed for being drunks? Perhaps it was their cheerlessness. All the Australian boredom and desperation was evident in Aboriginal drinking. They didn't sing when they were drunk, they didn't dance or become matey. They simply hurled up their supper and fell down and became comatose in a pool of their vomit. There was a furious singlemindedness about it all, and it was not unusual to see Aborigines under the gum trees getting through a four-liter box of Coolabah Moselle in a morning, and when money was short it was time for a "white lady"—methylated spirits and milk. All I had was anecdotal evidence, but statistics were available, and they were surprising. An authoritative report (by Pamela Lyon, for Tangentyere Council; June, 1990) on alcohol abuse by all racial groups in Alice Springs stated that Aborigines drank less than whites but were more affected by it, suffered more physical disability, and died earlier as a result.

I was told that David Gulpilil might have a thing or two to say on the subject of Aboriginal drinking. As the first Aboriginal movie star, he might also have views on fame and fortune. I had wondered about his life since that movie. He had apparently been given rather a raw deal by the makers of the movie "*Crocodile" Dundee*, his only other movie effort.

"He's gone walkabout," a woman in Sydney told me. That word again. Then I was told that he had been sighted in Darwin, and in Alice Springs. Everyone knew him.

"I saw him the other day walking down the street," someone else told me in Sydney. "A tall skinny bloke. Couldn't mistake him. He's such a beautiful dancer."

I was given a telephone number for him—the phone was in a reserve up north. I called but there was no answer. I tried a number of times, and then I was told that it was a public call box, somewhere on the reserve in Arnhem Land, another Woop Woop place. I had seen call boxes like that—dusty vandalized stalls, scratched with dates and nicknames and obscenities, baking in the sun, the phone almost too hot to hold. I never spoke to him—no one picked up the phone. Is it any wonder? But I kept imagining the phone ringing on a wooden post in Woop Woop, under a cloudless sky—ringing, ringing—and a tall black figure in the distance, not deaf, just not listening to the thing, and walking away.

● Applying a Postcolonial Frame

1. Does Theroux seem to you to write from a perspective influenced by postcolonial thought? He's often considered an equal-opportunity misanthrope, a writer who holds all people in equally low esteem. Do you see that kind of misanthropy evident here?

   • Does his work also function as a critique of colonialism, in your opinion? Consider his exchanges with his two taxi drivers in particular.

- He begins his trip by using a non-native film, *Walkabout*, as a guide. Do you think his writing is informed significantly by this frame?

2. How might you explain Theroux's depiction of the relationship of white Australians and Aborigines as a kind of mutual mimicry? How did you react to the rendition of the Twenty-Third Psalm in pidgin (para. 87)?

3. What means of silencing and erasure of Aboriginals and Aboriginal culture do Theroux's observations make obvious to you? How would you describe the white Australian discourse about Aboriginals?

4. Reread the section on Theroux's encounter with Darryl Pearce, director of the Institute on Aboriginal Development. How does Theroux's representation of him affect our sense of the Aboriginal issues of social justice he discusses? How does Pearce reflect postcolonial critiques, as you know them from Edward W. Said (p. 353) and others?

5. Theroux's book can be seen as itself one of many examples of Western commodification of Aboriginal culture—the process of transforming aspects of cultural life into consumable products for the producers' enrichment and for reproduction of the West's sense of its own "advanced" cultural status. Where else in the chapter do you see instances of Western commodification of Aboriginal culture? Consider the painter Michael's relationship to the shop owner, for example.

6. Theroux, like many from Western or Eurocentric cultures, finds the Aboriginal practice of walkabout alluring and perplexing. Examine how he goes about investigating it, considering the following questions:
   - What "Western" research practices does he employ?
   - What conclusions does he reach?
   - What sort of authorial voice does he employ in his account?
   - What about the practice of walkabout runs so counter to Western cultural assumptions?
   - How is its difference related to its exotic appeal?

Beyond the Veil: The Women of the Village of Khajuron

ELISABETH BUMILLER

This excerpt comes from Bumiller's book May You Be the Mother of a Hundred Sons: A Journey Among the Women of India *(1990), which Bumiller wrote after spending close to four years in India. She and her husband are U.S. journalists; she formerly wrote for the "Style" section of the Washington Post,* and he covered first the White House and then joined the foreign staff for the New York Times. *Bumiller's background and chosen subject make her work especially open to postcolonial critique, since she represents for consumption by a Western audience the lives of the subaltern women of India. This is the concept of the "gaze," in which the author/viewer from a more powerful cultural group renders another person and/or culture as a passive, voiceless object, and in which he/she/it is constructed according to the powerful culture's view.*

The village of Khajuron lies deep in a pocket of the fertile Ganges River plain, part of the "Hindi heartland" of northern India where some ways of life have not changed in thousands of years. Most of Khajuron's farming families still live in mud huts, segregated, like their ancestors, into neighborhoods by caste. They draw their water from wells, cook their meals over fires made from cow-dung cakes and go to the village sorcerer for magic spells when their cattle fall ill.

Over the course of a year, I lived in Khajuron during a half dozen visits, and sometimes at sunset, when I walked through the smoky, hazy light along the dirt road leading out of the village, I saw men crossing the fields, carrying their wooden plows home on their shoulders. I felt as if I had been dropped into a distant century. On one religious holiday, I watched as the head of a family, my host, put turmeric paste on a goat's forehead and a hibiscus blossom on its head. He then slit a bit of the goat's ear and threw the blood into a sacred fire as an offering. In the evenings, jackals howled in the surrounding fields. Later at night they stopped, but then I was kept awake by the snorts of the water buffalo tethered near my bed.

Khajuron is the village where I stayed with Bhabhiji, an upper-caste farmer's wife who lived in purdah. My purpose in Khajuron, which should not be confused with Khajuraho, the site of the erotic temple sculptures in central India, was to interview women of all castes in one village over the period of one year so that I could write about how they managed their lives. But I also wanted simply to live in Khajuron, to sleep, eat and work there, so that I could experience, to the extent that a foreigner could, a little bit of how most Indians live. Three fourths of the world's population live in villages; one seventh of the world's population live in the 560,000 villages in India. Khajuron lies almost in the dead center of the enormous Indian state of Uttar Pradesh, which has a population of more than 120 million. As a separate entity, U.P., as the Indians call it, would rank as the eighth largest country in the world. The ways of the 1,000 people of Khajuron are the ways of most of humanity.

One of the most important events that I saw that year, an event that in its own way revealed the true condition of the women of Khajuron, was the election of the village chief, who is called a pradhan. The campaign was in its final days when the summer monsoon arrived, forcing the six candidates on the last weekend before the Tuesday election to canvass through rain and the powerful kind of mud that sucked sandals off your feet and squished up cold and clammy between your toes. The battleground areas of the campaign were the outlying village hamlets, clusters of mud huts poking up from the flat fields, and the voters who lived in them had been subjected to the noisy candidates' processions all weekend. On Sunday at seven in the morning, Arvind Kumar Awasthi, a thirty-four-year-old Brahmin, was the first candidate through the hamlet of Ranjit Khera, leading his band of supporters in a chant of "Vote for the chair!" A few hours later, the dirt footpaths of Ranjit Khera were filled once again, this time with the supporters of Rameshwar Prasad, a sixty-year-old leader of Khajuron's Harijan community, who shouted "Vote for the tractor!" The tractor was his campaign symbol, and the chair was Awasthi's. The incumbent was represented by a camel. The symbols, which had been assigned to the candidates by the local election authorities, appeared on the ballot and enabled illiterate people to vote.

The night before, I sat under the neem tree outside Bhabhiji's house and   5 talked to the village elders about campaign developments. A few of the candidates had turned up to lobby for support and be interviewed by the press, which was me. I asked them about their qualifications, their platform and the issues, such as they were. Arvind Kumar Awasthi, the Brahmin candidate, said he was running against the incumbent, a middle-caste farmer named Shri Ram Choudhary, "because he harbors feelings of hatred toward Brahmins." He complained that when electricity was brought to the village, "persons of influence" had determined the site of the poles carrying the wires, and thus the Brahmin section of the village had no light. Shri Ram Choudhary, the incumbent, chose to ignore such allegations and merely said he was running on his record, which he considered impressive. "Whatever I have done in the past," he said, "I will do again." Rameshwar Prasad, the Harijan leader, told me the next day that he was running as a champion of the oppressed. "Always there is a fight between the rich people and the poor people in this village," he said, "I am the symbol of the poor people."

At the end of each interview, I tried asking each candidate a question he had never before heard in his political career: "What are you going to do for the women of the village?" This was clearly a misguided inquiry, and most of the candidates dismissed it. "The women of this village are not educated," said Choudhary, the incumbent. "Therefore whatever you tell them goes in one ear and out the other." As he answered, Choudhary pointed to his ears with great exasperation. His audience laughed appreciatively. Two to three years ago, Choudhary continued, adult education was offered for the women, and yet they weren't interested. "They were ashamed that they were so old and they couldn't read," he said.

Partly, I had been motivated to live in an Indian village by reading the accounts of a few other Western women who had done the same thing. Sarah Lloyd, a British landscape architect, had lived in villages in Punjab and written *An Indian Attachment* about her experiences there. It was a curious book, derided by Delhi's intellectuals, who found her account of her relationship with an uneducated opium-addicted Sikh both bizarre and condescending; I thought the story of "Jungli," the Sikh, was weird, too, but was impressed with Lloyd's unsentimental descriptions of village families in Punjab. "There was a superficial contentedness about the restful rhythms of their daily tasks and the constant chattering between neighbors which belied the bitterness and resignation often smouldering underneath," she wrote. "And somehow the conversation within families—and not just Jungli's family—seemed to lack the real friendship and understanding that is not uncommon in the supposedly arid family life in the West. Not once did I witness positive abandoned joy: it was as if there were wires straining at their hearts." Another English woman, Sarah Hobson, had written *Family Web*, a compelling account of the life of one Indian family in the southern state of Karnataka. Hobson, like Lloyd, discovered the tensions underneath the façade of simplicity.

But my real inspiration was Victor Zorza, an expert on Soviet politics and a former Washington columnist who had left his old life as a celebrated Kremlinologist to live in a remote Indian village high in the Himalayas. Zorza's five years there had been the basis for newspaper columns in *The Washington Post, The Guardian* and *The Times* (London). I interviewed Zorza in India in 1986 for a profile about him for the *Post*, and it was he who taught me the importance of living in a village rather than dropping by for the day. Villagers may be uneducated but they are extremely clever, he said, and very good at telling an outsider what they think she wants to hear. The truth about a village, Zorza believed, could come out only slowly, with time—time for trust to build between the villagers and the outsider, and time for the outsider to peel away all the layers to get at the truth. "Some of the things I'm writing now are the very opposite of what I used to say before," Zorza told me. "The people who in the past I regarded as good I've found are baddies, and vice versa." Zorza, who had undertaken his columns as a mission to explain the despair of the world's have-nots to the haves, was determined to involve his readers on an emotional level, to prove that the illiterate poor are rich when it comes to the complexities of emotion.

That said, I did not have five years. But I was able to spend as much as six days at a time in Khajuron, and during the course of a year I lived there for a total of three weeks. I was there for the blistering heat of May, the cold days at the end of December, the spring harvest festival and the July election for headman. When it was hot, I slept outside under mosquito netting on a charpoy, or string cot. When it was cold, I slept inside a brick-and-mud shed. I brought in my own water but ate Bhabhiji's chicken curries and rice sitting on a mat on the mud floor; not once did I have the stomach problems I frequently suffered after eating at restaurants and hotels. I took baths in a dark little room off the central courtyard, dipping a small urn into a cold bucket of well water and pouring it over myself. In the winter, the air inside the little room was so chilly I could see my breath. In the summer, it was so humid that the bath made no difference. I used the family latrine, a mud hut with a straw roof over a hole in the ground, built a few hundred feet away from the main house. At night, bats flew around in the hole or flapped overhead. And yet Bhabhiji and her husband were fortunate. Most families had no room for a latrine and had to make a long trip into the fields.

I spent my working hours in long interviews, sometimes two hours at a   10
time, with what eventually amounted to twenty-five women from the highest to
the lowest castes. By the end of the year, I came to two unqualified conclusions:
First, both men and women struggled in the village, but the women, because of
their gender, struggled and suffered twice as much as the men. Second, the
women of Khajuron had one of two lots in life, defined entirely by caste. If
a woman belonged to one of the upper or middle castes, she was virtually
a hostage, confined within the walls of her home to isolation and demanding
housework, which her husband did not consider work. Many men said their
wives did "nothing" all day, even though most women never stopped working
at physically exhausting household chores. If a woman belonged to the lower
castes, she was free to leave her house, usually to work at seasonal labor in the
fields for less than fifty cents a day. She was of course expected to handle all the
housework and child care as well. It may be too strident to say that a woman in
Khajuron was either a prisoner or a slave, but whatever one wants to call her,
she could never hope to escape from her fate nor determine it herself.

Susheela Bajpai was one of the first women I met. She was the wife of a
Brahmin landowner, plump from prosperity, with a round, soft face that had
been spared the effects of the sun and worries about feeding her two children.
She left her house only about once a month, usually for shopping or to see
friends in Lucknow. She covered her face with her sari until she was beyond the
limits of Khajuron and the neighboring village down the road. Only outside this
limit was she freed by her anonymity. The rest of the time, Susheela stayed
inside, confined to several small rooms and a central courtyard. Admittedly, it
was one of the best houses in Khajuron, with a courtyard made of brick instead
of the usual mud and a television set that kept her caught up with the programs
from Delhi. On Sunday mornings, she and her husband invited in about thirty
people, all from the upper castes, to watch the exploits of Ram and the anguish
of Sita in the *Ramayana*, a popular television series based on the great Hindu
epic. The first time I went to see Susheela, she gave me tea and cookies under
her ceiling fan and assured me she was happy with her life. "I don't want to go
out any more than I do," she said. Her husband, who had insisted on listening,
then spoke up. "I am a social person," he said. "I am a man. She is a woman.
So she cannot go anywhere. This is my rule."

At the other extreme was Sudevi, a fifty-year-old widow from one of the
lowest castes. She worked in the fields whenever one of the big landowners
would hire her and on other days received a few rupees from the rich families
for pulling water out of their wells. She never made more than fifty cents a
day and was lucky if she could find work fifteen days a month. Her husband had
died fifteen years earlier from tuberculosis, leaving her nothing. Many days she
was forced to beg at the big landowners' houses. When I first went to see her, in
her mud hut with a caved-in wall, she was embarrassed that she was wearing
no blouse underneath her rough cotton sari. She had only one, and she had
just washed it; I could see it hanging to dry in the sun. She was bony and

leather-skinned and told me she was living on flat bread and salt. She owned no land and said that as a widow she was sometimes called bad names. Her twenty-three-year-old son was living with her, but he had no work either, and his wife was eight months pregnant. "My boy doesn't have enough food," said Sudevi. "When I feel hungry, I drink water."

Between these two extremes was Asha Devi, the twenty-year-old wife of a son in a prosperous middle-caste farming family. She neither enjoyed the status of Susheela Bajpai, the Brahmin landowner's wife, nor suffered the widow's miseries of Sudevi. Yet in some ways, her life combined the worst of both worlds. She had married into a hardworking family that was on its way up, and its members kept her in purdah to further enhance their position in the community. Keeping women off the land had always been a mark of distinction; in Khajuron, as soon as a family could afford it, the women were brought indoors. Predictably, it was often these striving middle-caste families, the ones with the most to lose and the most to gain in their precarious new positions within the village hierarchy, who secluded their women the most rigidly. Asha Devi led an even more cloistered life than Susheela Bajpai, and with none of Susheela's relative luxuries as compensation. Asha Devi left the house only two or three times a year, to see her mother. The rest of the time she lived as a virtual servant in her in-laws' home. At the age of sixteen, she had been married to a man she had never seen before, and since then she had been cooking and cleaning for his parents, his three older brothers and their wives. She was up at six, in bed at midnight, and ate only after everyone else in the family had finished. I spoke to her on the top floor of the house but during the entire conversation never even saw her face; she had pulled her sari completely over her head, as a sign of deference, and probably of terror. I asked her what would happen if she walked out into the village. "My mother- and father-in-law would scold me," she said, "and my husband would also scold me." I turned to her mother-in-law, who was listening to every word, and asked the same question.

"If she went out," decreed the mother-in-law, "we would not get respect."

I found Khajuron by making careful plans that disintegrated, as they always did in India, into fate and serendipity. Since our first year in Delhi, Steve and I had been thinking about living and working in a village together. I wanted to use the material for this book, and he wanted to write a series of articles for *The New York Times* about life in one village in India. We talked about it on and off, finally deciding that no village in India was big enough for the two of us. We had covered the same story a few times in India in the past, and predictably *The New York Times* and *The Washington Post* had squabbled over turf and quotes. This time I wouldn't be writing for the *Post*, but nonetheless I wasn't in the mood to turn up at the door of a woman's mud hut and discover that the most interesting event of her week was that *The New York Times* reporter had been there the day before. And yet I did not want to go alone. Finally, Steve and I decided that a pair of villages within walking distance of each other might work.

15

We then settled on Lucknow, the capital of Uttar Pradesh, as a base. Lucknow had once been the center of a brilliant and then decadent Moghul court, but more important for us, it was in the heart of a vital northern farming belt and only a fifty-minute flight from Delhi. The people there spoke a Hindi that was similar to what we were learning in Delhi. We surmised, incorrectly, as it turned out, that therefore the Hindi spoken in the villages around Lucknow would be like our own.

One morning in May I landed in Lucknow as a one-woman advance team in search of two villages. My only contact there was a friend of a friend, who directed me to Lucknow University, where I was eventually sent to the office of Dr. Surendra Singh, a professor in the school of social work, who had done extensive research in the state's rural areas. (Readers may at this point be wondering why so many people in India are named Singh. *Singh* means "lion," and it is helpful to remember that all Sikhs use the name Singh, but not all Singhs are Sikhs. Dr. Surendra Singh was a Kshatriya, a member of the Hindu warrior caste, which had traditionally owned large tracts of land in Uttar Pradesh and frequently used Singh as a last name. In Rajasthan, many Rajputs also used Singh as a last name.)

I found Dr. Singh behind a large desk, surrounded on three sides by the usual gaggle of tea-drinking colleagues, students and hangers-on. I told him what I wanted: two predominantly Hindu villages, with a range of castes, each with a population of about one thousand, both of them a one-to-two-hour drive from Lucknow and a short walk apart. Dr. Singh, a round but compact man in his mid-forties with a cherubic face, thin mustache and courtly manner, was amused. Even then, I was aware that I was rattling off my specifications as if he were a short-order cook, but Dr. Singh made some notes and said he would consult the census. The next day he presented me with a list of a half dozen villages that met my requirements, but before I had a chance to be elated, Dr. Singh politely informed me that working in any of them would be nearly impossible.

"You are not known in these places," he said. "No one will trust you or tell you the truth. It would be better to live in my brother's village, where I could properly introduce you." Dr. Singh's elder brother, Sheo Singh, the husband of Bhabhiji, had stayed back in the village, to manage what remained of the family land. Dr. Singh had left years before. It was the story of independent India, an illustration of how land reform had shrunk the once-large holdings of feudal land-lords in rural India and compelled their sons to seek education and make their living in the burgeoning cities. Dr. Singh's story was also proof of the close ties to the land retained by the first generation of urban Indians, and why so many had kept to the ways of the village—arranged marriages, for example. Dr. Singh had distinguished himself from the millions of others by the remarkable success he had made of his life. Educated in village schools, he had gone on to Lucknow University, where he now was in line to become head of his department.

Dr. Singh's village turned out to be Khajuron, of course, an hour's drive from Lucknow. A twenty-minute walk from Khajuron was Gurha, a larger village, 20 where Steve could work. I went with Dr. Singh's wife, Reena, and his eldest daughter, Anu, to take a look at both the next day. As we headed south from Lucknow on one of the major arteries of central U.P., a two-lane paved road that led across fertile plains of wheat and under shady groves of enormous gnarled mango trees, Anu, a nineteen-year-old college student, quizzed me about America. She had been up all night studying for an English exam on Shakespeare, Browning and Auden, which she had taken early that morning. (One of the questions was "How much was Lady Macbeth responsible for her husband's death?") But now Anu wanted to know if we had a caste system in the United States and whether everyone was rich. Her state was one of the poorest in India, but the soil in that particular area was fed by canals, the land was benevolent, and the poverty not too wretched. We passed people on motor scooters, bicycles and horsecarts. Most of them seemed to have things to do and places to go.

At the town of Bachharawan, chiefly distinguished by dust and a chaotic roadside bazaar where bananas and tin pails were for sale, we turned east, onto a smaller paved highway, and came to the edge of Gurha. From there we turned right onto a bumpy dirt road that crossed marshy land and more fields. This road was only a mile long, and toward the end I could see Khajuron rising up as a little mound, surrounded on all sides by the plains. Within minutes we reached the outskirts—mud huts with thatched roofs, barefoot children, women breast-feeding babies on string cots, cows tethered near piles of long grasses. The car lumbered its way through, climbed up a small hill and came to a stop under the neem tree in Bhabhiji's front yard. To the right was the low-lying brick-and-mud shed where Steve and I would later sleep; in front of me was the main house, a large, weathered two-story brick structure with an open central courtyard and enormous double doors of heavy, rough wood that you opened and closed by pulling on brass rings. To me, the house looked like that of a prosperous farmer from Saxon times in England. I later learned that it was 150 years old and had changed little from the day it was built.

Bhabhiji and Dr. Singh's brother came out of the house to greet us, Bhabhiji smiling shyly, Sheo Singh talking nonstop. He was, in fact, the exact opposite of his brother—a tall, large, loud, boisterous man with a white mustache and skin darkened by the sun, who liked to smoke a hookah. Bhabhiji, slender and barefoot, was wearing a simple cotton print sari, red glass bangles, a nose stud and toe rings. She had gray hair, lovely dark eyes, workworn hands and a kind, comforting face. She gave us tea, and then Anu took me on a tour of Khajuron.

By this time I had been in enough villages in India to know that they are generally not quaint places brimming with interesting mud architecture and picturesque women in colorful saris. Most are depressing little collections of uncharming shacks, plagued by dust, heat, flies, open sewage and disease. Khajuron had all of that, too, but the upper- and middle-caste parts had meandering lanes, old brick houses with carved wooden doors, and pretty views looking out toward the green fields of young wheat. By Indian standards, Khajuron was poor but not desperate. It lay in the political district that had been represented for years by the Nehru dynasty, including Indira Gandhi when she was prime minister. Unlike other villages, Khajuron did not suffer from lack of water. In fact, the village had such access to irrigation canals that its surrounding fields suffered from the opposite problem: a poor drainage system, flooding and excessive salt deposits caused by waterlogging. There were hand pumps, and one tube well which pumped water from below the ground. Electricity had come five years earlier, and three of the 250 families now had television sets. Three farmers had tractors, and two had licenses to grow poppies for opium, which they sold at enormous profit to the government for medicine. People assumed they made even larger profits on the black market. On the edge of the fields there was a tall, narrow temple to the god Shiva, and a two-room brick schoolhouse stood nearby. On the Gurha side of the village lay a large pond, covered during parts of the year with white flowers. The bathing pool where I walked in the evenings had been built of brick by a Brahmin landowner more than a century before, but its two pavilions still stood and were reflected in the cool water below. I don't want to romanticize, but in truth, especially during the few temperate months of the year, Khajuron, for me, was a pleasant place to live.

The physical plan of the village was an indication of the complex social structure that lay underneath. The most powerful landlord, a mild-mannered college-educated Kshatriya farmer named Shardul Singh, lived in a large brick house on the highest spot in the village; around him were clustered tiny communities of houses belonging to the different castes and subcastes. There are four main castes in India, the highest being the Brahmins, who were traditionally teachers and priests. Next are the Kshatriyas, the warriors. Below them are the Vaisyas, who were traders and merchants, and after them come the Sudras, the farmers. The Harijans have no caste at all—hence they are considered outcastes. For thousands of years they were called Untouchables, but during the independence struggle Mahatma Gandhi gave them the name Harijans—"Children of God"—which paved the way for reform, including affirmative action quotas for Harijans and other low castes in jobs and education. Harijans, however, are still among the most impoverished and degraded people in India.

Within each caste are hundreds of subcastes, which change from region to region, and, like the main castes, were originally connected with specific professions. The Indian Constitution did not abolish caste, but it did outlaw discrimination on the basis of caste. In the cities, caste is to some extent disappearing, and people generally do not have to make their livings according to the accident of birth. But in the villages, caste was as insidious as ever and in large part predetermined the course of a person's life. The education of the younger generation was only slowly changing things.   25

The subcaste of mustard-oil makers in Khajuron, for example, lived together in their own little grouping of mud huts and still, for the most part, made oil from mustard seeds. The clay-pot makers still made clay pots and lived in a little community near one of the village hand pumps. The Kurmis, or large farmers, lived in relatively sizable houses not far from Shardul Singh's gates;

most of them still worked the land for a living, although some of their sons had found jobs in Lucknow. The Pasis, who traditionally had been pig tenders, were farmers, too, although with smaller holdings. They were one group whose occupation had changed, yet their former calling would forever classify them as Harijans. This had not prevented them, however, from creating castes within their outcaste. Those Pasis who had been born in Khajuron—the old families— lived in the heart of the Harijan section, called Pasitolla; those who had arrived only in the last few decades lived on the outskirts of the village, closer to the dirt road. The two Pasi groups did not mix much and even supported different candidates in the election for village pradhan.

Steve and I arrived in Khajuron to begin our work in September 1987, four months after I first met Dr. Singh. (A year later, even after sharing a shed with him, and putting our charpoys side by side under the stars, we never called him anything but Dr. Singh. We were always "Mrs. Elisabeth" and "Mr. Steve.") Dr. Singh and three of his daughters stayed with us at the home of his brother, who turned out to be the second-largest landowner in the village. Without our ever requesting it, the entire Singh family had become involved in our project. There were, I think, several reasons for this. Most of all, Dr. Singh wanted to make absolutely certain that his American guests were comfortable and stayed out of trouble. But I also think our research interested him and gave him a fresh glimpse of his roots.

Unfortunately, staying with the Singhs aligned us with the upper-caste landlords in the eyes of the rest of the villagers, and in the beginning I had trouble talking with some of the Harijan women because of our living arrangements. Rameshwar Prasad, the Harijan leader and, I later learned, a blood enemy of the landlords, actually went so far as to report Steve and me to the local police as possible American spies. It is difficult to know what the CIA might have learned in Khajuron, and, needless to say, nothing ever came of Prasad's harassment. Yet I fretted about our decision to live with the village landlords, even though I never figured out an alternative. Living with the Harijans would simply have aligned me with them, against the landlords, whose good graces I needed to remain in the village. Beyond that, it was unrealistic to think of living with anyone but a family that had space for us and could afford to feed us. Eventually it worked out. In the end, I was able to talk with plenty of Harijan women, I made peace with Prasad, and Bhabhiji and her husband could not have been more generous hosts.

Their house was one of the largest in Khajuron, built so that all family activity occurred in the central courtyard open to the sky. Once a week, the mud floor was smoothed with fresh greenish-brown cow dung, believed to be a disinfectant. In the hot weather, Bhabhiji and her husband slept on their charpoys in the courtyard; in the cold weather, they slept in one of the enclosed storage rooms off this courtyard, which contained five-foot-tall mud urns that held wheat and rice. Bhabhiji's mud stove, or chulha, was built into the floor of the courtyard in a protected corner. There was no electricity, and at night we ate by the light of an oil lamp.

In the mornings after breakfast (fried Indian bread and potatoes for Dr. Singh;   30
omelettes and white bread for us, because that is the sort of breakfast Americans
were supposed to eat), Steve would leave with Dr. Singh for Gurha. I would go
with one, two or three of Dr. Singh's five daughters—different ones came along on
each trip—to begin my interviews in Khajuron. My Hindi was passable for
Bhabhiji's house, but the lower castes spoke a local dialect and could scarcely
understand me. I had an easier time understanding them, but I still needed
Dr. Singh's daughters to translate. I selected the women by caste, so that I would
have a representative sampling. I would arrive at a woman's house, tell her I was
writing a book about women in India and ask if she would answer a few questions
for me. The "few questions" claim was not exactly accurate, but I needed to get my
foot in the door. The truth was that I had prepared a somewhat nightmarish list of
193 questions with my Hindi teacher in Delhi, covering work, education, living
conditions, family relationships, health, education, religion, politics, popular culture and knowledge of the world outside Khajuron and India. Only rarely had
I written out questions for interviews before, but then, I had never tried to
interview so many uneducated women, in a foreign language, and in depth.

Every single interview was excruciatingly slow and difficult. Many lasted
for two hours, the limit of my patience, and considerably beyond the limits of
patience of many of the women. Although a few were amazed that someone was
actually interested in their opinions, and appeared ready to talk all day, most
were shy and nervous. Many times a woman had to breast-feed her baby and
peel potatoes while she was talking to me. Sometimes her husband would try to
speak for her, although I usually asked the husbands to leave. Other times
friends would wander in and offer their opinions, or a swarm of kids would
stand around giggling. They called me "the Ameriki poochnee wallee," which
means "the American question-asking woman." The weather was usually suffo-
catingly hot, and flies buzzed incessantly around my head.

At times I lost heart and decided the questionnaire was a bad idea and was
not getting me anywhere. I knew a lot of the answers were made up, and that
the artificial situation I had constructed—an interview—was not the best way to
learn the truth about rural women's lives. And yet it was a beginning, a way of
getting to know them. The interviews allowed me to sit in their houses for
hours. I watched them knead the chapati dough, saw how they massaged their
babies with mustard oil and listened to them fight with their mothers-in-law.
The women were poor, but this did not mean they all had inhibited personalities. When I asked the village pradhan's daughter-in-law, Santosh Kumari, if she
had any say in her arranged marriage, she laughed and gestured toward the mud
floor and crumbling brick walls of her home. "If they had asked me, I wouldn't
have come to this house," she said. "I would have gone to a much better place."
When I asked if her mother-in-law treated her well, she laughed again. "If my
mother-in-law is bad," she said, "will you bring me a nice one?"

People I knew in rural development had advised me to be as specific as
possible in my questions. I would get nowhere, they said, dealing in abstract

concepts like fairness and equality. So I devised my questions as simple building blocks on basic themes. For example: "What is your education?" "Would you like to know how to read and write?" "Why did you not go to school?" "Do your children go to school?" "Who is it more important to educate—your son or your daughter?" Invariably, the sons were sent to school and the daughters stayed at home.

I also asked the women to tell me precisely how they had spent the day before, from the moment they got up to the time they went to bed. The minutiae always led me to the same conclusion: the women worked harder than the men. Phula, for example, was forty years old, a mother of four, the wife of a prosperous Pasi farmer who had lived in Khajuron all his life. He grew sugarcane, potatoes, rice, coriander and wheat. During the harvest, he employed up to fifteen people a day, and he made close to $1,000 each year. In the government census, a man like Phula's husband would be listed as the head of household, which he was, but a wife like Phula would be considered a nonworking dependent. And yet consider what she did all day: "Yesterday I got up at five in the morning," she told me as we sat in a dark, cramped room off her central courtyard. After rising, Phula walked half an hour into the fields, because the family had no latrine, then half an hour back. When she returned, she cleaned the pots used for the meal the night before. Soap was a luxury, so she used mud and water, scraping with her bare hands. She swept the floor of the house, squatting over a short-handled broom, then walked back to the fields to collect tall grasses for her cows to eat. This took several hours because she had to remove all the thorns. She fed the animals, then went into the house to make lunch for herself and her husband—the lentil stew called dal, and chapaties and rice. She rested during the heat of the afternoon, then got up to wash the pots before dinner. A dozen times during the day she had to fetch water from the well outside her house; she also had to make cow-dung cakes for fuel. And this was a leisurely time of year. In a few weeks, when the wheat was ready for harvesting, she would have to spend most of her time in the fields, managing her household chores in between. She felt her husband treated her well, although he was, after all, entitled to certain rights as the head of the family. "Sometimes he beats me if I make a mistake, or if I forget to give fodder to the animals," she said matter-of-factly. Phula had been married at seven and had begun living with her husband at fourteen. She had never learned to read and write because her parents had not sent her to school. "If I had been educated," she said, "I would have done some work." By "work" she meant paid work; she did not take into account the hard physical labor that she did all day.

Of the twenty-five women I interviewed, nineteen had never been to school. The other six had at least a grade-school education; three of them were Brahmins, and three were from prosperous middle-caste farming families. Almost all of the men had more education, however rudimentary, than the women, which meant they could at least read the local Hindi newspapers and participate in discussions about politics and other issues affecting their lives. It was almost always the men who went shopping, either by foot or bicycle, at the

35

wooden stalls that lined the main road through Gurha, and so it was the men who dealt quite literally in the ideas of the marketplace. Even the lower-caste women who ignored purdah rarely went to the market. When I asked why, they usually said they did not want to go, either because it was too far, or because they did not like the way the men treated them. Whatever the reason, it further isolated the women from society, and from each other.

Almost every illiterate woman I spoke to said she would have liked an education, and when I took that a step further and asked each woman what she thought an education might have done for her, a large number firmly believed that schooling would have pulled them out of the village and saved them from a life of drudgery. "If I had been educated, I would be a big person and I would not be doing all of this," said Sada Vati, the forty-year-old wife of a middle-caste farmer. I asked her what a "big person's" job would be. "Service," she replied, which was the village description for work in government service in an office in a town or city, perhaps even Lucknow, typically as a low-level clerk behind a desk with a salary guaranteed for life. In the village, any work that did not involve hard physical labor was considered almost glamorous. "I want to sit on a chair and do work," said Rajban, a tailor and the mother of five. It was naïve, of course, for the women to think education would have guaranteed them a job. One of India's biggest problems was its millions of young men with high school and college educations who could not find work.

The one encouraging sign was that the women of Khajuron were beginning to send their daughters to school, however sporadically. There were ninety-three boys and eighty-eight girls registered at the village's two-room schoolhouse. "At first, girls were not educated," Cheta Lal, the headmaster, told me. "But now they are coming a little bit more." That was just grade school, however; 80 percent of the boys went on to the high school in Gurha, but only 20 percent of the girls did. And although almost every woman I spoke to said it was important to educate sons and daughters equally—I am sure they said this because they thought it was what I wanted to hear—the reality, when I pressed, was that the boys were sent to school more often than the girls. It was practical economics in a country with no social security system. When money was scarce in a family, it made more sense to educate the boy, who would remain with his parents and support them in their old age. A girl was a wasted investment because she would leave her parents after her marriage and live at her in-laws' house. As Sada Vati, the farmer's wife who wanted to do "service," explained about her son and daughter: "The boy will live here, but my girl will go." Sada Vati had complained about her lack of education, and yet she was not sending her seven-year-old daughter to school, just as her mother had not sent her.

One of the more serious problems of the women in the village was their lack of access to adequate medical care. Although there was a government-trained midwife assigned to the village, she lived in Gurha and was so overburdened with her work there and in one other village that she rarely got to Khajuron. Only a third of the women I interviewed used her, even though her services were free.

Most of them went to a Dr. Kamlesh in Gurha, who charged more than one dollar—two days' wages for field work—per visit. On his wall he displayed a photograph of himself standing next to a cadaver in medical school. Those seriously ill had to go all the way to Bachharawan, or even Lucknow. Most women delivered their babies on the floors of their huts, and at least half had lost one or more children during childbirth or in the first few years of the baby's life. Three women I interviewed admitted they were trying to limit the size of their families, but two of them were doing it by only now and then taking birth control pills. The other woman, a Brahmin, had been given an IUD by a doctor in Bachharawan after the birth of her fifth child. The average number of living children per family appeared to be three or four, but Sheela, the thirty-year-old wife of the village silversmith, had eight. She was more than ready to stop, but her husband refused to allow her to have a government-funded sterilization operation. "There is no need," he insisted. Sheela, who was sitting on a nearby charpoy, just shrugged. "He is afraid it will make me weak," she said.

Not surprisingly, the women knew almost nothing about the village council, or panchayat, although they generally voted in elections, following their husbands' instructions. Seven claimed never to have heard of the panchayat. Of those who had, about half said it did some good. The rest complained. "There is no justice," said Rama Devi, a Harijan woman who served as one of the village midwives. "Only the rich people are given the facilities and we are not." Although the Uttar Pradesh state government had reserved places on every panchayat for women, the provision was widely ignored. As elsewhere, no woman served in Khajuron, and no women went to the meetings. But the women were clearly aware of where the real power lay in the village. When I asked who was the most powerful person in Khajuron, only one said it was Shri Ram Choudhary, the incumbent pradhan. Almost everyone else said it was Shardul Singh, the largest landlord. When I asked why, the answer was simple. "He has the most money and the most land," said Vidhya Devi, a thirty-five-year-old field laborer.

A number of women had never heard of Rajiv Gandhi, and of those who   40
had, there was some confusion about who he was. Most identified him not as prime minister but as Indira Gandhi's son, and most were unable to say whether he was good or bad. Indira Gandhi, however, was widely viewed as good. "She helped the poor people," several women told me. Some clearly identified with her as a woman and said that being a woman helped her become a good leader.

At the end of each interview, I asked each woman what her biggest problem was. The answers included not having enough money, worries about marrying off a daughter, needing a better house and fears about a husband's illness. Many women complained that the water from the wells and hand pumps was brackish, which it was, and that they did not have enough land. Only one woman owned land in her own name. The rest did not even own it jointly with their husbands. The pradhan's daughter-in-law complained that she did not have enough nice saris. Susheela Bajpai, the Brahmin landowner's wife, wanted better schools for her children. Sudevi, the widow, said she did not have enough money. But by far the most obvious, pressing problem, more than education and medical care, was lack of paid work. The women had no way to earn a living, no skills, no training. At the most, they could find field work only six months of the year. Every single woman I interviewed wanted to be taught a skill, but there was no factory near Khajuron, and no accessible market for goods she might produce in her home.

I also asked each woman this question: "If you could be anyone in the world you wanted, or have any job that you wanted, what would it be?" This stumped everyone—it was one of those abstractions I had been advised to avoid—but I was curious, and the answers were revealing. The immediate response of almost every woman was, "But I am not educated, so I cannot do anything." Then I would say, "No, imagine"—and "imagine" was the difficult word—"that anything is possible. What would you be?" It was nearly impossible for the women to make that leap. Finally, after prompting, a woman usually said she would like to be a teacher. It was one job they knew about. Teachers were usually Brahmins, and respected. Susheela Bajpai, the Brahmin landowner's wife, wanted to be a teacher, and so did Sudevi. Three women wanted to be doctors, and two wanted to do sewing at home. My favorite answer came from Phula, the prosperous Pasi farmer's wife. She wanted to be the village pradhan, which I took as a sign of great progress.

I often went back to the women who had been the most receptive to me and talked about other things. Susheela, the Brahmin landowner's wife, always liked to hear the news from Delhi and insisted I sit with her and have tea. Unlike the others, Susheela could talk to me about Indian film stars because she saw three or four movies a year during her trips to Lucknow. Sudevi, the widow, had never seen a movie in her life. When I went to see Sudevi again during Holi, the spring harvest festival in early March, she was in the middle of her hut, up to her knees in mud, at last repairing the crumbling wall of her house. The more exciting news was that her daughter-in-law had given birth to a little boy, who was now four months old. Amazingly, he looked plump and healthy. I asked Sudevi and her daughter-in-law to come outside with the baby, and I took a picture of all three of them in the afternoon light. I promised I would bring them a copy on my next trip.

At the end of each day in the village, just as it was getting dark, I would walk back to Bhabhiji's house, completely exhausted. Bhabhiji always gave me a cup of her sweet, milky tea and invited me to relax on the charpoy near her mud stove. So much smoke came out of it that I found it difficult to breathe—I suppose Bhabhiji, in all her years of cooking, had somehow become used to it—but I would sit there anyway, watching as she chopped onions for dinner on a small wooden board on the floor. As the guest, I was never allowed to help, but Bhabhiji was always interested to hear about my day. So I told her, and related just a little of what the women had said. I think she found my compilation of the obvious details of the women's lives quite odd; she must have wondered what possible use it was for me to know that Phula had spent several hours collecting fodder for her cows that morning. I imagined reversing the situation: Bhabhiji's daughter (her only child, who was married and living in another village) turning up at my mother's house in Cincinnati and interviewing my mother's friends about how long it took each of them to drive to the super-market.

As Bhabhiji and I talked, her husband was outside supervising either the 45 slaughter of the chickens or the plucking of the waterfowl that had been shot in a nearby marshland that afternoon. I never learned what kind of birds they were. Every time I asked, I was told they were "local birds," and from what I could see, they looked to be about the size of pigeons. Bhabhiji's husband brought them in, their bright red flesh all cut up, and Bhabhiji put them in a brass pot of onions, mustard oil and spices simmering on the stove. The spices—cinnamon, coriander, red chilies, bay leaf, cloves and cardamom—had been ground by one of her servants that afternoon. Because she was the wife of Khajuron's second-largest landowner, Bhabhiji had two or three servants who turned up a few hours each day to help her wash clothes, clean pots and, in this case, grind spices by crushing them with a cylinder-shaped stone used like a rolling pin over a flat slab of rock. It was miserable work, and Bhabhiji rarely did it herself. She made certain, however, to select the combination of spices for each meal herself.

While Bhabhiji cooked, the men gathered under the neem tree for the evening's conversation. Steve and Dr. Singh were usually back by this time, exhausted, too. Dr. Singh would go into the house to get a cup of tea from his sister-in-law, and Steve and I would go into the shed to compare notes on the day. Often we were overcome with frustration. "This is the hardest thing I've ever done," Steve said every evening. He was collecting, at what seemed to him a glacial pace, material for what eventually became a five-part series on caste, village politics, family planning, religion and the pressures of change in Gurha. I usually complained that I had just spent six hours in three interviews and had uncovered nothing more startling than the fact that my subjects had all eaten chapaties for lunch. On other days, Steve and I could only marvel at the elliptical evasions of the villagers. In one typical exchange, a man told Steve and Dr. Singh that he had no wife and children, but then excused himself a short time later because he said his wife and children were waiting for him at home. Steve pointed out the discrepancy in English to Dr. Singh. "Yes, first he was saying one thing," Dr. Singh said diplomatically, "and now he is saying this thing." That ended the discussion. Dr. Singh was above all an eternally polite man, who in any case had learned that there were some things in villages that took too much effort to understand.

By twilight the men had built the fire under the neem tree. It was by far the most pleasant time of day. Sometimes, when we sat around the fire, Dr. Singh would tell us a little about his childhood growing up in the village, including the story, my favorite, about the monkey that kidnapped him. When he first told us, we laughed, but Dr. Singh swore it was true. When he was a baby, he said, a female monkey had grabbed him from the house and escaped all the way up to the top of the neem tree with him in her arms. The family was beside itself.

"They called to the monkey but she would not come down," Dr. Singh said. "Fruits and allurements were given, but still she remained in the tree." Finally, after some time, the monkey relinquished the baby, returning him safe and sound on her own. "Yes," said Dr. Singh, pleased and amused, "she loved me." On other nights, the village pradhan from Gurha turned up, full of questions about the United States. "Are widows allowed to remarry in your country?" he once wanted to know. "Do villages in America have electricity? Do the rich people exploit the poor?" Dr. Singh had some questions of his own. "In America," he asked, "if a person is a cobbler"—cobblers in India were Harijans—"and he makes a lot of money, is he respected, despite his profession?"

If the conversation lagged, or bogged down too heavily in Gurha politics, I would go into the house to see how Bhabhiji was doing with dinner. One of Dr. Singh's daughters was always helping her, usually by rolling out the chapati dough. About nine or ten, we were called in to eat. Dr. Singh, Steve and I sat cross-legged on a grass mat in the middle of the courtyard while Bhabhiji and Sheo Singh served us bird, chicken or goat in little bowls. There were steaming chapaties to scoop up the sauce, and rice on the side. It was hot, spicy and utterly delicious.

● Applying a Postcolonial Frame

1. To what extent do you see Bumiller adopting the same methods of cultural study as Theroux (in the previous selection) does? What assumptions about how knowledge is produced are embedded in these? In paragraph 7, she cites a Western writer and a journalist ("who had undertaken his columns as a mission to explain the despair of the world's have-nots to the haves") as her "inspiration." From a postcolonial perspective, do you find using such figures as her cultural informants to be problematic?

2. Reread the opening two paragraphs. How has Bumiller framed the village rhetorically for your consumption as a Western reader?

3. In the fourth paragraph, she describes the use of icons for voting purposes—"Vote for the chair!" "Vote for the tractor!" If we consider the use of similar iconography in U.S. culture—the donkey and the elephant, for example—does that change your reading of this passage?

4. Homi Bhabha argues (in the Bertens reading, p. 368) that the colonizer finds in the colonized a means of establishing his or her own identity. Do we see such a psychological and cultural function in Bumiller's relations with her Indian contacts and interviewees?

   • What tensions in her own life emerge as she describes her experiences? Her preface to the book details the tension she felt when she agreed to accompany her husband to India for his work purposes; she writes, "I was already sensitive about my status as 'the wife' who had followed her husband halfway around the world. I certainly didn't want to write the predictable 'woman's book.'" To what extent do we see her subject (and subjects) used to address that tension?

- How do the Indian women she profiles help establish Bumiller's status?
- "The women worked harder than the men" is Bumiller's commonly stated conclusion. How do her Western values direct her repeatedly to this topic? Do we get a sense of how her female subjects view the apparent workload inequity?
- Do you see Bumiller create a system of values in which Western-style practices are coded as progressive, human, good, and Indian practices as the other part of this binary system—as primitive, bestial, bad?

5. Bumiller provides composite depictions of village women from three castes. What do you think Bumiller's rhetorical purpose is in producing a sense of each woman's daily routine?

6. Bumiller relies on ethos to a large extent in this chapter. Where do we see that in her prose, and why might ethos be crucial, given who she is and what she writes about?

- Why does she minimize her use of pathos? In particular, consider her depiction of the impoverished widow Sudevi.
- Bumiller mentions some of her subjects' "evasions" when she questions them. How might you explain their behavior?

Losing Robandi
ALEXANDRA FULLER

In her book Don't Let's Go to the Dogs Tonight: An African Childhood, *from which this chapter is taken, Fuller recounts her experience as a British-born white girl raised in then Rhodesia, the pre-independence Zimbabwe, whose farming family also later lived in Malawi and Zambia. Here she gives the child's perspective of the new black government's land distribution program, in which many of the farms of white colonists were reallocated to black citizens. The complicated ethics and administration of this redistribution is made even more challenging by political corruption, which resulted in prized land going to political supporters of the (still) President Robert Mugabe, recalling Edward W. Said's (p. 353) critique of corrupt postcolonial regimes. This political frame adds to the hostile relations of colonizer-colonized, illustrated in material form in the confrontation Fuller describes. In the end, she suggests, economic exploitation is the one form of unity the white family finds with the black Zimbabweans.*

Rhodesia has more history stuffed into its make-believe, colonial-dream borders than one country the size of a very large teapot should be able to amass in less than a hundred years. Without cracking.

But all the history of this land returns to the ground on which we stand, because all of us (black, white, coloured, Indian, old-timers, newcomers) are fighting for the same thing: tillable, rain-turned-over-fresh, fertile, worm-smelling soil. Land on which to grow tobacco, cattle, cotton, soybeans, sheep, women, children.

In Rhodesia, we are born and then the umbilical cord of each child is sewn straight from the mother onto the ground, where it takes root and grows. Pulling away from the ground causes death by suffocation, starvation. That's what the people of this land believe. Deprive us of the land and you are depriving us of air, water, food, and sex.

The Rudd Concession of 1888 tricked King Lobengula of the Matabeles into surrendering mineral rights to the British South African Company.

In 1889, the Lippert Concession allowed white settlers to appropriate land for 5
farms and townships in Lobengula's name—concessions that were supposed *to be valid only in Lobengula's lifetime.*

In 1894 a British Land Commission declared itself unable to remove white settlers from native land.

In 1898 the British government set up "sufficient" areas for the exclusive occupation of the African people.

In 1915 the boundaries of the "Native Reserves" were set up.

In 1920 a Southern Rhodesia Order-in-Council assigned 21.5 million acres (out of a possible 96 million acres) for the sole use of Africans.

The 1925 Morris Carter Commission recommended division of land among the 10
races.

The Land Apportionment Act of 1930 divided the country: 21.5 million acres for "Native Reserves"; 48 million acres for occupation and purchase only by Europeans; and 7.5 million acres for occupation and purchase only by Africans. Seventeen and a half million acres were unassigned.

The Land Apportionment Act was amended in 1941, 1946, and several times in the 1950s and 1960s, and the Native Reserves were renamed Tribal Trust Lands.

The Rhodesian government built its policy of racial segregation on the Land Tenure Act of 1969 (repealed in 1979 under growing international and internal pressure).

The Tribal Trust Lands Act is replaced by the Communal Land Act in 1982.

"To us the time has now come for those who have fought each other as 15 enemies to accept the reality of a new situation by accepting each other as allies who, in spite of their ideological, racial, ethnic, or religious differences are now being called upon to express loyalty to Zimbabwe." That's what the new "ZANU (PF)" government announces at the end of the war.

"I'll show them peace and re-bloody-conciliation," says Mum.

Piss and reconciliation, we call it.

Our farm is designated one of those that, under the new government, may be auctioned (but not to whites) by the government for the purpose of "land redistribution."

This is how land redistribution goes.

First, the nice farms, near the city, are given to Prime Minister Robert Mugabe's political allies.

Then, the nice farms far from the city are given to those politicians whom Mugabe must appease, but who are not best-beloved.

After that, the productive, tucked-away farms are given to worthy war veterans—to the men, and a few women, who showed themselves to be brave liberation strugglers.

Then farms like ours—dangerously close to existing minefields, without the hope of television reception and with sporadic rains, unreliable soil, a history of bad luck—are given to Mugabe's enemies, whom he is pretending to appease.

Our farm is a gift of badlands, eel-worm-in-the-bananas, rats-in-the-ceiling.

Our farm is a gift of the Dead Mazungu Baby.

Our farm is gone, whether we like it or not.

Dad shrugs. He lights a cigarette. He says, "Well, we had a good run of it, hey?"

But already, landless squatters from Mozambique have set themselves up on our farm. Before our farm has been officially auctioned, and the old crop has been pulled in, before the new owners can set foot on the road that leads, ribby and washed away, up to the squat barracks house (which Mum painted peach, years ago, to try and cheer us up), before our footsteps are cold on the shiny cement floors of the veranda, the squatters come.

No one invited the squatters to come and take over the farm and other farms close to the border. The squatters are mostly illiterate, unlikely to have been war heroes, but hungry. They are belly-hungry, home-hungry, land-hungry.

They have made themselves a camp up in the hills above the house, they have chopped down virgin forest and planted maize. Their cattle drink straight from hillside springs, crushing creek banks into red erosion, which comes out, in the end, like blood in our tap water.

Mum says, "I'll show them land re-bloody-distribution."

Dad says, "Too late now."

Mum grits her teeth and talks between them, so that the words are sharp and white-edged. She says, "It's not theirs yet. It's still our farm." She pours brandy straight into a glass and drinks it without pretending to be doing anything else. Straight brandy without water, Coke, lemon. She says, pointing her finger at Dad, "We fought for this land, Tim! We fought for it," and she makes her hand into a fist and shakes it. "And I'm not letting it go without a fight."

Dad sighs and looks tired. He stomps out his cigarette and lights another.

"I'll go and show those buggers," says Mum.

"Take it easy, Tub."

"Take it easy? Take it easy? Why should I take it easy?"

There is a baby, our fifth, swelling in her belly.

Mum started to throw up just after Christmas. She puked when she smelled

20

25

30

35

soap, petrol, diesel fumes, perfume, cooking meat. Which is how we knew she was pregnant again.

I had prayed so hard for another baby, this one might have been conceived out of my sheer willpower.

Now Mum says, "These bloody *munts* make me feel sick."

Which is not, apparently, anything to do with morning sickness and everything to do with losing the war.

She has closed down the little school which we used to run for the African children. "They can go to any school they like now." But there is no transport for the children, so they hang around under the big sausage tree near the compound, where their mothers have told them not to play. Mum will no longer run a clinic from the back door for the laborers or anyone else who happens through our farm and is ill or malnutritioned.

Now she says, "Don't you have your *comrades* at the hospital? We're all lovely socialists together now, didn't you know? If you go to the hospital, your *comrades* will treat you there."

"But, madam—"

"Don't 'But, madam' me. I'm not 'madam' anymore. I'm 'comrade.'"

"You are my mother—"

"I am not your bloody mother."

"We are seeking health."

"You should have thought of that in the first place."

The sick, the swollen-bellied, the bleeding, the malarial all sit at the end of the road, past the Pa Mazonwe store, and wait for a lift into town, where they will wait hours, maybe days, for the suddenly flooded, socialized health care system to take care of them.

Mum's belly makes it hard for her to get on her horse. She makes Flywell hold Caesar next to a big rock and she hops from the rock into her stirrup and eases herself up. Then she arranges her stomach over the pommel and kicks Caesar on.

"Wait for me!" I yank at Burma Boy's head. He is ear-deep in some yellow-flowered black-jacks. Mum doesn't even turn around. She whistles to the dogs, one short, sharp note. She is in a dangerous, quiet rage this morning.

We ride up, past the barns and past the turnoff to the cattle dip and past the compound where our laborers live in low-roofed redbrick houses or elaborately patterned huts. We ride up past the small plots where the laborers are allowed to grow their crops of cabbage, rape, beans, and tomatoes and up the newly blazed trails that lead to the new village erected by the squatters.

There is the acid-sweet smell of burning wood on damp air as we follow the patted-down red earth into the squatter village. We can hear the high, persistent wail of a small child and, as we get closer, the frantic yapping of dogs. The squatters built three mud huts in a circle around a wood fire over which a pot of *sadza* is bubbling. The curly-tailed African dogs run out at our pack and start to growl, their hackles raised high on bony backs.

"Call your dogs!" Mum shouts into the raw new village (the bush poles that have been cut to make the huts are still bleeding and wet; the thatched roofs smell green—they will not stop water from leaking into the huts when it rains).

The squatters are standing in a row in front of their huts. The baby that has been crying stops now and looks at us in silent astonishment. He is hanging from his mother's back. The other women have slung their small children onto soft, ready hips. The men stand in a row, chins high, mouths soft and sullen. One of the children is coughing, eyes bulging, hair fuzzed a telltale protein-deficient red: kwashiorkor hair. He is naked except for a pair of threadbare shorts through which I can see his shriveled penis and the tops of his stick-thin legs.

Mum circles around the huts; Caesar spins up the newly stripped earth as he paces. I pull Burma Boy up under one of the huts and sit, crouched into my saddle, watching.

"This is our land!"

The squatters stare back, their expressions not changing.   60

Mum spurs Caesar on, charging into the impassive group of men, women, and children. The African dogs yelp and flee, cowering, into the dark mouths of the huts. One of the young children, too big to be on a hip but too small to be far from his mother, screams and follows the dogs. The mother with the baby on her back is holding a gourd, used for carrying water or beer. She suddenly, in a rage of bravado, runs at Mum, shouting in a high, tremulous, singing voice, and strikes Caesar on the nose with the container. Caesar backs up, but Mum spins him around again, digs down into her saddle, legs tight. "Come on," she growls, and then as Caesar surges forward, his nostrils wide and red-rimmed with surprise, Mum screams at the woman, "Don't you hit my horse! You hear me? Don't you hit my bloody horse. . . ."

Mum charges at the squatters repeatedly, kicking Caesar fiercely and running indiscriminately at the women, the children, the men. And then she turns her horse onto the freshly planted maize field and begins tearing through it, between the still-bleeding stumps of the newly cut msasa trees. "You fucking kaffirs!" she screams. "Fucking, fucking kaffirs."

Some of the men break from the huddle around the huts and start to run after Caesar, shouting and waving their badzas and machetes. The children are all crying now. The women wrap the children in their arms and skirts and shield their faces.

"You bastards!" screams Mum. "You bloody, bloody bastards. This is our farm!"

One of the men starts to hurl clumps of earth at Mum. They fall damply   65
against Caesar's flank. He shies away, but Mum hunches down and clamps her legs onto him so that his breath comes out—*umph*—and she charges again and again at the squatters. The women scream and run into the huts with the children, shutting the flimsy bush-pole doors behind them. The men stand their ground, heaving whatever comes to hand at Mum and her horse. They are shouting at us in Shona.

I shout, "Come on, Mum!" Scared. "Mu-uuum."

Still she wheels Caesar around again and again; the white froths of sweat gathering in balls on his neck and flecking out from between his hind legs.

I stand up in my stirrups and scream as loudly as I can, "Mum! Let's go."

I start to cry, pleading, "Mum-umm, please."

Finally the fight seems to bleed out of her. She turns to the men one last   70
time and shakes her riding crop at them. "You get off my farm," she says in a beaten, broken voice, "you hear? You get the hell off my farm."

Mum has come back from the ride pale and with a light film of sweat on her top lip. She doesn't talk. When we get back to the yard, she slips off the horse, sliding down the saddle on her back, and then grimaces, holding her belly. She lets Caesar wander off, still saddled, reins looped and dragging on the ground, to graze in the garden. I shout for Flywell, frightened by the look of Mum.

Mum pours herself a glass of water and goes into her room. When I go in there, the curtains are drawn and it sounds as if Mum is breathing through her voice.

"Are you all right?"

"Uh-huh."

"Can I get you some tea?"

"That would be nice."   75

So I order the cook to make tea and I bring Mum a cup but she does not drink it.

When Dad comes in from the fields, he goes into the bedroom and stays there. I hear them talking softly to each other. It sounds as if Mum is crying.

Vanessa says, "Why don't we make a cake for Mum?"

I shake my head. "I don't feel like it." I go to my room and lie on my bed,   80
staring at the ceiling. It is a hot, sleepy afternoon and I am tired and salt-stinging from the excitement of the morning. My eyes are closing. Puncho, a rescued dog who has attached himself to me, sidles up to my head, licks my face, and settles himself happily next to me on the pillow. Sleepily, I start to search under his ears for ticks.

Suddenly, Puncho leaps off the bed, his hackles up, barking in high excitement, and I can hear the other dogs scrambling off the veranda and bursting outside with a volley of barking. An instant later I hear Dad shout, "You bloody baboons!"

I spring off my bed and run onto the veranda. Mum comes running out of her bedroom, still pale and holding her stomach. "Quick," she says, pressing herself against the front door, a simple wooden affair on a hook latch, but without a lock or bolt, "lean on the door."

"What's going on?" I ask, pinning my shoulder up against the door.

"Shhh," Mum hisses. She looks around wildly to see what dogs we have inside. "Hey Puncho!" Puncho is whining, his nose pressed to the bottom of the door. "Hsss," she says to Shea and Sam, "bark! Sound fierce."

I can hear Dad shouting on the other side of the door but I cannot hear 85 what he is saying.

"Who is it?"

"Soldiers," says Mum.

"Army guys?"

"No, not army guys. Soldiers."

Mum and I are losing the battle of the door. There are two of us leaning 90 with all our might against the door, but it is being pushed from the other side by three grown men. Suddenly, our resistance proves too feeble and the door collapses inward, sending Mum and me sprawling and a clatter of soldiers in on top of us.

I fall as I have been taught. Curl into a ball and cover your head. I bring my arms up and close my eyes. I take a deep, shaky breath.

I am going to die now. I wait. Does a bullet feel red hot coming into you? Do you feel it slicing into your flesh? Will I be dead before I feel pain?

Mum says, "*Fergodsake*, Bobo, get off the floor."

I open my eyes.

The Zimbabwean army soldiers are standing with their backs against the 95 door. They are staring down at me.

I sit up and find that I have not been shot. The soldiers' eyes are blazing red, and they smell strongly of ganja and native-brewed beer. Now that they have pushed our feeble wooden door open and have us at gunpoint, they look a bit sheepish.

Mum says, "Up!" And then she looks at me strangely. "Bobo, where's Vanessa?"

"Making a cake."

"Vanessa!" Suddenly Mum is screaming, "Vanessa!" and pushing her way past the three soldiers at the door. "Get out of my way you stupid bloody— Vanessa!"

Vanessa is still in the kitchen, where fright has turned into her habitual 100 seeming-calmness. Two soldiers are observing her from a polite distance, guns aimed casually at her belly, while she pours batter into a cake tin, scrapes the side of the bowl, puts the cake in the oven.

"Are you all right?" screams Mum, rushing toward Vanessa.

"Fine." Vanessa points to the cookbook lying open on the greasy-topped kitchen table. "It says forty minutes in a medium oven for the cake." The wood-stove is belching smoke. "Would you say that is a medium oven?"

"Oh, God," Mum says. She catches her breath sharply and holds the edge of the table.

"Are you all right, Mum?"

Mum nods. The soldiers look from Mum to Vanessa and back to Mum, 105 uncertainly. They wave their guns. "Come on, come on. Outside," says one of them. They herd Vanessa and Mum out onto the veranda.

"Don't let me forget. Forty minutes," says Vanessa.

Dad is negotiating with five or six more soldiers on the veranda. They are the new Zimbabwean army, fresh out of guerrilla troops. They are still war-minded. They are still war-trigger-happy.

"You called us baboons."

"You jumped into my bedroom window. That is not a civilized thing to do, that is a baboon thing to do."

The soldiers stare belligerently at Dad. There is a long, shuffling silence.   110

At last Dad says, "Look, either shoot me or put your fucking guns down and let's talk about this sensibly."

I want to say, "Dad was only joking about shooting him. And don't be touchy about being called a baboon. I'm their kid and they call *me* Bobo. Same thing."

One of the soldiers says, "Ah, comrade . . ."

Dad says, "And there's another thing. You can call me Mr. Fuller or Silly Old Bugger or Old Goat Fuller or any damn thing you like but comrade . . . never! You can never call me comrade."

The soldiers look at Dad in astonishment.   115

"I'm not your comrade." Dad takes the tip of one of the soldier's guns and moves the barrel out of the way. He says, "Didn't anyone teach you not to point these things at live targets?"

The afternoon turns into a thick mellow evening, the light filters syrup-yellow and as the heat of the day melts away, so does the anger in the men. The soldiers grow tired; some of them sprawl on the top of the wall, slouched over the barrels of their guns and watch, eyes hooded, as Dad speaks to the soldier who seems to be in charge. Vanessa and I sit on the steps with the dogs, picking ticks out of their coats and popping the little gray and red bodies on the stone flags. Mum is very pale, breathing in quick shallow breaths. At last the soldier in charge stands up and stretches, "Okay, okay. Let's leave this incident to sleep now. You just keep your wife under control from now on," he tells Dad. "This is Zimbabwe now. You can't just do as you please from now on. From now it is we who are in charge."

They drive away. We watch them until their lorry humps over the culvert at the bottom of the drive.

Dad says, "You okay, Tub?"

Mum nods. She says, "Let's have a drink."   120

Vanessa says, "Oh no! My cake."

That night we go out to the Club. While Vanessa and I sit on the black plastic chairs in the smoky bar sipping Cokes and crunching on salt-and-vinegar chips, kicking our heels against the chair legs, Mum and Dad drink and tell the story of their day's adventure. By the time deep night has come and the nocturnal creatures have started to sing and croak and screech, Mum and Dad are drunk and Vanessa and I are curled up in the back of the car, staring out of the windows at the slowly swinging bright stars as they make their way across the cloud-scudding sky. We are eating our third packet of chips and sipping on dumpy-sized bottles of Coke.

"Did you think you were going to die?" I ask Vanessa, carefully licking a chip to get the salt off it before I put the whole thing into my mouth.

"What?"

"Did you think we were going to be shot by those Affies?"   125

Vanessa yawns and scrunches up her chip packet. "Have you finished your chips?"

"No."

"Give them to me."

"No!"

"Do you want a Chinese bangle?"   130

I stuff the remaining chips into my mouth. My eyes sting and tears roll down my cheeks with the effort of it. Vanessa scrambles over the seat and squashes my cheeks together until the food squeezes out of my mouth.

I start to cry. "I'm telling on you," I weep. "I'm telling Mum and Dad."

Vanessa snorts. "Go ahead," she says.

Robandi is put up for mandatory auction under the new land distribution program. It is sold, in the loosest sense of the word, to a black Zimbabwean. The money that changes hands in this exchange doesn't even touch the sides of our pockets. Everything from the farm is given to the Farmers' Co-op, from which we had borrowed money to buy the farm in the first place.

Robandi never belonged to us, and it doesn't belong to the new Zimba-   135
bwean farmer. It belongs to the mortgage company. They, alone, seem unmoved by the fierce fight for land through which we have just come.

● Applying a Postcolonial Frame

1. Fuller opens and ends the chapter with what is an economic argument—that both white and black Africans need land to live. How do you think this rhetorical frame is being used to affect the reader's reaction to the hostile race relations of the incidents she recounts? What is the rhetorical effect of the section that follows—the listing of colonial and independence government policies on land use?

2. Fuller shows the shortcomings of the new government's policies on access to land, schooling, and medical care. How do you think these problems affect her mother's obvious racist views on the changes?

3. In the description of the incident in which Fuller's mother repeatedly charges her horse into the group of black "squatters," we see what might be called a reenactment of the colonial script, but changed to include native resistance.

Reread the scene from this postcolonial perspective: how is the image of the "other" altered by it?

4. How is the suddenly destabilized power relation of colonizer-to-colonized re-enacted again in through the arrival of the black soldiers in the white household?

  • During this incident, Fuller's mother suddenly starts screaming to find her older daughter, Vanessa, apparently in fear that she is in danger of being raped. How is this fear the product of cultural history as well as the mother's own racist views?

  • What do you see as "mixed" in Fuller's father's interactions with the soldiers? How is he both white colonist and new subaltern?

  • How do you see the power relations affecting the outcome of the incident, with the soldiers deciding to leave?

5. Why do you think Fuller includes the details of her conflict with her sister at the end, in which her sister uses force to try to get Alexandra/Bobo's share of chips?

The Fact of Blackness
FRANTZ FANON

Like Aimé Césaire (p. 374), Frantz Fanon (1925–1961) was a native of Martinique. A radical thinker and radical activist as well, Fanon was a psychiatrist who became deeply involved in the Algerian war of resistance against its French "masters." His work, especially The Wretched of the Earth *(1961), helped resistance movements throughout colonized Africa and elsewhere. In his writings he explores the problems of identity for blacks in a white-dominated world and analyzes the psychological effects of colonialism on the colonized subject. He was one of the earliest critics of what today we call assimilationist values. In this excerpt from* Black Skin, White Masks *(1952), Fanon, using a first-person voice, articulates the struggle of the colonized being to know himself outside the context of white colonial domination.*

Dirty nigger!" Or simply, "Look, a Negro!" |

I came into the world imbued with the will to find a meaning in things, my spirit filled with the desire to attain to the source of the world, and then I found that I was an object in the midst of other objects.

Sealed into that crushing objecthood, I turned beseechingly to others. Their attention was a liberation, running over my body suddenly abraded into nonbeing, endowing me once more with an agility that I had thought lost, and by taking me out of the world, restoring me to it. But just as I reached the other side, I stumbled, and the movements, the attitudes, the glances of the other fixed me there, in the sense in which a chemical solution is fixed by a dye: I was indignant; I demanded an explanation. Nothing happened. I burst apart. Now the fragments have been put together again by another self.

As long as the black man is among his own, he will have no occasion, except in minor internal conflicts, to experience his being through others. There is of course the moment of "being for others," of which Hegel speaks. But every ontology is made unattainable in a colonized and civilized society. It would seem that this fact has not been given sufficient attention by those who have discussed the question. In the *Weltanschauung* of a colonized people there is an impurity, a flaw that outlaws any ontological explanation. Someone may object that this is the case with every individual, but such an objection merely conceals a basic problem. Ontology—once it is finally admitted as leaving existence by the wayside—does not permit us to understand the being of the black man. For not only must the black man be black; he must be black in relation to the white man. Some critics will take it on themselves to remind us that this proposition has a converse. I say that this is false. The black man has no ontological resistance in the eyes of the white man. Overnight the Negro has been given two frames of reference within which he has had to place himself. His metaphysics, or, less pretentiously, his customs and the sources on which they were based, were wiped out because they were in conflict with a civilization that he did not know and that imposed itself on him.

The black man among his own in the twentieth century does not know at what moment his inferiority comes into being through the other. Of course I have talked about the black problem with friends, or, more rarely, with American Negroes. Together we protested, we asserted the equality of all men in the world. In the Antilles there was also that little gulf that exists among the almost-white, the mulatto, and the nigger. But I was satisfied with an intellectual understanding of these differences. It was not really dramatic. And then. . . .

And then the occasion arose when I had to meet the white man's eyes. An unfamiliar weight burdened me. The real world challenged my claims. In the white world the man of color encounters difficulties in the development of his bodily schema. Consciousness of the body is solely a negating activity. It is a third-person consciousness. The body is surrounded by an atmosphere of certain uncertainty. I know that if I want to smoke, I shall have to reach out my right arm and take the pack of cigarettes lying at the other end of the table. The matches, however, are in the drawer on the left, and I shall have to lean back slightly. And all these movements are made not out of habit but out of implicit knowledge. A slow composition of my *self* as a body in the middle of a spatial and temporal world—such seems to be the schema. It does not impose itself on me; it is, rather, a definitive structuring of the self and of the world—definitive because it creates a real dialectic between my body and the world.

For several years certain laboratories have been trying to produce a serum for "denegrification"; with all the earnestness in the world, laboratories have sterilized their test tubes, checked their scales, and embarked on researches that might make it possible for the miserable Negro to whiten himself and thus to throw off the burden of that corporeal malediction. Below the corporeal schema I had sketched a historico-racial schema. The elements that I used had been provided for me not by "residual sensations and perceptions primarily of a tactile, vestibular, kinesthetic, and visual character,"[1] but by the other, the white man, who had woven me out of a thousand details, anecdotes, stories. I thought that what I had in hand was to construct a physiological self, to balance space, to localize sensations, and here I was called on for more.

"Look, a Negro!" It was an external stimulus that flicked over me as I passed by. I made a tight smile.

"Look, a Negro!" It was true. It amused me.

"Look, a Negro!" The circle was drawing a bit tighter. I made no secret of my amusement.

"Mama, see the Negro! I'm frightened!" Frightened! Frightened! Now they were beginning to be afraid of me. I made up my mind to laugh myself to tears, but laughter had become impossible.

I could no longer laugh, because I already knew that there were legends, stories, history, and above all *historicity*, which I had learned about from Jaspers. Then, assailed at various points, the corporeal schema crumbled, its place taken by a racial epidermal schema. In the train it was no longer a question of being aware of my body in the third person but in a triple person. In the train I was given not one but two, three places. I had already stopped being amused. It was not that I was finding febrile coordinates in the world. I existed triply: I occupied space. I moved toward the other . . . and the evanescent other, hostile but not opaque, transparent, not there, disappeared. Nausea. . . .

I was responsible at the same time for my body, for my race, for my ancestors. I subjected myself to an objective examination, I discovered my blackness, my ethnic characteristics; and I was battered down by tom-toms, cannibalism, intellectual deficiency, fetichism, racial defects, slave-ships, and above all else, above all: "Sho' good eatin'."

On that day, completely dislocated, unable to be abroad with the other, the white man, who unmercifully imprisoned me, I took myself far off from my own presence, far indeed, and made myself an object. What else could it be for me but an amputation, an excision, a hemorrhage that spattered my whole body with black blood? But I did not want this revision, this thematization. All I wanted was to be a man among other men. I wanted to come lithe and young into a world that was ours and to help to build it together.

But I rejected all immunization of the emotions. I wanted to be a man, nothing but a man. Some identified me with ancestors of mine who had been enslaved or lynched: I decided to accept this. It was on the universal level of the intellect that I understood this inner kinship—I was the grandson of slaves in exactly the same way in which President Lebrun was the grandson of tax-paying, hard-working peasants. In the main, the panic soon vanished.

[1]Jean Lhermitte, *L'Image de notre corps* (Paris, Nouvelle Revue critique, 1939), p. 17.

In America, Negroes are segregated. In South America, Negroes are whipped in the streets, and Negro strikers are cut down by machine-guns. In West Africa, the Negro is an animal. And there beside me, my neighbor in the university, who was born in Algeria, told me: "As long as the Arab is treated like a man, no solution is possible."

"Understand, my dear boy, color prejudice is something I find utterly foreign. . . . But of course, come in, sir, there is no color prejudice among us. . . . Quite, the Negro is a man like ourselves. . . . It is not because he is black that he is less intelligent than we are. . . . I had a Senegalese buddy in the army who was really clever. . . ."

Where am I to be classified? Or, if you prefer, tucked away?

"A Martinican, a native of 'our' old colonies."

Where shall I hide?   20

"Look at the nigger! . . . Mama, a Negro! . . . Hell, he's getting mad. . . . Take no notice, sir, he does not know that you are as civilized as we. . . ."

My body was given back to me sprawled out, distorted, recolored, clad in mourning in that white winter day. The Negro is an animal, the Negro is bad, the Negro is mean, the Negro is ugly; look, a nigger, it's cold, the nigger is shivering, the nigger is shivering because he is cold, the little boy is trembling because he is afraid of the nigger, the nigger is shivering with cold, that cold that goes through your bones, the handsome little boy is trembling because he thinks that the nigger is quivering with rage, the little white boy throws himself into his mother's arms: Mama, the nigger's going to eat me up.

All round me the white man, above the sky tears at its navel, the earth rasps under my feet, and there is a white song, a white song. All this whiteness that burns me. . . .

I sit down at the fire and I become aware of my uniform. I had not seen it. It is indeed ugly. I stop there, for who can tell me what beauty is?

Where shall I find shelter from now on? I felt an easily identifiable flood   25
mounting out of the countless facets of my being. I was about to be angry. The fire was long since out, and once more the nigger was trembling.

"Look how handsome that Negro is! . . . "

"Kiss the handsome Negro's ass, madame!"

Shame flooded her face. At last I was set free from my rumination. At the same time I accomplished two things: I identified my enemies and I made a scene. A grand slam. Now one would be able to laugh.

The field of battle having been marked out, I entered the lists.

What? While I was forgetting, forgiving, and wanting only to love, my   30
message was flung back in my face like a slap. The white world, the only honorable one, barred me from all participation: A man was expected to behave like a man. I was expected to behave like a black man—or at least like a nigger. I shouted a greeting to the world and the world slashed away my joy. I was told to stay within bounds, to go back where I belonged.

They would see, then! I had warned them, anyway. Slavery? It was no longer even mentioned, that unpleasant memory. My supposed inferiority? A hoax that it was better to laugh at. I forgot it all, but only on condition that the world not protect itself against me any longer. I had incisors to test. I was sure they were strong. And besides. . . .

What! When it was I who had every reason to hate, to despise, I was rejected? When I should have been begged, implored, I was denied the slightest recognition? I resolved, since it was impossible for me to get away from an *inborn complex*, to assert myself as a BLACK MAN. Since the other hesitated to recognize me, there remained only one solution: to make myself known.

In *Anti-Semite and Jew* (p. 95), Sartre says: "They [the Jews] have allowed themselves to be poisoned by the stereotype that others have of them, and they live in fear that their acts will correspond to this stereotype. . . . We may say that their conduct is perpetually overdetermined from the inside."

All the same, the Jew can be unknown in his Jewishness. He is not wholly what he is. One hopes, one waits. His actions, his behavior are the final determinant. He is a white man, and, apart from some rather debatable characteristics, he can sometimes go unnoticed. He belongs to the race of those who since the beginning of time have never known cannibalism. What an idea, to eat one's father! Simple enough, one has only not to be a nigger. Granted, the Jews are harassed—what am I thinking of? They are hunted down, exterminated, cremated. But these are little family quarrels. The Jew is disliked from the moment he is tracked down. But in my case everything takes on a *new* guise. I am given no chance. I am overdetermined from without. I am the slave not of the "idea" that others have of me but of my own appearance.

I move slowly in the world, accustomed now to seek no longer for upheaval. I progress by crawling. And already I am being dissected under white eyes, the only real eyes. I am *fixed*. Having adjusted their microtomes, they objectively cut away slices of my reality. I am laid bare. I feel, I see in those white faces that it is not a new man who has come in, but a new kind of man, a new genus. Why, it's a Negro!   35

I slip into corners, and my long antennae pick up the catch-phrases strewn over the surface of things—nigger underwear smells of nigger—nigger teeth are white—nigger feet are big—the nigger's barrel chest—I slip into corners, I remain silent, I strive for anonymity, for invisibility. Look, I will accept the lot, as long as no one notices me!

"Oh, I want you to meet my black friend. . . . Aimé Césaire, a black man and a university graduate. . . . Marian Anderson, the finest of Negro singers. . . . Dr. Cobb, who invented white blood, is a Negro. . . . Here, say hello to my friend from Martinique (be careful, he's extremely sensitive). . . . "

Shame. Shame and self-contempt. Nausea. When people like me, they tell me it is in spite of my color. When they dislike me, they point out that it is not because of my color. Either way, I am locked into the infernal circle. . . .

● Applying a Postcolonial Frame

1. Work through the philosophical problem Fanon poses in the first four paragraphs. Which terms do you need to understand to grasp his point? Ontology, for example, is a philosophical term that refers to the fundamental categories of existence, and the ways of relating within a given category. So Fanon is talking about social interaction as a means of defining and knowing oneself. What interrupts this philosophical process, however, for the colonized being? Why is "every ontology (connection within a category) made unattainable in a colonized and civilized society"?

2. Note what happens to the black man once he is subjected to the eyes of the white man, as Fanon puts it.

   • How would you explain the concept of third-person consciousness, and how is it "negating," as you understand it?

   • Fanon focuses on the male subject; how well do you see his critique applying to the female subaltern?

3. Explain Fanon's point that the "white man . . . had woven me out of a thousand details, anecdotes, and stories." How is he made responsible for his body, his race, and his ancestors, as he argues? How do you see this colonialist/racist legacy as different from mainstream identity?

4. "I sit down at the fire and I become aware of my uniform. I had not seen it. It is indeed ugly" (para. 24). How has body consciousness as Fanon describes it affected him psychologically? How can you relate it to Sartre's notion of Jews being overdetermined, and what do you see as the difference, as Fanon experiences it? What makes the colonial gaze so powerful, for Fanon?

5. Reread Fuller's narrative (p. 430) from a Fanonian perspective. Does it change any of your understanding of the actions on the part of the black Zimbabweans?

t o p i c s   f o r   w r i t i n g

1. In Theroux, we see the "other" as a product of colonial domination in their own land; in Bumiller, as the exotic objects of a Western observer; in Fuller, as the resistant forces reclaiming their land; and in Fanon, as an alienated aspect of the self. Analyze the rhetorical construction of the "other" in each of the readings.

   • Do you find the categories "master" and "resistant" discourses satisfactory?

   • Do the authors see themselves as active participants in forming the "other" through their writing?

   • What are their differing rhetorical stances toward the "other"?

- How do Theroux and Bumiller differ in their stances from Fanon, and what is the rhetorical result of their difference? How do you see Fuller's stance in relation to these?

Consider how you see these authors in rhetorical relation to each other: Theroux and Bumiller can be seen as writing from the mainstream, Fuller as a child living through the transition of power, and Fanon from within a colonized position. How else might you formulate their rhetorical relationship?

2. Are the colonized figures in each of these readings feminized? If so, how are they made to seem voiceless, powerless, needy, dependent? Do we see any points of resistance in their words or acts?

    Rather than analyzing figures in each of the readings, try organizing your essay by a theory of feminization—by steps in the process. Is it fair to say that the colonized figure is feminized first by being depicted as an exotic being, some delicate, ethereal "other," and then by being silenced and represented by the more powerful voice; that the next step is . . . ? Focus on sketching out a process of feminization as the means to addressing the topic.

3. Fanon sees himself, a black man under colonial rule, as "overdetermined from without." How would you explain the condition of "overdetermination"? Where do you see means for creating a voice, a path of resistance?

- How is a set of social practices—how an individual is put in relation to others in his or her society—transformed into a psychological state in which the individual becomes aware of himself or herself as an "other," as a being defined by those outside her or him?

- How is language used to create this sense of being defined from without?

- Do we see this psychological state among the aborigines in Theroux's chapter? among the villagers in Bumiller? among the black Zimbabweans in Fuller?

- Do you see acts of resistance in each populace? What forms do these take, and how are they made possible?

**This Chapter's
Rhetorical Concepts**

- Understanding domestic forms
  of colonization
- Analyzing the ways in which
  difference is constructed
  rhetorically and materially
- Reading cultural "scripts"

Reading Critically About Domestic Colonization

An American of Color

VICTOR VILLANUEVA

*Victor Villanueva is a prominent scholar of rhetoric and a professor of English at Washington State
University. This selection is from his autobiographical book* Bootstraps: From an American
Academic of Color *(1993). He employs a range of voices and discourses, writing about his past in
the third person and present tense, moving from street language to conversational prose to academic
discourse. Villanueva critically constructs a narrative of his life as a Puerto Rican New Yorker; a
student, soldier, husband, father, worker; a student again; and, ultimately, a university faculty
member who nonetheless lived in poverty. In this chapter, Villanueva confronts us with the assumptions the academy makes about an academic of color.*

A **party, a bloody knife hanging from a hanging arm,** eye level, Mom and
Dad by the hand, running. Maybe three years old. Brooklyn. The picture
remains, forty years later.

Seated behind a pegboard desk in the middle of a furnitureless living room,
41 Bartlett Street, Williamsburg, Brooklyn, Mrs. Ashell nearby, Dad walking in
with a roll of linoleum. Why this memory? Maybe a three-year-old's sense of
affluence: a step up from the storefront flat.

Walking from Bartlett to John Lee's hand laundry, alone. Maybe aged four.
From Bartlett to somewhere near the Myrtle Avenue el. Shortest person on
street corners. The only one waiting for lights to turn green. No memory of
anyone asking where his Mommy is.

Just last week, 1992, Flagstaff, Arizona. A little three- or four-year-old
child is wandering around the supermarket. A concerned woman bends over:
"Did you lose your Mommy?" The same week, the same store, a little three- or
four-year-old American Indian child is wandering, bawling loudly. People stop
and stare. No one asks.

Sometime around six, the television. All kinds of kids, some of them strangers, congregate in the living room on Sunday evening for Walt Disney. The rest of the week, there are the Uncles who emcee cartoon shows, and there is Buffalo Bob, Lucy, Ralph Cramden. It was nice to see someone who lived like we did, maybe a little worse: loudmouth Ralph and his "one a dese days, Alice." He talked like the Micks, the Patties, the policemen. Some part of me has always been thankful that Ricky Ricardo was Cuban, even if he did sound portorican, what with his exaggerated accent, his complacency at the jibes on his accent. I stopped watching when Lucy and Ricky moved from the block to the 'burbs. I didn't need Ricky. I had Zorro. On Wednesday nights I could stay up past bedtime to watch Zorro. He was my special hero. On TV, he alone gave the Latino dignity for me. The Cisco Kid and Pancho were too foreign—another time, another place, another Spanish. Pancho was sillier than Ricky. But there was something Latino and not Mexican about Zorro, Don Diego, Don Alejandro—something old-world, Spaniard. Mami called my grandfather Don Basilio. Mami, especially, liked to claim Spain. I don't think I understood the colonial picture being presented in Zorro, just knew that the Latino could have a dashing, good-looking Robin Hood too.

Time and place and television didn't quite come together in the child's mind. I thought Beaver lived in another time, closer to the present than the Lone Ranger, even closer than Sky King, but not the present, not the 1950s I knew. It hadn't occurred to me that there would be Beavers in other places, neighbors on a global scale. The Cleavers, Sky King and Penny, the Lone Ranger and Tonto (Mami: "*Mira, tonto!*" when I would do something dumb; "Wake up, dummy," same thing). Not one of those TV folks fit my idea of contemporary Americans.

Before we got the neighborhood TV, before lessons on Liberty Statues and melting pots in school, the Americans I knew were the older folks who cared for me: portoricans from the family, Enchi's mom, *la comai*, portorican for *comadre*, godmother; and from as far back as I can remember, there was the old Jewish woman and the old Chinese man.

It wasn't a *barrio*, really, Williamsburg, Brooklyn, where I grew up before we moved up to Bed-Stuy. There was no one overriding ghetto culture, "ghetto" in the formal sense, an ethnic way-station to assimilation. We were portoricans, mostly, but not all alike: some of us *nuyorcinos*, natives to New York, Spanglish speakers: "*Dame la cuada*"; "Give me the quarter"; some of us from great cities on "the Island," like San Juan and Rio Piedras, pronouncing my name "*Vi-lya-nueva*"; some of us *jibaros*, country folk, with their strange Spanish: "*Bi-ja-nueba*." We were browns. We were black, the African Americans of the block, almost exclusively, it seemed, pouring out of one house on Bartlett Street, my street, the block. And we were many other colors, the world's poor. There was a *barrio* in Manhattan, Spanish Harlem, where *mi Tia Fela* lived, where there were more PRs hanging out on front stoops, and fewer broes, fewer of *los negros* who were not portorican, where there were more Cochifrito signs. So, it wasn't a *barrio*, but Bartlett Street and the Williamsburg district were the block.

The block had many hues and many sounds, mainly black and brown hues and sounds, but others as well, yellows and olives, and variations on white. Except for the Whites I would meet later, except for the middle class (having met the truly wealthy where my *abuela* lived as a resident cook for a Central Park family), I grew up among the poor, some passing through, some permanent residents.

Mrs. Ashell was never not an old woman: wrinkled face with wire-rimmed   10
glasses, white hair in a topknot, print housedresses that buttoned up the front, nun's shoes. She lived next door, the next apartment. Yet her home was older. Always dark. It even smelled of old. Milk bottles on the fire escape, an ice box, not a refrigerator. Mrs. Ashell would speak of the old country, of being a greenhorn, when Sol was a doughboy, the change in the neighborhood when the *schwartzes* moved in, her Sonny wanting to put her away (probably to a retirement community, Sonny, the successful lawyer). From Mrs. Ashell came the smell of potato pancakes, latkes, an offering on Sunday mornings, knishes on occasion, matzah balls and chicken fat (pronounced something like *fiat*) when I was sick, with a *gesundheit* or a "Bless you" but no "God bless you." From her I knew of *yarmulkes* and *sheitelah*. And I was *bubbela*, sometimes *bubby*.

Mrs. Ashell. She had likely lived in that third-floor apartment next to ours longer than my folks had been alive. And I knew that, what with the icebox and all. She was America, but she was not as American as my family and me. Mom and Dad would talk of life *en la isla*. *La isla* was part of America. The old country was not.

A tale from "the Island."

Story has it that my mother had been sold into servitude to a wealthy Chicago family. She had been shipped to Chicago to save her from my father, if I remember rightly. Dad, fresh out of the army, followed her there, and together they fled to New York. That was in 1947. I was born a year later. Their telling was not political; it was romantic. There was no "Can you imagine!?" My guess was that it was easily imaginable on the Island. I get the sense that they even felt they had committed a wrong in not having abided by the contract that had con-scripted my mother. Their telling is of a love story. And it is. A forty-four year marriage, as I write this, no trial separations.

So it was that I remember thinking that Mom was so American that she could be bought and sold; Dad so American that he could come and go. Mrs. Ashell had to have papers, a stay at Ellis Island, no talk of having gone back to the Jewish ghetto of London. She was foreign. I was American.

John Lee owned a Chinese hand laundry. I would go to his place during lunch   15
or after school. I think of John Lee whenever I see Edward G. Robinson in *Key Largo*. Few parallels in the personalities, likely. But there was something in the way John Lee and Edward G. Robinson wore their fifties, broad, pleated pants, the waist high over round bellies, so high that their torsos seemed short, still shorter by

broad ties; something in the way each held a cigar. Just that John Lee had the eyes of an Asian, but then, so did Edward G. Robinson. Stereotypes can be a bother.

Maybe age eight, I asked John Lee (who was never John or Mr. Lee) his age. "Sickty-fye Chinee; sickty-foe Amelican." Thick black hair, endless energy, laughing loudly when he would take me on amusement park rides in Coney Island: he didn't seem sixty-four or sixty-five to me. Mami explained that the Chinese counted life from inception. No conflict. That was their way, and it made sense. We had our way, and it made sense too.

That there are different worldviews, different notions of what constitutes reality, was always a given. That this is a heavy philosophical concern among academics today, even a radical rhetorical concern, only shows the limits of experience within a stratified society. Freire writes about "experts on Marx" who have never had a cup of coffee in a worker's home. How much can they know, really?

John Lee had a wife in Kowloon. He had supported her for years, thirty-five years or thereabouts. John Lee owned a high-rise apartment building in Kowloon, too. I have no idea what his wife looked like. There was a framed picture of his apartment building in the "almost-a-back room" of his laundry though.

The almost-a-back room was the social center. It was where we went when the laundry was closed. The kitchen was there, a table and chairs, a vinyl couch, the bathroom. The front room held a narrow entrance for customers, a counter with chicken wire to the ceiling, a small two-foot by two-foot opening with a little door where tickets and money and bundles of clothes wrapped in butcher paper would pass. I'd help wrap, sometimes count out change. On the other side of the counter were two large ironing tables, maybe six-feet square, with heavy irons, small tubs where the irons would be dipped before hitting a shirt, steam spewing out; beside the irons, copper bottles with what looked like kazoos attached for blowing mist over stubborn wrinkles, a tabletop steam roller, where starched collars and cuffs got pressed, a picture on the wall of Chiang Kai-Shek in full military regalia. Between the front and the back, "walls" of painted wood sheets on studs and a curtain, making four walls that surrounded a bed and a dresser. It always smelled of incense in that little area, the bed's room, not much larger than the bed. I would sleep there when I was still young enough to require naps.

The "real back room" held a coal-burning potbelly stove in the middle, four large tubs and a large washboard in one corner, a couple of saw horses that I would ride, wires strung from the ceiling. Laundry was washed there, then hung to dry from ceiling wires. John Lee's hand laundry smelled of clean and of steam and of Niagara starch in boiling water. Sometimes there would be a loud hiss, and the smell of soy sauce and soybeans and vegetables would pour in from the almost-a-back room. Sometimes a fried egg sandwich for my lunch. Sometimes egg foo yung, when fish-head soup was the specialty for Mom and Dad. Store fronts and store-front apartments, a laundry, a business, Chinese food unlike Chinatown's. This was part of my world, part of America—yet foreign, foreign to most Americans, I'd guess.

In the almost-a-back room: the picture of John Lee's apartment building back in China and a picture of John Lee himself, suit and tie, speaking into

20

a microphone. John Lee was a big shot in the Chinese community (which was larger than Chinatown). Other Chinese launderers seemed to seek his advice. John Lee was a merchant, with a "China-side wife," his own high rise, able to dispense silver dollars on my birthdays and on Christmases and Easters. He was the affluent among the poor. It was a sign of affluence that when John Lee would take us out to a Chinese restaurant, waiters would seat us in the back room among the silk-suited Chinese men and fur-collared Chinese women; a sign of affluence that waiters would bow often, that they would actually write down our order. Mom and Dad could claim none of that.

Mami on the assembly line at Standard Toycraft. Forty dollars a week—a dollar an hour. Dad, a machinist's assistant, then shop steward for a time, as well as working downstairs at Jimmy Vriniotis's deli in the evenings, short order at a greasy spoon. John Lee had more than we. But John Lee was an immigrant. He could never look American (thoughts of a child). He had an accent. So did Mom and Dad, but John Lee's was foreign. He'd say "fly lice" or "loose poke" instead of "fried rice" and "roast pork." He'd call me "Bobby," despite my lessons on calling me "Papi."

There is a point here that I'll get to in detail below. It is that we behave as if the minority problem is the immigrant problem. Two generations of learning the language and the ways of America, and all will be better, we hear. But two generations come and go and all that happens is that the minority's native tongue is gone. The African American lost his native tongue two hundred years ago. More on this too. For now, look to how far the analogy has been drawn. After sociolinguists posited a "language interference" to explain a transitional period in a foreign-language learner's acquisition of a new language, linguists and compositionists posited a dialect interference among Black English speakers. Learn the language and all will be better, they suggested, a promise to African Americans as well as non-English speakers. Two generations and blacks will melt? We need to look more broadly, historically, to the differences between minorities and immigrants, so as to break from the not helpful analogy between the two in the classroom and in our theorizing.

School.
All Saints, the Catholic school around the corner from Bartlett, across the   25
street from PS 168, the public school. All Saints charges a dollar a month for tuition (three a month in the seventh and eighth grades). It is my school from kindergarten till eighth-grade graduation. There I am filled with Catholicism, "Ave Maria," and with "Jingle Bells," maxims from Poor Richard, laws from Newton, the Beaver's neighbors—Dick and Jane, the parts of speech, times tables. There I play in the melting pot.
Or maybe it was a stewpot. A stew, not the easy mixes of the salad-bowl metaphor, the static coexistence of the mosaic metaphor. The stew metaphor maintains the violence of the melting-pot metaphor while suggesting that some

of the ingredients do not lose all of their original identity, though altered, taking in the juices from the other ingredients of the pot, adding to the juices; all of us this one thing, Americans, and all of us some things else; for some of us, never complete integration and never complete integrity. With the stewpot comes the sense that not all the ingredients are equally important, that the stew needs the beef of a Yankee pot roast cut more than fatback or red beans and *sofrito*.

As I saw it, prestige belonged to the Wattses, Andrew and Stephen. There were nuns and priests in their family. They lived in one of the brownstones, around the corner, not of the block. The kids on the block didn't look like the Wattses, didn't talk like them. I don't recall ever thinking they were better, in the sense of superior—they just had it better. And I don't recall ever thinking about what "having it better" meant; I just knew that they did.

There was something special about Jarapolk Cigash and his family too. But theirs was different from the Wattses. The Wattses were connected to All Saints, somehow, to culture, though that word—culture—only occurs to me now. Jara-polk, "Yacko," Jerry, was one of my two best friends (superlatives have no mean-ing for children). The Cigashes lived in the neighborhood, but there was some-thing special about their apartment: a piano that his sister played; a stand for sheet music alongside a violin case. Jerry practiced the violin. His parents would speak of their escape from the Ukraine, explain what it meant to be a satellite country. They had accents, thick accents, but there was an air about them. They were educated, in that special sense in which *educated* is sometimes used. It was clear to me even then that Brooklyn would only be a stopover for the Cigashes. It was not their home nor would it be. That wasn't clear about the Villanuevas.

I had the sense that there was something different about Charles Ber-mudez. He was kind of pale, allergic to milk. There was something strange about the way Charles's father held his cigarettes: palm up, the cigarette pinched between thumb and middle finger, like a movie old-world aristocrat or a monocle-wearing fascist general. Yet I didn't see prestige in the Bermudezes, really, just difference. Now as I look back, I wonder if the Bermudezes were Latin Americans on the run. Back then, I just assumed they were portoricans. Portoricans could not be foreign, like the foreignness of the very American Wattses or the foreignness of the Eastern European Cigashes.

Marie Engells, the German girl, was another stopover. We were in school   30 together from kindergarten through the eighth grade, yet I never knew her. Some of that was due to childish gender discrimination, no doubt, though Rose Marie, Peanuts, the Italian girl, was always a special friend, not boyfriend-girlfriend, not one of the boys, and not so as I feared being seen as a sissy, just a special friend. We'd buy each other knishes or soft, salted pretzels from the pushcart after school. But there was something about Marie Engells: an awfully erect back, the hint of a smile constantly on her lips. Maybe all this was in my imagination, but she seemed aloof to me. Marie Engells was the girl valedicto-rian at eighth-grade graduation. Jarapolk Cigash was the boy. They were immi-grants. And something was theirs that wasn't mine. Yet I was American and so were my parents and the generation before them, full citizens since 1919.

Some fell into a grey area between the immigrants and those like me, the spics or the blacks. I knew Peanuts wasn't like us, but she wasn't like Marie Engells or Jarapolk Cigash either. And I was less sure about Frankie Thompson, the Irish kid who introduced me to my first cigarette in one of the neighborhood abandoned lots where we jumped burning Christmas trees every year. I was less sure about Paul Caesar, "the Polack." I was less sure about their advantage despite the same school, the same neighborhood.

They would have been "new immigrants," not as easily assimilable, the bad-element immigrants that prompted the latent footnote to the Statue of Liberty: "in limited numbers." In terms of ethnicity, the Cigashes should have been "new immigrants" too, but pianos and violins suggested maybe these new immigrants came from higher in the class system. Class comes into the academic's thoughts. The child only knew that Peanuts and Frankie Thompson and Paul Caesar were not in the same league as Jerry or Marie Engells, the Wattses, maybe even Charles Bermudez. And it didn't have anything to do with brains. Yet I still believed they had something over Lana Walker and Irving Roach and me.

Irving Roach was the only African American kid I knew who didn't live on the same street I did. The African American kids went to PS 168. "You know we ain't Catholic," I was told once when Hambone said he wished he could read like I did, when I asked why his folks didn't send him to All Saints. Irving Roach didn't live on the block, but was of the block. I had a life on the block—with Butch, the black bully (stereotypes sometimes have bases in fact—Black Butch the Bad-ass Bully, Darnell the Dude, Lazy Leroy, Hambone with the thick glasses and bookish ways), Papo, the PR bully, Mike and Steven Figueroa and Enchi and Hershey. And I had a life at All Saints. And only Juan Torres, Johnny, my best friend from kindergarten till my family moved to California, and Irving Roach crossed over. And Irving Roach was kind, would bring his baby sister with him when he came to visit. And we would talk school things. He was smart. But I don't recall imagining him "making it."

Lana Walker might. She was as aloof as Marie Engells, as smart, too, I thought. And Lana Walker was beautiful, black and slender (but not skinny) and tall. I was short and chubby and all too insecure to do more than talk with her in passing in the nine years we were in school together. At eighth grade graduation Marie Engells would win the math award I really wanted. Lana Walker would get some special recognition, though I no longer remember what. I would get the spelling and the penmanship awards: the Merriam-Webster spelling bee champ that year. Jerry and Marie Engells went to the Catholic college-prep high school. Lana Walker made the alternate list. I never saw Irving Roach again. Juan Torres ended up in the vo-tech school in his area. I went to Alexander Hamilton Vocational-Technical High School.

So what had happened? I was an "A" student, third or fourth in the class, 35 able with language, Saturdays spent on special classes in preparation for the entrance exam to the college prep high school. Why hadn't I made it? Mom says the Bishop's Fund, but that seems inconsistent with a dollar tuition. Cultural bias in standardized tests is the more obvious answer.

I think of cultural bias in two ways. The first is a linguistic and rhetorical bias. It has to do with the test-makers' assumption that words have fixed meanings that are not arbitrary. The psychologist Lev Vygotsky, literary critic Mikhail Bakhtin, the philosopher Jacques Derrida, the archeologist and social critic Michel Foucault, as well as the Sophists of fifth-century B.C. Greece, and a score of others, call this into question, seeing language tied to time and place and culture and even ideology. So do kids who are bilingual and bidialectical. Sociolinguist Fernando Peñalosa sees the code switcher, the bidialectal speaker, as "the skillful speaker [who] uses his knowledge of how language choices are interpreted in his community to structure the interaction so as to maximize outcomes favorable to himself." In plain English: the code-switcher is a rhetorical power player. He knows language isn't fixed, has a relativistic perception of language, knows that words take on hues of meaning when colored by cognates; and for the bilingual there are words seeming the same in both languages, derived from the same sources, but nevertheless having undergone change through time and place. A relativistic notion of language is bound to be a problem for the standardized-test taker. A solution: English Only. One of the many problems with the solution: better writers have a heightened metalinguistic awareness, an awareness of language's multiplicity. So do the bidialectal and the bilingual. English Only could destroy the very metalinguistic awareness that could make for a better writer. Doomed if we teach to the test: doomed to lose the power of having a greater metalinguistic awareness. Doomed if we don't: doomed to be denied access.

The second way I think of cultural bias in standardized tests has to do with the differences between the minority and the immigrant. The immigrant seeks to take on the culture of the majority. And the majority, given certain preconditions, not the least of which is displaying the language and dialect of the majority, accepts the immigrant. The minority, even when accepting the culture of the majority, is never wholly accepted. There is always a distance.

The minority looked at the immigrants like John Lee and Mrs. Ashell, who had been on the continental United States far longer than his parents, who had some economic advantages (Mrs. Ashell through her Sonny, at least), and still felt they were less American than he. The minority looked at his immigrant school friends, second generation, maybe, and believed that theirs was the advantage.

More recent.

A discussion concerning a minority issue takes place at a national conference. It starts to get heated. One person tells of his sympathy. He says, "After all, we're all minorities in a sense." And in a sense he is right. In a sense. Relatively few these days can claim direct lineage to the majority culture of England. But he misses essential differences between immigrants and minorities.

40

A writing group in a graduate composition course. Martha Lopez's and Paul Reyes's group-work gets loud, drowning out the rest. Martha: black eyes, thick black hair, an accent to her voice. Paul: pale skinned, green eyed, red haired, no accent. Martha argues that her writing suffers from having learned English through grammar instruction, rather than through real conversation and writing practice. Paul argues that even after learning the language there is still the problem of thinking like white folks. He'd *be* white to anyone's eyes. He's drawing on contrastive rhetoric, the notion that different cultures display different rhetorical patterns in their discourse (more of which later). Yet there is more going on than Paul's contrastive rhetoric contention. Martha is arguing the case for assimilation through learning the language of the majority. Paul is arguing that learning the language isn't all there is. Both are Latinos, Spanish speakers. But Martha is Colombian; Paul is Puerto Rican. Martha, the immigrant. Paul, the minority. Martha believes in the possibilities for complete, structural assimilation; Paul is more cautious.

I think of those who try to calm others by saying that it takes two generations for ghetto dwellers to move on. This has been the pattern for immigrants. But what then do we do with the African American or the Latino, especially the Mexican-American, on American soil, in American society, far longer than two generations? What happens to them—to *us*—those of us who are of color, those of us normally labelled "minority"? The answer, I believe, comes in looking more closely at how one becomes assimilated.

Three factors affect the possibilities for complete structural assimilation:

1. The historical mode of entry into the dominant society;
2. The number and distribution of those attempting to take part in the overall society; and
3. The racial and cultural characteristics of those seeking equity with the majority.

I condense a list drawn by political scientist Mario Barrera. And even these three are interrelated. But let me continue with the convenience of the separation. To begin, if the mode of entry of the new group is voluntary, the new group does not carry the baggage of having become part of America through bloodshed. The bloodshed of the Civil War was the price paid for the admission of all African Americans as freed citizens ("all" because there were free blacks, as well as slaves, prior). Bloodshed marked the relationship to American Indians. There was the blood let at the Mexican War of 1846; at the Spanish-American War, the war which led to the acquisition of Puerto Rico. If the mode of entry is voluntary, the general attitude is that the new folks will attain full citizenship in time because they would most wish to do so (though we know that first-generation folks, especially refugees from war-torn countries, often hold dreams of returning).

If the mode of entry is voluntary, then the numbers entering would not be great enough to cause a threat to the majority. Should race become a factor, the numbers can be legally controlled.

The Chinese were granted only limited access from 1882, explaining John   45
Lee's China-side wife. Limited access also explains attitudes toward Southeast Asian refugees, Koreans, Filipinos (Asian and Polynesian and, often, Spanish-surnamed, and from a former colony).

Among Europeans, the "New Immigrants" were not welcomed with open arms. Liberty's torch of freedom burned low. In 1907, President Theodore Roosevelt appointed an immigration commission to study what was being per-ceived as an immigration problem. By 1911 the commission issued a forty-two volume report. Its findings were that "new immigrants," Eastern and Southern Europeans, were inherently inferior to old immigrants. The commission cited anthropologist Madison Grant:

> The new immigration contained a large and increasing number of the weak, the broken, and the mentally crippled of all races drawn from the lowest stra-tum of the Mediterranean basin and the Balkans, together with hordes of the wretched, submerged populations of the Polish ghettoes. Our jails, insane asylums, and almshouses are filled with human flotsam and the whole tone of American life, social, moral, and political, has been lowered and vulgarized by them.

By 1924 there were legal restrictions against the admission of ruddy-skinned Eastern European and Mediterranean new immigrants to the United States.

And so the numbers remain relatively small, the small numbers initially locating in ethnic pockets surrounded by the dominant group, ghettos, with smaller numbers moving out, for the most part, only after having achieved cul-tural assimilation. That is, if race weren't a factor. Chinatowns remain all through the country. There are fewer Little Italies, I think.

His first professional job, Kansas City. His co-workers, college professors, the middle class, mainly white, say he and his family have moved into the Italian neighborhood. And the old housing projects of the neighborhood do bear a faded wooden imitation of an Italian flag. There is an Italian deli, and the local warehouse supermarket bears an Italian name. But there are no Italians. The neighborhood belongs to the white working class with southern-like twangs to their speech, not Italians but folks claiming rural Arkansas, mainly.

When entry is by conquest, the numbers in the conquered land tend to be greater than the numbers of the conquerors, like the residents of Mexico or New Spain, or like those of Puerto Rico. The restricted landmass of Puerto Rico, a small island, pretty much assured that the numbers could not be turned around in the way the numbers were turned around in parts of conquered Mexico. Since the people are conquered in their own lands, they remain rooted to the land's history and culture.

New Mexico: denied statehood until Anglos outnumber the Hispanics.   50

Arizona: statehood denied, several times, because of the territory's Mexican "mongrel racial character."

From 1891, the Court of Private Claims overturns one land grant after another, until almost all Mexican landowners in New Mexico, Arizona, California, and Texas are displaced (Utah and Colorado never having had large numbers of Mexican landowners).

1928. Congressional hearings on Western Hemisphere Immigration. There is a concerted attempt at preventing the Mexican migrants from working farms, railroads, and mines, of damming the first wave of Mexican immigration which had begun in 1910 (and which would end in 1930). One speaker before the hearings describes Mexicans:

> Their minds run to nothing higher than animal functions—eat, sleep, and sexual debauchery. In every huddle of Mexican shacks one meets the same idleness, hordes of hungry dogs, and filthy children with faces plastered with flies, disease, lice, human filth, stench, promiscuous fornication, bastardy, lounging, apathetic peons and lazy squaws, beans and dried fruit, liquor, general squalor, and envy and hatred of the gringo. These people sleep by day and prowl by night like coyotes, stealing anything they can get their hands on, no matter how useless to them it may be. Nothing left outside is safe unless padlocked or chained down. Yet there are Americans clamoring for more of these human swine to be brought over from Mexico.

The description lumps the Mexicans with the American Indians ("lazy squaws"), another conquered people. Yet the bad-mouthing does not stop the solicitation of Mexican stoop laborers as long as there is profit in having them—and does not distinguish the Mexican from the Mexican American.

When the Great Depression hits, Mexicans and Mexican Americans who apply for relief are directed to "Mexican Bureaus." The Bureaus' job turns out to be *ex*patriation sold as *re*patriation. Mexicans are herded into cattle cars and railroaded to a home that for many has never been theirs. In 1933, a Los Angeles eyewitness to the expatriation process gives voice to the usual rationale:

> The repatriation programme is regarded locally as a piece of consummate statecraft. The average per family cost of executing it is $71.14, including food and transportation. It cost one Los Angeles County $77,249.29 to repatriate one shipment of 6,024. It would have cost $424,933.70 to provide this number with such charitable assistance as they would have been entitled to had they remained—a savings of $347,468.40.

From 1929 to 1934, the number of repatriated Mexicans exceeds 400,000. Approximately half are native to the United States—expatriated. The conquered (minorities) and the voluntary (immigrants) had gotten mixed.

Nor is the confusion of conquered and voluntary out of the ordinary. Others with the same racial and cultural attributes as the conquered, including language, enter voluntarily and follow the pattern of the voluntary immigrant. Puerto 55

Ricans solicited to work in New York and Chicago and Colorado get mixed with other Spanish West Indians and with Central Americans who voluntarily immigrate to the mainland. The same story for the Mexicans of the Southwest, shipped to Pennsylvania and to the Midwest to work mines and stockyards, for Mexicans of the West solicited to work the farms of California and Washington. All get mixed with the Mexican immigrant. And to the extent that structural assimilation is possible for the immigrant, those of the historically conquered who get confused for the Mexican join in the advantage sometimes. But this isn't the rule. More often, the voluntary share in the fate of the historically conquered.

Southeast Asian refugees suffer the historical fate of the Chinese excluded, the fate of the Japanese interred. Cuban refugees suffer the fate of the Puerto Rican and Mexican American. Haitians are black West Indians—a double whammy. I overgeneralize, I know, but I believe the distinction holds generally.

The voluntary of the same or similar cultural and racial attributes as the conquered share in the fate of the conquered. The depression-era expatriation of Mexican Americans with Mexicans was not an isolated instance. The post–Korean War economic recession saw "Operation Wetback" with 3.8 million Mexicans expelled. The series of economic recessions which began in the 1970s has seen a resurgence of "green card" checks. The rationale behind repatriation and expatriation involves the too great numbers, and underlying the rationale is the attitude of conquerors over the conquered. The result tends to exclusion rather than assimilation.

Race is the final factor affecting assimilation. The crackdowns on Mexicans in the 30s, the 50s, and the present have immigration authorities checking documents of those who "look Mexican." The closer the features of a minority correlate to the general features of the majority, the greater the chances for assimilation (and so the Jewish or East Indian or something-looking—but not Puerto Rican–looking—gets his Ph.D. and gets to write this book).

Tato Laviera, a Puerto Rican poet, describes the problem of race, culture, and language:

> i want to go back to puerto rico
> but i wonder if my kink could live
> in ponce, mayaguez and carolina
>
> tengo las venas aculturadas
> escribo in spanglish
> abraham in español
> abraham in english
> tato in spanish
> "taro" in english
> tonto in both languages

Acculturated veins ("*las venas aculturadas*"), yet not American and no longer quite Puerto Rican, linguistically a fool in both English and Spanish ("tonto in both languages"). The minority lives in a netherworld. Not quite American. No home to return to.

While the immigrant tends to become American in two generations, two generations only manages to erode the possibility for migration, for the Puerto Rican's return to the Island, or the Mexican American's (assuming the Mexican American's heritage is not from Mexico's ceded l~~~~~~exas and the like, but from present-day Mexico) return to Mexi~~

Puerto Rico is not my hom~~~~~~~~~~~~~ of its cultural ways are mine. Some of its language. ~~~~~~ ~~uklyn than anything else. The Nuyorcino, often racially clos~~~~~ ~~e African American than to the majority, takes on much of African-American culture.

Pathos-inbetween

Tato again:

> a blackness in spanish
> a blackness in english
> mixture-met on jam sessions in central park,
> there were no differences in
> the sounds merging inside.

And even when external attributes are not black or mulatto, the merging remains. I no longer speak with a blackness, not without the affected quality of white folks trying to sound black, but it resounds more of "home" within me nevertheless.

The new Teaching Assistant was videotaped. He saw and heard the sounds of a New York Jewish intellectual. He was shocked. Something had happened to the sounds of the Brooklyn boy. Yet he knew his portorican blackness remained within.

Nor am I alone in this. There remains Paul Reyes, the green-eyed, red-haired Puerto Rican who referred to "white folks." There remains the empirical—Paul and I are racially white. So Paul Reyes is a graduate student of English in Northern Arizona—and I am one of his English professors. And together we watch the more blatant instances of racism directed at the American Indians where we live: the conquered, their numbers great in Northern Arizona, near America's largest Indian reservation. And the local Navajos tend to be more racially distinct than Paul is or than I am. We have had chances not afforded other Puerto Ricans because we are racially closer to the majority, because we are not part of Northern Arizona's local memory and lore of conquest, because our numbers are so very few in the mountain city. And yet we know we are not assimilated. We are still "Hispanics," a word which says "other-American."

The immigrant enters; the minority is entered upon. Race and culture, sheer numbers and concentration, how one comes to be American: these are the factors that t[...] in the pot. The difference between the immigrant and the [...] difference between immigration and colonization.

N[...] p as well as colonial theory—not theories on biologic[...] cultural deficiency nor racial inequality. Biological deficienc[...] ᵤories no longer gather large followings. Few today would listen to the likes of the nineteenth-century Harvard naturalist, Louis Agassiz, who claimed that the brain of the Negro adult "never gets beyond that observable in the Caucasian in boyhood." Still, Arthur Jensen could argue the case that African Americans are genetically inferior to Whites in 1969 in the *Harvard Educational Review* and again in 1973 in the popular press—*Psychology Today*. And R. J. Herrnstein could provide the same argument in a 1971 *Atlantic Monthly*. Thomas Farrell's counter to biological deficiency theories would not be much better. In his version of cultural deficit theory, African Americans suffer a cognitive disadvantage because they reside in an oral culture. His counters would look at relativistic notions of what constitutes cognitive development—different ways of thinking for different social contexts: Scribner and Cole on the social determinants of cognitive functions, Shirley Brice Heath on the unlikelihood of an exclusively oral culture among African Americans, other counters. Biological and cultural deficit theories are not tenable.

Racial inequality theories, on the other hand, do have a kind of merit. They make sense to me. I think, in particular, of John Ogbu's assertion that there are different kinds of minorities, with some minorities suffering a castelike status. For Ogbu there are three different kinds of minorities in America: the castelike, the autonomous, and the immigrant minority. The immigrant minority is clear. Even if she maintains her ethnicity—like, say, Italians often do—the qualities ascribed to her ethnicity are not such that she would be necessarily excluded from the mainstream. The autonomous are those who are subject to ethnic or religious distinctiveness yet manage to accommodate the mainstream, even if not assimilate. Ogbu cites American Jews and Mormons as instances of autonomous minorities. The castelike are those who are regarded primarily on the basis of some particular birth ascription, in this country, race or a particular ethnicity, like Latinos. A while back the media focused less on Jesse Jackson's platform than on his race. Jackson, a castelike minority, was the black candidate. But Dukakis got the more usual coverage. Dukakis was not the second-generation Greek immigrant candidate, except when he himself asserted it. There can be no denying that some minorities cannot transcend their race or ethnicity, even when vying for the presidency of the United States or a seat on the Supreme Court.

For all their worth, however, racial inequality theories have a historical shortcoming. The ideology of racial difference, for instance, is relatively new historically, traceable to the eighteenth century. African Americans were savages; American Indians, noble savages—culturally inferior, not necessarily biologically. The cultural inferiority (or religious inferiority) of some races determined their suitability for slavehood or other forms of oppression. Racial inequality theory does not explain, for example, why East Indians are considered black by the British but not by Americans. The most suggestive answer: India was a British colony, not an American colony. The American East Indian is more often just another foreigner, another immigrant. Race alone is not the distinctive factor. Race and a history of subservience to those who remain dominant makes for the castelike minority.

Colonial theory refines the concept of the castelike minority by looking to the common feature in the castelike's histories—colonization or colonization's explicitly commodified form, slavery. The autonomous minority holds no memory of colonization in this country. There is no national memory of long-term subjugation of the autonomous minority or the immigrant, as there is of the Puerto Rican, the Mexican, the American Indian, the African American, the Asian (mainly by way of the Pacific Islands, colonies once). Looking to colonization makes a distinction not contained in race alone.

And we can look at present-day colonialism. Political scientists today speak   70
of neo-colonialism, when the colonial power, the metropole, exercises economic control over a colony, saving on having to provide resident military and political forces, using the military only as a final resort. Think of Panama. Think of the Philippine Islands, the former colony granted independence by the United States, but with the United States still managing to mess with Marcos and with Aquino. Then think of the numbers of American minorities who do not enjoy equal status with their peers, even when managing to move within the class system, the many who must remain dependent on financing from the State, the great numbers—an overwhelming majority—of minorities who people the prisons, not because of a pathology but because of money, political prisoners in an economic sense, as then Ambassador to the United Nations, Andrew Young, and then head of "Operation Push," Jesse Jackson, pointed out back in 1978. There is a kind of neo-colonialism at play right here in the United States.

Minorities remain a colonized people. Sociologist Gail Omvedt sees colonialism as "the economic, political and cultural domination of one cultural-ethnic group by another." And Gonzales Casanova goes a step further, writing in terms of the "domination and exploitation among culturally heterogeneous, distinct groups," thereby accounting for a colonialism even when the colonized live and work among the colonizers. Casanova is referring to internal colonialism. Colonial theory—internal colonialism—gives a historical precedent and gives a contemporary explanation for how minorities remain castelike, even when racially white, even when white and an expert, a practicing Ph.D. in the language of the dominant.

Mami believed in the traditional idea of language and assimilation. She and Dad had had English instruction in their schooling in Puerto Rico. It was required, an old-fashioned colonialism. Mami had gone as far as the third year of high school; Dad started high school under the GI Bill but switched to a trade school; still, there was the English of the army, though like most Puerto Ricans, his service was mainly on the Island, segregated forces, with the English coming mainly from the officers who were, more often than not, not Puerto Rican. There hasn't been a Villanueva yet who has completed high school (including the one with the Ph.D. and his twenty-one-year-old, GED-toting son).

Mami tells of her and Dad listening to radio shows in English and trying to read the American newspapers, tells of speaking to their Papi in both Spanish and English from the start. He remembers their insistence that he speak in English, that he teach it to them.

Sister Rhea Marie, his kindergarten teacher, visits his home. She is short, thin, plain, a little gap to her front teeth. She wears the traditional Dominican nun's habit: white starch circumscribing her face, seeming severe, as if it would cut off circulation to her face, topped by a black veil, long white apron in front, long rosary beads marking the contrast. For a many-generationed Catholic home, her apparel tells of authority. Her face tells of kindness.

She visits to speak with his Mami and Dad. And she tells them they should 75 speak to Papi in English because "Victor speaks with an accent." But a simple bit of logic has gotten by the good sister: *they* speak with an accent and the accent is passed on with the English. Victor (always "Victor" before Authority) spoke with an accent *because* they spoke in English. There was no verbal deprivation at play, just a process that takes time, "interlanguage," to use a sociolinguistic term.

It took TV for Papi to discover the ways of white language. Watching TV, he discovered that the dessert-that-there's-always-room-for and the rainbow color weren't pronounced the same. It would be a while longer before he stopped pronouncing the *e* when pronouncing certain words—like a fenc*e*d jard.

Then in college he's told to pronounce the *e* when reading Shakespeare, Donne, Marvell, and the like—wing*e*d steed. And he discovers that the British prestige dialect, the Received Pronunciation, prefers a trilled *r*: the rrain in Spain. He discovers this after having worked at removing the trill from the word *three* back in grrade thrree. His English was better than Sister Rhea Marie knew.

Bedtimes, before my mom started working swing and Dad started moonlighting, was reading time. Stories came from *Classics Illustrated*, a kind of comic book. The *Morte d'Arthur*, stories of King Arthur's court, stuck with me, the illustrations leaping to memory a quarter-century later, when reading Mallory in college. Comic books would be my reading supplement to the end of my teen years, a one-a-day within longer readings. And the readings would include Homer and Shelley and Sir Arthur Conan Doyle. Reading and TV and Saturday matinees filled my time more than anything else. And by the time eighth-grade graduation rolled around, I was a spelling-bee champ. And when the school-sponsored reading stopped, reading didn't. And the accent disappeared, and Spanish no longer came easily, sometimes going through French or through Latin in my head, the languages of my profession, searching for the Spanish with which to speak to my family. Assimilation.

And the immigrant went to college prep. And the minority didn't.

● Applying a Postcolonial Frame

1. We can call Villanueva's approach to depicting individual lives materialist in nature. To explore that claim, consider how he evokes the experience of Mrs. Ashell, John Lee, himself, and his parents: how are we to come to understand their lives?

2. The young Victor develops a taxonomy, a classification system, of the range of races, ethnicities, and immigrants that surrounds him in his neighborhood. How does he gather these groups, which include his schoolmates Jarapold Cigash, Charles Bermudez, Marie Engells, and others? What principle of social division do you see him beginning to learn inductively?

3. Explain in your own words the concept of *code-switching*, as Villanueva uses the term.

   - Why do you think it is so potentially valuable to understand it as a rhetorical tool, for a child in Villanueva's situation?

   - Are you aware of yourself switching codes in your own social environments? Under the pressure of what power systems might you consciously feel the need to switch to a different linguistic code?

4. How are "English only" laws (which specify that all instruction in public schools will be conducted in English) misguided, as you understand Villanueva's argument, if the argument for them is the benefit of accelerated assimilation? What sort of group is likely to suffer from such legislation, even if we accept this assimilation as a benefit?

   - Using the factors Villanueva analyzes for assessing the likelihood of a group gaining full assimilation into mainstream U.S. culture, consider how great a challenge the following groups (plus any of your own choosing) is likely to face.
     - Pakistanis
     - Iraqis
     - non-aboriginal Australians
     - white South Africans
     - Russians

   - How is the minority overdetermined, and how is the immigrant less likely to be so?

   - Is gender equivalent to a caste status, as Villanueva uses Ogbu's term? Is homosexuality?

5. What forms of resistant discourse can you identify Villanueva using in his chapter? What range of rhetorical techniques can you see in Villanueva's depiction and critique of the minority's internalized colonization?

   Explain how the chapter provides the logic for its final lines: "And the immigrant went to college prep. And the minority didn't." What rhetorical motives do you see employed?

6. Compare Villanueva's experience of internal colonization to that of the people depicted in Paul Theroux's "Walkabout in Woop Woop" (p. 395). Are the social realities significantly alike, despite their geographic and historical differences? How does Villanueva's chapter help account for any similarities?

Savage Inequalities

JONATHAN KOZOL

An educational critic famed for his devastating critique of mind-numbing curricula and pedagogy in U.S. schools (Death at an Early Age, 1985), Kozol revisited this topic with an economic critique as his framing method. He recounts the experiences of an array of students in privileged and impoverished schools; not surprisingly, his study reveals the many ways in which difference is built into schools as a kind of social tracking. He is expert at selecting the material details that defined and confined the lives of the students at a school in poverty-ridden Bronx, New York, in the 1980s (Kozol's Savage Inequalities appeared in 1991). The following selection is Chapter 3, "The Savage Inequalities of Public Education in New York." In it, quotations from the teachers and children reflect their clear sense of how they have been directed to a "special" path, a path of the internally colonized.

In a country where there is no distinction of class," Lord Acton wrote of the United States 130 years ago, "a child is not born to the station of its parents, but with an indefinite claim to all the prizes that can be won by thought and labor. It is in conformity with the theory of equality . . . to give as near as possible to every youth an equal state in life." Americans, he said, "are unwilling that any should be deprived in childhood of the means of competition."

It is hard to read these words today without a sense of irony and sadness. Denial of "the means of competition" is perhaps the single most consistent outcome of the education offered to poor children in the schools of our large cities; and nowhere is this pattern of denial more explicit or more absolute than in the public schools of New York City.

Average expenditures per pupil in the city of New York in 1987 were some $5,500. In the highest spending suburbs of New York (Great Neck or Manhasset, for example, on Long Island) funding levels rose above $11,000, with the highest districts in the state at $15,000. "Why . . . ," asks the city's Board of Education, "should our students receive less" than do "similar students" who live elsewhere? "The inequity is clear."

But the inequality to which these words refer goes even further than the school board may be eager to reveal. "It is perhaps the supreme irony," says the nonprofit Community Service Society of New York, that "the same Board of Education which perceives so clearly the inequities" of funding between separate towns and cities "is perpetuating similar inequities" right in New York. And, in comment on the Board of Education's final statement—"the inequity is clear"—the CSS observes, "New York City's poorest . . . districts could adopt that eloquent statement with few changes."

New York City's public schools are subdivided into 32 school districts. District 10 encompasses a large part of the Bronx but is, effectively, two separate districts. One of these districts, Riverdale, is in the northwest section of the Bronx. Home to many of the city's most sophisticated and well-educated families, its elementary schools have relatively few low-income students. The other section, to the south and east, is poor and heavily nonwhite.

The contrast between public schools in each of these two neighborhoods is obvious to any visitor. At Public School 24 in Riverdale, the principal speaks enthusiastically of his teaching staff. At Public School 79, serving poorer children to the south, the principal says that he is forced to take the "tenth-best" teachers. "I thank God they're still breathing," he remarks of those from whom he must select his teachers.

Some years ago, District 10 received an allocation for computers. The local board decided to give each elementary school an equal number of computers, even though the schools in Riverdale had smaller classes and far fewer students. When it was pointed out that schools in Riverdale, as a result, had twice the number of computers in proportion to their student populations as the schools in the poor neighborhoods, the chairman of the local board replied, "What is fair is what is determined . . . to be fair."

The superintendent of District 10, Fred Goldberg, tells the *New York Times* that "every effort" is made "to distribute resources equitably." He speculates that some gap might exist because some of the poorer schools need to use funds earmarked for computers to buy basic supplies like pens and paper. Asked about the differences in teachers noted by the principals, he says there are no differences, then adds that next year he'll begin a program to improve the quality of teachers in the poorer schools. Questioned about differences in physical appearances between the richer and the poorer schools, he says, "I think it's demographics."

Sometimes a school principal, whatever his background or his politics, looks into the faces of the children in his school and offers a disarming statement that cuts through official ambiguity. "These are the kids most in need," says Edward Flanery, the principal of one of the low-income schools, "and they get the worst teachers." For children of diverse needs in his overcrowded rooms, he says, "you need an outstanding teacher. And what do you get? You get the worst."

In order to find Public School 261 in District 10, a visitor is told to look for a mortician's office. The funeral home, which faces Jerome Avenue in the North Bronx, is easy to identify by its green awning. The school is next door, in a former roller-skating rink. No sign identifies the building as a school. A metal awning frame without an awning supports a flagpole, but there is no flag.

In the street in front of the school there is an elevated public transit line. Heavy traffic fills the street. The existence of the school is virtually concealed within this crowded city block.

In a vestibule between the outer and inner glass doors of the school there is a sign with these words: "All children are capable of learning."

Beyond the inner doors a guard is seated. The lobby is long and narrow. The ceiling is low. There are no windows. All the teachers that I see at first are middle-aged white women. The principal, who is also a white woman, tells me that the school's "capacity" is 900 but that there are 1,300 children here. The size of classes for fifth and sixth grade children in New York, she says, is "capped" at 32, but she says that class size in the school goes "up to 34." (I later see classes, however, as large as 37.) Classes for younger children, she goes on, are "capped at 25," but a school can go above this limit if it puts an extra adult in the room. Lack of space, she says, prevents the school from operating a pre-kindergarten program.

I ask the principal where her children go to school. They are enrolled in private school, she says.

"Lunchtime is a challenge for us," she explains. "Limited space obliges us   15
to do it in three shifts, 450 children at a time."

Textbooks are scarce and children have to share their social studies books. The principal says there is one full-time pupil counselor and another who is here two days a week: a ratio of 930 children to one counselor. The carpets are patched and sometimes taped together to conceal an open space. "I could use some new rugs," she observes.

To make up for the building's lack of windows and the crowded feeling that results, the staff puts plants and fish tanks in the corridors. Some of the plants are flourishing. Two boys, released from class, are in a corridor beside a tank, their noses pressed against the glass. A school of pinkish fish inside the tank are darting back and forth. Farther down the corridor a small Hispanic girl is watering the plants.

Two first grade classes share a single room without a window, divided only by a blackboard. Four kindergartens and a sixth grade class of Spanish-speaking children have been packed into a single room in which, again, there is no window. A second grade bilingual class of 37 children has its own room but again there is no window.

By eleven o'clock, the lunchroom is already packed with appetite and life. The kids line up to get their meals, then eat them in ten minutes. After that, with no place they can go to play, they sit and wait until it's time to line up and go back to class.

On the second floor I visit four classes taking place within another undi-   20
vided space. The room has a low ceiling. File cabinets and movable blackboards give a small degree of isolation to each class. Again, there are no windows.

The library is a tiny, windowless and claustrophobic room. I count approximately 700 books. Seeing no reference books, I ask a teacher if encyclopedias and other reference books are kept in classrooms.

"We don't have encyclopedias in classrooms," she replies. "That is for the suburbs."

The school, I am told, has 26 computers for its 1,300 children. There is one small gym and children get one period, and sometimes two, each week. Recess, however, is not possible because there is no playground. "Head Start," the principal says, "scarcely exists in District 10. We have no space."

The school, I am told, is 90 percent black and Hispanic; the other 10 percent are Asian, white or Middle Eastern.

In a sixth grade social studies class the walls are bare of words or decorations. There seems to be no ventilation system, or, if one exists, it isn't working.

The class discusses the Nile River and the Fertile Crescent.

The teacher, in a droning voice: "How is it useful that these civilizations developed close to rivers?"

A child, in a good loud voice: "What kind of question is that?"

In my notes I find these words: "An uncomfortable feeling—being in a building with no windows. There are metal ducts across the room. Do they give air? I feel asphyxiated. . . ."

On the top floor of the school, a sixth grade of 30 children shares a room with 29 bilingual second graders. Because of the high class size there is an assistant with each teacher. This means that 59 children and four grown-ups—63 in all—must share a room that, in a suburban school, would hold no more than 20 children and one teacher. There are, at least, some outside windows in this room—it is the only room with windows in the school—and the room has a high ceiling. It is a relief to see some daylight.

I return to see the kindergarten classes on the ground floor and feel stifled once again by lack of air and the low ceiling. Nearly 120 children and adults are doing what they can to make the best of things: 80 children in four kindergarten classes, 30 children in the sixth grade class, and about eight grown-ups who are aides and teachers. The kindergarten children sitting on the worn rug, which is patched with tape, look up at me and turn their heads to follow me as I walk past them.

As I leave the school, a sixth grade teacher stops to talk. I ask her, "Is there air conditioning in warmer weather?"

Teachers, while inside the building, are reluctant to give answers to this kind of question. Outside, on the sidewalk, she is less constrained: "I had an awful room last year. In the winter it was 56 degrees. In the summer it was up to 90. It was sweltering."

I ask her, "Do the children ever comment on the building?"

"They don't say," she answers, "but they know."

I ask her if they see it as a racial message.

"All these children see TV," she says. "They know what suburban schools are like. Then they look around them at their school. This was a roller-rink, you know. . . . They don't comment on it but you see it in their eyes. They understand."

On the following morning I visit P.S. 79, another elementary school in the same district. "We work under difficult circumstances," says the principal,

James Carter, who is black. "The school was built to hold one thousand students. We have 1,550. We are badly overcrowded. We need smaller classes but, to do this, we would need more space. I can't add five teachers. I would have no place to put them."

Some experts, I observe, believe that class size isn't a real issue. He dismisses this abruptly. "It doesn't take a genius to discover that you learn more in a smaller class. I have to bus some 60 kindergarten children elsewhere, since I have no space for them. When they return next year, where do I put them?

"I can't set up a computer lab. I have no room. I had to put a class into the   40
library. I have no librarian. There are two gymnasiums upstairs but they cannot be used for sports. We hold more classes there. It's unfair to measure us against the suburbs. They have 17 to 20 children in a class. Average class size in this school is 30.

"The school is 29 percent black, 70 percent Hispanic. Few of these kids get Head Start. There is no space in the district. Of 200 kindergarten children, 50 maybe get some kind of preschool."

I ask him how much difference preschool makes.

"Those who get it do appreciably better. I can't overestimate its impact but, as I have said, we have no space."

The school tracks children by ability, he says. "There are five to seven levels in each grade. The highest level is equivalent to 'gifted' but it's not a full-scale gifted program. We don't have the funds. We have no science room. The science teachers carry their equipment with them."

We sit and talk within the nurse's room. The window is broken. There are   45
two holes in the ceiling. About a quarter of the ceiling has been patched and covered with a plastic garbage bag.

"Ideal class size for these kids would be 15 to 20. Will these children ever get what white kids in the suburbs take for granted? I don't think so. If you ask me why, I'd have to speak of race and social class. I don't think the powers that be in New York City understand, or want to understand, that if they do not give these children a sufficient education to lead healthy and productive lives, we will be their victims later on. We'll pay the price someday—in violence, in economic costs. I despair of making this appeal in any terms but these. You cannot issue an appeal to conscience in New York today. The fair-play argument won't be accepted. So you speak of violence and hope that it will scare the city into action."

While we talk, three children who look six or seven years old come to the door and ask to see the nurse, who isn't in the school today. One of the children, a Puerto Rican girl, looks haggard. "I have a pain in my tooth," she says. The principal says, "The nurse is out. Why don't you call your mother?" The child says, "My mother doesn't have a phone." The principal sighs. "Then go back to your class." When she leaves, the principal is angry. "It's amazing to me that these children ever make it with the obstacles they face. Many *do* care and they *do* try, but there's a feeling of despair. The parents of these children want the same things for their children that the parents in the suburbs want. Drugs are not the cause of this. They are the symptom. Nonetheless, they're used by people in the suburbs and rich people in Manhattan as another reason to keep children of poor people at a distance."

I ask him, "Will white children and black children ever go to school together in New York?"

"I don't see it," he replies. "I just don't think it's going to happen. It's a dream. I simply do not see white folks in Riverdale agreeing to cross-bus with kids like these. A few, maybe. Very few. I don't think I'll live to see it happen."

I ask him whether race is the decisive factor. Many experts, I observe,   50
believe that wealth is more important in determining these inequalities.

"This," he says—and sweeps his hand around him at the room, the garbage bag, the ceiling—"would not happen to white children."

In a kindergarten class the children sit cross-legged on a carpet in a space between two walls of books. Their 26 faces are turned up to watch their teacher, an elderly black woman. A little boy who sits beside me is involved in trying to tie bows in his shoelaces. The children sing a song: "Lift Every Voice." On the wall are these handwritten words: "Beautiful, also, are the souls of my people."

In a very small room on the fourth floor, 52 people in two classes do their best to teach and learn. Both are first grade classes. One, I am informed, is "low ability." The other is bilingual.

"The room is barely large enough for one class," says the principal.

The room is 25 by 50 feet. There are 26 first graders and two adults on the   55
left, 22 others and two adults on the right. On the wall there is the picture of a small white child, circled by a Valentine, and a Gainsborough painting of a child in a formal dress.

"We are handicapped by scarcity," one of the teachers says. "One fifth of these children may be at grade level by the year's end."

A boy who may be seven years old climbs on my lap without an invitation and removes my glasses. He studies my face and runs his fingers through my hair. "You have nice hair," he says. I ask him where he lives and he replies, "Times Square Hotel," which is a homeless shelter in Manhattan.

I ask him how he gets here.

"With my father. On the train," he says.

"How long does it take?"   60

"It takes an hour and a half."

I ask him when he leaves his home.

"My mother wakes me up at five o'clock."

"When do you leave?"

"Six-thirty."   65

I ask him how he gets back to Times Square.

"My father comes to get me after school."

From my notes: "He rides the train three hours every day in order to attend this segregated school. It would be a shorter ride to Riverdale. There are rapid shuttle-vans that make that trip in only 20 minutes. Why not let him go to school right in Manhattan, for that matter?"

At three o'clock the nurse arrives to do her recordkeeping. She tells me she is here three days a week. "The public hospital we use for an emergency is called North Central. It's not a hospital that I will use if I am given any choice. Clinics in the private hospitals are far more likely to be staffed by an experienced physician."

She hesitates a bit as I take out my pen, but then goes on: "I'll give you an 70 example. A little girl I saw last week in school was trembling and shaking and could not control the motions of her arms. I was concerned and called her home. Her mother came right up to school and took her to North Central. The intern concluded that the child was upset by 'family matters'—nothing more— that there was nothing wrong with her. The mother was offended by the diag- nosis. She did not appreciate his words or his assumptions. The truth is, there was nothing wrong at home. She brought the child back to school. I thought that she was ill. I told her mother, 'Go to Montefiore.' It's a private hospital, and well respected. She took my advice, thank God. It turned out that the child had a neurological disorder. She is now in treatment.

"This is the kind of thing our children face. Am I saying that the city underserves this population? You can draw your own conclusions."

Out on the street, it takes a full half hour to flag down a cab. Taxi drivers in New York are sometimes disconcertingly direct in what they say. When they are contemptuous of poor black people, their contempt is unadorned. When they're sympathetic and compassionate, their observations often go right to the heart of things. "Oh . . . they neglect these children," says the driver. "They leave them in the streets and slums to live and die." We stop at a light. Outside the window of the taxi, aimless men are standing in a semicircle while another man is work- ing on his car. Old four-story buildings with their windows boarded, cracked or missing are on every side.

I ask the driver where he's from. He says Afghanistan. Turning in his seat, he gestures at the street and shrugs. "If you don't, as an American, begin to give these kids the kind of education that you give the kids of Donald Trump, you're asking for disaster."

Two months later, on a day in May, I visit an elementary school in Riverdale. The dogwoods and magnolias on the lawn in front of P.S. 24 are in full blossom on the day I visit. There is a well-tended park across the street, another larger park three blocks away. To the left of the school is a playground for small children, with an innovative jungle gym, a slide and several climbing toys. Behind the school there are two playing fields for older kids. The grass around the school is neatly trimmed.

The neighborhood around the school, by no means the richest part of 75 Riverdale, is nonetheless expensive and quite beautiful. Residences in the area— some of which are large, free-standing houses, others condominiums in solid red- brick buildings—sell for prices in the region of $400,000; but some of the larger

Tudor houses on the winding and tree-shaded streets close to the school can cost up to $1 million. The excellence of P.S. 24, according to the principal, adds to the value of these homes. Advertisements in the *New York Times* will frequently inform prospective buyers that a house is "in the neighborhood of P.S. 24."

The school serves 825 children in the kindergarten through sixth grade. This is approximately half the student population crowded into P.S. 79, where 1,550 children fill a space intended for 1,000, and a great deal smaller than the 1,300 children packed into the former skating rink; but the principal of P.S. 24, a capable and energetic man named David Rothstein, still regards it as excessive for an elementary school.

The school is integrated in the strict sense that the middle- and upper-middle-class white children here do occupy a building that contains some Asian and Hispanic and black children; but there is little integration in the classrooms since the vast majority of the Hispanic and black children are assigned to "special" classes on the basis of evaluations that have classified them "EMR"—"educable mentally retarded"—or else, in the worst of cases, "TMR"—"trainable mentally retarded."

I ask the principal if any of his students qualify for free-lunch programs. "About 130 do," he says. "Perhaps another 35 receive their lunches at reduced price. Most of these kids are in the special classes. They do not come from this neighborhood."

The very few nonwhite children that one sees in mainstream classes tend to be Japanese or else of other Asian origins. Riverdale, I learn, has been the residence of choice for many years to members of the diplomatic corps.

The school therefore contains effectively two separate schools: one of about 130 children, most of whom are poor, Hispanic, black, assigned to one of the 12 special classes; the other of some 700 mainstream students, almost all of whom are white or Asian.   80

There is a third track also—this one for the students who are labeled "talented" or "gifted." This is termed a "pull-out" program since the children who are so identified remain in mainstream classrooms but are taken out for certain periods each week to be provided with intensive and, in my opinion, excellent instruction in some areas of reasoning and logic often known as "higher-order skills" in the contemporary jargon of the public schools. Children identified as "gifted" are admitted to this program in first grade and, in most cases, will remain there for six years. Even here, however, there are two tracks of the gifted. The regular gifted classes are provided with only one semester of this specialized instruction yearly. Those very few children, on the other hand, who are identified as showing the most promise are assigned, beginning in the third grade, to a program that receives a full-year regimen.

In one such class, containing ten intensely verbal and impressive fourth grade children, nine are white and one is Asian. The "special" class I enter first, by way of contrast, has twelve children of whom only one is white and none is Asian. These racial breakdowns prove to be predictive of the schoolwide pattern.

In a classroom for the gifted on the first floor of the school, I ask a child what the class is doing. "Logic and syllogisms," she replies. The room is fitted with a planetarium. The principal says that all the elementary schools in District 10 were given the same planetariums ten years ago but that certain schools, because of overcrowding, have been forced to give them up. At P.S. 261, according to my notes, there was a domelike space that had been built to hold a planetarium, but the planetarium had been removed to free up space for the small library collection. P.S. 24, in contrast, has a spacious library that holds almost 8,000 books. The windows are decorated with attractive, brightly colored curtains and look out on flowering trees. The principal says that it's inadequate, but it appears spectacular to me after the cubicle that holds a meager 700 books within the former skating rink.

The district can't afford librarians, the principal says, but P.S. 24, unlike the poorer schools of District 10, can draw on educated parent volunteers who staff the room in shifts three days a week. A parent organization also raises independent funds to buy materials, including books, and will soon be running a fund-raiser to enhance the library's collection.

In a large and sunny first grade classroom that I enter next, I see 23 children, all of whom are white or Asian. In another first grade, there are 22 white children and two others who are Japanese. There is a computer in each class. Every classroom also has a modern fitted sink.

In a second grade class of 22 children, there are two black children and three Asian children. Again, there is a sink and a computer. A sixth grade social studies class has only one black child. The children have an in-class research area that holds some up-to-date resources. A set of encyclopedias (World Book, 1985) is in a rack beside a window. The children are doing a Spanish language lesson when I enter. Foreign languages begin in sixth grade at the school, but Spanish is offered also to the kindergarten children. As in every room at P.S. 24, the window shades are clean and new, the floor is neatly tiled in gray and green, and there is not a single light bulb missing.

Walking next into a special class, I see twelve children. One is white. Eleven are black. There are no Asian children. The room is half the size of mainstream classrooms. "Because of overcrowding," says the principal, "we have had to split these rooms in half." There is no computer and no sink.

I enter another special class. Of seven children, five are black, one is Hispanic, one is white. A little black boy with a large head sits in the far corner and is gazing at the ceiling.

"Placement of these kids," the principal explains, "can usually be traced to neurological damage."

In my notes: "How could so many of these children be brain-damaged?"

Next door to the special class is a woodworking shop. "This shop is only for the special classes," says the principal. The children learn to punch in time cards at the door, he says, in order to prepare them for employment.

The fourth grade gifted class, in which I spend the last part of the day, is humming with excitement. "I start with these children in the first grade," says the teacher. "We pull them out of mainstream classes on the basis of their test results and other factors such as the opinion of their teachers. Out of this group, beginning in third grade, I pull out the ones who show the most potential, and they enter classes such as this one."

The curriculum they follow, she explains, "emphasizes critical thinking, reasoning and logic." The planetarium, for instance, is employed not simply for the study of the universe as it exists. "Children also are designing their own galaxies," the teacher says.

A little girl sitting around a table with her classmates speaks with perfect poise: "My name is Susan. We are in the fourth grade gifted program."

I ask them what they're doing and a child says, "My name is Laurie and 95 we're doing problem-solving."

A rather tall, good-natured boy who is half-standing at the table tells me that his name is David. "One thing that we do," he says, "is logical thinking. Some problems, we find, have more than one good answer. We need to learn not simply to be logical in our own thinking but to show respect for someone else's logic even when an answer may be technically incorrect."

When I ask him to explain this, he goes on, "A person who gives an answer that is not 'correct' may nonetheless have done some interesting thinking that we should examine. 'Wrong' answers may be more useful to examine than correct ones."

I ask the children if reasoning and logic are innate or if they're things that you can learn.

"You know some things to start with when you enter school," Susan says. "But we also learn some things that other children don't."

I ask her to explain this. 100

"We know certain things that other kids don't know because we're *taught* them."

She has braces on her teeth. Her long brown hair falls almost to her waist. Her loose white T-shirt has the word TRI-LOGIC on the front. She tells me that Tri-Logic is her father's firm.

Laurie elaborates on the same point: "Some things you know. Some kinds of logic are inside of you to start with. There are other things that someone needs to teach you."

David expands on what the other two have said: "Everyone can think and speak in logical ways unless they have a mental problem. What this program does is bring us to a higher form of logic."

The class is writing a new "Bill of Rights." The children already know the 105 U.S. Bill of Rights and they explain its first four items to me with precision. What they are examining today, they tell me, is the very *concept* of a "right." Then they will create their own compendium of rights according to their own analysis and definition. Along one wall of the classroom, opposite the planetarium, are seven Apple II computers on which children have developed rather subtle color animations that express the themes—of greed and domination, for example—that they also have described in writing.

"This is an upwardly mobile group," the teacher later says. "They have exposure to whatever New York City has available. Their parents may take them to the theater, to museums. . . ."

In my notes: "Six girls, four boys. Nine white, one Chinese. I am glad they have this class. But what about the others? Aren't there ten black children in the school who could enjoy this also?"

The teacher gives me a newspaper written, edited and computer-printed by her sixth grade gifted class. The children, she tells me, are provided with a link to kids in Europe for transmission of news stories.

A science story by one student asks if scientists have ever falsified their research. "Gregor Mendel," the sixth grader writes, "the Austrian monk who founded the science of genetics, published papers on his work with peas that some experts say were statistically too good to be true. Isaac Newton, who formulated the law of gravitation, relied on unseemly mathematical sleight of hand in his calculations. . . . Galileo Galilei, founder of modern scientific method, wrote about experiments that were so difficult to duplicate that colleagues doubted he had done them."

Another item in the paper, also by a sixth grade student, is less esoteric: 110
"The Don Cossacks dance company, from Russia, is visiting the United States. The last time it toured America was 1976. . . . The Don Cossacks will be in New York City for two weeks at the Neil Simon Theater. Don't miss it!"

The tone is breezy—and so confident! That phrase—"Don't miss it!"—speaks a volume about life in Riverdale.

"What makes a good school?" asks the principal when we are talking later on. "The building and teachers are part of it, of course. But it isn't just the building and the teachers. Our kids come from good families and the neighborhood is good. In a three-block area we have a public library, a park, a junior high. . . . Our typical sixth grader reads at eighth grade level." In a quieter voice he says, "I see how hard my colleagues work in schools like P.S. 79. You have children in those neighborhoods who live in virtual hell. They enter school five years behind. What do they get?" Then, as he spreads his hands out on his desk, he says: "I have to ask myself why there should be an elementary school in District 10 with fifteen hundred children. Why should there be an elementary school within a skating rink? Why should the Board of Ed allow this? This is not the way that things should be."

● Applying a Postcolonial Frame

1. How does Kozol's rhetorical emphasis on the lack of windows in P.S. 261 connect to his argument about tracking?

2. A teacher at P.S. 26 comments that the students there "see TV [and] know what suburban schools are like. Then they look around them at their own school. . . .

They understand" (para. 37). What is it that they understand, in postcolonial terms, especially those of Fanon?

3. Analyze the rhetorical choices Principal James Carter faces when he must choose to speak either in terms of "violence and hope" or the "fair-play argument" to get resources for his school. How might a postcolonialist critic explain these choices? How might such a critic see the choice Carter ultimately makes?

4. How do the economic differences surrounding the schools Kozol profiles influence the quality of the education they offer? Is Kozol's a materialist critique?

5. Consider Kozol's rhetorical purposes in the following choices he makes:

   • including the curricular details for gifted students at P.S. 24—the focus on logic, on the Bill of Rights, on the student-written newspaper.

   • emphasizing the student line "Don't miss it!"

6. Does Kozol attempt to represent a range of voices? Does he "speak for" subalterns in ways that further marginalize them?

The Spirit Catches You and You Fall Down: A Hmong Child, Her American Doctors, and the Collision of Two Cultures

Anne Fadiman

Fadiman is the Francis Writer-in-Residence at Yale University. She is the author of two essay collections, At Large and At Small *and* Ex Libris: Confessions of a Common Reader. *The former editor of* The American Scholar, *Fadiman is also the editor of* Best American Essays 2003 *and* Rereadings: Seventeen Writers Revisit Books They Love. The Spirit Catches You and You Fall Down: A Hmong Child, Her American Doctors, and the Collision of Two Cultures, *published in 1997, won the National Book Critics Circle Award for Nonfiction. It is an account of one family of Hmong refugees in California and the devastating outcomes of cultural miscommunication and misunderstanding. The main narrative tells the story of Lia Lee, a young child whose epilepsy leads to an ultimately tragic intermingling of Hmong cultural beliefs and the U.S. medical system. Lia is left in a vegetative state after a massive seizure, with her parents believing her condition to be the result of the system's insistence on overtreating her and insisting on understanding her condition only in a scientific, physical way, instead of seeing it through the frame of their cultural belief that epilepsy is caused by a spirit who has "caught" her. Many of her doctors in turn blamed the terrible outcome on her parents' "noncompliance" with their directions (which included at one point forced removal from her home to ensure a regimen of "proper" medication). In a chapter toward the end of her book, Fadiman depicts the power struggle of differing cultural claims in their very material terms. A few notes on the characters mentioned in this chapter: Foua Yang is Lia's mother; Nao Kao Lee is her father; Jeanine Hilt is her social worker; Dee Korda is the foster mother who cared for Lia when she was removed from her parents' care; Neil Ernst and Peggy Philp are her pediatricians.*

Lia did not die, nor did she recover. Foua often dreamed that her daughter could walk and talk, but when she awoke, Lia lay curled next to her in bed, a slight, silent husk who hardly seemed big enough to contain her family's load of memory, anger, confusion, and grief. She lay suspended in time, growing only a few inches, gaining little weight, always looking far younger than her age, while the Lee siblings who still lived at home—six athletic, bilingual children who moved with ease between the Hmong and the American worlds—grew up around her. Cheng joined the Marine Reserves and was called to serve in the Gulf War, but to Foua's nearly hysterical relief, the war ended two days before his scheduled flight to Saudi Arabia. May went to Fresno State University, majoring in health science, a choice influenced by her childhood experiences, both positive and negative, as the ad hoc arbitrator between her parents and the medical establishment. Yer, a volleyball star who had won the award for Best Girl Athlete at Merced High School, joined May at Fresno State two years later, majoring in physical education. True became Merced High's student body treasurer and president of its Youth Culture Club, a Hmong social and service organization with more than 200 members. Mai became a stand-out soccer player and was known as one of the most beautiful teenagers in Merced, a reputation that caused boys to fight over her and girls all too frequently to resent her. Pang grew from a harum-scarum toddler into a self-possessed schoolgirl with a flair for traditional Hmong dance. There were a few tremors as the Lee children passed through adolescence, but never the rifts that American families accept almost as a matter of course. "My parents are the coolest parents in the world," True once wrote me. "We don't have everything in the world, but we do have the closeness of us eight sisters, one brother, and our parents. This is the coolest family ever and I would never trade it for anything else in this world."

Nao Kao gained weight and was troubled by high blood pressure. Foua felt tired much of the time. Seeing that their energies were waning, Jeanine Hilt urged the Lees to let Lia return to the Schelby Center for Special Education each day, not to educate her—that was a thing of the past—but to give her parents a few hours' respite each day. Because of their persistent fear that Lia might be stolen from them again by the government, the Lees were reluctant at first, but because they trusted Jeanine, they eventually agreed.

Dee Korda, one of whose foster children was severely retarded and also attended Schelby, frequently saw Lia there, lying on her back with her hands strapped to blocks in order to prevent her fingers from stiffening into claws. She could hardly bear to look. The Kordas had all taken Lia's neurological catastrophe hard. The entire family had gone through therapy at the Merced County Mental Health Department in order to deal with what Dee called "Lia being dead but alive." At their counselor's suggestion, the children—biological, foster, and adopted—drew pictures on butcher paper. "Wendy drew a mom and a baby, because Lia was with her mom," said Dee. "Julie drew a rainbow with clouds and birds, because Lia didn't have to cry anymore. Maria is real withdrawn, but when we told her about Lia she cried. Lia got through to her! She drew a broken heart with a jagged fence and an eye looking in from the outside. The heart was the sadness. The fence was the wall that Lia had gotten over by touching our lives. The eye was my eye, watching the sadness, with a tear that cried."

In 1993, while she was vacationing at Disneyland, Jeanine Hilt had an acute asthma attack, went into respiratory failure, and suffered oxygen deprivation so severe that she lost all brain function: in other words, she developed hypoxic ischemic encephalopathy, exactly the same fate that had befallen Lia. She died three days later with her partner of eighteen years, Karen Marino, at her side. "When I heard Jenny was dead, my heart broke," Foua told me. "I cried because Jenny had told me she wasn't going to get married and she would never have any children of her own, so she would help me raise my children. But she died, so she couldn't do that, and I felt I had lost my American daughter."

Neil Ernst won the MCMC residency program's first Faculty Teacher of the Year award. Peggy Philp became Merced's County Health Officer, a post her father had held more than forty years earlier. They continued to share their pediatric practice as well as housework and child care, scrupulously negotiating what one of their Christmas letters described as "a blur of laundry, lunches, cleaning, patient care, newborn resuscitation, and resident teaching." Their understanding of the Lees, and the Lees' understanding of them, deepened significantly when they, too, experienced a child's grave illness. During his last month of third grade, their elder son, Toby, was diagnosed with acute lymphocytic leukemia. When Neil tried to tell Dan Murphy about the diagnosis, he cried so hard he couldn't talk. After one of Lia's checkups, Neil wrote me:

> Mrs. Lee had heard that our son had leukemia. It was truly amazing how quickly she heard of this. When Peggy saw Lia in our clinic, Mrs. Lee was very concerned about Toby's health, how he was doing etc. There was very genuine concern expressed by her questions and facial expression. At the end of the visit Mrs. Lee was hugging Peggy and they were both shedding a few tears. Sorrows of motherhood cut through all cultural barriers.

Toby underwent three years of chemotherapy and achieved what seems to be a permanent remission. "Lia's mother continues to occupy a special place in our thoughts," wrote Neil in a later letter. "She always asks about Toby. Our contacts with her are very infrequent because her family provides excellent care for Lia, but they are special nonetheless."

Since Lia's brain death, whatever scant trust Foua and Nao Kao had once had in American medicine had shrunk almost to zero. (I say "almost" because Foua exempted Neil and Peggy.) When their daughter May broke her arm, and the doctors in the MCMC emergency room told them it needed a cast, Nao Kao marched her straight home, bathed her arm in herbs, and wrapped it in a poultice for a week. May's arm regained its full strength. When a pot of boiling oil fell from the electric stove onto Foua's skirt, setting it on fire and burning her right hip and leg, she sacrificed two chickens and a pig. When Foua got pregnant with her sixteenth child, and had an early miscarriage, she did nothing. When she got pregnant with her seventeenth child and had a complicated miscarriage in her fourth month, Nao Kao waited for three days, until she started to hemorrhage and fell unconscious to the living room floor, before he called an ambulance. He consented to her dilation and curettage only after strenuous—in fact, desperate—persuasion by the MCMC resident on obstetric rotation. Nao Kao also sacrificed a pig while Foua was in the hospital and a second pig after she returned home.

Before she was readmitted to Schelby, Lia was routinely vaccinated against diphtheria, pertussis, and tetanus. At about the same time, she started to develop occasional seizurelike twitches. Because they were brief, infrequent, and benign—and also, perhaps, because he had learned from bitter experience—Neil decided not to prescribe anticonvulsants. Foua and Nao Kao were certain that the shots had caused the twitches, and they told Neil that they did not want Lia to be immunized ever again, for anything.

Dan Murphy, who became the director of MCMC's Family Practice Residency Program, once told me that when you fail one Hmong patient, you fail the whole community. I could see that this was true. Who knew how many Hmong families were giving the hospital a wide berth because they didn't want their children to end up like the second-youngest Lee daughter? Everyone in Merced's Lee and Yang clans knew what had happened to Lia (those bad doctors!), just as everyone on the pediatric floor at MCMC knew what had happened to Lia (those bad parents!). Lia's case had confirmed the Hmong community's worst prejudices about the medical profession and the medical community's worst prejudices about the Hmong.

At the family practice clinic, the staff continued to marvel at the quality of care the Lees provided to their clean, sweet-smelling, well-groomed child. But at the hospital next door, where the nurses had had no contact with Lia since 1986, the case metastasized into a mass of complaints that grew angrier with each passing year. Why had the Lees been so ungrateful for their daughter's free medical care? (Neil—who did not share the nurses' resentment—once calculated that, over the years, Lia had cost the United States government about $250,000, not counting the salaries of her doctors, nurses, and social workers.) Why had the Lees always insisted on doing everything *their* way? Why—this was still the worst sin—had the Lees been noncompliant? As Sharon Yates, a nurse's aide, told me, "If only the parents had given Lia the medicine, she wouldn't be like this. I bet when she came back from that foster home, they just didn't give her any medicine."

But I knew that when she returned from foster care, Foua and Nao Kao *had* given Lia her medicine—4 ccs of Depakene, three times a day—exactly as prescribed. Hoping to clear up some questions about Lia's anticonvulsants, I went to Fresno to talk with Terry Hutchison, the pediatric neurologist who had overseen her care at Valley Children's Hospital. I had noticed that in one of his discharge notes, written nine months before her neurological crisis, he had described Lia as "a very pretty Hmong child" and her parents as "very interested and very good with Lia." I had never seen phrases like that in her MCMC chart.

10

Bill Selvidge had told me that Dr. Hutchison was "a known eccentric," beloved by his residents for his empathy but dreaded for his insistence on doing rounds at 4:00 a.m. He had an exiguous crewcut and on the day I met him was wearing a necktie decorated with a large bright-yellow giraffe. A sign in the hall outside his office, hung at toddler eye level, read:

KIDS ZONE
ENTER WITH CARE AND LOVE

When I asked him about the relationship between Lia's medications and her final seizure, he said, "Medications probably had nothing to do with it."

"Huh?" I said.

"Lia's brain was destroyed by septic shock, which was caused by the *Pseudomonas aeruginosa* bacillus in her blood. I don't know how Lia got it and I will never know. What I do know is that the septic shock caused the seizures, not the other way around. The fact that she had a preexisting seizure disorder probably made the status epilepticus worse or easier to start or whatever, but the seizures were incidental and not important. If Lia had not had seizures, she would have presented in a coma and shock, and the outcome would probably have been the same, except that her problem might have been more easily recognized. It was too late by the time she got to Valley Children's. It was probably too late by the time she got to MCMC."

"Did her parents' past noncompliance have anything to do with it?"

"Absolutely nothing. The only influence that medications could have had is   15
that the Depakene we prescribed might have compromised her immune system and made her more susceptible to the *Pseudomonas*." (Depakene occasionally causes a drop in white blood cells that can hamper the body's ability to fight infection.) "I still believe Depakene was the drug of choice, and I would prescribe it again. But, in fact, if the family was giving her the Depakene as instructed, it is conceivable that by following our instructions, they set her up for septic shock."

"Lia's parents think that the problem was caused by too much medicine."

"Well," said Dr. Hutchison, "that may not be too far from the truth."

I stared at him.

"Go back to Merced," he said, "and tell all those people at MCMC that the family didn't do this to the kid. We did."

Driving back to Merced, I was in a state of shock myself. I had known about   20
Lia's sepsis, but I had always assumed that her seizure disorder had been the root of the problem. *The Lees were right after all*, I thought. *Lia's medicine did make her sick!*

That night I told Neil and Peggy what Dr. Hutchison had said. As usual, their desire to ferret out the truth outweighed their desire—if indeed they had one—to defend their reputation for infallibility. They immediately asked for my photocopy of Lia's medical chart, and they sat together on Bill Selvidge's sofa, combing Volume 5 for evidence, overlooked during the crisis, that Lia might already have been septic at MCMC. Murmuring to each other in their shared secret language ("calcium 3.2," "platelets 29,000," "hemoglobin 8.4"), they might have been—in fact, were—a pair of lovers exchanging a set of emotionally charged intimacies.

"I always thought Lia got septic down at Children's when they put all those invasive lines in," said Peggy. "But maybe not. There are some signs here."

"I did too," said Neil. "If I'd thought she was septic here at MCMC, I would have done a lumbar puncture. I didn't start her on antibiotics because every single time Lia had come in before that, she was not septic. Every other time, the problem was her seizure disorder, and this was obviously the worst seizure of her life. I stabilized her, I arranged for her transport, and then I went home before all the lab results were back." He didn't sound defensive. He sounded curious.

After Neil and Peggy went home, I asked Bill Selvidge whether he thought Neil had made a mistake in not recognizing and treating Lia's sepsis, even though Dr. Hutchison believed that her fate was probably sealed before she arrived in the MCMC emergency room—and even though the increasing severity of her epilepsy might eventually have led to serious brain damage if sepsis had never entered the picture.

"Neil leaves no stone unturned," said Bill. "If Neil made a mistake, it's   25 because every physician makes mistakes. If it had been a brand-new kid walking off the street, I guarantee you Neil would have done a septic workup and he would have caught it. But this was Lia. *No one* at MCMC would have noticed anything but her seizures. Lia *was* her seizures."

To MCMC's residents, Lia continued to be her seizures—the memory of those terrifying nights in the emergency room that had taught them how to intubate or start IVs or perform venous cutdowns. They always spoke of Lia in the past tense. In fact, Neil and Peggy themselves frequently referred to "Lia's demise," or "what may have killed Lia" or "the reason Lia died." Dr. Hutchison did the same thing. He had asked me, "Was Lia with the foster parents when she died?" And although I reminded him that Lia was alive, five minutes later he said, "Noncompliance had nothing to do with her death." It wasn't just absentmindedness. It was an admission of defeat. Lia was dead to her physicians (in a way, for example, that she was never dead to her social workers) because medicine had once made extravagant claims on her behalf and had had to renounce them.

Once I asked Neil if he wished he had done anything differently. He answered as I expected, focusing not on his relationship with the Lees but on his choice of medication. "I wish we'd used Depakene sooner," he said. "I wish I'd accepted that it would be easier for the family to comply with one medicine instead of three, even if three seemed medically optimal."

Then I asked, "Do you wish you had never met Lia?"

"Oh, no, no, no!" His vehemence surprised me. "Once I might have said yes, but not in retrospect. Lia taught me that when there is a very dense cultural barrier, you do the best you can, and if something happens despite that, you have to be satisfied with little successes instead of total successes. You have to give up total control. That is very hard for me, but I do try. I think Lia made me into a less rigid person."

The next time I saw Foua, I asked her whether she had learned anything   30
from what had happened. "No," she said. "I haven't learned. I just feel confused." She was feeding Lia at the time, making baby noises as she spooned
puréed *zaub*, the spinachlike green she grew in the parking lot, into the slack
mouth. "I don't understand how the doctors can say she is going to be like this
for the rest of her life, and yet they can't fix her. How can they know the future
but not know how to change it? I don't understand that."

"Well, what do *you* think Lia's future will hold?" I asked.

"I don't know these things," said Foua. "I am not a doctor. I am not a *txiv
neeb*. But maybe Lia will stay hurt like this, and that makes me cry about what
will happen. I gave birth to Lia, so I will always take care of her with all my
heart. But when her father and I pass away, who will take care of Lia? Lia's
sisters do love her, but even though they love her, maybe they will not be able to
take care of her. Maybe they will need to study too hard and work too hard. I am
crying to think that they are just going to give Lia away to the Americans." Foua
wept soundlessly. May Ying embraced her and stroked her hair.

"I know where the Americans put children like Lia," she continued. "I saw
a place like that in Fresno where they took Lia once, a long time ago." (Foua
was recalling a chronic care facility for retarded and disabled children where Lia
had been temporarily placed, before her year in foster care, while her medications were monitored and stabilized.) "It was like a house for the dead. The children were so poor and so sad that they just cried. They cried all over. One child
had a big head and a really small body. Other children had legs that were all
dried up and they just fell on the floor. I have seen this. If the Americans take
Lia there she will want to die, but instead she will suffer."

Foua brushed her tears from her cheeks with the back of her hand, in a
quick, brusque gesture. Then she wiped Lia's mouth, far more gently, and
slowly started to rock her. "I am very sad," she said, "and I think a lot that if we
were still in Laos and not in the United States, maybe Lia would never be like
this. The doctors are very very knowledgeable, your high doctors, your best
doctors, but maybe they made a mistake by giving her the wrong medicine and
they made her hurt like this. If it was a *dab* that made Lia sick like this in Laos,
we would know how to go to the forest and get herbs to fix her and maybe
she could be able to speak. But this happened here in the United States, and
Americans have done this to her, and our medicine cannot fix that."

It was also true that if the Lees were still in Laos, Lia would probably have   35
died before she was out of her infancy, from a prolonged bout of untreated
status epilepticus. American medicine had both preserved her life and compromised it. I was unsure which had hurt her family more.

Since that night with Foua, I have replayed the story over and over again, wondering if anything could have made it turn out differently. Despite Dr. Hutchison's
revisionist emendation of the final chapter, no one could deny that if the Lees had
given Lia her anticonvulsants from the beginning, she might have had—might

still be having—something approaching a normal life. What was not clear was who, if anyone, should be held accountable. What if Neil *had* prescribed Depakene earlier? What if, instead of placing Lia in foster care, he had arranged for a visiting nurse to administer her medications? What if he had sought out Blia Yao Moua or Jonas Vangay or another Hmong leader who straddled both cultures, and had asked him to intervene with the Lees, thus transferring the issue of compliance to a less suspect source? What if MCMC had had better interpreters?

When I presented my "what if" list to Dan Murphy one day in the MCMC cafeteria, he was less interested in the Depakene than in the interpreters. However, he believed that the gulf between the Lees and their doctors was unbridgeable, and that nothing could have been done to change the outcome. "Until I met Lia," he said, "I thought if you had a problem you could always settle it if you just sat and talked long enough. But we could have talked to the Lees until we were blue in the face—we could have sent the Lees to *medical school* with the world's greatest translator—and they would still think their way was right and ours was wrong." Dan slowly stirred his lukewarm cocoa; he had been on all-night call. "Lia's case ended my idealistic way of looking at the world."

Was the gulf unbridgeable? I kept returning, obsessively, to the Lees' earliest encounters with MCMC during Lia's infancy, when no interpreters were present and her epilepsy was misdiagnosed as pneumonia. Instead of practicing "veterinary medicine," what if the residents in the emergency room had managed to elicit the Lees' trust at the outset—or at least managed not to crush it—by finding out what *they* believed, feared, and hoped? Jeanine Hilt had asked them for their version of the story, but no doctor ever had. Martin Kilgore had tried, but by then it was years too late.

Of course, the Lees' perspective might have been as unfathomable to the doctors as the doctors' perspective was to the Lees. Hmong culture, as Blia Yao Moua observed to me, is not Cartesian. Nothing could be more Cartesian than Western medicine. Trying to understand Lia and her family by reading her medical chart (something I spent hundreds of hours doing) was like deconstructing a love sonnet by reducing it to a series of syllogisms. Yet to the residents and pediatricians who had cared for her since she was three months old, there was no guide to Lia's world *except* her chart. As each of them struggled to make sense of a set of problems that were not expressible in the language they knew, the chart simply grew longer and longer, until it contained more than 400,000 words. Every one of those words reflected its author's intelligence, training, and good intentions, but not a single one dealt with the Lees' perception of their daughter's illness.

Almost every discussion of cross-cultural medicine that I had ever read   40
quoted a set of eight questions, designed to elicit a patient's "explanatory model," which were developed by Arthur Kleinman, a psychiatrist and medical anthropologist who chairs the department of social medicine at Harvard Medical School. The first few times I read these questions they seemed so obvious I hardly noticed them; around the fiftieth time, I began to think that, like many

obvious things, they might actually be a work of genius. I recently decided to call Kleinman to tell him how I thought the Lees might have answered his questions after Lia's earliest seizures, before any medications had been administered, resisted, or blamed, if they had had a good interpreter and had felt sufficiently at ease to tell the truth. To wit:

1. *What do you call the problem?*

   Qaug dab peg. That means the spirit catches you and you fall down.

2. *What do you think has caused the problem?*

   Soul loss.

3. *Why do you think it started when it did?*

   Lia's sister Yer slammed the door and Lia's soul was frightened out of her body.

4. *What do you think the sickness does? How does it work?*

   It makes Lia shake and fall down. It works because a spirit called a *dab* is catching her.

5. *How severe is the sickness? Will it have a short or long course?*

   Why are you asking us those questions? If you are a good doctor, you should know the answers yourself.

6. *What kind of treatment do you think the patient should receive? What are the most important results you hope she receives from this treatment?*

   You should give Lia medicine to take for a week but no longer. After she is well, she should stop taking the medicine. You should not treat her by taking her blood or the fluid from her backbone. Lia should also be treated at home with our Hmong medicines and by sacrificing pigs and chickens. We hope Lia will be healthy, but we are not sure we want her to stop shaking forever because it makes her noble in our culture, and when she grows up she might become a shaman.

7. *What are the chief problems the sickness has caused?*

   It has made us sad to see Lia hurt, and it has made us angry at Yer.

8. *What do you fear most about the sickness?*

   That Lia's soul will never return.

I thought Kleinman would consider these responses so bizarre that he would be at a loss for words. (When I had presented this same material, more or less, to Neil and Peggy, they had said, "Mr. and Mrs. Lee thought *what?*") But after each answer, he said, with great enthusiasm, "Right!" Nothing surprised him; everything delighted him. From his vantage point, a physician could encounter no more captivating a patient than Lia, no finer a set of parents than the Lees.

Then I told him what had happened later—the Lees' noncompliance with Lia's anticonvulsant regimen, the foster home, the neurological catastrophe—and asked him if he had any retroactive suggestions for her pediatricians.

"I have three," he said briskly. "First, get rid of the term 'compliance.' It's a lousy term. It implies moral hegemony. You don't want a command from a general, you want a colloquy. Second, instead of looking at a model of coercion, look at a model of mediation. Go find a member of the Hmong community, or go find a medical anthropologist, who can help you negotiate. Remember that a stance of mediation, like a divorce proceeding, requires compromise on both sides. Decide what's critical and be willing to compromise on everything else. Third, you need to understand that as powerful an influence as the culture of the Hmong patient and her family is on this case, the culture of biomedicine is equally powerful. If you can't see that your own culture has its own set of interests, emotions, and biases, how can you expect to deal successfully with someone else's culture?"

● Applying a Postcolonial Frame

1. "Lia *was* her seizures," says one of her health caregivers (para. 25). What do you think the effect was of this essentializing view of Lia?

2. The nurses who tended Lia through the years of her illness express great resentment once she is finally fully disabled. Why do you think they feel such anger? Where did your sympathies lie as you read of the conflict?

3. Dr. Kleinman states that the medical system should stop using the term *compliance* because "It implies moral hegemony" (para. 43). Thinking back to the readings on materialism, how can you define this phrase? Did a system of moral hegemony cause material damage to Lia and her parents, as you see the events? Why don't her parents just "get with the program"?

4. Some of Lia's doctors refer to her as having died, even though she is alive, though completely disabled. How does this view of her make sense within the medical culture? What rhetorical conventions of medical practice, as you know the system, might make this view logical for them to adopt?

5. Consider Victor Villanueva's (p. 446) categories of "immigrant" and "internally colonized."

   • How do you see Lia and her family—as immigrants or minorities, and for what reasons?

   • Compare the feelings of Lia's family to the experience of the mother in Jonathan Kozol's *Savage Inequalities* (p. 463) who takes her sick child to the local Bronx hospital. How do these incidents connect with Villanueva's immigrant vs. internally colonized distinctions?

Reading the Slender Body

Susan Bordo

Susan Bordo's book Unbearable Weight: Feminism, Western Culture, and the Body, *from which this chapter is taken, appeared in 1993. Bordo analyses the body as part of a larger cultural sign system that connects the physical body to the status and control of the individual within a larger social and economic system. She examines the way in which the female body throughout Western cultural history has been used as a sign for desire and the intense social need to control desire— echoes of Freud, but with a feminist lens that lets us consider how gender has figured into the demands for control within civilization. She examines as well the contemporary cultural context of the idealized body, which must at once respond to the social need for control and the economic need for consumption. The cultural pressure to discipline the body according to social norms falls especially hard on women, to the point of seeming to be another form of internal colonization—the woman's own alienation from her body and the objectification of it as a social measure of her worth.*

In the late Victorian era, arguably for the first time in the West, those who   ₁
could afford to eat well began systematically to deny themselves food in pursuit
of an aesthetic ideal. Certainly, other cultures had dieted. Aristocratic Greek
culture made a science of the regulation of food intake, as a road to self-mastery
and the practice of moderation in all things. Fasting, aimed at spiritual purifica-
tion and domination of the flesh, was an important part of the repertoire of
Christian practice in the Middle Ages. These forms of diet can clearly be viewed
as instruments for the development of a "self"—whether an "inner" self, for the
Christians, or a public self, for the Greeks—constructed as an arena in which
the deepest possibilities for human excellence may be realized. Rituals of fasting
and asceticism were therefore reserved for the select few, aristocratic or priestly,
who were deemed capable of achieving such excellence of spirit. In the late
nineteenth century, by contrast, the practices of body management begin to
be middle-class preoccupations, and concern with diet becomes attached to the
pursuit of an idealized physical weight or shape; it becomes a project in service
of body rather than soul. Fat, not appetite or desire, became the declared
enemy, and people began to measure their dietary achievements by the numbers
on the scale rather than by the level of their mastery of impulse and excess. The
bourgeois "tyranny of slenderness" (as Kim Chernin has called it) had begun its
ascendancy (particularly over women), and with it the development of numerous technologies—diet, exercise, and, later on, chemicals and surgery—aimed at
a purely physical transformation.

Today, we have become acutely aware of the massive and multifaceted
nature of such technologies and the industries built around them. To the degree
that a popular critical consciousness exists, however, it has been focused largely
(and not surprisingly) on what has been viewed as pathological or extreme—on
the unfortunate minority who become "obsessed" or go "too far." Television
talk shows feature tales of disasters caused by stomach stapling, gastric bubbles,

gastrointestinal bypass operations, liquid diets, compulsive exercising. Magazines warn of the dangers of fat-reduction surgery and liposuction. Books and articles about bulimia and anorexia nervosa proliferate. The portrayal of eating disorders by the popular media is often lurid; audiences gasp at pictures of skeletal bodies or at item-by-item descriptions of the mounds of food eaten during an average binge. Such presentations create a "side show" relationship between the ("normal") audience and those on view ("the freaks"). To the degree that the audience may nonetheless recognize themselves in the behavior or reported experiences of those on stage, they confront themselves as "pathological" or outside the norm.

Of course, many of these behaviors *are* outside the norm, if only because of the financial resources they require. But preoccupation with fat, diet, and slenderness are not abnormal. Indeed, such preoccupation may function as one of the most powerful normalizing mechanisms of our century, insuring the production of self-monitoring and self-disciplining "docile bodies" sensitive to any departure from social norms and habituated to self-improvement and self-transformation in the service of those norms. Seen in this light, the focus on "pathology," disorder, accident, unexpected disaster, and bizarre behavior obscures the normalizing function of the technologies of diet and body management. For women, who are subject to such controls more profoundly and, historically, more ubiquitously than men, the focus on "pathology" (unless embedded in a political analysis) diverts recognition from a central means of the reproduction of gender.

In this essay I examine the normalizing role of diet and exercise by analyzing popular representations through which their cultural meaning is crystallized, metaphorically encoded, and transmitted. More specifically, I pursue here Mary Douglas's insight that images of the "microcosm"—the physical body—may symbolically reproduce central vulnerabilities and anxieties of the "macrocosm"—the social body. I will explore this insight by reading, as the text or surface on which culture is symbolically written, some dominant meanings that are connected, in our time, to the imagery of slenderness.

The first step in my argument is a decoding of the contemporary slenderness ideal so as to reveal the psychic anxieties and moral valuations contained within it—valuations concerning correct and incorrect management of impulse and desire. In the process I describe a key contrast between two different symbolic functions of body shape and size: (1) the designation of social position, such as class status or gender role; and (2) the outer indication of the spiritual, moral, or emotional state of the individual. Next, aided by the significant work of Robert Crawford, I turn to the social body of consumer culture in order to demonstrate how the "correct" management of desire in that culture, requiring as it does a contradictory double-bind construction of personality, inevitably produces an unstable bulimic personality-type as its norm, along with the contrasting extremes of obesity and self-starvation. These symbolize, I will argue, the contradictions of the social body—contradictions that make self-management a continual and virtually impossible task in our culture. Finally, I introduce gender into this symbolic framework, showing how additional resonances (concerning the cultural management of female desire, on the one hand, and female flight from a purely reproductive destiny, on the other) have over-determined slenderness as the current ideal for women.

Contemporary Anxiety and the Enemy Flab

In the magazine show *20/20*, several ten-year-old boys were shown some photos of fashion models. The models were pencil-thin. Yet the pose was such that a small bulge of hip was forced, through the action of the body, into protuberance—as is natural, unavoidable on any but the most skeletal or the most tautly developed bodies. We bend over, we sit down, and the flesh coalesces in spots. These young boys, pointing to the hips, disgustedly pronounced the models to be "fat." Watching the show, I was appalled at the boys' reaction. Yet I could not deny that I had also been surprised at my own current perceptions while re-viewing female bodies in movies from the 1970s; what once appeared slender and fit now seemed loose and flabby. *Weight* was not the key element in these changed perceptions—my standards had not come to favor *thinner* bodies—rather, I had come to expect a tighter, smoother, more contained body profile. . . .

The self-criticisms of the anorectic, too, are usually focused on particular soft, protuberant areas of the body (most often the stomach) rather than on the body as a whole. Karen, in Ira Sacker and Marc Zimmer's *Dying to Be Thin*, tries to dispel what she sees as the myth that the anorectic misperceives her whole body as fat:

> I hope I'm expressing myself properly here, because this is important. You have to understand. I don't see my whole body as fat. When I look in the mirror I don't really see a fat person there. I see certain things about me that are really thin. Like my arms and legs. But I can tell the minute I eat certain things that my stomach blows up like a pig's. I know it gets distended. And it's disgusting. That's what I keep to myself—hug to myself.

Or Barbara, from Dalma Heyn's article on "Body Vision":

> Sometimes my body looks so bloated, I don't want to get dressed. I like the way it looks for exactly two days each month: usually, the eighth and ninth days after my period. Every other day, my breasts, my stomach—they're just awful lumps, bumps, bulges. My body can turn on me at any moment; it is an out-of-control mass of flesh.

Much has been made of such descriptions, from both psychoanalytic and feminist perspectives. But for now I wish to pursue these images of unwanted bulges and erupting stomachs in another direction than that of gender symbolism. I want to consider them as a metaphor for anxiety about internal processes out of control—uncontained desire, unrestrained hunger, uncontrolled impulse. Images of bodily eruption frequently function symbolically in this way in contemporary horror movies and werewolf films (*The Howling*, *A Teen-Age Werewolf in London*) and in David Cronenberg's remake of *The Fly*. The original *Fly* imagined a mechanical joining of fly parts and person parts, a variation on the standard "half-man, half-beast" image. In Cronenberg's *Fly*, as in the werewolf genre, a new, alien, libidinous, and uncontrollable self literally bursts through the seams of the victims' old flesh. (A related, frequently copied image occurs in *Alien*, where a parasite erupts from the chest of the human host.) In advertisements, the construction of the body as an alien attacker, threatening to erupt in an unsightly display of bulging flesh, is a ubiquitous cultural image.

Until the 1980s, excess weight was the target of most ads for diet products; today, one is much more likely to find the enemy constructed as bulge, fat, or flab. "Now," a typical ad runs, "get rid of those embarrassing bumps, bulges, large stomach, flabby breasts and buttocks. Feel younger, and help prevent cellulite buildup. . . . Have a nice shape with no tummy." To achieve such results (often envisioned as the absolute eradication of body, as in "no tummy") a violent assault on the enemy is usually required; bulges must be "attacked" and "destroyed," fat "burned," and stomachs (or, more disgustedly, "guts") must be "busted" and "eliminated." . . . The increasing popularity of liposuction, a far from totally safe technique developed specifically to suck out the unwanted bulges of people of normal weight (it is not recommended for the obese), suggests how far our disgust with bodily bulges has gone. The ideal here is of a body that is absolutely tight, contained, "bolted down," firm: in other words, a body that is protected against eruption from within, whose internal processes are under control. Areas that are soft, loose, or "wiggly" are unacceptable, even on extremely thin bodies. Cellulite management, like liposuction, has nothing to do with weight loss, and everything to do with the quest for firm bodily margins.

This perspective helps illuminate an important continuity of meaning in   10
our culture between compulsive dieting and body-building, and it reveals why it has been so easy for contemporary images of female attractiveness to oscillate between a spare, "minimalist" look and a solid, muscular, athletic look. The coexistence of these seemingly disparate images does not indicate that a postmodern universe of empty, endlessly differentiating images now reigns. Rather, the two ideals, though superficially very different, are united in battle against a common enemy: the soft, the loose; unsolid, excess flesh. It is perfectly permissible in our culture (even for women) to have substantial weight and bulk—so long as it is tightly managed. Simply to be slim is not enough—the flesh must not "wiggle." . . . Here we arrive at one source of insight into why it is that the image of ideal slenderness has grown thinner and thinner throughout the 1980s and early 1990s, and why women with extremely slender bodies often still see themselves as fat. Unless one takes to muscle-building, to achieve a flab-free, excess-free body one must trim very near the bone.

Slenderness and the Inner State of the Self

The moral—and, as we shall see, economic—coding of the fat/slender body in terms of its capacity for self-containment and the control of impulse and desire represents the culmination of a developing historical change in the social symbolism of body weight and size. Until the late nineteenth century, the central discriminations marked were those of class, race, and gender; the body indicated social identity and "place." So, for example, the bulging stomachs of successful mid-nineteenth-century businessmen and politicians were a symbol of bourgeois success, an outward manifestation of their accumulated wealth. By contrast, the gracefully slender body announced aristocratic status; disdainful of the bourgeois need to display wealth and power ostentatiously, it commanded social space invisibly rather than aggressively, seemingly above the commerce in appetite or the need to eat. Subsequently, this ideal began to be appropriated by the status-seeking middle class, as slender wives became the showpieces of their husbands' success.

Corpulence went out of middle-class vogue at the end of the century (even William Howard Taft, who had weighed over three hundred pounds while in office, went on a reducing diet). Social power had come to be less dependent on the sheer accumulation of material wealth and more connected to the ability to control and manage the labor and resources of others. At the same time, excess body weight came to be seen as reflecting moral or personal inadequacy, or lack of will. These associations are possible only in a culture of overabundance—that is, in a society in which those who control the production of "culture" have more than enough to eat. The moral requirement to diet depends on the material preconditions that make the *choice* to diet an option and the possibility of personal "excess" a reality. Although slenderness continues to retain some of its traditional class associations ("a woman can never be too rich or too thin"), the importance of this equation has eroded considerably since the 1970s. Increasingly, the size and shape of the body have come to operate as a market of personal, internal order (or disorder)—as a symbol for the emotional, moral, or spiritual state of the individual.

Consider one particularly clear example, that of changes in the meaning of the muscled body. Muscularity has had a variety of cultural meanings that have prevented the well-developed body from playing a major role in middle-class conceptions of attractiveness. Of course, muscles have chiefly symbolized and continue to symbolize masculine power as physical strength, frequently operating as a means of coding the "naturalness" of sexual difference. . . . But at the same time . . . they have been associated with manual labor and proletarian status, and they have often been suffused with racial meaning as well (as in numerous film representations of sweating, glistening bodies belonging to black slaves and prizefighters). Under the racial and class biases of our culture, muscles thus have been associated with the insensitive, unintelligent, and animalistic (recall the well-developed Marlon Brando as the emotionally primitive, physically abusive Stanley Kowalski in *A Streetcar Named Desire*). Moreover, as the body itself is dominantly imagined within the West as belonging to the "nature" side of a nature/culture duality, the *more* body one has had, the more uncultured and uncivilized one has been expected to be.

Today, however, the well-muscled body has become a cultural icon; "working out" is a glamorized and sexualized yuppie activity. No longer signifying inferior status (except when developed to extremes, at which point the old association of muscles with brute, unconscious materiality surfaces once more), the firm, developed body has become a symbol of correct *attitude*; it means that one "cares" about oneself and how one appears to others, suggesting willpower, energy, control over infantile impulse, the ability to "shape your life." . . . "You exercise, you diet," says Heather Locklear, promoting Bally Matrix Fitness Centre on television, "and you can do anything you want." Muscles express sexuality, but controlled, managed sexuality that is not about to erupt in unwanted and embarrassing display.

To the degree that the question of class still operates in all this, it relates to   15
the category of social mobility (or lack of it) rather than class *location*. So, for example, when associations of fat and lower-class status exist, they are usually mediated by moral qualities—fat being perceived as indicative of laziness, lack of discipline, unwillingness to conform, and absence of all those "managerial" abilities that, according to the dominant ideology, confer upward mobility. . . . Correspondingly, in popular teen movies such as *Flashdance* and *Vision Quest*, the ability of the (working-class) heroine and hero to pare, prune, tighten, and master the body operates as a clear symbol of successful upward aspiration, of the penetrability of class boundaries to those who have "the right stuff." These movies (as one title makes explicit) are contemporary "quest myths"; like their prototype, *Rocky*, they follow the struggle of an individual to attain a personal grail, against all odds and through numerous trials. But unlike the film quests of a previous era (which sent Mr. Smith to Washington and Mr. Deeds to town to battle the respective social evils of corrupt government and big business), *Flashdance* and *Vision Quest* render the hero's and heroine's commitment, will and spiritual integrity through the metaphors of weight loss, exercise, and tolerance of and ability to conquer physical pain and exhaustion. (In *Vision Quest*, for example, the audience is encouraged to admire the young wrestler's perseverance when he ignores the fainting spells and nosebleeds caused by his rigorous training and dieting.)

Not surprisingly, young people with eating disorders often thematize their own experience in similar terms, as in the following excerpt from an interview with a young woman runner:

> Well, I had the willpower, I could train for competition, and I could turn down food any time. I remember feeling like I was on a constant high. And the pain? Sure, there was pain. It was incredible. Between the hunger and the muscle pain from the constant workouts? I can't tell you how much I hurt.
>
> You may think I was crazy to put myself through constant, intense pain. But you have to remember, I was fighting a battle. And when you get hurt in

a battle, you're proud of it. Sure, you may scream inside, but if you're brave and really good, then you take it quietly, because you know it's the price you pay for winning. And I needed to win. I really felt that if I didn't win, I would die . . . all these enemy troops were coming at me, and I had to outsmart them. If I could discipline myself enough—if I could keep myself lean and strong—then I could win. The pain was just a natural thing I had to deal with.

As in *Vision Quest*, the external context is training for an athletic event. But here, too, that goal becomes subordinated to an internal one. The real battle, ultimately, is with the self. At this point, the limitations of the brief history presented in the opening paragraph of this essay are revealed. In that paragraph, the contemporary preoccupation with diet is contrasted to historical projects of body management that were suffused with moral meaning. In this section, however, I have suggested that examination of even the most shallow representations (teen movies) discloses a moral ideology—one, in fact, seemingly close to the aristocratic Greek ideal described by Foucault in *The Use of Pleasure*. The central element of that ideal, as Foucault describes it, is "an agonistic relation with the self"—aimed, not at the extirpation of desire and hunger in the interests of "purity" (as in the Christian strain of dualism), but at a "virile" mastery of desire through constant "spiritual combat."

For the Greeks, however, the "virile" mastery of desire took place in a culture that valorized moderation. The culture of contemporary body-management, struggling to manage desire in a system dedicated to the proliferation of desirable commodities, is very different. In cultural fantasies such as *Vision Quest* and *Flashdance*, self-mastery is presented as an attainable and stable state; but, as I argue in the next section of this essay, the reality of the contemporary agonism of the self is another matter entirely.

Slenderness and the Social Body

Mary Douglas, looking on the body as a system of "natural symbols" that reproduce social categories and concerns, has argued that anxiety about the maintenance of rigid bodily boundaries (manifested, for example, in rituals and prohibitions concerning excreta, saliva, and the strict delineation of "inside" and "outside") is most evident and intense in societies whose external boundaries are under attack. Let me hypothesize, similarly, that preoccupation with the "internal" management of the body (that is, management of its desires) is produced by instabilities in what could be called the macro-regulation of desire within the system of the social body.

In advanced consumer capitalism, as Robert Crawford has elegantly argued, an unstable, agonistic construction of personality is produced by the contradictory structure of economic life. On the one hand, as producers of goods and services we must sublimate, delay, repress desires for immediate gratification; we must cultivate the work ethic. On the other hand, as consumers we must display a boundless capacity to capitulate to desire and indulge in impulse; we must hunger for constant and immediate satisfaction. The regulation of desire thus becomes an ongoing problem, as we find ourselves continually besieged by temptation, while socially condemned for overindulgence. (Of course, those who cannot afford to indulge their desires as consumers, teased and frustrated by the culture, face a much harsher dilemma.)

Food and diet are central arenas for the expression of these contradictions.   20
On television and in popular magazines, with a flip of the page or barely a pause between commercials, images of luscious foods and the rhetoric of craving and desire are replaced by advertisements for grapefruit diets, low-calorie recipes, and exercise equipment. Even more disquieting than these manifest oppositions, however, are the constant attempts by advertisers to mystify them, suggesting that the contradiction doesn't really exist, that one can "have it all." Diets and exercise programs are accordingly presented with the imagery of instant gratification ("From Fat to Fabulous in 21 Days," "Size 22 to Size 10 in No Time Flat," "Six Minutes to an Olympic-Class Stomach") and effortlessness ("3,000 Sit-Ups Without Moving an Inch . . . 10 Miles of Jogging Lying Flat on Your Back" . . . , "85 Pounds Without Dieting," and even, shamelessly, "Exercise Without Exercise"). In reality, however, the opposition is not so easily reconciled. Rather, it presents a classic double bind, in which the self is torn in two mutually incompatible directions. The contradiction is not an abstract one but stems from the specific historical construction of a "consuming passion" from which all inclinations toward balance, moderation, rationality, and foresight have been excluded.

Conditioned to lose control at the mere sight of desirable products, we can master our desires only by creating rigid defenses against them. The slender body codes the tantalizing ideal of a well-managed self in which all is kept in order despite the contradictions of consumer culture. Thus, whether or not the struggle is played out in terms of food and diet, many of us may find our lives vacillating between a daytime rigidly ruled by the "performance principle" and nights and weekends that capitulate to unconscious "letting go" (food, shopping, liquor, television, and other addictive drugs). In this way, the central contradiction of the system inscribes itself on our bodies, and bulimia emerges as a characteristic modern personality construction. For bulimia precisely and explicitly expresses the extreme development of the hunger for unrestrained consumption (exhibited in the bulimic's uncontrollable food binges) existing in unstable tension alongside the requirement that we sober up, "clean up our act," get back in firm control on Monday morning (the necessity for purge—exhibited in the bulimic's vomiting, compulsive exercising, and laxative purges).

The same structural contradiction is inscribed in what has been termed (incorrectly) the "paradox" that we have an "epidemic" of anorexia nervosa in this country "despite the fact that we have an overweight majority." Far from paradoxical, the coexistence of anorexia and obesity reveals the instability of the contemporary personality construction, the difficulty of finding homeostasis between the producer and the consumer sides of the self. Bulimia embodies the unstable double bind of consumer capitalism, while anorexia and obesity embody an attempted resolution of that double bind. Anorexia could thus be seen as an extreme development of the capacity for self-denial and repression of desire (the work ethic in absolute control); obesity, as an extreme capacity to capitulate to desire (consumerism in control). Both are rooted in the same consumer-culture construction of desire as overwhelming and overtaking the self. Given that construction, we can only respond either with total submission or rigid defense.

Neither anorexia nor obesity is accepted by the culture as an appropriate response. The absolute conquest of hunger and desire (even in symbolic form) can never be tolerated by a consumer system—even if the Christian dualism of our culture also predisposes us to be dazzled by the anorectic's ability seemingly to transcend the flesh. Anorectics are proud of this ability, but, as the disorder progresses, they usually feel the need to hide their skeletal bodies from those around them. If cultural attitudes toward the anorectic are ambivalent, however, reactions to the obese are not. As Marcia Millman documents in *Such a Pretty Face*, the obese elicit blinding rage and disgust in our culture and are often viewed in terms that suggest an infant sucking hungrily, unconsciously at its mother's breast: greedy, self-absorbed, lazy, without self-control or willpower. People avoid sitting next to the obese (even when the space they take up is not intrusive); comics feel no need to restrain their cruelty; socially, they are considered unacceptable at public functions (one man wrote to "Dear Abby," saying that he was planning to replace his brother and sister-in-law as honor attendants at his wedding, because "they are both quite overweight"). Significantly, the part of the obese anatomy most often targeted for vicious attack, and most despised by the obese themselves, is the stomach, symbol of consumption (in the case of the obese, unrestrained consumption taking over the organism; one of Marcia Millman's interviewees recalls how the husband of a friend called hers "an awful, cancerous-looking growth").

Slenderness, Self-management, and Normalization

Self-management in consumer culture, I have been arguing, becomes more elusive as it becomes more pressing. The attainment of an acceptable body is extremely difficult for those who do not come by it "naturally" (whether aided by genetics, metabolism, or high activity-level) and as the ideal becomes firmer and tauter it begins to exclude more and more people. Constant watchfulness over appetite and strenuous work on the body itself are required to conform to this ideal, while the most popular means of "correction"—dieting—often insures its own failure, as the experience of deprivation leads to compensatory binging, with its attendant feelings of defeat, worthlessness, and loss of hope. Between the media images of self-containment and self-mastery and the reality of constant, everyday stress and anxiety about one's appearance lies the chasm that produces bodies habituated to self-monitoring and self-normalization.

Ultimately, the body (besides being evaluated for its success or failure at 25 getting itself in order) is seen as demonstrating correct or incorrect attitudes toward the demands of normalization itself. The obese and anorectic are therefore disturbing partly because they embody resistance to cultural norms. Bulimics, by contrast, typically strive for the conventionally attractive body shape dictated by their more "normative" pattern of managing desire. In the case of the obese, in particular, what is perceived as their defiant rebellion against normalization appears to be a source of the hostility they inspire. The anorectic at least pays homage to dominant cultural values, outdoing them in their own terms:

> I wanted people to look at me and see something special. I wanted to look in the face of a stranger and see admiration, so that I would know that I accomplished something that was just about impossible for most people, especially in our society. . . . From what I've seen, more people fail at losing weight than at any other single goal. I found out how to do what everyone else couldn't: I could lose as much or as little weight as I wanted. And that meant I was better than everyone else.

The anorectic thus strives to stand above the crowd by excelling at its own rules; in so doing, however, she exposes the hidden penalties. But the obese—particularly those who claim to be happy although overweight—are perceived as not playing by the rules at all. If the rest of us are struggling to be acceptable and "normal," we cannot allow them to get away with it; they must be put in their place, be humiliated and defeated.

A number of talk shows have made this abundantly clear. On one, much of the audience reaction was given over to disbelief and to the attempt to prove to one obese woman that she was *not* happy: "I can't believe you don't want to be slim and beautiful, I just can't believe it." "I heard you talk a lot about how you feel good about yourself and you like yourself, but I really think you're kidding yourself." "It's hard for me to believe that Mary Jane is really happy . . . you don't fit into chairs, it's hard to get through the doorway. My God, on the subway, forget it." When Mary Jane persisted in her assertion that she was happy, she was warned, in a viciously self-righteous tone, that it would not last: "Mary Jane, to be the way you are today, you had better start going on a diet soon, because if you don't you're going to get bigger and bigger and bigger. It's true." On another show, in an effort to subdue an increasingly hostile and offensive audience one of the doctor-guests kept trying to reassure them that the "fat and happy" target of their attacks did not *really* mean that she didn't *want* to lose weight; rather, she was simply tired of trying and failing. This construction allows people to give their sympathy to the obese, assuming as it does the obese person's acknowledgment that to be "normal" is the most desired goal, elusive only because of personal inadequacy. Those who are willing to present themselves as pitiable, in pain, and conscious of their own unattractiveness—often demonstrated, on these shows, by self-admissions about intimate physical difficulties, orgies of self-hate, or descriptions of gross consumption of food—win the sympathy and concern of the audience.

● Applying a Postcolonial Frame

1. Preoccupation with body weight, Bordo says, "may function as one of the most powerful normalizing mechanisms of our century, insuring the production of self-monitoring and self-disciplining 'docile bodies' sensitive to any departure from social norms." What other social norms does the vast media attention focused on the slender body reinforce? What other aspects of behavior and social identity do you think we are culturally led to "self-monitor" or else risk being classified as abnormal?

2. Bordo addresses the "microcosm" of the physical body and the "macrocosm" of how it functions culturally as a sign of the "spiritual, moral, or emotional state of the individual." What are some common connections you draw between the body and these areas of social judgment? How do such connections work to shape your views and values, do you think?

3. What in our cultural history do you think leads us to see as negative, even immoral, "the soft, the loose; unsolid, excess flesh"? If we gender this "unmanaged" flesh as female, what particularly female "sins" are we culturally influenced to connect to it?

4. Explain in your own words how the individual body ties to social class in contemporary culture, as Bordo argues. How does this connection work itself out in your daily experience?

5. Explain the cultural "double-bind" of being the controlled participant in economic life and the indulgent consumer. Again, where in your daily experience do you see this conflict emerge? What specific forms do you see it take for students?

6. Considering the readings you have read in this chapter, how would you situate yourself among the many cultural scripts that seem to direct the course of individual lives?

   • Which identity categories—gender, class, race, sexual orientation, religious affiliation, political affiliation, heritage, family history, and so on—stand out to you as the most powerful?

   • To what extent do you identify with the concept of the internally colonized in any of these categories?

   • How do you see your relation to cultural scripts intersecting with the script of American individualism, or the "bootstraps" script of opportunity and hard work?

   • Think about how your sense of your own cultural position might inform your rhetorical choices as a writer: What voices might you speak from? What forms might suit your various "stories" of your identity/identities?

topics for writing

1. The process of assimilation, through which "others" are to become more like the mainstream, in language use, customs, and attitudes, or through successful identification with the "norm," is complex and different for each of the figures/groups depicted in this chapter's readings (including gender as a category, though one inflected by race, class, and other cultural identity factors). Explore the view of assimilation that each seems to hold, and the problems that assimilation poses for each. Who wishes to resist the process? Who is less likely to become fully assimilated?

   - Clarify the different origins and path to a "successful" American life

   - Do you see assimilation as a positive goal for each? as a reachable goal?

   - What assumptions about assimilation did you bring to the readings? Has your view changed? Have you faced similar questions about "adapting" to mainstream culture that many of the authors pose?

2. Construct your own narrative of difference, based on personal experience and/or observation. Choose the audience you would most like to address. This could be a mainstream group or a more marginalized group; a pro-assimilation group or one that advocates cultural preservation; an activist postcolonial or a normative audience.

   - In what ways, if any, do you identify with an "other" position?

   - How have you experienced this otherness, or an awareness of the difference of others? Have you been on both sides of "the gaze"?

   - Did you view assimilation as an option, a conflict, something else?

      Draw on any of the readings in this section to help explain your ideas or persuade readers to accept your views.

3. What role do you think technology plays in either adding to an individual's marginalization or to her or his active participation in mainstream cultural life? How does one's relationship to technology reflect one's place in the mainstream? Consider the following:

   - *access* to technology (computers, the Internet, etc.).

   - *contact* with unfamiliar technology (through health care, for example, as in Lia's family's case, in the Anne Fadiman reading on page 474).

   - the *nature* of contact—active or passive; the intentional use of computers, cell phones, and so on, for example, versus the passive submission to technology used in medicine, financial affairs, educational settings, and so on.

   - the effect of *options* for using technology in communication (limited access to computers versus the ability to construct a Web site, for instance).

This Chapter's Rhetorical Concepts

● Engaging alternative discourses
● Working with rhetorically resistant voices and forms
● Connecting cultural difference and rhetorical choices

Reading Critically About Resistant Voices and Rhetorical Forms

La conciencia de la mestiza: Towards a New Consciousness

GLORIA ANZALDÚA

Gloria Anzaldúa's book Borderlands/La Frontera *was published in 1987, and was a breakthrough text for many kinds of voices. It helped open up the field of border studies—study of and from the social, psychological, and geographical borderlands where different cultures meet and overlap. Borderlands both threaten and help define the "mainland," the dominant culture. Anzaldúa (1942–2004) writes as Chicana, Tejana, feminist, lesbian, theorist, social critic, poet, and bilingual author, among other stances. She positions herself at the borders of her different identities, different cultures. Her work thus employs a variety of forms—verse, essay, history, autobiography; like her, it is* mestiza, *mixed. She argues for the power of the mixed, the queer, and sees hope in ambiguity, a way into a new, possibly liberating territory. Many students encountering Anzaldúa's rhetorical techniques for the first time find it alienating. Try reading this chapter from her book with the knowledge that she writes from a position of alienation, and that her purpose is to invite you into this border state.*

> Por la mujer de mi raza
> hablará el espíritu.

Jose **Vasconcelos,** Mexican philosopher, envisaged *una raza mestiza, una mezcla de razas afines, una raza de color—la primera raza síntesis del globo.* He called it a cosmic race, *la raza cósmica,* a fifth race embracing the four major races of the world. Opposite to the theory of the pure Aryan, and to the policy of racial purity that white America practices, his theory is one of inclusivity. At the confluence of two or more genetic streams, with chromosomes constantly "crossing over," this mixture of races, rather than resulting in an inferior being, provides hybrid progeny, a mutable, more malleable species with a rich gene pool. From

1

this racial, ideological, cultural and biological cross-pollinization, an "alien" consciousness is presently in the making—a new *mestiza* consciousness, *una conciencia de mujer*. It is a consciousness of the Borderlands.

Una lucha de fronteras / A Struggle of Borders

> Because I, a *mestiza*,
> continually walk out of one culture
> and into another,
> because I am in all cultures at the same time,
> *alma entre dos mundos, tres, cuatro,*
> *me zumba la cabeza con lo contradictorio.*
> *Estoy norteada por todas las voces que me hablan*
> *simultáneamente.*

The ambivalence from the clash of voices results in mental and emotional states of perplexity. Internal strife results in insecurity and indecisiveness. The mestiza's dual or multiple personality is plagued by psychic restlessness.

In a constant state of mental nepantilism, an Aztec word meaning torn between ways, *la mestiza* is a product of the transfer of the cultural and spiritual values of one group to another. Being tricultural, monolingual, bilingual, or multilingual, speaking a patois, and in a state of perpetual transition, the *mestiza* faces the dilemma of the mixed breed: which collectivity does the daughter of a darkskinned mother listen to?

El choque de un alma atrapado entre el mundo del espíritu y el mundo de la técnica a veces la deja entullada. Cradled in one culture, sandwiched between two cultures, straddling all three cultures and their value systems, *la mestiza* undergoes a struggle of flesh, a struggle of borders, an inner war. Like all people, we perceive the version of reality that our culture communicates. Like others having or living in more than one culture, we get multiple, often opposing messages. The coming together of two self-consistent but habitually incompatible frames of reference causes *un choque*, a cultural collision.

Within us and within *la cultura chicana*, commonly held beliefs of the white culture attack commonly held beliefs of the Mexican culture, and both attack commonly held beliefs of the indigenous culture. Subconsciously, we see an attack on ourselves and our beliefs as a threat and we attempt to block with a counterstance.

But it is not enough to stand on the opposite river bank, shouting questions, challenging patriarchal, white conventions. A counterstance locks one into a duel of oppressor and oppressed; locked in mortal combat, like the cop and the criminal, both are reduced to a common denominator of violence. The counterstance refutes the dominant culture's views and beliefs, and, for this, it is proudly defiant. All reaction is limited by, and dependent on, what it is reacting against. Because the counterstance stems from a problem with authority—outer as well as inner—it's a step towards liberation from cultural domination. But it is not a way of life. At some point, on our way to a new consciousness, we will have to leave the opposite bank, the split between the two mortal combatants somehow healed so that we are on both shores at once and, at once, see through serpent and eagle eyes. Or perhaps we will decide to disengage from the dominant culture, write it off altogether as a lost cause, and cross the border into a wholly new and separate territory. Or we might go another route. The possibilities are numerous once we decide to act and not react.

A Tolerance for Ambiguity

These numerous possibilities leave *la mestiza* floundering in uncharted seas. In perceiving conflicting information and points of view, she is subjected to a swamping of her psychological borders. She has discovered that she can't hold concepts or ideas in rigid boundaries. The borders and walls that are supposed to keep the undesirable ideas out are entrenched habits and patterns of behavior; these habits and patterns are the enemy within. Rigidity means death. Only by remaining flexible is she able to stretch the psyche horizontally and vertically. *La mestiza* constantly has to shift out of habitual formations; from convergent thinking, analytical reasoning that tends to use rationality to move towards a single goal (a Western mode), to divergent thinking, characterized by movement away from set patterns and goals and toward a more whole perspective, one that includes rather than excludes.

The new *mestiza* copes by developing a tolerance for contradictions, a tolerance for ambiguity. She learns to be an Indian in Mexican culture, to be Mexican from an Anglo point of view. She learns to juggle cultures. She has a plural personality, she operates in a pluralistic mode—nothing is thrust out, the good the bad and the ugly, nothing rejected, nothing abandoned. Not only does she sustain contradictions, she turns the ambivalence into something else.

She can be jarred out of ambivalence by an intense, and often painful, emotional event which inverts or resolves the ambivalence. I'm not sure exactly how. The work takes place underground—subconsciously. It is work that the soul performs. That focal point or fulcrum, that juncture where the mestiza stands, is where phenomena tend to collide. It is where the possibility of uniting all that is separate occurs. This assembly is not one where severed or separated pieces merely come together. Nor is it a balancing of opposing powers. In attempting to work out a synthesis, the self has added a third element which is greater than the sum of its severed parts. That third element is a new consciousness—a mestiza consciousness—and though it is a source of intense pain, its energy comes from continual creative motion that keeps breaking down the unitary aspect of each new paradigm.

En unas pocas centurias, the future will belong to the mestiza. Because the future depends on the breaking down of paradigms, it depends on the straddling of two or more cultures. By creating a new mythos—that is, a change in the way we perceive reality, the way we see ourselves, and the ways we behave—*la mestiza* creates a new consciousness.

The work of *mestiza* consciousness is to break down the subject-object duality that keeps her a prisoner and to show in the flesh and through the images in her work how duality is transcended. The answer to the problem between the white race and the colored, between males and females, lies in healing the split that originates in the very foundation of our lives, our culture, our languages, our thoughts. A massive uprooting of dualistic thinking in the individual and collective consciousness is the beginning of a long struggle, but one that could, in our best hopes, bring us to the end of rape, of violence, of war.

La encrucijada / The Crossroads

15

A chicken is being sacrificed
    at a crossroads, a simple mound of earth
a mud shrine for *Eshu*,
    Yoruba god of indeterminacy,
who blesses her choice of path.
    She begins her journey.

Su cuerpo es una bocacalle. La mestiza has gone from being the sacrificial goat to becoming the officiating priestess at the crossroads.

As a *mestiza* I have no country, my homeland cast me out; yet all countries are mine because I am every woman's sister or potential lover. (As a lesbian I have no race, my own people disclaim me; but I am all races because there is the queer of me in all races.) I am cultureless because, as a feminist, I challenge the collective cultural/religious male-derived beliefs of Indo-Hispanics and Anglos; yet I am cultured because I am participating in the creation of yet another culture, a new story to explain the world and our participation in it, a new value system with images and symbols that connect us to each other and to the planet. *Soy un amasamiento*, I am an act of kneading, of uniting and joining that not only has produced both a creature of darkness and a creature of light, but also a creature that questions the definitions of light and dark and gives them new meanings.

We are the people who leap in the dark, we are the people on the knees of the gods. In our very flesh, (r)evolution works out the clash of cultures. It makes us crazy constantly, but if the center holds, we've made some kind of evolutionary step forward. *Nuestra alma eltrabajo*, the opus, the great alchemical work;

spiritual *mestizaje*, a "morphogenesis," an inevitable unfolding. We have become the quickening serpent movement.

Indigenous like corn, like corn, the *mestiza* is a product of crossbreeding, [20] designed for preservation under a variety of conditions. Like an ear of corn—a female seed-bearing organ—the *mestiza* is tenacious, tightly wrapped in the husks of her culture. Like kernels she clings to the cob; with thick stalks and strong brace roots, she holds tight to the earth—she will survive the crossroads.

Lavando y remojando el maíz en agua de cal, despojando el pellejo. Moliendo, mixteando, amasando, haciendo tortillas de masa. She steeps the corn in lime, it swells, softens. With stone roller on *metate*, she grinds the corn, then grinds again. She kneads and moulds the dough, pats the round balls into *tortillas*.

We are the porous rock in the stone *metate*
squatting on the ground.
We are the rolling pin, *el maíz y agua,*
la masa harina. Somos el amasijo.
Somos lo molido en el metate.
We are the *comal* sizzling hot,
the hot *tortilla*, the hungry mouth.
We are the coarse rock.
We are the grinding motion,
the mixed potion, *somos el molcajete.*
We are the pestle, the *comino, ajo, pimienta,*
We are the *chile colorado,*
the green shoot that cracks the rock.
We will abide.

El camino de la mestiza / The Mestiza Way

Caught between the sudden contraction, the breath sucked in and the endless space, the brown woman stands still, looks at the sky. She decides to go down, digging her way along the roots of trees. Sifting through the bones, she shakes them to see if there is any marrow in them. Then, touching the dirt to her forehead, to her tongue, she takes a few bones, leaves the rest in their burial place.

She goes through her backpack, keeps her journal and address book, throws away the muni-bart metromaps. The coins are heavy and they go next, then the greenbacks flutter through the air. She keeps her knife, can opener and eyebrow pencil. She puts bones, pieces of bark, *hierbas*, eagle feather, snakeskin, tape recorder, the rattle and drum in her pack and she sets out to become the complete *tolteca*.

Her first step is to take inventory. *Despojando, desgranando, quitando paja.* 25
Just what did she inherit from her ancestors? This weight on her back—which is
the baggage from the Indian mother, which the baggage from the Spanish
father, which the baggage from the Anglo?

Pero es difícil differentiating between *lo beredado, lo adquirido, lo impuesto.*
She puts history through a sieve, winnows out the lies, looks at the forces that
we as a race, as women, have been a part of. *Luego bota lo que no vale, los
desmientos, los desencuentros, el embrutecimiento. Aguarda el juicio, bondo y
enraízado, de la gente antigua.* This step is a conscious rupture with all oppressive traditions of all cultures and religions. She communicates that rupture,
documents the struggle. She reinterprets history and, using new symbols, she
shapes new myths. She adopts new perspectives toward the darkskinned,
women and queers. She strengthens her tolerance (and intolerance) for ambiguity. She is willing to share, to make herself vulnerable to foreign ways of
seeing and thinking. She surrenders all notions of safety, of the familiar.
Deconstruct, construct. She becomes a *nabual*, able to transform herself into a
tree, a coyote, into another person. She learns to transform the small "I" into
the total Self. *Se bace moldeadora de su alma. Según la concepción que tiene de sí
misma, así será.*

Que no se nos olvide los bombres

"Tú no sirves pa' nada—
you're good for nothing.
Eres pura vieja"

"You're nothing but a woman" means you are defective. Its opposite is to
be *un macho.* The modern meaning of the word "machismo," as well as the concept, is actually an Anglo invention. For men like my father, being "macho"
meant being strong enough to protect and support my mother and us, yet being
able to show love. Today's macho has doubts about his ability to feed and protect his family. His "machismo" is an adaptation to oppression and poverty and
low self-esteem. It is the result of hierarchical male dominance. The Anglo,
feeling inadequate and inferior and powerless, displaces or transfers these feelings to the Chicano by shaming him. In the Gringo world, the Chicano suffers
from excessive humility and self-effacement, shame of self and self-deprecation.
Around Latinos he suffers from a sense of language inadequacy and its
accompanying discomfort; with Native Americans he suffers from a racial
amnesia which ignores our common blood, and from guilt because the Spanish
part of him took their land and oppressed them. He has an excessive compensatory hubris when around Mexicans from the other side. It overlays a deep
sense of racial shame.

The loss of a sense of dignity and respect in the macho breeds a false
machismo which leads him to put down women and even to brutalize them.

Coexisting with his sexist behavior is a love for the mother which takes precedence over that of all others. Devoted son, macho pig. To wash down the shame of his acts, of his very being, and to handle the brute in the mirror, he takes to the bottle, the snort, the needle, and the fist.

Though we "understand" the root causes of male hatred and fear, and the   30
subsequent wounding of women, we do not excuse, we do not condone, and we will no longer put up with it. From the men of our race, we demand the admission/acknowledgment/disclosure/testimony that they wound us, violate us, are afraid of us and of our power. We need them to say they will begin to eliminate their hurtful put-down ways. But more than the words, we demand acts. We say to them: We will develop equal power with you and those who have shamed us.

It is imperative that mestizas support each other in changing the sexist elements in the Mexican-Indian culture. As long as woman is put down, the Indian and the Black in all of us is put down. The struggle of the mestiza is above all a feminist one. As long as *los hombres* think they have to *chingar mujeres* and each other to be men, as long as men are taught that they are superior and therefore culturally favored over *la mujer*, as long as to be a *vieja* is a thing of derision, there can be no real healing of our psyches. We're halfway there—we have such love of the Mother, the good mother. The first step is to unlearn the *puta/virgen* dichotomy and to see *Coatlapopeuh-Coatlicue* in the Mother, *Guadalupe*.

Tenderness, a sign of vulnerability, is so feared that it is showered on women with verbal abuse and blows. Men, even more than women, are fettered to gender roles. Women at least have had the guts to break out of bondage. Only gay men have had the courage to expose themselves to the woman inside them and to challenge the current masculinity. I've encountered a few scattered and isolated gentle straight men, the beginnings of a new breed, but they are confused, and entangled with sexist behaviors that they have not been able to eradicate. We need a new masculinity and the new man needs a movement.

Lumping the males who deviate from the general norm with man, the oppressor, is a gross injustice. *Asombra pensar que nos hemos quedado en ese pozo oscuro donde el mundo encierra a las lesbianas. Asombra pensar que hemos, como femenistas y lesbianas, cerrado nuestros corazónes a los hombres, a nuestros hermanos los jotos, desheredados y marginales como nosotros.* Being the supreme crossers of cultures, homosexuals have strong bonds with the queer white, Black, Asian, Native American, Latino, and with the queer in Italy, Australia and the rest of the planet. We come from all colors, all classes, all races, all time periods. Our role is to link people with each other—the Blacks with Jews with Indians with Asians with whites with extraterrestrials. It is to transfer ideas and information from one culture to another. Colored homosexuals have more knowledge of other cultures; have always been at the forefront (although sometimes in the closet) of all liberation struggles in this country; have suffered more injustices and have survived them despite all odds. Chicanos need to acknowledge the political and artistic contributions of their queer. People, listen to what your *jotería* is saying.

The mestizo and the queer exist at this time and point on the evolutionary continuum for a purpose. We are a blending that proves that all blood is intricately woven together, and that we are spawned out of similar souls.

Somos una gente   35

Hay tantísimas fronteras
que dividen a la gente,
pero por cada frontera
existe también un puente.
—Gina Valdés

Divided Loyalties. Many women and men of color do not want to have any dealings with white people. It takes too much time and energy to explain to the downwardly mobile, white middle-class women that it's okay for us to want to own "possessions," never having had any nice furniture on our dirt floors or "luxuries" like washing machines. Many feel that whites should help their own people rid themselves of race hatred and fear first. I, for one, choose to use some of my energy to serve as mediator. I think we need to allow whites to be our allies. Through our literature, art, *corridos,* and folktales we must share our history with them so when they set up committees to help Big Mountain Navajos or the Chicano farmworkers or *los Nicaragüenses* they won't turn people away because of their racial fears and ignorances. They will come to see that they are not helping us but following our lead.

Individually, but also as a racial entity, we need to voice our needs. We need to say to white society: We need you to accept the fact that Chicanos are different, to acknowledge your rejection and negation of us. We need you to own the fact that you looked upon us as less than human, that you stole our lands, our personhood, our self-respect. We need you to make public restitution: to say that, to compensate for your own sense of defectiveness, you strive for power over us, you erase our history and our experience because it makes you feel guilty—you'd rather forget your brutish acts. To say you've split yourself from minority groups, that you disown us, that your dual consciousness splits off parts of yourself, transferring the "negative" parts onto us. (Where there is persecution of minorities, there is shadow projection. Where there is violence and war, there is repression of shadow.) To say that you are afraid of us, that to put distance between us, you wear the mask of contempt. Admit that Mexico is your double, that she exists in the shadow of this country, that we are irrevocably tied to her. Gringo, accept the doppelganger in your psyche. By taking back your collective shadow the intracultural split will heal. And finally, tell us what you need from us.

By Your True Faces We Will Know You

I am visible—see this Indian face—yet I am invisible. I both blind them with my beak nose and am their blind spot. But I exist, we exist. They'd like to think I have melted in the pot. But I haven't, we haven't.

The dominant white culture is killing us slowly with its ignorance. By taking away our self-determination, it has made us weak and empty. As a people we have resisted and we have taken expedient positions, but we have never been allowed to develop unencumbered—we have never been allowed to be fully ourselves. The whites in power want us people of color to barricade ourselves behind our separate tribal walls so they can pick us off one at a time with their hidden weapons; so they can whitewash and distort history. Ignorance splits people, creates prejudices. A misinformed people is a subjugated people.

Before the Chicano and the undocumented worker and the Mexican from   40 the other side can come together, before the Chicano can have unity with Native Americans and other groups, we need to know the history of their struggle and they need to know ours. Our mothers, our sisters and brothers, the guys who hang out on street corners, the children in the playgrounds, each of us must know our Indian lineage, our afro-*mestisaje*, our history of resistance.

To the immigrant *mexicano* and the recent arrivals we must teach our history. The 80 million *mexicanos* and the Latinos from Central and South America must know of our struggles. Each one of us must know basic facts about Nicaragua, Chile and the rest of Latin America. The Latinoist movement (Chicanos, Puerto Ricans, Cubans and other Spanish-speaking people working together to combat racial discrimination in the market place) is good but it is not enough. Other than a common culture we will have nothing to hold us together. We need to meet on a broader communal ground.

The struggle is inner: Chicano, *indio*, American Indian, *mojado*, *mexicano*, immigrant Latino, Anglo in power, working class Anglo, Black, Asian—our psyches resemble the border-towns and are populated by the same people. The struggle has always been inner, and is played out in the outer terrains. Awareness of our situation must come before inner changes, which in turn come before changes in society. Nothing happens in the "real" world unless it first happens in the images in our heads.

El día de la Chicana

I will not be shamed again
Nor will I shame myself.

I am possessed by a vision: that we Chicanas and Chicanos have taken back or uncovered our true faces, our dignity and self-respect. It's a validation vision.

Seeing the Chicana anew in light of her history. I seek an exoneration,   45
a seeing through the fictions of white supremacy, a seeing of ourselves in our true guises and not as the false racial personality that has been given to us and that we have given to ourselves. I seek our woman's face, our true features, the positive and the negative seen clearly, free of the tainted biases of male dominance. I seek new images of identity, new beliefs about ourselves, our humanity and worth no longer in question.

Estamos viviendo en la noche de la Raza, un tiempo cuando el trabajo se hace a lo quieto, en el oscuro. El día cuando aceptamos tal y como somos y para en donde vamos y porque—ese día será el día de la Raza. Yo tengo el conpromiso de expresar mi visión, mi sensibilidad, mi percepción de la revalidación de la gente mexicana, su mérito, estimación, honra, aprecio, y validez.

On December 2nd when my sun goes into my first house, I celebrate *el día de la Chicana y el Chicano.* On that day I clean my altars, light my *Coatlalopeuh* candle, burn sage and copal, take *el baño para espantar basura*, sweep my house. On that day I bare my soul, make myself vulnerable to friends and family by expressing my feelings. On that day I affirm who we are.

On that day I look inside our conflicts and our basic introverted racial temperament. I identify our needs, voice them. I acknowledge that the self and the race have been wounded. I recognize the need to take care of our personhood, of our racial self. On that day I gather the splintered and disowned parts of *la gente mexicana* and hold them in my arms. *Todas las partes de nosotros valen.*

On that day I say, "Yes, all you people wound us when you reject us. Rejection strips us of self-worth; our vulnerability exposes us to shame. It is our innate identity you find wanting. We are ashamed that we need your good opinion, that we need your acceptance. We can no longer camouflage our needs, can no longer let defenses and fences sprout around us. We can no longer withdraw. To rage and look upon you with contempt is to rage and be contemptuous of ourselves. We can no longer blame you, nor disown the white parts, the male parts, the pathological parts, the queer parts, the vulnerable parts. Here we are weaponless with open arms, with only our magic. Let's try it our way, the mestiza way, the Chicana way, the woman way.

On that day, I search for our essential dignity as a people, a people with   50
a sense of purpose—to belong and contribute to something greater than our

pueblo. On that day I seek to recover and reshape my spiritual identity. *Anímate! Raza, a celebrar el día de la Chicana.*

El retorno

All movements are accomplished in six stages,
and the seventh brings return.

—I Ching

*Tanto tiempo sin verte casa mía
mi cuna, mi hondo nido de la huerta.*

—*"Soledad"*

I stand at the river, watch the curving, twisting serpent, a serpent nailed to the fence where the mouth of the Rio Grande empties into the Gulf.

I have come back. *Tanto dolor me costó el alejamiento.* I shade my eyes and look up. The bone beak of a hawk slowly circling over me, checking me out as potential carrion. In its wake a little bird flickering its wings, swimming sporadically like a fish. In the distance the expressway and the slough of traffic like an irritated sow. The sudden pull in my gut, *la tierra, los aguaceros.* My land, *el viento soplando la arena, el lagartijo debajo de un nopalito. Me acuerdo como era antes. Una región desértica de vasta llanuras, costeras de baja altura, de escasa lluvia, de chaparrales formados por mesquites y huizaches.* If I look real hard I can almost see the Spanish fathers who were called "the cavalry of Christ" enter this valley riding their burros, see the clash of cultures commence.

Tierra natal. This is home, the small towns in the Valley, *los pueblitos* with   55 chicken pens and goats picketed to mesquite shrubs. *En las colonias* on the other side of the tracks, junk cars line the front yards of hot pink and lavender-trimmed houses—Chicano architecture we call it, self-consciously. I have missed the TV shows where hosts speak in half and half, and where awards are given in the category of Tex-Mex music. I have missed the Mexican cemeteries blooming with artificial flowers, the fields of aloe vera and red pepper, rows of sugar cane, of corn hanging on the stalks, the cloud of *polvareda* in the dirt roads behind a speeding pickup truck, *el sabor de tamales de rez y venado.* I have missed *la yegua colorada* gnawing the wooden gate of her stall, the smell of horse flesh from Carito's corrals. *He hecho menos las noches calientes sin aire, noches de linternas y lechuzas* making holes in the night.

I still feel the old despair when I look at the unpainted, dilapidated, scrap lumber houses consisting mostly of corrugated aluminum. Some of the poorest people in the U.S. live in the Lower Rio Grande Valley, an arid and semi-arid land of irrigated farming, intense sunlight and heat, citrus groves next to chaparral and cactus. I walk through the elementary school I attended so long ago, that remained segregated until recently. I remember how the white teachers used to punish us for being Mexican.

How I love this tragic valley of South Texas, as Ricardo Sánchez calls it; this borderland between the Nueces and the Rio Grande. This land has survived possession and ill-use by five countries: Spain, Mexico, the Republic of Texas, the U.S., the Confederacy, and the U.S. again. It has survived Anglo-Mexican blood feuds, lynchings, burnings, rapes, pillage.

Today I see the Valley still struggling to survive. Whether it does or not, it will never be as I remember it. The borderlands depression that was set off by the 1982 peso devaluation in Mexico resulted in the closure of hundreds of Valley businesses. Many people lost their homes, cars, land. Prior to 1982, U.S. store owners thrived on retail sales to Mexicans who came across the border for groceries and clothes and appliances. While goods on the U.S. side have become 10, 100, 1000 times more expensive for Mexican buyers, goods on the Mexican side have become 10, 100, 1000 times cheaper for Americans. Because the Valley is heavily dependent on agriculture and Mexican retail trade, it has the highest unemployment rates along the entire border region; it is the Valley that has been hardest hit.

"It's been a bad year for corn," my brother, Nune, says. As he talks, I remember my father scanning the sky for a rain that would end the drought, looking up into the sky, day after day, while the corn withered on its stalk. My father has been dead for 29 years, having worked himself to death. The life span of a Mexican farm laborer is 56—he lived to be 38. It shocks me that I am older than he. I, too, search the sky for rain. Like the ancients, I worship the rain god and the maize goddess, but unlike my father I have recovered their names. Now for rain (irrigation) one offers not a sacrifice of blood, but of money.

"Farming is in a bad way," my brother says. "Two to three thousand small and big farmers went bankrupt in this country last year. Six years ago the price of corn was $8.00 per hundred pounds," he goes on. "This year it is $3.90 per hundred pounds." And, I think to myself, after taking inflation into account, not planting anything puts you ahead.   60

I walk out to the back yard, stare at *los rosales de mamá*. She wants me to help her prune the rose bushes, dig out the carpet grass that is choking them. *Mamagrande Ramona también tenía rosales*. Here every Mexican grows flowers. If they don't have a piece of dirt, they use car tires, jars, cans, shoe boxes. Roses are the Mexican's favorite flower. I think, how symbolic—thorns and all.

Yes, the Chicano and Chicana have always taken care of growing things and the land. Again I see the four of us kids getting off the school bus, changing into our work clothes, walking into the field with Papí and Mamí, all six of us bending to the ground. Below our feet, under the earth lie the watermelon seeds. We cover them with paper plates, putting *terremotes* on top of the plates to keep them from being blown away by the wind. The paper plates keep the freeze away. Next day or the next, we remove the plates, bare the tiny green shoots to the elements. They survive and grow, give fruit hundreds of times the size of the seed. We water them and hoe them. We harvest them. The vines dry, rot, are plowed under. Growth, death, decay, birth. The soil prepared again and again, impregnated, worked on. A constant changing of forms, *renacimientos de la tierra madre.*

> This land was Mexican once
>   was Indian always
>   and is.
>   And will be again.

● Applying a Postcolonial Frame

1. What features of Anzaldúa's text can you identify as rhetorically resistant?
   - How does its form differ from conventional academic writing?
   - How does she "mark" its language as *mestiza*, or mixed?
   - Try giving names to the different voices she uses in her chapter.
   - How is the concept of a *mestiza* itself a resistant one?
   - How does the *mestiza* speak "differently"?

2. In what ways might tolerance for contradiction and ambiguity help strengthen one's consciousness? Were you able to read this essay "differently," more open-endedly? Why might it have been difficult for you to be tolerant of her experimental rhetoric?

3. What might be the historical origin of Anzaldúa's use of corn as a symbol of the *mestiza*? Why do you think she chooses it to illustrate the powers of the *mestiza*?

4. Anzaldúa helped define "border theory"—the idea that cultures, classes, genders overlap instead of being rigidly separated. What do you think might be the benefits of living and working at the borders of different cultures?
   - What do you think the effect might be on rules, laws, regulations?
   - What might the social effects be on the ways in which people interact?
   - What might the effect be on language use?

5. Think about the "border" regions that you live in and move through in the course of your daily life.
   - How is your sense of self affected?
   - Does your language use shift?
   - Is it a liberating experience, or a mixed one?
   - Are you frequently in locations that are primarily monocultural? If so, how do these feel "different" from borderland spaces?

6. Do you see rhetorical connections between Anzaldúa's styles and forms and those of Frantz Fanon's (p. 439)? To what extent can we apply the term *mestizo* to Fanon as a writer?

Language: Teaching New Worlds/New Words

bell hooks

Feminist critic bell hooks (b. 1952) has written on a wide variety of cultural topics, from the classroom, to film, to love, and is author of many critically acclaimed texts, including Talking Back: Thinking Feminist, Thinking Black; Yearning: Race, Gender, and Cultural Politics; Outlaw Culture: Resisting Representations; *and* Happy to Be Nappy, *a children's book.* Teaching to Transgress: Education as the Practice of Freedom *(1994), from which the following chapter is taken, is one of her most influential works. In it, she reworks Brazilian educational theorist Paulo Freire's theory of critical pedagogy to encompass gender, race, and class issues in the contemporary U.S. educational system. As a black feminist, hooks has critiqued both white feminist thought and black male sexism. Here she discusses language itself, and offers hope for its use as a positive means of disrupting oppressive relations.*

Like desire, language disrupts, refuses to be contained within boundaries. It speaks itself against our will, in words and thoughts that intrude, even violate the most private spaces of mind and body. It was in my first year of college that I read Adrienne Rich's poem, "The Burning of Paper Instead of Children." That poem, speaking against domination, against racism and class oppression, attempts to illustrate graphically that stopping the political persecution and torture of living beings is a more vital issue than censorship, than burning books. One line of this poem that moved and disturbed something within me: "This is the oppressor's language yet I need it to talk to you." I've never forgotten it. Perhaps I could not have forgotten it even if I tried to erase it from memory. Words impose themselves, take root in our memory against our will. The words of this poem begat a life in my memory that I could not abort or change.

When I find myself thinking about language now, these words are there, as if they were always waiting to challenge and assist me. I find myself silently speaking them over and over again with the intensity of a chant. They startle me, shaking me into an awareness of the link between languages and domination. Initially, I resist the idea of the "oppressor's language," certain that this construct has the potential to disempower those of us who are just learning to speak, who are just learning to claim language as a place where we make ourselves subject. *"This is the oppressor's language yet I need it to talk to you."* Adrienne Rich's words. Then, when I first read these words, and now, they make me think of standard English, of learning to speak against black vernacular, against the ruptured and broken speech of a dispossessed and displaced people. Standard

English is not the speech of exile. It is the language of conquest and domination; in the United States, it is the mask which hides the loss of so many tongues, all those sounds of diverse, native communities we will never hear, the speech of the Gullah, Yiddish, and so many other unremembered tongues.

Reflecting on Adrienne Rich's words, I know that it is not the English language that hurts me, but what the oppressors do with it, how they shape it to become a territory that limits and defines, how they make it a weapon that can shame, humiliate, colonize. Gloria Anzaldúa reminds us of this pain in *Borderlands/La Frontera* when she asserts, "So, if you want to really hurt me, talk badly about my language." We have so little knowledge of how displaced, enslaved, or free Americans who came or were brought against their will to the United States felt about the loss of language, about learning English. Only as a woman did I begin to think about these black people in relation to language, to think about their trauma as they were compelled to witness their language rendered meaningless with a colonizing European culture, where voices deemed foreign could not be spoken, were outlawed tongues, renegade speech. When I realize how long it has taken for white Americans to acknowledge diverse languages of Native Americans, to accept that the speech their ancestral colonizers declared was merely grunts or gibberish was indeed *language*, it is difficult not to hear in standard English always the sound of slaughter and conquest. I think now of the grief of displaced "homeless" Americans, forced to inhabit a world where they saw folks like themselves, inhabiting the same skin, the same condition, but who had no shared language to talk with one another, who needed "the oppressor's language." *"This is the oppressor's language yet I need it to talk to you."* When I imagine the terror of Americans on board slave ships, on auction blocks, inhabiting the unfamiliar architecture of plantations, I consider that this terror extended beyond fear of punishment, that it resided also in the anguish of hearing a language they could not comprehend. The very sound of English had to terrify. I think of black people meeting one another in a space away from the diverse cultures and languages that distinguished them from one another, compelled by circumstance to find ways to speak with one another in a "new world" where blackness or the darkness of one's skin and not language would become the space of bonding. How to remember, to reinvoke this terror. How to describe what it must have been like for Americans whose deepest bonds were historically forged in the place of shared speech to be transported abruptly to a world where the very sound of one's mother tongue had no meaning.

I imagine them hearing spoken English as the oppressor's language, yet I imagine them also realizing that this language would need to be possessed, taken, claimed as space of resistance. I imagine that the moment they realized the oppressor's language, seized and spoken by the tongues of the colonized, could be a space of bonding was joyous. For in that recognition was the understanding that intimacy could be restored, that a culture of resistance could be formed that would make recovery from the trauma of enslavement possible. I imagine, then, Americans first hearing English as "the oppressor's language" and then re-hearing it as a potential site of resistance. Learning English, learning to speak the alien tongue, was one way enslaved Americans began to reclaim their personal power within a context of domination. Possessing a shared language, black folks could find again a way to make community, and a means to create the political solidarity necessary to resist.

Needing the oppressor's language to speak with one another they neverthe-   5
less also reinvented, remade that language so that it would speak beyond the boundaries of conquest and domination. In the mouths of black Americans in the so-called "New World," English was altered, transformed, and became a different speech. Enslaved black people took broken bits of English and made of them a counter-language. They put together their words in such a way that the colonizer had to rethink the meaning of English language. Though it has become common in contemporary culture to talk about the messages of resistance that emerged in the music created by slaves, particularly spirituals, less is said about the grammatical construction of sentences in these songs. Often, the English used in the song reflected the broken, ruptured world of the slave. When the slaves sang "nobody knows de trouble I see—" their use of the word "nobody" adds a richer meaning than if they had used the phrase "no one," for it was the slave's *body* that was the concrete site of suffering. And even as emancipated black people sang spirituals, they did not change the language, the sentence structure, of our ancestors. For in the incorrect usage of words, in the incorrect placement of words, was a spirit of rebellion that claimed language as a site of resistance. Using English in a way that ruptured standard usage and meaning, so that white folks could often not understand black speech, made English into more than the oppressor's language.

An unbroken connection exists between the broken English of the displaced, enslaved American and the diverse black vernacular speech black folks use today. In both cases, the rupture of standard English enabled and enables rebellion and resistance. By transforming the oppressor's language, making a culture of resistance, black people created an intimate speech that could say far more than was permissible within the boundaries of standard English. The power of this speech is not simply that it enables resistance to white supremacy, but that it also forges a space for alternative cultural production and alternative epistemologies—different ways of thinking and knowing that were crucial to creating a counter-hegemonic worldview. It is absolutely essential that the revolutionary power of black vernacular speech not be lost in contemporary culture. That power resides in the capacity of black vernacular to intervene on the boundaries and limitations of standard English.

In contemporary black popular culture, rap music has become one of the spaces where black vernacular speech is used in a manner that invites dominant mainstream culture to listen—to hear—and, to some extent, be transformed. However, one of the risks of this attempt at cultural translation is that it will trivialize black vernacular speech. When young white kids imitate this speech in ways that suggest it is the speech of those who are stupid or who are only interested in entertaining or being funny, then the subversive power of this speech is undermined.

In academic circles, both in the sphere of teaching and that of writing, there has been little effort made to utilize black vernacular—or, for that matter, any language other than standard English. When I asked an ethnically diverse group of students in a course I was teaching on black women writers why we only heard standard English spoken in the classroom, they were momentarily rendered speechless. Though many of them were individuals for whom standard English was a second or third language, it had simply never occurred to them that it was possible to say something in another language, in another way. No wonder, then, that we continue to think, "This is the oppressor's language yet I need it to talk to you."

I have realized that I was in danger of losing my relationship to black vernacular speech because I too rarely use it in the predominantly white settings that I am most often in, both professionally and socially. And so I have begun to work at integrating into a variety of settings the particular Southern black vernacular speech I grew up hearing and speaking. It has been hardest to integrate black vernacular in writing, particularly for academic journals. When I first began to incorporate black vernacular in critical essays, editors would send the work back to me in standard English. Using the vernacular means that translation into standard English may be needed if one wishes to reach a more inclusive audience. In the classroom setting, I encourage students to use their first language and translate it so they do not feel that seeking higher education will necessarily estrange them from that language and culture they know most intimately.

Not surprisingly, when students in my Black Women Writers class began to speak using diverse language and speech, white students often complained. This seemed to be particularly the case with black vernacular. It was particularly disturbing to the white students because they could hear the words that were said but could not comprehend their meaning. Pedagogically, I encouraged them to think of the moment of not understanding what someone says as a space to learn. Such a space provides not only the opportunity to listen without "mastery," without owning or possessing speech through interpretation, but also the experience of hearing non-English words. These lessons seem particularly crucial in a multicultural society that remains white supremacist, that uses standard English as a weapon to silence and censor. June Jordan reminds us of this in *On Call* when she declares:

> I am talking about majority problems of language in a democratic state, problems of a currency that someone has stolen and hidden away and then homogenized into an official "English" language that can only express non-events involving nobody responsible, or lies. If we lived in a democratic state our language would have to hurtle, fly, curse, and sing, in all the common American names, all the undeniable and representative participating voices of everybody here. We would not tolerate the language of the powerful and, thereby, lose all respect for words, per se. We would make our language conform to the truth of our many selves and we would make our language lead us into the equality of power that a democratic state must represent.

That the students in the course on black women writers were repressing all longing to speak in tongues other than standard English without seeing this repression as political was an indication of the way we act unconsciously, in complicity with a culture of domination.

Recent discussions of diversity and multiculturalism tend to downplay or   10 ignore the question of language. Critical feminist writings focused on issues of difference and voice have made important theoretical interventions, calling for a recognition of the primacy of voices that are often silenced, censored, or marginalized. This call for the acknowledgment and celebration of diverse voices, and consequently of diverse language and speech, necessarily disrupts the primacy of standard English. When advocates of feminism first spoke about the desire for diverse participation in women's movement, there was no discussion of language. It was simply assumed that standard English would remain the primary vehicle for the transmission of feminist thought. Now that the audience for feminist writing and speaking has become more diverse, it is evident that we must change conventional ways of thinking about language, creating spaces where diverse voices can speak in words other than English or in broken, vernacular speech. This means that at a lecture or even in a written work there will be fragments of speech that may or may not be accessible to every individual. Shifting how we think about language and how we use it necessarily alters how we know what we know. At a lecture where I might use Southern black vernacular, the particular patois of my region, or where I might use very abstract thought in conjunction with plain speech, responding to a diverse audience, I suggest that we do not necessarily need to hear and know what is stated in its entirety, that we do not need to "master" or conquer the narrative as a whole, that we may know in fragments. I suggest that we may learn from spaces of silence as well as spaces of speech, that in the patient act of listening to another tongue we may subvert that culture of capitalist frenzy and consumption that demands all desire must be satisfied immediately, or we may disrupt that cultural imperialism that suggests one is worthy of being heard only if one speaks in standard English.

Adrienne Rich concludes her poem with this statement:

> I am composing on the typewriter late at night, thinking of today. How well we all spoke. A language is a map of our failures. Frederick Douglass wrote an English purer than Milton's. People suffer highly in poverty. There are methods but we do not use them. Joan, who could not read, spoke some peasant form of French. Some of the suffering are: it is hard to tell the truth; this is America; I cannot touch you now. In America we have only the present tense. I am in danger. You are in danger. The burning of a book arouses no sensation in me. I know it hurts to burn. There are flames of napalm in Cantonsville, Maryland. I know it hurts to burn. The typewriter is overheated, my mouth is burning, I cannot touch you and this is the oppressor's language.

To recognize that we touch one another in language seems particularly difficult in a society that would have us believe that there is no dignity in the experience of passion, that to feel deeply is to be inferior, for within the dualism of Western metaphysical thought, ideas are always more important than language. To heal the splitting of mind and body, we marginalized and oppressed people attempt to recover ourselves and our experiences in language. We seek to make a place for intimacy. Unable to find such a place in standard English, we create the ruptured, broken, unruly speech of the vernacular. When I need to say words that do more than simply mirror or address the dominant reality, I speak black vernacular. There, in that location, we make English do what we want it to do. We take the oppressor's language and turn it against itself. We make our words a counter-hegemonic speech, liberating ourselves in language.

● Applying a Postcolonial Frame

1. hooks repeatedly cites a line from an Adrienne Rich poem: "*This is the oppressor's language yet I need it to talk to you.*" How do you see that line rhetorically relating to hooks's purpose overall?

2. How can you explain standard English as a "language of domination and conquest," as hooks charges? How do you think language is tied to history? How does this connection make it a crucial issue from a postcolonial perspective?

3. hooks "flips the script" of the usual view of grammatical correctness, especially in relation to black English vernacular. How do you understand her challenge to the traditional view of standard usage as the norm?

   • How can vernacular speech connect with power, as hooks sees it?

   • How does she explain the white students' complaints in her class when black students use black vernacular?

   • hooks asks us to draw a connection between the end of Rich's poem and the use of black vernacular speech. How are both "ruptured, broken, [and] unruly"? How do both create "spaces" of/for resistance?

4. What connection can you draw between Bordo's argument about the body as sign embedded in the larger social and economic system and hooks's view of language as a cultural sign? Consider especially her discussion of rap music.

5. In *Decolonising the Mind: The Politics of Language in African Literature* (1986), Kenyan writer Ngugi wa Thiong'o describes his experience at an English-only colonial school he attended. He describes the fate of those caught using their home language, Gikuyu:

   The culprit was given corporal punishment—three to five strokes of the cane on bare buttocks—or was made to carry a metal plate around the neck with inscriptions such as I AM STUPID or I AM A DONKEY. Sometimes the culprits were fined money that they could hardly afford. And how did the teachers catch the culprits? A button was initially given to one pupil who was supposed to hand it over to whoever was caught speaking his mother tongue. Whoever had the button at the end of the day would sing who had given it to him and the ensuing process would bring out all the culprits of the day. Thus children were turned into witch-hunters and in the process were taught the lucrative value of being a traitor to one's immediate community (p. 11).

- How do you think the title of his essay connects to his argument, as you see one part of it here?
- Do you see differences between the explicitly colonialist purposes of Ngugi's boarding school and hooks's argument about required use of standard English?
- How do you think language ties to identity, self-image, and, to use one of hooks's recurrent points, love, or the realm of the affective?

Fault Lines in the Contact Zone: Assessing Homophobic Student Writing

RICHARD E. MILLER

Richard E. Miller is a professor of English at a large state university and a well-known scholar of rhetoric-composition. The original version of this article appeared in 1994 (the version reprinted here is the abridged form published in William J. Spurlin's 2000 collection Lesbian and Gay Studies and the Teaching English*). The article continues to be frequently cited in the critical literature of the field, and its topic continues to be debated—an excellent example of how transgressive writing is associated with the open-ended, not the definitive. While conventional in form, the essay directly addresses and argues for the place of oppositional, disruptive discourse as a fundamentally and deeply rhetorical issue. The essay treats a very troubling student essay that employs hate speech, in this case against gays. Miller draws on the concept of the contact zone, theorist Mary Louise Pratt's formulation of a space in which "cultures meet, clash, and grapple with each other, often in contexts of highly asymmetrical relations of power," to consider the challenges to the writing classroom to successfully function as such a space.*

What is the place of unsolicited oppositional discourse, parody, resistance, critique in the imagined classroom community?" Mary Louise Pratt asks in "Arts of the Contact Zone" (39). In Pratt's essay, this question is

I want to thank Scott Lankford for making this student essay available for discussion, Jean Ferguson Carr for providing me with materials related to this panel, and Mariolina Salvatori for introducing me to the idea of the "position paper" that appears here, in modified form, in my discussion of my students' responses to Gloria Anzaldúa's essay. An earlier, unabridged version of "Fault Lines in the Contact Zone" appeared in *College English* 56 (1994): 389–408.

occasioned by the fact that her son, Manuel, received "the usual star" from his teacher for writing a paragraph promoting a vaccine that would make school attendance unnecessary. Manuel's teacher, ignoring the critique of schooling leveled in the paragraph, registered only that the required work of responding to the assignment's questions about a helpful invention had been completed and, consequently, appended the silent, enigmatic star. For Pratt, the teacher's star labors to conceal a conflict in the classroom over what work is to be valued and why, presenting instead the image that everything is under control—students are writing and the teacher is evaluating. It is this other strategy for handling difficult material—namely, ignoring the content and focusing only on the outward forms of obedient behavior—that leads Pratt to wonder about the place of unsolicited oppositional discourse in the classroom. With regard to Manuel's real classroom community, the answer to this question is clear: the place of unsolicited oppositional discourse is no place at all.

Given Pratt's promising suggestion that the classroom be reconceived as a "contact zone," which she defines as a social space "where cultures meet, clash, and grapple with each other, often in contexts of highly asymmetrical relations of power" (34), this example of the kind of writing produced in such a contact zone seems oddly benign. One might expect that the writing Pratt's students did in Stanford University's Culture, Ideas, Values course, which she goes on to discuss, would provide ample evidence of more highly charged conflicts involving "unsolicited oppositional discourse, parody, resistance, critique." Unfortunately, however, although Pratt avows that this course "put ideas and identities on the line" (39), she offers no example of how her students negotiated this struggle in their writing or of how their teachers participated in and responded to their struggles on and over "the line." Instead, Pratt leaves us with just two images of writers in the contact zone—her son, Manuel, and Guaman Poma, author of a largely unread sixteenth-century bilingual chronicle of Andean culture. Both, to be sure, are readily sympathetic figures, obviously deserving better readers and more thoughtful respondents, but what about those who parody or critique the notion that we ought to value individual and cultural differences? And what exactly are we to say or do when the kind of racist, sexist, and homophobic sentiments now signified by the term "hate speech" surface in our classrooms? What "Arts of the Contact Zone" are going to help us learn how to read and respond to voices such as these?

By attending to a student essay that is much less likely to arouse our sympathies than Manuel's inventive critique, my concern in what follows is to examine the heuristic value of the notion of the contact zone when applied not only to student writing, but also to our own academic discussions of that writing. The student essay I begin with was so offensive that when it was first mentioned at an MLA workshop on "Composition, Multiculturalism, and Political Correctness" in December 1991, provisions were quickly made to devote an entire panel to the essay at the Conference on College Composition and Communication (hereafter

4C's) in 1992, and this in turn led to a follow-up workshop on "The Politics of Response" at 4C's in 1993. Thus I would hazard to guess that this student essay, titled "Queers, Bums, and Magic," has seized the attention of more teachers, taken up more institutional time, and provoked more debate than any other single piece of unpublished undergraduate writing in recent memory. Before beginning my discussion of "Queers, Bums, and Magic," I should note, however, that in the ensuing discussion I have intentionally allowed the content of the student's essay and the wider sweep of its context to emerge in fragments, as they did in the contact zone of the national conferences, where competing modes of response served alternately to reveal and obscure both the text and information about its writer. This partial, hesitant, contradictory motion defines how business gets transacted in the contact zones of our classrooms and our conferences, where important questions often do not get heard, are ignored, or simply do not get posed in the heat of the moment, with the result that vital contextual information often is either never disclosed or comes to light very late in the discussion. I believe that following this motion provides a stark portrait of the ways in which dominant assumptions about students and student writing allow unsolicited oppositional discourse to pass through the classroom unread and unaffected.

The essay I will discuss, "Queers, Bums, and Magic," was written in a pre-college-level community college composition class taught by Scott Lankford at Foothill College in Los Altos Hills, California, in response to an assignment taken from *The Bedford Guide for College Writers* that asked students to write a report on group behavior. One of Lankford's students responded with an essay detailing a drunken trip he and some friends made to "San Fagcisco" to study "the lowest class . . . the queers and the bums." The essay recounts how the students stopped a man on Polk Street, informed him that they were doing a survey and needed to know if he was "a fag." From here, the narrative follows the students into a dark alleyway where they discover, as they relieve themselves drunkenly against the wall, that they have been urinating on a homeless person. In a frenzy, the students begin to kick the homeless person, stopping after "30 seconds of non-stop blows to the body," at which point the writer says he "thought the guy was dead." Terrified, the students make a run for their car and eventually escape the city.

It is a haunting piece, one that gave Lankford many sleepless nights and 5
one that has traveled from conference to conference because it is so unsettling. When Lankford discussed it at 4C's in his paper titled "How Would You Grade a Gay-Bashing?" the engaged, provocative, and at times heated hour-long discussion that followed provided a forum for a range of competing commitments to, as Pratt might say, "meet, clash, and grapple" with one another. What was clear from this interchange was that part of what makes "Queers, Bums, and Magic" so powerful is that it disables the most familiar kinds of conference presentations and teacher responses. Here is writing that cannot easily be recuperated as somehow praiseworthy despite its numerous surface flaws, writing that

instead offers direct access to a voice from the margins that seems to belong there. The reactions given to Lankford's request to know how those present "would have handled such a situation" (5) varied considerably, both in intensity and in detail, but most of them, I would say, fell into one of three categories: read the essay as factual and respond accordingly; read the essay as fictional and respond accordingly; momentarily suspend the question of the essay's factual or fictional status and respond accordingly.

In the first category, by far the most popular, I place all suggestions that the student be removed from the classroom and turned over either to a professional counselor or to the police. Such a response, audience members argued repeatedly, would be automatic if the student had described suicidal tendencies, involvement in a rape, or having been the victim of incest. To substantiate this point, one member of the audience spoke passionately about Marc LeClerc, saying that the Canadian gunman had revealed his hatred of women to many of his college professors prior to his murderous rampage. As compelling as such examples were at the time, it is important to realize that this line of argument assumes that the described events really occurred and, therefore, that the essay contains evidence either of a serious crime or of a vivid and potentially dangerous fantasy life. This assessment of the student essay is striking because the audience members had little to go on beyond the kind of brief outline that has been provided here. In other words, although no one in the audience had actually read the student essay, many felt quite confident recommending that, based on brief excerpts and a summary of the essay's content alone, the student ought to be turned over either to the legal or psychological authorities! These respondents, starting with the assumption of a stable and unified subjectivity for Lankford's student, went on to construct a student writer incapable of dissimulation. Within such a paradigm, the actual text the student produced was of secondary importance at best in relation to a hasty and, as we will see, partial summary of the student text's contents.

Lankford chose another route entirely, electing "to respond to the essay exactly as if it were a fictional short story" (4). What this meant in practice was that he restricted himself to commenting on the student's word choice, querying the student about his imagined audience, acknowledging the text's "reasonable detail," and "favorably comparing the essay to *A Clockwork Orange* in its straightforward depictions of nightmarish 'megaviolence' and surrealistic detail" (4). According to these criteria, Lankford determined the essay merited a low B. Although this strategy provoked the wrath of a large portion of the audience, Lankford argued that it was not without its virtues: by focusing only on the formal features of the essay and its surface errors, Lankford was able to successfully deflect the student writer's use of his writing to "bash" his professor, with the unexpected result that the student not only stayed in the course, but actually chose to study with Lankford again the next semester. Thus, despite Lankford's own assessment of his approach as "spineless," he was in a position to insist that it was nevertheless a "qualified success," since the student in question "learned to cope with an openly gay instructor with some measure of civility" (5).

Among those present who had access to the student's paper, there were those on the panel who agreed with Lankford's approach but disagreed with the grade assigned. These respondents spoke of the essay's faulty organization, the problems evident in its plot development, the number of mechanical errors. On these grounds alone, one panelist assured the audience, the paper ought to have received a failing mark. If the first category of response displays a curious willingness to dispense with the formality of reading the student's essay, Lankford's strategy asks teachers to look away from what the student's writing is attempting to do—at the havoc it is trying to wreak in the contact zone—and restrict their comments to the essay's surface features and formal qualities, affixing the "usual star" or black mark as the situation warrants. Such a strategy itself invites parody: would changing the word choice/spelling errors/verb agreement problems/organization/etc. really "improve" this student's essay? Would such changes help inch it toward being, say, an excellent gay-bashing essay, one worthy of an A?

I intend this question to verge on being offensive. The problem, however, is not that this approach is "spineless." To the contrary, in Lankford's hands this kind of response made it possible for both the teacher and the student to remain in the contact zone of his classroom, allowing them to negotiate the difficult business of working with and through important issues of cultural and sexual difference. By suggesting that his difficulty in responding to the student essay is a personal problem, that it revolves around a question of "spine," Lankford obscures the ways in which the difficulty that confronted him as he struggled to find a way to respond to "Queers, Bums, and Magic" is the trace of a broader institutional conflict over what it means for a teacher to work with student writing. Lankford and the others who spoke of responding to the essay as "a piece of fiction" did not suddenly invent this curiously decontextualized way of responding to writing that can imagine no other approach to discussing a piece of writing than to speak of how it is organized, the aptness of the writer's word choice, and the fit between the text and its audience. Such an approach to writing instruction has been proffered in the majority of grammars, rhetorics, and readers that have filled English classrooms since before the turn of the century: it has been around for so long that, despite the grand "turn to process" in writing instruction, it continues to suggest itself as the most "natural" or "reasonable" way to define the work of responding to student writing. All of which leaves us with this profoundly strange state of affairs in which a discipline explicitly devoted to studying and articulating the power of the written word gets thrown into crisis when a student produces a powerful piece of writing.

To sum up, then, these two lines of response to the student essay—the one recommending the removal of the offending writer from circulation, and the other overlooking the offensive aspects of the student text in order to attend to its surface and structural features—taken together dramatize how little professional training in English studies prepares teachers to read and respond to the kinds of parodic, critical, oppositional, dismissive, resistant, transgressive, and

10

regressive writing that gets produced by students writing in the contact zone of the classroom. This absence of training, I would argue, actually comes into play every time a teacher sits down to comment on a student paper: it's just that the pedagogical shortcomings of restricting such commentary to the surface features and formal aspects of the writing are not as readily visible in a response to an essay on a summer vacation as they are in a response to an essay about beating up the homeless and bashing gays. Unfortunately, recent efforts to reimagine the work of responding to student writing provide little guidance for addressing this particular problem. Edward White's *Teaching and Assessing Writing*, for instance, argues for holistic scoring but offers no suggestions on how to go about holistically scoring essays that are racist, homophobic, misogynistic, and so forth. And, similarly, Anson's *Writing and Response: Theory, Practice, and Research*, which asserts that "real, substantive response is in one form or another fundamental to language development" (4), never gets around to the business of discussing how to produce a "real, substantive response" to the kind of unsolicited oppositional discourse discussed here. Since this is uncharted territory, it is not surprising that we often find ourselves at a loss, not knowing what to do, where to go, what to say.

And yet, granting this, one has to wonder why it is that, at a time when almost all of the current major theories on the rise celebrate partial readings, multiple subjectivities, marginalized positions, and subjugated knowledges, nearly all student essays remain essentially illegible, offered forth more often than not as the space in which error exercises its full reign, or, as here, the site where some untutored evil shows its face. There seems, in other words, to be little evidence of what one might call "poststructural" or "postcolonial" trickle down, little sign that the theoretical insights that carry so much weight in our journals actually make themselves known in the pedagogical practices deployed in classrooms across the country. There were, however, a few respondents to Lankford's presentation who saw a way to smuggle some of these insights into the classroom and thereby propose more fruitful responses than either expelling the student or ignoring the content of his essay. In proposing that "Queers, Bums, and Magic" be reproduced alongside legal definitions of hate speech for the entire class to read and discuss, one panelist found a way to pull the paper out of the private corridor running between the student writer and the teacher and move it into the public arena. This approach turns the essay into a "teachable object," enabling an investigation of the writing's performative aspect—how it does its work, what its imagined project might have been, and who or what might be the possible subjects of its critique. By situating the essay in relation to legal definitions of hate speech, this approach also puts the class in a position to consider both how words can work in the world and how and why that work has been regulated.

The prospect of having such a discussion would no doubt frighten some, since it would promise to be an explosive, tense, disturbing interchange. Some students would undoubtedly agree with the treatment meted out to the disenfranchised;

others might speak of it as being funny; others might point to the references to "Elm Street," "nightmares," and "magic" in the essay to argue that it was a piece of fiction; and still others might be horrified by the essay and express their feelings to the class. Such a discussion would, in other words, place one squarely in the act of teaching in the contact zone where, as Pratt says, "No one [is] excluded, and no one [is] safe" (39). The point of having such discussions, however, is neither to establish a community where a simple pluralism rules and hate speech is just one of its many voices, nor is it to create an environment that is relentlessly threatening, where not feeling safe comes to mean the same thing as feeling terrified. Pratt, in fact, is careful to maintain the importance of establishing "safe houses" in the curriculum, courses in which a different kind of talk is supported and sustained. But for those courses that take as their subject how language works in the world, the central concern should be to provide students with moments taken from their own writing as well as from the writing collected in published texts where the written word is powerful. In such classrooms, "teaching the conflicts" is not simply an empty slogan plastered over a practice that means "business as usual," but an actual set of practices whereby the conflicts that capture and construct both the students and their teachers become the proper subject of study for the course.

This third category of response argues for the necessity of seeing the way we structure our courses and the kinds of texts we read with our students as potential resources for commenting on the writing our students produce. Thinking along these lines, another member of the audience suggested responding to this essay with a revisionary assignment that required the student to rewrite the story from the perspective of either the gay man whom the students had harassed on Polk Street or the homeless person whom the students had beaten in the alleyway. This strategy of having the student do more writing about this event seems particularly appropriate in a discipline that believes in the heuristic power of the composing process, and the further requirement to have the student shift perspective provides a meaningful avenue for re-seeing the described events. As useful as I believe it is to see the assignment of revision as a way of responding to student writing, though, I think the response called for in this instance is so obvious that it is most likely to solicit a seamless parody, one of those acts of hyperconformity regularly produced by those writing in the contact zone. In other words, while producing a writing situation in which the student is advised to mime the teacher's desired position would probably succeed in sweeping the most visible manifestations of the student's hateful thoughts and actions out of the classroom, it would not, I think, actually address the roots of that hatred. That hatred would simply curl up and go underground for the duration of the course.

At this point, it may seem that in assessing the range of reactions to "Queers, Bums, and Magic" I am holding out for some magical form of response that would not only make this student stop writing such things, but would actually put an end to his thinking them as well. My central concern, however, is not with this particular student essay or with what the student writer as an individual

thinks, but with what this student essay and the professional activity that surrounds it can tell us about the cultural, political, and pedagogical complexities of
composition instruction. With this distinction in mind, I would go so far as to
argue that adopting any classroom strategy that isolates this essay and treats it as
an anomaly misreads both the essay's cultural significance and its pedagogical
possibilities. As the debate over military service's "don't ask, don't tell" policy
made abundantly clear, Lankford's student has not expressed a unique and private
hatred of gays, nor, to be sure, has he voiced a peculiar antipathy for the homeless. Rather, the homophobia this student articulates and the violence he
describes as perpetrating against the disenfranchised are cultural commonplaces,
drawn from the national symbolic imaginary. For these reasons, it seems much
more important to me to produce a classroom in which part of the work involves
articulating, investigating, and questioning the affiliated cultural forces that
underwrite the ways of thinking that find expression in this student's essay—
a classroom, in short, that studies the forces that make such thoughts not only
permissible but prevalent.

From this perspective, one could say that the only truly surprising thing   15
about "Queers, Bums, and Magic" is that it voices this particular set of cultural
commonplaces in the classroom, since most students practiced in the conventions of reading teacher expectations know not to commit themselves to positions their teachers clearly oppose. In this regard, the following facts are not
insignificant: the student writer grew up in Kuwait; English is his second language; he was writing during the onset of the Persian Gulf War. An outsider
himself, Lankford's student almost certainly did not understand what was
intended by the examples that accompanied the assignment in the *Bedford Guide*
to: "Station yourself in a nearby place where you can mingle with a group of
people gathered for some reason or occasion. Observe the group's behavior and
in a short paper report on it. Then offer some insight" (Kennedy and Kennedy
41). Following these instructions, the student is informed that one writer "did
an outstanding job of observing a group of people nervously awaiting a road test
for their driver's licenses"; another observed a bar mitzvah; another an emergency room; and another a group of people looking at a luna moth on a telephone pole "including a man who viewed it with alarm, a wondering toddler,
and an amateur entomologist" (42). Unschooled in the arts of reading the textbook, this student failed to pick up on the implicit directions: when you write
this essay, report only on the behavior of a group that is of no particular interest
or importance to you. Had the student been able to read the cues in the suggested examples, he might well have selected a less explosive topic and thereby
kept his most familiar ways of knowing the world out of view.

If the assignment's examples direct students to topics guaranteed not to
provoke offense, the assignment, by refraining from using any kind of critical
terminology, encourages students not to wander beyond the business of reporting their immediate experiences. In lieu of inviting students to work with any of
the central terms taken from anthropology, sociology, or cultural studies, say,

the assignment merely informs the students that, after observing the behavior of their selected group, they are "to form some general impression of the group or come to some realization about it" (Kennedy and Kennedy 42). They can expect, the assignment concludes, that it will take at least two written pages "to cover" their subject. Grasping the import of these directives, Lankford's student did even more than was required, performing the kind of hyperconformity I suggested earlier characterizes one of the arts of the contact zone: he wrote, as required, for his "fellow students" (41); he handed in not two but four typed pages; and he made sure his essay concluded with "some realization." His final paragraph reads as follows:

> Although this night was supposed to be an observation on the people of the streets, it turned out that we were walking on "Elm Street," and it was a "nightmare." I will always remember one thing, next time I see bums and fags walking on the streets, I will never make fun of them or piss on them, or anything like that, because they did not want to be bums or fags. It was society that forced them out of their jobs and they could not beat the system. Now when I think about that bum we beat up I can't understand how he managed to follow us the whole time, after being kicked and being down for so long. I think it was one of two things; he is either psychic or it was just plain magic.

In miming the requisite better understanding that is supposed to come from studying groups, the student's essay concludes by disrupting all that has come before: did the beating actually take place or has the writer simply fabricated it, recasting the assignment within the readily available narrative frame of the film *Nightmare on Elm Street*? Is the student having one over on the system, manufacturing both the material for his response and his consequent realization, and thus, in one fell swoop, parodying, resisting, and critiquing the values that hold the classroom community together? Or—and this is obviously the more frightening possibility—is his conclusion some kind of penitential confession for events that really did happen?

These questions, slightly rephrased, are of central importance to any writing classroom: How does a writer establish authority? How does one distinguish between fact and fiction in a written document? What does it mean to read and to write dialogically? And yet it is important to realize that, had the assignment worked as it was supposed to, these questions would never have surfaced with the urgency they have here. That is, had Lankford's student been a better reader of classroom norms and textbook procedures, he might well have written about beekeepers or people at hair salons and left the surface calm of the educational community undisturbed. If we step back from "Queers, Bums, and Magic" for a moment and consider the fact that the mixture of anger, rage, ignorance, and confusion that produced this student essay are present in varying degrees on college and secondary school campuses across the country, what is truly significant about this event is not that it occurred, but that it occurs so rarely. This, surely, is a testament to the immense pressures exerted by the classroom environment, the presentation of the assigned readings, the directions included in the writing assignments, and the range of teaching practices which work together to ensure that conflicts about or contact between fundamental beliefs and prejudices do not arise. The classroom does not, in other words, automatically function as a contact zone in the positive ways Pratt discovered in the Stanford course, where, she asserts: "Along with rage, incomprehension, and pain there were exhilarating moments of wonder and revelation, mutual understanding, and new wisdom—the joys of the contact zone" (39). As the conclusion of Pratt's article makes clear, and the foregoing discussion of "Queers, Bums, and Magic" vividly illustrates, there is still a great deal of work to be done in constructing the "pedagogical arts of the contact zone." Thus, having acknowledged that, from this distance, we will never be able to resolve the question of whether or not "Queers, Bums, and Magic" is a factual or fictional account, I would like to turn now to my own efforts to create a place where more contact between the competing interpretive systems of the classroom and the worlds outside the classroom occurs and is made available for discussion.

There is a paradox, of course, in trying to establish a classroom that solicits "unsolicited oppositional discourse." There is also an attendant danger of a kind of "intellectual slumming," whereby investigating the disjunction between the ways of knowing fostered inside and outside the classroom might result in students deeming the former kind of knowledge "artificial" and the latter "authentic." Rather than perish in the abyss created by this killer dichotomy or put myself in the pedagogically questionable position of inviting my students to vent on the page so that we can discuss their feelings afterward, I have tried to develop a pedagogical practice that allows the classroom to function as a contact zone, where the central activity is investigating the range of literate practices available to those within asymmetrical power relationships. My primary concern as a composition instructor, in other words, is with the kinds of issues raised in Pratt's article and Lankford's student's essay insofar as they shape the ways of reading and writing that occur inside and outside the classroom. And, given the heightened racial tensions following the O. J. Simpson verdicts, the ongoing fear and ignorance about AIDS and the means of its transmission, the backlash against feminism, and a climate of diminished expectations and violence, it should come as no surprise that students bring to our classrooms the ill-formed, irrational, and even dangerous ideas fostered by the surrounding environment. The challenge, for teachers who are interested in teaching rather than indoctrinating their students, is to learn how to respond when such potentially threatening material makes its way into the classroom.

I would like to turn to one such instance, drawn from my own classroom, that emerged when my students set out to respond to Gloria Anzaldúa's "Entering the Serpent." Now, for many of the students in my class, the introduction of this text was itself perceived as a threatening act: in "Entering the Serpent," excerpted from Anzaldúa's *Borderlands/La Frontera*, Anzaldúa shifts back and forth between

Anglo-American English, Castilian Spanish, Tex-Mex, Northern Mexican dialect, and Nahualt, writing in a mélange of languages to express the diversity of her heritage and her own unique position as lesbian, feminist, Chicana poet, and critic. While Anzaldúa's multilingual text places special—and many of the students argued, unfair—linguistic demands on its readers, it also makes relatively unique generic demands, moving between poetry and prose, personal narrative and revisionist history. Thus Anzaldúa occupies a range of positions, some of them contradictory, as she relates her efforts to reclaim the Aztec goddess Coatlicue, the "serpent goddess," split from the goddess Cihuacoatl by the "male dominated Azteca-Mexica culture" in order to drive "the powerful female deities underground" (26–27). After the Spanish Conquest, Cihuacoatl was further domesticated by the Christian Church and transformed by stages into the figure now known as the Virgin of Guadalupe. While Anzaldúa admires La Virgen de Guadalupe as "the symbol of ethnic identity and of the tolerance for ambiguity that Chicanos-*mexicanos*, people of mixed race, people who have Indian blood, people who cross cultures, by necessity possess" (29), she nevertheless insists on the importance of regaining access to Coatlicue, "the symbol of the dark sexual drive, the chthonic (underworld), the feminine, the serpentine movement of sexuality, of creativity, the basis of all energy and life" (33). Recovering this contact with the supernatural provides one with "*la facultad* . . . the capacity to see in surface phenomena the meaning of deeper realities, to see the deep structure below the surface" (36). Anzaldúa concludes this section by asserting that "[t]hose who are pounced on the most have [*la facultad*] the strongest—the females, the homosexuals of all races, the darkskinned, the outcast, the persecuted, the marginalized, the foreign" (36).

Here's how one of my students described his experience reading "Entering the Serpent":   20

> Even though I had barely read half of the first page, I was already disgusted. I found myself reading onward only to stop and ask "What is she trying to prove?" Scanning the words and skipping over the ones that were not english, I went from an egocentric personal story to a femo-nazi account of central american mythology that was occasionally interrupted by more poems. . . .
>
> From what I gather, she is trying to exorcise some personal demons. Her feelings of inadequacy and insecurity drove her to project her own problems not only onto the world, but into history and mythology. I'm surprised she didn't call history "herstory." It seems that she had no sense of self or worth. To overcome this, she fabricated a world, a past, and a scapegoat in her own image. Although her accusations do hold some truth, her incredible distortion of the world would lead me to believe that she has lost touch with reality and is obsessively driven by her social psychosis. She views herself as a gallant and brilliant member of a great culture that has been oppressed by the world. Her continuous references to females, sex, and the phallic symbols of snakes is most likely brought out by the lack of a man in her life. Rather than admit her faults, she cherishes them and calls them friends.

This was not an uncommon response to my assignment that began by asking the students to discuss the difficulties they encountered reading Anzaldúa's essay. This student, having made his way past the language barrier of the text, confronts the description of a world and a way of being in that world that he finds personally repugnant. Beginning with a variant of the Rush Limbaughism, "femo-nazi," the student then proceeds to document the many ways that "Entering the Serpent" offended him: it contains Anzaldúa's effort to "exorcise some personal demons"; it includes "her incredible distortion of the world"; the writer claims to be "a gallant and brilliant member of a great culture" of which the student is not a part. Given this reading, it is not too surprising that the student concludes that all the faults in the text are produced by "the lack of a man in [Anzaldúa's] life."

Taking offense with this response to Anzaldúa's essay strikes me as being exactly the wrong tactic here. It is of paramount importance, I believe, to begin where students are, rather than where one thinks they should or ought to be, and this student, by my reading, is trapped between the desire to produce a stereotypical critique of any feminist text ("I'm surprised she didn't call history 'herstory'") and the necessity of responding to this particular feminist text. He negotiates the tension between this desire and this necessity by producing a fairly detailed outline of Anzaldúa's essay and, simultaneously, mocking its argument ("Rather than admit her faults, she cherishes them and calls them friends."). However rudimentary or sophisticated one deems this kind of multivocalic writing to be, it is, as I have said, only a starting point for beginning more detailed work with Anzaldúa's text. For this reason, the assignment that elicited this response does not simply ask the students to revel in the difficulties they experienced reading Anzaldúa's essay; it also requests that they outline "a plan of action for addressing the difficulties [they] encountered." The goal, thus, is not to invite students simply to record their various levels of rage, incomprehension, and despair with an admittedly difficult text, but rather to have them reflect on how they might adjust their own ways of reading to meet the text halfway.

The results of having the students read their own readings and chart alternative ways of returning to the text can be startling indeed. Although this writer began by accusing Anzaldúa of being a "femo-nazi," he concluded by reflecting on what he had done with her text in the following way:

> If not for searching for her hidden motives and then using them to criticize/bash Anzaldúa and her story, I would not have been able to read the story in its entirety. Although my view is a bit harsh, it has been a way that allows me to counter Anzaldúa's extremities. In turn, I can now see her strategy of language and culture choice and placement to reveal the contact zone in her own life. All of my obstacles previously mentioned, (not liking the stories, poems, or their content) were overcome by "bashing" them. Unfortunately, doing that in addition to Anzaldúa's ridiculous disproportionism and over-intense, distorted beliefs created a mountain which was impossible for me to

climb. This in effect made it impossible to have taken any part of her work seriously or to heart. I feel I need to set aside my personal values, outlook and social position in order to escape the bars of being offended and discouraged. Not only must I lessen my own barriers of understanding, but I must be able to comprehend and understand the argument of the other. It is these differences between people and groups of people that lead to the conflicts and struggles portrayed and created by this selection.

This strikes me as being an extraordinarily astute assessment of the strengths and weaknesses of this writer's initial reading strategy: "bashing" Anzaldúa enabled a certain kind of work to be accomplished (the reading was completed, the writing assignment could be fulfilled), but it also prevented the writer from taking "any part of her work seriously or to heart." Thus, by "bashing" Anzaldúa, the student inadvertently ended up showing himself that her description of her trying experiences within the straight white world was, at least partly, accurate. The writer's proposed solution to this problem—setting aside his "personal values, outlook and social position"—attests to the magnitude of the challenge Anzaldúa's position holds for him. Whether this proposed solution proves, in practice, to be a workable plan can only be known when the writer returns to Anzaldúa's essay to begin his revision. What is important to notice here, however, is that the writer's plan does make returning to her text an imaginable activity with an unforeseeable outcome. Given the way this student's essay began, this is no small accomplishment.

Required self-reflexivity does not, of course, guarantee that repugnant positions will be abandoned. At best, it ensures only that the students' attention will be focused on the interconnections between the ways they read and the ways they write. This can be a salutary experience, as in the previous example, where it provided the student with an avenue for renegotiating a relationship with a difficult text and the wide range of concerns affiliated with that text, but it does not mean that this approach wields sufficient power to transform the matrix of beliefs, values, and prejudices that students (and teachers alike) bring to the classroom. This kind of wholesale transformation (or, to be more precise, the *appearance* of this kind of wholesale transformation) is only possible in classrooms where the highly asymmetrical relations of power are fully reinstated and students are told either implicitly or explicitly (as I was during a course in graduate school), "No language that is racist, sexist, homophobic, or that degrades the working class will be allowed in our discussions." Reimagining the classroom as a contact zone is a potentially powerful pedagogical intervention only so long as it involves resisting the temptation either to silence or to celebrate the voices that seek to oppose, critique, and/or parody the work of constructing knowledge in the classroom. Scott Lankford achieved the kind of partial, imperfect, negotiated microvictory available to those who work in the contact zone when he found a way to respond to his student's essay that not only kept the student in his course, but eventually led to the student signing up to work with him in another course as well. By having my students interrogate literate practices inside and outside the classroom, by having them work with challenging essays that speak about issues of difference from a range of perspectives, and by having them pursue this work in the ways I have outlined here, I have been trying to create a course that allows the students to use their writing to investigate the cultural conflicts that serve to define and limit their lived experience.

In the uncharted realms of teaching and studying in the contact zone, the teacher's traditional claim to authority is thus constantly undermined and reconfigured, which, in turn, enables the real work of learning how to negotiate and to place oneself in dialogue with different ways of knowing to commence. This can be strangely disorienting work, requiring as it does the recognition that in many places what passes for reason is not something separate from rhetoric, but rather one of many rhetorical devices. This in turn quickly leads to the corollary concession that, in certain situations, reason exercises little or no persuasive force when vying against the combined powers of rage, fear, and prejudice, which together forge innumerable hateful ways of knowing the world that have their own internalized systems, self-sustaining logics, and justifications. For teachers who believe in education as a force for positive social change, the appropriate response to these new working conditions is not to exile students to the penitentiaries or the psychiatric wards for writing offensive, antisocial papers. Nor is it to give free rein to one's self-righteous indignation and call the resultant interchange a "political intervention." The most promising pedagogical response lies, rather, in closely attending to what our students say and write in an ongoing effort to learn how to read, understand, and respond to the strange, sometimes threatening, multivocal texts they produce while writing in the contact zone.

Works Cited

Anson, Chris, ed. *Writing and Response: Theory, Practice, and Research*. Urbana, IL: NCTE, 1989.

Anzaldúa, Gloria. "Entering into the Serpent." *Ways of Reading*. Ed. David Bartholomae and Anthony Petrosky. Boston: Bedford, 1993. 25–38.

Kennedy, X. J., and Dorothy M. Kennedy. *The Bedford Guide for College Writers*. Boston: Bedford, 1990. 41–42.

Lankford, Scott. "'Queers, Bums, and Magic': How Would You Grade a Gay-Bashing?" Myths of Correctness: Approaches to Grammar and Politics. Conference on College Composition and Communication. Cincinnati. 19 Mar. 1992.

Pratt, Mary Louise. "Arts of the Contact Zone." *Profession 91* (MLA 1991): 33–40.

White, Edward M. *Teaching and Assessing Writing*. San Francisco: Jossey-Bass, 1985.

● **Applying a Postcolonial Frame**

1. Clarify the three categories of teacher response to the homophobic essay that Miller outlines.

   • Did your own initial response as you first encountered the student essay fall into one of these? Or did you find yourself having some other kind of response?

   • How does your position as a student in a writing course inform your reaction?

   • As you read Miller's argument, why do you think he rejects the first two categories as ineffective responses?

2. Miller argues that teachers are poorly prepared to "respond to the kinds of parodic, critical, oppositional, dismissive, resistant, transgressive, and regressive writing that gets produced by students writing in the contact zone of the classroom." He also argues that he sees "little evidence of . . . 'postcolonial' trickle down, little sign that the theoretical insights that carry so much weight in [professional] journals actually make themselves known in the pedagogical practices deployed in the classrooms across the country" (para. 11). What cultural forces may be at work to deter attention to such writing in formal education? Consider how bell hooks (p. 509) or Gloria Anzaldúa (p. 496) might explain this absence. What do you think might be at stake, and for whom?

3. Explain what you think makes Miller reject the idea of having the student rewrite the essay from the perspective of one or both victims. What does the term *seamless parody* mean, as you interpret it in the context of his argument and of postcolonial critique?

   • Have you as a writer "mimed" what you took to be the expected response to an assignment? If so, how does this experience lead you to see Miller's position?

   • Why does Miller seek to avoid "hyperconformity"?

   • What is the role of the "asymmetrical power relations" of student-teacher in such mimicry?

   • Do you believe students/student bodies are "administered" in and by the school system, in a colonialist sense?

4. Miller advocates the kind of classroom that encourages "articulating, investigating, and questioning the affiliated cultural forces that underwrite the ways of thinking that find expression in [the homophobic] essay—a classroom, in short, that studies the forces that make such thoughts not only permissible but prevalent" (para. 14). What values do you see him advocating in this stance?

   • What does it say about the role of the writer's authority? The ability to use evidence? To address an audience?

   • Why do you think Miller turns to rhetorical issues as a means of addressing oppositional, disruptive, transgressive discourse?

5. How does Miller's student "renegotiat[e] a relationship with a difficult text" as he rereads the Anzaldúa chapter? Consider doing the same by revisiting one of the readings in this chapter (or in another) that you initially found alienating. How might you read it dialogically—that is, read it with a conscious awareness of your own resistance to it as a means to develop a strategy for entering it/engaging with it?

topics for writing

1. Of the three essays in this chapter, which did you react to with the deepest feeling (whether a positive, negative, or mixed one)? Examine that author's rhetorical choices: how do they help create your emotional reaction? Consider:

   - the author's purpose in writing.
   - the author's persona(s).
   - the "intertextual" elements—the other authors, voices, writings the authors connect to their own text.
   - the author's stance in relation to you as an individual reader. (Is she or he speaking to you? Are you included? What role does she or he cast you in?)
   - the voices the author uses.
   - the critical frames she or he adopts.
   - the nature and the evidence she or he employs.

2. In question 5, in "Applying a Postcolonial Frame" (above), you were asked to revisit a reading you found alienating at first and then to consider a strategy for engaging with it critically. Treat that topic in more complete form: take your reader through the resistance, analyzing the causes as you may now see them, and explain possible ways of renegotiating your engagement with the text. Then flip the script: take the reader through a piece that he or she may resist recognizing as making rhetorical sense. Help the reader find a possible critical reading strategy. Consider popular texts that often are the object of hostility from mainstream culture: rap songs, for instance, or some kind of graffiti/tagging; or consider the pidgin version of the Twenty-Third Psalm in Paul Theroux's essay (p. 395), or another piece you are familiar with that uses a dialect.

3. Drawing on the ideas and styles of the authors where useful, experiment with alternative discourses to treat a topic that, as bell hooks (p. 509) says, lets you "do more that simply mirror or address the dominant reality."

   - How will you generate such a topic? Consider the authors' sources: personal/cultural, a woman seeking to write from her many identities; historical, a topic exploring an oppressed figure resisting her "masters"; personal/critical, an academic including her racial and linguistic experiences to analyze and resist colonized language use.

- What of Richard E. Miller's (p. 515) critique of topics that generate the "usual star"?

- What might your purpose(s) be in this writing? How can you use the process illustrated by Miller's student as he attempts to work with his resistance to Anzaldúa's writing, for instance? How can you use this topic to explore, revisit, connect with/resist dominant culture and your position in it? What can you teach yourself, in other words, about your use of language beyond the conventions of academic discourse?

- How will you frame your ideas? What theoretical concepts can help? How many voices/languages will you speak from? Whose voices will you introduce (as hooks uses Adrienne Rich, for example)?

Framing and Composing
from a Postcolonial Perspective

1. Focusing on one of the topics listed below, explain how contact between the United States and "other" cultures frequently becomes an exercise in a power imbalance, reification, and misreading. Draw on the ideas presented in Edward W. Said (p. 353), Hans Bertens (p. 368), Aimé Césaire (p. 374), David Henry Hwang (p. 383), and Frantz Fanon (p. 439) to explore the topic: how are the relations of the two cultures, the contact made, informed by assumptions about center/margin; masculine/feminine; progressive/backward; and other binaries that establish dominant and submissive roles? For the third topic, consider the perspective of internal colonialism, drawing from Villanueva in particular.

   - Third-world tourism
   - The Peace Corps
   - Service learning

2. Resistant voices "speak back" to the dominant discourse. One can easily see academic discourse as an elite form that demonstrates and reproduces dominant language. How might you work from within academic discourse to create a resistant voice?

   - How can you use and then write against its conventions, creating an alternative discourse? Perhaps begin by considering the "*mestiza* rhetoric" of Anzaldúa, the "street" of Villanueva, the psychically divided persona of Fanon. Then consider your position as student, member of an ethnic group, social class, or other identity base, or a nonmainstream style you find appealing (for example, hip hop; tattoos; body piercing).

   - How can you assert the validity of your role/style in a way that both enables others to understand, but claims a new discursive mode for it?

   - What are your essay's rhetorical features? How can you represent these in written language? For a musical style, for example, rhythm and sound are essential; how will the form you choose capture essential traits of this sort? Will your voice remain stable, or will you move into and out of different voices, dialects, personae? Will you bring other voices in—the voice of the dominant group, the voice of postcolonial theorists?

   - Why might your text be hybrid?

3. Colonialism historically is accompanied by exploitation of natural resources— it is often as environmentally as culturally devastating. Choose one country that has been subject to colonial exploitation at the environmental level and gather information on pre- and postcolonial conditions. Focus your research on establishing the reasons for the colonial interest; the means of exploiting the

target resource; the environmental effects, including the effects on the population; and the success of any attempts to remediate damage. Add to the following list of possible topics:

- Bhopal, India
- Bikini Atoll atomic testing
- diamond mining
- Central American coffee production
- oil exploration

4. Some cultural groups in the United States have undertaken the difficult task of reclaiming their pre-U.S., precolonization identity. Native Americans and ethnic Hawaiians are two of the most active cultures seeking to reestablish cultural and linguistic traditions. The term *rhetorical sovereignty* is critical to their efforts.

- From your understanding of rhetoric, what might this term signify?
- How might it tie to material cultural practices?
- How would rhetorical sovereignty affect communities—in how schools are organized and how the curriculum is defined; in language practices; in relations to those outside the ethnic group?
- What challenges are likely to arise to the idea and practice of rhetorical sovereignty?

You might begin by gathering information from Internet sources on the concept of rhetorical sovereignty and related material efforts. The bell hooks (p. 509), Gloria Anzaldúa (p. 496), and Anne Fadiman (p. 474) readings may be useful sources.

part five

Working with a Semiotics Frame

Introduction and Historical Origins

A **recurrent fantasy that's shared across time and** cultures is that we'll discover some powerful object, ritual, or phrase that will provide us with all the answers—the access to total knowledge, the ability to be omniscient, all-seeing, all-knowing, and thus all-powerful. Such wish fulfillment comes in a vast variety of shapes: decoder rings, X-ray glasses, magic 8 balls, Ouija boards, superheroes, fortune-tellers, love potions, magical spells, astrology, Tarot cards, and a long list of similar objects, images, and practices that offer us or enable us to identify with some heightened form of power. The interpretive frame of semiotics theory can be seen as a kind of realistic entry in this list of power-enhancing tools. While perhaps not as cool as having X-ray vision, understanding semiotics does provide a powerful way of revealing otherwise invisible worlds of meaning. And as in many stories of fantastic powers, there is a dark side to such knowledge: once you're able to read cultural signs through semiotics, you may lose a certain naïve innocence, a blissful unawareness of cultural manipulation and the operations of cultural power that saturate communication in all its forms.

In tales of unexpected magical powers, the source of the power often appears innocuous, plain, or even tedious, from Mary Poppins's carpetbag to Superman's mild-mannered alter ego, Clark Kent. The origins of semiotics might be seen as similar on this score as well, for semiotics derives from highly technical linguistic and philosophical theories developed independently but in roughly the same era (the early twentieth century) by Swiss scholar Ferdinand de Saussure and American scholar Charles Sanders Peirce (his last name is pronounced "purse"; after you've read this section, you should be able to explain why the "right" pronunciation matters, and what "right" means, semiotically). From what might seem a dry diagram of how language works comes a system that enables us to read, or decode, how words bristle with a multiplicity of meanings, images, and ideological messages. And more disturbingly, perhaps, how *we*, by using words, are formed in and by semiotic webs.

The theories of Saussure and Peirce basically argue that words are arbitrary pointers embedded in a social system, not isolated containers of set meanings. Meaning is not a one-to-one relationship between "signifier" and "signified," to use the formal terminology of semiotics. In simpler terms, the word *beer* is not the same thing as the actual foamy, yellowish liquid we understand the word to name. Its meaning depends on our knowing many other kinds of liquids that are not beer, and so the meaning depends on a network of other meanings, not on the substance we mean by "beer" in itself. The sign "beer" also carries with it many cultural associations, or "myths," and these aspects of its meaning are also not contained in and by the word *beer* itself, but depend again on that network of meanings that a language community creates and shares. That means that language is not transparent: words don't simply and solely mean the things they name, and words aren't derived from those things but from the social use of language. Words are **conventional** and **arbitrary** signs: we agree that a certain sound indicates one thing by excluding others, and the sound itself is not the meaning or thing it signifies ("beer" could just as well be "yatsap," if the language community members agree).

This recognition of the arbitrary nature of signs matters because it helps us see that meaning is not stable—it is not finite, containable, nor unchanging over time and place. Words and images carry histories with them, in a sense. Any word/sign we use is full of cultural baggage that we don't get to define or control fully. That "baggage" is what semiotic theory calls a "myth"—not a false notion, nor an ancient tale, but a set of beliefs and values that serve competing cultural interests. So the communication we receive and send—the images, speech, and written texts we consume and produce—is part of a cultural web, and no word or image exists in isolation from it. Thus all words, images, practices, environments, clothing styles, and so on are open to semiotic interpretation. Those who can decode cultural myths—who can read semiotically—have the critical ability to understand how cultural interests pervade everyday experience. And that's a kind of special power, one centered in awareness: you become more aware of how you're influenced by and are influencing the special interests of our culture.

The following chapters include images along with written texts; the written word is, after all, just one kind of image. Looking at texts in this way helps us consider the visual nature of rhetoric. From document design—how written texts appear on a page or screen—to pictures, photographs, landscapes, outfits, traffic signs, we read the visual display of texts each time we open our eyes. We can read our own bodies semiotically, for example, in relation to their physical surroundings. Our bodies are cultural texts, and it may be very surprising to see how infrequently we're the author of their "meaning." Our cultural myths about attractiveness, for instance, prepare us to read others' bodies as well as direct us in how to display our own, if we seek such social approval.

We also use our bodies in ways that correspond with social relations of power—in a classroom, for example. Consider the many ways in which authority in a classroom is assigned to the body of the teacher, regardless of the individual teacher's beliefs about his or her relation to students. In the conventional classroom, we can see, through semiotic interpretation, many cultural signs of the teacher's power over students:

Bodies in Relation to Space

There is one teacher, but many students

The teacher stands; the students sit

The teacher can move about; the students sit in fixed rows/desks, facing the teacher and the board

Style and Appearance as Status Markers

The teacher is usually dressed professionally, the students casually

The teacher has a briefcase; the students have backpacks

The teacher is usually older, the students younger

Behaviors

The teacher writes on the board; the students copy the teacher's words

The teacher asks questions; the students answer them

The teacher speaks at will; students raise their hand for permission to speak

The teacher determines the course content and syllabus; the students follow the directions

The teacher determines grades; the students are examined and graded

The design and rituals of the conventional classroom work to make teachers the center of social action, literally and figuratively. In our long experience as students, we are schooled in knowing our "place," which, according to our dominant cultural myth of education, is subordinate to the teacher. Students come into the college classroom and follow the conventions of their own subservient status without any need for direction—even if no instructor is in the classroom, students sit down, face front, and follow the rules of classroom behavior. Semiotics allows us to see how the environment of the classroom and its cultural meanings direct student (and teacher) bodies. The image on the next page of an empty classroom shows how its design, from the way student seating is arranged to the articles that are (and are not) present, tells the story of traditional teaching and learning. Semiotics lets us see its cultural, not just practical, functions.

Our continued exposure to and participation in social systems such as schooling has another effect beyond directing our behavior: **naturalization**.

We are so much *in* cultural codes that we can't typically recognize them as *constructed*. Instead, they come to seem natural, or just the way things are. We "naturally" associate pink with girls and blue with boys (or see ourselves as female or male); we "naturally" respect elders, teachers, ministers, and so on, "naturally" want to increase our incomes, own big houses, go on vacations. Cultural myths help disguise the historical grounds for our desires and behaviors and direct attention away from the ideological purposes and interests that benefit from them. A commercial for a sports car, for example, appeals to a "natural" desire for speed, power, freedom, all treated as "natural" masculine values. Reinforcing a connection between competition and masculinity serves many cultural purposes, however, that are not overt elements of the myths the commercial employs—capitalism and male dominance, for instance. We're encouraged to identify such consumption with pleasure and status, to experience it as a "natural" relationship rather than a historically produced and continuously reinforced linkage.

What semiotic analysis can show is how the myth takes the place of historical reality. The elements of the myth—the words that call it into existence as a meaningful and familiar reference—help detach the particulars of the cultural story from its material reality and ideological interests. Sometimes a cultural myth is "outed," made visible, by a challenge from those who detect in it a damaging social agenda or reproduction of historical injustice. You can see a kind of semiotic undoing of cultural myths in objections activist groups have made to the mainstream use of "American Indian" images as sports mascots or the display of the Confederate flag as "just" a symbol of a region or heritage, not a historical reality that included slavery; in resistance by early feminists to "Miss/Mrs." as social designations tied to women's marital status; in court cases about enforced reciting of the Pledge of Allegiance because it includes the amendment "under God." Less controversial are shifts in the signs that indicate shifts in cultural styles and target audiences: the NBA's change in its symbol from a basketball player coded as white (and modeled on a white player, Jerry West) dribbling a ball to an image of Michael Jordan airborne, dunking the ball. The different images reflect the changing elements of the sport, the cultural narrative shifting from one kind of player and play to another. The change in just about any famous company logo or product design is equally a kind of social history: the updated images of Betty Crocker and Aunt Jemima; the design progression of vans to SUVs to Hummers. Semiotics can help us disrupt naturalization and question the cultural codes that otherwise remain invisible and trace the ways in which society and its myths change.

A cautionary note: just as with psychoanalytic theory, semiotic analysis can produce real resistance, denial, and disbelief. Decoding deeply ingrained, long-accepted "natural" truths is less challenging, often, than persuading others to see your analysis as credible. In our classroom experience, more students resist these two critical frames than any others, and one of the most common comments is "Aren't you reading too far into this?" Semiotic theory shows that signs don't operate as one-way indicators of meaning, which leaves us with language as always open-ended. To try to delimit meaning, at least from a semiotic perspective, is an impossible task. The idea of reading "too far" requires a point of final, fixed meaning—something we may always desire, but, according to poststructural theory, a lack that always defines us as language users. Objections of this sort seem often to mean "too far for comfort."

● Adding to the Conversation

Most of us are quite aware of the manipulative ways of advertising—the fantasies it evokes to seduce us into spending our money. The ability to read the subtexts of ads is a good way into sophisticated semiotic analysis. Semiotics lets us take a further step beyond the logic (or illogic) of an advertisement to see the larger cultural interests at work in an image and slogan. We can then use this very familiar frame to read other kinds of images in equally critical ways. Just as a magazine ad is a design, a purposefully organized relation of its elements, so most of our daily environments are as well. A residence, car, bus stop, parking lot, department store, park, jail—these social spaces can be "read' for the cultural myths they reproduce and the directions they give to us for our behavior and relations with others.

Try reading some of these familiar signs semiotically:

✓ a police uniform
✓ a diploma
✓ a cereal box
    five randomly chosen newspaper film ads
✓ the cover of your college catalog or home page of its Web site
    a mall
    the outfit you wore in public today; the outfits you did not
✓ a "Dr. Barbie" doll

Rhetorical Issues in Semiotics

As a critical frame, semiotics provides an analytic method that produces interpretive data. What you do with that data is not prescribed—semiotics does not provide a value system, a way of judging what you uncover. As a writer, you'll find semiotics a useful investigative tool, but one that also leaves you responsible for deciding on the nature and extent of the argument you make from your results. You become a kind of detective in search of the cultural myths and special interests served by your object of study, and you then have to decide if you'll take on a further role as cultural commentator or critic. The credibility of any commentary you add—any judgment you make using the data of your semiotic analysis—depends on the thoroughness of your analysis. Thus a semiotics-based argument requires a careful, detailed, specific mapping of how your object of study connects to larger cultural myths/stories.

Semiotics is therefore a valuable *invention* device. It lets you discover cultural codes, the larger semiotic web in which your subject of study exists. By analyzing your subject semiotically, you reveal connections, identify myths, and map out the cultural interests at work behind the "natural" or "common-sense" conventional meaning of an object, place, event, or text. Semiotics also foregrounds the *dialogic*, or social, nature of language, and so a semiotics-based analysis calls for careful attention to voice, audience, and form. You need to be especially semiotically aware, that is, of how you position yourself in relation to your subject of study, your audience/reader, your medium of presentation (written language, in print form, with academic discourse conventions, or some alternative genre and/or style), and your consciousness of all these as parts of a "web," a culturally constructed system of meaning that no one speaker/writer knows in its entirety.

Since semiotics does not provide a plan for presenting your findings, an organizational method, you have to decide on a rhetorically effective form once you've "read" the data you've produced. You can emphasize your subject as part of a historical narrative, one more version of a familiar cultural story whose difference really serves to emphasize the unchanging nature of the story itself. For example, Jack Solomon, author of *The Signs of Our Time* (excerpted below), presents a semiotic reading of the then-current *Cosby Show* to demonstrate how its surface differences are subsumed to the larger cultural myth it reflects.

Reading Bill Cosby

Throughout the 1980s, Bill Cosby has emerged as something of an American institution. The subject of a *Time* magazine cover story (September 28, 1987), Cosby looms as the most successful entertainer of his generation, black or white. There are a number of reasons for Cosby's success. First, as one of his early comedy albums puts it, he is a very funny man. More importantly, perhaps, Cosby has succeeded in restoring to television the image of the "strong father" after years of paternal buffoonery. Shows like "All in the Family" and "The Jeffersons" featured weak and foolish fathers who presented a contrast to the dignified fathers of the fifties. The undercutting of the seventies' TV father was deliberate: it reflected the iconoclastic mood of a country suspicious, for the moment, of authority. But with the advent of the new decade, paternal authority—symbolized for many by Ronald Reagan's paternalistic presidency—came back into popular fashion. Once more, American audiences were looking for TV father figures, men who were sensitive, nurturing, yet authoritative and masculine. Cosby fit the role perfectly, quickly emerging as America's favorite father.

Bill Cosby is not only America's favorite father, he is America's favorite symbol of the American dream, one that his success seems to establish as color blind. Cosby has embraced this symbolic interpretation of his career and incorporated it into his show, which has been self-consciously designed to project an image of black success, a black version of the American dream. But behind the image lurks a concealed semiotic reality.

The explicit symbolism of "The Cosby Show" is something that Cosby himself has done much to promote in the press. The Huxtables, he insists, are "an *American* family," an exemplary model of "the American way of life." Cosby continues: "If you want to live like they do, and you're willing to work, the opportunity is there." Cosby is defending himself against the common criticism that his show is an unrealistic representation of what life is really like for most black Americans in the 1980s. His defense—that he isn't trying to represent what life is like for most black families but is only trying to present a model family that all Americans can aspire toward—is perfectly justified. There's always room for the presentation of admirable examples, of positive images for others to imitate. Cosby seems to be succeeding in this very nicely, if we can judge from recent matriculation surveys at UCLA that indicate a high proportion of minority freshmen plan to become pediatricians and lawyers.

The semiotic question, then, is not whether "The Cosby Show" is a realistic picture of black American life. The question is, what does the creation and presentation of the Huxtable family say about America in the 1980s? Consider how "The Cosby Show" resembles the "Father Knows Best"–style sitcoms of the fifties. True, the skin color is different, and Mom has a career of her own, but in "Cosby," as in its predecessors, it is the family home that constitutes the focus of everyone's attention. Dad's a pediatrician, Mom's a lawyer, the kids all have outside interests and activities, but the psychic and moral center of the family is the living room. There, child meets with father—who, like Ozzie Nelson, always seems to find time away from his job to lounge around the house—to settle his or her little problems. Dad is funny, often adorably self-mocking, but he's always there and his advice always works.

What is striking about this is not so much the similarity between "Cosby" and the family sitcoms of the fifties and sixties but the astonishing success of the program among audiences who are well aware of the artificiality of the mode. Americans are nostalgic not for "Father Knows Best" but for the family-centered mythology that show reflected. "Cosby" only adds a new layer of mythology to the old mythology, presenting a black family in the place of the white originals. Viewers of the show are thus doubly reassured on the one hand by images of a tightly knit family group even as the real nuclear family continues to come apart in American life, and on the other hand by the iconic representation of a successful black family at a time when black America is falling further behind white America. For black Americans, "Cosby" is a sign of promise, of economic desires that *can* be fulfilled. For white Americans, it is a sign of progress, of social desires that *have* been fulfilled. And for all the Americans who faithfully watch it week after week, it is a sign of continuity, of the continuing desirability of a close-knit family home.

But the fact that, semiotically speaking, these signs signify the state of American *desires* in the 1980s more than they do American *realities* is the most significant sign of all. College freshmen may want to become pediatricians, but few will make it, especially when financial aid resources for college tuition are shrinking. We may still want families in which the home is the center of activity, but for the kinds of families that the Huxtables represent, the focus of parental interest tends to be the career that got them their money, not their kids, who are being raised by professional surrogates, from nannies to day-care workers and school teachers.

"The Cosby Show," one could say, realistically represents our desires for a world that is practically the inverse of the one in which we actually live. It is perfectly true at the level of desire, but is desire a substitute for the real thing?

Solomon situates Cosby, the focus of his study, as familiar not only as a very funny and successful entertainer but also as occupying a cultural role in a familiar American myth, the "strong father"; as embodying a second common myth, the "American dream"; and as a color-blind representation of that dream, in an era that experienced great racial tension. Judging from the popularity of the show in reruns, it continues to reproduce and reinforce a still-valued and valuable myth that anyone can make it, and that assimilation into mainstream culture—the "melting pot" myth—is the way to do so. Solomon seeks to explain rather than critique the myth. But his analysis could easily be made a part of a cultural and social critique: he could embed it in an argument about the validity of assimilation as a social goal, for one example.

Semiotics, because it does not make a distinction between signs (written language, images, objects, landscapes, practices are all signs), helps us imagine producing academic texts that are themselves multimedia, in a sense. We can play with form, adding to the conventional elements other forms of communication, such as the visual (and, depending on how much access you have to computer technology, sound, moving images, hypertext, etc.). Incorporating images and visual document designs is like moving from one-dimensional painting to textures, mixed materials, installation art, and other shifts and enrichments of format, even as a basic coherence among elements remains a typical assumption. The different media used—let's say written language and illustrations—exist in a varying relationship according to rhetorical purpose.

In basic document design, we can use the layout of published texts as an organizing device: title page, table of contents, headings and subheadings, end matter (appendices, etc.), along with accompanying charts and illustrations. The written text is typically the primary means of communicating, and the design elements support the written argument. But we can also compose visual arguments in which the image is equal to written text or even the primary medium. In the painting on the next page, image and words work together to refer to a well-known product advertisement. Together, the image and words form a powerful visual argument against the use of industrial poisons in farming as well as the exploitation of farm workers.

Some students find writing from a semiotic frame difficult precisely because it requires a strong authorial voice and consideration of more than conventional forms/media. Unlike a more text-based method, such as postcolonial critique, for example, the author writing from a semiotic frame is responsible for finding and framing his or her subject; presenting it in descriptive detail; and sometimes researching its historical contexts. As a writer in this frame, you have to make the subject visible, render it familiar, rather than refer to lines in a text or a historical event, for instance. You have to serve as the primary authority via your analysis, and

you can't really rely on citation of semiotic theorists ("Peirce argues . . .") because your subject is a material cultural text from your own time and place in the cultural web. And you have to take an ethical stand if you're going to move from a semiotic analysis into a specific critique of your findings. In some ways, this critical frame requires more of a writer as a mature public voice than some other critical frames may. But we can soften that judgment by invoking the myth of no pain/no gain; try, try again; never say never; or other cultural code intended to make hard work palatable. And, by the way, instead of excerpting the works of Saussure and Peirce in the next section, we've drawn from secondary discussions of semiotics for a more accessible entry into this critical frame.

Exploring Semiotics

● Enhancing your critical reading
ability by applying semiotic
theory to visual texts, physical
spaces, and cultural practices

● Understanding the social,
historical, and cultural nature
of words and language

● Considering the rhetorical role
of visual elements in your
written work

How much of your day is entirely print-based? Your alarm clock is probably digital, and it's certainly got some kind of material design features that are more than just functional—color, layout, product name, setting options. You may have woken up wearing some specific article of clothing associated with sleep, which you knew to select even though they didn't have a label saying WEAR THIS FOR SLEEPING. You probably didn't wash at the kitchen sink but went into a room whose *contents* said "bathroom," not kitchen or other living space. Even before you opened a newspaper—itself filled with photographs and layout designs—you were operating in a realm of signs that are complex and more cultural and visual than they are print-based. Considering how dependent we are on visual understanding of the world, the theory of semiotics seems a critically useful frame for reading the world around us.

As you might expect, many of the readings and rhetorical projects of this chapter mix print and visual signs. Having a rhetorical understanding of the visual is another critical tool for the academic and professional writer.

Introducing Semiotics

PAUL COBLEY and LITZA JANSZ

The following excerpt explains the history of theoretical study of the "sign," from ancient Western philosophy through the work of twentieth-century French theorist Roland Barthes (p. 566). Paul Cobley summarizes the major theoretical ideas, and Litza Jansz has produced a visual display of them, accompanied by dialogue Cobley provides. Their 1997 book, Introducing Semiotics, *is one in a series of "popularized" treatments of major thinkers and theoretical frames; the use of written and visual argument is especially appropriate for their purpose of introducing semiotics. You can read word and image to gain a sense of the foundational concepts of semiotics: the "sign"—words, images, and so on—is not a natural but conventional and arbitrary way of indicating meaning; meaning is a mental concept that is never the same thing as the sign signifies; signs "mean" within or refer to larger social systems, or "myths," which come to seem "natural" or "commonsense" truths, even though they are always socially constructed.*

The Pre-History of Semiotics

Early precursors of semiotics include **Plato** (c. 428-348 BCE*) whose *Cratylus* ponders the origin of language; and **Aristotle** (384-322 BCE) who considers nouns in his *Poetics* and *On Interpretation*.

The word "semiotics" comes from the Greek root, *seme*, as in *semeiotikos*, an interpreter of signs. Semiotics as a discipline is simply the analysis of signs or the study of the functioning of sign systems.

The idea that sign systems are of great consequence is easy enough to grasp; yet the recognition of the need to study sign systems is very much a modern phenomenon.

*BCE - Before the Common Era

4

One of the most notable debates on signs in the Ancient world took place between the Stoics and the Epicureans (around 300 BCE in Athens).

The crux of the matter concerned the difference between "natural signs" (freely occurring throughout nature) and "conventional" signs (those designed precisely for the purpose of communication).

For the Stoics especially, the quintessential sign was what we know as the medical symptom.

5

The symptom remained the model sign for the Western era.

The major foundation for the Western interrogation of signs was laid in the Middle Ages with the teachings of **St. Augustine** (354-430).

Augustine developed his theory of *signa data* - conventional signs. Contrary to Classical commentators, he promoted such signs as the proper objects of philosophical scrutiny.

He also served to narrow the focus of sign study by pronouncing on the way in which words seem to be the correlates of "mental words".

Augustine's narrowing of the focus was to have a serious impact on subsequent sign study.

Other scholars, such as the English Franciscan, **William of Ockham** (c. 1285-1349) exacerbated this version of the sign.

This, in turn, underpinned the work of **John Locke** (1632-1704) in his *Essay Concerning Human Understanding* (1690).

Although these figures in European philosophy are in some senses proto-semioticians, it is not until the 20th century that a full-blown semiotic awareness appears, under the auspices of two founding fathers.

6

7

In 1906 the University of Geneva, by fluke, provided the catalyst for him to produce a landmark in linguistics and, subsequently, semiotics.

Saussure was assigned the task of teaching a course in general linguistics (1906-11), a task he had not previously undertaken, and dealing with a topic upon which he would not publish in his lifetime.

Nevertheless, when Saussure died in 1913, his students and colleagues thought the course was so innovative that they reassembled it from their preserved notes and published it in 1916 as the *Cours de linguistique générale*.

In opposition to a "historical" - **diachronic** - linguistics which looks at the changes which take place over time in specific languages, Saussure pursued a **synchronic** linguistics. He presented an analysis of the state of language in general; an understanding of the conditions for existence of *any* language.

9

Ferdinand de Saussure (1857-1913)

Saussure was born into an academic Geneva family in 1857.

At the age of 19 he went to study languages at the University of Leipzig where he was to publish, two years later, a famous paper on the "Primitive System of Vowels in Indo-European Languages".

Following completion of his thesis, Saussure left for the École Pratique des Hautes Études in Paris where he was to teach Sanskrit, Gothic and Old High German.

Here he stayed for ten years before being enticed back to Geneva to teach Sanskrit and historical linguistics.

8

Inseparable from the signifier in any sign - and, indeed, engendered by the signifier - is what Saussure calls the **signified.**

This is a **mental concept.**

If we take the word "dog" in English (made up of the signifiers /d/, /o/ and /g/), what is engendered for the hearer is not the "real" dog but a mental concept of "dogness":

The "real" dog might be a Great Dane, West Highland terrier, a lurcher, a wolfhound etc. rather than a general dog.

The *Cours* focussed on the nature of the linguistic sign, and Saussure made a number of crucial points which are integral to any understanding of the European study of sign systems.

Saussure defined the linguistic sign as a two-sided entity, a **dyad.** One side of the sign was what he called the **signifier.** A signifier is the thoroughly material aspect of a sign: if one feels one's vocal cords when speaking, it is clear that sounds are made from vibrations (which are undoubtedly material in nature). Saussure described the verbal signifier as a "sound image".

Alternatively, in writing . . .

10

Central to Saussure's understanding of the linguistic sign is the **arbitrary nature** of the bond between signifier and signified.

The mental concept of a dog need not necessarily be engendered by the signifier which consists of the sounds /d/, /o/ and /g/. In fact, for French people the concept is provoked by the signifier *"chien"*, while for Germans, the signifier *"hund"* does the same job.

For English speakers, the signifier "dog" could, if enough people agreed to it, be replaced by "woofer", or even "blongo" or "glak".

That is to say, there is no natural reason why the signifier "dog" should engender the signified. The connection between the two is arbitrary.

A SCIENCE THAT STUDIES THE LIFE OF SIGNS WITHIN SOCIETY IS CONCEIVABLE; IT WOULD BE A PART OF SOCIAL PSYCHOLOGY AND CONSEQUENTLY OF GENERAL PSYCHOLOGY; I SHALL CALL IT SEMIOLOGY.

Saussure uses the term *semiology* as opposed to *semiotics*. The former word will become associated with the European school of sign study, while the latter will be primarily associated with American theorists. Later, "semiotics" will be used as the general designation for the analysis of sign systems.

THE CONCEPT IS GIVEN PRIMACY IN SAUSSURE'S SCHEMA

The inseparability of the signified (mental concept) and the signifier (material aspect) leads Saussure to offer the following diagram:

signified
signifier

Clearly, Saussure believes that the process of communication through language involves the transfer of the contents of minds:

The signs which make up the **code** of the circuit between the two individuals "unlock" the contents of the brain of each.

It is this combination of the contents of mind with a special kind of sign code which encourages Saussure to posit a new science.

But how do these signs which semiology studies actually work?

He describes the way in which the general phenomenon of language (in French, *langage*) is made up of two factors:

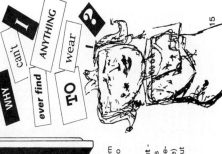

parole - individual acts of speech

langue - a system of differences between signs

Langue can be thought of as a communal cupboard, housing all the possible different signs which might be pulled out and utilized in the construction of an instance of *parole*.

Clearly, the fact that language is a system (*langue*) used by all, means that it is also a social phenomenon through and through.

But note also that the system is **abstract** - like a successful game of chess, there is rarely the need to stop and consult a rule-book to check if a move (or an utterance) is legitimate. The rules are known without necessarily needing to be continually tangible.

15

The only reason that the signifier does entail the signified is because there is a **conventional relationship** at play.

Agreed rules govern the relationship (and these are in action in any speech community).
But if the sign does not contain a "natural" relationship which signifies, then how is it that signs function?

For Saussure, the sign signifies by virtue of its **difference** from other signs. And it is this difference which gives rise to the possibility of a speech community.

LANGUAGE IS NOT COMPLETE IN ANY SPEAKER, IT EXISTS PERFECTLY ONLY WITHIN A COLLECTIVITY

Note: This principle of difference that gives rise to a system should be remembered when we go on to consider post-structuralism.

14

For the European thinkers that follow Saussure, however, the concept of *langue* represents the major breakthrough.

A Danish linguist, **Louis Hjelmslev** (1899-1965), embarked on Saussure's task of forging "a science that studies the life of signs within society". The crucial first move in this project involved the promotion of *langue* to the level of a master system of signs that governed *all* sign production above and beyond that described by linguistics alone.

Saussure and Semiology

One of the most penetrating critiques of Saussure acts as evidence of the spread of his influence.

The Soviet theorist, **Valentin Volósinov** (1895-1936), names the school of Saussure as a key player in Russian linguistics. However, he chides it for its "abstract objectivism": that is to say, he disagrees that *langue* (used by all, yet intangible) is where we might find the true social nature of communication.

Connotation is by no means an unfamiliar phenomenon.

In fact, probably one of the most gifted and entertaining analysts of connotation presented his most famous insights into signs *before* becoming immersed in semiology.

From 1954-56, a series of essays appeared in a French magazine, *Les Lettres nouvelles*. In each one, their author, **Roland Barthes** (1915-80), set out to expose a "Mythology of the Month", largely by showing how the denotations in the signs of popular culture betray connotations which are themselves "myths" generated by the larger sign system that makes up society.

I HOPE TO ACCOUNT IN DETAIL FOR THE MYSTIFICATION WHICH TRANSFORMS PETIT-BOURGEOIS CULTURE INTO A UNIVERSAL NATURE.

43

What strikes the reader of these two words - if he or she is sufficiently versed in history - is a whole set of associations to do with American expansion (the frontier, the 19th century, heroic pioneers, the railroad, the claiming of land from the East to the Pacific, the removal of Native Americans).

"Manifest destiny", coined in 1845, was a cliché used by successive U.S. presidents in the 19th century to refer to and justify the colonization of a continent.

The sign, then, can be said to have the power of **connotation**. Like all signs, it can - potentially - invoke the action of existing sign-systems.

DESTINY

MANIFEST

AS AMERICA'S TERRITORY SPREADS, SO WILL DEMOCRACY!

42

554

The book which contains these essays - appropriately entitled *Mythologies* and published in 1957 - presents meditations on striptease, the New Citroën, the foam that is a product of detergents, the face of Greta Garbo, steak and chips, and so on.

In each essay, Barthes takes a seemingly unnoticed phenomenon from everyday living and spends time deconstructing it, showing how the "obvious" connotations which it carries have usually been carefully constructed.

> IN "THE WORLD OF WRESTLING" I DESCRIBE HOW, FAR FROM BEING A SPORT, WRESTLING IS A COMPLEX SPECTACLE OF SIGNS MADE UP OF THE WRESTLERS' BODIES AND EXCESSIVE GESTURES.

Even though everybody knows that wrestling is "fixed" it does not stop people (often old ladies) getting carried away with certain bouts.

More subtly, in "The Romans in Films", Barthes shows that the means by which connotations of "Roman-ness" are produced in Joseph Mankiewicz's film of *Julius Caesar* are minute.

Apart from the obvious things (togas, sandals, swords etc.), Barthes notes that all the characters are wearing fringes.

> EVEN THOSE WHO HAVE LITTLE HAIR HAVE NOT BEEN LET OFF FOR ALL THAT, AND THE HAIRDRESSER - THE KING-PIN OF THE FILM - HAS STILL MANAGED TO PRODUCE ONE LAST LOCK WHICH DULY REACHES THE TOP OF THE FOREHEAD, ONE OF THOSE ROMAN FOREHEADS, WHOSE SMALLNESS HAS AT ALL TIMES INDICATED A SPECIFIC MIXTURE OF SELF-RIGHTEOUSNESS, VIRTUE AND CONQUEST.

44

45

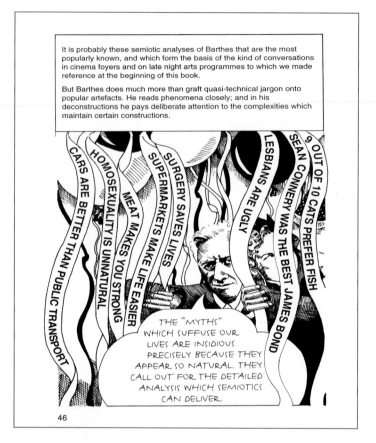

It is probably these semiotic analyses of Barthes that are the most popularly known, and which form the basis of the kind of conversations in cinema foyers and on late night arts programmes to which we made reference at the beginning of this book.

But Barthes does much more than graft quasi-technical jargon onto popular artefacts. He reads phenomena closely; and in his deconstructions he pays deliberate attention to the complexities which maintain certain constructions.

● Building the Frame Through Writing

1. Saussure drew a critical distinction between the **sign** and the **signified**. What happens when we recognize that a word—*dog, tree, book*—as a sound image is not equivalent to the mental concept, the signified, that we intend? How does this distinction "open up" meaning and make communication unstable?

2. We're all part of many speech communities (groups joined together by shared social experience and language conventions). Think of a "sign" you use in one speech community you belong to that would not work in another—in other words, where the meaning would not be conventionally known and so the sign would not communicate a shared mental concept. For example, in which speech communities might you not conventionally use the word *semiotics*?

3. The sign "contains a relation between itself and systems of signs *outside itself*." Even this apparently literal term *homework* also refers to a system of education; authority or unequal power relations; personal responsibility and work ethic; unstable borders of school/domestic or personal life, among other systems. What systems do you see the following signs referring to in this same way?

- the right to arms
- the frontier
- turn the other cheek
- girdles
- remedial writing
- the war on drugs
- hip hop
- other terms you identify

4. Myths, Roland Barthes (p. 566) argues, are "insidious" (subtly causing trouble or harm) because they seem *natural*, not socially constructed. What are some myths that you see commonly accepted in daily life without critical examination? Add to the following examples, and analyze each: to what extent is each natural or commonsensical, and to what extent can we see that it promotes specific social/cultural purposes? Has each been constant over time, or can you begin to trace a social history for it?

- 18 as the age of legal adulthood
- the nuclear family
- fast food
- office cubicles; job interviews; retirement
- freeways
- pets
- lawns; fences; garages
- virtues: punctuality; abstinence; others?

5. Try reading your classroom as a cultural landscape. What myths lead to its design, contents, arrangement of bodies, and/or other features?

Semiotics: The Science of the Sign
JACK SOLOMON

The following chapter opens Jack Solomon's book The Signs of Our Time *(1988). Like Cobley and Jansz (p. 545), Solomon offers a "popularized" version of semiotics in the belief that being able to decode cultural texts of all kinds gives us critical and material agency—the ability to act with greater choice and freedom than we'd otherwise have. He voices this goal in his introduction:*

> *As long as you are unable to decode the significance of ordinary things, and as long as you take the signs of your culture at face value, you will continue to be mastered by them and by those who have constructed them. But once you see behind the surface of a sign into its*

hidden cultural significance, you can free yourself from that sign and perhaps find a new way of looking at the world. You will control the signs of your culture rather than having them control you. (p. 8)

Semiotics is concerned with everything that can he taken as a sign.

—Umberto Eco

It is not an exaggeration to say that we are confronted by signs everywhere we turn, but in spite of their ubiquity—or perhaps because of it—we are often unaware of them *as signs,* and so are unaware of the significant network in which they move. There is a science dedicated to the study of this network, but it is not yet well known outside of the academic circles in which it began. This science is called semiotics, an unfortunately frightening-looking word that will be as familiar to you by the time you finish reading this book as the much more common science known as semantics. Both sciences are devoted to the study of meaning, but the latter explores only the linguistic significance of word-signs, while the former delves into their social and political significance. Semanticists are concerned only with words. Semioticians are concerned with *us,* and though they do analyze words, their analyses also explore the ways that clothes, buildings, TV programs, toys, food, and other ordinary objects are signs of hidden cultural interests.

There is a single commanding reason why you should want to learn to think like a semiotician: so you won't get hoodwinked. For example, when you are made to feel inadequate because you don't have a lot of money, you have been duped by a culture that measures everything in monetary terms. When you are told that a "woman's place is in the home," your culture is trying to conceal a patriarchal interest behind the veil of "nature" and "common sense." You can find alternatives to such beliefs by employing what I call the Six Principles of Semiotics:

1. Always question the "commonsense" view of things, because common sense is really "communal sense": the habitual opinions and perspectives of the tribe.

2. The "commonsense" viewpoint is usually motivated by a cultural interest that manipulates our consciousness for ideological reasons.

3. Cultures tend to conceal their ideologies behind the veil of nature, defining what they do as "natural" and condemning contrary cultural practices as "unnatural."

4. In evaluating any system of cultural practices, one must take into account the interests behind it.

5. We do not perceive our world directly but view it through the filter of a semiotic code or mythic frame.

6. A sign is a sort of cultural barometer, marking the dynamic movement of social history.

The first principle tells us to distrust what is called "common sense." To a semiotician, "common sense" is really *communal sense*, the set of beliefs that is shared by the members of a group or culture. Most Americans, for example, believe that it is only "common sense" to prepare themselves financially for the future, accumulating whatever stores they can against the advent of an accident or old age. We "save for a rainy day," hoard our resources, and generally conform to the materialistic slogan "You can't be too rich" rather than to the more spiritual "You can't take it with you." In orthodox Hindu society, by contrast, a man may give up all the security he has accumulated during the first three stages of his life—youth, manhood, and middle age—and become *sannyasa* in old age, abandoning his family and former ties to wander India with a begging bowl and staff in order to acquire religious merit. Let the rain fall, the orthodox Hindu believes, because no amount of wealth will free you from life's illusions and bring eternal peace.

A semiotician looks at these two different systems of belief and explores the cultural motivations behind them. He views saving money for retirement as "common sense" because Americans live in such a competitive environment. There is little comfort for the destitute in a country that equates one's quality of life with one's level of consumption. America's "commonsense" notions about retirement have been determined by an economic system that stresses material consumption rather than spiritual exploration. In the cultural codes of traditional Hindu society, where this ideology is lacking, a different set of values *can* motivate a man to abandon everything and throw himself upon the charity of his neighbors.

This doesn't mean that Leisure World is necessarily any better or any worse than *sannyasa*. What it does mean is that the "normal" attitude toward something as basic as retirement is actually only a social attitude; behind the "norm" lies a cultural interest, in this case, the interest a consumerist society has in encouraging its members to a lifetime of consumption.   5

According to the second principle of semiotics, a cultural interest lurks behind our most fundamental beliefs. However, if we were aware of this interest, we might not conform to it, so cultures tend to cover up their ideological investments by making them appear to be the only ones that conform to nature. For example, sexual activity is both "natural" and also governed by cultural interests. Of all the possible sexual acts that occur between men and women, men and men, and women and women, only those that take place between men and women are considered "natural" in mainstream American culture. Homosexual acts are labeled "unnatural" and are still forbidden by law in many states. Furthermore, some statutes declare the so-called "missionary position" as the only acceptable heterosexual practice.

To call one sexual act "natural" and another "unnatural" is to conceal what is in fact an ancient set of ideological interests that can be traced to the founders of Judeo-Christian culture. For the ancient Hebrews, the strident condemnation of homosexuality was one way to maintain their distinct cultural identity. Under Alexander the Great, Hellenic culture, which tolerated and even endorsed homosexuality, began spreading and threatened to engulf the indigenous cultures in the Middle East. Thus, the Hebrews were led to reject the new Hellenic social mores for the purposes of cultural survival. Other sexual prohibitions, such as those forbidding nonprocreative sexuality, have similar origins. Christianity began to rise during the decline and fall of ancient Rome. As Edward Gibbon writes in *The Decline and Fall of the Roman Empire*, the men and women of the early Church, reacting to Rome's notorious licentiousness, sought a purity beyond all measure. During the long Roman nights, they often tested themselves by lying naked side by side without touching. I can't help but say that if anything is "unnatural" it's that, but it's through these traditions that we have inherited many of our notions of sexual "naturalness."

Culture often conceals its own ideological interests behind the veil of "nature," naturalizing beliefs that are, in fact, only social and conventional. This is the third principle of semiotic thinking. The implications of this principle are not, as you might expect, that we must find some values that are truly "natural" and objective; on the contrary, what is implied is that no set of cultural beliefs can claim logical superiority over another set because all such beliefs are motivated by subjective interests. Of course, we *do* make moral distinctions between different cultural practices, but such judgments are not an ordinary part of semiotic analysis. The semiotician doesn't try to choose between cultural systems, he or she only demystifies them, revealing the ideological origins of human values. Hence, we come to the fourth principle of semiotics.

To a committed ideologue, the semiotician may look like a fence sitter, but that can't be helped. Semiotics never tells you *what* to think, only *how* to think and how to probe beneath the surface. This doesn't mean that you can't take a position of your own when thinking semiotically; it only means that to be consistent the semiotician should reveal and be aware of his or her own ideological stand before pursuing an analysis. My own stand in the analyses to follow is to take a fundamentally progressive line, venting occasional aggravation at the excesses of capitalism, suggesting a greater sensitivity to the rights of animals, and often taking a position that might be characterized as "soft-core" feminism. "Hard-core" feminists and committed Marxists—who, it should be added, are among the most distinguished of contemporary academic semioticians—may be disappointed by some of my analyses, but so be it. I'm not trying to peddle my beliefs beyond the one central semiotic belief that it is better to analyze what is going on around you than to take everything at face value, even if this means acknowledging the relativity of your own position.

There is something liberating in the semiotic rejection of the absolute, 10 however. Once you open up to a plurality of possible perspectives, you can be free to choose those which are most suited to you. I don't mean to efface the distinction between good and evil, but I do mean to suggest that there are more ways of looking at things than our culture ordinarily admits.

The Circle of Signs

The modern science of semiotics traces its descent to two late nineteenth-century philosophers who, working independently of each other, first began to elaborate the conceptual framework on which contemporary semioticians rely. Charles Sanders Peirce, a logician and physicist by training, inaugurated the science of the sign in America, while Ferdinand de Saussure, a Swiss linguist and psychologist, worked on the Continent. Although they called their sciences by different names (Peirce coined the word *semiotics* while Saussure called his science "semiology"), both men arrived at strikingly similar conclusions in strikingly similar ways.

It is rather poignant to note that semiotics, or semiology, is a posthumous science. Despite the close parallels between their research, neither Peirce nor Saussure ever learned of each other's work, for they both died in relative obscurity before the full range of their ideas appeared in print. Saussure died shortly after completing a series of lectures on linguistics, which he delivered between 1906 and 1911. It was this series on which the science of semiology was to be founded. We owe our knowledge of these lectures wholly to the devotion of his students, who together compiled their notes and published them in 1915 as the *Course in General Linguistics*.

Peirce's story is sadder still. He labored for more than forty years, producing page after page of largely unpublished speculations, but he could never collect his thoughts into a single, master text (if the complete collection of his papers is ever published, it may run to a hundred volumes). When he died in 1914, his work was still unfinished. Years later, editors began to sift through the mass and made portions of it available to scholars who are now energetically developing the science that Peirce did not live to see blossom.

Together Peirce and Saussure established the foundation for the fundamental semiotic conviction that the meaning of a sign is not to be found in the *object* to which it appears to refer but in a *concept* that functions within a culturally constituted system. For Saussure, the "signified" (or meaning) referred to by the "signifier" *dog*, for instance, is not a flesh-and-blood animal but a concept that can be distinguished from our concepts of, say, foxes, wolves, and even cats. The meaning of each concept—dog, wolf, cat—lies in its *difference* from every other concept in the system of English-language classification. Thus, a wolf is a wild, doglike animal that is neither a dog nor a fox, and a fox is a wild, doglike animal that is neither a dog nor a wolf. In each case, the semiotic definition of the concept lies not in some biological entity but in the coils of a conceptual system.

Similarly, when Ronald Reagan calls a soldier a "freedom fighter," the meaning of the sign belongs to a conceptual system that distinguishes between gunmen sponsored by the Soviet Union and gunmen backed by the United States. Reagan calls Afghan guerrillas and Contra rebels "freedom fighters" but does not put the same label on SWAPO guerrillas in South Africa who are 15 presumably fighting for freedom too but who are not supported by America. The difference, then, between U.S.-backed and non-U.S.-backed forces provides the real meaning of the name. On the other side of the political spectrum, the Soviets call members of the Polish labor union Solidarity "hooligans," which really means "opponents of Soviet hegemony" in the conceptual system of the Soviet Union and has no intrinsic relation to the character of the union members themselves. The Soviets also label Russian dissidents "insane," a concept similarly defined by a conceptual system rather than by reality.

Semiotic systems, in other words, are self-enclosed codes in which meaning is determined by a movement from sign to concept rather than from sign to thing. Within the terms of this movement, the continuum of reality is divided up into the culturally defined categories of objects that we call "dogs," "wolves," and "foxes," or "freedom fighters," "liberation organizations," and "terrorists," depending on the interests behind the system. . . . In this way, semiotic systems are closed off from any competing views, self-reflexively defining all things only in terms of their own conceptual and ideological beliefs. Think of these systems as labyrinths, or as those wooden Russian matrushka dolls that you open up only to find another doll, which you then open only to find another doll, and so forth. Or think of the way a Bible-thumping evangelist answers every challenge by referring back to the Bible. You never get out of the system.

The implications can be rather disconcerting. If the meanings of our signs reside in a closed system of concepts, then it seems that we can never break out of the circle to see our world as it "really is." Systems of signs always intervene between our perceptions and what we perceive. A sign system thus forms a kind of *frame* that determines the shape of our knowledge in advance. As the American anthropologist and linguist Edward Sapir said: "Human beings do not live in the objective world alone . . . but are very much at the mercy of the particular language which has become the medium of exchange for their society. . . . We see and hear and otherwise experience very largely as we do because the language habits of our community predispose certain choices of interpretation."

Semioticians refer to these interpretive frames as "myths." According to the fifth semiotic principle, a myth is not a fanciful story but a code that informs an entire structure of belief. There are gender myths that shape our conceptions of the relation between the sexes. The American presumption that free enterprise is an absolute necessity for a thriving economy is an example of an economic myth. Historical myths include the belief that all human history is progressive and is constantly moving upward toward better things. Such myths are not necessarily right or wrong, and they can be countered only with another myth, but it is only by recognizing them *as* myths that we can begin to consider how to interpret them.

Living within the terms of a cultural myth is like coming into the world with permanently attached violet-colored eyeglasses. We'd never know that the lavender-tinted world around us was really an artificial effect. The nature of the frame in which we live and move can accordingly be of the utmost importance in our lives, and it is one of the major tasks of semiotics to expose the ordinarily hidden contours of such frames.

Americans, for example, tend to conceive their relation to the natural   20
environment according to one of the dominant cultural myths of the West. This myth predisposes us to view the world in the terms of an opposition between the natural world and the human world and to judge all things by virtue of their relation to human needs. The meaning of our own sign of *Homo sapiens* within this mythic code is determined by a hierarchical structure that defines humans as the earth's dominant and sole important species. All other creatures are defined only as they relate to us. This viewpoint stems from a biblical culture whose code tells us that the earth and everything on it are ours to control. Such a system can be and is being used to justify everything from industrial pollution to animal vivisection. But if we change frames and look at things from another perspective, we may see new ways of perceiving our relationship to the natural world, causing us to drop the hierarchical scheme of things and see ourselves on equal terms with other species, as dwellers on earth, not rulers.

Semiotics, then, can be of great practical use to those who wish to dislodge the ordinary way of viewing things. To a certain extent, it is a potentially subversive science in that it can enable you to challenge the status quo by revealing its systematic presuppositions. Almost any cultural object can be read as a sign whose significance can be traced to a larger social system. For example, what is the significance of a high-heeled shoe? To the women who wear them, they may be merely fashionable articles of dress, but to feminist decoders the shoes signify the desire of a male-dominated culture to disable its women physically, to keep them jacked up on heels that prevent them from running away. A less extreme interpretation is that high heels tend to make a woman look as if she were trying to attract sexual attention. This fact does, at any rate, point to a common gender myth that defines women as sexual objects and requires them to appear sexually attractive. Men are not subjected to the same pressures within the terms of the myth; rather, they are expected to appear sexually aggressive. This division of labor is not the outcome of nature; it is the result of a gender myth. The propagation of the species would still continue even if women were expected to be the sexual aggressors and men the sexual objects. In fact, in most animal species the males are the beautiful sex. Think of the difference between a drab brown peahen and her iridescent mate, the peacock.

Academic semioticians have been probing both linguistic and nonlinguistic sign systems for many years but have been doing so largely among themselves, publishing their findings in technical articles and books aimed primarily at professional audiences, thus writing *of* but not *to* the cultures in which they live. Although semiotics has not yet been made widely accessible, there is nothing inherently obscure about it. It is actually the most intimately familiar of all the sciences, focusing on what we do and say. You only need to be introduced to it to become a semiotician yourself.

What the Apple Said

Because the system to which a given cultural sign belongs is often a historical one, referring to a cross section of the life and times of the society that produces it, semiotics is a profoundly historical science. To be a semiotician one must have a keen awareness of the dynamics of popular culture. This brings us to semiotic principle number six.

Consider the significance of the Apple Computer logo. At one level, it simply signifies an American corporation, like the RCA dog ("His Master's Voice"), the Chrysler star, or McDonald's golden arches. In recognizing this sign, you have already performed a sophisticated act of semiotic analysis that has been made possible by the corporate trademark code. It's easy to take this act for granted, but a visitor from a foreign culture who is unacquainted with the system of symbols that informs the trademark code might see only a rainbow-colored, half-eaten apple. To read this symbol you must be versed in the code, just as centuries ago a medieval knight could identify the family of a strange knight by the heraldric symbols on his shield. Knowing this code was essential to a knight's survival. Although one might survive without knowing the meaning of the trademark code, life in a consumer society does require a certain facility in corporate signs, lest we confuse a Chrysler with a Mercedes-Benz.

The Apple Computer logo can tell us more than the mere identity of the   25
corporation it symbolizes, however. To discover its entire message, we must see the logo in its original historical context. First, we might ask why a computer company emerging in the mid-seventies chose to represent itself with a rainbow-striped apple. The answer lies in the subculture to which the company's young founders belonged and in the market they envisioned.

Steven Jobs and Stephen Wozniak, along with the generation that responded to their product, were not comfortable with the impersonal artificiality of the unadorned machine. Machines were for the "Establishment," not for the newly emerging generation (eventually called "yuppies") who by the mid-seventies were abandoning the campus and commune for the corporate boardroom but were feeling rather uneasy about it. The Woodstock generation was entering the Establishment at full speed but did not like to be reminded of it, as was dramatized in the film *The Big Chill*. This generation was thus perfectly primed to respond to a bearded and sandaled Jobs, whose appearance was in itself a sign of his belonging to the counterculture. Jobs offered not a mechanical Establishment computer with a cold, impersonal name like IBM but a mellow little "Apple" sporting a Peter Max rainbow. The yuppie market liked the way a machine could be associated with the natural world, as well as the sly irony of the bite taken out of the apple (shades of Eden here?). The Beatles' company, Apple Records, was another association. Colored a soothing, non-threatening adobe gray, the Apple computer was calculated to appeal to the nostalgic sentimentality of its initial market, consumers who were fonder of rock 'n' roll than of technological wizardry but who needed that wizardry to get ahead.

The full meaning of the Apple logo emerges when we see it in its social and historical context. It does not refer only to a computer (which could have just as easily been called a "wozniak") but to a system of signs that expresses the consciousness of the mid-seventies, charting a trend that was among the most profound cultural movements of the era.

Not only social activists can benefit from semiotics. Business people can also read their cultures to spot emerging trends that may either be exploited or ridden out. In a sense, Steven Jobs might be considered one of the premier semioticians of his generation—if only unconsciously so—because he was able to take the pulse of his time and determine which sort of signs best fit the system then emerging. Of course, by choosing an apple, Jobs was manipulating his market, which is why the semiotic sword can always be said to cut two ways. Semiotically astute businesspeople can use signs to manipulate consumers, but semiotically astute consumers can, in turn, read these signs to determine how much manipulation is going on.

By carefully reading cultural signs, we can see how much more sensitive they are to rapid changes in our popular sensibility than the more conservative linguistic signs that we are taught in school. Words can keep their meanings for centuries; cultural images can change their meanings overnight. When Peter Fonda painted an American flag on his motorcycle helmet in *Easy Rider*, for example, the flag signified the sixties' ironic attitude toward blind patriotism. When Sylvester Stallone wrapped himself in the same symbol in *Rocky IV*, its meaning had changed dramatically to an *approval* of the same patriotism that had been questioned in *Easy Rider*. What you do with this knowledge is up to you. Remember, semiotics doesn't tell you what to do, only what things signify.

● Building the Frame Through Writing

1. You can create a semiotic methodology for your own use by identifying the key concepts in each one of the Six Principles of Semiotics that Jack Solomon outlines (para. 2). Try writing them in one sentence, in your own words, to create sequential steps in a semiotic analysis. Begin, perhaps, with "The common-sense view embodies. . . ."

2. Pick an aspect of common social experience that you're familiar with—education, friendship, marriage, or some other social connection.

   - What are some commonsense views or, as Solomon defines the term, *communal* views on these institutions/connections?

   - Look at the resulting list. Are the views consistent?

   - Now consider possible cultural motivations for differing views: in whose interest, for instance, is a positive view? In whose interest is a more negative one?

3. Solomon "reads" the social value of retirement planning as motivated by the interests of a consumer culture. What other "commonsense" behaviors might be motivated by consumerism, and how are they "cloaked"? Think of holiday purchases, for one example, or home decor, or fashion.

4. To demystify is to reveal the cultural interests that naturalize a practice (that is, that make it seem natural and commonsensical). Demystify a common social celebration from the list below. How are we persuaded to participate and to see the practice as a natural part of daily life? In which events does pathos play a major role? ethos? logos?

   • a baby shower
   • a bachelor party
   • a birthday party
   • Valentine's Day

5. In the introduction to Part Five, we noted that the correct pronunciation of the name "Peirce" is "purse." Now that you've read some semiotics theory, how would you address our earlier questions: why does "correct" pronunciation matter, and what does "correct" mean, semiotically?

Mythologies
ROLAND BARTHES

Roland Barthes's book, in which he reads common cultural events and images as signs that point to and evoke cultural myths, first appeared in 1957. Barthes is among the earliest of French theorists whose work led to the age of poststructural/postmodern thought. His analysis of how meaning operates as a complex system of cultural myths helped to create a new era in cultural thought, showing how signs operate in a system that the speaker or author does not fully control. Note: We have highlighted key phrases.

It **is now time to give one or two examples of mythical speech.** I shall borrow the first from an observation by Valery. I am a pupil in the second form in a French *lycee.* I open my Latin grammar, and I read a sentence, borrowed from Aesop or Phaedrus: *quia ego nominor leo.* I stop and think. There is something ambiguous about this statement: on the one hand, the words in it do have a simple meaning: *because my name is lion.* And on the other hand, the sentence is evidently there in order to signify something else to me. Inasmuch as it is addressed to me, a pupil in the second form, it tells me clearly: I am a grammatical example meant to illustrate the rule about the agreement of the predicate. I am even forced to realize that the sentence in no way *signifies* its meaning to me, that it tries very little to tell me something about the lion and what sort of name he has; its true and fundamental signification is to impose itself on me as the presence of a certain agreement of the predicate. I conclude that I am faced with a particular, greater, semiological system, since it is co-extensive with the language: there is, indeed, a signifier, but this signifier is itself formed by a sum of signs, it is in itself a first semiological system (*my name is lion*). Thereafter, the formal pattern is correctly unfolded: **there is a signified** (*I am a grammatical example*) **and there is a global signification**, which is none other than the correlation of the signifier and the signified; for neither the naming of the lion nor the grammatical example are given separately.

And here is now another example: I am at the barber's, and a copy of *Paris-Match* is offered to me. On the cover, a young Negro in a French uniform is saluting, with his eyes uplifted, probably fixed on a fold of the tricolour. All this is the *meaning* of the picture. But, whether naively or not, I see very well what it signifies to me: that France is a great Empire, that all her sons, without any colour discrimination, faithfully serve under her flag, and that there is no better answer to the detractors of an alleged colonialism than the zeal shown by this Negro in serving his so-called oppressors. I am therefore again faced with a greater semiological system: there is a signifier, itself already formed with a previous system (*a black soldier is giving the French salute*); there is a signified (it is here a purposeful mixture of Frenchness and militariness); finally, there is a presence of the signified through the signifier.

Before tackling the analysis of each term of the mythical system, one must agree on terminology. We now know that **the signifier can be looked at, in myth, from two points of view: as the final term of the linguistic system, or as the first term of the mythical system**. We therefore need two names. On the plane of language, that is, as the final term of the first system, I shall call the signifier: meaning (*my name is lion, a Negro is giving the French salute*); on the plane of myth, I shall call it *form*. In the case of the signified, no ambiguity is possible: we shall retain the name *concept*. The third term is the correlation of the first two: in the linguistic system, it is the *sign*; but it is not possible to use this word again without ambiguity, since in myth (and this is the chief peculiarity of the latter), **the signifier is already formed by the *signs* of the language**. I shall call the third term of myth the *signification*. This word is here all the better justified since myth has in fact a double function: it points out and it notifies, it makes us understand something and it imposes it on us.

The Form and the Concept

The signifier of myth presents itself in an ambiguous way: it is at the same time meaning and form, full on one side and empty on the other. As meaning, the signifier already postulates a reading, I grasp it through my eyes, it has a sensory reality (unlike the linguistic signifier, which is purely mental), there is a richness in it: the naming of the lion, the Negro's salute are credible wholes, they have at their disposal a sufficient rationality. **As a total of linguistic signs, the meaning of the myth has its own value**, it belongs to a history, that of the lion or that of the Negro: **in the meaning, a signification is already built, and**

could very well be self-sufficient if myth did not take hold of it and did not turn it suddenly into an empty, parasitical form. The meaning is already complete, it postulates a kind of knowledge, a past, a memory, a comparative order of facts, ideas, decisions.

When it becomes form, the meaning leaves its contingency behind; it empties itself, it becomes impoverished, history evaporates, only the letter 5 remains. **There is here a paradoxical permutation in the reading operations, an abnormal regression from meaning to form, from the linguistic sign to the mythical signifier.** If one encloses *quia ego nominor leo* in a purely linguistic system, the clause finds again there a fullness, a richness, a history: I am an animal, a lion, I live in a certain country, I have just been hunting, they would have me share my prey with a heifer, a cow and a goat; but being the stronger, I award myself all the shares for various reasons, the last of which is quite simply that *my name is lion*. But as the form of the myth, the clause hardly retains anything of this long story. **The meaning contained a whole system of values: a history, a geography, a morality, a zoology, a Literature. The form has put all this richness at a distance: its newly acquired penury calls for a signification to fill it.** The story of the lion must recede a great deal in order to make room for the grammatical example, one must put the biography of the Negro in parentheses if one wants to free the picture, and prepare it to receive its signified.

But the essential point in all this is that **the form does not suppress the meaning, it only impoverishes it, it puts it at a distance, it holds it at one's disposal**. One believes that the meaning is going to die, but it is a death with reprieve; the meaning loses its value, but keeps its life, from which the form of the myth will draw its nourishment. The meaning will be for the form like an instantaneous reserve of history, a tamed richness, which it is possible to call and dismiss in a sort of rapid alternation: the form must constantly be able to be rooted again in the meaning and to get there what nature it needs for its nutriment; above all, it must be able to hide there. It is this constant game of hide-and-seek between the meaning and the form which defines myth. The form of myth is not a symbol: the Negro who salutes is not the symbol of the French Empire: he has too much presence, he appears as a rich, fully experienced, spontaneous, innocent, *indisputable* image. But at the same time this presence is tamed, put at a distance, made almost transparent; it recedes a little, it becomes the accomplice of a concept which comes to it fully armed, French imperiality: once made use of, it becomes artificial.

Let us now look at the signified: this history which drains out of the form will be wholly absorbed by the concept. As for the latter, it is determined, it is at once historical and intentional; it is the motivation which causes the myth to be uttered. Grammatical exemplarity, French imperiality, are the very drives behind the myth. **The concept reconstitutes a chain of causes and effects, motives and intentions. Unlike the form, the concept is in no way abstract: it is filled with a situation. Through the concept, it is a whole**

new history which is implanted in the myth. Into the naming of the lion, first drained of its contingency, the grammatical example will attract my whole existence: Time, which caused me to be born at a certain period when Latin grammar is taught; History, which sets me apart, through a whole mechanism of social segregation, from the children who do not learn Latin; pedagogic tradition, which caused this example to be chosen from Aesop or Phaedrus; my own linguistic habits, which see the agreement of the predicate as a fact worthy of notice and illustration. The same goes for the Negro-giving-the-salute: as form, its meaning is shallow, isolated, impoverished; as the concept of French imperiality, here it is again tied to the totality of the world: to the general History of France, to its colonial adventures, to its present difficulties. Truth to tell, **what is invested in the concept is less reality than a certain knowledge of reality**; in passing from the meaning to the form, the image loses some knowledge: the better to receive the knowledge in the concept. In actual fact, the knowledge contained in a mythical concept is confused, made of yielding, shapeless associations. One must firmly stress this open character of the concept; it is not at all an abstract, purified essence; it is a formless, unstable, nebulous condensation, whose unity and coherence are above all due to its function.

In this sense, we can say that **the fundamental character of the mythical concept is to be *appropriated***: grammatical exemplarity very precisely concerns a given form of pupils, French imperiality must appeal to such and such group of readers and not another. The concept closely corresponds to a function, it is defined as a tendency. This cannot fail to recall the signified in another semiological system, Freudianism. In Freud, the second term of the system is the latent meaning (the content) of the dream, of the parapraxis, of the neurosis. Now Freud does remark that the second-order meaning of behaviour is its real meaning, that which is appropriate to a complete situation, including its deeper level; it is, just like the mythical concept, the very intention of behaviour.

A signified can have several signifiers: this is indeed the case in linguistics and psycho-analysis; It is also the case in the mythical concept: it has at its disposal an unlimited mass of signifiers: I can find a thousand Latin sentences to actualize for me the agreement of the predicate, I can find a thousand images which signify to me French imperiality. This means that *quantitively*, the concept is much poorer than the signifier, it often does nothing but re-present itself. . . . This repetition of the concept through different forms is precious to the mythologist, it allows him to decipher the myth: it is the insistence of a kind of behaviour which reveals its intention. This confirms that there is no regular ratio between the volume of the signified and that of the signifier. In language, this ratio is proportionate, it hardly exceeds the word, or at least the concrete unit. In myth, on the contrary, **the concept can spread over a very large expanse of signifier**. For instance, a whole book may be the signifier of a single concept; and conversely, a minute form (a word, a gesture, even incidental, so long as it is noticed) can serve as signifier to a concept filled with a very rich history. Although unusual in language, this disproportion between signifier and signified is not specific to myth: in Freud, for instance, the parapraxis is a signifier whose thinness is out of proportion to the real meaning which it betrays.

● Building the Frame Through Writing

1. Roland Barthes's writing is dense, but his reasoning is linear, a step-by-step analysis of how the sign works. Give yourself a simplified version of his argument by outlining the steps of semiotic reasoning. Use the boldfaced lines in the passage to explain the system of myth.
   - Signifier/signified/signification
   - Meaning, history and form/myth
   - Form impoverishes meaning
   - Appropriation is the purpose of the mythical concept

   You can use Solomon's explanation of semiotics to help put these ideas in your own words. And in places you can draw on your knowledge of Freudian theory to clarify some of the key points, as Barthes himself does.

2. Barthes's first example of a "mythical speech" is a line typically studied by a student in a mid-twentieth century French high school (a lycée). What can we "read" about the cultural myths shaping his life? He is studying Latin grammar; the line chosen is "because my name is lion." What signs do you see that show he is immersed in cultural practices that relate to class and gender?

3. "[M]yth has in fact a double function: it points out and it notifies, it makes us understand something and it imposes it on us." Barthes makes this point in his analysis of the black soldier saluting the French flag. How do you see them directing us away from a postcolonial understanding of the image?

4. Barthes explains how signs/signifiers are "emptied of" their historical connections, how myths replace history with their own narrative. Consider some common images in the following categories. How are they "emptied" of history and "put at a distance"?
   - food packaging: images of cows on dairy products; cattle and other animals on meat products
   - candy
   - gas stations
   - "gold' and "platinum" credit cards
   - blue jeans
   - a female body
   - a diamond ring
   - a flag

Writing from a Semiotics Frame

a sample drafting process

In the final part of this book, we turn perhaps fittingly to the final frames of *Jurassic Park*. The ending of the film invites a semiotic approach precisely because it consists of images and music only, no dialogue, and to interpret it we must work from visual and aural data. Let's take that as our grounds for writing: what conclusion to the problems of the story does the film's ending suggest? We'll start by observing the images in the final sequence of the film. (A somewhat arbitrary demarcation—we could construct a case for identifying the ending in many ways; here, we choose the portion of the final scenes by the end of dialogue and the characters' physical departure from the island.)

The survivors—John Hammond, Ian Malcolm, Alan Grant, Ellie Sattler, and the children, Lex and Tim—have boarded a helicopter, the same mode of transport on which they arrived. They ascend past the same waterfall we earlier saw. Hammond gazes at the amber tip of his cane (the amber from which dinosaur DNA had been extracted); then he and Malcolm stare out the window. Ellie sits between them, smiling. We then see what she is gazing at: Alan Grant, across from her in the center seat, his arms around the two sleeping children. The camera moves back and forth three times between Ellie's smiling gaze and Grant's returned smile, establishing their wordless exchange as the center of attention. Ellie then looks out the window; he follows her eyes. We see a flock of birds flying across the ocean, then a single bird, then a shot of the helicopter itself. All fly into the shining sun, and then the screen goes dark. The swelling sounds of John Williams's orchestral score has played throughout.

The steps that Jack Solomon outlines for a semiotic analysis can help us begin to shape a reading of these final scenes. First, we can read the sequence commonsensically: these are people who have survived a range of traumatic events and are happy to be headed home, alive and safe. They are exhausted, and so they are quiet; they are in a helicopter, and so they "naturally" look out the window at the scenery. And the music emphasizes their relief, even exhilaration, to be returning home. But remember that semiotics tells us that the common-sense reading both evokes and masks deeper cultural narratives or myths, and these serve the interests, the ideological frame, of powerful cultural groups or belief systems. The masking of these interests results from an alliance of the sign with a "natural" meaning—with happiness to be going home, with the peace that comes with safety, even the "natural fact" that both birds and helicopters fly in the air together. Yet we know that the scenes were all constructed, not natural; a writer, director, cinematographer, and editor made choices about what we would see. The story is fiction, and the events depicted were selected from a huge range of possibilities. What mythical frames were used in the selection process?

We noticed that the exchange of smiling gazes between Ellie and Alan form the center of attention—we are led to watch them, not Hammond or Malcolm.

That means that the grandfather/dreamer/entrepreneur and the scientist are both made peripheral—they are *not* central, not important, not worthy of our attention. It's the female character, Ellie, who is our guide, and we follow her gaze to see what is worth looking at. What she and we see that is valuable and important is first the man, Alan, who smiles back, and who then looks down at the sleeping children; we return to Ellie, who smiles approvingly. Yes, this is what's important: the family unit, the man who was once hostile to children brought back to his natural role as father and protector, allied to the woman who knew all the time that this is the ultimate scene of cultural goodness. All are happy, content, and peaceful as members of this social unit, and we sense that Ellie's earlier acknowledged desire to have children of her own with Alan is now a likelihood. The music underscores the completeness of the scene, its natural harmony. Business schemes, altering nature, speaking about theory—these have been shown to be either secondary, useless, or outright destructive. In the end, we see, the best state is the nuclear family, with the father in his rightful place, the mother in hers as guardian angel or moral guide, the innocent children sleeping within the protective gaze of father and mother, seen but not heard. The myth of the patriarchal family unit is clearly invoked and approved. The proper roles of the male and female within this unit are reconfirmed. Those who don't conform—Hammond and Malcolm, and even more certainly the lawyer, gamekeeper, computer technician, minority worker, who are all killed on the island—are losers, figuratively, literally, or both.

Note that the family unit has been coded as white, blue-eyed, and American. The lawyer is coded as ethnic through his Italian last name and as unethical through the cultural frame popularly applied to lawyers. The gamekeeper is Australian and single. The worker is Latino and one of a mass of workers. Hammond is Scottish and apparently unmarried, but he is a devoted grandfather; he survives. Malcolm is coded as a straight white male, but one who has been unable to establish a family; we learn earlier that he has been divorced several times, and he flirts with Ellie, potentially disrupting her relationship with Alan, who has to "protect" his interest in her at one point by letting Malcolm know they are romantically involved. Malcolm survives; we don't see a complete dismissal of his worth, perhaps because the film does not completely reject science as a progressive force (or entrepreneurship, either, since Hammond survives). But clearly those who align themselves with the traditional family and traditional means of procreation (as opposed to cloning) are the proper objects of our attention and approval.

When Ellie and Alan gaze out at the birds, when even in a helicopter they are flying in synch with these creatures, we are told once again that they are allied with nature and its beauty, balance, and rightness. They leave the dangerous, primitive world of the foreign, and home is a sunlit, happy, safe place on the mainland. These are the simple, good pleasures of life. Birds, not dinosaurs—in the film the relationship of the two species is emphasized—are the natural, best form of life, reinforcing, not challenging, the natural superiority of humans. The island is left behind, and any indigenous culture and damage to it is simply unrecorded and so erased. Such places can be forgotten, will be forgotten, in the myth of the nuclear, Anglo Saxon, American family, "emptying out" any history of colonization, or of social change in the composition of families. Even in a story about a wildly new form of technology, what remains is the "eternal" truth of the traditional family, just as Solomon showed in his analysis of *The Cosby Show*.

The principles of semiotics that Solomon has given us work very well as an invention process for reading these scenes. You could certainly go through the scenes again and add to the data, noting connections, changes in the musical score, in lighting and other visual effects. Now come the rhetorical decisions.

Who will be the audience for your semiotic analysis? Let's assume you're writing for an academic one. What will readers need to follow your reading? Some shared context on the film is likely needed, even given the film's massive audience over time. You may want your readers to imagine the film from a common-sense perspective—an action film about cloning for profit, a technological adventure that goes fatally wrong—which would set you up as the semiotic authority revealing the cultural myth that leads to such an interpretation. You may want to explain your method—what semiotics is and how a semiotic reading works. You can then go through the scenes using Solomon's principles as an organizing guide.

But do you also want to take up the voice of a social commentator? Do you want to comment on the film's cultural value or effect based on the analysis you've given it? Your thesis then might include a claim about the film as a whole, which you'll demonstrate logically through your analysis. To move to a critical voice would not be hard: the film is clearly conservative, given the cultural myths it relies on, and it seems to reproduce assumptions about our culture as dominant and, within that culture, one group as the privileged ideal. If you choose to approach the essay from this critical perspective, you may want to employ several voices—analytic, questioning, assertive, critical. You may choose to rely primarily on logos, or reasoned statement; or, if you find the film offensive in its cultural coding, you may employ pathos as well, since any text that excludes also likely does damage, making those who differ from the film's privileged model resistant to the cultural interests it serves.

Would graphics have an important place in the essay? Including stills from the film to show the progression of signifiers you analyze can function as effective visual evidence. Or they can be used to chart the steps in the film's own visual argument: we can see the successive frames that establish Ellie's approving gaze as she surveys Alan and the children, and the repetition of her gazing and them being observed as demonstration of the film's rhetorical emphasis. The same is true for showing how the technological—the helicopter—is integrated back into the natural world of the birds, water, and sun. You could also use historical visual evidence—photographs of the effects of colonization and/or technological exploitation on islands in the Caribbean or Pacific, for example—to show what is *not* represented, what is "emptied out," by the cultural myth invoked in the film. You'd be constructing a visual counterargument to the film.

topics for writing

1. Depicted here are two enduring images of the terrorist attacks on the World Trade Center towers in New York on September 11, 2001. One shows a plane approaching the second tower, with the first tower already on fire; the other shows the second tower after the impact. Applying your understanding of semiotics, explain why these images have emerged as a crucial way in which we frame our cultural memory of the event. What cultural myths are activated? Focus on the following visual elements:

   • the towers themselves, rising above surrounding buildings, whose roofs are barely visible; what was the main type of work that went on there?

   • the gaping hole made by the exploding airplane.

   • the smoke coming from the tower.

   The images are frequently reproduced in the media. To what extent do the images now evoke a cultural myth rather than the historical event? How has any "emptying out" of historical content occurred?

2. Explain the fundamental semiotic claim that the sign is not equal to the signified by using both print and visual argument. Your goal is to show that a given word for an object is not the same, not equivalent to or able to delimit, the concept it names. Show this instability in the relationship between language and meaning, perhaps moving from obvious examples ("body" along with images of the widely varying concepts the word can name—a variety of human bodies; a body of water; a police chalk outline of a body, etc.). Then consider instances in

which this inequivalence has assumed social and/or material importance. Following are some possible examples:

- The line in the Declaration of Independence asserting that "all men are created equal," along with images of enslaved Africans, unenfranchised women, or child laborers of the period; analyze the logic of the restricted meaning of "men."

- Advertisements whose graphic content limits the concept they use to pitch a product (for example, claims of freedom attached to sports car ads; promises of security attached to family scenes in insurance company ads).

- The image of the all-American family or all-American home and the variety of family structures and non-suburban domiciles.

3. Through the use of historical images, you can create a visual argument that depicts the changing social history of a particular concept, even as its name remains the same. Choose a topic that you want to explore from this semiotic perspective of a visual history. What historical forces help account for the shift, and how can you illustrate the change over time? Following are some possible topics:

- transportation
- women's professions
- mental illness
- "cool," "hipness"
- rural life

Reading Critically
About Cultural Myths

**This Chapter's
Rhetorical Concepts**

- Reading closely for semiotic signs
- Reading to connect text and cultural narratives
- Writing to analyze conflicting cultural narratives

Anthony Robbins—Motivational
Speaker and Author

DOMINICK A. MISERANDINO

The following interview focuses on Anthony Robbins, author of self-help programs and positive-thinking books, beginning with Unlimited Power *(1986). He appears frequently on television talk shows and late-night infomercials. Robbins became a multimillionaire by "training" others in his methods of success through self-programming. The blurb on one of his books sounds much like this section's opening point about our common desire to be all-powerful: we're told we can "reprogram" our mind "in minutes," enjoy "spectacular health and energy," be "persuasive," have "instant rapport" with others, and enjoy "wealth and happiness," all through learning his "ultimate success formula." Here he details the myth he has so successfully sold.*

Motivational Guru Anthony Robbins goes over his coaching techniques and theories, and explains why people put themselves in bad states, and how to get out of them.

> **DM)** Do you ever have a bad day where you aren't as productive as you'd like to be?
>
> **AR)** (Laughs) That's the most commonly asked question anybody ever asks me! They usually say something a little bit more direct like, "Come on, you can't be UP all of the time?!? Don't you get depressed? Even on the weekends, where you grow your beard, read Penthouse, and eat Cheetos?" Honestly, I have times where I get frustrated, or I feel a bit overwhelmed, or whatever the case may be, but I just don't stay there. Those are normal human emotions, and you certainly experience them. They used to be the dominant force in my life, and now they're pretty

rare. And when they happen, I just don't live in that place. That's really my message for people. I think all human emotions are valuable—disappointment is a valuable emotion if it's invested—but painful emotions are destined to call us out, to find something within us we're not using. To try to ignore them, to sit and dwell with them can be disastrous. I try to find the message, use it, and move on.

DM) I'd imagine for most people it's common to be in one of those states . . .

AR) I don't think I'd be B.S.ing you to say it's not a common occurrence for me; and the reason is, it's like an athlete. Your nervous system is something you train. You can train yourself to be fat, or frustrated, or depressed—or you can train yourself to be certain, hopeful, committed, dedicated, or loving—whatever the case may be. You've probably had people who laugh all the time—they even laugh at the dumb jokes—but that person has conditioned their nervous system to find the humor in things. I've conditioned myself to find out how to utilize whatever life tends to bring me. That's like an athlete. It's my life—although it wasn't my life until I chose to operate it that way.

One of the reasons I entered this as a business is I went to a seminar by a man named Jim Rohn, and I remember listening and saying, "Everything this guy is teaching you: if you lived it, your life would be extraordinary." So I thought the best way to live it was to be in that life in that business, so you'd have to live it. My life was focused on it, so it was the dominant experience in my life.

DM) Is there that much of a similarity between training yourself mentally as you would physically?

AR) That's exactly what I'm talking about—in fact, you can't separate the two. The mind and the body are totally related. If I'm going to help anybody, whether it's a child or an athlete, the first thing I do with everybody is put them in a peak state of mind. We all have states of mind where you say something; and then after you've said it you think, "I can't believe I said that. That was so stupid. That was so dumb." Then we have other times where afterwards we say, "Wow, I like it. I don't know how I did it, but I like it." Well, it's not based on ability, but it's based on the state you're in. The state you're in is directly related to the way you use your physiology, your body. If you take somebody who's depressed, and you look at their body, they always have similar physiology: Their head and shoulders are down. Their breathing is shallow. They talk slowly, they don't punctuate their words, and their voice trails off. If you take that same person and stand them up, put their shoulders back, and talk to them with an explosive breath, you will have them talking quicker, they will start to punctuate their words or their gestures, and you will see an instant change in their biochemistry. It's not just the way they feel in the moment; it's knowing the triggers in the body that will put the person in that state. That's why when people work out, they tend to be in a much stronger emotional state, which they will become physically as well. That's why the two cannot be separated.

DM) How long does such a process take then?

AR) Well, you can do something in a matter of seconds and change somebody in a moment. I was just dealing recently with a woman who was on Prozac and two other anti-depressants. She's maxed out on medications; the doctor had told her she just has to adjust, but she's still depressed. The ultimate change can happen in your body. The best drugs in the world are inside your body. You can change in a matter of seconds.

There was a study done at Harvard University, where they took people and didn't give them placebos—they gave them barbiturates instead, but told them they were amphetamines in a convincing manner. The people's bodies sped up (even though the drugs were telling them to slow down) and the same effect happened in the other direction. 10

What we can create is instantaneous. Now if you want lasting change and not just a spark, you've got to build that into your physiology. How fast can that be? It depends on the individual. It's something you can build enormous momentum on in a weekend if you do it day and night. That's what I do in a live seminar. It can take you 21 days, or three months, or six months if you do it once a week, or once an hour.

People often say, "How long does it take to get good at something?" I always tell them, "How long do you want it to take?" If you do it once a month, maybe it will take you twelve months; if you do it once a week, maybe it will take you four weeks. If you do it a couple of times a day, maybe it will take you two weeks. If you do it all day long, you can do it in two or three days and anchor it in.

That's why in seminars, it's a total immersion, a day and night immersion. People discover what it is that they want, what's stopping them, what's preventing them, and most importantly, they discover how to turn themselves on to produce that result right away.

That's one of the reasons I use the fire walk. You get somebody in front of a fire, and they don't know how confident they are. When they are in front of a 2,000-degree fire, they get an emotional state change. The ability to instantly change your state of mind, so that you're absolutely certain and get yourself to take action in that moment when everything in your body is freaking out—it's what it's all about. It's being in the emotional state to get yourself to step through anything you're afraid of, and storm through it. People can use it for the rest of their lives. And they come to that end and condition their body, so they can use it at will.

DM) Why do you think people get stuck in these negative states at times? Wouldn't it be natural for the body to want to be in a more natural state?   15

AR) No, here's the truth. Your body chemistry, way of life, and way of breathing will reflect your emotional states. We live in a society that doesn't exactly encourage us to be in the fittest state physically, mentally, or emotionally. Closer to none of the above.

Here's another reason: If you said to me, "Tony, how's your life in the last three or four years?" And I say, "Oh my g-d, it's been the most incredible time of my life. My oldest son has his own business now; he's doing incredibly well. My daughter is an actress who's done all of these different shows. My youngest one started a business. My other boy is just going into college; he's a straight A student. I'm the happiest I've ever been; I'm traveling around the world. I'm advising some of the greatest leaders of the world in politics, business and sports. Oh, and by the way, I took my company public, and I made $400 million dollars last year." You'd think under your breath, "Who does this guy think he is?"

But if I responded, "I have four kids. It's a battle that never ends. It doesn't matter where they are; they're still your kids. I have eight companies . . . no matter what I do, there's a demand on me constantly. I decided to get divorced three years ago, and it's the toughest thing in your life . . . I got married when I was 17. Nobody's happy when you make a decision like this." Your reaction would be to go, "Hey buddy, I know how you feel," and hug me.

We are a culture that rewards people for pain and failure with attention; and initially we reward people for success, but then our favorite thing is to jab them back down. If they are so successful, and we don't feel we are, we begin to feel insignificant. So to gain our significance, there's two ways to do it: build the tallest building in town, or burn it down, or blow up everybody else's buildings.

September 11th shows you don't have to have much intelligence,   20
background, or education to be able to feel like you're insignificant. That's how people operate. In our culture, we tend to give pain to people who succeed if they appreciate their successes, and we give pleasure to people as they fail. And that rewards people to be there. It also takes the risk of facing your greatest fear—the greatest fear everybody has is they're not enough, and they won't be loved.

Well, the goal for us in life requires the fear of failure. If you fail, you're going to feel like you're rejected, you're not enough, and you won't be loved. People feel like they're worthless, and they won't be loved. These are unconscious fears in everybody, so it's much easier to have a big reason why you can't do something. It's easier to claim it's not your fault than it is to acknowledge you're gutless and don't want to put something on the line.

In our culture, you're seen as naïve. I don't believe in positive thinking. I don't think you should go to your garden and start chanting, "There's no weeds . . . there's no weeds." There are weeds there, and they're going to take your garden. But I also don't believe you should come up with this illusion or this escape hatch of "I'm skeptical or I'm pessimistic." Most who say they're skeptical or pessimistic are really gutless because they don't want to get their hopes up . . . they don't want to be disappointed. They don't want to look naïve or fail.

I believe, "See it as it is." No worse than it is, but just as it is, so you have a reason to try or make it better. Just see it as it really is. And secondly, you've got to see it better than it is because without a vision, people perish. Once you have that vision, you've got to make the vision a reality by action on a consistent basis.

● Applying a Semiotics Frame

1. To what extent is Anthony Robbins's "vision" a version of the American "can-do" attitude or similar cultural narrative of individual success?

2. Robbins argues that "painful emotions are destined to call us out." Explain the logic, or common sense, of his argument. Why might people find it appealing, compared to the Freudian view of human discontent, for example?

3. Robbins emphasizes the connection of mind and body. Why is this view essential to his "personal power" message? Does it challenge or does it comply with cultural narratives about the body, attractiveness, "normalcy," health?

4. Robbins often appears in late-night television commercials amid scenery that calls attention to his wealth. How does wealth enter into the code he promotes, even as he does not verbally refer to it?

5. "It's easier to claim it's not your fault than it is to acknowledge you're gutless." How does this line erase social realities of difference?

   • How would Robbins likely see social movements such as the women's movement, federal equal opportunity laws, welfare programs?

   • Does his narrative encourage certain political orientations and discourage others?

   • Are some social groups more likely than others to succeed in his program?

Speaking of Courage

TIM O'BRIEN

This story is one of the many interconnected pieces that make up Tim O'Brien's 1990 collection of stories, The Things They Carried, *which is considered one of the most powerful works of fiction on the Viet Nam war. The stories collectively present readers with the material experiences of a company of young soldiers, beginning with the literal objects they "humped" through the countryside of Viet Nam. Many of the stories recount the same events—the violent deaths of many of the men, the particularities of the gunfire and explosions that killed them as the other men witnessed their deaths, the cruelties they suffered and committed, and the efforts they make to connect things and events to some larger meaning. Where Anthony Robbins (p. 576) carefully constructs a myth of individual power, O'Brien shows how cultural myths deconstruct when placed side by side with the material details of the soldier's war experience. Although fictionalized, the stories are semi-autobiographical, and O'Brien purposely calls into question how we can know what a "true" story is. Semiotics asks a similar question.*

The war was over and there was no place in particular to go. Norman Bowker followed the tar road on its seven-mile loop around the lake, then he started all over again, driving slowly, feeling safe inside his father's big Chevy, now and then looking out on the lake to watch the boats and water-skiers and scenery. It was Sunday and it was summer, and the town seemed pretty much the same. The lake lay flat and silvery against the sun. Along the road the houses were all low-slung and split-level and modern, with big porches and picture windows facing the water. The lawns were spacious. On the lake side of the road, where real estate was most valuable, the houses were handsome and set deep in, well kept and brightly painted, with docks jutting out into the lake, and boats moored and covered with canvas, and neat gardens, and sometimes even gardeners, and stone patios with barbecue spits and grills, and wooden shingles saying who lived where. On the other side of the road, to his left, the houses were also handsome, though less expensive and on a smaller scale and with no docks or boats or gardeners. The road was a sort of boundary between the affluent and the almost affluent, and to live on the lake side of the road was one of the few natural privileges in a town of the prairie—the difference between watching the sun set over cornfields or over water.

It was a graceful, good-sized lake. Back in high school, at night, he had driven around and around it with Sally Kramer, wondering if she'd want to pull into the shelter of Sunset Park, or other times with his friends, talking about urgent matters, worrying about the existence of God and theories of causation. Then, there had not been a war. But there had always been the lake, which was the town's first cause of existence, a place for immigrant settlers to put down their loads. Before the settlers were the Sioux, and before the Sioux were the vast open prairies, and before the prairies there was only ice. The lake bed had been dug out by the southernmost advance of the Wisconsin glacier. Fed by neither streams nor springs, the lake was often filthy and algaed, relying on fickle prairie rains for replenishment. Still, it was the only important body of water within forty miles, a source of pride, nice to look at on bright summer days, and later that evening it would color up with fireworks. Now, in the late afternoon, it lay calm and smooth, a good audience for silence, a seven-mile circumference that could be traveled by slow car in twenty-five minutes. It was not such a good lake for swimming. After high school, he'd caught an ear infection that had almost kept him out of the war. And the lake had drowned his friend Max Arnold, keeping him out of the war entirely. Max had been one who liked to talk about the existence of God. "No, I'm not saying *that*," he'd argue against the drone of the engine. "I'm saying it's possible as an *idea*, even necessary as an idea, a final cause in the whole structure of causation." Now he knew, perhaps. Before the war, they'd driven around the lake as friends, but now Max was just an idea, and most of Norman Bowker's other friends were living in Des Moines or Sioux City, or going to school somewhere, or holding down jobs. The high school girls were mostly gone or married. Sally Kramer, whose pictures he had once carried in his wallet, was one who had married. Her name was now Sally Gustafson and she lived in a pleasant blue house on the less expensive side of the lake road. On his third day home he'd seen her out mowing the lawn, still pretty in a lacy red blouse and white shorts. For a moment he'd almost pulled over, just to talk, but instead he'd pushed down hard on the gas pedal. She looked happy. She had her house and her new husband, and there was really nothing he could say to her.

The town seemed remote somehow. Sally was married and Max was drowned and his father was at home watching baseball on national TV.

Norman Bowker shrugged. "No problem," he murmured.

Clockwise, as if in orbit, he took the Chevy on another seven-mile turn   5
around the lake.

Even in late afternoon the day was hot. He turned on the air conditioner, then the radio, and he leaned back and let the cold air and music blow over him. Along the road, kicking stones in front of them, two young boys were hiking with knapsacks and toy rifles and canteens. He honked going by, but neither boy looked up. Already he had passed them six times, forty-two miles, nearly three hours without stop. He watched the boys recede in his rearview mirror. They turned a soft grayish color, like sand, before finally disappearing.

He tapped down lightly on the accelerator.

Out on the lake a man's motorboat had stalled; the man was bent over the engine with a wrench and a frown. Beyond the stalled boat there were other boats, and a few water-skiers, and the smooth July waters, and an immense flatness everywhere. Two mud hens floated stiffly beside a white dock.

The road curved west, where the sun had now dipped low. He figured it was close to five o'clock—twenty after, he guessed. The war had taught him to tell time without clocks, and even at night, waking from sleep, he could usually place it within ten minutes either way. What he should do, he thought, is stop at Sally's house and impress her with this new time-telling trick of his. They'd talk for a while, catching up on things, and then he'd say, "Well, better hit the road, it's five thirty-four," and she'd glance at her wristwatch and say, "Hey! How'd you *do* that?" and he'd give a casual shrug and tell her it was just one of those things you pick up. He'd keep it light. He wouldn't say anything about anything. "How's it being married?" he might ask, and he'd nod at whatever she answered with, and he would not say a word about how he'd almost won the Silver Star for valor.

He drove past Slater Park and across the causeway and past Sunset Park. 10 The radio announcer sounded tired. The temperature in Des Moines was eighty-one degrees, and the time was five thirty-five, and "All you on the road, drive extra careful now on this fine Fourth of July." If Sally had not been married, or if his father were not such a baseball fan, it would have been a good time to talk.

"The Silver Star?" his father might have said.

"Yes, but I didn't get it. Almost, but not quite."

And his father would have nodded, knowing full well that many brave men do not win medals for their bravery, and that others win medals for doing nothing. As a starting point, maybe, Norman Bowker might then have listed the seven medals he did win: the Combat Infantryman's Badge, the Air Medal, the Army Commendation Medal, the Good Conduct Medal, the Vietnam Campaign Medal, the Bronze Star, and the Purple Heart, though it wasn't much of a wound and did not leave a scar and did not hurt and never had. He would've explained to his father that none of these decorations was for uncommon valor. They were for common valor. The routine, daily stuff—just humping, just enduring—but that was worth something, wasn't it? Yes, it was. Worth plenty. The ribbons looked good on the uniform in his closet, and if his father were to ask, he would've explained what each signified and how he was proud of all of them, especially the Combat Infantryman's Badge, because it meant he had been there as a real soldier and had done all the things soldiers do, and therefore it wasn't such a big deal that he could not bring himself to be uncommonly brave.

And then he would have talked about the medal he did not win and why he did not win it.

"I almost won the Silver Star," he would have said.   15

"How's that?"

"Just a story."

"So tell me," his father would have said.

Slowly then, circling the lake, Norman Bowker would have started by describing the Song Tra Bong. "A river," he would've said, "this slow flat muddy river." He would've explained how during the dry season it was exactly like any other river, nothing special, but how in October the monsoons began and the whole situation changed. For a solid week the rains never stopped, not once, and so after a few days the Song Tra Bong overflowed its banks and the land turned into a deep, thick muck for a half mile on either side. Just muck—no other word for it. Like quicksand, almost, except the stink was incredible. "You couldn't even sleep," he'd tell his father. "At night you'd find a high spot, and you'd doze off, but then later you'd wake up because you'd be buried in all that slime. You'd just sink in. You'd feel it ooze up over your body and sort of suck you down. And the whole time there was that constant rain. I mean, it never stopped, not ever."

"Sounds pretty wet," his father would've said, pausing briefly. "So what   20
happened?"

"You really want to hear this?"

"Hey, I'm your *father*."

Norman Bowker smiled. He looked out across the lake and imagined the feel of his tongue against the truth. "Well, this one time, this one night out by the river . . . I wasn't very brave."

"You have seven medals."

"Sure."   25

"Seven. Count 'em. You weren't a coward either."

"Well, maybe not. But I had the chance and I blew it. The stink, that's what got to me. I couldn't take that goddamn awful *smell*."

"If you don't want to say any more—"

"I do want to."

"All right then. Slow and sweet, take your time."   30

The road descended into the outskirts of town, turning northwest past the junior college and the tennis courts, then past Chautauqua Park, where the picnic tables were spread with sheets of colored plastic and where picnickers sat in lawn chairs and listened to the high school band playing Sousa marches under the band shell. The music faded after a few blocks. He drove beneath a canopy of elms, then along a stretch of open shore, then past the municipal docks, where a woman in pedal pushers stood casting for bullheads. There were no other fish in the lake except for perch and a few worthless carp. It was a bad lake for swimming and fishing both.

He drove slowly. No hurry, nowhere to go. Inside the Chevy the air was cool and oily-smelling, and he took pleasure in the steady sounds of the engine and air-conditioning. A tour bus feeling, in a way, except the town he was touring seemed dead. Through the windows, as if in a stop-motion photograph, the place looked as if it had been hit by nerve gas, everything still and lifeless, even the people. The town could not talk, and would not listen. "How'd you like to hear about the war?" he might have asked, but the place could only blink and shrug. It had no memory, therefore no guilt. The taxes got paid and the votes got counted and the agencies of government did their work briskly and politely. It was a brisk, polite town. It did not know shit about shit, and did not care to know.

Norman Bowker leaned back and considered what he might've said on the subject. He knew shit. It was his specialty. The smell, in particular, but also the numerous varieties of texture and taste. Someday he'd give a lecture on the topic. Put on a suit and tie and stand up in front of the Kiwanis club and tell the fuckers about all the wonderful shit he knew. Pass out samples, maybe.

Smiling at this, he clamped the steering wheel slightly right of center, which produced a smooth clockwise motion against the curve of the road. The Chevy seemed to know its own way.

The sun was lower now. Five fifty-five, he decided—six o'clock, tops.

Along an unused railway spur, four workmen labored in the shadowy red heat, setting up a platform and steel launchers for the evening fireworks. They were dressed alike in khaki trousers, work shirts, visored caps, and brown boots. Their faces were dark and smudgy. "Want to hear about the Silver Star I almost won?" Norman Bowker whispered, but none of the workmen looked up. Later they would blow color into the sky. The lake would sparkle with reds and blues and greens, like a mirror, and the picnickers would make low sounds of appreciation.

"Well, see, it never stopped raining," he would've said. "The muck was everywhere, you couldn't get away from it."

He would have paused a second.

Then he would have told about the night they bivouacked in a field along the Song Tra Bong. A big swampy field beside the river. There was a ville nearby, fifty meters downstream, and right away a dozen old mama-sans ran out and started yelling. A weird scene, he would've said. The mama-sans just stood there in the rain, soaking wet, yapping away about how this field was bad news. Number ten, they said. Evil ground. Not a good spot for good GIs. Finally Lieutenant Jimmy Cross had to get out his pistol and fire off a few rounds just to shoo them away. By then it was almost dark. So they set up a perimeter, ate chow, then crawled under their ponchos and tried to settle in for the night.

But the rain kept getting worse. And by midnight the field turned into soup.

"Just this deep, oozy soup," he would've said. "Like sewage or something. Thick and mushy. You couldn't sleep. You couldn't even lie down, not for long, because you'd start to sink under the soup. Real clammy. You could feel the crud coming up inside your boots and pants."

Here, Norman Bowker would have squinted against the low sun. He would have kept his voice cool, no self-pity.

"But the worst part," he would've said quietly, "was the smell. Partly it was the river—a dead-fish smell—but it was something else, too. Finally somebody figured it out. What this was, it was a shit field. The village toilet. No indoor plumbing, right? So they used the field. I mean, we were camped in a goddamn *shit* field."

He imagined Sally Kramer closing her eyes.

If she were here with him, in the car, she would've said, "Stop it. I don't like that word."

"That's what it *was*."

"All right, but you don't have to use that word."

35

40

45

"Fine. What should we call it?"

She would have glared at him. "I don't know. Just stop it."

Clearly, he thought, this was not a story for Sally Kramer. She was Sally   50
Gustafson now. No doubt Max would've liked it, the irony in particular, but
Max had become a pure idea, which was its own irony. It was just too bad. If his
father were here, riding shotgun around the lake, the old man might have
glanced over for a second, understanding perfectly well that it was not a question of offensive language but of fact. His father would have sighed and folded
his arms and waited.

"A shit field," Norman Bowker would have said. "And later that night
I could've won the Silver Star for valor."

"Right," his father would've murmured, "I hear you."

The Chevy rolled smoothly across a viaduct and up the narrow tar road.
To the right was open lake. To the left, across the road, most of the lawns were
scorched dry like October corn. Hopelessly, round and round, a rotating sprinkler scattered lake water on Dr. Mason's vegetable garden. Already the prairie
had been baked dry, but in August it would get worse. The lake would turn
green with algae, and the golf course would burn up, and the dragonflies would
crack open for want of good water.

The big Chevy curved past Centennial Beach and the A&W root beer stand.
It was his eighth revolution around the lake.   55

He followed the road past the handsome houses with their docks and
wooden shingles. Back to Slater Park, across the causeway, around to Sunset
Park, as though riding on tracks.

The two little boys were still trudging along on their seven-mile hike.

Out on the lake, the man in the stalled motorboat still fiddled with his engine.
The pair of mud hens floated like wooden decoys, and the water-skiers looked
tanned and athletic, and the high school band was packing up its instruments, and
the woman in pedal pushers patiently rebaited her hook for one last try.

Quaint, he thought.

A hot summer day and it was all very quaint and remote. The four work-   60
men had nearly completed their preparations for the evening fireworks.

Facing the sun again, Norman Bowker decided it was nearly seven o'clock.
Not much later the tired radio announcer confirmed it, his voice rocking itself
into a deep Sunday snooze. If Max Arnold were here, he would say something
about the announcer's fatigue, and relate it to the bright pink in the sky, and the
war, and courage. A pity that Max was gone. And a pity about his father, who
had his own war and who now preferred silence.

Still, there was so much to say.

How the rain never stopped. How the cold worked into your bones. Sometimes the bravest thing on earth was to sit through the night and feel the cold
in your bones. Courage was not always a matter of yes or no. Sometimes it came
in degrees, like the cold; sometimes you were very brave up to a point and then
beyond that point you were not so brave. In certain situations you could do

incredible things, you could advance toward enemy fire, but in other situations, which were not nearly so bad, you had trouble keeping your eyes open. Sometimes, like that night in the shit field, the difference between courage and cowardice was something small and stupid.

The way the earth bubbled. And the smell.

In a soft voice, without flourishes, he would have told the exact truth.

"Late in the night," he would've said, "we took some mortar fire."

He would've explained how it was still raining, and how the clouds were pasted to the field, and how the mortar rounds seemed to come right out of the clouds. Everything was black and wet. The field just exploded. Rain and slop and shrapnel, nowhere to run, and all they could do was worm down into slime and cover up and wait. He would've described the crazy things he saw. Weird things. Like how at one point he noticed a guy lying next to him in the sludge, completely buried except for his face, and how after a moment the guy rolled his eyes and winked at him. The noise was fierce. Heavy thunder, and mortar rounds, and people yelling. Some of the men began shooting up flares. Red and green and silver flares, all colors, and the rain came down in Technicolor.

The field was boiling. The shells made deep slushy craters, opening up all those years of waste, centuries worth, and the smell came bubbling out of the earth. Two rounds hit close by. Then a third, even closer, and immediately, off to his left, he heard somebody screaming. It was Kiowa—he knew that. The sound was ragged and clotted up, but even so he knew the voice. A strange gargling noise. Rolling sideways, he crawled toward the screaming in the dark. The rain was hard and steady. Along the perimeter there were quick bursts of gunfire. Another round hit nearby, spraying up shit and water, and for a few moments he ducked down beneath the mud. He heard the valves in his heart. He heard the quick, feathering action of the hinges. Extraordinary, he thought. As he came up, a pair of red flares puffed open, a soft fuzzy glow, and in the glow he saw Kiowa's wide-open eyes settling down into the scum. Briefly, all he could do was watch. He heard himself moan. Then he moved again, crabbing forward, but when he got there Kiowa was almost completely under. There was a knee. There was an arm and a gold wristwatch and part of a boot.

He could not describe what happened next, not ever, but he would've tried anyway. He would've spoken carefully so as to make it real for anyone who would listen.

There were bubbles where Kiowa's head should've been.

The left hand was curled open; the fingernails were filthy; the wristwatch gave off a green phosphorescent shine as it slipped beneath the thick waters.

He would've talked about this, and how he grabbed Kiowa by the boot and tried to pull him out. He pulled hard but Kiowa was gone, and then suddenly he felt himself going, too. He could taste it. The shit was in his nose and eyes. There were flares and mortar rounds, and the stink was everywhere—it was inside him, in his lungs—and he could no longer tolerate it. Not here, he thought. Not like this. He released Kiowa's boot and watched it slide away.

Slowly, working his way up, he hoisted himself out of the deep mud, and then he lay still and tasted the shit in his mouth and closed his eyes and listened to the rain and explosions and bubbling sounds.

He was alone.

He had lost his weapon but it did not matter. All he wanted was a bath.

Nothing else. A hot soapy bath.   75

Circling the lake, Norman Bowker remembered how his friend Kiowa had disappeared under the waste and water.

"I didn't flip out," he would've said. "I was cool. If things had gone right, if it hadn't been for that smell, I could've won the Silver Star."

A good war story, he thought, but it was not a war for war stories, nor for talk of valor, and nobody in town wanted to know about the terrible stink. They wanted good intentions and good deeds. But the town was not to blame, really. It was a nice little town, very prosperous, with neat houses and all the sanitary conveniences.

Norman Bowker lit a cigarette and cranked open his window. Seven thirty-five, he decided.

The lake had divided into two halves. One half still glistened, the other was   80
caught in shadow. Along the causeway, the two little boys marched on. The man in the stalled motorboat yanked frantically on the cord to his engine, and the two mud hens sought supper at the bottom of the lake, tails bobbing. He passed Sunset Park once again, and more houses, and the junior college and the tennis courts, and the picnickers, who now sat waiting for the evening fireworks. The high school band was gone. The woman in pedal pushers patiently toyed with her line.

Although it was not yet dusk, the A&W was already awash in neon lights.

He maneuvered his father's Chevy into one of the parking slots, let the engine idle, and sat back. The place was doing a good holiday business. Mostly kids, it seemed, and a few farmers in for the day. He did not recognize any of the faces. A slim, hipless young carhop passed by, but when he hit the horn, she did not seem to notice. Her eyes slid sideways. She hooked a tray to the window of a Firebird, laughing lightly, leaning forward to chat with the three boys inside.

He felt invisible in the soft twilight. Straight ahead, over the take-out counter, swarms of mosquitoes electrocuted themselves against an aluminum Pest-Rid machine.

It was a calm, quiet summer evening.

He honked again, this time leaning on the horn. The young carhop turned   85
slowly, as if puzzled, then said something to the boys in the Firebird and moved reluctantly toward him. Pinned to her shirt was a badge that said EAT MAMA BURGERS.

When she reached his window, she stood straight up so that all he could see was the badge.

"Mama Burger," he said. "Maybe some fries, too."

The girl sighed, leaned down, and shook her head. Her eyes were as fluffy and airy-light as cotton candy.

"You blind?" she said.

She put out her hand and tapped an intercom attached to a steel post.   90

"Punch the button and place your order. All I do is carry the dumb trays."

She stared at him for a moment. Briefly, he thought, a question lingered in her fuzzy eyes, but then she turned and punched the button for him and returned to her friends in the Firebird.

The intercom squeaked and said, "Order."

"Mama Burger and fries," Norman Bowker said.

"Affirmative, copy clear. No rootie-tootie?"   95

"Rootie-tootie?"

"You know, man—*root* beer."

"A small one."

"Roger-dodger. Repeat: one Mama, one fries, one small beer. Fire for effect. Stand by."

The intercom squeaked and went dead.   100

"Out," said Norman Bowker.

When the girl brought his tray, he ate quickly, without looking up. The tired radio announcer in Des Moines gave the time, almost eight-thirty. Dark was pressing in tight now, and he wished there were somewhere to go. In the morning he'd check out some job possibilities. Shoot a few buckets down at the Y, maybe wash the Chevy.

He finished his root beer and pushed the intercom button.

"Order," said the tinny voice.

"All done."   105

"That's *it*?"

"I guess so."

"Hey, loosen up," the voice said. "What you really need, friend?"

Norman Bowker smiled.

"Well," he said, "how'd you like to hear about—"   110

He stopped and shook his head.

"Hear *what*, man?"

"Nothing."

"Well, hey," the intercom said, "I'm sure as fuck not *going* anywhere. Screwed to a post, for God sake. Go ahead, try me."

"Nothing."   115

"You sure?"

"Positive. All done."

The intercom made a light sound of disappointment. "Your choice, I guess. Over an' out."

"Out," said Norman Bowker.

On his tenth turn around the lake he passed the hiking boys for the last time.   120
The man in the stalled motorboat was gone; the mud hens were gone. Beyond the lake, over Sally Gustafson's house, the sun had left a smudge of purple on the horizon. The band shell was deserted, and the woman in pedal pushers quietly reeled in her line, and Dr. Mason's sprinkler went round and round.

On his eleventh revolution he switched off the air-conditioning, opened up his window, and rested his elbow comfortably on the sill, driving with one hand.

There was nothing to say.

He could not talk about it and never would. The evening was smooth and warm.

If it had been possible, which it wasn't, he would have explained how his friend Kiowa slipped away that night beneath the dark swampy field. He was folded in with the war; he was part of the waste.

Turning on his headlights, driving slowly, Norman Bowker remembered   125
how he had taken hold of Kiowa's boot and pulled hard, but how the smell was simply too much, and how he'd backed off and in that way had lost the Silver Star.

He wished he could've explained some of this. How he had been braver than he ever thought possible, but how he had not been so brave as he wanted to be. The distinction was important. Max Arnold, who loved fine lines, would've appreciated it. And his father, who already knew, would've nodded.

"The truth," Norman Bowker would've said, "is I let the guy go."

"Maybe he was already gone."

"He wasn't."

"But maybe."   130

"No, I could feel it. He wasn't. Some things you can feel."

His father would have been quiet for a while, watching the headlights against the narrow tar road.

"Well, anyway," the old man would've said, "there's still the seven medals."

"I suppose."

"Seven honeys."   135

"Right."

On his twelfth revolution, the sky went crazy with color.

He pulled into Sunset Park and stopped in the shadow of a picnic shelter. After a time he got out, walked down to the beach, and waded into the lake without undressing. The water felt warm against his skin. He put his head under. He opened his lips, very slightly, for the taste, then he stood up and folded his arms and watched the fireworks. For a small town, he decided, it was a pretty good show.

● Applying a Semiotics Frame

1. The story opens with Norman Bowker driving the "seven-mile loop around the lake." As you see it, how does this image reflect the suburban world he has returned to?

   • In how many ways can you see that world as itself a repetition of cultural patterns?

   • Why do you think Norman is unable to enter into the pattern? Why does he "circle" it?

- Why do you think he does not stop to speak to his old girlfriend Sally? How do you read his parallel sense that "Sally was married and Max was drowned," making them both "remote" from him?

- How should we read the image of the two boys walking along the road who do not look up when Norman honks as he passes them for the sixth time?

2. Another recurring image is the "Silver Star" he "almost won for valor." What are medals signs of, semiotically?

- Why do you think the Silver Star is set apart from the other medals? Would Norman's reentry into "normal" society have been different if he had won it, do you believe?

- Norman has a Purple Heart, awarded to wounded soldiers; why do you think we are told his wound was not painful and left no scar? What are the rhetorical and semiotic effects?

- What cultural myth do you see embedded in the phrase "[medals] for common valor"?

- How might you connect the cultural sign of the medals to the town's lake, good neither for fishing nor swimming, but used as a sign dividing the more from the less affluent?

- How does the image of the workers preparing the Fourth of July fireworks connect semiotically to the soldiers during the nighttime firefight, with its red, green, and silver flares?

3. Norman imagines telling Sally the story of the "shit field," which was the village toilet; her imagined response is, "Stop it. I don't like that word." Using Barthes's reading (p. 566), can you explain this as a critical semiotic moment when history is replaced by myth?

   Using the same device, Norman imagines talking to his father, but we're told the father is a man who "had his own war, and who now preferred silence." How should we read the noncommittal answers that are part of the conversation Norman fantasizes, and the role of silence between father and son in the face of war experiences?

4. We read about the Silver Star again when Norman recalls the nighttime battle scene and his friend Kiowa being shot and sinking into the waste. Would having won the medal, and being able to invoke the cultural myth attached to the medal, have helped Norman cope with the memory, do you think?

5. At the A&W hamburger stand, the exchange Norman has with the order clerk mimics military communication. How can you use Barthes's theory (p. 566) to explain Norman's outsider status in this world that makes myth out of his historical experiences?

6. Re-read the ending, in which Norman goes under the lake water fully clothed while the fireworks go off over his head. Is this scene reminiscent of an earlier one in the story? Is this Norman's attempt to empty out the historical reality of his experience? If so, how successful do you think he will be?

Dead Man Walking

SISTER HELEN PREJEAN

Published in 1993, Dead Man Walking *is Catholic nun Sister Helen Prejean's account of her experience working with convicts on death row. Her religious values and her experiences with the condemned confirm her belief that as humans we are "worth more than the worst thing we've ever done," and she argues against the right of the state to put citizens to death. In this chapter, she tells of her first encounter with Pat Sonnier, convicted along with his brother Eddie for kidnapping, rape, and murder; their victims, David LeBlanc and Loretta Bourque, were 17 and 18 at the time of their deaths. Although Eddie was likely the gunman, Pat received the death penalty and Eddie a sentence of life in prison. In the following excerpt, which is Chapter 2 of her book, Prejean details the environment in which they meet and the ways in which the daily routine and physical treatment of the condemned set Pat Sonnier off from others, rendering him "a thing waiting to be handled by the executioners," as Prejean quotes from French existential philosopher Albert Camus. After several stays, Sonnier was executed in 1984, with Prejean a witness to his death. (The phrase "dead man walking" is uttered by guards as the prisoner is led to the death chamber.)*

Pat's return letter brims with excitement and he explains that he must   1
put me on his visitor list so the prison can do a security check. I am to send my birth date and social security number. He tells me that he went back and forth in his mind about which category of visitor to put me in—friend or spiritual adviser—but he has decided on spiritual adviser. I have no idea what difference the category will make. I later learn that a spiritual adviser may remain with the condemned man in the death house after 6:00 P.M., when relatives and friends must leave. The spiritual adviser is allowed to witness the execution.

Nothing happens for months, and then I receive a letter from a Catholic priest who serves as chaplain at the prison. He says he has to interview me before I can become Pat's spiritual adviser. I drive to Angola for the interview.

It is July 1982. I set out around nine in the morning. My interview is set for the early afternoon. I have a poor sense of direction, so I have carefully written down the route to the prison, which is at the end of a circuitous road, about three hours from New Orleans.

It feels good to get out of the steamy housing project onto the open road, to see sky and towering clouds and the blue, wide waters of Lake Pontchartrain.

Highway 66, which dead-ends at the gates of the prison, snakes through   5
the Tunica hills, a refreshing change of terrain in pancake-flat Louisiana. It is cooler and greener in the hills, and some of the branches of the trees arch across the road and bathe it in shadow.

I think of the thousands of men who have been transported down this road since 1901, when this 18,000-acre prison was established. About 4,600 men are locked up here now, half of them, practically speaking, serving life sentences. "Wide-stripes," they used to call the lifers.

Louisiana deals out harsh sentences. In 1977, when the death penalty was reinstated by the state legislature, the life-imprisonment statute was reformulated, effectively eliminating probation, parole, or suspension of sentence for first- and second-degree murder. An eighteen-year-old first-time offender convicted of distributing heroin faces a life sentence without possibility of probation or parole; and the habitual-offender law, aimed at reducing "career criminals," imposes a life sentence on offenders even for nonviolent crimes.

About five miles from the prison I see a hand-painted sign nailed to a tree: "Do not despair. You will soon be there." I make a sharp S-curve in the road and see a clearing, an open sky, and the Louisiana State Penitentiary—Angola. I drive up to the front gate. Several armed, blue-uniformed guards occupy a small, glassed-in office and one of them comes to the car and I show him the letter from the chaplain. They inspect my car—trunk, glove compartment, seats—put a visitor's sign on my dashboard, and direct me to the administration building about a quarter of a mile inside the prison grounds.

There are red and yellow zinnias all along the road, and the grass is neatly trimmed. Mottled black-and-white cattle browse in a field of green. I see a column of inmates, most of them black, marching out to soybean and vegetable fields, their hoes over their shoulders. Behind and in front of the marching men, guards on horseback with rifles watch their charges. In antebellum days three cotton plantations occupied these 18,000 acres, worked by slaves from Angola in Africa. The name Angola stuck. Since its beginnings in 1901, abuse, corruption, rage, and reform have studded its history.

In 1951 eight inmates, known as the "Heel-string Gang," inaugurated the first   10
reform at Angola by slitting their Achilles tendons with razor blades rather than go to the "long line" in the fields, where they were systematically beaten or shot by guards. The *Shreveport Times* and the New Orleans *Times-Picayune* carried the heel-slashing story, and the ensuing publicity brought a gubernatorial investigative commission to the prison and the first rudimentary reforms. But as recently as 1975 it took a federal court to prod state officials to enact needed reforms of Louisiana penal institutions. Before then, at Angola, men were still being kept in the "Red Hat," a disciplinary cell block made of tiny concrete cells (including a cement bunk) with only a slit of a window near the ceiling. After prisoners were moved out, prison authorities converted the facility into a dog kennel.

I wait in the front foyer of the administration building for the chaplain. Soon he comes in from one of the offices along the side wing of the building. He is an elderly man. His face is kind. His voice seems tired. Why, he asks, do I want to become Sonnier's spiritual adviser? I say I want to visit him because he has no one else and visiting prisoners is a Christian work of mercy.

The chaplain says that "these people," I must remember, are the "scum of the earth," and that I must be very, very careful because they are all con men and will try to take advantage of me every way they can. "You can't trust them," he says emphatically. "Your job is to help this fellow save his soul by receiving the sacraments of the church before he dies," he says.

He is strictly an old-school, pre–Vatican Catholic, and he shows me a pamphlet on sexual purity and modesty of dress that he distributes to the prisoners. Later I will be the source of such stress to this man that the warden will tell me, "That old man is going to have a heart attack because of you." Later, the chaplain will try to bar me and other women from serving as spiritual advisers to death-row inmates.

But for now, on this July afternoon, we chat pleasantly. As I am leaving he urges me to wear my habit when I visit the inmates. It's the modesty thing, I think, but, no, it isn't that. "The inmates know," he says, "that the Pope has requested nuns to wear the habit, and for you to flout authority will only encourage them to do the same." Which amazes me. I have serious doubts that Angola inmates know—or care—what dress code the Pope recommends for nuns.

I have not had one of these "habit" conversations in a long while. There   15
had been much discussion when we had changed to ordinary clothes back in 1968. Seeing us dress like regular people had been upsetting for many Catholics, who said that when they saw us in our long, flowing robes, dressed like "angels," it had made them think of God.

Actually, for me, discarding the habit probably increased my life expectancy. As a student teacher my veil had caught on fire from a candle during a prayer service and I had almost gone up in smoke before my wide-eyed class. I tend to move quickly, and more than once my long black veil, flowing behind me, had caught on a door knob and stopped me dead in my tracks. The garb had covered us completely—except for face and hands—and once, when a member of my community, Sister Alice Macmurdo, was in a fabric shop she felt small tugs at her veil and turned to face an embarrassed woman who had mistaken her for a bolt of material.

But this dear old priest will not like these stories. I thank him for his time and his advice and on the drive home I take some of his wariness of prisoners to heart. I could never call inmates "scum," but I know I'm inexperienced and he's right—I do need to be on guard against being conned. Until today I have never been inside a prison, except for a brief foray into the Orleans Parish Jail in the late sixties during the days of the "singing nuns" ("*Dominique-nique, nique*"— that crowd). I could plunk out a few chords on my guitar and another Sister and I had gone once or twice to entertain the prisoners. When I suggested "If I Had a Hammer" for our opening number, the inmates sang it with great relish, and, as the song progressed, made up spirited verses of their own: "If I had a crowbar; If I had a switchblade . . ." The guards rolled their eyes.

And I think again of the sliver of fear I felt when I first saw the photo of Patrick Sonnier, the cruel slant of the eyebrows. What will he be like in person? My heart tightens. How did I get involved in this bizarre affair? Where is this going to take me?

Early in September I receive approval from prison authorities to become Elmo Patrick Sonnier's spiritual adviser. I set a date for our first visit: September 15, 1982.

Along with the letter of approval, I receive the Louisiana Department of   20
Corrections regulations for visitors. The most alarming rule is that by entering

the corrections facility, you are subject to "searches of your property, automobile, and person" including "pat-down searches, inspection by dogs, and strip searches of your body, including your body cavities."

Maybe I'm an exception since I'm a nun. But I can't be sure. I have heard ugly stories of strip searches of visitors in Georgia. But I remind myself that I have been in other scary situations. Shoot-outs in the neighborhood, for instance. I am learning to face things as they come, not stepping out ahead of grace, as one of the spiritual maxims of my community counsels.

On September 15 I drive to Angola for my first visit with Pat. The summer heat has not yet lifted, though some of the trees along the highway are looking dry and yellow. I have a thermos of coffee. I have my approval papers and a picture ID.

I arrive at the prison at about 10:00 A.M. There are mostly women guards inside the visitor center, and they seem friendly, respectful. There are several bouquets of plastic flowers on the wall, probably their warming touch. A sign on a trash can catches my attention. It says, "It will be grateful if you throw your butts in the butt can."

I show the guards my ID and letter of approval. One of the women searches my billfold (no purses are allowed) and the pockets of my suit. She does a few quick pats of my front and sides. Not bad. I breathe easier. I notice my fingertips are cold.

Death row is located in a building near the prison entrance. I walk past the guard's station and wait outside the gate of the fenced-in yard surrounding the death-row building. A woman guard in a nearby watchtower opens the gate electronically from a control switch. I hear a loud click. I walk through and the gate clangs shut behind me. There are flowers along the sidewalk leading to the building, and a small pond with ducks swimming. It looks like a quiet little park.

Inside the building I am accompanied by a guard through a series of gates down a hallway. "Woman on the tier," he yells, warning prisoners to steer clear of the hallway. Gate one, *clang*, gate two, *clang*, gate three. Metal on metal. It is all green and cement and bars. And it is stiflingly hot. Too many blocked-off spaces. No way for the air to circulate. I see a green metal door with a barred window and above it red block letters: "Death Row."

The guard is unlocking a door to my right. I am to go inside. "Wait here. They'll get your man for you," he says, then closes the door and locks me in the room.

I look around. I feel a tight band of ice around my stomach. In the room are six visiting booths the size of telephone booths constructed of heavy plywood painted stark white. A heavy mesh screen separates visitors from inmates. On the visitor side is a loud, whirring fan. There are plastic chairs stacked in a corner and several large tin cans painted red which serve as trash cans. I am the only one in the room. The place gives me the creeps.

The reality of this waiting place for death is difficult to grasp. It's not a ward in a hospital where sick people wait to die. People here wait to be taken out of their cells and killed. This is the United States of America and these are government officials in charge and there's a law sanctioning and upholding what is going on here, so it all must be legitimate and just, or so one compartment of my brain tells me, the part that studied civics in high school, the part that wants to trust that my country would never violate the human rights of its citizens.

The red block letters say "Death Row."   30

My stomach can read the letters better than my brain.

I pace slowly back and forth in the room and keep trying to take deep breaths, to settle down. I am allowed two hours for my visit. That seems like a very long time. I'm doubly tense. One, I am locked behind four—I count them—doors in this strange, unreal place. Two, I'm about to meet and talk to someone who killed two people. Letters are one thing, but just the two of us like this talking for two hours?

I hear him before I see him. I can hear the rattle of chains on his legs scraping across the floor and I can hear his voice. He is laughing and teasing the guard. I detect a Cajun accent.

"Hi, Pat, I made it," I say.

"Am I glad to see *you*, Sister," he says.   35

He is freshly shaven and his black hair is combed into a wave in the front. A handsome face, open, smiling. Not the face I had seen in the photo. He has on a clean blue denim shirt and jeans. His hands are cuffed to a wide brown leather belt at his waist. He has brought me a gift: a picture frame made out of intricately folded cigarette packages. "I made it for you," he says, and he explains that the biggest challenge had been collecting enough of the wrappers from the others on the tier. He is bright and talkative and tells me of some recent letters from college students whom I have referred to him.

"I was always a loner growing up. I've never had so many friends," he says, and he tells in detail what each pen pal has said and how he has responded. He keeps a checklist: "letters received—letters answered" and the date next to each.

He smokes one cigarette after another and he has to lean his head far down to reach the cigarette because his hands are cuffed to the belt. He is obviously very happy to have someone to talk to. Contact with someone in the outside world goes a long way in this place, where, as I soon learn, mail is rare and visits rarer.

As we talk I find myself looking at his hands—clean, shapely hands, moving expressively despite the handcuffs as he talks. These hands that made the nice picture frame for me also held a rifle that killed. The fingernails are bitten down to the quick.

He tells again of receiving the first letter from me and how the name Helen   40
had made him think at first it was from his ex–"old lady," and he wanted to have nothing to do with her because she was the one who had told the sheriff where to find him, warning that he was dangerous and heavily armed, and the scowl is there and he stares past me as he talks. He can't believe his good fortune, he says, that I have come into his life out of the blue like this, and he thanks me profusely for making the long drive to come and see him.

The way he was teasing the guard and the way he thanks me and is talking to me now—I can tell he likes to please people.

He hasn't done well with women, he admits—lived with several but always "busted up." He has a little girl, Star, eleven years old, but she is with foster parents and her mother is in Texas and he says that his child was born when he was serving time in Angola for stealing a truck, and the first time he laid eyes on her was the day he got out of prison because he went right to where his "first old lady" was living and there was the child, playing in the front yard, and he had swooped her into his arms and said, "I'm your daddy," and her mother had appeared at the front door with a shotgun because she thought someone was trying to kidnap the child and he had called out to her, "It's me. I'm back. I want to see my kid." But the first thing he had done when he stepped out of the gates at Angola was to get a case of beer, and by the time the Greyhound bus had pulled into St. Martinville he was pretty "tanked" and he and the woman had "gotten into it" that night and he smashed up some furniture and she threw him out and he had gone to his mother's.

He never has been one to share his feelings, he says, because when he was a kid growing up his mother and father used to fight a lot and they separated when he was six and his sister was three and Eddie was just a baby. His mother went on welfare because his daddy never did come through with child support and the welfare check would run out and they'd be hungry and he and Eddie would hunt deer and rabbit. He chuckles remembering how his mother would help them with the rabbit hunt and it was always her job to put the dead rabbits in a sack and to "finish them off" with a stick if they weren't dead yet. "And we'd be stalking along and behind us we'd hear *whack, whack, whack*—Mama beating the hell out of those rabbits."

I cringe, but he tells the incident nonchalantly. I am thinking of the clobbered rabbits. He is thinking of the food.

Once, he says, he and Eddie couldn't find a deer so they shot a neighbor's 45 cow and skinned it and brought it home. "Mama knew this was no more a deer than the man in the moon, but she didn't say nothing 'cause we were all so hungry. She fixed us up a good roast that night and you could smell it cooking all through the house."

They often hunted at night. "Isn't it against the law to hunt at night?" I ask. "Yeah," he says, "but we didn't worry about that."

As kids they moved from mother to father and back again, he says, and by the time he was fourteen he had changed schools seven or eight times. He got only as far as eighth grade, dropped out when he was fifteen, forged his mother's signature on an application form, and went to work as a roustabout on the oil rigs. Later, he got his license and drove eighteen-wheelers and he had liked that best. From the age of nine, he says, he was on probation with juvenile authorities for burglaries, disturbing the peace, trespassing. "Mama couldn't do anything with me and she'd have Daddy come get me out of trouble."

His daddy was a sharecropper and one of the best things he got from him, he says, is his love of work. At the age of seven he picked cotton, potatoes, and peppers alongside his father, and as he got older, when it was harvesting time for the sugar cane, "there I'd be walking to school and see those open fields and I'd drop my books on the side of the road and head out into the fields." He hopes that maybe some day he can "hand back the chair" and work in the fields here, driving one of the tractors.

He stands up and I try to adjust my view of him because it is hard to see through the heavy mesh screen and he tells me to look down sometimes. "This screen can really do a number on your eyes."

He talks and talks and talks, and I am easing up inside because I was   50 wondering how much I'd have to keep the conversation going, and now I can see that all I have to do is listen.

"Daddy took me to a bar when I was twelve and told me to pick my whiskey and there were all these bottles behind the bar and I pointed and said I'd take the one with the pretty turkey on it and the guys in the bar laughed and Daddy laughed too." He laughs. "We got drunk as a couple of coots and there we were at one in the morning trying to make it home on our bicycles, weaving and hitting every garbage can along the road."

He has feelings for his father, I can tell by the way he speaks of him, and he says that when he and his cousin, Robert, had been arrested for stealing a truck (the plan was to run away to Texas and start a new life) Robert's father had come to the jail to talk to the authorities and had gotten his boy off, but by then his own father was dead—cancer of the liver—and so Pat served time in Angola. "But you can bet your bottom dollar that if Daddy had been living, he'd been there to get me out," he says.

The guard announces that visiting time is over.

I rise to leave. I thank him for the picture frame and promise to come back in a month, and again he thanks me for making the long drive. "Be careful on that highway," he says. "People drive crazy."

I have a roaring headache when I emerge from the prison, and I take two   55 Bufferins before I begin the drive back. Pure tension. I have never been in such a strange place in my life. When I get home, I promise myself, I'm going to take a bath to wash the place off me.

Freedom. How blessed it is to be outside the bars, and the windows are down in the car and the road is open before me and I take deep gulps of the fresh, good air. I wonder how I would bear up day after day, month after month in such a tiny cell.

I notice—the omission is glaring—that Pat said nothing about the crime. Maybe he's blocked it out or feels no remorse for what he did. Or maybe he just can't talk about the worst thing he ever did in his life to someone he meets for the first time. I have no right to demand that he confess to me his terrible sin. That kind of revelation demands trust and should be freely offered. I respect that.

His words drift back: what he said about his ex-wife turning him in to the police and his getting drunk and smashing furniture and her warning the sheriff that he was dangerous. If I had lived in St. Martinville I probably would have been terrified to meet him on the streets.

But I am not meeting him on the streets. I am meeting him in a crucible, and I am surprised by how human, even likable, he is. Despite his friendly letters I had half expected Charles Manson—brutish, self-absorbed, paranoid, incapable of normal human encounter.

But even if he were unlikable and repulsive, even if he were Manson, I still 60 maintain that the state should not kill him. For me, the unnegotiable moral bedrock on which a society must be built is that killing by anyone, under any conditions, cannot be tolerated. And that includes the government.

Ten years have passed since I first met Patrick Sonnier. Over the years I have clarified my perspective. Back in 1982 I was an exuberant activist, having just joined the fray against social injustice, and I see now that I devoted my energies exclusively to Pat Sonnier's plight when I should have shouldered the struggles of victims' families as well. I should have reached out to the Bourques and LeBlancs immediately and offered them love and comfort, even if they chose to reject it. Now, as I befriend each new man on death row, I always offer my help to his victim's family. Some accept my offer. Most angrily reject it. But I offer.

I also realize how naive I was about the criminal justice system. I had always known, of course, that there were imperfections in the system, but I honestly thought that when a person faced death, he or she would at least be given adequate legal defense. I thought the Constitution promised that. It took me longer than it should have to realize the shamefully inadequate legal counsel that Pat Sonnier and others like him get. By the time I sought remedial legal help for him it was too late. If I had acted sooner, I believe he would be alive today— imprisoned at Angola where he should be, but alive.

"The truth arrives disguised; therein the sorrow lies." So wrote Jimmy Glass, executed by the state of Louisiana in 1987.

Pat Sonnier and I continue to write, and every month I visit. He talks to me often about Eddie. The prison doesn't allow the brothers to visit each other, and I figure that since I'm making the long trip to the prison I can visit two people instead of one. Eddie keeps receiving disciplinary write-ups, which land him in the "hole," a stripped-down disciplinary cell with no TV or radio, nothing to read except the Bible, minimal writing materials.

"He's got to learn to control his temper in this place. He blows up too easy," 65 Pat says. "That'll get you killed here, you can't afford to have enemies, but he just won't learn, and I can't be there to calm him down the way I used to on the streets."

Since his arrival on death row three years ago, Pat has never received a disciplinary write-up. No small feat in such a confined space where tensions run high, not only between inmates and guards, but among inmates as well.

"You have to learn each 'free man' [guard]," he says. "You learn which ones you can tease and which ones you can't and which ones blow hot one day and cold the next."

Pat has written to Eddie about me, preparing the way for my first visit. "She's a nun, but she talks natural and doesn't quote the Bible all the time."

In March of 1983 I visit Eddie for the first time. He reminds me of a caged panther. He is thin, tight, his eyes narrow slits. His hands tremble. He makes me feel tense, wary. I feel afraid of him and sorry for him at the same time. Clearly he's a tortured man.

He's on a lock-down tier, not yet in a "big yard," where inmates sleep in a   70
sixty-man dormitory, eat in a cafeteria, and have access to a recreation room.
He shares a cell with one other person and he stays in this cell at all times except
when he works in the fields. Meals are served in the cell. This is the normal
track when inmates first come to Angola. Prison authorities keep a man in the
fields until he "adjusts."

"Adjusting" does not come easily to Eddie Sonnier. Later, when I know
him well, I will ask him why he got all those write-ups and he will answer with
a wry smile, "Because I didn't have no understandin'."

A stack of Eddie's disciplinary reports will be among Pat's personal possessions, shipped to me by prison authorities after his execution.

The visiting room in the main prison where I visit Eddie is much more
agreeable than the death-row visiting room. The room is spacious and air-
conditioned. You can have a private conversation at a small table at the far end
of the large room. You can touch. You can get a hot dog or hamburger and a
cold drink at one of the concession stands run by inmate clubs. You can get
a Polaroid picture taken. You can get an ice-cream cone.

But the visiting room does not give Eddie much consolation. First of all,
because he doesn't see much of it. I am his first visitor. Prison is torture for him. He
hates waiting while guards do the "count." He tells me how every inmate at every
minute of the day has to be accounted for. Before going to work you wait for the
count. After work you wait for the count. Before eating, before you go to sleep,
when you first wake up at 5 A.M. He hates being thrown side by side with "all kinds
of people." On the streets he had kept to himself, avoided crowds. He is afraid in
"this place." You never know, he says, when someone might "lose it" and stab you
with a radio antenna or a blade someone's buddy made for him in the welding
shop. He's already been sent to the "hole" because someone with a grievance had
put contraband under his mattress. He had protested his innocence but to no avail.
"You got no defense in this place." And he says it's okay with him if they keep him
on a lock-down tier forever "because you only have to deal with one cellmate, but
in the dorms, if you have enemies, they can follow you when you go to the bathroom at two or three in the morning and beat you up or stab you or rape you and if
the free man on duty isn't quick to intervene, you're dead meat, you're history."

Periodically, inmates are strip-searched. Eddie points to the door in the vis-   75
iting room through which inmates return to the prison. Behind that door is a
room and a guard. After a visit the inmate removes all of his clothes. He opens
his mouth and sticks out his tongue. He turns his head from side to side so the
guard can check his ears. He raises his arms above his head and stands spread-
eagled, then he turns his back to the guard, bends over, and opens the cheeks of
his buttocks. Finally, his back still toward the guard, he raises his feet one at a
time for the guard to inspect the soles of his feet, his toes. If a guard suspects
drugs he may do a "finger wave" of the inmate's rectum.

I shudder to think of myself in this type of situation, and I remember reading
Dorothy Day's account of her experience in jail for civil disobedience. She told

how the woman who conducted her physical exam had been "brutal" and how shocking it was to hear other women inmates shouting vulgar invitations to her and her young companions as they were led down the tier to their cells.

I can't imagine.

Sometime in July 1983, I receive a phone call from Pat. That morning a guard had entered the tier, stopped in front of his cell, and handed him a paper to read and sign. The paper was entitled "Warrant of Execution in Capital Case," and he had found himself reading his own name after the words "the condemned person to be put to death," and the date of his death, "the 19th day of August, 1983."

His voice cracks. "This is my second date," he tells me, and I remember that Chava had mentioned his receiving an execution date shortly after his arrival at Angola.

On my fingers as I talk to him I count the days. How many Fridays left? Thursdays? Sundays? 80

"I'll be moving to Cell 1 any time now," he tells me. An inmate on "countdown" for execution is put in the cell nearest the guard station. That way the guards, trained to spot desperate behavior—suicide, escape—can look in on him and make notes in a log book on how he is bearing up. Tranquilizing medication is offered to the inmate if he desires it. Pat refuses medication.

I step up the visits and begin seeing Pat once a week. I write to him more often and tell his other pen pals about the execution date so they can write to him also. A week or so after the delivery of the death warrant he tells me that a couple of guards had appeared unannounced at his cell one morning. They had shackled his hands and feet and taken him to a scale. "What's this for?" he asked. "Y'all starting a Weight Watchers program around here?" But the guards had not answered and did not smile. One guard recorded his weight while another measured his height. Then the guards returned him to his cell.

"What was that all about?" I ask.

"They wouldn't say," he answers. "Some of the guys on the Row say they're measuring us for our coffins."

Later, Warden Frank Blackburn will explain to me that a guard, matching 85 the inmate's height and weight, does a dry run from the cell to the chair to make sure the "Tactical Team" can "contain" the condemned prisoner should he put up a fight. "Some of these guys are pretty big and strong," he explains. "Once the guards get the inmate in the chair, they use the leather straps on the chair to hold him, then remove the leg irons and handcuffs."

Albert Camus:

Long in advance the condemned man knows that he is going to be killed and that the only thing that can save him is a reprieve . . . In any case, he cannot intervene, make a plea outside himself, or convince. Everything goes on outside him. He is no longer a man but a thing waiting to be handled by the executioners . . . This explains the odd submissiveness that is customary in the condemned at the moment of their execution.

● Applying a Semiotics Frame

1. What differing cultural scripts do you see at play in Sister Helen Prejean's interview with the Catholic priest who serves as the prison's chaplain?

   - Do you see gender myths involved?
   - Both Prejean and the priest are Catholic; how can you account for their conflicting views on Sonnier?
   - What forms of authority can you identify being deployed during her first visit?

2. In addition to serving the interests of prison security, the search policies Prejean encounters define her relationship to the prison system as well. How do you see the process affecting her, in terms of her autonomy, her relationship to the state, her own sense of self?

3. Reread the description of the physical location of death row within the prison and the interior visiting area. Using Jack Solomon's semiotic steps (p. 557), try "reading" the cultural meanings attaching to the "quiet little park" setting and the interior "waiting place for death."

4. Prejean relates the details of Pat Sonnier's background. What is the rhetorical effect of his story?

   - Do you think the details are intended to elicit pathos?
   - How does the account of his life connect to Prejean's larger argument that the individual is "worth more than the worst thing he has done"?
   - Why do you think Prejean wants to take a bath after the first visit? What cultural myths might lead to such a need?

5. What do you think might be some cultural reasons for the differences between the visiting rooms in death row and the regular prison?

   Consider the line at the end of the reading from Camus describing condemned prisoners as "thing[s] waiting to be handled by the executioners." Do you see differences in how the inmates in the two areas are treated? How would you articulate the cultural signs attached to the bodies of the regular prison inmates, given the details of daily life as Sonnier's brother Eddie relates them?

6. Do you see ways in which Prejean's argument could be supported from other critical perspectives you can apply?

   - Freud held a very dark view of inherent human aggression, but he also asserted the role of Eros in the human community. How might some of Freud's theories be used to support Prejean's view that the individual should not be reduced to the worst act he is capable of committing?
   - In the same way, consider whether a materialist view would be useful in supporting Prejean's argument. What ideological scripts may have helped the state complete the order of execution? How might socioeconomic class have influenced the outcome?

- Can Sonnier be seen as a kind of colonized subject, reading from a postcolonial perspective? Is he "owned" by the state, in a system that defines him as lesser? How would such a view account for his crimes?

topics for writing

1. One of the purposes of a semiotic analysis is to make clear the often hidden code of power relations. Choose two of the readings in Part Five that depict unequal social relations. Analyze how the less powerful person perceives her or his role:
   - What are the semiotic signs of unequal relations?
   - How aware is the person of the power relations that tie her or him to some more powerful person or entity? How aware is the more powerful party?
   - Is the individual made to accept or even see positively her or his position of dependence or lesser authority?
   - Does the individual seek any means of resistance?

   Your analysis should result in an argument about the ways in which we are assigned social roles of greater and lesser authority with or without explicit statements regarding our "place." Consider Norman Bowker in his hometown (p. 581); Sister Helen Prejean or Pat Sonnier in the prison system (p. 592).

2. If we consider the myth of success commonly held in our culture, the figure in the part readings who comes closest to embodying it may be Anthony Robbins (p. 576)—the rich, self-made man, a version of the myth of success that is still a dominant one. Think of other contemporary figures who embody this myth (Donald Trump, for example, or Oprah Winfrey, or various celebrities and athletes).
   - What are the common signs used to indicate this version of success?
   - What role do the media play in promoting the myth as a positive and "true" story?
   - What cultural values are being promoted, and in whose interest?
   - What realities are suppressed or ignored?

3. Choose an individual who represents a local campus myth or code and analyze this figure semiotically. Think about how this cultural sign has affected you—how it helped attract you to the institution, how it influences your academic and social decisions, and/or how you support or resist the cultural myth that this figure represents.
   - What "story" about the institution does he or she represent?
   - What are the signs of his or her status?
   - In whose interest is the myth perpetuated?
   - What is the intended effect on you?
   - Are there consequences to questioning the myth?

Reading Critically
About Visual Signs

- Reading form and image
  semiotically
- Reading visual texts
- Writing with mixed media

Cultural Texts: A Syllabus

The syllabus is one of the most common and familiar genres in academic discourse. Its elements typically include a description of course content and requirements; a schedule of course work; instructor contact information; course policies; exam dates. But, like any genre, it has a social function as well beyond its informational details. A syllabus is written by an instructor for students (among other audiences). It thus invokes a construct, or model, of students, as the instructor imagines them, consciously or not. Read the following syllabus for the assumptions it makes about students: how they are to behave, to interact with the instructor and other students—how they are semiotically defined into existence by the elements of the syllabus itself. We have reprinted the syllabus in substantially original form.

Comparative Immigration

1. Course Description

This course surveys and *compares* the immigration of Europeans, Asians, and Latin Americans to the United States since the late nineteenth century. To a large extent, this comparison focuses on European immigration of the period 1880–1920 in comparison with the Mexican, Central American, Middle Eastern, and Asian immigration since 1965, hoping thereby to command the major issues. However, the course also offers some comparative coverage of current immigration to Europe as well. The purpose of this course is to provide a factually grounded survey of immigration experience of ethno-racial groups that migrated voluntarily to this country with some comparison to contemporary immigration to Europe. The criterion of voluntary migration distinguishes whites, Asians, and Latin Americans from African Americans, whose "immigration" was involuntary. However, the course will pay some attention to the relationship of African Americans to various immigrant groups.

This course deals with immigration and with immigration's immediate consequences. It contrasts and compares cultural backgrounds, the context and causes of migration, the migration process, immediate settlement issues, and immigrant generation conflict and accommodation with American society. However, it does not deal with assimilation issues among the descendants of immigrants. We try to balance discussions of the historic past and the present, avoiding narrowly technical discussions of legislative details or research methodology while sketching the causes and immediate consequences of the migrations treated. We also try to balance treatments of Europeans, Asians, Middle Easterners, Mexicans, and Central Americans so that the course contains exposure to each region's emigrants.

2. Administrative Details

Instructor:	XXX, Professor of Sociology
Mailing Address:	*Department of Sociology*
Office Hours	Thursdays 10:30 a.m. to 12:30 p.m.
Telephone:	xxx-xxx-xxxx
Email	x@x.edu
Instructor's Office:	xxx
Class Meetings:	Tues & Thurs. 2:00 to 3:15 p.m.
Classroom:	xxx 000
Teaching Assistant:	XXXX

3. Required Reading

You are not required to *buy* any reading. You are only required to read it. All reading is on reserve in the library. You can read it there without having to purchase it. Starred (*) books are also for sale in the bookstore. Doublestarred (**) works are included in the reader. Students can buy books online from www.amazon.com or www.barnesandnoble.com. These companies will deliver books ordered in three days to you by mail.

1. **Immigrants in the USA, 1880–1924**

   ***"Revisiting the New Immigration, 1880–1920: Documents and Commentary"* (in reader).

   *John Bodnar. 1985. *The Transplanted*. Bloomington: Indiana University. Chs 1–8. Bookstore.

2. **Current American Migration**

   *Roger Waldinger and Mehdi Bozorgmehr, eds., *Ethnic Los Angeles*. Cornell University. Chs 5, 9–12

   *Ueda, Reed. *Postwar Immigrant America*. Boston: Bedford Books, 1994. Chs. 1–6. Bookstore.

   *Alejandro Portes and Reuben Rumbaut. *Immigrant America, 2d edition*. Los Angeles: Univ. of California, 1990. Chs 1–7. Bookstore.

3. Migration to Other Countries

*Stephen Castles and Mark J. Miller, *The Age of Migration*, rev. ed. NY: Guilford, 1998. Chs. 3, 4, 5, 6, 10. Bookstore.

4. Sequence of Reading/Discussion by Week

Lecture Meeting

09-26 Instructor's Introduction

Pt I Immigration to the USA, 1880–1924

10-01 Ueda's Introduction; Bodnar, 1–2

10-03 Bodnar, 3–4

10-08 Bodnar, 5

10-10 Bodnar, 6

Pt II Current Immigration to the USA

10-15 Ueda, 1–3

10-17 TBA Video

10-22 Ueda, 4–6

10-24 Waldinger, ed., 9 & 10

10-29 Waldinger, ch 11

10-31 Waldinger, 12

11-05 Midterm Examination: Pt 1 only

Pt III Acculturation and Assimilation

11-07 Waldinger, 5

11-12 Portes and Rumbaut, 2

11-14 P&R, 3

11-19 P&R, 4

11-21 P&R, 5

11-26 P&R, 6–7

11-28 Thanksgiving Holiday

Pt IV Immigration to Other Countries

12-03 Castles and Miller, 3–4

12-05 C&M, 5–6

12-12 Final Examination: 11:30 a.m.–2:30 p.m.

Section Meetings and Assignments

Week Beginning	Assignments
09-23	No section meetings
09-30	Reader, 2–46

10-07	Reader, 47–86
10-14	Ueda, ch 1, 2
10-21	Census overview
10-28	Waldinger, chs 5, 9, 10
11-04	Waldinger, chs 11, 12
11-11	P&R, 2–4
11-18	P&R, 5–7
11-25	Ueda, 3–6
12-02	C&M

5. Grading

Instructor awards final letter grade on the basis of total points earned on the scale below. There are 10 extra-credit points available. No one need fail.

Students write a final examination based on the required reading and lectures. They also complete an external written assignment with the option of either (a) a book review or (b) a life history.

A+ 95+
A 92.5–94.4 points
A– 90–92.4
B+ 88–89.4
B 83–87.4
B– 80–82.4
C+ 78–79.4
C 73–77.4 P/NP grade requires C for P
C– 65–72.4
D 60–64.4
F Less than 60

	Book Review Option	**Life History Option**
Final Examination	60	60
Midterm examination	20	20
Book Review	20	0
Life History	0	20
1 Extra Credit Book Report	10	10
Total	110 max	110 max

6. Writing Assignment Options

A. Book Review Option

Students must complete a written assignment of up to 10 typewritten pages. They have a choice of how to complete the assignment. They may *either* write a book review *or* they can write up an immigrant's life history from a personally conducted interview, following the course format in their write-up.

Please follow this format for the required reviews as well as for the extra credit reviews. Papers should be double-spaced, typewritten, and submitted on 8.5 × 11-inch white paper. Number pages. None should exceed 12 pages including title page and list of references. All students should keep copies of their papers on disk. Label each section:

1. *Title page* should contain your name and the title, plus bibliographical details (author's name, title of book, publisher, place of publication, date of publication, and date of first publication if different) of what you are reviewing. You do not need to footnote references to course texts.

2. *Description of contents* explains the book's orienting problem, its methods, data, and research design. The orienting problem is the big question at issue, which the book seeks to answer. Try to define in your own mind what that big question is. This task requires you to synthesize. Methods, data, and research design refer to the manner by which authors obtained the information necessary to reach their conclusions. Sometimes methods, data, and design are not clear in the text, and you have to characterize them on your own. In such cases, just explain how authors know about their subject if, in fact, they do know anything about it. Sad but true, authors sometimes don't know enough about their subject. The instructor wants you to ask how the author knows what he or she claims to know, and to evaluate the likelihood that the author's information is correct. This section should be 2–4 pages long.

3. *Analysis.* This is the main section. It describes the author's results and compares these results with what you learned in class and from prior readings about the same or similar problems. This is the most important part of your review. Example: does the book you reviewed say something different than anything you read or heard in class? If so, was the lecture/text book/section wrong? If not, does your book amplify or expand the aforesaid without contradicting same? If so, how (4–6 pages long)? The instructor wants you to relate the contents of the book you read to the general course content, and to explain what you learned there that you did not already know or know so well from other reading.

4. *Evaluation.* Is this book/set convincing or unconvincing? Is it important or trivial? Does it represent a worthwhile contribution to your knowledge (1–2 pages long)? The instructor wants you to reach a conclusion

about how good a book this was. You are not required to like the book you evaluate, but you are asked to have thoughtful reasons for rejecting or praising it.

B. Life History Option

Instead of a book review, students find and interview an immigrant who is at least 31 years of age. Interview should last at least two hours. Then they write up that immigrant's life history following the 3 section guidelines below. Students have the responsibility for finding a qualifying immigrant who is willing to be interviewed; instructor does not provide an interviewee.

1. The interviewee must have entered the United States as an adult, e.g., must have been 21 years of age or older when he or she entered the USA for the first time. Additionally, interviewees must have resided in the USA for at least ten years at the time of the interview. Therefore, the immigrant must be at least 31 years of age. The intent here is to guarantee that interviewees have an adult perspective on their experience and enough experience in this country to have a story to tell.

2. The interviewee should be of a different race *or* ethnicity *or* gender (any one is enough) from the student interviewer. Reason: objectivity. Student interviewers will identify overmuch with people too much like them; and they will lose their objectivity.

3. Interview reports must follow these guidelines. Papers should not exceed 12 pages, including section 1. Number your pages. Include all sections below.

   Section 1: One page. Contains: the full name of your interviewee, his/her age, date of immigration, country of origin, and the date(s) when you interviewed that person, interviewee's telephone number. —

   Section 2: 5–6 pages. Interviewee's Life History. What the interviewee told you about (a) his/her overseas household's reasons for emigration, and how they made the decision to emigrate; (b) how the international travel was arranged for the interviewee and others of his/her household; (c) initial settlement experience in the USA including occupations, residences, community, and hardships; (d) interviewee's current socioeconomic status in the USA compared to status in country of origin; (e) interviewee's current satisfaction with her/his decision to come to the United States.

   Section 3: 4–5 pages. Analysis. This is the hardest section. You should analyze the life history in terms of the sociology of immigration, pointing out any points of compatibility and incompatibility between what you learned from course lectures and texts and what this person's life history taught you. The idea is to see your immigrant's story in the context of theoretical knowledge about immigration, not just as someone's idiosyncratic story. Anyone can do the latter; it takes training to do the former.

C. Extra Credit Book Report

Regardless of which one chosen above, interview or book review, any student can earn up to 10 points extra credit by reviewing a book from the accredited list below. If you have already done one book report, this will be your second. If you selected the Life History option, this review will be your first. Follow the format indicated in section A above.

7. List of Books for Review

This is a list of approved books for review and extra credit. If you have a book you would prefer to review it may be OK. You are at liberty to introduce books of your own choice and preference here, but they must first be approved by the instructor or TA. Please obtain written permission from either, and submit same with your book review.

Stalker, Peter. 2000. *Workers Without Frontiers: The Impact of Globalization on International Migration*. Boulder: Lynne Rienner. A neo-classical economist addresses contemporary world migration. Reading this book will considerably expand and enhance your understanding of migration outside the United States, materials covered in our course by C&M.

Higham. John. 1988. *Strangers in the Land: Patterns of American Nativism, 1860–1925*. 2d edition. New Brunswick: Rutgers University. An exceptionally fine book: The definitive history of anti-immigrant movement and ideology up to 1925.

Peter Brimelow. *Alien Nation*. This is a suggested book just because, although polemical, it is timely and controversial. It makes a vigorous political case against immigration, and it attracted much debate. Reading Brimelow, and dealing with his arguments, will certainly sharpen your views, pro or conimmigration. Popular bookstores carry this book.

Jeffrey G. Reitz. *Warmth of the Welcome: The Social Causes of economic Success for Immigrants in Different Nations and Cities*. Boulder: Westview. 1998. Compares Australia, Canada, and the USA.

Barbara Jordan, Chair. US Immigration Policy: Restoring Credibility. Washington, DC: US Commission on Immigration Reform.

Edna Bonacich and Richard P. Appelbaum. 2000. Behind the Label: Inequality in the Los Angeles Apparel Industry. Los Angeles: University of California.

John F. Kennedy. *A Nation of Immigrants*. Any edition. President Kennedy's ghost-written book promoted a liberal and compassionate immigration policy.

Susan Baker. 1990. *The Cautious Welcome: The Legalization Programs of the Immigration Reform and Control Act*. Santa Monica: RAND Corporation.

Eliz. Rolph and Abby Robyn. 1990. A Window on Immigration Reform: Implementing the Immigration Reform and Control Act in Los Angeles. Santa Monica: RAND Corp.

Unauthorized Migration. Report of the Commission for the Study of International Migration and Cooperative Economic Development. 1990.

Leslie Page Moch. *Moving Europeans*. Bloomington: Indiana University Press. 1993.

John Bodnar, et al. Lives of their Own: Blacks, Italians, and Poles in Pittsburgh, 1900–1960.

Peter Gottlieb. Making Their Own Way. 1987.

Leonard Covello. The Social Background of the Italo-American School Child. Leiden, Brill. 1967.

Philip Kasinitz. Caribbean New Yorkers. Cornell University Press. 1991.

Guillermina Jasso and Mark Rosenzweig. The New Chosen People: Immigrants in the United States. 1990.

Roger Waldinger. Through the Eye of the Needle. New York University.

Stanley Lieberson. *A Piece of the Pie: Blacks and White Immigrants*. Berkeley and Los Angeles: University of California Press, 1980. Rest of book.

Jan Lucassen and Rinus Penninx. *Newcomers: Immigrants and their Descendants in the Netherlands, 1550–1995*. Amsterdam: Het Spinhuis. 1997.

Camarota, Steven A. 1999. "Importing Poverty: Immigration's Impact on the Size and Growth of the Poor Population in the United States." [www.cis .org/povstudy/] You will have to download from the Web.

Ivan Light and Edna Bonacich. *Immigrant Entrepreneurs: Koreans in Los Angeles, 1965–1982*. Berkeley & Los Angeles: Univ. of California, 1988.

Ivan Light and Steven Gold. Ethnic Economies. (San Diego: Academic Press, 2000). Stresses economic integration of immigrants and native minorities.

Douglas Massey, et al. *Return to Aztlan* (Berkeley and Los Angeles: University of California, 1987). Rest of book.

Ewa Morawska. *For Bread with Butter* (New York: Columbia University, 1987). Rest of book.

Thomas Kessner. *The Promised City*. New York: Oxford University Press, 1978.

David Ward. *Poverty, ethnicity, and the American city, 1840–1925*. Cambridge: Cambridge University Press, 1987, Chapter 5.

Min Zhou. *Chinatown: The Socioeconomic Potential of an Ethnic Enclave*. Philadelphia: Temple University Press. 1991, Chapter 7.

John Bodnar, Roger Simon, and Michael Weber. *Lives of Their Own*. Urbana and Chicago: University of Illinois Press, 1982.

Pyong-Gap Min. *Caught in the Middle: Korean Communities in New York and Los Angeles*. Los Angeles: University of California, 1996.

Alejandro Portes and Robert Bach. *Latin Journey: Cuban and Mexican Immigrants* (Berkeley and Los Angeles: University of California. 1985)

Leslie Page Moch. *Moving Europeans: Migration in Western Europe since 1650*. Bloomington: Indiana University Press. 1992.

Saskia Sassen, *Guest and Aliens*. New York: New Press. 1999 Macro-level review of American and world immigration since 1970.

Peggy Levitt. *Transnational Villagers*. Los Angeles: University of California. 2001. Dominicans in contemporary New York. This book won second place in the Znaniescki-Thomas book award competition, 2002.

Alejandro Portes and Ruben Rumbaut. *Legacies*. University of California, 2001. This book won first prize in the 2002 T-Z book contest.

8. Classroom Good Manners

Please observe the following decorum for everyone's comfort:

Shoes and shirts are required attire.

No pets, except seeing-eye dogs.

No smoking, drinking, sleeping, or eating during class.

If you must leave early, please sit near the door to minimize distraction.

Please fill in the front rows when empty.

No disruptive infants are permitted.

● Applying a Semiotics Frame

1. What image of the student emerges from references to students in the syllabus? When does the first reference to students appear, and in what connection? What assumptions are made about their material conditions, motivations, personal backgrounds, manners?

2. Are students the audience for this text? Consider the shifting voice—direct address in some places ("you"), and third-person references in others ("they"). How does the instructor's voice shape the instructor–student relationship?

3. Analyze the rhetorical effect of the syllabus—its major elements, organizational categories, the sequencing of these, and so on. How do the rhetorical choices form a kind of cultural narrative about education—about what's important, how we learn, where knowledge comes from?

Cultural Texts: A Brochure

A brochure, like any advertisement, is a marketing device that sells an image and lifestyle along with the activities it promises. What are the different myths that the brochure that appears on the following pages depends on, and how do the verbal and visual elements evoke these cultural narratives? To what sort of audience is the brochure pitched, and what is the connection between the myths and the intended audience? Applying the steps in semiotic analysis to the advertisements that bombard in all media can help make us critically aware of the cultural beliefs we endorse through our consumer behavior.

● Applying a Semiotics Frame

1. Read the gun range brochure—the print, the visuals, and the document design,
    - What is the story or "myth" the brochure constructs about the purposes of the shooting range?
    - Who is pictured? How does this selection add to or change the cultural narratives presented verbally?
    - How are competing narratives about guns addressed? Consider narratives that criminalize guns/gun owners, for example, or narratives that tie guns and violence.

2. What elements of the gun range brochure connect gun use and leisure? gun use and status? Articulate the reasoning of such narratives.

3. The gun range includes a gym with exercise equipment. How does the presence of an area devoted to physical exercise frame gun use?

Visual Texts

The two images that follow work in a visual way to parody revered figures: the ancient Greek philosopher Plato and the likenesses of early U.S. presidents, in their official portraits reprinted on U.S. tender (or paper money). The images "work" as arguments because they evoke both the conventional meaning, or cultural script—Plato as great thinker, Washington, Lincoln, and Jackson as great historical leaders—and the author's ability to "even out" the cultural script. How does the bust of Plato made of Play-Doh change the conventional view of him? And how do the "Groucho glasses" imposed on the presidents' portraits do the same? We're deep into the realm of the intertextual here—the semiotic relationship of images and myths, with these visual signs pointing to a tangle of cultural meanings.

● Applying a Semiotics Frame

1. What cultural myth attaches to the image and word *Plato* today?
   - Do you think people "know" the myth from having read his works?
   - Trace the semiotic web: what is knowing or not knowing who Plato is a sign of?
   - What view of Plato and his works is the "cultured" person supposed to have? In whose interest is this view promoted?

2. The Play-Doh bust of Plato is an actual sculpture modeled after an actual sculpture. What is the rhetorical effect of the artist using a child's clay product on how we perceive Plato's image? What is the rhetorical effect of the word play on "Plato" and "Play-Doh"?

3. One of Plato's foundational theories calls art or any representation a distortion of truth. Plato was an idealist: he argued that ideas exist in perfect form in a realm of pure abstraction, one we can attain only through a transcendental mental process. Our senses lie, and so material objects, including works of art, lead us astray. How do you think the author of the Play-Doh bust is playing with this idealist rejection of representation?
   - What argument might the author be making, in your view? Do you see her as seeking to refute or support Plato's point about representation, or do you perceive a different kind of purpose?

4. The image of the presidents in Groucho glasses is, at first, amusing, perhaps. Groucho glasses have been common comic objects in our culture since the 1930s, when Groucho Marx, of the Marx Brothers, became a familiar comic image in very popular films. They've become naturalized as gag objects. But Groucho glasses have specific characteristics: attached to thick black frames, they have a big nose, heavy eyebrows, and a bushy moustache. Read these visual elements in connection with the cultural text of Groucho Marx.
   - How does each connect with the fact that the Marx Brothers were Jewish? For example, the Jewish religion was and is known for its hermeneutic tradition—for its long historical practice of extensive textual interpretation. The thick glasses thus connect with the intellectualism in the Jewish tradition. What cultural myths connect with the other physical features of Groucho glasses?
   - What was the social and cultural situation of Jews in the 1930s Western world? How do the Groucho glasses connect to the cultural myths of the era?
   - Are Groucho glasses an anti-Semitic cultural sign?

5. Put the glasses on the presidents' images on U.S. paper money, and what further cultural myth is foregrounded? How does the background—a map of the U.S. with a flag design—fit into the emerging argument the image promotes?

topics for writing

1. Alter a well-known image—a photograph, painting, or product logo, for example—to create an argument about its place in our culture. You have an example in the Sun Maid Raisin parody at the start of this part.

   - Be sure that you have a sense of its semiotic meaning to begin with—go through Jack Solomon's (p. 557) analytic steps first.

   - Think about the argument you'd make: do you seek to endorse, critique, or emphasize its "message"?

   - What contextual information, in visual form, will help readers follow your argument? Can you use color, verbal elements, borders, or other formal visual signs to clarify your purpose?

   - Who will your audience be, and how are they likely to view the original?

2. Compose a syllabus that embodies your sense of how the student, and the student–instructor relationship, ought to be represented. Choose an actual course you've taken or are taking now, or develop a course you'd like to take. The syllabus genre ought to be recognizable to your readers, or you should find some means to help readers understand that you're working against the form, if that's your choice.

   - First analyze the generic elements of a syllabus—the sample included here (p. 604) or one from another class.

   - Decide what your syllabus's purpose will be: how do you see the construct of "the student"? The teacher–student relationship?

   - How can you use the form of the syllabus genre to foreground these? What elements should you give rhetorical emphasis to through visual signs?

   - How will you design the overall document? Will it be strictly print-based? How will the order of its elements be related to each other logically to support your overall argument?

   - What voice(s) will you use to create the desired rhetorical effect?

Framing and Composing
from a Semiotics Perspective

1. Examine competing cultural narratives by pairing ads or other images that promote conflicting messages. Read each rhetorically for its argument, means of persuasion, and the cultural myths it engages. To what extent are their mythic codes different, and do we see them "agree" at points? Consider the following possibilities:

   - Ads for cigarettes/antismoking ads

   - Ads depicting female roles: professional women, housewives, sexual objects, mothers, other roles; another approach would be to examine a bridal magazine and a working woman's magazine

2. Observe and take notes on a class meeting (English, math, etc.). What education myths can you identify? Do you see resistant elements—practices or statements that challenge, directly or indirectly, the traditional cultural narratives of the classroom?

3. Visit your school's Web site for first-year or prospective students. What cultural narratives are used to represent the school, its students, its faculty, its physical location and grounds?

   - How do the visual components help create the "story" of a student's experience as part of the school community?

   - How does the site design, the ways one can navigate its links, help compose the narrative?

   - What types of student activities and interests are encouraged?

   - Who speaks to the site visitor? other students? administrators? faculty?

   - How closely does your experience at the institution follow the narratives?

4. The anonymous narrative below appears in *Comp Tales*, a collection of stories told by writing teachers. Sketch out the cultural myth in this narrative that outlines the expected teacher role. Trace the different cultural frames evoked in the opening of the main anecdote, beginning with the campus deserted for Thanksgiving vacation.

You fail occasionally—just fail. And you can't say it was not your fault. And you can't forget, either.

It was the Friday before Thanksgiving vacation. Students had left in droves the day before because a storm had been predicted, and indeed it was snowing hard. It was late in the afternoon, and I too wanted to get home, to my wife and a fire. But a student, one I did not much like, had come into the office and was not picking up on my hints that it was time to go. A loner, the kind the women in class laugh about. He had brought a draft, but he had once before conferenced with me about it and done nothing to it in the meantime. Finally I got up, put on my coat. He followed me out into the snow. He was telling me how he had done well in the university chess competition. At the edge of campus I shook his hand, glove on glove, and pointed toward the street I had to go down. He said he would walk with me a ways. It was 5:30 and dark already and the snow was nearly suffocating. He explained that his parents were divorced, that he was remaining in the dorms over vacation rather than deal with his stepfather. After several blocks, I stopped and said, "Look, you seem like you need someone to talk to about all this. You know, there are good counselors in Student Services. All you have to do is walk in." He said he would think about it. Then he said, "Thanks." We parted. I didn't turn around but I can still see him heading back through the snow to the dorms.

After vacation he wasn't in class. I never saw him again.
I've told my wife about this. A shrink. That's it (82–83).

- What cultural frames inform our perception of the student?
- How did the student's sense of the teacher's role transgress the teacher's sense of it?
- The teacher ends with a kind of confessional statement. What does this ending tell us about the power of cultural myths to frame individual experience?
- How might Anthony Robbins see this anecdote? What advice might he give to the student? to the teacher?

5. Design a brochure for an event you'd like to attend or have some experience with—a music concert, for example, or a community service fundraiser, church-related gathering, or student club meeting.

- Look at the genre of brochures that advertise an event: what are the conventional elements?
- What audience will you appeal to, and what sort of voice and visual elements are likely to be rhetorically effective?
- Work with the form of a trifold brochure (a single piece of 8.5 × 11-inch paper held horizontally and folded into thirds). What will appear on the front of the brochure? Will you use images, or both images and words? What will appear to readers when they open to view the inside pages?
- Will there be an argument to address, and if so, how will you engage your intended audience's interest in it?

WPA Outcomes Statement for First-Year Composition

Introduction

This statement describes the common knowledge, skills, and attitudes sought by first-year composition programs in American postsecondary education. To some extent, we seek to regularize what can be expected to be taught in first-year composition; to this end the document is not merely a compilation or summary of what currently takes place. Rather, the following statement articulates what composition teachers nationwide have learned from practice, research, and theory. This document intentionally defines only "outcomes," or types of results, and not "standards," or precise levels of achievement. The setting of standards should be left to specific institutions or specific groups of institutions.

Learning to write is a complex process, both individual and social, that takes place over time with continued practice and informed guidance. Therefore, it is important that teachers, administrators, and a concerned public do not imagine that these outcomes can be taught in reduced or simple ways. Helping students demonstrate these outcomes requires expert understanding of how students actually learn to write. For this reason we expect the primary audience for this document to be well-prepared college writing teachers and college writing program administrators. In some places, we have chosen to write in their professional language. Among such readers, terms such as "rhetorical" and "genre" convey a rich meaning that is not easily simplified. While we have also aimed at writing a document that the general public can understand, in limited cases we have aimed first at communicating effectively with expert writing teachers and writing program administrators.

These statements describe only what we expect to find at the end of first-year composition, at most schools a required general education course or sequence of courses. As writers move beyond first-year composition, their writing abilities do not merely improve. Rather, students' abilities not only diversify along disciplinary and professional lines but also move into whole new levels where expected outcomes expand, multiply, and diverge. For this reason, each statement of outcomes for first-year composition is followed by suggestions for further work that builds on these outcomes.

Rhetorical Knowledge

By the end of first-year composition, students should

- Focus on a purpose
- Respond to the needs of different audiences
- Respond appropriately to different kinds of rhetorical situations
- Use conventions of format and structure appropriate to the rhetorical situation
- Adopt appropriate voice, tone, and level of formality
- Understand how genres shape reading and writing
- Write in several genres

Faculty in all programs and departments can build on this preparation by helping students learn

- The main features of writing in their fields
- The main uses of writing in their fields
- The expectations of readers i

Critical Thinking, Reading, and Writing

By the end of first-year composition, students should

- Use writing and reading for inquiry, learning, thinking, and communicating
- Understand a writing assignment as a series of tasks, including finding, evaluating, analyzing, and synthesizing appropriate primary and secondary sources
- Integrate their own ideas with those of others
- Understand the relationships among language, knowledge, and power

Faculty in all programs and departments can build on this preparation by helping students learn

- The uses of writing as a critical thinking method
- The interactions among critical thinking, critical reading, and writing
- The relationships among language, knowledge, and power in their fields

Processes

By the end of first-year composition, students should

- Be aware that it usually takes multiple drafts to create and complete a successful text
- Develop flexible strategies for generating, revising, editing, and proof-reading
- Understand writing as an open process that permits writers to use later invention and re-thinking to revise their work
- Understand the collaborative and social aspects of writing processes
- Learn to critique their own and others' works
- Learn to balance the advantages of relying on others with the responsibility of doing their part
- Use a variety of technologies to address a range of audiences

Faculty in all programs and departments can build on this preparation by helping students learn

- To build final results in stages
- To review work-in-progress in collaborative peer groups for purposes other than editing
- To save extensive editing for later parts of the writing process
- To apply the technologies commonly used to research and communicate within their fields

Knowledge of Conventions

By the end of first-year composition, students should

- Learn common formats for different kinds of texts
- Develop knowledge of genre conventions ranging from structure and paragraphing to tone and mechanics
- Practice appropriate means of documenting their work
- Control such surface features as syntax, grammar, punctuation, and spelling

Faculty in all programs and departments can build on this preparation by helping students learn

- The conventions of usage, specialized vocabulary, format, and documentation in their fields
- Strategies through which better control of c̶o̶n̶v̶e̶n̶tions can be achieved

credits

Photo Credits

p. 177, Curtis Publishing and Norman Rockwell Family Agency, Inc.
p. 275, © Joel Pett
p. 311, Photograph: Brant Ward/ San Franciso Chronicle; Headline: Kathleen Pender/San Francisco Chronicle Staff Writer
p. 339, © Matt Groening
p. 538, Richard Ross/Getty Images
p. 544, Ester Hernandez
p. 574, Masatomo Kurlya/Corbis
p. 575, Reuters/Corbis
p. 616, top: Eva David
p. 616, bottom: Denis Scott/Corbis

Reading Credits

Anyon, Jean. "Social Class and the Hidden Curriculum of Work," *Journal of Education*, 162:1 (Winter 1987): 67–92. Reprinted by permission of the *Journal of Education* and the author, p. 251.

Anzaldúa, Gloria. From *Borderlands/La Frontera: The New Mestiza*. Copyright © 1987, 1999 by Gloria Anzaldúa. Reprinted by permission of Aunt Lute Books, p. 496.

Barthes, Roland. From *Mythologies*, published by Jonathan Cape. Reprinted by permission of The Random House Group Ltd.; "Myth Today," *Mythologies*, Trans. by Annette Lavers, Hill and Wang/Farrar, Straus & Giroux, 1972. Used by permission, p. 566.

Bertens, Hans. *Literary Theory: The Basics*, Routledge, 2004. Copyright © 2004 Routledge. Reproduced by Taylor & Francis UK, p. 368.

Bordo, Susan. "Exploring the Slender Body" from the book *Unbearable Weight: Feminism, Western Weight, and the Body*. University of California Press, 1993. Used by permission of the University of California Press, p. 484.

Bumiller, Elisabeth. *May You Be the Mother of a Hundred Sons: A Journey Among the Women of India*, Fawcett Columbine, 1990. Used by permission of Random House, p. 413.

Catton, Bruce. From *Reflections on the Civil War*, copyright © 1981 by Gerald Dickler as the executor of the estate of Bruce Catton and John Leckley. Used by permission of Doubleday, a division of Random House, Inc., p. 276.

Césaire, Aimé. Copyright © 1972 by MR Press. Reprinted by permission of Monthly Review Foundation, p. 374.

Cobley, Paul, and Litza Jansz. *Introducing Semiotics*, Totem Books, 1997. Used by permission, p. 545.

Council of Writing Program Administrators. Reprinted with permission of the Council of Writing Program Administrators. The original can be found at http://wpacouncil.org/positions/outcomes.html, p. 625.

Decker, Scott H., and Barrik Van Winkle, *Life in the Gang*, Cambridge University Press, 2004. Reprinted with the permission of Cambridge University Press, p. 133.

de Zengotita, Thomas. Copyright © 2002 by *Harper's Magazine*. All rights reserved. Reproduced from the April issue by special permission, p. 322.

DFW Gun Range brochure. Used by permission, p. 613.

Eagleton, Terry. "Psychoanalysis," *Literary Theory: An Introduction*, University of Minnesota Press, 1983. Used by permission of University of Minnesota Press, p. 91.

Fadiman, Anne. *The Spirit Catches You and You Fall Down: A Hmong Child, Her American Doctors, and the Collision of Two Cultures*, Farrar, Straus and Giroux, 1997. Used by permission, p. 474.

Fanon, Frantz. From *Black Skin, White Masks*. Copyright © 1967 by Grove Press, Inc. Used by permission of Grove/Atlantic, Inc., p. 439.

Freud, Sigmund. From *Civilization and Its Discontents*, translated by James Strachey. Copyright © 1961 by James Strachey, renewed 1989 by Alix Strachey. Used by permission of W. W. Norton & Company, Inc.; Sigmund Freud © Copyrights, The Institute of Psycho-Analysis and The Hogarth Press for permission to quote from *Civilization and Its Discontents* from *The Standard Edition of the*

Complete Psychological Works of Sigmund Freud translated and edited by James Strachey. Reprinted by permission of The Random House Group Ltd., p. 80.

Fuller, Alexandra. From *Don't Let's Go to the Dogs Tonight*, copyright © 2001 by Alexandra Fuller. Used by permission of Random House, Inc., p. 430.

Grinker, Roy Richard. "Pygmalion," *In the Arms of Africa: The Life of Colin M. Turnbull*, St. Martin's, 2000. Used by permission of Palgrave, p. 121.

Hirsch, E. D. Jr. "Literacy and Cultural Literacy," from *Cultural Literacy*. Copyright © 1987 by Houghton Mifflin Company. Reprinted by permission of Hougton Mifflin Company. All rights reserved, p. 237.

hooks, bell. "Language: Teaching New Worlds/New Words," *Teaching to Transgress*, Routledge, 1994, pp. 167–75. Used by permission, p. 509.

Hwang, David Henry. "Afterword," copyright © 1988 by David Henry Hwang, from *M. Butterfly*. Used by permission of Dutton Signet, a division of Penguin Group (USA) Inc., p. 383.

Kagan, Jerome, and Ernest Havemann. From *Psychology: An Introduction*. 1968. Reprinted with permission of Thomson Learning: www.thomsonrights.com. Fax 800 730-2215, p. 75.

Karier, Clarence J. From *The Individual, Society, and Education: A History of American Educational Ideas*. Copyright 1967, 1986 by the Board of Trustees of the University of Illinois. Used with permission of the University of Illinois Press, p. 228.

Kozol, Jonathan. From *Savage Inequalities*, copyright © 1991 by Jonathan Kozol. Used by permission of Crown Publishers, a division of Random House, Inc., p. 463.

Krakauer, Jon. From *Into the Wild*, copyright © 1996 by Jon Krakauer. Used by permission of Villard Books, a division of Random House, Inc., p. 143.

Lens, Sidney. Reprinted by permission of Spectrum Literary Agency, p. 282.

Mairs, Nancy. *Plaintext*, University of Arizona Press, 1986. Reprinted by permission of University of Arizona Press, p. 129.

Martín-Baró, Ignacio. Reprinted by permission of the publisher from "Political Socialization: Two Critical Themes," translated by Adrianne Aron in *Writings for a Liberation Psychology*. Edited by Adrianne Aron and Shawn Corne, pp. 68–69, 72–78, Cambridge, Mass.: Harvard University Press, Copyright © 1994 by the President and Fellows of Harvard College, p. 197.

Miller, Richard, "Fault Lines in the Contact Zone: Assessing Homophobic Student Writing." *Lesbian and Gay Studies and the Teaching of English*. Ed. William J. Spurlin. Urbana: NCTE, 2000. Used by permission of NCTE, p. 515.

Miserandino, Dominick A. From TheCelebrityCafe.com. Used by permission, p. 576.

O'Brien, Tim. "Speaking of Courage," *The Things They Carried*, Random House, 1990. Used by permission, p. 581.

Postman, Neil. "The Age of Show Business," from *Amusing Ourselves to Death*, copyright © 1985 by Neil Postman. Used by permission of Viking Penguin, a division of Penguin Group (USA) Inc., p. 312.

Power, Samantha. From *A Problem from Hell*. Reprinted by permission of Basic Books, a member of Perseus Books Group, p. 153.

Prejean, Sister Helen. Chap. 2, *Dead Man Walking*, Random House, 1993. Used by permission, p. 592.

Reich, Charles A. *The Greening of America*, Random House, 1970. Used by permission of the author, p. 299.

Said, Edward W. From *Culture and Imperialism*, copyright © 1993 by Edward W. Said. Used by permission of Alfred A. Knopf, a division of Random House, Inc., p. 353.

Schaefer, Jack. From *Shane*. Copyright 1949 by Jack Schaefer, renewed © 1976 by Jack Schaefer. Reprinted by permission of Houghton Mifflin Company. All rights reserved, p. 109.

Solomon, Jack. "Semiotics: The Science of the Sign," from *The Signs of Our Time*, copyright © 1988 by Jack Solomon. Used by permission of Jeremy P. Tarcher, an imprint of Penguin Group (USA) Inc., p. 557.

Staten, Clark. "Three Days of Hell in Los Angeles, A Series of Reports prepared by the Emergency-net News Service (ENN) in 'real-time' as the events were unfolding," http://www.emergency.com/la-riots.htm. Emergency Response & Research Institute. Used by permission, p. 289.

Syllabus. Used by permission of Ivan Light, p. 604.

Theroux, Paul. "Walkabout in Woop Woop," *The Happy Isles of Oceania: Paddling the Pacific*, Ballantine, 1992. Used by permission of The Wylie Agency, p. 395.

Villanueva, Victor. "An American of Color," *Bootstraps: From an American Academic of Color*, NCTE, 1993. Reprinted by permission of the National Council for Teacher's of English, p. 446.

Wertz, Richard W., and Dorothy C. Wertz. *Lying-In: A History of Childbirth in America*, Yale University Press. Used by permission, p. 207.

index

Note: Essays, interviews, stories, syllabus, and chapter titles appear in quotes; book titles are italicized.